CRITICAL THINKING, READING, and WRITING

A Brief Guide to Argument

SIXTH EDITION

CRITICAL THINKING, READING, and WRITING

A Brief Guide to Argument

SYLVAN BARNET
Professor of English, Tufts University

HUGO BEDAU
Professor of Philosophy, Tufts University

Bedford/St. Martin's   BOSTON ◆ NEW YORK

For Bedford / St. Martin's
Senior Developmental Editor: John E. Sullivan III
Production Editor: Kerri A. Cardone
Production Supervisor: Jennifer Peterson
Senior Marketing Manager: Karita dos Santos
Editorial Assistant: Jennifer Lyford
Copyeditor: Lisa Wehrle
Text Design: Linda M. Robertson, LMR Designs
Cover Design: Donna Lee Dennison
Cover Art: Jordan, by Charles Arnoldi. Courtesy of the artist and Charles Cowles Gallery, NY.
Composition: TexTech
Printing and Binding: R.R. Donnelley and Sons Company

President: Joan E. Feinberg
Editorial Director: Denise B. Wydra
Editor in Chief: Karen S. Henry
Director of Marketing: Karen Melton Soeltz
Director of Editing, Design, and Production: Marcia Cohen
Managing Editor: Elizabeth M. Schaaf

Library of Congress Control Number: 2007921373

For information, write: Bedford/St. Martin's, 75 Arlington Street, Boston, MA 02116
(617-399-4000)

ISBN-10: 0–312–45987–4
ISBN-13: 978–0–312–45987–1

Acknowledgments

Derek Bok. "Protecting Freedom of Expression on the Campus" (editor's title). Originally titled "Protecting Freedom of Expression at Harvard." From the *Boston Globe*, May 25, 1991. Copyright © 1991 by Derek Bok. Reprinted by permission of the author.

Susan Brownmiller. "Let's Put Pornography Back in the Closet." Originally published in *Newsday*, 1979. © 1979 by Susan Brownmiller. Later included in *Take Back the Night* edited by Laura Lederer (1980). Reprinted by permission of Susan Brownmiller.

Randy Cohen. "Suffer the Little Children," From *The New York Times* May 11, March 16 and 30, 2003. Copyright © 2003 Randy Cohen. Reprinted by permission of McCormick and Williams, agents for Randy Cohen.

Alan M. Dershowitz. "Why Fear National ID Cards?" From *The New York Times*, September 13, 2001. Copyright © 2001 The New York Times Company, Inc. Reprinted by permission.

Acknowledgments and copyrights are continued at the back of the book on pages 547–48, which constitute an extension of the copyright page. It is a violation of the law to reproduce these selections by any means whatsoever without the written permission of the copyright holder.

Preface

This book is a text about critical thinking and argumentation —a book about getting ideas, using sources, evaluating kinds of evidence, and organizing material. It also includes about fifty readings, with a strong emphasis on contemporary arguments. In a moment we will be a little more specific about what sorts of readings we include, but first we want to mention our chief assumptions about the aims of a course that might use *Critical Thinking, Reading, and Writing: A Brief Guide to Argument.*

Probably most students and instructors would agree that, as **critical readers,** students should be able to

- Summarize accurately an argument they have read;
- Locate the thesis (the claim) of an argument;
- Locate the assumptions, stated and unstated;
- Analyze and evaluate the strength of the evidence and the soundness of the reasoning offered in support of the thesis; and
- Analyze, evaluate, and account for discrepancies among various readings on a topic (for example, explain why certain facts are used, why others are ignored, why probable consequences of a proposed action are examined or ignored, or why two sources might interpret the same facts differently).

Probably, too, students and instructors would agree that, as *thoughtful writers,* students should be able to

- Imagine an audience and write effectively for it (for instance, by using the appropriate tone and providing the appropriate amount of detail);
- Present information in an orderly and coherent way;
- Be aware of their own assumptions;

- Locate sources and incorporate them into their own writing, not simply by quoting extensively or by paraphrasing but also by having digested material so that they can present it in their own words;
- Properly document all borrowings—not merely quotations and paraphrases but also borrowed ideas; and
- Do all these things in the course of developing a thoughtful argument of their own.

In the first edition of this book we quoted Edmund Burke and John Stuart Mill. Burke said,

> He that wrestles with us strengthens our nerves, and sharpens our skill. Our antagonist is our helper.

Mill said,

> He who knows only his own side of the cause knows little.

These two quotations continue to reflect the view of argument that underlies this text: In writing an essay one is engaging in a serious effort to know what one's own ideas are and, having found them, to contribute to a multisided conversation. One is not setting out to trounce an opponent, and that is partly why such terms as *marshaling evidence, attacking an opponent,* and *defending a thesis* are misleading. True, on television talk shows we see right-wingers and left-wingers who have made up their minds and who are concerned only with pushing their own views and brushing aside all others. But in an academic community, and indeed in our daily lives, we learn

- by listening to others and also
- by listening to ourselves.

We draft a response to something we have read, and in the very act of drafting we may find—if we think critically about the words we are putting down on paper—we are changing (perhaps slightly, perhaps radically) our own position. In short, one reason that we write is so that we can improve our ideas. And even if we do not drastically change our views, we and our readers at least come to a better understanding of why we hold the views we do.

FEATURES

The Text

Parts One and Two   Part One, Critical Thinking and Reading (Chapters 1–4), and Part Two, Critical Writing (Chapters 5–7), together offer a short course in methods of thinking about and writing arguments. By "thinking" we mean serious analytic thought, including analysis of one's own assumptions (Chapter 1); by "writing" we mean the use of effective, respectable techniques, not gimmicks (such as the notorious note a politician scribbled in the margin of the text of his speech: "Argument weak; shout here"). For a delightfully wry account of the use of gimmicks, we recommend that you consult "The Art of Controversy" in *The Will to Live* by the nineteenth-century German philosopher Arthur Schopenhauer. Schopenhauer reminds readers that a Greek or Latin quotation (however irrelevant) can be impressive to the uninformed and that one can knock down almost any proposition by loftily saying, "That's all very well in theory, but it won't do in practice."

We offer lots of advice about how to set forth an argument, but we do not offer instruction in one-upmanship. Rather, we discuss responsible ways of arguing persuasively. We know, however, that before one can write a persuasive argument, one must clarify one's own ideas—a process that includes arguing with oneself—to find out what one really thinks about a problem. Therefore, we devote Chapter 1 to critical thinking, Chapters 2, 3, and 4 to critical reading (Chapter 4 is about reading images), and Chapters 5, 6, and 7 to critical writing.

Parts One and Two together contain twenty-eight readings (nine are student papers) for analysis and discussion. Some of these essays originated as op-ed newspaper pieces, and we reprint some of the letters to the editor that they generated, so students can easily see several sides to a given issue and in their own responses they can, so to speak, join the conversation. (We have found, by the way, that the format of a letter helps students to frame their ideas, and therefore in later chapters we occasionally suggest writing assignments in the form of a letter to the editor. In Chapter 10 we reprint three letters written by Randy Cohen of the *New York Times Magazine,* and we invite students to write their own responses.)

All of the essays in the book are accompanied by Topics for Critical Thinking and Writing.[1] This is not surprising, given the emphasis we place on asking questions in order to come up with ideas for writing. Among the chief questions that writers should ask, we suggest, are "What is X?" and "What is the value of X?" (pp. 224–28). By asking such questions—for instance (to look only at these two types of questions), "Is the fetus a person?" or "Is Arthur Miller a better playwright than Tennessee Williams?"— a writer probably will find ideas coming, at least after a few moments of head scratching. The device of developing an argument by identifying issues is, of course, nothing new. Indeed, it goes back to an ancient method of argument used by classical rhetoricians, who identified a *stasis* (an issue) and then asked questions about it: Did X do such-and-such? If so, was the action bad? If bad, how bad? (Finding an issue or *stasis*—a position where one stands—by asking questions is discussed in Chapter 6.)

---

[1]With a few exceptions, the paragraphs in the essays are, for ease of reference, numbered in increments of five (5, 10, 15, and so on). The exceptions involve essays in which paragraphs are uncommonly long: In such cases, every paragraph is numbered.

In keeping with our emphasis on writing as well as reading, we raise issues not only of what can roughly be called the "content" of the essays but also of what can (equally roughly) be called the "style"—that is, the *ways* in which the arguments are set forth. Content and style, of course, cannot finally be kept apart. As Cardinal Newman said, "Thought and meaning are inseparable from each other. . . . *Style is thinking out into language.*" In our Topics for Critical Thinking and Writing we sometimes ask the student

- to evaluate the effectiveness of an essay's opening paragraph,
- to explain a shift in tone from one paragraph to the next, or
- to characterize the persona of the author as revealed in the whole essay.

In short, the book is not designed as an introduction to some powerful ideas (though in fact it is that, too); it is designed as an aid to *writing* thoughtful, effective arguments on important political, social, scientific, ethical, legal, and religious issues.

The essays reprinted in this book also illustrate different styles of argument that arise, at least in part, from the different disciplinary backgrounds of the various authors. Essays by journalists, lawyers, judges, social scientists, policy analysts, philosophers, critics, activists, and other writers—including first-year undergraduates—will be found in these pages. The authors develop and present their views in arguments that have distinctive features reflecting their special training and concerns. The differences in argumentative styles found in these essays foreshadow the differences students will encounter in the readings assigned in many of their other courses. Part Three, which offers a philosopher's view, a logician's view, a moralist's view, a lawyer's view, a psychologist's view, a literary critic's view, and a forensic view, also reveals differences in argumentative styles.

Parts One and Two, then, are a preliminary (but we hope substantial) discussion of such topics as

- *identifying assumptions*
- *getting ideas by means of invention strategies*
- *using printed and electronic sources*
- *interpreting visual sources*
- *evaluating kinds of evidence, and*
- *organizing material*

as well as an introduction to some ways of thinking.

Part Three   Part Three, Further Views on Argument, consists of Chapters 8 through 14. The first of these,

- Chapter 8, A Philosopher's View: The Toulmin Model, is a summary of the philosopher Stephen Toulmin's method for analyzing arguments. This summary will assist those who wish to apply Toulmin's methods to the readings in our book.

- Chapter 9, A Logician's View: Deduction, Induction, Fallacies, offers a more rigorous analysis of these topics than is usually found in composition courses and reexamines from a logician's point of view material already treated briefly in Chapter 3.

- Chapter 10, A Moralist's View: Ways of Thinking Ethically, consists of a discussion of amoral, immoral, and moral reasoning, A Checklist for Moral Reasoning, three challenging essays, and three short responses to highly specific moral questions.

- Chapter 11, A Lawyer's View: Steps toward Civic Literacy, introduces students to some basic legal concepts such as the distinction between civil and criminal cases, and then gives majority and minority opinions in three cases covering current topics: burning the flag, searching students for drugs, and establishing the right to an abortion. We accompany these judicial opinions with questions that invite the student to participate in these exercises in democracy.

- Chapter 12, A Psychologist's View: Rogerian Argument, with an essay by psychotherapist Carl R. Rogers and an essay by a student, complements the discussion of audience, organization, and tone in Chapter 6.

- Chapter 13, A Literary Critic's View: Arguing about Literature, should help students to see the things literary critics argue about and *how* they argue. Students can apply what they learn not only to the literary readings that appear in the chapter (poems by Robert Frost and Andrew Marvell and a story by Kate Chopin) but also to the readings that appear in Part Six, Enduring Questions: Essays, a Story, Poems, and a Play. Finally, Part Three concludes with

- Chapter 14, A Forensic View: Oral Presentation and Debate, which introduces students to standard debate format and presentation.

Part Four   Finally, Part Four is a casebook on the state and the individual, with Chapter 15 on the question, "What is the Ideal Society?" The voices here include Thomas More, Niccolò Machiavelli, Thomas Jeferson, Elizabeth Cady Stanton, Martin Luther King Jr., and Ursula K. Le Guin.

The Companion Web Site

The companion Web site at bedfordstmartins.com/barnetbedau offers students and instructors an extensive set of annotated links on argument and on the controversial topics in the book. Brainteasers allow students to test their understanding of logic and analysis.

TWO OTHER VERSIONS

For instructors who do *not* require a text with a substantial number of essays, a *very* brief version is also available: *From Critical Thinking to Argument*, Second Edition, contains Parts One and Two, plus three Further Views on Argument: A Philosopher's View (on Toulmin argument); A Logician's View (Deduction, Induction, and Logical Fallacies); and A Psychologist's View (on Rogerian argument). It contains a dozen readings throughtout the text.

For instructors who require a text with a *large* number of essays, a longer edition of this book, *Current Issues and Enduring Questions*, Eighth Edition, is also available. The longer version contains Parts One, Two, and Three (Chapters 1-14) of the present book as well as its own anthology of eighty-eight additional readings.

WHAT'S NEW IN THE SIXTH EDITION

We have made some significant changes in the Sixth Edition that we believe enrich the book and make the content more accessible:

Fresh and timely new readings. One third of the essays are new, as are a dozen topics such as a peacetime draft, extermination of wild horses, immigration, intelligent design, polygamy, college sports teams' use of Indian mascots, banning laptops in college classrooms, and the point of a college education.

Five new checklists (twenty-eight total), including "A Checklist for a Thesis Statement" and "A Checklist for Imagining an Audience."

Updated research features. Chapter 7, Using Sources, has been revised to provide the latest information on finding, evaluating, and documenting electronic as well as print sources. It also includes a discussion of plagiarism, with A Checklist for Avoiding Plagiarism.

Expanded discussion of summary, paraphrase, and plagiarism. Recognizing that many students do not easily grasp the distinctions between summarizing and paraphrasing, we have expanded our discussion, and we have also expanded our discussion of the relationship between paraphrase and plagiarism.

Expanded coverage of visual rhetoric. Chapter 4, Visual Rhetoric: Images and Arguments, now discusses political cartoons as well as advertisements, photographs, and visual aids to clarity (maps, graphs, tables, and pie charts). The chapter also discusses the visual impact produced by the layout in a student's essay.

A dramatially redesigned book. It now features a second color that heightens readability as it makes it easier to navigate the text.

Additional student writing. The book now includes eleven essays by students writing about current issues (five are new), as well as two essays by students writing about literature.

In preparing the sixth edition we were aided by suggestions from instructors using the fifth edition. In response, we have done the following:

- In Part One, Critical Thinking and Reading, we have clarified some passages concerning logic, fallacies, and summarizing, amplified the discussions of plagiarism, and added seven readings (three of these seven new readings are accompanied by nine letters of response, thus giving readers a better sense of varying positions on a given issue).

- Part Two, Critical Writing, includes new essays (among them a casebook on diversity) and three new checklists (on analyzing a text, on using charts and graphs, and on using quotations and summaries).

- Part Three, Further Views on Argument, now includes a revised discussion of fallacies, with an extensive exercise on the topic. The chapter on the Toulmin method now includes an essay for analysis, with helpful prompts; and the chapter on Rogerian thinking now includes an essay by a student.

There can be no argument about the urgency of the topics that we have retained and have added or about the need to develop civic literacy and visual literacy, but there can be lots of argument about the merits of the positions offered in the selections. That's where the users of the book—students and instructors—come in.

ACKNOWLEDGMENTS

Finally, it is our pleasant duty to thank those who have strengthened the book by their comments and advice on the sixth edition: Connie S. Adair, Marshalltown Community College; Larry Beason, University of South Alabama; Maggie Christensen, University of Nebraska, Omaha; Michelle Dowd, Chaffey College; Margaret Fox, Oregon State University; Alexis Khoury, Reedley College; Elma Kronemeijer, Valdosta State University; Nicole Montoya, University of Texas at El Paso; Saleem Peeradina, Siena Heights University; Bonnie Pickett, Viterbo University; John Regan, Boston University; and Linda Tetzlaff, Normandale Community College.

We also appreciate the helpful suggestions given in response to the fourth edition: Kathryn Bartle Angus, California State University; Larry Beason, University of South Alabama; Patricia Brooke, Fontbonne University; Charles Fisher, Aims Community College; Terri Lowry, Longview Community College; Janette L. MacDonald, University of Colorado at Denver; Michael Muscat, Fullerton College; Ling Na, University of Texas at El Paso; Peter Potamianos, Roosevelt University; Kathellen Raphael, University of Texas at El Paso; Ed Reber, Dixie State College of Utah; John Regan, Boston university; Claudio Stranger, Fullerton College; Maria K. Bachman, Coastal Carolina University; and Joanne Carter-Wells, California State University–Fullerton.

We would also like to thank those instructors who reviewed previous editions: Lawrence Anderson, Louisiana State University–Shreveport; Evelyn D. Asch, DePaul University; Larry Beason, University of South Alabama; Donavin Bennes, University of North Dakota; Karla Block, Iowa State University; Earnest Cox, Texas Christian University; Ian Crawford, Berry College; Tracy A. Crouch, Stephen F. Austin State University; Jonathan M. DeLisle, Ohio University; Gloria Dyc, University of New Mexico; Ann Ellsworth, University of Washington; Elaine Elmo, Stanley Community College; Larry D. Engel, Rochester Community and Technical College; James M. Ewing, Fresno City College; Jill Fieldkamp, Wartburg College; Charles Fisher, Aims Community College; Karl Fornes, University of Minnesota–Morris; Paula F. Furr, United States Military Academy; Lillis Gilmartin, Sierra Heights College; Gary Grieve-Carlson, Lebanon Valley College; Eric H. Hobson, St. Louis College of Pharmacy; William T. Hope, Jefferson Technical College; Jane Janssen, Bellevue Community College; K. Kaleta, Roawn College; Cathy Kaye, University of Wisconsin–Milwaukee; Janice Kollity, Riverside Community College; Mary R. Lamb, Texas Christian University; Teresa K. Lehr, SUNY at Brockport; Anne Lockwood, Limestone College; Thomas Loe, SUNY at Oswego; Mary Macaluso, New Mexico Highlands University; Barry Mauer, University of Central Florida; Samuel A. McCool, Florida International University; Barbara McGuire, University of Wisconsin; Jonathan Murrow, West Virginia University; Alison Preston, California Polytechnic State University; Jeanne Purdy, University of Minnesota–Morris; Linsy J. Rawling, Moorpark College; Ed Reben, Dixie College; Warren G. Rochelle, Limestone College; Howard Sage, New York University; Sally Scholz, Purdue University; Christine M. Smith, Butler University; Matt Smith, Chattanooga State Technical Community College; John E. Stowe, Fordham University; Judith Swartout, Palm Beach Atlantic College; Charles Tita, Shaw University; Allen Wall, Chabot College; Lori Ann Wallin, North Idaho College; Eric A. Weil, Shaw University; Norman Weiner, SUNY at Oswego; Henry L. Wilson, Lebanon Valley College; Joann L. Yost, Bethel College; John W. Daugherty, Barstow Community College.

We would like especially to thank Barbara Fister, Academic Librarian at Gustavus Adolphus College, who revised the research chapter to encompass the latest advice and information on using electronic sources. We would also like to thank Naomi Kornhauser and Sandy Schechter, who adeptly managed art research and text permissions respectively.

We are also indebted to the people at Bedford/St. Martin's, especially to our editor, John Sullivan, who is wise, patient, supportive, and unfailingly helpful. Steve Scipione and Maura Shea, our editors of the preceding editions, have left a lasting impression on us and on the book; without their work on earlier editions, there probably would not be a sixth. Others at Bedford/St. Martin's to whom we are deeply indebted include Charles H. Christensen, Joan E. Feinberg, Elizabeth Schaaf, Kerri Cardone, Lisa Wehrle, and Jennifer Lyford, all of whom have offered countless valuable (and invaluable) suggestions. Intelligent, informed, firm yet courteous, persuasive—these folks know how to think and how to argue.

Contents

3 Critical Reading: Getting Deeper into Arguments   75

14 A Forensic View: Oral Presentation and Debate   495

PART FOUR   A CASEBOOK ON THE STATE AND THE INDIVIDUAL   503

15 What Is the Ideal Society?   505

PART ONE

CRITICAL THINKING
and READING

Critical Thinking

What is the hardest task in the world? To think.

—RALPH WALDO EMERSON

I write entirely to find out what I'm thinking, what I'm looking at, what I see and what it means. What I want and what I fear.

—JOAN DIDION

In all affairs it's a healthy thing now and then to hang a question mark on the things you have long taken for granted.

—BERTRAND RUSSELL

Although Emerson said simply "to think," he pretty clearly was using the word *think* in the sense of *critical thinking*. By itself, *thinking* can mean almost any sort of mental activity, from idle daydreaming ("During the chemistry lecture I kept thinking about how I'd like to go camping") to careful analysis ("I'm thinking about whether I can afford more than one week—say two weeks—of camping in the Rockies," or even "I'm thinking about whether Emerson's comment is true").

In short, when we add the adjective *critical* to the noun *thinking*, we pretty much eliminate reveries, just as we also eliminate snap judgments. We are talking about searching for hidden assumptions, noticing various facets, unraveling different strands, and evaluating what is most significant. The word *critical* comes from a Greek word, *krinein*, meaning "to separate," "to choose"; it implies conscious, deliberate inquiry, and especially it implies adopting a skeptical state of mind. To say that it implies a skeptical state of mind is by no means to say that it implies a self-satisfied fault-finding state of mind. Quite the reverse: Because critical thinkers seek to draw intelligent conclusions, they are sufficiently open-minded that they can adopt a skeptical attitude

- Toward *their own* ideas,
- Toward *their own* assumptions, and
- Toward the evidence *they themselves* tentatively offer,

as well as toward the assumptions and evidence offered by others. When they reread a draft they have written, they read it with a skeptical frame of mind, seeking to improve the thinking that has gone into it.

THINKING ABOUT DRIVERS' LICENSES AND PHOTOGRAPHIC IDENTIFICATION

By way of illustration, let's think about a case that was in the news in 2003. When Sultaana Freeman, an American Muslim woman in Florida, first applied for a driver's license, she refused on religious grounds to unveil her face for the photograph that Florida requires. She was allowed to remain veiled for the photo, with only her eyes showing. Probably in a response to the terrorist attacks of September 11, 2001, she was informed in 2002 that her license would be revoked if she refused to allow the Department of Motor Vehicles to photograph her face. She sued the state of Florida, saying that unveiling would violate her Islamic beliefs. "I'm fighting for the principle and the religious freedom of all people in the country," she said. "It's not about me."

Well, let's think about this—let's think critically, and to do this, we will use a simple aid that is equal to the best word processor, a pencil.

"It sort of makes you stop and think, doesn't it."

Your own experience has already taught you that thinking is largely a matter of association; one thought leads to another, as when you jot down "peanut butter" on a shopping list and then add "bread," and "bread" somehow reminds you—you don't know why—that you also need paper napkins. As the humorist Finley Peter Dunne observed, philosophers and cows have the gift of meditation, but "others don't begin to think till they begin to talk or write." So what are some thoughts that come to mind when we begin to talk or write about this Florida case?

Critical thinking means questioning not only the assumptions of others, but also questioning *your own* assumptions. We will discuss this point at some length later in this chapter, but here we want to say only that when you write an argument, you ought to be *thinking*, evaluating evidence and assumptions, not merely collecting evidence to support a preestablished conclusion.

Back to the Florida case: Here is what we came up with in a few minutes, using a process called *clustering*. (We illustrate clustering again on page 223.)

In the center of a sheet of paper, we jotted down a phrase summarizing the basic issue, and then we began jotting down what must be the most obvious justification for demanding the picture—national safety. (We might equally well have begun with the most obvious justifications for refusing to be photographed—religious belief and perhaps privacy, to think of arguments that Sultaana Freeman—or, more likely, her lawyer—might set forth.) Then we let our minds work, and one thought led to another. Sometimes almost as soon as we jotted down an idea we saw that it wasn't very good, but we made considerable progress.

In the illustration, we have added numbers to the ideas, simply so that you can see how our minds worked, which is to say how we jumped around. Notice, for instance, that our fifth point—our fifth idea—is connected to our second point. When we were rereading our first four jottings, the fifth idea—that she is not being discriminated against as a Muslim—came to mind, and we saw that it should be linked with the second point. Our sixth point—a modification of our fifth, occurred to us even before we finished writing the fifth. The sixth point, that temporary licenses in Florida are issued without photographs, prompted us to start thinking more vigorously about the arguments that Ms. Freeman, or her lawyer, might offer.

A very brief digression: A legal case is pretty much a matter of guilty or not guilty, right or wrong, yes or no. Of course in some trials a defendant can be found guilty of certain charges and innocent of others, but, again, it is usually an either/or situation: The prosecution wins, or the defense wins. But in many other aspects of life, there is room for compromise, and it may well be that *both* sides win—by seeing what ground they share and by developing additional common ground. We go into this topic at greater length on p. 453, where we discuss Rogerian argument (named for Carl Rogers, a psychotherapist) and in our introduction to several chapters that offer pairs of debates.

Now back to *Freeman v. State of Florida, Department of Highway Safety and Motor Vehicles*, where we began by trying to list arguments on one side versus arguments on the other.

After making our seventh note, which goes directly back to the central issue (hence we connected it, with a line, to the central issue) and which turned out to be an argument that the government rather than the plaintiff might make, we decided to keep thinking about government positions, and wrote the eighth note—that some states do not require pictures on drivers' licenses. The ninth note—that the government is prohibiting a belief, not a harmful action—in some degree refutes our seventh note, so we connected it to the seventh. Again, if you think with a pencil and a sheet of paper and let your mind make associations, you will find, perhaps to your surprise, that you have plenty of interesting ideas. Doubtless you will also have some not-so-interesting ones. We

4. Not the point: She believes her face ought not to be seen by a cop who might ask for her license.

3. Compromise: Maybe have a woman photographer take the picture in private.

7. Maybe infringement. But the gov't sometimes prohibits beliefs it considers harmful to society. It does not permit the use of drugs in religious ceremonies, or sacrifice.

2. National security is more important than private beliefs.

1. Infringement on one's religious beliefs.

9. But those things are harmful actions that the believer engages in. In the case at issue, the believer is not engaging in harmful action. It's the gov't that is doing the acting — taking a picture.

5. She is not being discriminated against, as a Muslim. All people who want a Florida license need a photo.

6. Not quite true. Temporary licenses are issued without a photo.

8. Some states do not require pictures on licenses.

10. Florida itself issues temporary licenses without photos.

confess that we have slightly edited our notes; originally they included two points that we are ashamed we thought of:

- "What is she complaining about? In some strict Islamic countries they don't even let women drive, period."
- "Being deprived of a license isn't a big deal. She can take the bus."

It will take only a moment of reflection to decide that these thoughts can scarcely be offered as serious arguments: What people do in strict Islamic countries has nothing to do with what we should do in ours, and that bus service is available is utterly irrelevant to the issue of whether this woman's rights are being infringed. Still, if a fear of making fools of ourselves had prevented us from jotting down ideas, we would not have jotted down any decent ideas, and the page would not have gotten written.

Plaintiff in *Freeman v. State of Florida, Department of Highway Safety and Motor Vehicles.*
(Peter Cosgrove/© AP/Worldwide Photos.)

> **A RULE FOR WRITERS:** One good way to start writing an essay is to
> start generating ideas—and at this point don't worry that some of
> them may be nonsense. Just get ideas down on paper, and evaluate
> them later.

The outcome of the driver's license photo case? Judge Janet C. Thorpe
ruled against the plaintiff, explaining that "the State has always had a
compelling interest in promoting public safety. That interest is served by
having the means to accurately and swiftly determine identities in given
circumstances." (You can read Judge Thorpe's entire decision online—
sixteen highly readable double-spaced pages—by going to Google and
typing in "Sultaana Lakiana.")

Topics for Critical Thinking and Writing

1. Think about Judge Thorpe's comment, quoted in the preceding paragraph. Even if we agree that a photograph establishes identity—itself a
   debatable point—one might raise a question: Given the fact that Florida
   has not passed a law requiring a photo ID, why should it say that the
   driver of a vehicle must provide a photo ID? Isn't a driver's license a
   mere certification of permission to drive?

2. Judge Thorpe wrote the following as part of her explanation for her decision:

> Although the Court acknowledges that Plaintiff herself most likely poses no threat to national security, there likely are people who would be willing to use a ruling permitting the wearing of fullface cloaks in driver's license photos by pretending to ascribe to religious beliefs in order to carry out activities that would threaten lives.

Is the judge in effect saying that we should infringe on Sultaana Freeman's religious beliefs because someone else might do something wicked?

3. In England in 2006 a Muslim woman—a British citizen—was removed from her job as a schoolteacher because she wore a veil. The stated reason was that the veil prevented her from effectively communicating with children. What do you think of the view that a woman has a right to wear a veil, but when she enters the marketplace she may rightly be denied certain jobs? Your reasons?

THINKING ABOUT ANOTHER ISSUE CONCERNING DRIVERS' LICENSES: IMAGINATION, ANALYSIS, EVALUATION

Let's think critically about a law passed in West Virginia in 1989. The law provides that although students may drop out of school at the age of sixteen, no dropout younger than eighteen can hold a driver's license. (Several states now have comparable laws.)

What ought we to think of such a law?

- Is it fair?
- What is its purpose?
- Is it likely to accomplish its purpose?
- Might it unintentionally cause some harm?
- If so, can we weigh the potential harm against the potential good?

Suppose you had been a member of the West Virginia state legislature in 1989: How would you have voted?

In thinking critically about a topic, we try to see it from all sides before we come to our conclusion. We conduct an argument with ourselves, advancing and then questioning opinions:

- What can be said *for* the proposition, and
- What can be said *against* it?

Our first reaction may be quite uncritical, quite unthinking: "What a good idea!" or "That's outrageous!" But critical thinking requires us to reflect further, trying to support our position *and also* trying to see the other side. One can almost say that the heart of critical thinking is a *willingness to face objections to one's own beliefs,* a willingness to adopt a skeptical attitude not only toward authority and toward views opposed to our own but also toward common sense—that is, toward the views that seem obviously right to us. If we assume we have a monopoly on the truth and we dismiss as bigots those who oppose us, or if we say our opponents are acting merely out of self-interest and we do not in fact analyze their views, we are being critical but we are not engaged in critical thinking.

> **A RULE FOR WRITERS:** Early in the process of jotting down your ideas on a topic, stop to ask yourself, "What might reasonably be offered as an *objection* to my view?"

Critical thinking requires us to use our *imaginations,* seeing things from perspectives other than our own and envisioning the likely consequences of our positions. (This sort of imaginative thinking—grasping a perspective other than our own and considering the possible consequences of positions—is, as we have said, very different from daydreaming, an activity of unchecked fantasy.)

Thinking critically involves, along with imagination (so that we can see our own beliefs from another point of view), a twofold activity:

analysis, finding the parts of the problem and then separating them, trying to see how things fit together; and

evaluation, judging the merit of our claims and assumptions and the weight of the evidence in their favor.

If we engage in imaginative, analytic, and evaluative thought, we will have second and third ideas; almost to our surprise we may find ourselves adopting a position that we initially couldn't imagine we would hold. As we think about the West Virginia law, we might find ourselves coming up with a fairly wide variety of ideas, each triggered by the preceding idea but not necessarily carrying it a step further. For instance, we may think *X* and then immediately think, "No, that's not quite right. In fact, come to think of it, the opposite of *X* is probably true." We haven't carried *X* further, but we have progressed in our thinking.

WRITING AS A WAY OF THINKING

"To learn to write," Robert Frost said, "is to learn to have ideas." But how do we get ideas? One way, practiced by the ancient Greeks and Romans and still regarded as among the best ways, is to consider what the ancients called **topics,** from the Greek word *topos,* meaning "place," as in our word *topography* (a description or representation of a place). For the ancients, certain topics, put into the form of questions, were in effect places where one went to find ideas. Among the classical *topics* were

- Definition (What is it?);
- Comparison (What is it like or unlike?);
- Relationship (What caused it, and what will it cause?); and
- Testimony (What is said about it, for instance, by experts?).

All of these topics or idea-generating places will be treated in detail in later chapters, but here we can touch briefly on a few of them.

If we are talking about the West Virginia law, it's true that we won't get ideas by asking questions concerning definition, but we may generate ideas by asking ourselves if this law is like any other (and, if so, how well did the corresponding law work) and by asking what caused this law and what it may in turn cause. Similarly, if we go to the topic of testimony, we may want to find out what some students, teachers, parents, police officers, and lawmakers have to say.

If you think you are at a loss for ideas when confronted with an issue (and when confronted with an assignment to write about it), you probably will find ideas coming to you if you turn to the relevant classical topics and begin jotting down your responses. (In classical terminology, you are engaged in the process of **invention,** from the Latin *invenire,* "to come upon," "to find.") Seeing your ideas on paper—even in the briefest form—will help bring other ideas to mind and will also help you to evaluate them. For instance, after jotting down ideas as they come and responses to them,

1. You might go on to organize them into two lists, pro and con;
2. Next, you might delete ideas that, when you come to think about them, strike you as simply wrong or irrelevant; and
3. Then you might develop those ideas that strike you as pretty good.

You probably won't know where you stand until you have gone through some such process. It would be nice if we could make a quick decision, immediately justify it with three excellent reasons, and then give three further reasons showing why the opposing view is inadequate. In fact, however, we almost never can come to a reasoned decision without a good deal of preliminary thinking.

Consider again the West Virginia law. Here is a kind of inner dialogue that you might engage in as you think critically about it:

The purpose is to give students an incentive to stay in school by making them pay a price if they choose to drop out.

Adolescents will get the message that education really is important. But come to think of it, *will* they? Maybe they will see this as just another example of adults bullying young people.

According to a newspaper article, the dropout rate in West Virginia decreased by 30 percent in the year after the bill was passed.

Well, that sounds good, but is there any reason to think that kids who are pressured into staying really learn anything? The *assumption* behind the bill is that if would-be dropouts stay in school, they—and society—will gain. But is the assumption sound? Maybe such students will become resentful, will not learn anything, and may even be so disruptive that they will interfere with the learning of other students.

Notice how part of the job is *analytic*, recognizing the elements or complexities of the whole, and part is *evaluative*, judging the adequacy of all of these ideas, one by one. Both tasks require *imagination*.

So far we have jotted down a few thoughts and then immediately given some second thoughts contrary to the first. Of course, the counter-thoughts might not immediately come to mind. For instance, they might not occur until we reread the jottings, or try to explain the law to a friend, or until we sit down and begin drafting an essay aimed at supporting or undermining the law. Most likely, in fact, some good ideas won't occur until a second or third or fourth draft.

Here are some further thoughts on the West Virginia law. We list them more or less as they arose and as we typed them into a computer—not sorted out neatly into two groups, pro and con, or evaluated as you would want to do in further critical thinking of your own. And of course, a later step would be to organize the material into some useful pattern. As you read, you might jot down your own responses in the margin.

Education is <u>not</u> optional, something left for the individual to take or not to take--like going to a concert, jogging, getting annual health checkups, or getting eight hours of sleep each night. Society has determined that it is <u>for the public good</u> that citizens have a substantial education, so we require education up to a certain age.

Come to think about it, maybe the criterion of age doesn't make much sense. If we want an educated citizenry, it would make more sense to require people to attend school until they demonstrated competence in certain matters rather than until they reached a certain age. Exceptions, of course, would be made for mentally retarded persons and perhaps for certain other groups.

What is needed is not legal pressure to keep teenagers in school but schools that hold the interest of teenagers.

A sixteen-year-old usually is not mature enough to make a decision of this importance.

Still, a sixteen-year-old who finds school unsatisfying and who therefore drops out may become a perfectly useful citizen.

Denying a sixteen-year-old a driver's license may work in West Virginia, but it would scarcely work in a state with great urban areas, where most high school students rely on public transportation.

We earn a driver's license by demonstrating certain skills. The state has no right to take away such a license unless we have demonstrated that we are unsafe drivers.

To prevent a person of sixteen from having a driver's license prevents that person from holding certain kinds of jobs, and that's unfair.

A law of this sort deceives adults into thinking that they have really done something constructive for teenage education, but it may work <u>against</u> improving the schools. It may be <u>counterproductive:</u> If we are really serious about educating youngsters, we have to examine the curriculum and the quality of our teachers.

Doubtless there is much that we haven't said, on both sides, but we hope you will agree that the issue deserves thought. In fact, several states now revoke the driver's license of a teenager who drops out of school, and four of these states go even further and revoke the licenses of students whose academic work does not reach a given standard. On the other hand, Louisiana, which for a while had a law like West Virginia's, dropped it in 1997.

If you were a member of a state legislature voting on this proposal, you would *have* to think about the issue. But just as a thought experiment, try to put into writing your tentative views.

One other point about this issue. If you had to think about the matter *today,* you might also want to know whether the West Virginia legislation of 1989 is considered a success and on what basis. That is, you would want to get answers to such questions as the following:

- What sort of evidence tends to support the law or tends to suggest that the law is a poor idea?
- Did the reduction in the dropout rate continue, or did the reduction occur only in the first year following the passage of the law?
- If indeed students who wanted to drop out did not, was their presence in school a good thing, both for them and for their classmates?
- Have some people emerged as authorities on this topic? What makes them authorities, and what do they have to say?

✓ A CHECKLIST FOR CRITICAL THINKING

Attitudes

☐ Does my thinking show imaginative open-mindedness and intellectual curiosity?

   ☐ Am I willing to examine my assumptions?

   ☐ Am I willing to entertain new ideas—both those that I encounter while reading and those that come to mind while writing?

   ☐ Am I willing to exert myself—for instance, to do research—to acquire information and to evaluate evidence?

Skills

☐ Can I summarize an argument accurately?

☐ Can I evaluate assumptions, evidence, and inferences?

☐ Can I present my ideas effectively—for instance, by organizing and by writing in a manner appropriate to my imagined audience?

- Has the constitutionality of the bill been tested? With what results?

Some of these questions require you to do **research** on the topic. The questions raise issues of fact, and some relevant evidence probably is available. If you are to arrive at a conclusion in which you can have confidence, you will have to do some research to find out what the facts are.

Even without doing any research, however, you might want to look over the ideas, pro and con, perhaps adding some totally new thoughts or perhaps modifying or even rejecting (for reasons that you can specify) some of those already given. If you do think a bit further about this issue, and we hope that you will, notice an interesting point about *your own* thinking: It probably is not *linear* (moving in a straight line from *A* to *B* to *C*) but *recursive*, moving from *A* to *C* and back to *B* or starting over at *C* and then back to *A* and *B*. By zigging and zagging almost despite yourself, you'll get to a conclusion that may finally seem correct. In retrospect it seems obvious; *now* you can chart a nice line from *A* to *B* to *C*—but that was not at all evident to you at the start.

A SHORT ESSAY ILLUSTRATING CRITICAL THINKING

When we read an essay, we expect the writer to have thought things through, at least to a considerable degree. We do not want to read every false start, every fuzzy thought, every ill-organized paragraph that the writer knocked off. Yes, writers make false starts, put down fuzzy thoughts, write ill-organized paragraphs, but then they revise and revise yet again, and they end by giving us a readable essay that seems effort-lessly written. Still—and here we get to our real point—in argumenta-tive essays, writers need to show their readers that they have made some effort; they need to show us *how* they got to their final (for the moment) views. It is not enough for the writer to say, "I believe *X*"; rather, the writer must in effect say, "I believe *X*—and I hope you will believe it also—because *Y* and *Z*, though attractive, just don't stand up to inquiry as well as *X* does. *Y* is superficially plausible, but . . . , and *Z*, which is an attractive alternative to *Y*, nevertheless fails because . . ."

Notice in the following short essay that Alan Dershowitz frequently brings up objections to his own position; that is, he shows his awareness of other views, and then tries to show why he thinks his position is preferable. In the very first paragraph he speaks of "a tradeoff between privacy and convenience." That is, he sees that the course he is advocat-ing ("convenience") has its cost, its downside. And in the third para-graph he says, "As a civil libertarian, I am instinctively skeptical of such tradeoffs. But . . ." In the fourth paragraph he says, "I can hear the ob-jections." He may not convince you, but we think you will probably grant that he does a pretty good job (though maybe not a perfect job) of scrutinizing his own thoughts.

Alan Dershowitz

Alan Dershowitz, educated at Brooklyn College and Yale Law School, is a profes-sor at the Harvard Law School. Among his books are Why Terrorism Works *(2002) and* Shouting Fire: Civil Liberties in a Turbulent Era *(2002). The fol-lowing essay was published in the* New York Times *on September 13, 2001—two days after the destruction of the Twin Towers at the World Trade Center.*

Why Fear National ID Cards?

At many bridges and tunnels across the country, drivers avoid long delays at the toll booths with an unobtrusive device that fits on a car's dashboard. Instead of fumbling for change, they drive right through; the device sends a radio signal that records their passage. They are billed later. It's a tradeoff between privacy and convenience: the toll-takers know more about you—when you entered and left Manhattan for instance—but you save time and money.

An optional national identity card could be used in a similar way, of-fering a similar kind of tradeoff: a little less anonymity for a lot more se-curity. Anyone who had the card could be allowed to pass through airports or building security more expeditiously, and anyone who opted out could be examined much more closely.

As a civil libertarian, I am instinctively skeptical of such tradeoffs. But I support a national identity card with a chip that can match the holder's fingerprint. It could be an effective tool for preventing terrorism, reducing the need for other law-enforcement mechanisms—especially racial and ethnic profiling—that pose even greater dangers to civil liberties.

I can hear the objections: What about the specter of Big Brother? What about fears of identity cards leading to more intrusive measures? (The National Rifle Association, for example, worries that a government that registered people might also decide to register guns.) What about fears that such cards would lead to increased deportation of illegal immigrants?

First, we already require photo IDs for many activities, including fly-   5
ing, driving, drinking and check-cashing. And fingerprints differ from photographs only in that they are harder to fake. The vast majority of Americans routinely carry photo IDs in their wallets and pocketbooks. These IDs are issued by state motor vehicle bureaus and other public and private entities. A national card would be uniform and difficult to forge or alter. It would reduce the likelihood that someone could, intentionally or not, get lost in the cracks of multiple bureaucracies.

The fear of an intrusive government can be addressed by setting criteria for any official who demands to see the card. Even without a national card, people are always being asked to show identification. The existence of a national card need not change the rules about when ID can properly be demanded. It is true that the card would facilitate the deportation of illegal immigrants. But President Bush has proposed giving legal status to many of the illegal immigrants now in this country. And legal immigrants would actually benefit from a national ID card that could demonstrate their status to government officials.

Finally, there is the question of the right to anonymity. I don't believe we can afford to recognize such a right in this age of terrorism. No such right is hinted at in the Constitution. And though the Supreme Court has identified a right to privacy, privacy and anonymity are not the same. American taxpayers, voters and drivers long ago gave up any right of anonymity without loss of our right to engage in lawful conduct within zones of privacy. Rights are a function of experience, and our recent experiences teach that it is far too easy to be anonymous—even to create a false identity—in this large and decentralized country. A national ID card would not prevent all threats of terrorism, but it would make it more difficult for potential terrorists to hide in open view, as many of the September 11 hijackers apparently managed to do.

A national ID card could actually enhance civil liberties by reducing the need for racial and ethnic stereotyping. There would be no excuse for hassling someone merely because he belongs to a particular racial or ethnic group if he presented a card that matched his print and that permitted his name to be checked instantly against the kind of computerized criminal-history retrieval systems that are already in use. (If there is too much personal information in the system, or if the information is being used improperly, that is a separate issue. The only information the card need contain is name, address, photo, and print.)

From a civil liberties perspective, I prefer a system that takes a little bit of freedom from all to one that takes a great deal of freedom and dignity from the few—especially since those few are usually from a racially or ethnically disfavored group. A national ID card would be much more effective in preventing terrorism than profiling millions of men simply because of their appearance.

Topics for Critical Thinking and Writing

1. One might say that Dershowitz doesn't recognize that an ID might serve not simply to *identify* but to *authorize*. That is, some people fear that if the government issues national identity cards, the government would soon be regulating whether we can buy knives or fertilizer or any other substance that the government considers dangerous, whether we can take flying lessons, and whether we can travel to certain destinations. Does Dershowitz take account of this objection—or is the objection so far-fetched that there is no reason for him to face it?

2. To the best of your knowledge, would an ID card such as Dershowitz advocates have helped to avert the disaster of September 11, 2001? If not, does his argument lose all force? Explain.

3. Dershowitz admits (para. 4) that one might argue against a national identity card on the grounds that it raises "the specter of Big Brother." What is Dershowitz's reply to this objection, and how convincing do you find it? By the way, where does the expression "Big Brother" come from?

4. Dershowitz mentions the "right to anonymity" (para. 7). Do we really have such a right? If so, can other morally important considerations conflict with this right? If they can, which should prevail, and why? Explain in an essay of 500 words.

5. Dershowitz says that the kind of national ID card he favors would have on it only the bearer's "name, address, photo, and [finger]print" (para. 8). Do you think the bearer's social security card number should be on it as well? Explain in an essay of 100 words.

6. Dershowitz's essay was first published as an op-ed piece in a newspaper. Write a letter to the editor explaining why you disagree with some or all of his points, or explaining why, although you accept some or all of his points, you think he has neglected others.

EXAMINING ASSUMPTIONS

In Chapter 3 we will discuss **assumptions** in some detail, but here we want to introduce the topic by emphasizing the importance of *identifying* and *examining* assumptions—the assumptions you will encounter in the writings of others and the assumptions you will rely on in your own essays.

With this in mind, let's return to considering the West Virginia driver's license law. What assumptions did the legislature make in enacting this statute? We earlier mentioned one such assumption: If the law helped to keep teenagers from dropping out of school, then that was a good thing for them and for society in general. For all we know, the advocates of this legislation may have made this assumption *explicit* in the course of their argument in favor of the statute. Perhaps they left this assumption *tacit*, believing that the point was obvious and that everyone shared this assumption. The assumption may be obvious, but it was not universally shared; the many teenagers who wanted to drop out of school at sixteen and keep their drivers' licenses did not share it.

Another assumption that the advocates of this legislation may have made is this:

> The provisions of this statute are the most efficient way to keep teenagers in high school.

Defending such an assumption is no easy task because it requires identifying other possible legislative strategies and evaluating their merits against those of the proposed legislation.

Consider now two of the assumptions involved in the Sultaana Freeman case. Thanks to the "clustering" exercise (pp. 5–7), these and other assumptions are already on display. Perhaps the most important and fundamental assumption Ms. Freeman made is this:

> Where private religious beliefs conflict with duly enacted laws, the former should prevail.

This assumption is widely shared in our society and is by no means unique to Muslim women seeking drivers' licenses in Florida after September 11, 2001. Freeman's opponents probably assumed a very different but equally fundamental proposition:

> Private religious practices and beliefs must yield to the demands of national security.

Obviously these two assumptions were on a collision course and neither side could hope to prevail so long as the key assumptions of the other side were ignored.

Finally, let us examine Dershowitz's essay defending a national ID card with an eye to identifying some of the assumptions made in the course of his argument. In his second paragraph, he asserts that "a lot more security" than we have at present is available to us through a national ID card. This assertion verges on being only an assumption, since it really isn't argued for. In paragraph 3, Dershowitz assumes that the in-

---

✓ A CHECKLIST FOR EXAMINING ASSUMPTIONS

□ What assumptions does the writer's argument presuppose?

□ Are these assumptions explicit or implicit?

□ Are these assumptions important to the author's argument or only incidental?

□ Does the author give any evidence of being aware of the hidden assumptions in her or his argument?

□ Would a critic be likely to share these assumptions, or are they exactly what a critic would challenge?

□ What sort of evidence would be relevant to supporting or rejecting these assumptions?

□ Am I willing to grant the author's assumptions?

   □ If not, why not?

---

vasion of privacy such a card would allow would make unnecessary "other law enforcement mechanisms" that are far more invasive (though he gives no examples). Finally, he assumes that it is better to take "a little bit of freedom from all" rather than "a great deal of freedom and dignity from the few."

Remember, also, to ask these questions (except the last two) when you are reading your own drafts. And remember to ask yourself why some people may *not* grant your assumptions.

Thinking about Wild Horses

And now for something completely different. Well, not really completely different, because we are still concerned with writing arguments, but let's get a breath of fresh air.

The following short essay by Deanne Stillman appeared in a newspaper, and it reports a piece of news—that the president of the United States had recently signed a bill that, in the words of the writer, "will destroy our greatest icon—the wild horse." We follow her essay with two letters that readers wrote, and we follow the letters with some topics for you to think and write about.

Deanne Stillman

Deanne Stillman, the author of *Twentynine Palms* (2001), is working on a book called *Horse Latitudes: Last Stand for the Wild Horse in the American West*. The essay that follows was originally published in the *Boston Globe* (March 5, 2006).

Last roundup for wild horses

People keep comparing George W. Bush to Richard Nixon. But that's wrong.

In 2005, President Bush signed legislation that will destroy our greatest icon—the wild horse. In 1971, President Nixon signed legislation protecting it. This was the Wild Free-Roaming Horses and Burro Act, a hard-fought bill brought to lawmakers by "Wild Horse Annie," a Nevada character who saw blood spilling from a truck hauling mustangs to the slaughterhouse, then dropped everything and spent the rest of her life trying to save them.

Now those trucks are revving their engines again. Starting on March 10, 7,200 wild horses in government pipelines will begin to make their way to the three horse slaughterhouses in this country—which are owned by France and Belgium.

In 1900, about 2 million wild horses roamed the West. By 1950, there were 50,000. Today, there are about 25,000—perhaps spelling doom for the mustang. What happened? World War I, the pet food industry, and cattle ranchers, who contend that the remaining wild horses steal food from 3 million cows on the range. In the old days, they hired contractors to gun down mustangs and bring them the ears. Today, Big Beef still hires guns—politicians who set policy for the Bureau of Land Management, the agency that presided over a recent fixed grazing study yet is supposed to protect the wild horse. Now, the animal America rode in on is facing its meanest battle.

Last year, Senator Conrad Burns of Montana, a Republican who 5 once referred to Bush as "the man who wears the spurs," attached a rider to the 2005 appropriations bill, permitting the Bureau of Land Management to sell horses it has rounded up that are over ten years old or haven't been adopted by the third try through its own program to be sold to the lowest bidder. But ten is not old for a horse, and it's not unusual for a horse to remain unadopted on the third try—there are barely enough adopters to take in the thousands of available horses (but those who do include the US Marine Corps Color Guard, which trains palominos from the Nevada range for parade duty—naming some after famous battles, including Montezuma Willy and Peking).

Days after Bush signed the bill, thirty-six horses criminalized as "three-strikers" ended up at the killer plants. A nationwide outcry led to a new bill, temporarily halting such sales by cutting off funding for federal meat inspectors at the slaughterhouses. But Department of Agriculture Secretary Mike Johanns—a friend to the meat lobby—has done an end-run around the legislation, granting petitioners of the slaughterhouses permission to hire their own inspectors, beginning on March 10.

Wild horses run through the California desert. Only about 25,000 wild horses remain.

Last week, the second bell for the mustang tolled. With thousands of wild horses about to hit the market, the Bureau of Land Management announced a partnership with the Public Lands Council, urging public lands ranchers to buy wild horses for $10 each and put them back on the range. But the Public Lands Council consists of the National Cattlemen's Beef Association, the American Sheep Industry, and the Association of National Grasslands—the very people who have been trying to expunge wild horses for years.

Wild horse advocates fear that some ranchers, businessmen after all, will turn around and sell the horses to the slaughterhouse. Making the plan even more suspicious is the fact that the wild horses are simply not returned to the land, which supposedly could not support them in the first place.

Conrad Burns is right—the president is wearing the spurs. And he's driving our greatest partner off a cliff. So next time you see Montezuma Willy and Peking at a parade, take a picture and say goodbye. Or, join the posse and stop the horse thief at the pass.

"Wild horses and burros merit man's protection historically," Nixon 10 said, "for they are a living link with the days of the conquistadors, through the heroic times of the western Indians and pioneers, to our own day when the tonic of wilderness seems all too scarce. More than

---

✓ A CHECKLIST FOR EVALUATING LETTERS OF RESPONSE

After reading the letters responding to an editorial or to a previous letter, go back and read each letter with the following questions in mind:

☐ What assumption(s) does the letter-writer make? Do you share the assumption(s)?

☐ What is the writer's claim?

☐ What evidence, if any, does the writer offer to support the claim?

☐ Is there anything about the style of the letter—the distinctive use of language, the tone—that makes the letter especially engaging or especially annoying?

---

that, they merit it as a matter of ecological right—as anyone knows who has ever stood awed at the indomitable spirit and sheer energy of a mustang running free."

TOPICS FOR CRITICAL THINKING AND WRITING

1. Suppose a reader of Stillman's essay were to argue that all she has done is assemble a bunch of sentimental feelings rather than give any cogent reasons to support the government policy toward wild horses that she favors. How might you respond on her behalf?

2. On what grounds does Stillman assert that wild horses "'merit [survival] as a matter of ecological right'" (para. 10)? Do you agree? Why, or why not?

With these questions in mind—and others of your own invention—read the following two letters of response to Stillman.

Letters of Response
by Holly Williams and Tom Burke

To the Editor:

It is astonishing that legislation has been signed that will destroy the wild horse in America (op-ed, March 6). Next to the flag and the bald eagle, the wild mustang is the greatest symbol of America that we have. The wild horse is the very symbol of the West, and not only of the West but of the entire country, because it was through the West, by means of the horse, that the East extended exploration to the Pacific. Do the growers of beef not realize that without the cowboys' horses there would be no cattle industry today?

This is not a Democratic issue or a Republican issue; it is an American issue, and historically both parties have realized that we have a duty to protect these creatures that are a living link with our past. It is high noon but it is still not too late for Congress to pass new legislation that will protect the animal that in effect is a national symbol.

Holly Williams
Boston, Mass., March 6, 2006

To the Editor:

Deanne Stillman's argument essentially appeals to our emotions, with talk about "the indomitable spirit and sheer energy of a mustang running free" and "driving our greatest partner off a cliff," and that's probably OK, but really, who considers a horse "our greatest partner"? It's fine to talk about our great American heritage, and it's fine to express our love of animals (I myself have a dog and my wife has a cat), but let's also try to be reasonable.

First of all, as Stillman admits, only three-time losers and only older horses are selected for harvesting. Second, Stillman never tells the reader that the land is overgrazed and that the horses deprive cattle of forage. Nor does Stillman recognize the fact that because the land is overgrazed, some horses will probably starve to death. Yes, the government might collect the older (weaker) horses who might starve, and the government could put them in pens, but is this solution—weak old horses kept in pens until they die—really preferable to the quick clean death of a bullet, a bullet that allows *younger horses to live?*

Let's be reasonable. Let's value our heritage, and let's respect the wild horses by recognizing that a humane death for a few will allow the others to run free.

Tom Burke
Cambridge, Mass., March 6, 2006

Topics for Critical Thinking and Writing

1. Consider the first letter as an argument. Does it offer any appeals to reason? To emotion? Does the writer present himself as the sort of person with whom a reader would want to agree? How effective do you think the letter is? Please explain your response.

2. Consider the second letter, again from the point of view of the nature of its appeal—to reason, to the emotions, to the reader's sense that the writer is a person of intelligence and goodwill.

3. Write your own letter to the editor, indicating your reasons for supporting Stillman, or for supporting the view that the number of horses should be reduced. Or, perhaps in the light of Stillman's essay and the two responses, you might take a different position. For instance, you might suggest an alternative way to save the horses.

Here is an essay submitted early in the semester by a student in a first-year writing course. Students were asked to write 750 to 1,000 words on some issue that they had read about in the newspapers, such as legalizing gay marriage, allowing prayer in school, raising the minimum wage, or criminalizing the burning of the American flag.

Luke Saginaw

Why Flag-Burning Should Not Be Permitted

As recently as a year and a half ago, on June 27, 2006, the Senate defeated—by a single vote—a proposed constitutional amendment to prohibit desecration of the flag. The text of the proposed amendment was this: "The Congress shall have power to prohibit the physical desecration of the flag of the United States" (qtd. in Hulse A1). I want to explain why, if I had been in the Senate, I would have voted for the proposed amendment.

First, let's look at the reasons offered *against* the proposal. Newspaper editorials made two points against the proposed amendment. First, they argued that flag-burning is passé; it was fairly common during the Vietnam era, but there has been only a handful of reported instances in the last year or two. But if we were talking about, say, torturing a gay man or a lesbian woman, who would say that that the *number* of offenses was relevant? A single case would be one more than enough to criminalize the action.

Second, the editorials arguing against the proposal claimed that it was incompatible with the protection of freedom of speech that the Constitution offers. In fact, however, the Constitution says nothing at all about desecrating the flag. The First Amendment guarantees freedom of speech, but burning a flag is not speech by any reasonable definition. Yes, the Supreme Court ruled that it is "symbolic speech" (*Texas v. Johnson*) but "speech" means (or should mean) something like the coherent use of words. Further, the Constitution guarantees free speech because it wants to guarantee the free exchange of political ideas. It does *not* guarantee "free expression"; if it did, people who believed that they can express themselves best by walking naked through the streets or by urinating in public would have a constitutional right to do so. Suppose someone said that, by way of freedom of expression, as a protest against the war in Iraq he wanted to dance on the grave of a buried American soldier in Arlington National Cemetery. Would we say that this action is "symbolic speech" and is therefore protected by the Constitution? Surely not; flag-burning is *conduct*, not speech.

Probably most people will agree that the Constitution does not guarantee all kinds of conduct including conduct that is said to be "self-expression." The flag-burners by their behavior may well be expressing their feelings, but they are hardly engaging in political argument, hardly behaving in a way that might conceivably change someone's mind. In fact, flag-burning is counterproductive; far from changing the opinions of someone who (for instance) supports the war in Iraq, flag-burning is likely to cause such a person to support it even more strongly.

Flag-burning, in short, is *not* speech, and we should recognize that to call it speech is to use words in a Humpty Dumpty *Alice in Wonderland* fashion: "When I use a word . . . it means just what I choose it to mean—neither more nor less" (Carroll). But let's now look at arguments supporting the amendment to forbid burning the flag. First of all, various polls indicate that at least 70 percent of the people of the United States support it. Many articles in newspapers say that *if* the Congress does pass such a bill and then allows state legislatures to vote, the states will surely approve. It seems to be widely agreed that a vast majority of Americans would like to see flag-burning criminalized. In short, members of Congress should support the proposal because they are the representatives of the people, and their constituents support it.

Second, the flag is something very special. No one argues that protesters should not be allowed to burn an effigy of the president of the United Sates, or that stand-up comics should not be allowed to make political jokes about politicians, or that the general public should not be allowed to write angry letters to newspapers. No, we are talking about something very special, the American flag. Yes, it is only a piece of cloth, and it may even have been manufactured in China, but it is something that people have literally died for, *literally* died for. We have all seen the photograph of marines raising the American flag on Iwo Jima, a battle that cost hundreds of American lives. And we have seen flag-draped coffins of Americans who died in battle and whose bodies are being returned to the country they gave their lives for. Respect for the dead, and for their families and friends, would be a good enough reason to criminalize flag-burning. There are other ways of protesting, such as speaking and writing, and even burning the Constitution. That is, if someone wants to argue that a particular action of the government shows disregard for the Constitution—for example, wire-tapping—they might burn a copy, indicating that in their view the present administration no longer respects the Constitution. Such action would be disturbing and thought-provoking, but probably no one would call it sacrilegious. But the flag, perhaps because it has literally been carried into battle and has draped the coffins of fallen soldiers, is something richer in symbolism, richer in the emotional chords that it touches, than even the Constitution.

Our nation recognizes that certain kinds of violation of the emotions of others should indeed be criminalized. We recognize what are called "hate crimes"; we recognize that there is something criminal about assaulting people because of their race or their religion or their sexual identity. Surely the attachment that most Americans have to their flag, like their attachment to their religion, is something that our government ought to protect against assaults. Again, no one is saying that protesters cannot say whatever they want about any issue, or any politician, or any particular political administration, or even about America in general. If someone wants to say that they think America has lost its way, is no longer the America envisioned by the Founding Fathers, they are free to say so and we will listen, and respond. We may even be persuaded. But they should not be free to burn our flag, to desecrate the symbol that Americans have died for.

WORKS CITED

Carroll, Lewis. *Alice's Adventures in Wonderland. Project Gutenberg.* Project Guten-
berg Literary Archive Foundation, 1 Jan. 1991. Web. 13 Feb. 2006.
Hulse, Carl. "Flag Amendment Narrowly Fails in Senate Vote." *New York Times* 28
June 2006, natl. ed.: A1+. Print.
Texas v. Johnson. 491 US 397. Supreme Court of the US. 1989. *Supreme Court Col-
lection.* Legal Information Inst., Cornell U Law School, n.d. Web. 13 Feb. 2006.

TOPICS FOR CRITICAL THINKING AND WRITING

1. In a short paragraph explain the difference between favoring freedom of speech and favoring freedom of expression.

2. Saginaw insists that "flag-burning is *conduct,* not 'speech'" (para. 3). Do you agree? Why, or why not?

3. Why not concede that it is wrong to desecrate the flag but insist that it is a bad idea to make it a criminal offense?

4. How persuasive an argument is it that "a vast majority of Americans would like to see flag-burning criminalized" (para. 5)?

5. In the third paragraph Saginaw uses the word *desecrating,* in the seventh *sacrilegious,* and in the final sentence *desecrate.* Are these words appropriate, and are they effective? (If you are uncertain about their exact meanings, consult a dictionary.)

6. Does Saginaw omit any counterarguments that you think demand attention? If so, what are the counterarguments, and how might the writer have attempted to respond to them?

7. What assumptions — explicit or implicit — does Saginaw make?

8. Is flag-burning antipatriotic? Explain your response.

9. Putting aside your own views on the issue, what grade would you give this essay as a work of argumentative writing? Support your evaluation with reasons.

FIVE EXERCISES IN CRITICAL THINKING

1. Think further about the 1989 West Virginia law that prohibits high school dropouts younger than eighteen from holding a driver's license. Jot down pros and cons, and then write a balanced dialogue between

two imagined speakers who hold opposing views on the merits of the law. You'll doubtless have to revise your dialogue several times, and in revising your drafts you will find that further ideas come to you. Present *both* sides as strongly as possible. (You may want to give the two speakers distinct characters; for instance, one may be a student who has dropped out and the other a concerned teacher, or one a parent—who perhaps argues that he or she needs the youngster to work full-time driving a delivery truck—and one a legislator. But do not write as if the speakers must present the arguments they might be expected to hold. A student might argue *for* the law, and a teacher *against* it.)

2. Take one of the following topics and jot down all the pro and con arguments you can think of in, say, ten minutes. Then, at least an hour or two later, return to your jottings and see whether you can add to them. Finally, as in Exercise 1, write a balanced dialogue, presenting each idea as strongly as possible. (If none of these topics interests you, talk with your instructor about the possibility of choosing a topic of your own.) Suggested topics:

   a. Colleges should not award athletic scholarships.
   b. Bicyclists and motorcyclists should be required by law to wear helmets.
   c. High school teachers should have the right to search students for drugs on school grounds.
   d. Smoking should be prohibited in all parts of all college buildings.
   e. College administrators should take no punitive action against students who use racist language or language that offends any minority.
   f. Students should have the right to drop out of school at any age.
   g. In rape trials, the names of the alleged victims should not be released to the public.
   h. The United States ought to require a national identity card.

3. On the evening of July 31, 2001, after court employees had left the Alabama Judicial Building in Montgomery, Chief Justice Roy S. Moore of the Alabama Supreme Court and his supporters installed in the lobby of the courthouse a four-foot high, 5,200 pound granite block bearing the text of the Ten Commandments. Moore had not discussed his plan with other justices. Civil liberties groups complained that the monument was an unconstitutional attempt to endorse a specific religion (the First Amendment to the U.S. Constitution says, "Congress shall make no law respecting an establishment of religion"), and in 2002 a federal judge ordered Moore to remove the monument. He refused, saying that the monument is a symbol of the roots of American law. He also said, "To do my duty, I must obey God." His supporters have offered several arguments on his behalf, notably that (a) the Founding Fathers often spoke of God; (b) every courtroom has a Bible to swear in witnesses and jurors; (c) the U.S. Supreme Court has a frieze of lawgivers, including Moses with the Ten Commandments, Hammurabi, Confucius, and Muhammad. In August 2003, Moore was suspended from his position on the court, and the monument was removed from view. Your views?

4. Since 1937, when San Francisco's Golden Gate Bridge opened, some 1,200 people have leaped from it to their deaths. The board of the Golden Gate Bridge, Highway and Transportation District periodically contemplates plans to make it suicide-proof. It discusses the kinds of devices proposed (railings, nets, or a combination), the cost (an estimated $15.25 million, which could be used for other civic purposes), the aesthetic factor (the devices may spoil the appearance of this renowned art deco work), and the engineering uncertainties (some engineers express reservations about the aerodynamic drag the barrier may create). And now consider these additional arguments against altering the bridge: (a) the government has no business paternalistically interfering with the free will of persons who wish to commit suicide; (b) if the Golden Gate Bridge is made suicide-proof, persons who wish to commit suicide will easily find some other site, such as the nearby Bay Bridge; (c) only 3 percent of the persons who commit suicide in the Bay Area do so by leaping from the bridge.

   The assignment: You are on the board of the Golden Gate Bridge. Suicides on the bridge are now averaging two a month, and a proposal to make the bridge suicide-proof has come up. Taking account of the arguments just mentioned, and any others—pro and con—that you can think of, what is your well-reasoned 500-word response?

5. In September 2004, the year of a presidential election, the Bush-Cheney campaign approached Allegheny College (in northwest Pennsylvania), asking to rent for October 13 the college's gymnasium, the largest enclosed space in the area. Because the electoral votes of Pennsylvania were uncertain, Vice President Cheney's appearance at Allegheny was likely to get national attention, at least briefly. The college did *not* have in place a policy against renting space to a political organization, so refusal to rent the gymnasium might seem like discrimination against the Republican Party. Further, the college faculty and administrators involved in making the decision concluded that the event would strengthen

town/gown relationships and energize the students to participate in the political process. The gymnasium was therefore rented to the Bush-Cheney campaign, so that the vice president could appear.

The event was a sort of town-hall-style presentation, but tickets were limited: The campaign personnel distributed most of the six hundred tickets to local Republican activists; forty tickets were given to a group called College Republicans, who could distribute the tickets as they saw fit. Obviously the idea was to keep out hecklers and demonstrators, an entirely reasonable plan from the Republican point of view. Why should Republicans rent a hall and stage an event that might get national coverage if the opposing party could use it to get TV attention?

The issue: Should a college—supposedly a site where inquiry is open, where ideas are exchanged freely in robust debate—allow its facilities to be used by those who would stifle debate? Professor Daniel M. Shea, who initially favored the decision to rent the gymnasium, ultimately concluded that he was mistaken. In an essay in the *Chronicle of Higher Education* (August 4, 2006), Shea discusses the affair, and he suggests that colleges and universities ought to band together to "form an open-event alliance." Candidates might have at their disposal half of the available seats, but the other half would be for the college to distribute through some sort of open procedure, perhaps a lottery.

The assignment: Assume that a political party wanted to rent your institution's gymnasium or a large lecture hall. What would your position be? Why? In a letter of about 500 words addressed to the college paper, set forth your views.

2

Critical Reading: Getting Started

Some books are to be tasted, others to be chewed, and some few to be chewed and digested.

— FRANCIS BACON

ACTIVE READING

In the passage that we quote at the top of this page, Bacon makes at least two good points. One is that books are of varying worth; the second is that a taste of some books may be enough.

But even a book (or an essay) that you will chew and digest is one that you first may want to taste. How can you get a taste—that is, how can you get some sense of a piece of writing *before* you sit down to read it carefully?

Previewing

Even before you read a work, you may have some ideas about it, perhaps because you already know something about the **author.** You know, for example, that a work by Martin Luther King Jr. will probably deal with civil rights. You know, too, that it will be serious and eloquent. On the other hand, if you pick up an essay by Woody Allen, you will probably expect it to be amusing. It may be serious—Allen has written earnestly about many topics, especially those concerned with the media— but it's your hunch that the essay will be at least somewhat entertaining and probably will not be terribly difficult to understand. In short, a reader who has some knowledge of the author probably has some idea of what the writing will be like, and so the reader reads it in a certain mood. Admittedly, most of the authors represented in this book are not widely known, but we give biographical notes that may provide you with some sense of what to expect.

The **place of publication** may also tell you something about the essay. For instance, the *National Review* is a conservative journal. If you notice that an essay on affirmative action was published in the *National*

Review, you are probably safe in tentatively assuming that the essay will not endorse affirmative action. On the other hand, *Ms. Magazine* is a liberal publication, and an essay on affirmative action published in *Ms.* will probably be an endorsement.

The **title** of an essay, too, may give you an idea of what to expect. Of course, a title may announce only the subject and not the author's thesis or point of view ("On Gun Control," "Should Drugs Be Legal?"), but fairly often it will indicate the thesis too, as in "Give Children the Vote" and "Gay Marriages: Make Them Legal." Knowing more or less what to expect, you can probably take in some of the major points even on a quick reading.

Skimming: Finding the Thesis

Although most of the material in this book is too closely argued to be fully understood by merely skimming, still, skimming can tell you a good deal. Read the first paragraph of an essay carefully because it may announce the author's **thesis** (chief point, major claim), and it may give you some sense of how the argument for that thesis will be conducted. (What we call the *thesis* can also be called the *main idea,* the *point,* or even the *argument,* but in this book we use *argument* to refer not only to the thesis statement but also to the entire development of the thesis in the essay.) Run your eye over the rest, looking for key expressions that indicate the author's conclusions, such as "It follows, then, that . . ." Passages of this sort often occur as the first or last sentence in a paragraph. And of course, pay attention to any headings within the text. Finally, pay special attention to the last paragraph because it probably will offer a summary and a brief restatement of the writer's thesis.

Having skimmed the work, you probably know the author's thesis, and you may detect the author's methods—for instance, whether the author supports the thesis chiefly by personal experience, by statistics, or by ridiculing the opposition. You also have a clear idea of the length and some idea of the difficulty of the piece. You know, then, whether you can read it carefully now before dinner or whether you had better put off a careful reading until you have more time.

Reading with a Pencil: Underlining, Highlighting, Annotating

Once you have a general idea of the work—not only an idea of its topic and thesis but also a sense of the way in which the thesis is argued—you can then go back and start reading it carefully.

As you read, **underline** or **highlight** key passages, and make **annotations** in the margins (but not in library books, please). Because you are reading actively, or interacting with the text, you will not simply let your eye rove across the page. You will underline or highlight what seem to be the chief points, so that later when you review the essay you can easily locate the main passages. But don't overdo a good thing. If you find yourself underlining or highlighting most of a page, you are probably not thinking carefully enough about what the key points are. Similarly, your marginal annotations should be brief and selective. Probably they will consist of hints or clues, things like "really?," "doesn't follow," "!!!," "???," "good," "compare with Jones," and "check this." In short, in a paragraph you might underline or highlight a key definition, and in the margin you might write "good" or, on the other hand, "?," if you think the definition is fuzzy or wrong. You are interacting with the text and laying the groundwork for eventually writing your own essay on what you have read.

What you annotate will depend largely on your **purpose.** If you are reading an essay in order to see the ways in which the writer organizes an argument, you will annotate one sort of thing. If you are reading in order to challenge the thesis, you will annotate other things. Here is a passage from an essay entitled "On Racist Speech," with a student's rather skeptical, even aggressive annotations. But notice that at least one of the annotations—"Definition of 'fighting words'"—apparently was made chiefly in order to remind the reader of where an important term appears in the essay. The essay, printed in full on page 55, is by Charles R. Lawrence III, a professor of law at Georgetown University. It originally appeared in the *Chronicle of Higher Education* (October 25, 1989), a publication read chiefly by college and university faculty members and administrators.

Example of such a policy?

University officials who have formulated <u>policies</u> to respond to incidents of racial harassment have been characterized in the press as "thought police," but such policies generally do nothing more than impose ⟨sanctions⟩ against intentional face-to-face insults. When *What about* racist speech takes the form of <u>face-to-face insults</u>, catcalls, or other *sexist speech?* assaultive speech aimed at an <u>individual or small</u> group of persons, *ample?* it falls directly within the "fighting words" exception to First Amend- *Definition* ment protection. The Supreme Court has held that <u>words which</u> *of "fighting* "<u>by their very utterance inflict injury</u> or tend to <u>incite an immediate *words"*</u> breach of the peace" are not protected by the First Amendment.

If the purpose of the First Amendment is to foster the greatest amount of speech, racial insults disserve that purpose. Assaultive racist speech functions as a preemptive strike. The <u>invective is</u> <u>experienced as a blow, not as a proffered idea,</u> and once the blow is *Really?* struck, it is unlikely that a dialogue will follow. Racial insults are *Probably* particularly undeserving of First Amendment protection because *depends on* *ay must* the perpetrator's <u>intention is not to discover truth</u> or initiate *the individual.* *eech* dialogue but to injure the victim. <u>In most situations,</u> members *vays* of minority groups realize that they are likely to lose if they *How does he* *ek "to* respond to epithets by fighting and are forced to remain silent *know?* *cover* and submissive. *th"?*

"This; Therefore, That"

To arrive at a coherent thought or a coherent series of thoughts that will lead to a reasonable conclusion, a writer has to go through a good deal of preliminary effort. And if the writer is to convince the reader that the conclusion is sound, the reasoning that led to the conclusion must be set forth in detail, with a good deal of "This; therefore, that"; If this, then that"; and "It might be objected at this point that . . ." The arguments in this book require more comment than President Calvin Coolidge provided when his wife, who hadn't been able to go to church on a Sunday, asked him what the preacher's sermon was about. "Sin," he said. His wife persisted: "What did the preacher say about it?" Coolidge's response: "He was against it."

But, again, when we say that most of the arguments in this book are presented at length and require careful reading, we do not mean that they are obscure; we mean, rather, that the reader has to take the sentences thoughtfully, one by one. And speaking of one by one, we are reminded of an episode in Lewis Carroll's *Through the Looking-Glass:*

> "Can you do Addition?" the White Queen asked. "What's one and one and one and one and one and one and one and one and one and one?"
> "I don't know," said Alice. "I lost count."
> "She can't do Addition," the Red Queen said.

It's easy enough to add one and one and one and so on, and Alice can, of course, do addition, but not at the pace that the White Queen sets. Fortunately, you can set your own pace in reading the cumulative thinking set forth in the essays we reprint. Skimming won't work, but slow reading — and thinking about what you are reading — will.

When you first pick up an essay, you may indeed want to skim it, for some of the reasons mentioned on page 32, but sooner or later you have to settle down to read it and to think about it. The effort will be worthwhile. John Locke, the seventeenth-century English philosopher, said,

> *Reading* furnishes the mind with materials of knowledge; it is *thinking* [that] makes what we read ours. We are of the ruminating kind, and it is not enough to cram ourselves with a great load of collections; unless we chew them over again they will not give us strength and nourishment.

First, Second, and Third Thoughts

Suppose you are reading an argument about pornographic pictures. For the present purpose, it doesn't matter whether the argument favors or opposes censorship. As you read the argument, ask yourself whether *pornography* has been adequately defined. Has the writer taken the trouble to make sure that the reader and the writer are thinking about the same thing? If not, the very topic under discussion has not been adequately fixed; and therefore further debate over the issue may well be so unclear as to be futile. How, then, ought a topic such as this be defined for effective critical thinking?

It goes without saying that pornography can't be defined simply as pictures of nude figures or even of nude figures copulating, for such a definition would include not only photographs taken for medical, sociological, and scientific purposes but also some of the world's great art. Nobody seriously thinks that such images should be called pornography.

Is it enough, then, to say that pornography "stirs lustful thoughts" or "appeals to prurient interests"? No, because pictures of shoes probably stir lustful thoughts in shoe fetishists, and pictures of children in ads for underwear probably stir lustful thoughts in pedophiles. Perhaps, then, the definition must be amended to "material that stirs lustful thoughts in the average person." But will this restatement do? First, it may be hard to agree on the characteristics of "the average person." In other matters, the law often does assume that there is such a creature as "the reasonable person," and most people would agree that in a given situation there might be a reasonable response—for almost everyone. But we cannot be so sure that the same is true about the emotional responses of this "average person." In any case, far from stimulating sexual impulses, sadomasochistic pictures of booted men wielding whips on naked women probably turn off "the average person," yet this is the sort of material that most people would agree is pornographic.

Something must be wrong, then, with the definition that pornography is material that "stirs lustful thoughts in the average person." We began with a definition that was too broad ("pictures of nude figures"), but now we have a definition that is too narrow. We must go back to the drawing board. This is not nitpicking. The label "average person" was found to be inadequate in a pornography case argued before the Supreme Court; because the materials in question were aimed at a homosexual audience, it was agreed that the average person would not find them sexually stimulating.

One difficulty has been that pornography is often defined according to its effect on the viewer ("genital commotion," Father Harold Gardiner, S.J., called it, in *Catholic Viewpoint on Censorship*), but different people, we know, may respond differently. In the first half of the twentieth century, in an effort to distinguish between pornography and art—after all, most people don't want to regard Botticelli's *Venus* or Michelangelo's *David* as "dirty"—it was commonly said that a true work of art does not stimulate in the spectator ideas or desires that the real object might stimulate. But in 1956, Kenneth Clark, probably the most influential English-speaking art critic of the twentieth century, changed all that; in a book called *The Nude* he announced that "no nude, however abstract, should fail to arouse in the spectator some vestige of erotic feeling."

SUMMARIZING AND PARAPHRASING

Perhaps the best approach to a fairly difficult essay is, after first reading, to reread it and simultaneously to take notes on a sheet of paper, perhaps summarizing each paragraph in a sentence or two. Writing a summary will help you to

- Understand the contents and
- See the strengths and weaknesses of the piece.

Don't confuse a summary with a paraphrase. A paraphrase is a word-by-word or phrase-by-phrase rewording of a text, a sort of translation of the author's language into your own. A paraphrase is therefore as long as the original or even longer; a summary is much shorter. A book may be summarized in a page, or even in a paragraph or a sentence. Obviously the summary will leave out all detail, but—if the summary is a true summary—it accurately states the gist, the essential thesis or claim or point of the original.

Why would anyone ever summarize, and why would anyone ever paraphrase? Because, as we have already said, these two activities—in different ways—help readers follow the original author's ideas. But, again, summarizing and paraphrasing are not the same.

- **When you summarize,** you are standing back, saying very briefly what the whole adds up to; you are seeing the forest, not the individual trees.
- **When you paraphrase,** you are inching through the forest, scrutinizing each tree—that is, finding a synonym for almost every word in the original, in an effort to make sure that you know exactly what you are dealing with. (*Caution:* Do not incorporate a summary or a paraphrase into your own essay without acknowledging your source and stating that you are summarizing or paraphrasing.)

Let's examine the distinction between summary and paraphrase in connection with the first two paragraphs of Paul Goodman's essay, "A Proposal to Abolish Grading," which is excerpted from Goodman's book, *Compulsory Miseducation and the Community of Scholars* (1966). The two paragraphs run thus:

> Let half a dozen of the prestigious universities—Chicago, Stanford, the Ivy League—abolish grading, and use testing only and entirely for pedagogic purposes as teachers see fit.
>
> Anyone who knows the frantic temper of the present schools will understand the transvaluation of values that would be effected by this modest innovation. For most of the students, the competitive grade has come to be the essence. The naive teacher points to the beauty of the subject and the ingenuity of the research; the shrewd student asks if he is responsible for that on the final exam.

A **summary** of these two paragraphs might run thus:

> If some top universities used tests only to help students to learn, students would stop worrying about grades and might share the teacher's interest in the beauty of the subject.

We hope we have accurately summarized Goodman's point, though we know we have lost his flavor, his style—for instance, the wry tone in his pointed contrast between "the naive teacher" and "the shrewd student."

Now for a **paraphrase**. Suppose you are not quite sure what Goodman is getting at, maybe because you are uncertain about the meanings of some words (perhaps *pedagogic* and *transvaluation*?), or maybe just because the whole passage is making such a startling point that you want to make sure that you have understood it. In such a case, you may want to move slowly through the sentences, translating them (so to speak) into your own English. For instance, you might turn Goodman's "pedagogic purposes" into "goals in teaching" or "attempts to help students to learn," or some such thing. Here is a paraphrase—not a summary but an extensive rewording—of Goodman's paragraphs:

> Suppose some of the top universities—such as Chicago, Stanford, Harvard, and Yale, and whatever other schools are in the Ivy League—stopped using grades and used tests only in order to help students to learn.
>
> Everyone who is aware of the hysterical mood in schools today will understand the enormous change in views of what is good and bad that would come about by this small change. At present, instructors, unworldly folk, talk about how beautiful their subjects are, but smart students know that grades are what count, so they listen to instructors only if they know that the material the instructor is talking about will be on the exam.

In short, you may want to paraphrase an important text that your imagined reader may find obscure because it is written in specialized, technical language, for instance, the language of psychiatry or of sociology. You want the reader to see the passage itself—you don't want to give just the gist, just a summary—but you know that the full passage will puzzle the reader, so you offer help, giving a paraphrase before going on to make your own point about the author's point.

A second good reason to offer a paraphrase is if there is substantial disagreement about what the text says. The Second Amendment to the U.S. Constitution is a good example of this sort of text:

> A well regulated Militia being necessary to the security of a free State, the right of the people to keep and bear Arms shall not be infringed.

Exactly what, one might ask, is a "Militia"? And what does it mean for a militia to be "well regulated"? And does "the people" mean each individual, or does it mean—something very different—the citizenry as some sort of unified group? After all, elsewhere in the document, when the Constitution speaks of individuals, it speaks of a "man" or a "person," not "the people." To speak of "the people" is to use a term (some argue) that sounds like a reference to a unified group—perhaps the citizens of each of the thirteen states?—rather than a reference to individuals. On the other hand, if Congress did mean a unified group rather than individuals, why didn't it say "Congress shall not prohibit the states from organizing militias"?

In fact, thousands of pages have been written about this sentence, and if you are going to talk about it, you certainly have to let your reader know exactly what you make out of each word. In short, you almost surely will paraphrase it, going word by word, giving your reader your sense of what each word or phrase says. Here is one paraphrase:

> Because an independent society needs the protection of an armed force if it is to remain free, the government may not limit the right of the individuals (who may some day form the militia needed to keep the society free) to possess weapons.

In this interpretation, the Constitution grants individuals the right to possess weapons, and that is that. Other students of the Constitution, however, offer very different paraphrases, usually along these lines:

> Because each state that is now part of the United States may need to protect its freedom [from the new national government], the national government may not infringe on the right of each state to form its own disciplined militia.

This second paraphrase says that the federal government may not prevent each state from having a militia; it says nothing about every individual person having a right to possess weapons. The first of these two paraphrases, or something like it, is one that might be offered by the National Rifle Association or any other group that interprets the Constitution as guaranteeing individuals the right to own guns. The second paraphrase, or something like it, might be offered by groups that seek to limit the ownership of guns.

Why paraphrase? Here are two reasons (perhaps the *only* two reasons) why you might paraphrase a passage:

- To help yourself to understand it. In this case, the paraphrase does not appear in your essay.

- To help your reader to understand a passage that is especially important but that for one reason or another is not immediately clear. In this case, you paraphrase the passage to let the reader know exactly what it means. This paraphrase, of course, does appear in your essay.

A Note about Paraphrase and Plagiarism

If you offer a paraphrase, be sure to tell the reader, explicitly, what you are doing and why you are doing it. If you do not explicitly say that you are paraphrasing Jones's material, you are plagiarizing. If you merely cite the author ("As Jones says") and then you give a paraphrase, you are plagiarizing. How, you may ask, can you be accused of plagiarism if you cite your source? Here is how: If you do not explicitly say that you are paraphrasing Jones, the reader assumes you have digested Jones's point and are giving it in a summary form, entirely in your own words; the reader does not think (unless you *say* that you are paraphrasing) that you are merely following Jones's passage phrase by phrase, sentence by sentence, changing some words but not really writing *your own* sentences. In short, when you paraphrase you are translating, not writing. (For a further comment on plagiarism, see page 269.)

> **A RULE FOR WRITERS:** Your essay is *likely to include brief summaries* of points of view that you are agreeing or disagreeing with, but it will *rarely include a paraphrase* unless the original is obscure and you think you need to present a passage at length but in words that are clearer than those of the original. If you do paraphrase, explicitly identify the material as a paraphrase.

Last Words (Almost) about Summarizing

Summarizing each paragraph or each group of closely related paragraphs will help you to follow the thread of the discourse and, when you are finished, will provide you with a useful map of the essay. Then, when you reread the essay yet again, you may want to underline passages that you now understand are the author's key ideas—for instance, definitions, generalizations, summaries—and you may want to jot notes in the margins, questioning the logic, expressing your uncertainty, or calling attention to other writers who see the matter differently. Here is a paragraph from a 1973 decision of the U.S. Supreme Court, written by Chief Justice Warren Burger, setting forth reasons that the government may censor obscene material. We follow it with a sample summary.

> If we accept the unprovable assumption that a complete education requires the reading of certain books, and the well-nigh universal belief that good books, plays, and art lift the spirit, improve the mind, enrich the human personality, and develop character, can we then say that a state legislature may not act on the corollary assumption that commerce in obscene books, or public exhibitions focused on obscene conduct, have a tendency to exert a corrupting and debasing impact leading to antisocial

behavior? The sum of experience, including that of the past two decades, affords an ample basis for legislatures to conclude that a sensitive, key relationship of human existence, central to family life, community welfare, and the development of human personality, can be debased and distorted by crass commercial exploitation of sex. Nothing in the Constitution prohibits a State from reaching such a conclusion and acting on it legislatively simply because there is no conclusive empirical data.

Now for a student's summary. Notice that the summary does not include the reader's evaluation or any other sort of comment on the original; it is simply an attempt to condense the original. Notice too that, because its purpose is merely to assist the reader to grasp the ideas of the original by focusing on them, it is written in a sort of shorthand (not every sentence is a complete sentence), though, of course, if this summary were being presented in an essay, it would have to be grammatical.

> Unprovable but acceptable assumption that good books etc. shape character, so that legislature can assume obscene works debase character. Experience lets one conclude that exploitation of sex debases the individual, family, and community. Though "there is no conclusive empirical data" for this view, the Constitution lets states act on it legislatively.

Notice that

- A few words (in the last sentence of the summary) are quoted exactly as in the original. They are enclosed within quotation marks.
- For the most part, the original material is drastically reduced. The first sentence of the original, some eighty words, is reduced in the summary to nineteen words.

Of course, the summary loses much of the detail and flavor of the original: "Good books etc." is not the same as "good books, plays, and art"; and "shape character" is not the same as "lift the spirit, improve the mind, enrich the human personality, and develop character." But the statement in the summary will do as a rough approximation, useful for a quick review. More important, the act of writing a summary forces the reader to go slowly and to think about each sentence of the original. Such thinking may help the reader-writer to see the complexity — or the hollowness — of the original.

The sample summary in the preceding paragraph was just that, a summary; but when writing your own summaries, you will often find it useful to inject your own thoughts ("seems far-fetched," "strong point," "I don't get it"), enclosing them within square brackets or in some other way to keep these responses distinct from your summary of the writer's argument.

Review: If your instructor asks you to hand in a summary,

- It should not contain ideas other than those found in the original piece.

- You can rearrange these, add transitions as needed, and so forth, but the summary should give the reader nothing but a sense of the original piece.
- If the summary includes any of the original wording, these words should be enclosed within quotation marks.
- In your notes, keep a clear distinction between *your* writing and the writing of your *source*. For the most part you will summarize, but if you paraphrase, indicate that the words are a paraphrase, and if you quote directly, indicate that you are quoting.

We don't want to nag you, but we do want to emphasize the need to read with a pencil in hand. If you read slowly and take notes, you will find that what you read will give you the "strength and nourishment" that John Locke spoke of.

> **A RULE FOR WRITERS:** Remember that when you write a summary, you are putting yourself into the author's shoes.

Having insisted that the essays in this book need to be read slowly because the writers build one reason on another, we will now seem to contradict ourselves by presenting an essay that can almost be skimmed. Susan Jacoby's essay originally appeared in the *New York Times*, a thoroughly respectable newspaper but not one that requires its readers to linger over every sentence. Still, compared with most of the news accounts, Jacoby's essay requires close reading. When you read the essay, you will notice that it zigs and zags, not because Jacoby is careless or wants to befuddle her readers but because she wants to build a strong case to support her point of view and must therefore look at some widely held views that she does *not* accept; she must set these forth and then give her reasons for rejecting them.

Susan Jacoby

Susan Jacoby (b. 1946), a journalist since the age of seventeen, is well known for her feminist writings. "A First Amendment Junkie" (our title) appeared in the Hers column in the New York Times *in 1978.*

A First Amendment Junkie

It is no news that many women are defecting from the ranks of civil libertarians on the issue of obscenity. The conviction of Larry Flynt, publisher of *Hustler* magazine—before his metamorphosis into a born-again Christian—was greeted with unabashed feminist approval. Harry Reems, the unknown actor who was convicted by a Memphis jury for conspiring to distribute the movie *Deep Throat,* has carried on his legal battles with almost no support from women who ordinarily regard themselves as supporters of the First Amendment. Feminist writers and scholars have even discussed the possibility of making common cause against pornography with adversaries of the women's movement—including opponents of the equal rights amendment and "right-to-life" forces.

All of this is deeply disturbing to a woman writer who believes, as I always have and still do, in an absolute interpretation of the First Amendment. Nothing in Larry Flynt's garbage convinces me that the late Justice Hugo L. Black was wrong in his opinion that "the Federal Government is without any power whatsoever under the Constitution to put any type of burden on free speech and expression of ideas of any kind (as distinguished from conduct)." Many women I like and respect tell me I am wrong; I cannot remember having become involved in so many heated discussions of a public issue since the end of the Vietnam War. A feminist writer described my views as those of a "First Amendment junkie."

Many feminist arguments for controls on pornography carry the implicit conviction that porn books, magazines, and movies pose a greater threat to women than similarly repulsive exercises of free speech pose to other offended groups. This conviction has, of course, been shared by everyone—regardless of race, creed, or sex—who has ever argued in favor of abridging the First Amendment. It is the argument used by some Jews who have withdrawn their support from the American Civil Liberties Union because it has defended the right of American Nazis to march through a community inhabited by survivors of Hitler's concentration camps.

If feminists want to argue that the protection of the Constitution should not be extended to *any* particularly odious or threatening form of speech, they have a reasonable argument (although I don't agree with it). But it is ridiculous to suggest that the porn shops on 42nd Street are more disgusting to women than a march of neo-Nazis is to survivors of the extermination camps.

The arguments over pornography also blur the vital distinction be- 5 tween expression of ideas and conduct. When I say I believe unreservedly in the First Amendment, someone always comes back at me with the issue of "kiddie porn." But kiddie porn is not a First Amendment issue. It is an issue of the abuse of power—the power adults have over children—and not of obscenity. Parents and promoters have no more right to use their children to make porn movies than they do to send them to work in coal mines. The responsible adults should be prosecuted, just as adults who use children for back-breaking farm labor should be prosecuted.

Susan Brownmiller, in *Against Our Will: Men, Women and Rape,* has described pornography as "the undiluted essence of antifemale propaganda." I think this is a fair description of some types of pornography, especially of the brutish subspecies that equates sex with death and portrays women primarily as objects of violence.

The equation of sex and violence, personified by some glossy rock record album covers as well as by *Hustler,* has fed the illusion that censorship of pornography can be conducted on a more rational basis than other types of censorship. Are all pictures of naked women obscene? Clearly not, says a friend. A Renoir nude is art, she says, and *Hustler* is trash. "Any reasonable person" knows that.

But what about something between art and trash—something, say, along the lines of *Playboy* or *Penthouse* magazines? I asked five women for their reactions to one picture in *Penthouse* and got responses that ranged from "lovely" and "sensuous" to "revolting" and "demeaning." Feminists, like everyone else, seldom have rational reasons for their preferences in erotica. Like members of juries, they tend to disagree when confronted with something that falls short of 100 percent vulgarity.

In any case, feminists will not be the arbiters of good taste if it becomes easier to harass, prosecute, and convict people on obscenity charges. Most of the people who want to censor girlie magazines are equally opposed to open discussion of issues that are of vital concern to women: rape, abortion, menstruation, contraception, lesbianism—in fact, the entire range of sexual experience from a women's viewpoint.

Feminist writers and editors and filmmakers have limited financial 10 resources: Confronted by a determined prosecutor, Hugh Hefner[1] will fare better than Susan Brownmiller. Would the Memphis jurors who convicted Harry Reems for his role in *Deep Throat* be inclined to take a more positive view of paintings of the female genitalia done by sensitive feminist artists? *Ms.* magazine has printed color reproductions of some of those art works; *Ms.* is already banned from a number of high school libraries because someone considers it threatening and/or obscene.

Feminists who want to censor what they regard as harmful pornography have essentially the same motivation as other would-be censors: They want to use the power of the state to accomplish what they have been unable to achieve in the marketplace of ideas and images. The impulse to censor places no faith in the possibilities of democratic persuasion.

It isn't easy to persuade certain men that they have better uses for $1.95 each month than to spend it on a copy of *Hustler?* Well, then, give the men no choice in the matter.

I believe there is also a connection between the impulse toward censorship on the part of people who used to consider themselves civil libertarians and a more general desire to shift responsibility from individuals

[1]**Hugh Hefner** Founder and longtime publisher of *Playboy* magazine. [Editors' note.]

to institutions. When I saw the movie *Looking for Mr. Goodbar,* I was stunned by its series of visual images equating sex and violence, coupled with what seems to me the mindless message (a distortion of the fine Judith Rossner novel) that casual sex equals death. When I came out of the movie, I was even more shocked to see parents standing in line with children between the ages of ten and fourteen.

I simply don't know why a parent would take a child to see such a movie, any more than I understand why people feel they can't turn off a television set their child is watching. Whenever I say that, my friends tell me I don't know how it is because I don't have children. True, but I do have parents. When I was a child, they did turn off the TV. They didn't expect the Federal Communications Commission to do their job for them.

I am a First Amendment junkie. You can't OD on the First Amend-   15 ment, because free speech is its own best antidote.

Summarizing Jacoby, Paragraph by Paragraph

Suppose we want to make a rough summary, more or less paragraph by paragraph, of Jacoby's essay. Such a summary might look something like this (the numbers refer to Jacoby's paragraphs):

1. Although feminists usually support the First Amendment, when it comes to pornography, many feminists take pretty much the position of those who oppose ERA and abortion and other causes of the women's movement.

2. Larry Flynt produces garbage, but I think his conviction represents an unconstitutional limitation of freedom of speech.

3, 4. Feminists who want to control (censor) pornography argue that it poses a greater threat to women than similar repulsive speech poses to other groups. If feminists want to say that all offensive speech should be restricted, they can make a case, but it is absurd to say that pornography is a "greater threat" to women than a march of neo-Nazis is to survivors of concentration camps.

5. Trust in the First Amendment is not refuted by kiddie porn; kiddie porn is not a First Amendment issue but an issue of child abuse.

6, 7, 8. Some feminists think censorship of pornography can be more "rational" than other kinds of censorship, but a picture of a nude woman strikes some women as base and others as "lovely." There is no unanimity.

9, 10. If feminists censor girlie magazines, they will find that they are unwittingly helping opponents of the women's movement to censor discussions of rape, abortion, and so on. Some of the art in the feminist magazine Ms. would doubtless be censored.

11, 12. Like other would-be censors, feminists want to use the power of
the state to achieve what they have not achieved in "the marketplace
of ideas." They display a lack of faith in "democratic persuasion."

13, 14. This attempt at censorship reveals a desire to "shift responsibility from individuals to institutions." The responsibility--for instance,
to keep young people from equating sex with violence--is properly
the parents'.

15. We can't have too much of the First Amendment.

Jacoby's **thesis**, or major claim, or chief proposition—that any form
of censorship of pornography is wrong—is clear enough, even as early
as the end of her first paragraph, but it gets its life or its force from the
reasons offered throughout the essay. If we want to reduce our summary even further, we might say that Jacoby supports her thesis by arguing several subsidiary points. We will merely assert them briefly, but
Jacoby **argues** them—that is, she gives reasons:

a. Pornography can scarcely be thought of as more offensive than
   Nazism.

b. Women disagree about which pictures are pornographic.

c. Feminists who want to censor pornography will find that they help
   antifeminists to censor discussions of issues advocated by the
   women's movement.

d. Feminists who favor censorship are in effect turning to the government
   to achieve what they haven't achieved in the free marketplace.

e. One sees this abdication of responsibility in the fact that parents allow
   their children to watch unsuitable movies and television programs.

If we want to present a brief summary in the form of one coherent
paragraph—perhaps as part of our own essay to show the view we are
arguing in behalf of or against—we might write something like this
summary. (The summary would, of course, be prefaced by a **lead-in**
along these lines: "Susan Jacoby, writing in the *New York Times*, offers a
forceful argument against censorship of pornography. Jacoby's view,
briefly, is . . .".)

When it comes to censorship of pornography, some feminists take a position shared by opponents of the feminist movement. They argue that
pornography poses a greater threat to women than other forms of offensive speech offer to other groups, but this interpretation is simply a mistake. Pointing to kiddie porn is also a mistake, for kiddie porn is an issue
involving not the First Amendment but child abuse. Feminists who support censorship of pornography will inadvertently aid those who wish to
censor discussions of abortion and rape or censor art that is published in

magazines such as <u>Ms.</u> The solution is not for individuals to turn to institutions (that is, for the government to limit the First Amendment) but for individuals to accept the responsibility for teaching young people not to equate sex with violence.

Whether we agree or disagree with Jacoby's thesis, we must admit that the reasons she sets forth to support it are worth thinking about. Only a reader who closely follows the reasoning with which Jacoby buttresses her thesis is in a position to accept or reject it.

TOPICS FOR CRITICAL THINKING AND WRITING

1. What does Jacoby mean when she says she is a "First Amendment junkie" (para. 15)?

2. The essay is primarily an argument against the desire of some feminists to try to censor pornography of the sort that appeals to some heterosexual adult males, but the next-to-last paragraph is about television and children. Is the paragraph connected to Jacoby's overall argument? If so, how?

3. Evaluate the final paragraph as a final paragraph. (Effective final paragraphs are not, of course, all of one sort. Some, for example, round off the essay by echoing something from the opening; others suggest that the reader, having now seen the problem, should think further about it or even act on it. But a good final paragraph, whatever else it does, should make the reader feel that the essay has come to an end, not just broken off.)

4. This essay originally appeared in the *New York Times*. If you are unfamiliar with this newspaper, consult an issue or two in your library. Next, in a paragraph, try to characterize the readers of the paper—that is, Jacoby's audience.

5. Jacoby claims in paragraph 2 that she "believes . . . in an absolute interpretation of the First Amendment." What does such an interpretation involve? Would it permit shouting "Fire!" in a crowded theater even though the shouter knows there is no fire? Would it permit shouting racist insults at blacks or immigrant Vietnamese? Spreading untruths about someone's past? If the "absolutist" interpretation of the First Amendment does permit these statements, does that argument show that nothing is morally wrong with uttering them? (*Does* the First Amendment, as actually interpreted by the Supreme Court today, permit any or all of these claims? Consult your reference librarian for help in answering this question.)

6. Jacoby implies that permitting prosecution of persons on obscenity charges will lead eventually to censorship of "open discussion" of important issues such as "rape, abortion, menstruation, contraception, lesbianism" (para. 9). Do you find her fears convincing? Does she give any evidence to support her claim?

✓ A CHECKLIST FOR GETTING STARTED

☐ Have I adequately previewed the work?
☐ Can I state the thesis?
☐ If I have jotted down a summary,
  ☐ Is the summary accurate?
  ☐ Does the summary mention all the chief points?
  ☐ If there are inconsistencies, are they in the summary or the original selection?
  ☐ Will the summary be clear and helpful?

Gwen Wilde

This essay was written for a composition course at Tufts University.

Why the Pledge of Allegiance Should Be Revised

All Americans are familiar with the Pledge of Allegiance, even if they cannot always recite it perfectly, but probably relatively few know that the *original* Pledge did *not* include the words "under God." The original Pledge of Allegiance, published in the September 8, 1892, issue of the *Youth's Companion,* ran thus:

> I pledge allegiance to my flag, and to the Republic for which it stands: one Nation indivisible, with Liberty and justice for all. (Djupe 329)

In 1923, at the first National Flag Conference in Washington, DC, it was argued that immigrants might be confused by the words "my Flag," and it was proposed that the words be changed to "the Flag of the United States." The following year it was changed again, to "the Flag of the United States of America," and this wording became the official—or, rather, unofficial—wording, unofficial because no wording had ever been nationally adopted (Djupe 329).

In 1942, the United States Congress included the Pledge in the United States Flag Code (4 USC 4, 2006), thus for the first time officially sanctioning the Pledge. In 1954, President Dwight D. Eisenhower approved adding the words "under God." Thus, since 1954 the Pledge reads:

> I pledge allegiance to the flag of the United States of America, and to the Republic for which it stands: one nation under God, indivisible,with Liberty and Justice for all. (Djupe 329)

In my view, the addition of the words "under God" is inappropriate, and they are needlessly divisive—an odd addition indeed to a Nation that is said to be "indivisible."

Very simply put, the Pledge in its latest form requires all Americans to say something that some Americans do not believe. I say "requires" because although the courts have ruled that students may not be compelled to recite the Pledge, in effect peer pressure does compel all but the bravest to join in the recitation. When President Eisenhower authorized the change, he said,

> In this way we are reaffirming the transcendence of religious faith in America's heritage and future; in this way we shall constantly strengthen those spiritual weapons which forever will be our country's most powerful resource in peace and war. (Sterner)

Exactly what did Eisenhower mean when he spoke of "the transcendence of faith in America's heritage," and when he spoke of "spiritual weapons"? I am not sure what "the transcendence of faith in America's heritage" means. Of course many Americans have been and are deeply religious—no one doubts it—but the phrase certainly goes far beyond saying that many Americans have been devout. In any case, many Americans have *not* been devout, and many Americans have *not* believed in "spiritual weapons," but they have nevertheless been patriotic Americans. Some of them have fought and died to keep America free.

In short, the words "under God" cannot be uttered in good faith by many Americans. True, something like 70 or even 80% of Americans say they are affiliated with some form of Christianity, and approximately another 3% say they are Jewish. I don't have the figures for persons of other faiths, but in any case we can surely all agree that although a majority of Americans say they have a religious affiliation, nevertheless several million Americans do *not* believe in God.

If one remains silent while others are reciting the Pledge, or even if one remains silent only while others are speaking the words "under God," one is open to the charge that one is unpatriotic, is "unwilling to recite the Pledge of Allegiance." In the Pledge, patriotism is connected with religious belief, and it is this connection that makes it divisive and (to be blunt) un-American. Admittedly the belief is not very specific: one is not required to say that one believes in the divinity of Jesus, or in the power of Jehovah, but the fact remains, one is required to express belief in a divine power, and if one doesn't express this belief one is—according to the Pledge—somehow not fully an American, maybe even un-American.

Please notice that I am not arguing that the Pledge is unconstitutional. I understand that the First Amendment to the Constitution says that "Congress shall make no law respecting an establishment of religion, or prohibiting the free exercise thereof." I am not arguing that the words "under God" in the Pledge add up to the "establishment of religion," but they certainly do assert a religious doctrine. Like the words "In God we trust," found on all American money, the words "under God" express an idea that many Americans do not hold, and there is no reason why these Americans—loyal people who may be called upon to defend the country with their lives — should be required to say that America is a nation "under God."

It has been argued, even by members of the Supreme Court, that the words "under God" are not to be taken terribly seriously, not to be taken to say what they seem to say. For instance, Chief Justice Rehnquist wrote,

> To give the parent of such a child a sort of "heckler's veto" over a patriotic ceremony willingly participated in by other students, simply because the Pledge of Allegiance contains the descriptive phrase "under God," is an unwarranted extension of the establishment clause, an extension which would have the unfortunate effect of prohibiting a commendable patriotic observance. (qtd. in Mears)

Chief Justice Rehnquist here calls "under God" a "descriptive phrase," but descriptive of *what*? If a phrase is a "descriptive phrase," it describes something, real or imagined. For many Americans, this phrase does *not* describe a reality. These Americans may perhaps be mistaken — if so, they may learn of their error at Judgment Day — but the fact is, millions of intelligent Americans do not believe in God.

Notice, too, that Chief Justice Rehnquist goes on to say that reciting the Pledge is "a commendable patriotic observance." Exactly. That is my point. It is a *patriotic* observance, and it should not be connected with religion. When we announce that we respect the flag — that we are loyal Americans — we should not also have to announce that we hold a particular religious belief, in this case a belief in monotheism, a belief that there is a God and that God rules.

One other argument defending the words "under God" is often heard: the words "In God We Trust" appear on our money. It is claimed that these words on American money are analogous to the words "under God" in the Pledge. But the situation really is very different. When we hand some coins over, or some paper money, we are concentrating on the business transaction, and we are not making any affirmation about God or our country. But when we recite the Pledge — even if we remain silent at the point when we are supposed to say "under God" — we are very conscious that we are supposed to make this affirmation, an affirmation that many Americans cannot in good faith make, even though they certainly can unthinkingly hand over (or accept) money with the words "In God We Trust."

Because I believe that *reciting* the Pledge is to be taken seriously, with 10 a full awareness of the words that is quite different from when we hand over some money, I cannot understand the recent comment of Supreme Court Justice Souter, who in a case said that the phrase "under God" is "so tepid, so diluted, so far from compulsory prayer, that it should, in effect, be beneath the constitutional radar" (qtd. in "Guide"). I don't follow his reasoning that the phrase should be "beneath the constitutional radar," but in any case I am willing to put aside the issue of constitutionality. I am willing to grant that this phrase does not in any significant sense signify the "establishment of religion" (prohibited by the First Amendment) in the United States. I insist, nevertheless, that the phrase is neither "tepid" nor "diluted." It means what it says—it *must* and *should* mean what it says, to everyone who utters it—and, since millions of loyal Americans cannot say it, it should not be included in a statement in which Americans affirm their loyalty to our great country.

In short, the Pledge, which ought to unite all of us, is divisive; it includes a phrase that many patriotic Americans cannot bring themselves to utter. Yes, they can remain silent when others recite these two words, but, again, why should they have to remain silent? The Pledge of Allegiance should be something that *everyone* can say, say out loud, and say with pride. We hear much talk of returning to the ideas of the Founding Fathers. The Founding Fathers did not create the Pledge of Allegiance, but we do know that they never mentioned God in the Constitution. Indeed the only reference to religion, in the so-called establishment clause of the First Amendment, says, again, that "Congress shall make no law respecting an establishment of religion, or prohibiting the free exercise thereof." Those who wish to exercise religion are indeed free to do so, but the place to do so is not in a pledge that is required of all schoolchildren and of all new citizens.

WORKS CITED

Djupe, Paul A. "Pledge of Allegiance." *Encyclopedia of American Religion and Politics.* Ed. Paul A. Djupe and Laura R. Olson. New York: Facts on File, 2003. Print.

"Guide to Covering 'Under God' Pledge Decision." *ReligionLink.* Religion Newswriters Foundation, 17 Sept. 2005. Web. 9 Feb. 2007.

Mears, Bill. "Court Dismisses Pledge Case." *CNN.com.* Cable News Network 15 June 2004. Web. 9 Feb. 2007.

Sterner, Doug. "The Pledge of Allegiance." *Home of Heroes.* N.p., n.d. Web. 9 Feb. 2007.

Topics for Critical Thinking and Writing

1. Summarize the essay in a paragraph.

2. Does the background material about the history of the pledge serve a useful purpose? Should it be deleted? Why, or why not?

3. Does the writer give enough weight to the fact that no one is compelled to recite the pledge? Explain your answer.

4. What arguments does the writer offer in support of her position?

5. Does the writer show an adequate awareness of other counterarguments?

6. Which is the writer's strongest argument? Is any argument notably weak, and, if so, how could it be strengthened? (If you cannot think of how it might be strengthened, should it have been omitted?)

7. What assumptions—tacit or explicit—does the author make? Do you agree or disagree with them? Please explain.

8. What do you take the words "under God" to mean? Do they mean "under God's special protection"? Or "acting in accordance with God's rules"? Or "accountable to God"?

9. Chief Justice Rehnquist wrote that the words "under God" are a "descriptive phrase." What do you think he meant by this?

10. What is the purpose of the Pledge of Allegiance? Does the phrase "under God" promote or defeat that purpose? Explain your answer.

11. What do you think about substituting "with religious freedom" for "under God"? Set forth your response, supported by reasons, in about 250 words.

12. Wilde makes a distinction between the reference to God on U.S. money and the reference to God in the Pledge. Do you agree with her that the two cases are not analogous? Explain.

13. Putting aside your own views on the issue, what grade would you give this essay as a work of argumentative writing? Support your evaluation with reasons.

A CASEBOOK FOR CRITICAL READING:
Should Some Kinds of Speech Be Censored?

Now we present a series of essays that we think are somewhat more difficult than Jacoby and Wilde's but that address in more detail some of the issues of free speech that she raises. We suggest you read each one through to get its gist and then read it a second time, jotting down after each paragraph a sentence or two summarizing the paragraph. Keep in mind the First Amendment to the Constitution, which reads, in its entirety,

> Congress shall make no law respecting an establishment of religion, or prohibiting the free exercise thereof; or abridging the freedom of speech, or of the press; or the right of the people peaceably to assemble, and to petition the government for a redress of grievances.

> For links related to free speech, see the companion Web site
> **bedfordstmartins.com/barnetbedau.**

Susan Brownmiller

Susan Brownmiller (b. 1935), a graduate of Cornell University, is the founder of Women against Pornography and the author of several books, including **Against**

Our Will: Men, Women, and Rape *(1975). The essay reprinted here is from* Take Back the Night *(1980), a collection of essays edited by Laura Lederer. The book has been called "the manifesto of antipornography feminism."*

Let's Put Pornography Back in the Closet

Free speech is one of the great foundations on which our democracy rests. I am old enough to remember the Hollywood Ten, the screenwriters who went to jail in the late 1940s because they refused to testify before a congressional committee about their political affiliations. They tried to use the First Amendment as a defense, but they went to jail because in those days there were few civil liberties lawyers around who cared to champion the First Amendment right to free speech, when the speech concerned the Communist party.

The Hollywood Ten were correct in claiming the First Amendment. Its high purpose is the protection of unpopular ideas and political dissent. In the dark, cold days of the 1950s, few civil libertarians were willing to declare themselves First Amendment absolutists. But in the brighter, though frantic, days of the 1960s, the principle of protecting unpopular political speech was gradually strengthened.

It is fair to say now that the battle has largely been won. Even the American Nazi party has found itself the beneficiary of the dedicated, tireless work of the American Civil Liberties Union. But—and please notice the quotation marks coming up—"To equate the free and robust exchange of ideas and political debate with commercial exploitation of obscene material demeans the grand conception of the First Amendment and its high purposes in the historic struggle for freedom. It is a misuse of the great guarantees of free speech and free press."

I didn't say that, although I wish I had, for I think the words are thrilling. Chief Justice Warren Burger said it in 1973, in the United States Supreme Court's majority opinion in *Miller v. California.* During the same decades that the right to political free speech was being strengthened in the courts, the nation's obscenity laws also were undergoing extensive revision.

It's amazing to recall that in 1934 the question of whether James   5
Joyce's *Ulysses* should be banned as pornographic actually went before the Court. The battle to protect *Ulysses* as a work of literature with redeeming social value was won. In later decades, Henry Miller's *Tropic* books, *Lady Chatterley's Lover,* and the *Memoirs of Fanny Hill* also were adjudged not obscene. These decisions have been important to me. As the author of *Against Our Will,* a study of the history of rape that does contain explicit sexual material, I shudder to think how my book would have fared if James Joyce, D. H. Lawrence, and Henry Miller hadn't gone before me.

I am not a fan of *Chatterley* or the *Tropic* books, I should quickly mention. They are not to my literary taste, nor do I think they represent female sexuality with any degree of accuracy. But I would hardly suggest that we ban them. Such a suggestion wouldn't get very far anyway. The battle to protect these books is ancient history. Time does march on, quite methodically. What, then, is unlawfully obscene, and what does the First Amendment have to do with it?

In the *Miller* case of 1973 (not Henry Miller, by the way, but a porn distributor who sent unsolicited stuff through the mails), the Court came up with new guidelines that it hoped would strengthen obscenity laws by giving more power to the states. What it did in actuality was throw everything into confusion. It set up a three-part test by which materials can be adjudged obscene. The materials are obscene if they depict patently offensive, hard-core sexual conduct; lack serious scientific, literary, artistic, or political value; and appeal to the prurient interest of an average person—as measured by contemporary community standards.

"Patently offensive," "prurient interest," and "hard-core" are indeed words to conjure with. "Contemporary community standards" are what we're trying to redefine. The feminist objection to pornography is not based on prurience, which the dictionary defines as lustful, itching desire. We are not opposed to sex and desire, with or without the itch, and we certainly believe that explicit sexual material has its place in literature, art, science, and education. Here we part company rather swiftly with old-line conservatives who don't want sex education in the high schools, for example.

No, the feminist objection to pornography is based on our belief that pornography represents hatred of women, that pornography's intent is to humiliate, degrade, and dehumanize the female body for the purpose of erotic stimulation and pleasure. We are unalterably opposed to the presentation of the female body being stripped, bound, raped, tortured, mutilated, and murdered in the name of commercial entertainment and free speech.

These images, which are standard pornographic fare, have nothing 10 to do with the hallowed right of political dissent. They have everything to do with the creation of a cultural climate in which a rapist feels he is merely giving in to a normal urge and a woman is encouraged to believe that sexual masochism is healthy, liberated fun. Justice Potter Stewart once said about hard-core pornography, "You know it when you see it," and that certainly used to be true. In the good old days, pornography looked awful. It was cheap and sleazy, and there was no mistaking it for art.

Nowadays, since the porn industry has become a multimillion dollar business, visual technology has been employed in its service. Pornographic movies are skillfully filmed and edited, pornographic still shots using the newest tenets of good design artfully grace the covers of *Hustler*, *Penthouse*, and *Playboy*, and the public—and the courts—are sadly confused.

The Supreme Court neglected to define "hard-core" in the *Miller* decision. This was a mistake. If "hard-core" refers only to explicit sexual intercourse, then that isn't good enough. When women or children or men—no matter how artfully—are shown tortured or terrorized in the service of sex, that's obscene. And "patently offensive," I would hope, to our "contemporary community standards."

Justice William O. Douglas wrote in his dissent to the *Miller* case that no one is "compelled to look." This is hardly true. To buy a paper at the corner newsstand is to subject oneself to a forcible immersion in pornography, to be demeaned by an array of dehumanized, chopped-up parts of the female anatomy, packaged like cuts of meat at the supermarket. I happen to like my body and I work hard at the gym to keep it in good shape, but I am embarrassed for my body and for the bodies of all women when I see the fragmented parts of us so frivolously, and so flagrantly, displayed.

Some constitutional theorists (Justice Douglas was one) have maintained that any obscenity law is a serious abridgement of free speech. Others (and Justice Earl Warren was one) have maintained that the First Amendment was never intended to protect obscenity. We live quite compatibly with a host of free-speech abridgements. There are restraints against false and misleading advertising or statements—shouting "fire" without cause in a crowded movie theater, etc.—that do not threaten, but strengthen, our societal values. Restrictions on the public display of pornography belong in this category.

The distinction between permission to publish and permission to display publicly is an essential one and one which I think consonant with First Amendment principles. Justice Burger's words which I quoted above support this without question. We are not saying "Smash the presses" or "Ban the bad ones," but simply "Get the stuff out of our sight." Let the legislatures decide—using realistic and humane contemporary community standards—what can be displayed and what cannot. The courts, after all, will be the final arbiters.   15

TOPICS FOR CRITICAL THINKING AND WRITING

1. Objecting to Justice Douglas's remark that no one is "'compelled to look'" (para. 13), Brownmiller says, "This is hardly true. To buy a paper at the corner newsstand is to subject oneself to a forcible immersion in pornography, to be demeaned by an array of dehumanized, chopped-up parts of the female anatomy, packaged like cuts of meat at the supermarket." Is this true at your local newsstand, or are the sex magazines kept in one place, relatively remote from the newspapers?

2. When Brownmiller attempts to restate the "three-part test" for obscenity established by the Supreme Court in *Miller v. California,* she writes (para. 7): "The materials are obscene if they depict . . ." and so on. She should have written: "The materials are obscene if and only if they de-

pict . . ." and so on. Explain what is wrong here with her "if," and why "if and only if" is needed.

3. In her next-to-last paragraph, Brownmiller reminds us that we already live quite comfortably with some "free-speech abridgements." The examples she gives are that we may not falsely shout "fire" in a crowded theater and may not issue misleading advertisements. Do you think that these widely accepted restrictions are valid evidence in arguing on behalf of limiting the display of what Brownmiller considers pornography? Why, or why not?

4. Brownmiller insists that defenders of the First Amendment, who will surely oppose laws that interfere with the freedom to publish, need not go on to condemn laws that regulate the freedom to publicly display pornographic publications. Do you agree? Suppose a publisher insists that he cannot sell his product at a profit unless he is permitted to display it to advantage and that restriction on the latter amounts to interference with his freedom to publish. How might Brownmiller reply?

5. In her last paragraph Brownmiller says that "contemporary community standards" should be decisive. Can it be argued that because standards vary from one community to another and from time to time even in the same place, her recommendation subjects the rights of a minority to the whims of a majority? The Bill of Rights, after all, was supposed to safeguard the constitutional rights of the minority from the possible tyranny of the majority.

6. When Brownmiller accuses "the public . . . and the courts" of being "sadly confused" (para. 11), what does she think they are confused about? The definition of *pornography* or *obscenity*? The effects of such literature on men and women? Or is it something else?

Charles R. Lawrence III

Charles R. Lawrence III (b. 1943), author of numerous articles in law journals and coauthor of We Won't Go Back: Making the Case for Affirmative Action *(1997), teaches law at Georgetown University. This essay originally appeared in the* Chronicle of Higher Education *(October 25, 1989), a publication read chiefly by faculty and administrators at colleges and universities. An amplified version of the essay appeared in* Duke Law Journal *(February 1990).*

On Racist Speech

I have spent the better part of my life as a dissenter. As a high school student, I was threatened with suspension for my refusal to participate in a civil defense drill, and I have been a conspicuous consumer of my First Amendment liberties ever since. There are very strong reasons for protecting even racist speech. Perhaps the most important of these is that such protection reinforces our society's commitment to tolerance as a value, and that by protecting bad speech from government regulation, we will be forced to combat it as a community.

But I also have a deeply felt apprehension about the resurgence of racial violence and the corresponding rise in the incidence of verbal and symbolic assault and harassment to which blacks and other traditionally subjugated and excluded groups are subjected. I am troubled by the way the debate has been framed in response to the recent surge of racist incidents on college and university campuses and in response to some universities' attempts to regulate harassing speech. The problem has been framed as one in which the liberty of free speech is in conflict with the elimination of racism. I believe this has placed the bigot on the moral high ground and fanned the rising flames of racism.

Above all, I am troubled that we have not listened to the real victims, that we have shown so little understanding of their injury, and that we have abandoned those whose race, gender, or sexual preference continues to make them second-class citizens. It seems to me a very sad irony that the first instinct of civil libertarians has been to challenge even the smallest, most narrowly framed efforts by universities to provide black and other minority students with the protection the Constitution guarantees them.

The landmark case of *Brown v. Board of Education* is not a case that we normally think of as a case about speech. But *Brown* can be broadly read as articulating the principle of equal citizenship. *Brown* held that segregated schools were inherently unequal because of the *message* that segregation conveyed—that black children were an untouchable caste, unfit to go to school with white children. If we understand the necessity of eliminating the system of signs and symbols that signal the inferiority of blacks, then we should hesitate before proclaiming that all racist speech that stops short of physical violence must be defended.

University officials who have formulated policies to respond to incidents of racial harassment have been characterized in the press as "thought police," but such policies generally do nothing more than impose sanctions against intentional face-to-face insults. When racist speech takes the form of face-to-face insults, catcalls, or other assaultive speech aimed at an individual or small group of persons, it falls directly within the "fighting words" exception to First Amendment protection. The Supreme Court has held that words which "by their very utterance inflict injury or tend to incite an immediate breach of the peace" are not protected by the First Amendment.

If the purpose of the First Amendment is to foster the greatest amount of speech, racial insults disserve that purpose. Assaultive racist speech functions as a preemptive strike. The invective is experienced as a blow, not as a proffered idea, and once the blow is struck, it is unlikely that a dialogue will follow. Racial insults are particularly undeserving of First Amendment protection because the perpetrator's intention is not to discover truth or initiate dialogue but to injure the victim. In most situations, members of minority groups realize that they are likely to lose if they respond to epithets by fighting and are forced to remain silent and submissive.

Courts have held that offensive speech may not be regulated in public forums such as streets where the listener may avoid the speech by moving on, but the regulation of otherwise protected speech has been permitted when the speech invades the privacy of the unwilling listener's home or when the unwilling listener cannot avoid the speech. Racist posters, fliers, and graffiti in dormitories, bathrooms, and other common living spaces would seem to clearly fall within the reasoning of these cases. Minority students should not be required to remain in their rooms in order to avoid racial assault. Minimally, they should find a safe haven in their dorms and in all other common rooms that are a part of their daily routine.

I would also argue that the university's responsibility for ensuring that these students receive an equal educational opportunity provides a compelling justification for regulations that ensure them safe passage in all common areas. A minority student should not have to risk becoming the target of racially assaulting speech every time he or she chooses to walk across campus. Regulating vilifying speech that cannot be anticipated or avoided would not preclude announced speeches and rallies — situations that would give minority-group members and their allies the chance to organize counterdemonstrations or avoid the speech altogether.

The most commonly advanced argument against the regulation of racist speech proceeds something like this: We recognize that minority groups suffer pain and injury as the result of racist speech, but we must allow this hate mongering for the benefit of society as a whole. Freedom of speech is the lifeblood of our democratic system. It is especially important for minorities because often it is their only vehicle for rallying support for the redress of their grievances. It will be impossible to formulate a prohibition so precise that it will prevent the racist speech you want to suppress without catching in the same net all kinds of speech that it would be unconscionable for a democratic society to suppress.

Whenever we make such arguments, we are striking a balance on 10 the one hand between our concern for the continued free flow of ideas and the democratic process dependent on that flow, and, on the other, our desire to further the cause of equality. There can be no meaningful discussion of how we should reconcile our commitment to equality and our commitment to free speech until it is acknowledged that there is real harm inflicted by racist speech and that this harm is far from trivial.

To engage in a debate about the First Amendment and racist speech without a full understanding of the nature and extent of that harm is to risk making the First Amendment an instrument of domination rather than a vehicle of liberation. We have not known the experience of victimization by racist, misogynist, and homophobic speech, nor do we equally share the burden of the societal harm it inflicts. We are often quick to say that we have heard the cry of the victims when we have not.

The *Brown* case is again instructive because it speaks directly to the psychic injury inflicted by racist speech by noting that the symbolic message of segregation affected "the hearts and minds" of Negro children "in a way unlikely ever to be undone." Racial epithets and harassment often cause deep emotional scarring and feelings of anxiety and fear that pervade every aspect of a victim's life.

Brown also recognized that black children did not have an equal opportunity to learn and participate in the school community if they bore the additional burden of being subjected to the humiliation and psychic assault contained in the message of segregation. University students bear an analogous burden when they are forced to live and work in an environment where at any moment they may be subjected to denigrating verbal harassment and assault. The same injury was addressed by the Supreme Court when it held that sexual harassment that creates a hostile or abusive work environment violates the ban on sex discrimination in employment of Title VII of the Civil Rights Act of 1964.

Carefully drafted university regulations would bar the use of words as assault weapons and leave unregulated even the most heinous of ideas when those ideas are presented at times and places and in manners that provide an opportunity for reasoned rebuttal or escape from immediate injury. The history of the development of the right to free speech has been one of carefully evaluating the importance of free expression and its effects on other important societal interests. We have drawn the line between protected and unprotected speech before without dire results. (Courts have, for example, exempted from the protection of the First Amendment obscene speech and speech that disseminates official secrets, that defames or libels another person, or that is used to form a conspiracy or monopoly.)

Blacks and other people of color are skeptical about the argument   15
that even the most injurious speech must remain unregulated because, in an unregulated marketplace of ideas, the best ones will rise to the top and gain acceptance. Our experience tells us quite the opposite. We have seen too many good liberal politicians shy away from the issues that might brand them as being too closely allied with us.

Whenever we decide that racist speech must be tolerated because of the importance of maintaining societal tolerance for all unpopular speech, we are asking blacks and other subordinated groups to bear the burden for the good of all. We must be careful that the ease with which we strike the balance against the regulation of racist speech is in no way influenced by the fact that the cost will be borne by others. We must be certain that those who will pay that price are fairly represented in our deliberations and that they are heard.

At the core of the argument that we should resist all government regulation of speech is the ideal that the best cure for bad speech is good, that ideas that affirm equality and the worth of all individuals will ultimately prevail. This is an empty ideal unless those of us who would fight racism are vigilant and unequivocal in that fight. We must look for ways to offer assistance and support to students whose speech and political participation are chilled in a climate of racial harassment.

Civil rights lawyers might consider suing on behalf of blacks whose right to an equal education is denied by a university's failure to ensure a nondiscriminatory educational climate or conditions of employment. We must embark upon the development of a First Amendment jurisprudence grounded in the reality of our history and our contemporary experience. We must think hard about how best to launch legal attacks against the most indefensible forms of hate speech. Good lawyers can create exceptions and narrow interpretations that limit the harm of hate speech without opening the floodgates of censorship.

Everyone concerned with these issues must find ways to engage actively in actions that resist and counter the racist ideas that we would have the First Amendment protect. If we fail in this, the victims of hate speech must rightly assume that we are on the oppressors' side.

TOPICS FOR CRITICAL THINKING AND WRITING

1. Summarize Lawrence's essay in a paragraph. (You may find it useful first to summarize each paragraph in a sentence and then to revise these summary sentences into a paragraph.)

2. In a sentence state Lawrence's thesis (his main point).

3. Why do you suppose Lawrence included his first paragraph? What does it contribute to his argument?

4. Paragraph 7 argues that "minority students" should not have to endure "racist posters, fliers, and graffiti in dormitories, bathrooms, and other common living spaces." Do you think that Lawrence would also argue that straight white men should not have to endure posters, fliers, or graffiti that speak of "honkies" or "rednecks"? On what do you base your answer?

5. In paragraph 8 Lawrence speaks of "racially assaulting speech" and of "vilifying speech." It is easy to think of words that fit these descriptions, but what about other words? Is *Uncle Tom*, used by an African American about another African American who is eager to please whites, an example of "racially assaulting speech"? Or take the word *gay*. Surely this word is acceptable because it is widely used by homosexuals, but what about *queer* (used by some homosexuals but usually derogatory when used by heterosexuals)? A third example: There can be little doubt that women are demeaned when males speak of them as *chicks* or *babes*, but are these terms "assaulting" and "vilifying"?

6. For a start, you might think about some provisions in the Code of Conduct of Shippensburg University in Pennsylvania. The code says that

each student has a "primary" right to be free from harassment, intimidation, physical harm, and emotional abuse, and has a "secondary" right to express personal beliefs in a manner that does not "provoke, harass, demean, intimidate, or harm" another. The code prohibits conduct that "annoys, threatens, or alarms a person or group," such as sexual harassment, "innuendo," "comments, insults," "propositions," "humor/jokes about sex or gender-specific traits," and "suggestive or insulting sounds, leering, whistling, [and] obscene gestures." The president of the university has said (according to the *New York Times,* April 24, 2003, p. A23) that the university encourages free speech as a means to examine ideas and that the university is "committed to the principle that this discussion be conducted appropriately. We do have expectations that our students will conduct themselves in a civil manner that allows them to express their opinions without interfering with the rights of others." Again, you may find that some of this material helps you to generate your own thoughts.

7. Find out if your college or university has a code governing hate speech. If it does, evaluate it. If your college has no such code, imagine that you are Lawrence, and draft one of about 250 words. (See especially his paras. 5, 7, and 14.)

Derek Bok

Derek Bok was born in 1930 in Bryn Mawr, Pennsylvania, and educated at Stanford University and Harvard University, where he received a law degree. From 1971 to 1991 he served as president of Harvard University. The following essay, first published in the Boston Globe *in 1991, was prompted by the display of Confederate flags hung from a window of a Harvard dormitory.*

Protecting Freedom of Expression on the Campus

For several years, universities have been struggling with the problem of trying to reconcile the rights of free speech with the desire to avoid racial tension. In recent weeks, such a controversy has sprung up at Harvard. Two students hung Confederate flags in public view, upsetting students who equate the Confederacy with slavery. A third student tried to protest the flags by displaying a swastika.

These incidents have provoked much discussion and disagreement. Some students have urged that Harvard require the removal of symbols that offend many members of the community. Others reply that such symbols are a form of free speech and should be protected.

Different universities have resolved similar conflicts in different ways. Some have enacted codes to protect their communities from forms of speech that are deemed to be insensitive to the feelings of other groups. Some have refused to impose such restrictions.

It is important to distinguish between the appropriateness of such communications and their status under the First Amendment. The fact that speech is protected by the First Amendment does not necessarily mean that it is right, proper, or civil. I am sure that the vast majority of Harvard students believe that hanging a Confederate flag in public view—or displaying a swastika in response—is insensitive and unwise because any satisfaction it gives to the students who display these symbols is far outweighed by the discomfort it causes to many others.

I share this view and regret that the students involved saw fit to be- 5 have in this fashion. Whether or not they merely wished to manifest their pride in the South—or to demonstrate the insensitivity of hanging Confederate flags, by mounting another offensive symbol in return— they must have known that they would upset many fellow students and ignore the decent regard for the feelings of others so essential to building and preserving a strong and harmonious community.

To disapprove of a particular form of communication, however, is not enough to justify prohibiting it. We are faced with a clear example of the conflict between our commitment to free speech and our desire to foster a community founded on mutual respect. Our society has wrestled with this problem for many years. Interpreting the First Amendment, the Supreme Court has clearly struck the balance in favor of free speech.

While communities do have the right to regulate speech in order to uphold aesthetic standards (avoiding defacement of buildings) or to protect the public from disturbing noise, rules of this kind must be applied across the board and cannot be enforced selectively to prohibit certain kinds of messages but not others.

Under the Supreme Court's rulings, as I read them, the display of swastikas or Confederate flags clearly falls within the protection of the free-speech clause of the First Amendment and cannot be forbidden simply because it offends the feelings of many members of the community. These rulings apply to all agencies of government, including public universities.

Although it is unclear to what extent the First Amendment is enforceable against private institutions, I have difficulty understanding why a university such as Harvard should have less free speech than the surrounding society—or than a public university.

One reason why the power of censorship is so dangerous is that it is 10 extremely difficult to decide when a particular communication is offensive enough to warrant prohibition or to weigh the degree of offensiveness against the potential value of the communication. If we begin to forbid flags, it is only a short step to prohibiting offensive speakers.

I suspect that no community will become humane and caring by restricting what its members can say. The worst offenders will simply find other ways to irritate and insult.

In addition, once we start to declare certain things "offensive," with all the excitement and attention that will follow, I fear that much ingenuity will be exerted trying to test the limits, much time will be expended trying to draw tenuous distinctions, and the resulting publicity will eventually attract more attention to the offensive material than would ever have occurred otherwise.

Rather than prohibit such communications, with all the resulting risks, it would be better to ignore them, since students would then have little reason to create such displays and would soon abandon them. If this response is not possible—and one can understand why—the wisest course is to speak with those who perform insensitive acts and try to help them understand the effects of their actions on others.

Appropriate officials and faculty members should take the lead, as the Harvard House Masters have already done in this case. In talking with students, they should seek to educate and persuade, rather than resort to ridicule or intimidation, recognizing that only persuasion is likely to produce a lasting, beneficial effect. Through such effects, I believe that we act in the manner most consistent with our ideals as an educational institution and most calculated to help us create a truly understanding, supportive community.

TOPICS FOR CRITICAL THINKING AND WRITING

1. Bok sketches the following argument (paras. 8 and 9): The First Amendment protects free speech in public universities and colleges; Harvard is not a public university; therefore, Harvard does not enjoy the protection of the First Amendment. This argument is plainly invalid. Bok clearly rejects the conclusion ("I have difficulty understanding why . . . Harvard should have less free speech . . . than a public university"). What would need to be revised in the premises to make the argument valid? Do you think Bok would accept or reject such a revision?

2. Bok objects to censorship that simply prevents students from being "offended." He would not object to the campus police preventing students from being harmed. In an essay of 100 words, explain the difference between conduct that is *harmful* and conduct that is (merely?) *offensive*.

3. Bok advises campus officials (and students) simply to "ignore" offensive words, flags, and so forth (para. 13). Do you agree with this advice? Or do you favor a different kind of response? Write a 250-word essay on the theme "How We Ought to Respond to the Offensive Misconduct of Others."

Stanley Fish

Stanley Fish (b. 1938) established his reputation as a student of English literature—he has taught literature at the University of California–Berkeley, Johns Hopkins University, and Duke University—but he has also published on legal issues, and now teaches at Florida International University's College of Law.

Conspiracy Theories 101

Kevin Barrett, a lecturer at the University of Wisconsin at Madison, has now taken his place alongside Ward Churchill of the University of Colorado as a college teacher whose views on 9/11 have led politicians and ordinary citizens to demand that he be fired.

Mr. Barrett, who has a one-semester contract to teach a course titled "Islam: Religion and Culture," acknowledged on a radio talk show that he has shared with students his strong conviction that the destruction of the World Trade Center was an inside job perpetrated by the American government. The predictable uproar ensued, and the equally predictable battle lines were drawn between those who disagree about what the doctrine of academic freedom does and does not allow.

Mr. Barrett's critics argue that academic freedom has limits and should not be invoked to justify the dissemination of lies and fantasies. Mr. Barrett's supporters (most of whom are not partisans of his conspiracy theory) insist that it is the very point of an academic institution to entertain all points of view, however unpopular. (This was the position taken by the university's provost, Patrick Farrell, when he ruled on July 10 that Mr. Barrett would be retained: "We cannot allow political pressure from critics of unpopular ideas to inhibit the free exchange of ideas.")

Both sides get it wrong. The problem is that each assumes that academic freedom is about protecting the content of a professor's speech; one side thinks that no content should be ruled out in advance; while the other would draw the line at propositions (like the denial of the Holocaust or the flatness of the world) considered by almost everyone to be crazy or dangerous.

But in fact, academic freedom has nothing to do with content. It is 5 not a subset of the general freedom of Americans to say anything they like (so long as it is not an incitement to violence or is treasonous or libelous). Rather, academic freedom is the freedom of academics to *study* anything they like; the freedom, that is, to subject any body of material, however unpromising it might seem, to academic interrogation and analysis.

Academic freedom means that if I think that there may be an intellectual payoff to be had by turning an academic lens on material others consider trivial—golf tees, gourmet coffee, lingerie ads, convenience stores, street names, whatever—I should get a chance to try. If I manage to demonstrate to my peers and students that studying this material yields insights into matters of general intellectual interest, there is a new topic under the academic sun and a new subject for classroom discussion.

In short, whether something is an appropriate object of academic study is a matter not of its content—a crackpot theory may have had a history of influence that well rewards scholarly scrutiny—but of its availability to serious analysis. This point was missed by the author of a comment posted to the blog of a University of Wisconsin law professor, Ann Althouse: "When is the University of Wisconsin hiring a professor of astrology?" The question is obviously sarcastic; its intention is to equate the 9/11-inside-job theory with believing in the predictive power of astrology, and to imply that since the university wouldn't think of hiring someone to teach the one, it should have known better than to hire someone to teach the other.

But the truth is that it would not be at all outlandish for a university to hire someone to teach astrology—not to profess astrology and recommend it as the basis of decision-making (shades of Nancy Reagan), but to teach the history of its very long career. There is, after all, a good argument for saying that Shakespeare, Chaucer, and Dante, among others, cannot be fully understood unless one understands astrology.

The distinction I am making—between studying astrology and proselytizing for it—is crucial and can be generalized; it shows us where the line between the responsible and irresponsible practice of academic freedom should always be drawn. Any idea can be brought into the classroom if the point is to inquire into its structure, history, influence, and so forth. But no idea belongs in the classroom if the point of introducing it is to recruit your students for the political agenda it may be thought to imply.

And this is where we come back to Mr. Barrett, who, in addition to 10 being a college lecturer, is a member of a group calling itself Scholars for 9/11 Truth, an organization with the decidedly political agenda of persuading Americans that the Bush administration "not only permitted 9/11 to happen but may even have orchestrated these events."

Is the fact of this group's growing presence on the Internet a reason for studying it in a course on 9/11? Sure. Is the instructor who discusses the group's arguments thereby endorsing them? Not at all. It is perfectly possible to teach a viewpoint without embracing it and urging it. But the moment a professor does embrace and urge it, academic study has ceased and been replaced by partisan advocacy. And that is a moment no college administration should allow to occur.

Provost Farrell doesn't quite see it that way, because he is too hung up on questions of content and balance. He thinks that the important thing is to assure a diversity of views in the classroom, and so he is reassured when Mr. Barrett promises to surround his "unconventional" ideas and "personal opinions" with readings "representing a variety of viewpoints."

But the number of viewpoints Mr. Barrett presents to his students is not the measure of his responsibility. There is, in fact, no academic requirement to include more than one view of an academic issue, although it is usually pedagogically useful to do so. The true requirement is that no matter how many (or few) views are presented to the students, they should be offered as objects of analysis rather than as candidates for allegiance.

There is a world of difference, for example, between surveying the pro and con arguments about the Iraq war, a perfectly appropriate academic assignment, and pressing students to come down on your side. Of course the instructor who presides over such a survey is likely to be a partisan of one position or the other—after all, who doesn't have an opinion on the Iraq war?—but it is part of a teacher's job to set personal conviction aside for the hour or two when a class is in session and allow the techniques and protocols of academic research full sway.

This restraint should not be too difficult to exercise. After all, we re-   15 quire and expect it of judges, referees and reporters. And while its exercise may not always be total, it is both important and possible to make the effort.

Thus the question Provost Farrell should put to Mr. Barrett is not "Do you hold these views?" (he can hold any views he likes) or "Do you proclaim them in public?" (he has that right no less that the rest of us) or even "Do you surround them with the views of others?"

Rather, the question should be: "Do you separate yourself from your partisan identity when you are in the employ of the citizens of Wisconsin and teach subject matter—whatever it is—rather than urge political action?" If the answer is yes, allowing Mr. Barrett to remain in the classroom is warranted. If the answer is no (or if a yes answer is followed by classroom behavior that contradicts it), he should be shown the door. Not because he would be teaching the "wrong" things, but because he would have abandoned teaching for indoctrination.

The advantage of this way of thinking about the issue is that it outflanks the sloganeering and posturing both sides indulge in; on the one hand, faculty members who shout "academic freedom" and mean by it an instructor's right to say or advocate anything at all with impunity; on the other hand, state legislators who shout "not on our dime" and mean by it that they can tell academics what ideas they can and cannot bring into the classroom.

All you have to do is remember that academic freedom is just that: the freedom to do an academic job without external interference. It is not the freedom to do other jobs, jobs you are neither trained for nor paid to perform. While there should be no restrictions on what can be taught—no list of interdicted ideas or topics—there should be an absolute restriction on appropriating the scene of teaching for partisan political ideals. Teachers who use the classroom to indoctrinate make the enterprise of higher education vulnerable to its critics and shortchange students in the guise of showing them the true way.

Topics for Critical Thinking and Writing

1. What does Fish believe is the erroneous assumption that "both sides" accept (para. 4)?

2. Explain why you agree or disagree with Fish's definition of academic freedom (paras. 5, 6, 19).

3. How would you explain the difference between teaching and indoctrination (para. 17)?

4. Explain and evaluate the title of Fish's essay.

5. Basing your response on the style and content of this essay, would you like to take a course with Professor Fish? Why, or why not?

Letters of Response by Jonah Seligman, Richard DiMatteo, Miriam Cherkes-Julkowski, Joseph Kyle, and Patrick Ward

To the Editor:

Re "Conspiracy Theories 101," by Stanley Fish (Op-Ed, July 23):

As a recent high school graduate, I often endured teachers who spouted their personal political views on topics unrelated to course material without allowing for other opinions to be voiced.

While a teacher's opinions can be of interest, the educators who inspired me the most were those who articulated each side's argument in a debate and the possible fallacies underpinning those arguments, without inserting their own beliefs, allowing the students to make informed decisions.

I want to be taught, not indoctrinated!

Jonah Seligman
Livingston, N.J., July 24, 2006

To the Editor:

Stanley Fish seems to think that the sterile presentation of opposing attitudes and the detached study of the abstractions involved are the legitimate boundaries for academic courses. This kind of stenography is something that can be accomplished by simple reading assignments, without even the need of a teacher in the classroom.

Education is the free interchange and expression of ideas and concepts, and as long as no one crosses the line into the advocacy of criminal behavior or destruction of the social order, just about anything is fair game.

Kevin Barrett, a lecturer at the University of Wisconsin at Madison whose case is discussed by Mr. Fish, shared with his students his belief that the Bush administration may have countenanced the attacks on the World Trade Center and the Pentagon. This view may seem outlandish to some, but the fact is that a full examination of such suspicions has never been conducted.

Journalism has succumbed all too often to the expediency of stenography as reportage. Mr. Fish is advocating the same for academia.

Richard DiMatteo
San Diego, July 24, 2006

To the Editor:

Academic freedom is precisely about the content of speech that takes place in our universities. Stanley Fish might call it "proselytizing"; others might call it presenting an argument for a hard-to-accept position.

Academic freedom is meant to protect ideas, not people; and to maintain diversity within the idea pool and thus to increase the chance of discovering what is actually true.

Miriam Cherkes-Julkowski
Ocean Grove, N.J., July 23, 2006

To the Editor:

The litmus question in Stanley Fish's argument would have a teacher ask: "Do you separate yourself from your partisan identity when you are in the employ of the citizens of [your state] and teach subject matter—whatever it is—rather than urge political action?'

This is mere sophistry.

Perhaps the question should be does one "pretend" to do so, because a skilled instructor can claim objectivity and still use many measures to indoctrinate students.

When Mr. Fish discusses academic freedom in the coming semester, will he miraculously be able to distance himself from his opinions, which are now part of public discourse?

Why not simply be honest with our students—let them know that we all have opinions—and get to work on the investigation and analysis of evidence?

Joseph Kyle
Maplewood, N.J., July 23, 2006

The writer teaches Advanced Placement history in high school.

To the Editor:

Students' ability to learn from or to form contrary opinions to the teachings of an opinionated professor should not be doubted.

Some of the United States' best teachers have been and will continue to be those who hold and share strong convictions in their beliefs.

So long as our professors don't punish students for opposing views, nothing is lost in professors' expressing their beliefs: nothing is lost except classrooms dead from intellectual boredom and hallways silent of enlivened debate.

Inquiry without judgment is not the role of the American scholar. If our universities are truly to be places of learning and scholarship, and not of mere training or rote instruction, professors should be encouraged in their diverse and divergent views; college students should be trusted to make their own opinions; and our nation, a nation of ideas, should be left to benefit.

Patrick Ward
Lusaka, Zambia, July 24, 2006

The writer is a student at Yale.

Topics for Critical Thinking and Writing

1. What differences do you detect in the five letter-writers' tone?

2. What's the difference between being taught something, say, about global warming, and being indoctrinated in the matter?

3. In insisting that "academic freedom is precisely about the content of speech," Cherkes-Julkowski obviously disagrees with Fish. With which writer do you agree, and why?

4. Write a letter (but don't mail it) to one of the letter-writers, responding to his or her letter and indicating whether you agree or disagree with the position taken.

Jean Kilbourne

A graduate of Wellesley College, Jean Kilbourne is the author of Deadly Persuasion: Why Women and Girls Must Fight the Addictive Power of Advertising *(1999), issued in paperback as* Can't Buy My Love: How Advertising Changes the Way We Think and Feel *(2000). In her book she argues that advertising contributes to health problems—including those traced to cigarette smoking, eating disorders, and alcoholism. In the following extract from her book, Kilbourne argues that it is immoral for advertisers to target children. The title of the extract is the editors', and the notes have been renumbered.*

"Own This Child"

Some [Web] sites offer prizes to lure children into giving up the e-mail addresses of their friends too.[1] Online advertising targets children as young as four in an attempt to develop "brand loyalty" as early as possible. Companies unrelated to children's products have Web sites for children, such as Chevron's site, which features games, toys, and videos touting the importance of—surprise!—the oil industry.[2] In this way, companies can create an image early on and can also gather marketing data. As one ad says to advertisers, "Beginning this August, Kidstar will be able to reach every kid on the planet. And you can, too."

The United States is one of the few industrialized nations in the world that thinks that children are legitimate targets for advertisers. Belgium, Denmark, Norway, and the Canadian province of Quebec ban all advertising to children on television and radio,[3] and Sweden and Greece are pushing for an end to all advertising aimed at children throughout the European Union.[4] An effort to pass similar legislation in the United States in the 1970s was squelched by a coalition of food and toy companies, broadcasters, and ad agencies. Children in America appear to have value primarily as new consumers. As an ad for juvenile and infant bedding and home accessories says, "Having children is so rewarding. You get to buy childish stuff and pretend it's for them." Our public policy—

or lack thereof—on every children's issue, from education to drugs to teen suicide to child abuse, leaves many to conclude that we are a nation that hates its children.

However, the media care about them. The Turner Cartoon Network tells advertisers, "Today's kids influence over $130 billion of their parents' spending annually. Kids also spend $8 billion of their own money. That makes these little consumers big business."[5] Not only are children influencing a lot of spending in the present, they are developing brand loyalty and the beginnings of an addiction to consumption that will serve corporations well in the future. According to Mike Searles, president of Kids 'Я' Us, "If you own this child at an early age, you can own this child for years to come. Companies are saying, 'Hey, I want to own the kid younger and younger.'"[6] No wonder Levi Strauss & Co. finds it worthwhile to send a direct mailing to seven- to twelve-year-old girls to learn about them when they are starting to form brand opinions.[7] According to the senior advertising manager, "This is more of a long-term relationship that we're trying to explore." There may not seem much harm in this until we consider that the tobacco and alcohol industries are also interested in long-term relationships beginning in childhood—and are selling products that can indeed end up "owning" people.

Advertisers are willing to spend a great deal on psychological research that will help them target children more effectively. Nintendo U.S. has a research center which interviews at least fifteen hundred children every week.[8] Kid Connection, a unit of the advertising agency Saatchi & Saatchi, has commissioned what the company calls "psychocultural youth research" studies from cultural anthropologists and clinical psychologists.[9] In a recent study, psychologists interviewed young people between the ages of six and twenty and then analyzed their dreams, drawings, and reactions to symbols. Meanwhile, the anthropologists spent over five hundred hours watching other children use the Internet.

Children are easily influenced. Most little children can't tell the difference between the shows and the commercials (which basically means they are smarter than the rest of us). The toys sold during children's programs are often based on characters in the programs. Recently the Center for Media Education asked the Federal Trade Commission to examine "kidola," a television marketing strategy in which toy companies promise to buy blocks of commercial time if a local broadcast station airs programs associated with their toys.[10]

One company has initiated a program for advertisers to distribute samples, coupons, and promotional materials to a network of twenty-two thousand day care centers and 2 million preschool children.[11] The editor-in-chief of *KidStyle,* a kids' fashion magazine that made its debut in 1997, said, "It's not going to be another parenting magazine. This will be a pictorial magazine focusing on products."[12]

Perhaps most troubling, advertising is increasingly showing up in our schools, where ads are emblazoned on school buses, scoreboards, and book covers, where corporations provide "free" material for teachers, and where many children are a captive audience for the commercials on Channel One, a marketing program that gives video equipment to desperate schools in exchange for the right to broadcast a "news" program studded with commercials to all students every morning. Channel One is hardly free, however—it is estimated that it costs taxpayers $1.8 billion in lost classroom time.[13] But it certainly is profitable for the owners who promise advertisers "the largest teen audience around" and "the undivided attention of millions of teenagers for twelve minutes a day." Another ad for Channel One boasts, "Our relationship with 8.1 million teenagers lasts for six years [rather remarkable considering most of theirs last for . . . like six days]."[14] Imagine the public outcry if a political or religious group offered schools an information package with ten minutes of news and two minutes of political or religious persuasion.[15] Yet we tend to think of commercial persuasion as somehow neutral, although it certainly promotes beliefs and behavior that have significant and sometimes harmful effects on the individual, the family, the society, and the environment.

"Reach him at the office," says an ad featuring a small boy in a business suit, which continues, "His first day job is kindergarten. Modern can put your sponsored educational materials in the lesson plan." Advertisers are reaching nearly 8 million public-school students each day.[16]

Cash-strapped and underfunded schools accept this dance with the devil. And they are not alone. As many people become less and less willing to pay taxes to support public schools and other institutions and services, corporations are only too eager to pick up the slack—in exchange for a captive audience, of course. As one good corporate citizen, head of an outdoor advertising agency, suggested, "Perhaps fewer libraries would be closing their doors or reducing their services if they wrapped their buildings in tastefully done outdoor ads."[17]

According to the Council for Aid to Education, the total amount corporations spend on "educational" programs from kindergarten through high school has increased from $5 million in 1965 to about $500 million today.[18] The Seattle School Board recently voted to aggressively pursue advertising and corporate sponsorship.[19] "There can be a Nike concert series and a Boeing valedictorian," said the head of the task force. We already have market-driven educational materials in our schools,[20] such as Exxon's documentary on the beauty of the Alaskan coastline or the McDonald's Nutrition Chart and a kindergarten curriculum that teaches children to "Learn to Read through Recognizing Corporate Logos."[21] 10

No wonder so many people fell for a "news item" in *Adbusters* (a Canadian magazine that critiques advertising and commercialism) about a new program called "Tattoo You Too!", which pays schools a fee in exchange for students willing to be tattooed with famous corporate logos, such as the Nike "swoosh" and the Guess question mark. Although the item was a spoof, it was believable enough to be picked up by some major media. I guess nothing about advertising seems unbelievable these days.

There are penalties for young people who resist this commercialization. In the spring of 1998 Mike Cameron, a senior at Greenbrier High School in Evans, Georgia, was suspended from school.[22] Why? Did he bring a gun to school? Was he smoking in the boys' room? Did he assault a teacher? No. He wore a Pepsi shirt on a school-sponsored Coke day, an entire school day dedicated to an attempt to win ten thousand dollars in a national contest run by Coca-Cola.

Coke has several "partnerships" with schools around the country in which the company gives several million dollars to the school in exchange for a long-term contract giving Coke exclusive rights to school vending machines. John Bushey, an area superintendent for thirteen schools in Colorado Springs who signs his correspondence "The Coke Dude," urged school officials to "get next year's volume up to 70,000 cases" and suggested letting students buy Coke throughout the day and putting vending machines "where they are accessible all day." Twenty years ago, teens drank almost twice as much milk as soda. Today they drink twice as much soda as milk. Some data suggest this contributes to broken bones while they are still teenagers and to osteoporosis in later life.

NOTES

1. F. Rich, "howdydoody.com," *New York Times* 8 June 1997: E15.
2. I. Austen, "But First, Another Word from Our Sponsors," *New York Times* 18 Feb. 1999: E1, E8.
3. M. F. Jacobson and L. A. Mazur, "Marketing Madness: A Survival Guide for a Consumer Society," *Westview Press* 1995: 28. Also J. Weber, "Selling to Kids: At What Price?" *Boston Globe* 18 May 1997: F4.
4. J. Koranteng, "Sweden Presses EU for Further Ad Restrictions," *Advertising Age International* 12 April 1999: 2.
5. Ad, *New York Times* (Calif. ed.) 8 Feb. 1993: C7.
6. R. Harris, "Children Who Dress for Excess: Today's Youngsters Have Become Fixated with Fashion," *Los Angeles Times* 12 Nov. 1989: A1.
7. C. Krol, "Levi's Reach Girls as They Develop Their Opinions on Brands," *Advertising Age* 20 April 1998: 29.
8. Stephen Kline, author of *Out of the Garden: Toys and Children's Culture in the Age of TV Marketing*, interview with McLaren, "The Babysitter's Club," *Stay Free!* Spring 1997: 10.
9. I. Austen, "But First, Another Word from Our Sponsors," *New York Times* 18 Feb. 1999: E1, E8.
10. Center for Media Education, 1511 K Street N.W., Suite 518, Washington, D.C. 20005, 202-628-2620.
11. J. Carroll, "Adventures into New Territory," *Boston Globe* 24 Nov. 1996: D5.
12. A. M. Kerwin, "'KidStyle' Crafts Customized Ad Opportunities," *Advertising Age* 28 April 1997: 46.
13. "Reading, Writing . . . and TV Commercials," *Enough!* Spring 1999: 10.
14. "Our Relationship with 8.1 Million Teenagers . . . ," *Advertising Age* 29 June 1998: S27.

15. H. Rank, "Channel One: Misconceptions Three," *English Journal* 81.4 (April 1992): 31-32.
16. Some corporations sponsor contests and incentive programs, such as an essay-writing contest sponsored by Reebok shoes, which then uses the information to fine-tune the appeal of its advertisements to youth (*Not for Sale!* [Center for Commercial-Free Public Education, Oakland, CA: Spring 1997]: 1), and a Kellogg's contest which had kids make sculptures out of Rice Krispies and melted marshmallows (N. Labi, "Classrooms for Sale," *Time* 19 April 1999: 44). Schools can earn points for every Campbell's soup label or AT&T long-distance phone call, which can then be redeemed for athletic and educational equipment. And a math textbook introduces a decimal division problem as follows: "Will is saving his allowance to buy a pair of Nike shoes that cost $68.25. If Will earns $3.25 per week, how many weeks will Will need to save?" Beside the text is a full-color picture of Nikes (C. L. Hays, "Math Book Salted with Brand Names Raises New Alarm," *New York Times* 21 March 1999: 1).
17. B. Wilkins, "Moving from Blight to Blessing," *Advertising Age* 2 June 1997: 32.
18. K. Zernike, "Let's Make a Deal: Business Seek Classroom Access," *Boston Globe* 2 Feb. 1997: A1, B6.
19. *Not for Sale!* (Center for Commercial-Free Public Education, Oakland, CA) Spring 1997: 1.
20. J. Carroll, "Adventures into New Territory," *Boston Globe* 24 Nov. 1996: D1, D5.
21. *Not for Sale!* (Center for Commercial-Free Public Education, Oakland, CA) Winter 1999: 1.
22. Associated Press, "Pepsi Prank Goes Flat," *Boston Globe* 26 March 1998: A3.
23. J. Foreman, "Sugar's 'Empty Calories' Pile Up," *Boston Globe* 1 March 1999: C1, C4.

TOPICS FOR CRITICAL THINKING AND WRITING

1. In her second paragraph, Kilbourne tells us that some countries "ban all advertising to children on television and radio." Do you favor such a law? Why, or why not?

2. In her third paragraph, Kilbourne indicates her distress that children "are developing brand loyalty and the beginnings of an addiction to consumption." Are you loyal to certain brands? If so, do you think this loyalty is a bad thing? Explain. And are you addicted to consumption? (*Addicted*, of course, implies a loss of self-control. Elsewhere in her book Kilbourne argues, perhaps rightly, that most of us are more deeply influenced by advertising than we are willing to grant or than we are aware.)

3. Beginning in paragraph 7, Kilbourne calls our attention to the practice of allowing companies to donate materials to schools in exchange for ads. The schools accept these materials—with the ads—because they cannot afford to buy the materials. Should such a practice be forbidden? For instance, should a school reject funds that are offered on behalf of "a Nike concert series" (para. 10)? If you are aware that your secondary school accepted material, along with the accompanying advertisements, do you think the ads influenced your behavior? Explain.

4. Do you think Mike Cameron ought to have been suspended for wearing a Pepsi shirt on a Coke day (para. 12)? Should he have been repri-

manded by the school authorities? Would it make any difference if (a) he didn't know it was a Coke day, (b) he knew it was a Coke day and refused to go along because he strongly opposed commercial sponsorship of this sort, or (c) he knew it was a Coke day but thought it would be amusing to be the only holdout?

5. Is there really such a thing as an "addiction to consumption" (para. 3)? Write a 500-word essay on the theme "Excessive Juvenile Consumption, Yes; Addiction to Consumption, No."

6. In her final paragraph, Kilbourne expresses her unhappiness that young people today drink more soda than milk. Are you convinced that they should drink more milk than soda? If so, where did you get the idea that milk is more healthful than soda?

EXERCISE: LETTER TO THE EDITOR

Your college newspaper has published a letter that links a hateful attribute to a group and that clearly displays hate for the entire group. (For instance, the letter charges that interracial marriages should be made illegal because "African Americans contain a criminal gene," or that "Jews should not be elected to office because their loyalty is to Israel, not the United States," or that "Muslims should not be allowed to enter the country because they are intent on destroying America.") The letter generates many letters of response; some responses, supporting the editor's decision to publish the letter, make these points:

- The writer of the offending letter is a student in the college, and she has a right to express her views.
- The point of view expressed is probably held only by a few persons, but conceivably it expresses a view held by a significant number of students.
- Editors should not act as censors.
- The First Amendment guarantees freedom of speech.
- Freedom of expression is healthy, i.e., society gains.

On the other hand, among the letters opposing the editor's decision to publish, some make points along these lines:

- Not every view of every nutty student can be printed; editors must make responsible choices.
- The First Amendment, which prohibits the government from controlling the press, has nothing to do with a college newspaper.
- Letters of this sort do not foster healthy discussion; they merely heat things up.

Write a 250- to 500-word letter to the editor, expressing your view of the editor's decision to publish the first letter. (If you wish, you can assume that the letter was on one of the topics we specify in the second sentence of this exercise. But in any case, address the general issue of the editor's decision, not only the specific issue of the charge or charges made in the first letter.)

3

Critical Reading: Getting Deeper into Arguments

He that wrestles with us strengthens our nerves, and sharpens our skill. Our antagonist is our helper.

—EDMUND BURKE

PERSUASION, ARGUMENT, DISPUTE

When we think seriously about an argument (not name calling or mere rationalization), not only do we hear ideas that may be unfamiliar, but we are also forced to examine closely our own cherished opinions, and perhaps for the first time really come to see the strengths and weaknesses of what we believe. As John Stuart Mill put it, "He who knows only his own side of the case knows little."

It is customary, and useful, to distinguish between persuasion and argument. **Persuasion** has the broader meaning. To persuade is to win over—whether by giving reasons (that is, by argument), by appealing to the emotions, or, for that matter, by using torture. **Argument,** one form of persuasion, relies on reason; it offers statements as reasons for other statements. Rhetoricians often use the Greek word **logos,** which merely means "word" or "reason," to denote this aspect of persuasive writing—the appeal to reason. An appeal to reason may include such things as an appeal to

- Physical evidence;
- The testimony of experts;
- Common sense; and
- Probability.

The appeal to the emotions is known as **pathos.** Strictly speaking, *pathos* is Greek for "feeling," and especially for "suffering," but it now covers all sorts of emotional appeal—for instance, to one's sense of pity or sympathy (Greek for "feeling with") or one's sense of patriotism.

Notice that an argument, in the sense of statements that are offered as reasons for other statements, does not require two speakers or writers who represent opposed positions. The Declaration of Independence is an argument, setting forth the colonists' reasons for declaring their independence. In practice, of course, someone's argument usually advances reasons for a claim in opposition to someone else's position or belief. But even if one is writing only for oneself, trying to clarify one's thinking by setting forth reasons, the result is an argument. **Dispute,** however, is a special kind of argument in which two or more people express views that are at odds.

Most of this book is about argument in the sense of the presentation of reasons in support of claims, but of course, reason is not the whole story. If an argument is to be effective, it must be presented persuasively. For instance, the writer's **tone** (attitude toward self, topic, and audience) must be appropriate if the discourse is to persuade the reader. The careful presentation of the self is not something disreputable, nor is it something that publicity agents or advertising agencies invented. Aristotle (384–22 B.C.) emphasized the importance of impressing on the audience that the speaker is a person of good sense and high moral character. (He called this aspect of persuasion **ethos,** the Greek word for "character," as opposed to *logos,* which we have noted is the word for persuasion by appealing to reason.)

Writers convey their trustworthiness by

- Avoiding vulgar language;
- Showing an awareness of the complexity of the issue (for instance, by granting the goodwill of those offering other points of view and by recognizing that there may be some merit to contrary points of view); and
- Showing attention to detail (for instance, by citing relevant statistics).

In short, writers who are concerned with *ethos* — and all writers should be — employ devices that persuade readers that the writers are trustworthy, are persons in whom the reader can have confidence.

We talk at length about tone, along with other matters such as the organization of an argument, in Chapter 5, but here we deal with some of the chief devices used in reasoning, and we glance at emotional appeals.

We should note at once, however, that an argument presupposes a fixed **topic.** Suppose we are arguing about Thomas Jefferson's assertion, in the Declaration of Independence, that "all men are created equal." Jones subscribes to this statement, but Smith says it is nonsense and argues that one has only to look around to see that some people are brighter than others, or healthier, or better coordinated, or whatever. Jones and Smith, if they intend to argue the point, will do well to examine what Jefferson actually wrote:

> We hold these truths to be self-evident, that all men are created equal:
> that they are endowed by their Creator with certain unalienable rights;
> and that among these are life, liberty, and the pursuit of happiness.

There is room for debate over what Jefferson really meant and about whether he is right, but clearly he was talking about *equality of rights.* If Smith and Jones wish to argue about Jefferson's view of equality—that is, if they wish to offer their reasons for accepting, rejecting, or modifying it—they will do well first to agree on what Jefferson said or what he probably meant to say. Jones and Smith may still hold different views; they may continue to disagree on whether Jefferson was right and proceed to offer arguments and counterarguments to settle the point. But only if they can agree on *what* they disagree about will their dispute get somewhere.

REASON VERSUS RATIONALIZATION

Reason may not be our only way of finding the truth, but it is a way we often rely on. The subway ran yesterday at 6:00 A.M. and the day before at 6:00 A.M. and the day before, and so I infer from this evidence that it will also run today at 6:00 A.M. (a form of reasoning known as **induction**). Bus drivers require would-be passengers to present the exact change; I do not have the exact change; therefore, I infer I cannot ride on the bus (**deduction**). (The terms *deduction* and *induction* are discussed in more detail on pages 84–88 and 88–90.)

We also know that, if we set our minds to a problem, we can often find reasons (not necessarily sound ones but reasons nevertheless) for almost anything we want to justify. Here is an entertaining example from Benjamin Franklin's *Autobiography:*

> I believe I have omitted mentioning that in my first voyage from
> Boston, being becalmed off Block Island, our people set about catching
> cod and hauled up a great many. Hitherto I had stuck to my resolution
> of not eating animal food, and on this occasion, I considered with my
> master Tryon the taking of every fish as a kind of unprovoked murder,
> since none of them had or ever could do us any injury that might justify
> the slaughter. All this seemed very reasonable. But I had formerly been
> a great lover of fish, and when this came hot out of the frying pan, it
> smelt admirably well. I balanced some time between principle and
> inclination, till I recollected that when the fish were opened I saw
> smaller fish taken out of their stomachs. Then thought I, if you eat one
> another, I don't see why we mayn't eat you. So I dined upon cod very
> heartily and continued to eat with other people, returning only now
> and then occasionally to a vegetable diet. So convenient a thing it is to
> be a *reasonable creature,* since it enables one to find or make a reason for
> everything one has a mind to do.

Franklin is being playful; he is *not* engaging in critical thinking. He tells us that he loved fish, that this fish "smelt admirably well," and so we are prepared for him to find a reason (here one as weak as "Fish eat fish, therefore people may eat fish") to abandon his vegetarianism. (But think: Fish also eat their own young. May we therefore eat ours?)

Still, Franklin touches on a truth: If necessary, we can find reasons to justify whatever we want. That is, instead of reasoning we may *rationalize* (devise a self-serving but dishonest reason), like the fox in Aesop's fables who, finding the grapes he desired were out of his reach, consoled himself with the thought they were probably sour.

Perhaps we can never be certain that we are not rationalizing, except when, like Franklin, we are being playful — but we can seek to think critically about our own beliefs, scrutinizing our assumptions, looking for counterevidence, and wondering if different conclusions can reasonably be drawn.

SOME PROCEDURES IN ARGUMENT

Definition

Definition, we mentioned in our first chapter, is one of the classical topics, a "place" to which one goes with questions; in answering the questions, one finds ideas. When we define, we are answering the question "What is it?" and in answering this question as precisely as we can, we will find, clarify, and develop ideas.

We have already glanced at an argument over the proposition that "all men are created equal," and we saw that the words needed clarification. *Equal* meant, in the context, not physically or mentally equal but something like "equal in rights," equal politically and legally. (And of course, "men" meant "white men and women.") Words do not always mean exactly what they seem to: There is no lead in a lead pencil, and a standard 2-by-4 is currently $1^5/8$ inches in thickness and $3^3/8$ inches in width.

Definition by Synonym   Let's return, for a moment, to *pornography*, a word that, we saw, is not easily defined. One way to define a word is to offer a **synonym.** Thus, pornography can be defined, at least roughly, as "obscenity" (something indecent). But definition by synonym is usually only a start because we find that we will have to define the synonym and, besides, that very few words have exact synonyms. (In fact, *pornography* and *obscenity* are not exact synonyms.)

Definition by Example   A second way to define something is to point to an example (this is often called **ostensive definition,** from the Latin *ostendere*, "to show"). This method can be very helpful, ensuring that both writer and reader are talking about the same thing, but it also has its limitations. A few decades ago many people pointed to James Joyce's *Ulysses* and D. H. Lawrence's *Lady Chatterley's Lover* as examples of obscene novels, but today these books are regarded as literary masterpieces. Possibly they can be obscene and also be literary masterpieces. (Joyce's wife is reported to have said of her husband, "He may have been a great writer, but . . . he had a very dirty mind.")

One of the difficulties of using an example, however, is that the example is richer and more complex than the term it is being used to define, and this richness and complexity get in the way of achieving a clear definition. Thus, if one cites Lawrence's *Lady Chatterley's Lover* as an example of pornography, a listener may erroneously think that pornography has something to do with British novels or with heterosexual relationships outside of marriage. Yet neither of these ideas is part of the concept of pornography.

We are not trying here to formulate a satisfactory definition of *pornography*. Our object is to show that

- An argument will be most fruitful if the participants first agree on what they are talking about;
- One way to secure such agreement is to define the topic ostensively; and
- Choosing the right example, one that has all the central or typical characteristics, can make a topic not only clear but also vivid.

Definition by Stipulation   In arguing, you can legitimately offer a **stipulative definition,** saying, perhaps, that by *Native American* you mean any person with any Native American blood; or you might say, "For the purpose of the present discussion, I mean by a *Native American* any person who has at least one grandparent of pure Native American blood." A stipulative definition is appropriate where

- No fixed or standard definition is available, and
- Some arbitrary specification is necessary to fix the meaning of a key term in the argument.

Not everyone may be willing to accept your stipulative definition, and alternatives can probably be defended. In any case, when you stipulate a definition, your audience knows what *you* mean by the term thus defined.

It would *not* be reasonable, of course, to stipulate that by *Native American* you mean anyone with a deep interest in North American aborigines. That's just too idiosyncratic to be useful. Similarly, an essay on Jews in America will have to rely on some definition of the key idea. Perhaps the writer will stipulate the definition used in Israel: A Jew is a person who has a Jewish mother or, if not born of a Jewish mother, a person who has formally adopted the Jewish faith. Or perhaps the writer

will stipulate another meaning: Jews are people who consider themselves to be Jews. Some sort of reasonable definition must be offered.

To stipulate, however, that by *Jews* you mean "persons who believe
that the area formerly called Palestine rightfully belongs to the Jews"
would hopelessly confuse matters. Remember the old riddle and the answer: If you call a dog's tail a leg, how many legs does a dog have? Answer: Four. Calling a tail a leg doesn't make it a leg.

In Chapter 2 we saw an effective use of a stipulative definition in
Stanley Fish's discussion of academic freedom, when Fish talks about a
professor at the University of Wisconsin who believes that the U.S. government may have caused the destruction of the World Trade Center.
Some people have called for the university to fire the professor, but others have defended him on the grounds of academic freedom. Fish argues
that both sides misinterpret the concept of academic freedom:

> Both sides get it wrong. The problem is that each assumes that aca-
> demic freedom is about protecting the content of a professor's speech;
> one side thinks that no content should be ruled out in advance; while
> the other would draw the line at propositions (like the denial of the
> Holocaust or the flatness of the world) considered by almost everyone
> to be crazy or dangerous.
>
> But in fact, academic freedom has nothing to do with content. It is
> not a subset of the general freedom of Americans to say anything they like
> (so long as it is not an incitement to violence or is treasonous or libelous).
> Rather, academic freedom is the freedom of academics to *study* anything
> they like; the freedom, that is, to subject any body of material, however
> unpromising it might seem, to academic interrogation and analysis.

Fish goes on to give examples: Astrology is discredited as a science, but
one might well *study* it because of its enormous influence on the thought
of the past. Fish emphasizes the distinction is between *studying* a subject
and *advocating* it. "There is a world of difference . . . between surveying
the pro and con arguments about the Iraq war, a perfectly appropriate
academic assignment, and pressing students to come down on your
side." Readers might disagree with Fish, but at least they understand exactly what he means when he speaks of academic freedom.

A stipulation may be helpful and legitimate. Here is the opening
paragraph of an essay by Richard B. Brandt titled "The Morality and Rationality of Suicide" (from *A Handbook for the Study of Suicide*, edited by
Seymour Perlin). Notice that

- The author first stipulates a definition, and
- Then, aware that the definition may strike some readers as too
  broad and therefore unreasonable or odd, he offers a reason on
  behalf of his definition:

> "Suicide" is conveniently defined, for our purposes, as doing something
> which results in one's death, either from the intention of ending one's
> life or the intention to bring about some other state of affairs (such as

relief from pain) which one thinks it certain or highly probable can be achieved only by means of death or will produce death. It may seem odd to classify an act of heroic self-sacrifice on the part of a soldier as suicide. It is simpler, however, not to try to define "suicide" so that an act of suicide is always irrational or immoral in some way; if we adopt a neutral definition like the above we can still proceed to ask when an act of suicide in that sense is rational, morally justifiable, and so on, so that all evaluations anyone might wish to make can still be made.

Sometimes a definition that at first seems extremely odd can be made acceptable, if strong reasons are offered in its support. Sometimes, in fact, an odd definition marks a great intellectual step forward. For instance, in 1990 the U.S. Supreme Court recognized that *speech* includes symbolic nonverbal expression such as protesting against a war by wearing armbands or by flying the American flag upside down. Such actions, because they express ideas or emotions, are now protected by the First Amendment. Few people today would disagree that *speech* should include symbolic gestures. (We include an example of controversy over precisely this issue, in Derek Bok's "Protecting Freedom of Expression on the Campus," in Chapter 2.)

A definition that seems notably eccentric to many readers and thus far has not gained much support is from page 94 of Peter Singer's *Practical Ethics*, in which the author suggests that a nonhuman being can be a *person*. He admits that "it sounds odd to call an animal a person" but says that it seems so only because of our bad habit of sharply separating ourselves from other species. For Singer, *persons* are "rational and self-conscious beings, aware of themselves as distinct entities with a past and a future." Thus, although a newborn infant is a human being, it is not a person; on the other hand, an adult chimpanzee is not a human being but probably is a person. You don't have to agree with Singer to know exactly what he means and where he stands. Moreover, if you read his essay, you may even find that his reasons are plausible and that by means of his unusual definition he has enlarged your thinking.

The Importance of Definitions   Trying to decide on the best way to define a key idea or a central concept is often difficult as well as controversial. *Death*, for example, has been redefined in recent years. Traditionally, a person was dead when there was no longer any heartbeat. But with advancing medical technology, the medical profession has persuaded legislatures to redefine *death* as cessation of cerebral and cortical functions— so-called brain death.

Some scholars have hoped to bring clarity into the abortion debate by redefining *life*. Traditionally, human life begins at birth or perhaps at viability (the capacity of a fetus to live independently of the uterine environment). However, some have proposed a "brain birth" definition, in the hope of resolving the abortion controversy. A *New York Times* story of November 8, 1990, reported that these thinkers want abortion to be prohibited by law at the point where "integrated brain functioning begins to emerge—about seventy days after conception." Whatever the merits of such a redefinition, the debate is convincing evidence of just how important the definition of certain terms can be.

Last Words about Definition   Since Plato's time, in the fourth century B.C., it has often been argued that the best way to give a definition is to state the *essence* of the thing being defined. Thus, the classic example defines *man* as "a rational animal." (Today, to avoid sexist implications, instead of *man* we would say *human being* or *person*.) That is, the property of *rational animality* is taken to be the essence of every human creature, and so it must be mentioned in the definition of *man*. This statement guarantees that the definition is neither too broad nor too narrow. But philosophers have long criticized this alleged ideal type of definition, on several grounds, one of which is that no one can propose such definitions without assuming that the thing being defined has an essence in the first place—an assumption that is not necessary. Thus, we may want to define *causality*, or *explanation*, or even *definition* itself, but it is doubtful whether it is sound to assume that any of these things has an essence.

A much better way to provide a definition is to offer a set of **sufficient and necessary conditions.** Suppose we want to define the word *circle* and are conscious of the need to keep circles distinct from other geometrical figures such as rectangles and spheres. We might express our definition by citing sufficient and necessary conditions as follows: "Anything is a circle *if and only if* it is a closed plane figure and all points on the circumference are equidistant from the center." Using the connective "if and only if" (called the *biconditional*) between the definition and what is being defined helps to force into our consciousness the need to make the definition neither too exclusive (too narrow) nor too inclusive (too broad). Of course, for most ordinary purposes we don't require such a formally precise and explicit definition. Nevertheless, perhaps the best criterion to keep in mind when assessing a proposed definition is whether it can be stated in the "if and only if " form, and whether, if it is so stated, it is true; that is, if it truly specifies *all and only* the things covered by the word being defined.

Thus, to summarize, definitions can be given by

- Synonym,
- Example,
- Stipulation,
- Mention of the essence, and
- Statement of necessary and sufficient conditions.

Assumptions

In Chapter 1 we discussed the **assumptions** made by the authors of two essays on campus discipline. But we have more to say about assumptions. We have already said that in the form of discourse known as argument certain statements are offered as reasons for other statements. But even the longest and most complex chain of reasoning or proof is fastened to assumptions—one or more *unexamined beliefs*. (Even if such a belief is shared by writer and reader, it is no less an assumption.) Benjamin Franklin argued against paying salaries to the holders of executive offices in the federal government on the grounds that men are moved by ambition (love of power) and by avarice (love of money) and that powerful positions conferring wealth incite men to do their worst. These assumptions he stated, though he felt no need to argue them at length because he assumed that his readers shared them.

An assumption may be unstated. A writer, painstakingly arguing specific points, may choose to keep one or more of the argument's assumptions tacit. Or the writer may be as unaware of some underlying assumption as of the surrounding air. For example, Franklin didn't even bother to state another assumption. He must have assumed that persons of wealth who accept an unpaying job (after all, only persons of wealth could afford to hold unpaid government jobs) will have at heart the interests of all classes of people, not only the interests of their own class. Probably Franklin did not state this assumption because he thought it was perfectly obvious, but if you think critically about the assumption, you may find reasons to doubt it. Surely one reason we pay our legislators is to make certain that the legislature does not consist only of people whose incomes may give them an inadequate view of the needs of others.

An Example: Assumptions in the Argument Permitting Abortion

1. Ours is a pluralistic society, in which we believe that the religious beliefs of one group should not be imposed on others.
2. Personal privacy is a right, and a woman's body is hers, not to be violated by laws that tell her she may not do certain things to her body.

But these (and other) arguments *assume* that a fetus is not—or not yet—a person and therefore is not entitled to the same protection against assaults that we are. Virtually all of us assume that it is usually wrong to kill a human being. Granted, we may find instances in which we believe it is acceptable to take a human life, such as self-defense against a would-be murderer. But even here we find a shared assumption that persons are ordinarily entitled not to be killed.

The argument about abortion, then, usually depends on opposed assumptions: For one group, the fetus is a human being and a potential person—and this potentiality is decisive. But for the other group it is not. Persons arguing one side or the other of the abortion issue ought to be aware that opponents may not share their assumptions.

Premises and Syllogisms

Premises are stated assumptions used as reasons in an argument. (The word comes from a Latin word meaning "to send before" or "to set in front.") A premise thus is a statement set down—assumed—before the argument is begun. The joining of two premises—two statements taken to be true—to produce a conclusion, a third statement, is called a **syllogism** (Greek for "a reckoning together"). The classic example is this:

> Major premise: All human beings are mortal.
> Minor premise: Socrates is a human being.
> Conclusion: Socrates is mortal.

Deduction

The mental process of moving from one statement ("All human beings are mortal") through another ("Socrates is a human being") to yet a further statement ("Socrates is mortal") is called **deduction,** from Latin for "lead down from." In this sense, deductive reasoning does not give us any new knowledge, although it is easy to construct examples that have so many premises, or premises that are so complex, that the conclusion really does come as news to most who examine the argument. Thus, the great detective Sherlock Holmes was credited by his admiring colleague, Dr. Watson, with unusual powers of deduction. Watson meant in part that Holmes could see the logical consequences of apparently disconnected reasons, the number and complexity of which left others at a loss. What is common in all cases of deduction is that the reasons or premises offered are supposed to contain within themselves, so to speak, the conclusion extracted from them.

Often a syllogism is abbreviated. Martin Luther King Jr., defending a protest march, wrote in "Letter from Birmingham Jail":

> You assert that our actions, even though peaceful, must be condemned because they precipitate violence.

Fully expressed, the argument that King attributes to his critics would be stated thus:

> Society must condemn actions (even if peaceful) that precipitate violence.

> This action (though peaceful) will precipitate violence.

> Therefore, society must condemn this action.

An incomplete or abbreviated syllogism in which one of the premises is left unstated, of the sort found in King's original quotation, is called an **enthymeme** (Greek for "in the mind").

Here is another, more whimsical example of an enthymeme, in which both a premise and the conclusion are left implicit. Henry David Thoreau

remarked that "circumstantial evidence can be very strong, as when you find a trout in the milk." The joke, perhaps intelligible only to people born before 1930 or so, depends on the fact that milk used to be sold "in bulk"—that is, ladled out of a big can directly to the customer by the farmer or grocer. This practice was finally prohibited in the 1930s because for centuries the sellers, in order to increase their profit, were diluting the milk with water. Thoreau's enthymeme can be fully expressed thus:

Trout live only in water.

This milk has a trout in it.

Therefore, this milk has water in it.

These enthymemes have three important properties: Their premises are *true,* the form of their argument is *valid,* and they leave *implicit* either the conclusion or one of the premises.

Sound Arguments

The purpose of a syllogism is to present reasons that establish its conclusion. This is done by making sure that the argument satisfies both of two independent criteria:

- First, all of the premises must be *true.*
- Second, the syllogism must be *valid.*

Once these criteria are satisfied, the conclusion of the syllogism is guaranteed. Any such argument is said to establish or to prove its conclusion, or to use another term, it is said to be **sound.** Here's an example of a sound argument, a syllogism that proves its conclusion:

> Extracting oil from the Arctic Wildlife Refuge would adversely affect the local ecology.
>
> Adversely affecting the local ecology is undesirable, unless there is no better alternative fuel source.
>
> Therefore, extracting oil from the Arctic Wildlife Refuge is undesirable, unless there is no better alternative fuel source.

Each premise is **true,** and the syllogism is **valid,** so it establishes its conclusion.

But how do we tell in any given case that an argument is sound? We perform two different tests, one for the truth of each of the premises and another for the validity of the argument.

The basic test for the **truth** of a premise is to determine whether what it asserts corresponds with reality; if it does, then it is true, and if it doesn't, then it is false. Everything depends on the content of the premise — what it asserts — and the evidence for it. (In the preceding syllogism, the truth of the premises can be tested by checking the views of experts and interested parties, such as policymakers, environmental groups, and experts on energy.)

The test for **validity** is quite different. We define a valid argument as one in which the conclusion follows from the premises, so that if all the premises are true then the conclusion *must* be true, too. The general test for validity, then, is this: If one grants the premises, one must also grant the conclusion. Or to put it another way, if one grants the premises but denies the conclusion, is one caught in a self-contradiction? If so, the argument is valid; if not, the argument is invalid.

The preceding syllogism passes this test. If you grant the information given in the premises but deny the conclusion, you have contradicted yourself. Even if the information were in error, the conclusion in this syllogism would still follow from the premises — the hallmark of a valid argument! The conclusion follows because the validity of an argument is a purely formal matter concerning the *relation* between premises and conclusion based on what they mean.

This relationship can be seen more clearly by examining an argument that is valid but that, because one or both of the premises are false, does *not* establish its conclusion. Here is an example of such a syllogism:

> The whale is a large fish.
>
> All large fish have scales.
>
> Therefore, whales have scales.

We know that the premises and the conclusion are false: Whales are mammals, not fish, and not all large fish have scales (sharks have no scales, for instance). But when the validity of the argument is being determined, the truth of the premises and the conclusion is beside the point. Just a little reflection assures us that *if* both of these premises were true, then the conclusion would have to be true as well. That is, anyone who grants the premises of this syllogism and yet denies the conclusion has contradicted herself. So the validity of an argument does not in any way depend on the truth of the premises or the conclusion.

A sound argument, as we said, is an argument that passes both the test of true premises and the test of valid inference. To put it another way, a sound argument passes the test of *content* (the premises are true, as a matter of fact) and the test of *form* (its premises and conclusion, by virtue of their very meanings, are so related that it is impossible for the premises to be true and the conclusion false).

Accordingly, an unsound argument, an argument that fails to prove its conclusion, suffers from one or both of two defects. First, not all of the premises are true. Second, the argument is invalid. Usually, we have in mind one or both of these defects when we object to someone's argument as "illogical." In evaluating someone's deductive argument, therefore, you must always ask: Is it vulnerable to criticism on the ground that one (or more) of its premises is false? Or is the inference itself vulnerable because even if all the premises are all true, the conclusion still wouldn't follow?

A deductive argument *proves* its conclusion if and only if *two conditions* are satisfied: (1) All the premises are *true,* and (2) it would be *inconsistent to assert the premises and deny the conclusions.*

A Word about False Premises   Suppose that one or more of the premises of a syllogism is false but the syllogism itself is valid. What does that tell us about the truth of the conclusion? Consider this example:

All Americans prefer vanilla ice cream to other flavors.

Tiger Woods is an American.

Therefore, Tiger Woods prefers vanilla ice cream to other flavors.

The first (or major) premise in this syllogism is false. Yet the argument passes our formal test for validity; it is clear that if one grants both premises, then one must accept the conclusion. So we can say that the conclusion *follows from* its premises, even though the premises *do not prove* the conclusion. This is not as paradoxical as it may sound. For all we know, the conclusion of this argument may in fact be true; Tiger Woods may indeed prefer vanilla ice cream, and the odds are that he does because consumption statistics show that a majority of Americans prefer vanilla. Nevertheless, if the conclusion in this syllogism is true, it is not because this argument proved it.

A Word about Invalid Syllogisms   Usually, one can detect a false premise in an argument, especially when the suspect premise appears in someone else's argument. A trickier business is the invalid syllogism. Consider this argument:

All terrorists seek publicity for their violent acts.

John Doe seeks publicity for his violent acts.

Therefore, John Doe is a terrorist.

In the preceding syllogism, let us grant that the first (major) premise is true. Let us also grant that the conclusion may well be true. Finally, the person mentioned in the second (minor) premise could indeed be a terrorist. But it is also possible that the conclusion is false; terrorists are not the only ones who seek publicity for their violent acts; think, for example, of the violence committed against doctors, clinic workers, and patients at clinics where abortions are performed. In short, the truth of the two premises is no guarantee that the conclusion is also true. It is possible to assert both premises and deny the conclusion without self-contradiction.

How do we tell, in general and in particular cases, whether a syllogism is valid? Chemists use litmus paper to enable them to tell instantly whether the liquid in a test tube is an acid or a base. Unfortunately, logic has no litmus test to tell us instantly whether an argument is valid or invalid. Logicians beginning with Aristotle have developed techniques that enable them to test any given argument, no matter how complex or subtle, to determine its validity. But the results of their labors cannot be expressed in a paragraph or even a few pages; not for nothing are semester-long courses devoted to teaching formal deductive logic. Apart from advising you to consult Chapter 9, A Logician's View: Deduction, Induction, Fallacies, all we can do here is repeat two basic points.

First, validity of deductive arguments is a matter of their *form* or *structure*. Even syllogisms like the one on the Arctic Wildlife Refuge on page 86 come in a large variety of forms (256 different ones, to be precise), and only some of these forms are valid. Second, all valid deductive arguments (and only such arguments) pass this test: If one accepts all the premises, then one must accept the conclusion as well. Hence, if it is possible to accept the premises but reject the conclusion (without self-contradiction, of course), then the argument is invalid.

Let us exit from further discussion of this important but difficult subject on a lighter note. Many illogical arguments masquerade as logical. Consider this example: If it takes a horse and carriage four hours to go from Pinsk to Chelm, does it follow that a carriage with two horses will get there in two hours?

Note: In Chapter 9, we discuss at some length other kinds of deductive arguments, as well as **fallacies,** which are kinds of invalid reasoning.

Induction

Whereas deduction takes our beliefs and assumptions and extracts their hidden consequences, **induction** uses information about observed cases to reach a conclusion about unobserved cases. (The word comes from the Latin *in ducere*, "to lead into" or "to lead up to.") If we observe that the bite of a certain snake is poisonous, we may conclude on this evidence that another snake of the same general type is also poisonous. Our inference might be even broader. If we observe that snake after snake of a certain type has a poisonous bite and that these snakes are all rattlesnakes, we are tempted to **generalize** that all rattlesnakes are poisonous.

By far the most common way to test the adequacy of a generalization is to confront it with one or more **counterexamples.** If the counterexamples are genuine and reliable, then the generalization must be false. For example, Ronald Takaki's essay on the "myth" of Asian racial superiority (p. 117) is full of examples that contradict the alleged superiority of Asians; they are counterexamples to that thesis, and they help to expose it as a "myth." What is true of Takaki's reasoning is true generally in argumentative writing. We are constantly testing our generalizations against actual or possible counterexamples.

Unlike deduction, induction gives us conclusions that go beyond the information contained in the premises used in their support. Not surprisingly, the conclusions of inductive reasoning are not always true, even when all the premises are true. On page 77, we gave as an example our observation that on previous days a subway has run at 6:00 A.M. and that therefore we believe that it runs at 6:00 A.M. every day. Suppose, following this reasoning, we arrive at the subway platform just before 6:00 A.M. on a given day and wait an hour without a train. What inference should we draw to explain this? Possibly today is Sunday, and the subway doesn't run before 7:00 A.M. Or possibly there was a breakdown earlier this morning. Whatever the explanation, we relied on a sample that was not large enough (a larger sample might have included some early morning breakdowns) or not representative enough (a more representative sample would have included the later starts on holidays).

A Word about Samples   When we reason inductively, much depends on the size and the quality of the sample. We may interview five members of Alpha Tau Omega and find that all five are Republicans, yet we cannot legitimately conclude that all members of ATO are Republicans. The problem is not always one of failing to interview large numbers. A poll of ten thousand college students tells us very little about "college students" if all ten thousand are white males at the University of Texas. Such a sample, because it leaves out women and minority males, obviously is not sufficiently *representative* of "college students" as a group. Further, though not all of the students at the University of Texas are from Texas or even from the Southwest, it is quite likely that the student body is not fully representative (for instance, in race and in income) of American college students. If this conjecture is correct, even a truly representative sample of University of Texas students would not allow one to draw firm conclusions about American college students.

In short: An argument that uses samples ought to tell the reader how the samples were chosen. If it does not provide this information, the argument may rightly be treated with suspicion.

Evidence: Experimentation, Examples, Authoritative Testimony, Statistics

Different disciplines use different kinds of evidence:

- In literary studies, the texts are usually the chief evidence.
- In the social sciences, field research (interviews, surveys) usually provides evidence.

In the sciences, reports of experiments are the usual evidence; if an assertion cannot be tested — if an assertion is not capable of being shown to be false — it is a *belief*, an *opinion*, not a scientific hypothesis.

Experimentation   Induction is obviously useful in arguing. If, for example, one is arguing that handguns should be controlled, one will point to specific cases in which handguns caused accidents or were used to commit crimes. If one is arguing that abortion has a traumatic effect on women, one will point to women who testify to that effect. Each instance constitutes **evidence** for the relevant generalization.

In a courtroom, evidence bearing on the guilt of the accused is introduced by the prosecution, and evidence to the contrary is introduced by the defense. Not all evidence is admissible (hearsay, for example, is not, even if it is true), and the law of evidence is a highly developed subject in jurisprudence. In the forum of daily life, the sources of evidence are less disciplined. Daily experience, a particularly memorable observation, an unusual event we witnessed — any or all of these may be used as evidence for (or against) some belief, theory, hypothesis, or explanation. The systematic study of what experience can yield is what science does, and one of the most distinctive features of the evidence that scientists can marshal on behalf of their claims is that it is the result of **experimentation.** Experiments are deliberately contrived situations that are often complex in their technology and designed to yield particular observations. What the ordinary person does with unaided eye and ear, the scientist does, much more carefully and thoroughly, with the help of laboratory instruments.

The variety, extent, and reliability of the evidence obtained in daily life and in the laboratory are quite different. It is hardly a surprise that in our civilization much more weight is attached to the "findings" of scientists than to the corroborative (much less the contrary) experiences of the ordinary person. No one today would seriously argue that the sun really does go around the earth just because it looks that way; nor would we argue that because viruses are invisible to the naked eye they cannot cause symptoms such as swellings and fevers, which are quite plainly visible.

Examples   One form of evidence is the **example.** Suppose that we argue that a candidate is untrustworthy and should not be elected to public office. We point to episodes in his career—his misuse of funds in 1998 and the false charges he made against an opponent in 2002— as examples of his untrustworthiness. Or if we are arguing that President Truman ordered the atom bomb dropped to save American (and, for that matter, Japanese) lives that otherwise would have been lost in a hard-fought invasion of Japan, we point to the stubbornness of the Japanese defenders in battles on the islands of Saipan, Iwo Jima, and Okinawa, where Japanese soldiers fought to the death rather than surrender.

These examples, we say, show us that the Japanese defenders of the main islands would have fought to their deaths without surrendering, even though they knew they would be defeated. Or if we argue that the war was nearly won when Truman dropped the bomb, we can cite secret peace feelers as examples of the Japanese willingness to end the war.

An example is a sample; these two words come from the same Old French word, *essample,* from the Latin *exemplum,* which means "something taken out"—that is, a selection from the group. A Yiddish proverb shrewdly says that "'For example' is no proof," but the evidence of well-chosen examples can go a long way toward helping a writer to convince an audience.

In arguments, three sorts of examples are especially common:

- Real events,
- Invented instances (artificial or hypothetical cases), and
- Analogies.

We will treat each of these briefly.

REAL EVENTS   In referring to Truman's decision to drop the atom bomb, we have already touched on examples drawn from real events— the battles at Saipan and elsewhere. And we have also seen Ben Franklin pointing to an allegedly real happening, a fish that had consumed a smaller fish. The advantage of an example drawn from real life, whether a great historical event or a local incident, is that its reality gives it weight. It can't simply be brushed off.

On the other hand, an example drawn from reality may not provide as clear-cut an instance as could be wished for. Suppose, for instance, that someone cites the Japanese army's behavior on Saipan and on Iwo Jima as evidence that the Japanese later would have fought to the death in an American invasion of Japan and would therefore have inflicted terrible losses on themselves and on the Americans. This example is open to the response that in June and July 1945, Japanese diplomats sent out secret peace feelers, so that in August 1945, when Truman authorized dropping the bomb, the situation was very different.

Similarly, in support of the argument that nations will no longer resort to atomic weapons, some people have offered as evidence the fact that since World War I the great powers have not used poison gas. But the argument needs more support than this fact provides. Poison gas was not decisive or even highly effective in World War I. Moreover, the invention of gas masks made it obsolete.

In short, any *real* event is so entangled in its historical circumstances that it might not be adequate or even relevant evidence in the case being argued. In using a real event as an example (and real events certainly can be used), the writer ordinarily must demonstrate that the event can be taken out of its historical context and be used in the new context of argument. Thus, in an argument against using atomic weapons in warfare, the many deaths and horrible injuries inflicted on the Japanese at Hiroshima and Nagasaki can be cited as effects of nuclear weapons that would invariably occur and did not depend on any special circumstances of their use in Japan in 1945.

INVENTED INSTANCES   **Artificial** or **hypothetical cases—invented instances**—have the great advantage of being protected from objections of the sort just given. Recall Thoreau's trout in the milk; that was a colorful hypothetical case that nicely illustrated his point. An invented instance ("Let's assume that a burglar promises not to shoot a householder if the householder swears not to identify him. Is the householder bound by the oath?") is something like a drawing of a flower in a botany textbook or a diagram of the folds of a mountain in a geology textbook. It is admittedly false, but by virtue of its simplifications it sets forth the relevant details very clearly. Thus, in a discussion of rights, the philosopher Charles Frankel says,

> Strictly speaking, when we assert a right for *X*, we assert that *Y* has a duty. Strictly speaking, that *Y* has such a duty presupposes that *Y* has the capacity to perform this duty. It would be nonsense to say, for example, that a nonswimmer has a moral duty to swim to the help of a drowning man.

This invented example is admirably clear, and it is immune to charges that might muddy the issue if Frankel, instead of referring to a wholly abstract person, *Y*, talked about some real person, Jones, who did not rescue a drowning man. For then he would get bogged down over arguing about whether Jones *really* couldn't swim well enough to help, and so on.

Yet invented cases have their drawbacks. First and foremost, they cannot be used as evidence. A purely hypothetical example can illustrate a point or provoke reconsideration of a generalization, but it cannot substitute for actual events as evidence supporting an inductive inference. Sometimes such examples are so fanciful, so remote from life that they fail to carry conviction with the reader. Thus the philosopher Judith Jarvis Thomson, in the course of her argument entitled "A Defense of Abortion," asks you to imagine that you wake up one day and find that against your will a celebrated violinist whose body is not adequately functioning has been hooked up into your body, for life support. Do you have the right to unplug the violinist? Readers of the essays in this book will have to decide for themselves whether the invented cases proposed by various authors are helpful or whether they are so remote that they hinder thought. Readers will have to decide, too, about when they can use invented cases to advance their own arguments.

But we add one point: Even a highly fanciful invented case can have the valuable effect of forcing us to see where we stand. We may say that we are, in all circumstances, against vivisection. But what would we say if we thought that an experiment on one mouse would save the life of someone we love? Or conversely, if one approves of vivisection, would one also approve of sacrificing the last giant panda to save the life of a senile stranger, a person who in any case probably would not live longer than another year? Artificial cases of this sort can help us to see that, well, no, we didn't really mean to say such-and-such when we said so-and-so.

ANALOGIES   The third sort of example, **analogy,** is a kind of comparison. An analogy asserts that things that are alike in some ways are alike in yet another way. Example: "Before the Roman Empire declined as a world power, it exhibited a decline in morals and in physical stamina; our culture today shows a decline in morals (look at the high divorce rate, and look at the crime rate) and we also show a decline in physical culture (just read about obesity in children). America, like Rome, will decline as a world power."

Strictly, an analogy is an extended comparison in which different things are shown to be similar in several ways. Thus, if one wants to argue that a head of state should have extraordinary power during wartime, one can argue that the state at such a time is like a ship in a storm: The crew is needed to lend its help, but the decisions are best left to the captain. (Notice that an analogy compares things that are relatively *unlike*. Comparing the plight of one ship to another or of one government to another is not an analogy; it is an inductive inference from one case of the same sort to another such case.)

Or take another analogy: We have already glanced at Judith Thomson's hypothetical case in which the reader wakes up to find himself or herself hooked up to a violinist. Thomson uses this situation as an analogy in an argument about abortion. The reader stands for the mother, the violinist for the unwanted fetus. Whether this analogy is close enough to pregnancy to help illuminate our thinking about abortion is something that you may want to think about.

The problem with argument by analogy is this: Two admittedly different things are agreed to be similar in several ways, and the arguer goes on to assert or imply that they are also similar in another way—the point that is being argued. (That is why Thomson argues that if something is true of the reader-hooked-up-to-a-violinist, it is also true of the pregnant mother-hooked-up-to-a-fetus.) But the two things that are said to be analogous and that are indeed similar in characteristics *A, B,* and *C* are also different—let's say in characteristics *D* and *E.* As Bishop Butler is said to have remarked in the early eighteenth century, "Everything is what it is, and not another thing."

Analogies can be convincing, especially because they can make complex issues simple. "Don't change horses in midstream," of course, is not a statement about riding horses across a river but about choosing leaders in critical times. Still, in the end, analogies do not necessarily prove anything. What may be true about riding horses across a stream may not be true about choosing leaders in troubled times or about deciding on a given change of leadership. Riding horses across a stream and choosing leaders are, at bottom, different things, and however much these activities may be said to resemble one another, they remain different, and what is true for one need not be true for the other.

Analogies can be helpful in developing our thoughts. It is sometimes argued, for instance—on the analogy of the doctor-patient or the lawyer-client, or the priest-penitent relationship—that newspaper and television reporters should not be required to reveal their confidential sources. That is worth thinking about: Do the similarities run deep enough, or are there fundamental differences? Or take another example: Some writers who support abortion argue that the fetus is not a person any more than the acorn is an oak. That is also worth thinking about. But one should also think about this response: A fetus is not a person, just as an acorn is not an oak, but an acorn is a potential oak, and a fetus is a potential person, a potential adult human being. Children, even newborn infants, have rights, and one way to explain this claim is to call attention to their potentiality to become mature adults. And so some people argue that the fetus, by analogy, has the rights of an infant, for the fetus, like the infant, is a potential adult.

Three analogies for consideration: First, let's examine a brief comparison made by Jill Knight, a member of the British Parliament, speaking about abortion:

> Babies are not like bad teeth, to be jerked out because they cause suffering.

Her point is effectively put; it remains for the reader to decide whether or not fetuses are *babies* and if a fetus is not a baby, *why* it can or can't be treated like a bad tooth. Now, a second bit of analogical reasoning, again about abortion: Thomas Sowell, an economist at the Hoover Institute, grants that women have a legal right to abortion, but he objects to a requirement that the government pay for abortions:

Because the courts have ruled that women have a legal right to an abortion, some people have jumped to the conclusion that the government has to pay for it. You have a constitutional right to privacy, but the government has no obligation to pay for your window shades. (*Pink and Brown People*, 1981, p. 57)

We leave it to the reader to decide whether the analogy is compelling— that is, if the points of resemblance are sufficiently significant to allow one to conclude that what is true of people wanting window shades should be true of people wanting abortions.

And one more: A common argument on behalf of legalizing gay marriage draws an analogy between gay marriage and interracial mar- riage, a practice that was banned in sixteen states until 1967, when the Supreme Court declared miscegenation statutes unconstitutional. The gist of the analogy is this: Racism and discrimination against gay and les- bian people are the same. If marriage is a fundamental right—as the Supreme Court held in its 1967 decision when it struck down bans on miscegenation—then it is a fundamental right for gay people as well as heterosexual people.

Authoritative Testimony   Another form of evidence is **testimony,** the citation or quotation of authorities. In daily life we rely heavily on au- thorities of all sorts: We get a doctor's opinion about our health, we read a book because an intelligent friend recommends it, we see a movie be- cause a critic gave it a good review, and we pay at least a little attention to the weather forecaster.

In setting forth an argument, one often tries to show that one's view is supported by notable figures, perhaps Jefferson, Lincoln, Martin Luther King Jr., or scientists who won the Nobel Prize. You may recall that in the second chapter, in talking about definitions of pornography, we referred to Kenneth Clark. To make certain that you were impressed by his testimony even if you had never heard of him, we described him as "probably the most influential English-speaking art critic of our time." But heed some words of caution:

- Be sure that the authority, however notable, is an authority on the topic in question (a well-known biologist might be an author- ity on vitamins but not on the justice of a war).
- Be sure that the authority is not biased. A chemist employed by the tobacco industry isn't likely to admit that smoking may be harmful, and a "director of publications" (that means a press agent) for a hockey team isn't likely to admit that watching or even playing ice hockey stimulates violence.
- Beware of nameless authorities: "a thousand doctors," "leading educators," "researchers at a major medical school."
- Be careful when using authorities who indeed were great authori- ties in their day but who now may be out of date (Adam Smith

on economics, Julius Caesar on the art of war, Louis Pasteur on medicine).

• Cite authorities whose opinions your readers will value. William F. Buckley Jr.'s conservative/libertarian opinions mean a good deal to readers of the magazine that he founded, the *National Review*, but probably not to most liberal thinkers. Gloria Steinem's liberal/feminist opinions carry weight with the readers of the magazines that she cofounded, *New York* and *Ms.* magazine, but probably not to most conservative thinkers. If you are writing for the general reader, your usual audience, cite authorities who are likely to be accepted by the general reader.

One other point: *You* may be an authority. You probably aren't nationally known, but on some topics you perhaps can speak with the authority of personal experience. You may have been injured on a motorcycle while riding without wearing a helmet, or you may have escaped injury because you wore a helmet; you may have dropped out of school and then returned; you may have tutored a student whose native language is not English, or you may be such a student and you may have received tutoring. You may have attended a school with a bilingual education program. In short, your personal testimony on topics relating to these issues may be invaluable, and a reader will probably consider it seriously.

Statistics   The last sort of evidence we discuss here is quantitative or statistical. The maxim "More is better" captures a basic idea of quantitative evidence. Because we know that 90 percent is greater than 75 percent, we are usually ready to grant that any claim supported by experience in 90 percent of the cases is more likely to be true than an alternative claim supported by experience only 75 percent of the time. The greater the difference, the greater our confidence. Consider an example. Honors at graduation from college are often computed on a student's cumulative grade-point average (GPA). The undisputed assumption is that the nearer a student's GPA is to a perfect record (4.0), the better scholar he or she is and therefore the more deserving of highest honors. Consequently, a student with a GPA of 3.9 at the end of her senior year is a stronger candidate for graduating summa cum laude than another student with a GPA of 3.6. When faculty members on the honors committee argue over the relative academic merits of graduating seniors, we know that these quantitative, statistical differences in student GPAs will be the basic (even if not the only) kind of evidence under discussion.

GRAPHS, TABLES, NUMBERS   Statistical information can be marshaled and presented in many forms, but it tends to fall into two main types: the graphic and the numerical. Graphs, tables, and pie charts are familiar ways of presenting quantitative data in an eye-catching manner. (See page 161.) To prepare the graphics, however, one first has to get the numbers themselves under control, and for some purposes it may be acceptable simply to stick with the numbers themselves.

But should the numbers be presented in percentages or in fractions? Should one report, say, that the federal budget underwent a twofold increase over the decade, that it increased by 100 percent, that it doubled, or that the budget at the beginning of the decade was one-half what it was at the end? Taken strictly, these are equivalent ways of saying the same thing. Choice among them, therefore, in an example like this perhaps will rest on whether one's aim is to dramatize the increase (a 100 percent increase looks larger than a doubling) or to play down the size of the increase.

THINKING ABOUT STATISTICAL EVIDENCE   Statistics often get a bad name because it is so easy to misuse them, unintentionally or not, and so difficult to be sure that they have been correctly gathered in the first place. (We remind you of the old saw "There are lies, damned lies, and statistics.") Every branch of social science and natural science needs statistical information, and countless decisions in public and private life are based on quantitative data in statistical form. It is important, therefore, to be sensitive to the sources and reliability of the statistics and to develop a healthy skepticism when confronted with statistics whose parentage is not fully explained.

Consider, for instance, statistics that kept popping up during the baseball strike of 1994. The owners of the clubs said that the average salary of a major-league player was $1.2 million. (The **average** in this case — technically the **mean** — is the result of dividing the total number of salary dollars by the number of players.) The players' union, however, did not talk about the average; rather, the union talked about the **median,** which was less than half of the average, a mere $500,000. (The *median* is the middle value in a distribution. Thus, of the 746 players, 363 earned less than $500,000, 361 earned more, and 22 earned exactly $500,000.) The union said, correctly, that *most* players earned a good deal less than the $1.2 million figure that the owners kept citing; but the $1.2 million average sounded more impressive to the general public, and that is the figure that the guy in the street mentioned when asked for an opinion about the strike.

Consider this statistic: In Smithville in 2005, 1 percent of the victims in fatal automobile accidents were bicyclists. In 2006 the percent of bicyclists killed in automobile accidents was 2 percent. Was the increase 1 percent (not an alarming figure), or was it 100 percent (a staggering figure)? The answer is both, depending on whether we are comparing (a) bicycle deaths in automobile accidents with *all* deaths in automobile accidents (that's an increase of 1 percent), or (b) bicycle deaths in automobile accidents *only with other bicycle deaths* in automobile accidents (an increase of 100 percent). An honest statement would say that bicycle deaths due to automobile accidents doubled in 2006, increasing from 1 to 2 percent. But here's another point: Although every such death is lamentable, if there was one such death in 2005 and two in 2006, the increase from one death to two (an increase of 100 percent!) hardly suggests that there is a growing problem that needs attention. No one would be surprised to learn that in the next year there were no deaths, or only one or even two.

One other example may help to indicate the difficulties of interpreting statistics. According to the San Francisco police department, in 1990 the city received 1,074 citizen complaints against the police. Los Angeles received only half as many complaints in the same period, and Los Angeles has five times the population of San Francisco. Does this mean that the police of San Francisco are much rougher than the police of Los Angeles? Possibly. But some specialists who have studied the statistics not only for these two cities but also for many other cities have concluded that a department with proportionately more complaints against it is not necessarily more abusive than a department with fewer complaints. According to these experts, the more confidence that the citizens have in their police force, the more the citizens will complain about police misconduct. The relatively small number of complaints against the Los Angeles police department thus may indicate that the citizens of Los Angeles are so intimidated and have so little confidence in the system that they are afraid to complain or they do not bother to complain.

If it is sometimes difficult to interpret statistics, it is often at least equally difficult to establish accurate statistics. Consider this example:

> Advertisements are the most prevalent and toxic of the mental pollutants. From the moment your radio alarm sounds in the morning to the wee hours of late-night TV, microjolts of commercial pollution flood into your brain at the rate of about three thousand marketing messages per day. (Kalle Lasn, *Culture Jam,* 1999, pp. 18–19)

Lasn's book includes endnotes as documentation, so, curious about the statistics, we turn to the appropriate page and we find this information concerning the source of his data:

> "three thousand marketing messages per day." Mark Landler, Walecia Konrad, Zachary Schiller, and Lois Therrien, "What Happened to Advertising?" *BusinessWeek,* September 23, 1991, page 66. Leslie Savan in *The Sponsored Life* (Temple University Press, 1994), page 1, estimated that "16,000 ads flicker across an individual's consciousness daily." I did an informal survey in March 1995 and found the number to be closer to 1,500 (this included all marketing messages, corporate images, logos, ads, brand names, on TV, radio, billboards, buildings, signs, clothing, appliances, in cyberspace, etc., over a typical twenty-four hour period in my life). (219)

Well, this endnote is odd. In the earlier passage, you will recall, the author asserted that "about three thousand marketing messages per day" flood into a person's brain. Now, in the documentation, he helpfully cites a source for that statistic, from *BusinessWeek*—though we have not the faintest idea of how the authors of the article in *BusinessWeek* came up with that figure. Oddly, he goes on to offer a very different figure (16,000 ads), and then, to our utter confusion, he offers yet a third figure, 1,500, based on his own "informal survey."

Probably the one thing we can safely say about all three figures is that none of them means very much. Even if the compilers of the statistics told us exactly how they counted—let's say that among countless other criteria they assumed that the average person reads one magazine per day and that the average magazine contains 124 advertisements—it would be hard to take them seriously. After all, in leafing through a magazine, some people may read many ads, some may read none. Some people may read some ads carefully—but perhaps to enjoy their absurdity. Our point: Although the author in his text said, without implying any uncertainty, that "about three thousand marketing messages per day" reach an individual, it is evident (if one checks the endnote) that even he is confused about the figure he gives.

We are not suggesting that everyone who uses statistics is trying to deceive or even that many who use statistics are unconsciously deceived

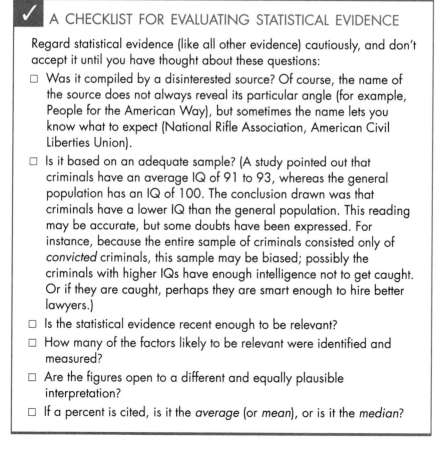

✓ A CHECKLIST FOR EVALUATING STATISTICAL EVIDENCE

Regard statistical evidence (like all other evidence) cautiously, and don't accept it until you have thought about these questions:

☐ Was it compiled by a disinterested source? Of course, the name of the source does not always reveal its particular angle (for example, People for the American Way), but sometimes the name lets you know what to expect (National Rifle Association, American Civil Liberties Union).

☐ Is it based on an adequate sample? (A study pointed out that criminals have an average IQ of 91 to 93, whereas the general population has an IQ of 100. The conclusion drawn was that criminals have a lower IQ than the general population. This reading may be accurate, but some doubts have been expressed. For instance, because the entire sample of criminals consisted only of *convicted* criminals, this sample may be biased; possibly the criminals with higher IQs have enough intelligence not to get caught. Or if they are caught, perhaps they are smart enough to hire better lawyers.)

☐ Is the statistical evidence recent enough to be relevant?

☐ How many of the factors likely to be relevant were identified and measured?

☐ Are the figures open to a different and equally plausible interpretation?

☐ If a percent is cited, is it the *average* (or *mean*), or is it the *median*?

by them. We mean to suggest only that statistics are open to widely different interpretations and that often those columns of numbers, so precise with their decimal points, are in fact imprecise and possibly even worthless because they may be based on insufficient or biased samples.

QUIZ

What is wrong with the following statistical proof that children do not have time for school?

> One-third of the time they are sleeping (about 122 days);
>
> One-eighth of the time they are eating (three hours a day, totaling 45 days);
>
> One-fourth of the time is taken up by summer and other vacations (91 days);
>
> Two-sevenths of the year is weekends (104 days).
>
> Total: 362 days—so how can a kid have time for school?

NONRATIONAL APPEALS

Satire, Irony, Sarcasm, Humor

In talking about definition, deduction, and evidence, we have been talking about means of rational persuasion. But as mentioned earlier, there are also other means of persuasion. Take force, for example. If *X* kicks *Y*, threatens to destroy *Y*'s means of livelihood, or threatens *Y*'s life, *X* may persuade *Y* to cooperate. One form of irrational but sometimes highly effective persuasion is **satire**—that is, witty ridicule. A cartoonist may persuade viewers that a politician's views are unsound by caricaturing (and thus ridiculing) the politician's appearance or by presenting a grotesquely distorted (funny, but unfair) picture of the issue.

Satiric artists often use caricature; satiric writers, also seeking to persuade by means of ridicule, often use **verbal irony.** Irony of this sort contrasts what is said and what is meant. For instance, words of praise may be meant to imply blame (when Shakespeare's Cassius says, "Brutus is an honorable man," he means his hearers to think that Brutus is dishonorable), and words of modesty may be meant to imply superiority ("Of course, I'm too dumb to understand this problem"). Such language, when heavy-handed, is called **sarcasm** ("You're a great guy," said to someone who will not lend the speaker ten dollars). If it is witty—if the jeering is in some degree clever—it is called irony rather than sarcasm.

Although ridicule is not a form of argument (because it is not a form of reasoning), passages of ridicule, especially verbal irony, sometimes appear in essays that are arguments. These passages, like reasons, or for that matter like appeals to the emotions, are efforts to persuade the hearer to accept the speaker's point of view. For example, in Judy Brady's essay "I Want a Wife" (p. 978), the writer, a woman, does not really mean that she wants a wife. The pretense that she wants a wife gives the essay a playful, joking quality; her words must mean something other than what they seem to mean. But that she is not merely joking (satire has been defined as "joking in earnest") is evident; she is seeking to persuade. She has a point, and she could argue it straight, but that would produce a very different sort of essay.

We have said that Brady's essay has a playful quality—which is not to say that it merely clowns around. She clearly is serious, but she is also entertaining. The great trick in using humor in an argument is, on the one hand, to avoid mere wisecracking, which makes the writer seem like a smart aleck, and, on the other hand, to avoid mere clownishness, which makes the writer seem like a fool. Later in this chapter (p. 106), we print an essay by George F. Will, that is (or seeks to be?) humorous in places. You be the judge.

Emotional Appeals

It is sometimes said that good argumentative writing appeals only to reason, never to emotion, and that any sort of emotional appeal is illegitimate, irrelevant. "Tears are not arguments," the Brazilian writer Machado de Assis said. Logic textbooks may even stigmatize with Latin labels the various sorts of emotional appeal—for instance, *argumentum ad populam* (appeal to the prejudices of the mob, as in "Come on, we all know that schools don't teach anything anymore") and *argumentum ad misericordiam* (appeal to pity, as in "No one ought to blame this poor kid for stabbing a classmate because his mother was often institutionalized for alcoholism and his father beat him").

True, appeals to emotion may get in the way of the facts of the case; they may blind the audience by, in effect, throwing dust in its eyes or by stimulating tears.

Learning from Shakespeare   A classic example is found in Shakespeare's *Julius Caesar*, when Marc Antony addresses the Roman populace after Brutus, Cassius, and others have assassinated Caesar. The real issue is whether Caesar was becoming tyrannical (as the assassins claim) and would therefore curtail the freedom of the people. Antony turns from the evidence and stirs the mob against the assassins by appealing to its emotions. In the ancient Roman biographical writing that Shakespeare drew on, Sir Thomas North's translation of Plutarch's *Lives of the Noble Grecians and Romans*, Plutarch says that Antony,

> perceiving that his words moved the common people to compassion, . . .
> framed his eloquence to make their hearts yearn [that is, grieve] the
> more, and, taking Caesar's gown all bloody in his hand, he laid it open
> to the sight of them all, showing what a number of cuts and holes it had
> upon it. Therewithal the people fell presently into such a rage and
> mutiny that there was no more order kept.

Here are a few extracts from Antony's speeches in Shakespeare's play. Antony begins by asserting that he will speak only briefly:

> Friends, Romans, countrymen, lend me your ears;
> I come to bury Caesar, not to praise him.

After briefly offering some rather insubstantial evidence that Caesar gave no signs of behaving tyrannically (for example, "When that the poor have cried, Caesar hath wept"), Antony begins to play directly on the emotions of his hearers. Descending from the platform so that he may be in closer contact with his audience (like a modern politician, he wants to work the crowd), he calls attention to Caesar's bloody toga:

> If you have tears, prepare to shed them now.
> You all do know this mantle; I remember
> The first time ever Caesar put it on:
> 'Twas on a summer's evening, in his tent,
> That day he overcame the Nervii.
> Look, in this place ran Cassius' dagger through;
> See what a rent the envious Casca made;
> Through this, the well-belovèd Brutus stabbed. . . .

In these few lines Antony first prepares the audience by suggesting to them how they should respond ("If you have tears, prepare to shed them now"), then flatters them by implying that they, like Antony, were intimates of Caesar (he credits them with being familiar with Caesar's garment), then evokes a personal memory of a specific time ("a summer's evening")—not just any old specific time but a very important one, the day that Caesar won a battle against the Nervii (a particularly fierce tribe in what is now France). In fact, Antony was *not* at the battle, and he did not join Caesar until three years later.

Antony does not mind being free with the facts; his point here is not to set the record straight but to stir the mob against the assassins. He goes on, daringly but successfully, to identify one particular slit in the garment with Cassius's dagger, another with Casca's, and a third with Brutus's. Antony cannot know which slit was made by which dagger, but his rhetorical trick works.

Notice, too, that Antony arranges the three assassins in climactic order, since Brutus (Antony claims) was especially beloved by Caesar:

> Judge, O you gods, how dearly Caesar loved him!
> This was the most unkindest cut of all;
> For when the noble Caesar saw him stab,
> Ingratitude, more strong than traitor's arms,
> Quite vanquished him. Then burst his mighty heart. . . .

Nice. According to Antony, the noble-minded Caesar—Antony's words have erased all thought of the tyrannical Caesar—died not from the wounds inflicted by daggers but from the heartbreaking perception of

Brutus's ingratitude. Doubtless there was not a dry eye in the house. We can all hope that if we are ever put on trial, we have a lawyer as skilled in evoking sympathy as Antony.

Are Emotional Appeals Fallacious?   The oration is obviously successful in the play and apparently was successful in real life, but it is the sort of speech that prompts logicians to write disapprovingly of attempts to stir feeling in an audience. (As mentioned earlier in this chapter, the evocation of emotion in an audience is called **pathos,** from the Greek word for "emotion" or "suffering.") There is nothing inherently wrong in stimulating our audience's emotions, but when an emotional appeal confuses the issue that is being argued about or shifts the attention away from the facts of the issue, we can reasonably speak of the fallacy of emotional appeal.

No fallacy is involved, however, when an emotional appeal heightens the facts, bringing them home to the audience rather than masking them. If we are talking about legislation that would govern police actions, it is legitimate to show a photograph of the battered, bloodied face of an alleged victim of police brutality. True, such a photograph cannot tell the whole truth; it cannot tell us if the subject threatened the officer with a gun or repeatedly resisted an order to surrender. But it can tell us that the victim was severely beaten and (like a comparable description in words) evoke in us emotions that may properly enter into our decision about the permissible use of police evidence. Similarly, an animal rights activist who is arguing that calves are cruelly confined might reasonably tell us about the size of the pen in which the beast—unable to turn around or even to lie down—is kept. Others may argue that calves don't much care about turning around or have no right to turn around, but the verbal description, which unquestionably makes an emotional appeal, can hardly be called fallacious or irrelevant.

In appealing to emotions then, the important things are

- Not to falsify (especially by oversimplifying) the issue and
- Not to distract attention from the facts of the case.

Focus on the facts and concentrate on offering reasons (essentially, statements linked with "because"), but you may also legitimately bring the facts home to your readers by seeking to induce in them the appropriate emotions. Your words will be fallacious only if you stimulate emotions that are not rightly connected with the facts of the case.

DOES ALL WRITING CONTAIN ARGUMENTS?

Our answer to the question we have just posed is no—but probably *most* writing *does* contain an argument of sorts. Or put it this way: The writer wants to persuade the reader to see things the way the writer sees

✓ A CHECKLIST FOR ANALYZING AN ARGUMENT

□ What is the writer's claim or thesis? Ask yourself:
  □ What claim is being asserted?
  □ What assumptions are being made — and are they acceptable?
  □ Are important terms satisfactorily defined?
□ What support (evidence) is offered on behalf of the claim? Ask yourself:
  □ Are the examples relevant, and are they convincing?
  □ Are the statistics (if any) relevant, accurate, and complete? Do they allow only the interpretation that is offered in the argument?
  □ If authorities are cited, are they indeed authorities on this topic, and can they be regarded as impartial?
  □ Is the logic — deductive and inductive — valid?
  □ If there is an appeal to emotion — for instance, if satire is used to ridicule the opposing view — is this appeal acceptable?
□ Does the writer seem to you to be fair? Ask yourself:
  □ Are counterarguments adequately considered?
  □ Is there any evidence of dishonesty or of a discreditable attempt to manipulate the reader?
  □ How does the writer establish the image of himself or herself that we sense in the essay? What is the writer's tone, and is it appropriate?

them — at least until the end of the essay. After all, even a recipe for a cherry pie in a food magazine — a piece of writing that is primarily expository (how to do it) rather than argumentative (how a reasonable person ought to think about this topic) — probably includes, near the beginning, a sentence with a hint of an argument in it, such as "*Because* [a sign that a *reason* will be offered] this pie can be made quickly and with ingredients (canned cherries) that are always available, give it a try, and it will surely become one of your favorites." Clearly, such a statement cannot stand as a formal argument — a discussion that takes account of possible counterarguments, that relies chiefly on logic and little if at all on emotional appeal, and that draws a conclusion that seems irrefutable.

Still, the statement is something of an argument on behalf of making a pie with canned cherries. In this case, a claim is made (the pie will become a favorite), and two *reasons* are offered in support of this claim:

- It can be made quickly, and
- The chief ingredient—because it is canned—can always be at hand.

The underlying *assumptions* are

- You don't have a great deal of time to waste in the kitchen, and
- Canned cherries are just as tasty as fresh cherries—and even if they aren't, well, you wouldn't know the difference.

When we read a lead-in to a recipe, then, we won't find a formal argument, but we probably will get a few words that seek to persuade us to keep reading. And most writing does contain such material—sentences that give us a reason to keep reading, that engage our interests, and that make us want to stay with the writer for at least a little longer. If the recipe happens to be difficult and time-consuming, the lead-in may say, "Although this recipe for a cherry pie, using fresh cherries that you will have to pit, is a bit more time-consuming than the usual recipe that calls for canned cherries, once you have tasted it you will never go back to canned cherries." Again, although the logic is scarcely compelling, the persuasive element is evident. The assumption here is that you have a discriminating palate; once you have tasted a pie made with fresh cherries, you will never again enjoy the canned stuff. The writer is not giving us a formal argument, with abundant evidence and with a detailed refutation of counterarguments, but we do know where the writer stands and how the writer wishes us to respond.

AN EXAMPLE: AN ARGUMENT AND A LOOK AT THE WRITER'S STRATEGIES

This essay concerns President George W. Bush's proposal that drilling be allowed in part of the Arctic National Wildlife Refuge (ANWR, pronounced "An-war"). The section of the ANWR that is proposed for drilling is called the "1002 area," as defined by Section 1002 of the Alaska National Interest Lands Conservation Act of 1980. In March 2003, the Senate rejected the Bush proposal, but the issue remains alive.

We follow George F. Will's essay with some comments about the ways in which he constructs his argument.

George F. Will

George F. Will, a syndicated columnist whose writing appears in 460 newspapers, was born in Champaign, Illinois, in 1941, and educated at Trinity College (Hartford), Oxford University, and Princeton University. Will has served as the Washington, D.C., editor of the National Review *and now writes a regular column for* Newsweek. *His essays have been collected in several books.*

Being Green at Ben and Jerry's

Some Environmental Policies Are Feel-Good Indulgences for an Era of Energy Abundance

If you have an average-size dinner table, four feet by six feet, put a dime on the edge of it. Think of the surface of the table as the Arctic National Wildlife Refuge in Alaska. The dime is larger than the piece of the coastal plain that would have been opened to drilling for oil and natural gas. The House of Representatives voted for drilling, but the Senate voted against access to what Sen. John Kerry, Massachusetts Democrat and presidential aspirant, calls "a few drops of oil." ANWR could produce, for 25 years, at least as much oil as America currently imports from Saudi Arabia.

Six weeks of desultory Senate debate about the energy bill reached an almost comic culmination in . . . yet another agriculture subsidy. The subsidy is a requirement that will triple the amount of ethanol, which is made from corn, that must be put in gasoline, ostensibly to clean America's air, actually to buy farmers' votes.

Over the last three decades, energy use has risen about 30 percent. But so has population, which means per capita energy use is unchanged. And per capita GDP has risen substantially, so we are using 40 percent less energy per dollar output. Which is one reason there is no energy crisis, at least none as most Americans understand such things—a shortage of, and therefore high prices of, gasoline for cars, heating oil for furnaces and electricity for air conditioners.

In the absence of a crisis to concentrate the attention of the inattentive American majority, an intense faction—full-time environmentalists—goes to work. Spencer Abraham, the secretary of Energy, says "the previous administration . . . simply drew up a list of fuels it *didn't* like—nuclear energy, coal, hydropower, and oil—which together account for 73 percent of America's energy supply." Well, there are always windmills.

Sometimes lofty environmentalism is a cover for crude politics. The 5 United States has the world's largest proven reserves of coal. But Mike Oliver, a retired physicist and engineer, and John Hospers, professor emeritus of philosophy at USC, note that in 1996 President Clinton put 68 billion tons of America's cleanest-burning coal, located in Utah, off-limits for mining, ostensibly for environmental reasons. If every existing U.S. electric power plant burned coal, the 68 billion tons could fuel them for 45 years at the current rate of consumption. Now power companies must import clean-burning coal, some from mines owned by Indonesia's Lippo Group, the heavy contributor to Clinton, whose decision about Utah's coal vastly increased the value of Lippo's coal.

The United States has just 2.14 percent of the world's proven reserves of oil, so some people say it is pointless to drill in places like ANWR because "energy independence" is a chimera. Indeed it is. But domestic supplies can provide important insurance against uncertain foreign supplies. And domestic supplies can mean exporting hundreds of billions of dollars less to oil-producing nations, such as Iraq.

Besides, when considering proven reserves, note the adjective. In 1930 the United States had proven reserves of 13 billion barrels. We then fought the Second World War and fueled the most fabulous economic expansion in human history, including the electricity-driven "New Economy." (Manufacturing and running computers consume 15 percent of U.S. electricity. Internet use alone accounts for half of the growth in demand for electricity.) So by 1990 proven reserves were . . . 17 billion barrels, not counting any in Alaska or Hawaii.

In 1975 proven reserves in the Persian Gulf were 74 billion barrels. In 1993 they were 663 billion, a ninefold increase. At the current rate of consumption, today's proven reserves would last 150 years. New discoveries will be made, some by vastly improved techniques of deep-water drilling. But environmental policies will define opportunities. The government estimates that beneath the U.S. outer continental shelf, which the government owns, there are at least 46 billion barrels of oil. But only 2 percent of the shelf has been leased for energy development.

Opponents of increased energy production usually argue for decreased consumption. But they flinch from conservation measures. A new $1 gasoline tax would dampen demand for gasoline, but it would stimulate demands for the heads of the tax increasers. After all, Americans get irritable when impersonal market forces add 25 cents to the cost of a gallon. Tougher fuel-efficiency requirements for vehicles would save a lot of energy. But who would save the legislators who passed those requirements? Beware the wrath of Americans who like to drive, and autoworkers who like to make cars that are large, heavy and safer than the gasoline-sippers that environmentalists prefer.

Some environmentalism is a feel-good indulgence for an era of energy abundance, which means an era of avoided choices. Or ignored choices—ignored because if acknowledged, they would not make the choosers feel good. Karl Zinsmeister, editor in chief of the *American Enterprise* magazine, imagines an oh-so-green environmentalist enjoying the most politically correct product on the planet—Ben & Jerry's ice cream. Made in a factory that depends on electricity-guzzling refrigeration, a gallon of ice cream requires four gallons of milk. While making that much milk, a cow produces eight gallons of manure, and flatulence with another eight gallons of methane, a potent "greenhouse" gas. And the cow consumes lots of water plus three pounds of grain and hay, which is produced with tractor fuel, chemical fertilizers, herbicides and insecticides, and is transported with truck or train fuel:

"So every time he digs into his Cherry Garcia, the conscientious environmentalist should visualize (in addition to world peace) a pile of grain, water, farm chemicals, and energy inputs much bigger than his ice cream bowl on one side of the table, and, on the other side of the table, a mound of manure eight times the size of his bowl, plus a balloon of methane that would barely fit under the dining room table."

Cherry Garcia. It's a choice. *Bon appétit.*

George F. Will's Strategies

Now let's look at Will's essay, to see some of the techniques that he uses, techniques that enable him to engage a reader's interest and perhaps enable him to convince the reader, or at least make the reader think, that Will probably is on to something.

The title, "Being Green at Ben and Jerry's," does not at all prepare the reader for an argument about drilling in the National Arctic Wildlife Refuge, but if you have read any of Will's other columns in *Newsweek,* you probably know that he is conservative and that he will be poking some fun at the green folk—the environmentalists. Will can get away with using a title that is not focused because he has a body of loyal readers—people who will read him because they want to read him, whatever the topic is—but the rest of us writers have to give our readers some idea of what we will be talking about. In short, let your readers know early, perhaps in the title, where you will be taking them.

The subtitle, "Some Environmental Policies Are Feel-Good Indulgences for an Era of Energy Abundance" perhaps added by an editor of the magazine, does suggest that the piece will concern energy, and the words "feel-good indulgence" pretty clearly tell readers that Will believes the environmentalists are indulging themselves.

Paragraph 1 offers a striking comparison. Will wants us to believe that the area proposed for drilling is tiny, so he says that if we imagine the entire Arctic National Wildlife Refuge as a dinner table, the area proposed for drilling is the size of a dime. We think you will agree that this opening seizes a reader's attention. Assuming the truth of the figure—but there seems to be some dispute, since opponents have said that the area would be more like the size of a dinner plate—the image is highly effective. A dime is so small! And is worth so little! Still, one might ask—but probably one doesn't, because Will's figure is so striking—if the tininess of the area really is decisive. One might easily, and apparently with reason, dismiss as absurd the idea that a minuscule tsetse fly could kill a human being, or that the plague is spread by fleas that have bitten rats, because these proposals sound ridiculous—but they are true. One other point about the first paragraph: Will's voice sounds like a voice you might hear in your living room: "If you have an average-size dinner table," "the dime is larger," "at least as much oil." Don't think that in your own essays you need to adopt a highly formal style. Your reader should think of you as serious but not solemn.

Will goes on to say that Senator John Kerry, an opponent of drilling and therefore on the side that Will opposes, dismisses the oil in the refuge as "a few drops." Will replies that it "could produce, for 25 years, at least as much oil as America currently imports from Saudi Arabia." Kerry's "a few drops" is, of course, not to be taken literally; he means, in effect, that the oil is a drop in the bucket. But when one looks into the issue, one finds that estimates by responsible sources vary considerably, from 3.2 billion barrels to 11.5 billion barrels.

Paragraph 2 dismisses the Senate's debate ("almost comic," "actually to buy farmers' votes").

Paragraph 3 offers statistics to make the point that "there is no energy crisis." Here, as in the first paragraph, where he showed his awareness of Kerry's view, Will indicates that he is familiar with views other than his own. In arguing a case, it is important for the writer to let readers know that indeed there are other views—which the writer then goes on to show are less substantial than the writer's. Will is correct in saying that "per capita energy use is unchanged," but those on the other side might say, "Yes, per capita consumption has not increased, but given the population increase, the annual amount has vastly increased, which means that resources are being depleted and that pollution is increasing."

Paragraph 4 asserts again that there is no energy crisis, pokes at "full-time environmentalists" (perhaps there is a suggestion that such people really ought to get a respectable job), and ends with a bit of whimsy: These folks probably think we should go back to using windmills.

Paragraph 5, in support of the assertion that "Sometimes lofty environmentalism is a cover for crude politics," cites an authority (often an effective technique), and, since readers are not likely to recognize the name, it also identifies him ("professor emeritus of philosophy at USC"), and it then offers further statistics (again effective). The paragraph begins by talking about "crude politics" and ends with the assertion that "Now power companies must import clean-burning coal, some from mines owned by Indonesia's Lippo Group, the heavy contributor to Clinton." In short, Will does what he can to suggest that the views of at least some environmentalists are rooted in money and politics.

Paragraph 6 offers another statistic ("The United States has just 2.14 percent of the world's proven reserves of oil"), and he turns it *against* those who argue that therefore it is pointless for us to drill in Alaska. In effect, he is replying to people like Senator Kerry who say that the Arctic refuge provides only "a few drops of oil." The point, Will suggests, is not that we can't achieve independence; the point is that "domestic supplies can provide important insurance against uncertain foreign supplies."

Paragraph 7 begins nicely with a transition, "Besides," and then offers additional statistics concerning the large amount of oil that we have. It was, for instance, enough to fuel "the most fabulous economic expansion in human history."

Paragraph 8 offers additional statistics, first about "proven reserves" in the Persian Gulf and then about an estimate—but it is only an estimate—of oil "beneath the U.S. outer continental shelf." We are not certain of Will's point, but in any case the statistics suggest to a reader that the author has done his homework.

Paragraph 9 summarizes the chief position (as Will sees it) of those on the other side: They usually argue for decreased consumption, but they are afraid to argue for the sort of tax on gasoline that might indeed decrease consumption because they know that many Americans want to drive large, heavy cars. Further, the larger, heavier cars that the environmentalists object to are in fact "safer than the gasoline-sippers that environmentalists prefer."

Paragraph 10 uses the term "feel-good indulgence," which is also found in the subtitle of the essay, and now, in the third sentence of the paragraph, we hear again of Ben and Jerry, who have not been in our minds since the title of the essay, "Being Green at Ben and Jerry's." Perhaps we have been wondering all this while why Ben and Jerry are in the title. Almost surely the reader knows that Ben and Jerry are associated with ice cream and therefore with cows and meadows, and probably many readers know, at least vaguely, that Ben and Jerry are somehow associated with environmentalism and with other causes often thought to be on the left. Will (drawing on an article by Karl Zinsmeister, editor of the *American Enterprise*), writes what we consider an extremely amusing paragraph in which he points out that the process of making ice cream "depends on electricity-guzzling refrigeration" and that the cows are, so to speak, supported by fuel that transports fertilizers, herbicides, and insecticides. Further, in the course of producing the four gallons of milk that are required for one gallon of ice cream, the cows themselves — those darlings of environmentalists — contribute "eight gallons of manure, and flatulence with another eight gallons of methane, a potent 'greenhouse' gas." As we see when we read Will's next paragraph, the present paragraph is in large measure a lead-in for the following quotation. Will knows it is is *not* enough to give a quotation; a writer has to *make use* of the quotation — has to lead in to it or, after quoting, has to comment on it, or do both.

Paragraph 11 is entirely devoted to quoting Zinsmeister, who imagines an environmentalist digging into a dish of one of Ben and Jerry's most popular flavors, Cherry Garcia. We are invited to see the bowl of ice cream on one side of the table — here Will effectively evokes the table of his first paragraph — and a pile of manure on the other side, "plus a balloon of methane that would barely fit under the dining room table." Vulgar, no doubt, but funny too. George Will knows that humor as well as logic (and statistics and other kinds of evidence) can be among the tools a writer uses in getting an audience to accept or at least to consider an argument.

Paragraph 12 consists of three short sentences, adding up to less than a single line of type: "Cherry Garcia. It's a choice. *Bon appétit.*" None of the sentences mentions oil or the Arctic Refuge or statistics, and therefore this ending might seem utterly irrelevant to the topic, but we think Will is very effectively saying, "Sure, you have a choice about drilling in the Arctic Refuge; any sensible person will choose the ice cream (drilling) rather than the manure and the gas (not drilling).

Topics for Critical Thinking and Writing

1. What, if anything, makes Will's essay interesting? What, if anything, makes it highly persuasive? How might it be made more persuasive?

2. In paragraph 10, Will clowns a bit about the gas that cows emit, but apparently this gas, which contributes to global warming, is no laughing matter. The government of New Zealand, in an effort to reduce livestock emissions of methane and nitrous oxide, proposed a tax that would subsidize future research on the emissions. The tax would cost the average farmer $300 a year. Imagine that you are a New Zealand farmer. Write a letter to your representative, arguing for or against the tax.

3. Senator Barbara Boxer, campaigning against the proposal to drill in ANWR, spoke of the refuge as "God's gift to us" (*New York Times*, March 20, 2002). How strong an argument is she offering? Some opponents of drilling have said that drilling in ANWR is as unthinkable as drilling in Yosemite or the Grand Canyon. Again, how strong is this argument? Can you imagine circumstances in which you would support drilling in these places? Do we have a moral duty to preserve certain unspoiled areas?

4. The Inupiat (Eskimo) who live in and near ANWR by a large majority favor drilling, seeing it as a source of jobs and a source of funding for schools, hospitals, and police. But the Ketchikan Indians, who speak of themselves as the "Caribou People," see drilling as a threat to the herds that they depend on for food and hides. How does one balance the conflicting needs of these two groups?

5. Opponents of drilling in ANWR argue that over its lifetime of fifty years, the area would produce less than 1 percent of the fuel we need during the period and that therefore we should not risk disturbing the area. Further, they argue that drilling in ANWR is an attempt at a quick fix to U.S. energy needs, whereas what is needed are sustainable solutions, such as the development of renewable energy sources (e.g., wind and sun) and fuel-efficient automobiles. How convincing do you find these arguments?

6. Proponents of drilling include a large majority—something like 75 percent of the people of Alaska, including its governor and its two senators. How much attention should be paid to their voices?

Gloria Jiménez

Gloria Jiménez married immediately after she graduated from high school, worked briefly, had two children, and then, after her younger child started school, continued her own formal education. This essay, written for a composition course at Tufts University in 2003, is her first publication.

Against the Odds, and Against the Common Good

[Student Essay]

State-run lotteries are now so common—thirty-nine states and Washington, D.C., operate lotteries—that the states probably will never get out of the lottery business. Still, when all is said and done about lotteries bringing a bit of excitement into the lives of many people and bringing a vast amount of money into the lives of a few, the states should not be in the business of urging people to gamble.

And they *do* urge people. Consider a slogan used in Maryland, "Play Today. Cash Tomorrow." If the statement were, "Get a job today and you will have cash tomorrow," it would be true; it would make sense, however small the earnings might be. But "Play Today. Cash Tomorrow" falsely suggests that the way to have money tomorrow is to buy a ticket today. In fact, buying a ticket is an almost sure-fire way of getting nothing for something.

Maryland is not the only state that uses a clever slogan to get its citizens to part with hard-earned money. New York's ads say, "You Can't Win If You Don't Play," and Oregon's ads say, "There Is No Such Thing as a Losing Ticket." This last slogan—which at first glance seems to say that every ticket will benefit the purchaser—is built on the idea that the state's share of the money goes to a worthy cause, usually education or some social service. But no matter how you look at it, this slogan, like the others, urges people to buy a product—a jackpot—that they have almost no chance of receiving.

The chief arguments *in favor* of state-run lotteries seem to be these: (1) people freely choose to participate; (2) funds are used for education or for other important services; (3) if this source of funding disappears, the states will have to compensate by imposing taxes of one sort or another; (4) operation by the government ensures that the lotteries are run honestly; and (5) lotteries create jobs. We can respond briefly to the last two points, and then concentrate on the first three.

It probably is true that the lotteries are run honestly (though I seem to recall reading in the newspaper about one state in which corruption was found in administering the lottery), but that is not the point. If it is wrong to encourage people to gamble, it is hardly relevant to say that the game is run honestly. The other point that can be dismissed briefly is that lotteries create jobs. This argument is usually advanced in connection with the creation of casinos, which surely do create jobs, not only in the casinos but also in nearby restaurants, parking lots, movie theaters, and so forth. But lottery tickets are sold in places where the clerks are already employed. Presumably the only new jobs created by the lottery are the relatively few jobs of the people who dream up the slogans or who are in charge of collecting and processing the receipts.

The three other claims require more attention. The first, that people freely choose to participate, probably is largely true. Although some buy-

ers are compulsive gamblers, people who are addicted and therefore cannot really be said to choose freely, I grant that most people do have a free
choice — although, as I have already said, I think that some of the slogans that states use are deceptive, and if this is the case, purchasers who
are misled by the ads are not entirely free. Consider a slogan that Illinois
used on billboards, especially in poor neighborhoods: "This Could Be
Your Ticket Out." Yes, a person might hit the jackpot and get out of
poverty, but the chances are one in several million, and to imply that the
lottery is a reasonable option to get out of present poverty is to be deceptive. Further, the message is essentially unwholesome. It implies that the
way out is luck, rather than education and hard work. Of course, luck
plays a part in life, but 99.99 percent of the people who rely on the ticket
as the "ticket out" of poverty are going to be terribly disappointed. But
again, we can grant that except for gambling addicts, people who buy
lottery tickets are freely doing so.

Probably the strongest claim is that the funds are used for important
purposes, usually education. This claim apparently is true: The legislators
are smart enough to package the lottery bills this way. And the revenue
gained seems enormous — $20 billion in 2002, according to the *New York
Times* (May 18, 2003, sec. 4, p. 1). On the other hand, this amount is
only about 4 percent of the total revenue of the states. That is, this
amount *could* be raised by other means, specifically by taxation, but legislators understandably do not want to be associated with increasing
taxes. And so, again, advocates of state lotteries emphasize the voluntary
nature of the lottery: By buying lottery tickets, they say, people are in effect volunteering to give money to the states, in exchange for the chance
(however remote) of getting a ticket out. Buying a ticket, in this view,
is paying an optional tax; if you don't want to pay the tax, don't buy the
ticket.

I now get to the point in my argument where I may sound condescending, where I may offend decent people. The point is this: Studies
show that most of the tickets are bought by people who don't have
much money, people who are near the bottom of the economic scale.
According to one study, adults whose income was under $10,000 spent
nearly three times as much buying lottery tickets as did adults who
earned $50,000 or more.[1] I say that this argument is delicate because
anyone who advances it is liable to be accused of being snobbish and paternalistic, of saying, in effect, "Poor people don't know how to manage
their money, so we ought to remove temptation from their eyes." But
such a reply does not get to the central issues: The central issues are
(1) that the state should not tempt people, rich or poor, with dreams of
an easy buck and (2) that education and social services are immensely
important to the whole of society, so they should not be disproportionately financed by the poor and the addicted.

---

[1] Verna V. Gehring, "The American State Lottery: Sale or Swindle?" *Report from the Institute
for Philosophy and Public Policy* 20 (Winter/Spring 2000): 15.

Let me end a bit indirectly. Surely everyone will grant that tobacco is a harmful product. Yes, it is legal, but everyone knows it is harmful. The state puts very heavy taxes on it, presumably not to raise revenue but to discourage the use of tobacco. We agree, surely, that it would be almost criminal if, in an effort to increase its revenues, the state *enticed* people to smoke—for example, by posting billboards showing attractive people smoking or cartoon characters that appealed to children. Would we say, "Oh, well, we need the revenue (from the taxes) to provide services, so let's make smoking as attractive as we can to get people to buy cigarettes"? No, we would say, "People should not smoke, but if they will, well, let's use the revenue from the taxes for two chief purposes: *to dissuade* people from smoking and *to treat* people who have become ill from smoking."

State legislators who genuinely have the interests of their constituents at heart will not pass bills that put the state into the lottery business and that cause the state to engage in an activity that is close to pickpocketing. Rather, they will recognize that, however unpopular taxes are, taxes may have to be raised to support education and social services that the people rightly expect the state to provide. It's against the odds to expect politicians to act this way, but let's hope that some politicians will do the right thing and will vote for the common good.

TOPICS FOR CRITICAL THINKING AND WRITING

1. Jiménez omits at least one important argument that advocates of state-run lotteries sometimes offer: If our state doesn't run a lottery, residents will simply go to nearby states to buy tickets, so we will just be losing revenue that other states pick up; poor people will still be spending money that they can't afford, and our state will in no way benefit. What do you suppose Jiménez might say in reply? And what is your own view of this argument?

2. A bit of humor appears at the end of Jiménez's second paragraph. Is it appropriate? Or is the essay too solemn, too preachy? If you think it is too preachy, cite some sentences, and then revise them to make them more acceptable.

3. What would you say are the strengths and the weaknesses of this essay? What grade would you give it, and why? If you were the instructor in this first-year composition course, what comment (three or four sentences) would you write at the end of the essay?

Anna Lisa Raya

Daughter of a second-generation Mexican American father and a Puerto Rican mother, Anna Lisa Raya grew up in Los Angeles. While an undergraduate at Columbia University in New York, she wrote and published this essay on identity.

It's Hard Enough Being Me

[Student Essay]

When I entered college, I *discovered* I was Latina. Until then, I had never questioned who I was or where I was from: My father is a second-generation Mexican-American, born and raised in Los Angeles, and my mother was born in Puerto Rico and raised in Compton, California. My home is El Sereno, a predominantly Mexican neighborhood in L.A. Every close friend I have back home is Mexican. So I was always just Mexican. Though sometimes I was just Puerto Rican—like when we would visit Mamo (my grandma) or hang out with my Aunt Titi.

Upon arriving in New York as a first-year student, 3,000 miles from home, I not only experienced extreme culture shock, but for the first time I had to define myself according to the broad term "Latina." Although culture shock and identity crisis are common for the newly minted collegian who goes away to school, my experience as a newly minted Latina was, and still is, even more complicating. In El Sereno, I felt like I was part of a majority, whereas at the College I am a minority.

I've discovered that many Latinos like myself have undergone similar experiences. We face discrimination for being a minority in this country while also facing criticism for being "whitewashed" or "sellouts" in the countries of our heritage. But as an ethnic group in college, we are forced to define ourselves according to some vague, generalized Latino experience. This requires us to know our history, our language, our music, and our religion. I can't even be a content "Puerto Mexican" because I have to be a politically-and-socially-aware-Latina-with-a-chip-on-my-shoulder-because-of-how-repressed-I-am-in-this-country.

I am none of the above. I am the quintessential imperfect Latina. I can't dance salsa to save my life, I learned about Montezuma and the Aztecs in sixth grade, and I haven't prayed to the *Virgen de Guadalupe* in years.

Apparently I don't even look Latina. I can't count how many times people have just assumed that I'm white or asked me if I'm Asian. True, my friends back home call me *güera* ("whitey") because I have green eyes and pale skin, but that was as bad as it got. I never thought I would wish my skin were a darker shade or my hair a curlier texture, but since I've been in college, I have—many times.

Another thing: my Spanish is terrible. Every time I call home, I berate my mama for not teaching me Spanish when I was a child. In fact, not knowing how to speak the language of my home countries is the biggest problem that I have encountered, as have many Latinos. In Mexico there is a term, *pocha,* which is used by native Mexicans to ridicule Mexican-Americans. It expresses a deep-rooted antagonism and dislike for those of us who were raised on the other side of the border. Our failed attempts to speak pure, Mexican Spanish are largely responsible for the dislike. Other Latin American natives have this same attitude. No matter how well a Latino speaks Spanish, it can never be good enough.

Yet Latinos can't even speak Spanish in the U.S. without running the risk of being called "spic" or "wetback." That is precisely why my mother refused to teach me Spanish when I was a child. The fact that she spoke Spanish was constantly used against her: It prevented her from getting good jobs, and it would have placed me in bilingual education—a construct of the Los Angeles public school system that has proved to be more of a hindrance to intellectual development than a help.

To be fully Latina in college, however, I *must* know Spanish. I must satisfy the equation: Latina [equals] Spanish-speaking.

So I'm stuck in this black hole of an identity crisis, and college isn't making my life any easier, as I thought it would. In high school, I was being prepared for an adulthood in which I would be an individual, in which I wouldn't have to wear a Catholic school uniform anymore. But though I led an anonymous adolescence, I knew who I was. I knew I was different from white, black, or Asian people. I knew there was a language other than English that I could call my own if I only knew how to speak it better. I knew there were historical reasons why I was in this country, distinct reasons that make my existence here easier or more difficult than other people's existence. Ultimately, I was content.

Now I feel pushed into a corner, always defining, defending, and proving myself to classmates, professors, or employers. Trying to understand who and why I am, while understanding Plato or Homer, is a lot to ask of myself.

A month ago, I heard three Nuyorican (Puerto Ricans born and raised in New York) writers discuss how New York City has influenced their writing. One problem I have faced as a young writer is finding a voice that is true to my community. I was surprised and reassured to discover that as Latinos, these writers had faced similar pressures and conflicts as myself; some weren't even taught Spanish in childhood. I will never forget the advice that one of them gave me that evening: She said that I need to be true to myself. "Because people will always complain about what you are doing—you're a 'gringa' or a 'spic' no matter what," she explained. "So you might as well do things for yourself and not for them."

I don't know why it has taken 20 years to hear this advice, but I'm going to give it a try. *Soy yo* and no one else. *Punto.*[1]

TOPICS FOR CRITICAL THINKING AND WRITING

1. When Raya says she "discovered" she was Latina (para. 1), to what kind of event is she referring? Was she coerced or persuaded to declare herself as Latina, or did it come about in some other way?

[1]*Soy yo . . . Punto.* I'm me . . . Period (Spanish). [Editors' note.]

2. Is Raya on balance glad or sorry that she did not learn Spanish as a child? What evidence can you point to in her essay one way or the other?

3. What is an "identity crisis" (para. 9)? Does everyone go through such a crisis about the time one enters college? Did you? Or is this an experience that only racial minorities in predominantly white American colleges undergo?

Ronald Takaki

Ronald Takaki, the grandson of agricultural laborers who had come from Japan, is professor of ethnic studies at the University of California at Berkeley. He is the editor of From Different Shores: Perspectives on Race and Ethnicity in America *(1987) and the author of (among other writings)* Strangers from a Different Shore: A History of Asian-Americans *(1989). The essay that we reprint appeared originally in the* New York Times *on June 16, 1990.*

The Harmful Myth of Asian Superiority

Asian Americans have increasingly come to be viewed as a "model minority." But are they as successful as claimed? And for whom are they supposed to be a model?

Asian Americans have been described in the media as "excessively, even provocatively" successful in gaining admission to universities. Asian American shopkeepers have been congratulated, as well as criticized, for their ubiquity and entrepreneurial effectiveness.

If Asian Americans can make it, many politicians and pundits ask, why can't African Americans? Such comparisons pit minorities against each other and generate African American resentment toward Asian Americans. The victims are blamed for their plight, rather than racism and an economy that has made many young African American workers superfluous.

The celebration of Asian Americans has obscured reality. For example, figures on the high earnings of Asian Americans relative to Caucasians are misleading. Most Asian Americans live in California, Hawaii, and New York—states with higher incomes and higher costs of living than the national average.

Even Japanese Americans, often touted for their upward mobility,   5 have not reached equality. While Japanese American men in California earned an average income comparable to Caucasian men in 1980, they did so only by acquiring more education and working more hours.

Comparing family incomes is even more deceptive. Some Asian American groups do have higher family incomes than Caucasians. But they have more workers per family.

The "model minority" image homogenizes Asian Americans and hides their differences. For example, while thousands of Vietnamese American young people attend universities, others are on the streets. They live in motels and hang out in pool halls in places like East Los Angeles; some join gangs.

Twenty-five percent of the people in New York City's Chinatown lived below the poverty level in 1980, compared with 17 percent of the city's population. Some 60 percent of the workers in the Chinatowns of Los Angeles and San Francisco are crowded into low-paying jobs in garment factories and restaurants.

"Most immigrants coming into Chinatown with a language barrier cannot go outside this confined area into the mainstream of American industry," a Chinese immigrant said. "Before, I was a painter in Hong Kong, but I can't do it here. I got no license, no education. I want a living; so it's dishwasher, janitor, or cook."

Hmong and Mien refugees from Laos have unemployment rates that 10 reach as high as 80 percent. A 1987 California study showed that three out of ten Southeast Asian refugee families had been on welfare for four to ten years.

Although college-educated Asian Americans are entering the professions and earning good salaries, many hit the "glass ceiling"—the barrier through which high management positions can be seen but not reached. In 1988, only 8 percent of Asian Americans were "officials" and "managers," compared with 12 percent for all groups.

Finally, the triumph of Korean immigrants has been exaggerated. In 1988, Koreans in the New York metropolitan area earned only 68 percent of the median income of non-Asians. More than three-quarters of Korean greengrocers, those so-called paragons of bootstrap entrepreneurialism, came to America with a college education. Engineers, teachers, or administrators while in Korea, they became shopkeepers after their arrival. For many of them, the greengrocery represents dashed dreams, a step downward in status.

For all their hard work and long hours, most Korean shopkeepers do not actually earn very much: $17,000 to $35,000 a year, usually representing the income from the labor of an entire family.

But most Korean immigrants do not become shopkeepers. Instead, many find themselves trapped as clerks in grocery stores, service workers in restaurants, seamstresses in garment factories, and janitors in hotels.

Most Asian Americans know their "success" is largely a myth. They 15 also see how the celebration of Asian Americans as a "model minority" perpetuates their inequality and exacerbates relations between them and African Americans.

Topics for Critical Thinking and Writing

1. What is the thesis of Takaki's essay? What is the evidence he offers for its truth? Do you find his argument convincing? Explain your answers to these questions in an essay of 500 words.

2. Takaki several times uses statistics to make a point. Do some of the statistics seem more convincing than others? Explain.

3. Consider Takaki's title. To what group(s) is the myth of Asian superiority harmful?

4. Suppose you believed that Asian Americans are economically more successful in America today, relative to white Americans, than African Americans are. Does Takaki agree or disagree with you? What evidence, if any, does he cite to support or reject the belief?

5. Takaki attacks the "myth" of Asian American success and thus rejects the idea that they are a "model minority" (recall the opening and closing paragraphs). What do you think a genuine model minority would be like? Can you think of any racial or ethnic minority in the United States that can serve as a model? Explain why or why not in an essay of 500 words.

James Q. Wilson

James Q. Wilson is Collins Professor of Management and Public Policy at the University of California at Los Angeles. Among his books are Thinking about Crime *(1975),* Bureaucracy *(1989),* The Moral Sense *(1993), and* Moral Judgment *(1997). The essay that we reprint appeared originally in the* New York Times Magazine *on March 20, 1994.*

Just Take Away Their Guns

The president wants still tougher gun control legislation and thinks it will work. The public supports more gun control laws but suspects they won't work. The public is right.

Legal restraints on the lawful purchase of guns will have little effect on the illegal use of guns. There are some 200 million guns in private ownership, about one-third of them handguns. Only about 2 percent of the latter are employed to commit crimes. It would take a Draconian, and politically impossible, confiscation of legally purchased guns to make much of a difference in the number used by criminals. Moreover, only about one-sixth of the handguns used by serious criminals are purchased from a gun shop or pawnshop. Most of these handguns are stolen, borrowed, or obtained through private purchases that wouldn't be affected by gun laws.

What is worse, any successful effort to shrink the stock of legally purchased guns (or of ammunition) would reduce the capacity of law-abiding people to defend themselves. Gun control advocates scoff at the importance of self-defense, but they are wrong to do so. Based on a household survey, Gary Kleck, a criminologist at Florida State University, has estimated that every year, guns are used—that is, displayed or fired—for defensive purposes more than a million times, not counting their use by the police. If his estimate is correct, this means that the number of people who defend themselves with a gun exceeds the number of arrests for violent crimes and burglaries.

Our goal should not be the disarming of law-abiding citizens. It should be to reduce the number of people who carry guns unlawfully, especially in places—on streets, in taverns—where the mere presence of a gun can increase the hazards we all face. The most effective way to reduce illegal gun-carrying is to encourage the police to take guns away from people who carry them without a permit. This means encouraging the police to make street frisks.

The Fourth Amendment to the Constitution bans "unreasonable   5 searches and seizures." In 1968 the Supreme Court decided (*Terry v. Ohio*) that a frisk—patting down a person's outer clothing—is proper if the officer has a "reasonable suspicion" that the person is armed and dangerous. If a pat-down reveals an object that might be a gun, the officer can enter the suspect's pocket to remove it. If the gun is being carried illegally, the suspect can be arrested.

The reasonable-suspicion test is much less stringent than the probable-cause standard the police must meet in order to make an arrest. A reasonable suspicion, however, is more than just a hunch; it must be supported by specific facts. The courts have held, not always consistently, that these facts include someone acting in a way that leads an experienced officer to conclude criminal activity may be afoot; someone fleeing at the approach of an officer; a person who fits a drug courier profile; a motorist stopped for a traffic violation who has a suspicious bulge in his pocket; a suspect identified by a reliable informant as carrying a gun. The Supreme Court has also upheld frisking people on probation or parole.

Some police departments frisk a lot of people, but usually the police frisk rather few, at least for the purpose of detecting illegal guns. In 1992 the police arrested about 240,000 people for illegally possessing or carrying a weapon. This is only about one-fourth as many as were arrested for public drunkenness. The average police officer will make *no* weapons arrests and confiscate *no* guns during any given year. Mark Moore, a professor of public policy at Harvard University, found that most weapons arrests were made because a citizen complained, not because the police were out looking for guns.

It is easy to see why. Many cities suffer from a shortage of officers, and even those with ample law-enforcement personnel worry about having their cases thrown out for constitutional reasons or being accused of police harassment. But the risk of violating the Constitution or engaging in actual, as opposed to perceived, harassment can be substantially reduced.

Each patrol officer can be given a list of people on probation or parole who live on that officer's beat and be rewarded for making frequent stops to insure that they are not carrying guns. Officers can be trained to recognize the kinds of actions that the Court will accept as providing the "reasonable suspicion" necessary for a stop and frisk. Membership in a gang known for assaults and drug dealing could be made the basis, by statute or Court precedent, for gun frisks.

The available evidence supports the claim that self-defense is a legiti- 10 mate form of deterrence. People who report to the National Crime Survey that they defended themselves with a weapon were less likely to lose property in a robbery or be injured in an assault than those who did not defend themselves. Statistics have shown that would-be burglars are threatened by gun-wielding victims about as many times a year as they are arrested (and much more often than they are sent to prison) and that the chances of a burglar being shot are about the same as his chances of going to jail. Criminals know these facts even if gun control advocates do not and so are less likely to burgle occupied homes in America than occupied ones in Europe, where the residents rarely have guns.

Some gun control advocates may concede these points but rejoin that the cost of self-defense is self-injury: Handgun owners are more likely to shoot themselves or their loved ones than a criminal. Not quite. Most gun accidents involve rifles and shotguns, not handguns. Moreover, the rate of fatal gun accidents has been declining while the level of gun ownership has been rising. There are fatal gun accidents just as there are fatal car accidents, but in fewer than 2 percent of the gun fatalities was the victim someone mistaken for an intruder.

Those who urge us to forbid or severely restrict the sale of guns ignore these facts. Worse, they adopt a position that is politically absurd. In effect, they say, "Your government, having failed to protect your person and your property from criminal assault, now intends to deprive you of the opportunity to protect yourself."

Opponents of gun control make a different mistake. The National Rifle Association and its allies tell us that "guns don't kill, people kill" and urge the Government to punish more severely people who use guns to commit crimes. Locking up criminals does protect society from future crimes, and the prospect of being locked up may deter criminals. But our experience with meting out tougher sentences is mixed. The tougher the prospective sentence the less likely it is to be imposed, or at least to be imposed swiftly. If the Legislature adds on time for crimes committed with a gun, prosecutors often bargain away the add-ons; even when they do not, the judges in many states are reluctant to impose add-ons.

Worse, the presence of a gun can contribute to the magnitude of the crime even on the part of those who worry about serving a long prison sentence. Many criminals carry guns not to rob stores but to protect themselves from other armed criminals. Gang violence has become more threatening to bystanders as gang members have begun to arm themselves. People may commit crimes, but guns make some crimes worse. Guns often convert spontaneous outbursts of anger into fatal encounters. When some people carry them on the streets, others will want to carry them to protect themselves, and an urban arms race will be underway.

And modern science can be enlisted to help. Metal detectors at airports 15 have reduced the number of airplane bombings and skyjackings to nearly zero. But these detectors only work at very close range. What is needed is a device that will enable the police to detect the presence of a large lump of metal in someone's pocket from a distance of ten or fifteen feet. Receiving such a signal could supply the officer with reasonable grounds for a pat-down. Underemployed nuclear physicists and electronics engineers in the post-cold-war era surely have the talents for designing a better gun detector.

Even if we do all these things, there will still be complaints. Innocent people will be stopped. Young black and Hispanic men will probably be stopped more often than older white Anglo males or women of any race. But if we are serious about reducing drive-by shootings, fatal gang wars and lethal quarrels in public places, we must get illegal guns off the street. We cannot do this by multiplying the forms one fills out at gun shops or by pretending that guns are not a problem until a criminal uses one.

Topics for Critical Thinking and Writing

1. If you had to single out one sentence in Wilson's essay as coming close to stating his thesis, what sentence would that be? Why do you think it states, better than any other sentence, the thesis of the essay?

2. In his third paragraph Wilson reviews some research by a criminologist purporting to show that guns are important for self-defense in American households. Does the research as reported show that displaying or firing guns in self-defense actually prevented crimes? Or wounded aggressors? Suppose you were also told that in households where guns may be used defensively, thousands of innocent people are injured, and hundreds are killed—for instance, children who find a loaded gun and play with it. Would you regard these injuries and deaths as a fair tradeoff? Explain. What does the research presented by Wilson really show?

3. In paragraph 12 Wilson says that people who want to severely restrict the ownership of guns are in effect saying, "'Your government, having failed to protect your person and your property from criminal assault, now intends to deprive you of the opportunity to protect yourself.'" What reply might an advocate of severe restrictions make? (Even if you strongly believe Wilson's summary is accurate, try to put yourself in the shoes of an advocate of gun control, and come up with the best reply that you can.)

4. Wilson reports in paragraph 7 that the police arrest four times as many drunks on the streets as they do people carrying unlicensed firearms. Does this strike you as absurd, reasonable, or mysterious? Does Wilson explain it to your satisfaction?

5. In his final paragraph Wilson grants that his proposal entails a difficulty: "Innocent people will be stopped. Young black and Hispanic men will probably be stopped more often than older white Anglo males or

women of any race." Assuming that his predictions are accurate, is Wilson's proposal therefore fatally flawed and worth no further thought, or (to take the other extreme view) do you think that innocent people who fall into certain classifications will just have to put up with frisking, for the public good?

6. In an essay of no more than 100 words, explain the difference between the "reasonable-suspicion" test (para. 5) and the "probable-cause standard" (para. 6) that the courts use in deciding whether a street frisk is lawful. (You may want to organize your essay into two paragraphs, one on each topic, or perhaps into three if you want to use a brief introductory paragraph.)

7. Wilson criticizes both gun control advocates and the National Rifle Association for their ill-advised views. In an essay of 500 words, state his criticisms of each side, and explain whether and to what extent you agree.

Nadya Labi

A reporter and staff writer for Time, *Nadya Labi published this essay in* Time *on April 19, 1999. The research was based on reporting by Richard Woodbury (Denver), Melissa August (Washington), and Maggie Sleger (Chicago).*

Classrooms for Sale

Solve this problem: the staff and students of School District 11 in Colorado Springs, Colorado, drank 30,000 cases of Coke beverages last year. District 11 has a 10-year, $8 million contract with the soft-drink company that calls for the yearly consumption of 1.68 million bottles of Coke products. If a case contains 24 bottles, which answer is correct? (A) District 11 met its goal, and its students will sing back-up to Aretha Franklin in a new ad campaign. (B) District 11 is 960,000 bottles in the red. (C) Students should drink lots more Coke.

The best answer is B, but a District 11 administrator chose C. "If 35,439 staff and students buy one Coke product every other day for a school year," wrote John Bushey in a September missive to area principals, "we will double the required quota." His advice: allow Coke products in class and place vending machines in easily accessible areas. "Location, location, location is the key," he wrote, signing his memo "the Coke Dude."

Schools need money. Students have plenty of it to spend: $72 billion for all kids through high school, according to the most recent figures from Consumers Union. Those twin economic pressures have led to a disturbing trend on school grounds. In the past nine months, public school exclusivity deals with cola companies have soared 300 percent to a record 150. And that's just the most obvious signal that schools are

open for business. Calvin Klein models pout on the covers of textbooks; homecoming may be sponsored by Dr. Pepper; Taco Bell dishes up burritos at a school cafeteria near you; and that new overhead projector may be just one company's way of saying thanks — for eating Campbell's soup.

Commercialism in classrooms has become so rampant that last week a California education committee voted to restrict the use of brand names in taxpayer-funded textbooks. Parents were upset about a McGraw-Hill math textbook that is filled with references to products like Volkswagen automobiles, Jif peanut butter, and Beanie Babies. McGraw-Hill representatives point out that the company receives no compensation for mentioning the products, which are used simply to get kids' attention. "The practice of using real-life examples is a technique that's been around for 12 to 15 years," says Roger Rogalin, president of the publishing company's school division. "We live in a branded society, and these are the things kids are talking about."

The product placements in textbooks do seem innocent of any overt 5 commercial intent. Still, if you think Toys "R" Us and MTV are the only places where kids are being trained as consumers, take a walk through any elementary school or high school. Those splashy book covers? Chances are they're distributed by Cover Concepts, a company that sells advertising space on book covers to companies like Nestlé and Calvin Klein. That new weight-lifting machine? The school may participate in any of the incentive programs run by General Mills, Campbell's soup, or AT&T. Schools earn points for every box top, soup label, or long-distance phone call — which can then be redeemed for athletic and educational equipment. Or the school may be flush with prize money won in a contest sponsored by Chips Ahoy!, which asked students to confirm that there really are 1,000 chips in each bag, or Kellogg's, which had kids make sculptures out of Rice Krispies and melted marshmallows. "Is it proper for public institutions to become salespeople and build brand loyalty?" asks Andrew Hagelshaw, senior program director at the Center for Commercial-Free Public Education in Oakland, California. "Advertisers realize that schools are the perfect place to develop new markets. Kids can't switch the channel."

That's literally true in the case of ZapMe! Corp., which gives schools a free ride on the information superhighway, providing high-speed PCs, Internet access, laser printers and technical support. The catch? Students must use the computers for a minimum of four hours daily, while staring at a 2-in. × 4-in. billboard of rotating ads. Students earn "ZapPoints" that can be redeemed at an e-commerce mall. "There's a huge gap between what schools need and what they can afford," says Frank Vigil, president of the San Ramon–based company. "We want to provide the solution." He has signed up five thousand schools in his first four months of marketing.

School resistance to these kinds of ventures has been steadily worn down, ever since Channel One began offering schools free video equipment in return for showing kids a daily TV newscast filled with commercials. Now some companies are allowed into schools to do their market research. Noggin, an interactive TV network created by Nickelodeon and the Children's Television Network, meets with more than three hundred students at a New Jersey school during lunch and recess for the express purpose of finding out "what sparks kids." To thank Watchung School for its cooperation, the network has "contributed" $7,000 worth of keyboards. Education Market Resources conducts focus groups in schools on behalf of Kentucky Fried Chicken, McDonald's, Mattel, and advertising giant Leo Burnett. "We are strictly a kids' market-research firm," says Bob Reynolds, president of the Kansas-based company. "We never promote or market goods." But the information it collects is provided to other companies that then promote and market their own goods.

Secretary of Education Richard Riley is fond of saying, "Better education is everybody's business." In Plymouth, Michigan, they take that slogan to heart. District administrators are considering auctioning off school names to the highest-bidding corporation. No takers yet, but it could be the ultimate product placement: imagine your kid one day graduating from McDonald's Middle School and heading off to Coke High.

TOPICS FOR CRITICAL THINKING AND WRITING

1. The whole tone of Labi's essay shows that she is strongly opposed to turning public school classrooms into billboards for commercial products.

Do you think she exaggerates the harm done by such practices? By the way, what exactly *is* the harm done? Explain in an essay of about 250 words.

2. Labi titles her essay "Classrooms for Sale." Suppose she had titled it "Classrooms for Rent." What, if anything, would she have had to change in her argument?

3. What's the difference between attending Coke High or McDonald's Middle School (para. 8) and attending Duke University or Stanford University—institutions named after major donors?

Nadine Strossen

Nadine Strossen, president of the American Civil Liberties Union since 1991 and professor of law at New York Law School, published the following essay on IntellectualCapital.com in 1998. It evoked an abundant response, from which we reprint (following her essay) a selection of e-mails, including a response by Strossen.

Everyone Is Watching You

In 1949, a young English author named Eric Blair opened his latest novel with a scene in an apartment building where on each landing, a poster with an "enormous face gazed from the wall. It was so contrived that the eyes follow you about when you move."

You probably know Blair better by his pen name—George Orwell. The book, of course, was *1984*, and the poster bore the now-clichéd caption, "Big Brother is watching you." But even Blair's vivid imagination did not accurately predict the future. Today, the more appropriate caption would be, "Everyone Is Watching You."

"Everyone" includes banks, automated teller machines, parking lots, shopping centers, stadiums, and convenience stores. Also government offices, schools, businesses, and workplaces. Whether cruising through a toll booth, or buying a gallon of milk, or strolling in the park, private citizens increasingly are forfeiting their privacy whenever they venture out of their homes—or even, for that matter, while we are at home.

Consider the chilling story of Barbara Katende, who recently told the *New York Times* that she had spotted a camera on a rooftop about 200 yards from her apartment. A rooftop she had seen, but not thought about, every time she stood before her sixth-floor window with the blinds open, lounging around in her underwear or in nothing at all. The camera monitors traffic. But it has a powerful zoom lens and can turn in any direction. A technician who controls traffic cameras from a Manhattan studio told the *Times*, "If you can see the Empire State Building, we can see you."

Cities all over the country, including our nation's capital, are installing 5 cameras to record citizens' every coming-and-going on the streets, side-

walks, and parks. In Tempe, Arizona, officials struck a rotating camera—
nicknamed "Sneaky Peak"—atop the municipal building.

Why? Why not? "It's the biggest hit on our Web page," a Tempe official told the *Washington Post*.

Even more chillingly, new "face recognition" technology makes it
possible to instantly identify individuals who are captured on video
through complicated searches of facial images stored in government
databases. As CNN commented, this is "a wonderful way for government
to spy on its citizens who went to the antigovernment rally."

Why the mania for surveillance? Many claim that we need to trade
privacy for safety. But even many law-enforcement officials believe,
based on their actual experience, that video surveillance does not effectively detect or deter crime.

A number of cities that previously used video cameras—for
example, Miami Beach, Florida, Newark, New Jersey, White Plains, New
York, and Fredricksburg, Virginia—have abandoned them, concluding
that they were not worth the expense. Surveillance cameras that had
been mounted for twenty-two months in New York City's Times Square
led to only ten arrests before they were dismantled, prompting the *New
York Times* to dub them "one of the greatest flops along the Great White
Way."

Even in Blair's United Kingdom, where video-surveillance cameras 10
are the most pervasive and powerful, the government itself has concluded that they have not demonstrably improved public safety. As
noted by a report in the *Telegraph*, "A series of studies, including one by
the Home Office itself, suggest that" video surveillance "has merely
pushed crime into others areas or that its initial impact fades rapidly."

Just last September, the police department in Oakland, California,
urged the city council to reject a video-surveillance project that the police department itself initially had recommended, but about which it had
second thoughts—in terms of both privacy and efficiency. As Oakland's
police chief told the city council, "There is no conclusive way to establish
that the presence of video surveillance cameras resulted in the prevention or reduction of crime."

Moreover, responding to a detailed letter of concern from the American Civil Liberties Union, the Oakland city attorney concluded that a
"method of surveillance may be no greater than that which can be
achieved by the naked eye. [T]he California Supreme Court has held
that 'precious liberties' . . . do not simply shrink as the government ac-
quires new means of infringing upon them.'"

I applaud the California supreme court's ruling, which echoes the
pro-privacy principles first declared by U.S. Supreme Court Justice Louis
Brandeis in a famous 1928 dissent. Unfortunately, the Brandeisian view
of privacy—which he defined as "the right to be let alone, the most
comprehensive of rights"—remains a minority position among current
judges. The Supreme Court, for example, has held that the Constitution

only protects expectations of privacy that society considers "reasonable." This creates a downward spiral: The more government and others invade our privacy, the fewer "reasonable expectations" of privacy we have, which means that government and others may intrude even further into our privacy, etc., etc.

Given the foreshortened view of constitutional privacy that is currently enforced by our courts, we have to develop other avenues of legal protection—most importantly, federal and state statutes. Here, too, we now have only a patchwork of protection.

We must, therefore, take political and other direct action to remedy   15
the current lack of legal protection against the ubiquitous electronic "peeping Toms." Urge your community to oppose cameras in public places. If you notice a camera in an odd place, find out why it is there and what it is supposed to be recording. Tell businesses that record every transaction on camera that you will not be shopping there anymore. Before taking a job, let the employer know that you object to secret taping. And, most importantly, urge your elected officials to introduce laws limiting surveillance.

E-mail Responses to Nadine Strossen

Here we give a selection of e-mail responses that Strossen's article evoked. Typographical errors have not been corrected.

5/28/98
Dave
We have had the cop on the corner for over a hundred years, watching. He had a circle of vision of about 200 yards diameter. If the young lady in the story had lived in that 200 yard circle, she would have been observed by the government. What has changed is that the circle of vision is now about 2000 yards diameter. That and the cop on the corner of 50–100 years ago would have walked over to the womans house and ask her to act responsibly. All a camera can do is replace 100 cops on the corner with one. The garantee of the government is to be secure in our person and our homes, and it was done to provide for the pursuit of happiness. A camera can help to provide that security and that avenue of pursuit. The real question I have is this: is the decision of police departments to abandon video surveillance an outcome of Rodney King?

5/29/98
Merwyn R. Markel
There still are some situations where individuals may have no reasonable expectation of privacy. These include public areas and unshaded 6th floor windows in urban areas, where they may easily be seen, and may want to be seen, by others. Government has as much right to post cameras as to patrol police officers in the former areas, and for some

strange reason I can't get too concerned about people parading semi-nude and nude and then complaining when they are observed in the latter areas.

5/29/98
Merwyn R. Markel

By insisting government curtail its observation in public areas does ACLU really want to protect the right of persons to conduct criminal activities out of sight of law enforcement personnel?

5/29/98
Wilson Lee, San Diego

Merwyn, I don't think the ACLU is arguing that criminals should be allowed to commit crimes, but rather that there are better ways—which don't infringe upon our privacy rights—to enforce laws against criminal behavior than using blanket video surveillance. Those cameras are pretty much equivalent to warrantless searches of innocent people.

5/30/98
Merwyn R. Markel

Wilson Lee: I don't think you adequately dealt with my first post. Cameras in public places don't "search" innocent people; they mearly record what is there for anyone present to see. I can't escape the conclusion that the ACLU just wants goverment to give criminals what the ACLU considers a sporting chance. Of course without using video cameras, government has and continues to unjustifiably if not illegally intrude on the privacy of its citizens. Some of the ways it does so include: (a) gathering information about them that they do not vluntarily disclose, whether or not it then discloses that information to unauthorized parties for political or other unauthorized purposes, and (b) obtaining information from citizens under the promise that it will not be used to their detrament, and then breaking that promise. Category (a) includes EEOC's requirement that all employers of 15 or more persons gather and report the percentages of "minorities" and females they employ, and the 500 FBI files on political opponents that just happened to be turned over to White House personnel. Example (b) includes a government agency asking an employment applicant to disclose his race and sex on a document it promises to use only for "statistical puropses" and then managing to associate it with the applicant anyway to deny him a job he was better qualified for than the successful applicant. Now why, do you suppose, Nadine and the ACLU don't mention such intrusions of our privacy?

5/30/98
Wilson Lee, San Diego

Merwyn: Perhaps calling surveillance cameras warrantless searches may have been hyperbolic on my part. But I still think we have some reasonable expectations of privacy, even in public places. And I'm not sure a surveillance camera is equivalent in power to posting police officers. For one, a police officer wouldn't be able to search databases to instantly identify the faces of those being surveilled. The point is not that criminals will get away with more without surveillance. That may be true, to a certain extent. But having some crimes go unpunished costs our society less than giving the government more power. Even if you ignore the issue of constitutional rights, on purely pragmatic terms, surveillance fails the test because its efficacy in preventing crime is unproven, simlar to how capital punishment fails as a deterrent (but that's a debate for another article). I agree that we should be able to keep control over our private information. I can't speak for the ACLU, but I imagine that the lack of mention of such other privacy violations in the article does not imply that they don't take issue with them.

5/31/98
Merwyn R. Markel

Wilson Lee: You say "surveilence fails the test [of fairness or constitutionality, I assume] because its efficacy in preventing crime is unproven." I humbly suggest that we don't need "proof" to justify doing what seems reasonable, even when its constutionality is challenged. I'd like to see a judicial decision that says otherwise. It is reasonable to believe that many if not all criminals would not commit their crimes if they thought they were being observed doing so by law enforcement officers or recorded doing so by law enforcement cameras. It is also resonable to believe that such surveilence will assist government law enforcement personnel to detect and apprehend criminals, which is still a prime responsibility of government. The "proof" Nadine mentions is, assumining her claims about it are correct, merely "proof" that in specific past situations electronic surveilence was found—correctly or incorrectly—to deter crime less than certain government officials thought justified by the cost. That says nothing about the efficacy of other past or future surveilence programs or situations. The efficacy of science to prove something today and the opposite tomorrow hardly needs proof. For similar reasons, I welcome future discussions about capital punishment.

6/1/98
Nadine Strossen

A couple of you...make a point that is often raised in opposition to pro-privacy arguments, namely: If you've got nothing to hide, why should you care about privacy? This is a variation on the theme that only criminals would benefit from increasing privacy protection. Nothing could be further from the truth. I pride myself on being a law-abiding person, and on holding myself to high moral standards even in arenas where no one can observe my behavior. In other words, it is extremely important to me that I conduct myself consistent with my own moral standards especially when I am being judged only by my own conscience, rather than for the benefit of some outside observer/evaluator. . . . So, when I want to stop someone from observing my behavior, it's not because I believe my behavior is illegal or immoral. Rather, it's because my behavior is my private business—and that of the others with whom I affirmatively choose to share it. Think of this analogy: I'm not ashamed of my nude body, but that doesn't mean I want government or private Peeping Toms to look at it! In short, I—and every other law-abiding citizen—has something very important to hide: our privacy.

TOPICS FOR CRITICAL THINKING AND WRITING

1. Do you consider surveillance cameras in "banks, automated teller machines, parking lots, shopping centers, stadiums, and convenience stores" (para. 3) an unreasonable invasion of your privacy? Explain.

2. Strossen refers to "a famous 1928 dissent" by Justice Brandeis (para. 13). The case is *Olmstead v. United States*. With the help of your reference librarian, locate a copy of this case, and read Brandeis's dissent. Then summarize it in an essay of 250 words.

3. The U.S. Supreme Court has held, Strossen tells us, "that the Constitution only protects expectations of privacy that society considers 'reasonable'" (para. 13). Look back at paragraph 4, in which Strossen tells us that Barbara Katende sometimes stood nude before her sixth-floor window. Would you say that Katende had a "reasonable" expectation of privacy? Why, or why not?

4. "Dave" offers a comparison with "50–100 years ago." How convincing do you find this argument? Why?

5. "Dave" also mentions Rodney King. Who is he, and why is it apt to mention him in the context?

6. Two of the letter writers, "Dave" and "Merwyn R. Markel," draw an analogy between police observation and camera observation. Do you think the analogy is a good one? Explain your view in an essay of 250 words.

7. Do you agree with "Wilson Lee" (5/29/98) that surveillance "cameras are pretty much equivalent to warrantless searches of innocent people"? In your response, consider also the later postings that we print.

8. "Merwyn R. Markel" ends his posting of 5/30/98 with a question. What do you think his own answer to the question would be?

9. "Wilson Lee" (5/30/98) says that "having some crimes go unpunished costs our society less than giving the government more power." How would you support or refute this assertion?

10. Write a response to Nadine Strossen's posting of 6/1/98 (but don't send it). Consider especially the analogy that she offers.

11. Strossen recommends that you "tell businesses that record every transaction on camera that you will not be shopping there anymore" (para. 15). Is this reasonable advice? Are you prepared to follow it? Why, or why not?

Sally Satel

Sally Satel, a psychiatrist and resident scholar at the American Enterprise Institute, is a lecturer at the Yale University School of Medicine. Satel is the author of PC, MD: How Political Correctness Is Corrupting Medicine *(2000), and the coauthor of* One Nation under Therapy *(2005). We reprint an op-ed piece that she wrote for the* New York Times *in 2006, and we follow it with several letters written in response.*

Death's Waiting List

March was National Kidney Month. I did my part: I got a new one. My good fortune, alas, does not befall nearly enough people, and the federal government deserves much of the blame.

Today 70,000 Americans are waiting for kidneys, according to the United Network for Organ Sharing, which maintains the national waiting list. Last year, roughly 16,000 people received one (about 40 percent are from living donors, the others from cadavers). More are waiting for livers, hearts, and lungs, which mostly come from deceased donors, bringing the total to about 92,000. In big cities, where the ratio of acceptable organs to needy patients is worst, the wait is five to eight years and is expected to double by 2010. Someone on the organ list dies every ninety seconds. Tick. Tick. Tick.

Until my donor came forward, I was desperate. I had been on the list only for a year and was about to start dialysis. I had joined a Web site, MatchingDonors.com, and found a man willing to give me one of his kidneys, but he fell through. I wished for a Sears organ catalog so I could find a well-matched kidney and send in my check. I wondered about going overseas to become a "transplant tourist," but getting a black market organ seemed too risky.

Paradoxically, our nation's organ policy is governed by a tenet that closes off a large supply of potential organs—the notion that organs from any donor, deceased or living, must be given freely. The 1984 National Organ Transplantation Act makes it illegal for anyone to sell or acquire an organ for "valuable consideration."

In polls, only 30 percent to 40 percent of Americans say they have 5 designated themselves as donors on their driver's licenses or on state-run donor registries. As for the remainder, the decision to donate will fall to their families who are as likely as not to deny the hospital's request. In any event, only a small number of bodies of the recently deceased, perhaps 13,000 a year, possess organs healthy enough for transplanting.

The verdict is in: Relying solely on altruism is not enough. Charities rely on volunteers to help carry out their good works but they also need paid staff. If we really want to increase the supply of organs, we need to try incentives—financial and otherwise.

Many transplant experts recognize this, proposing initiatives that would allow people to give their organs in exchange for tax breaks, guaranteed health insurance, college scholarships for their children, deposits in their retirement accounts, and so on: Ethics committees of United Network for Organ Sharing, the American Society of Transplant Surgeons, and the World Transplant Congress, along with the President's Council on Bioethics and others, have begun discussing the virtues of such incentives.

Against this backdrop of mounting frustration, the Institute of Medicine, part of the National Academy of Sciences, this month issued a report titled, "Organ Donation: Opportunities for Action." Unfortunately, the report more properly should be subtitled "Recommendations for Inaction."

Basically, it recommended only one new initiative: expanding donor eligibility to patients who died of cardiac arrest. (Organs now can be retrieved only from those who suffer brain death.) This makes sense, as more people die because their heart stops than because of brain damage.

But even so, this new supply will fall far short of need. At the very 10 least, the report should have shown enthusiasm for other initiatives. One is the popular and effective European practice of "presumed consent" in which citizens are considered donors at death unless they sign an anti-donor (or opt-out) card.

Another possibility it could have recommended was pilot studies using incentives in a regulated market. One model resembles a "futures" market in cadaver organs. A potential donor could receive compensation—outright payment, a sizable contribution to a charity of his choice, or lifetime health insurance—in installments before death or to his estate afterwards in exchange for permission to recover his organs at death.

Why so timid? The Institute of Medicine cautioned against treating the body as if it were "for sale." But that's outdated thinking: we've accepted markets for human eggs, sperm, and surrogate mothers. A recent poll by researchers in Pennsylvania found that 59 percent of respondents favored the general idea of incentives, with 53 percent saying direct payments would be acceptable.

Some critics worry that compensation for kidney donation by the living would be most attractive to the poor and hence exploit them. But if it were government-regulated we could ensure that donors would receive education about their choices, undergo careful medical and psychological screening, and receive quality follow-up care. We could even make a donation optior that favors the well-off by rewarding donors with a tax credit. Besides, how is it unfair to poor people if compensation enhances their quality of life?

Paying for organs, from the living or deceased, may seem distasteful. But a system with safeguards, begun as a pilot to resolve ethical and practical aspects, is surely preferable to the status quo that allows thousands to die each year. As the International Forum for Transplant Ethics put it: "The well-known shortage of kidneys for transplantation causes much suffering and death. If we are to deny treatment to the suffering and dying, we need better reasons than our own feelings of disgust."

Topics for Critical Thinking and Writing

1. How would you characterize Satel's tone? Businesslike? Wimpy? Or what? Come up with a characterization in a word or two, and then point to two or three sentences to support your view.

2. In a reasoned essay of 250–500 words, set forth your view of "presumed consent" (para. 9).

3. If you have not signed a donor card, explain why you have not. You just haven't gotten around to it? You don't like the idea? Religious reasons?

4. In a reasoned essay of 250–500 words, set forth your view of the proposal that Satel offers in paragraph 11, which involves payment. By the way, do the statistics offered in paragraph 12 play any role in shaping your opinion of the proposal?

5. In 250 words, specify and evaluate the argumentative techniques that Satel uses in her final paragraph.

6. In the United States it is legal and widely acceptable to sell blood, sperm, and eggs. Is there any significant difference between selling such things and selling a kidney? Between selling a kidney and renting a womb? Explain your answer.

7. Suppose that you have a recently signed organ-donor card in your wallet. Then suppose that you die in an accident. On what grounds, if any, would you think it reasonable for a family member to veto your organ donation?

8. Given the great need for organ donors, should the federal government mount a massive (and costly) campaign to alert the public to the need? Give your reasons pro or con, in an essay of 250–500 words.

9. Some doctors and some hospitals make a great deal of money from donated organs. Should doctors and hospitals that receive free organs be required to implant them without charge, or receive, at most, minimal compensation?

Letters of Response by Dorothy H. Hayes, Charles B. Fruit, and Michelle Goodwin

To the Editor:

Re "Death's Waiting List," by Sally Satel (Op-Ed, May 15):

As a kidney donor, I consider cash for organs an obscene proposal. I donated a kidney to a loved one in 2002 and would do it again in a heartbeat. It was a gift to me to offer new life.

But cash for body parts? This option has the potential to promote donor trafficking, and to germinate guilt on a grand scale.

Even in life-and-death situations, some may not be able to risk the pain and their own health for a loved one in need of an organ transplant, no matter how much they love.

But for tax breaks, guaranteed health insurance, college scholarships, and deposits in retirement accounts, as Dr. Satel suggests?

Europe's "presumed consent" is the humane answer and decades overdue.

Dorothy H. Hayes
Stamford, Conn., May 16, 2006

To the Editor:

Sally Satel and I were both lucky enough to have found donors for kidney transplants that saved our lives. But I disagree with her endorsement of a market-based incentive strategy that would pay organ donors or their family members. That would set a dangerous precedent.

In 2005, a national survey found that 10.8 percent of those polled would be less likely to grant consent for the organs of a deceased family member to be used for transplant if they were offered payment; 68 percent said they would be neither more nor less likely to grant consent.

Thus, there is little data to show that financial incentives would increase donation rates. More likely, "paying for organs" would lead people to view organs as commodities.

The National Kidney Foundation has long maintained that financial incentives for donation would not allow the United States to maintain its values as a society, and that a voluntary system of organ donation, free of commercialization, is the only ethical way transplantation can be practiced in the United States.

The foundation is working to attack the organ shortage through improvement in organ-donation education for families and the establishment of standards to ensure the health and safety of living donors. A wholesale sellout to the law of supply and demand is not the answer.

Charles B. Fruit
Atlanta, May 17, 2006

The writer is chairman of the National Kidney Foundation.

To the Editor:

Sally Satel offers a provocative solution to the American organ transplant system failure: try incentives. She's right.

African-Americans are disproportionately affected by the organ shortage. They represent 40 percent of people on the kidney transplant waiting list, have the longest waits, and experience the highest death rates on lists.

For years, commentators have suggested that African-Americans would suffer most under a system with incentives. Their arguments verge on the paternalistic and polemical, and their rationales are out-moded and incendiary.

Such thinking ignores the fact that blacks might benefit from the in-troduction of incentives into the current transplantation system, because African-Americans need kidneys more than any other group.

The consequences of ignoring the possible advantages of cadaveric sales for curing organ deficits and thereby enhancing the health oppor-tunities for all Americans, especially black Americans, are extreme.

Michele Goodwin
Chicago, May 15, 2006

The writer, a professor at DePaul University College of Law, is the author of a book about the supply and demand of body parts.

Topics for Critical Thinking and Writing

1. Hayes says in her second paragraph, "I consider cash for organs an ob-scene proposal." Do you agree? Why, or why not?

2. Fruit offers statistics concerning financial rewards to the families of the deceased, but he does not address the points Satel raises in paragraph 11 — outright payments to the donor, or to a charity of the donor's choice, or to the donor's estate. Would any of these plans influence you to become a donor after your death? Why, or why not?

3. Goodwin in her third paragraph mentions "paternalistic" arguments, but she doesn't describe them. What do you suppose a paternalistic ar-gument would be?

4. Write a response (250 words, in the form of a letter) to one of the pre-ceding letters.

Paul Kane

Paul Kane served as a marine in Iraq. At the time that he published this essay, he was a fellow at the Kennedy School of Government. Kane is writing a book about national service and sacrifice. Kane's essay was originally published as a New York Times *op-ed piece (April 20, 2006).*

A Peaceful Call to Arms

The American public needs to be prepared for what is shaping up to be a clash of colossal proportions between the West and Iran.

President Franklin D. Roosevelt masterfully prepared Americans be-fore the United States entered World War II by initiating a peacetime draft under the Selective Training and Service Act of 1940.

Now, President Bush and Congress should reinstitute selective service under a lottery without any deferments.

This single action will send a strong message to three constituencies in the crisis over Iran's nuclear intentions—Iran, outside powers like China and Russia, and Americans at home—and perhaps lead to a peaceful resolution.

Iran's leaders and public will see that the United States is serious 5 about ensuring that they never possess a nuclear weapon. The Chinese and Russian governments will see that their diplomatic influence should be exercised sooner rather than later and stop hanging back. But most important, America's elites and ordinary citizens alike will know that they may be called upon for wartime service and sacrifice.

President Bush has the perfect credentials overseas to execute this move, and little political capital at home to lose at this stage. Polls confirm that a wide majority of people in many countries view him and the United States as the major threat to global peace. Why let them down on this count? Go with the flow.

President Ronald Reagan was the past master of using this strategy during the cold war. Reagan capitalized on his image as the madman at the helm to keep the Russians off balance, using the signs of war to dissuade our foes and avert actual war. President Bush should take a page from Reagan's playbook.

Iran's leaders are highly sensitive to Iranian public attitudes about the nuclear program. That, at least, is the impression one gets from a speech given behind closed doors to Iran's Supreme Cultural Revolution Council by Hassan Rowhani, the former chief nuclear negotiator with the Europeans. In the text of his remarks published last year by an Iranian policy journal, Mr. Rowhani said the nuclear issue had already created too many headlines, and that "whatever we do, we must have the support of the public."

Engaging Iranian public opinion at a deeper level can only enhance the prospects for a peaceful settlement. By signaling to Iranians that the cost of a clandestine nuclear program will be expensive—in blood, treasure, time, and standing—reinstitution of selective national service in the United States will alter the calculus of the crisis with Iran.

As it now stands, we have an American administration that is deter- 10 mined to deny the Iranians nuclear weapons but needs time to effect regime change in Tehran. Iran's hard-line leadership, meanwhile, needs time to solve the technological challenge of enriching enough uranium to make an atomic bomb.

Unfortunately, with time in short supply for both sides, the clash of national wills is escalating, and a military conflict seems more likely.

President Bush should therefore consult with Congress about reinstituting selective national service by lottery for all young males and females. After 9/11, President Bush missed an opportunity to ask America's citizenry to make sacrifices in the form of military service, homeland defense, and conservation that many would have accepted. Instead, he asked people to continue shopping to prop up the flagging economy.

We should not fumble the opportunity now to begin selective service again, while the Iranians and others are watching. It may be our last best chance to avoid war with Iran.

TOPICS FOR CRITICAL THINKING AND WRITING

1. The United States has never had a draft system without any deferments. Why does Kane think the nation is ready and willing to have one now (paras. 3, 12)?

2. How analogous is the current situation in the Middle East to the international situation of 1940 when President Roosevelt created the draft (para. 2)—a year after war had broken out in Europe?

Letters of Response by Julie E. Dinnerstein, Murray Polner, Joan Z. Greiner, and Jonathan Zimmerman

To the Editor:

President Bush has turned me into someone I never thought I would become; a supporter of the Selective Service.

My support is not based, as Paul Kane ("A Peaceful Call to Arms," Op-Ed, April 20) would have it, on a belief that we Americans are willing to "make sacrifices in the form of military service, homeland defense, and conservation," at least not for dubious adventures in distant nations whose internal workings we do not understand and whose direct threat to our own well-being is far from clear.

Rather, if all of us across the nation faced losing partners and children and brothers and sisters and neighbors and perhaps our own lives, we would think long and hard about whether a war was worth fighting.

Julie E. Dinnerstein
New York, April 20, 2006

To the Editor:

"A Peaceful Call to Arms" advances an absurd reason for reinstating the draft of young men and women on the grounds that it will deter Iran's nuclear program and conceivably an American attack on Iran.

A draft will only create more potential American cannon fodder and eventual war memorials to the dead, sharpen antiwar protests everywhere, awaken renewed civil strife at home, and add ever more billions to our national debt, not to mention whetting the appetite of our bellicose administration and its neoconservative allies eager to promote yet another war in the volatile Middle East.

Rather than a draft, what may prevent another American military adventure in the Middle East is for Washington to stop threatening Iran, recall the bulk of our troops in Iraq, work hard to establish a just peace between Israelis and Palestintans, and, of course, learn to control our insatiable appetite for oil and the demands it makes on our nation's military.

Murray Polner
Great Neck, N.Y., April 20, 2006

To the Editor:

As the mother of two twentysomething daughters, I have no intention of standing quietly by if the military draft is reinstated. I, and a number of others, do not support women in the military, on the front lines, despite the louder voices of my feminist sisters pushing this as a vehicle for equality.

Female soldiers and interrogators at Guantanamo and Abu Ghraib, used to soften up prisoners for interrogation by engaging in sexually demeaning acts directed at the prisoners, were sexually exploited in the most vile way.

These behaviors are not the acts of a few renegades but the policies of our new streamlined military under the tutelage of Defense Secretary Donald H. Rumsfeld and the cooperation of Maj. Gen. Geoffrey D. Miller. The treatment of our soldiers and our prisoners under this regime is devoid of moral consciousness.

As for calming down the Iranian nuclear wildfire, I think reinstating the draft would only fan the flames.

Joan Z. Greiner
Flemington, N.J., April 20, 2006

To the Editor:

By focusing upon an imaginary future conflict with Iran, Paul Kane misses the best argument in favor of national conscription: it would bring our present-day misadventure in Iraq to a hasty conclusion.

Most of my students are vehemently opposed to American involvement in the Iraq war, but very few of them have engaged in organized protest against it. If they knew that they could be drafted, however, they'd take to the streets. So would millions of other young people, along with their parents and grandparents.

Our elected officials would sit up and take notice, ending the war in Iraq before their own daughters and sons faced the terrifying prospect of fighting and dying there. Fear has a way of concentrating the mind.

Jonathan Zimmerman
New York, April 20, 2006

The writer is a professor of education and history at New York University.

Topics for Critical Thinking and Writing

1. Explain whether you agree with Dinnerstein that a draft would have the benefit of discouraging military adventures like those we have initiated in Iraq and elsewhere in the Middle East.

2. How might Kane reply to Polner's defense of alternatives to a military draft?

3. Greiner speaks "as the mother of two twentysomething daughters." During wartime, people do things that are almost inconceivable. For instance, they kill people who have in no way harmed them. Is Greiner too protective of her daughters' innocence, too unwilling to recognize that war requires us to do dreadful things? Explain in 250 words.

4. What is "the best argument in favor of national conscription" to which Zimmerman refers? Do you agree that it is the best argument? Why, or why not?

4

Visual Rhetoric: Images as Arguments

A picture is worth a thousand words.
— CHINESE PROVERB

"What is the use of a book," thought Alice, "without pictures or conversations?"
— LEWIS CARROLL

SOME USES OF IMAGES

Most visual materials that accompany written arguments serve one of two functions—they appeal to the emotions (a photograph of a calf in a pen so narrow that the calf cannot turn, in an essay on animal liberation) or they clarify numerical data (a graph showing five decades of male and female law school enrollments). There are of course additional uses for pictures, for example cartoons may add a welcome touch of humor or satire, but in this chapter we concentrate on appeals to emotion and briefly on graphs and related images.

APPEALS TO THE EYE

We began the preceding chapter by distinguishing between *argument,* which we said relies on reason (*logos*), and *persuasion,* which we said is a broad term that can include appeal to the emotions (*pathos*)—for example, an appeal to pity. Threats, too, can be persuasive. As Al Capone famously said, "You can get a lot more done with a kind word and a gun than with a kind word alone." Indeed, most of the remarks that we can think of link persuasion not with the power of reason but with the power of emotional appeals, of flattery, of threats, and of appeals to self-interest. We have in mind passages spoken not only by the likes of the racketeer Al Capone, but by more significant figures. Consider these two remarks, which both use the word *interest* in the sense of "self-interest":

> Would you persuade, speak of Interest, not Reason.
> —Ben Franklin

> There are two levers for moving men—interest and fear.
> —Napoleon Bonaparte

An appeal to self-interest is obviously at the heart of most advertisements: "Buy *X* automobile, and members of the opposite sex will find you irresistible," "Use *Y* instant soup, and your family will love you more," "Try *Z* cereal and enjoy regularity." We will look at advertisements later in this chapter, but first let's talk a bit more about the use and abuse of visual material in persuasion.

When we discussed the appeal to emotion (p. 101), we quoted from Mark Antony's speech to the Roman populace in Shakespeare's *Julius Caesar.* You will recall that Antony stirred the mob by displaying Caesar's blood-stained mantle, that is, by supplementing his words with visual material:

> Look, in this place ran Cassius' dagger through;
> See what a rent the envious Casca made;
> Through this, the well-belovèd Brutus stabbed. . . .

In courtrooms today, trial lawyers and prosecutors still do this sort of thing when

- They exhibit photos of a bloody corpse, or
- They introduce as witnesses small children who sob as they describe the murder of their parents.

The appeal clearly is not to reason but to the jurors' emotions—and yet, can we confidently say that this sort of visual evidence—this attempt to stir anger at the alleged perpetrator of the crime and pity for the victims —is irrelevant? Why shouldn't jurors vicariously experience the assault?

When we think about it—and it takes only a moment of thinking—the appeal in the courtroom to the eye and then to the heart or mind is evident even in smaller things, such as the clothing that the lawyers wear and the clothing that they advise their clients to wear. To take the most obvious, classic example: The mugger who normally wears jeans, a T-shirt, and a leather jacket appears in court in a three-piece suit, dress shirt, and necktie. Lawyers know that in arguing a case, visuals make statements—perhaps not logical arguments but nevertheless meaningful statements that will attract or repel jurors.

Another sort of visual appeal connected with some arguments should be mentioned briefly—the visual appeal of the specific setting in which

Martin Luther King Jr. delivering his "I Have a Dream" speech on August 28, 1963, from the steps of the Lincoln Memorial. The visual aspects — the setting (the Lincoln Memorial with the Washington Monument and the Capitol in the distance) and King's gestures — are part of the persuasive rhetoric of the speech.

the argument occurs. Martin Luther King Jr.'s great speech of August 28, 1963, "I Have a Dream," still reads very well on the page, but part of its immense appeal when it was first given was due to its setting: King spoke to some 200,000 people in Washington, D.C., as he stood on the steps of the Lincoln Memorial. That setting was part of King's argument.

Pictures—and here we get to our chief subject—are also sometimes used as parts of arguments because pictures make statements. Some pictures, like Edvard Munch's *The Scream* (below), make obvious statements: The swiftly receding diagonal lines of the fence and the walkway, the wavy sky, and the vibrating vertical lines to the right of the figure all convey the great agitation experienced by the figure in the woodcut. Some pictures, like the photographs shown to members of Congress during the debate over whether permission should be given to drill in the Arctic National Wildlife Refuge are a bit less obvious:

- Opponents of drilling showed beautiful pictures of polar bears frolicking, wildflowers in bloom, and caribou on the move.

- Proponents of drilling showed bleak pictures of what they called "barren land" and "a frozen wasteland."

Both sides knew very well that images are powerful persuaders, and they did not hesitate to use images as supplements to words.

We again invite you to think about the appropriateness of using images in arguments. Should argument be entirely a matter of reason, of logic, without appeals to the emotions? Or can images of the sort that we

(Edvard Munch, *The Scream.* © 2007 The Munch Museum/The Munch-Ellingsen Group/Artists Rights Society (ARS), NY. Digital Image ©/The Museum of Modern Art, NY. Licensed by SCALA/Art Resource.)

have already mentioned provide visual (and emotional) support for reasons that are offered? The statement that "the Arctic National Wildlife Refuge is a home for abundant wildlife, notably polar bears, caribou, and wildflowers" may not mean much until it is reinforced with breathtaking images. (And, similarly, the statement that "most of the ANWR land is barren" may not mean much until it is corroborated by images of the vast bleakness.)

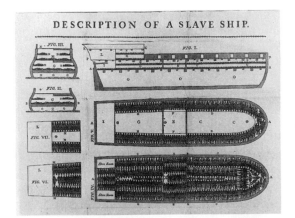
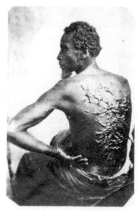

Images played an important role in the activities of the antislavery movement in the nineteenth century. On the top left is a diagram that shows how human cargo was packed into a slave ship; it was distributed with Thomas Clarkson's *Essay on the Slavery and Commerce of the Human Species* (1804). On the top right is Frederick W. Mercer's photograph (April 2, 1863) of Gordon, a "badly lacerated" runaway slave. Images such as the slave ship and Gordon were used against the claims of slaveowners that slavery was a humane institution—claims that also were supported by illustrations, such as the woodcut at the bottom, titled *Attention Paid to a Poor Sick Negro*, from Josiah Priest's *In Defense of Slavery*.

> **A RULE FOR WRITERS:** If you think that pictures will help you to make the point you are arguing, include them with captions explaining sources and relevance.

ARE SOME IMAGES NOT FIT TO BE SHOWN?

Images of suffering—human or, as animal rights activists have made us see, animal—can be immensely persuasive. In the nineteenth century, for instance, the antislavery movement made extremely effective use of images in its campaign. We reproduce two antislavery images here, as well as a counterimage that sought to assure viewers that slavery is a beneficent system. But are there some images not fit to print?

Until recently, many newspapers did not print pictures of lynched African Americans, hanged and burned and maimed. The reasons for not printing such images probably differed in the South and North: Southern papers may have considered the images to be discreditable to whites, while Northern papers may have deemed the images too revolting. Even today, when it is commonplace to see in newspapers and on television

Huynh Cong (Nick) Ut, *The Terror of War: Children on Route 1 near Trang Bang*

Eddie Adams, *Execution of Viet Cong prisoner, Saigon, 1968*

screens pictures of dead victims of war, or famine, or traffic accidents, one rarely sees bodies that are horribly maimed. (For traffic accidents, the body is usually covered, and we see only the smashed car.) The U.S. government has refused to release photographs showing the bodies of American soldiers killed in the war in Iraq, and it has been most reluctant to show pictures of dead Iraqi soldiers and civilians. Only after many Iraqis refused to believe that Saddam Hussein's two sons had been killed did the U.S. government reluctantly release pictures showing the blood-spattered faces of the two men — and some American newspapers and television programs refused to use the images.

There have been notable exceptions to this practice, such as Huynh Cong (Nick) Ut's 1972 photograph of children fleeing a napalm attack in Vietnam (p. 146), which was widely reproduced in the United States and won the photographer a Pulitzer Prize in 1973. The influence of this particular photograph cannot be measured, but it is widely felt to have played a substantial role in increasing public pressure to end the Vietnam War. Another widely reproduced picture of horrifying violence is Eddie Adams's picture (1968) of a South Vietnamese chief of police firing a pistol into the head of a Viet Cong prisoner.

The issue remains: Are some images unacceptable? For instance, although capital punishment is legal in parts of the United States — by methods including lethal injection, hanging, shooting, and electrocution — every state in the Union prohibits the publication of pictures showing a criminal being executed. (On this topic, see Wendy Lesser, *Pictures at an Execution* [1993].)

The most famous recent example of an image widely thought to be unprintable concerns the murder of Daniel Pearl, a Jewish reporter for the *Wall Street Journal.* Pearl was captured and murdered in June 2002 by Islamic terrorists in Pakistan. His killers videotaped Pearl reading a statement denouncing American policy, and being decapitated. The video also shows a man's arm holding Pearl's head. The video ends with the killers making several demands (such as the release of the Muslim prisoners being held by the United States in Guantánamo Bay, Cuba) and asserting that "if our demands are not met, this scene will be repeated again and again."

The chief arguments against reproducing in newspapers material from this video were that

- The video and even still images from it are unbearably gruesome;
- Showing the video would traumatize the Pearl family; and
- The video is propaganda by an enemy.

Those who favored broadcasting the video on television and printing still images from it in newspapers tended to argue that

- The photo will show the world what sort of enemy the United States is fighting;
- Newspapers have published pictures of other terrifying sights (notably, people leaping out of windows of New York's twin towers and endless pictures of the space shuttle *Challenger* exploding); and
- No one was worried about protecting the families of these other victims from seeing painful images.

But ask yourself if the comparison of the Daniel Pearl video to the photos of the twin towers and of the *Challenger* is valid. You may respond that the individuals in the twin towers pictures are not specifically identifiable and that the images of the *Challenger,* though horrifying, are not as visually revolting as the picture of a severed head held up for view.

The *Boston Phoenix,* a weekly newspaper, published some images from the Daniel Pearl video and also put a link to the video (with a warning that the footage is "extremely graphic") on its Web site. The editor of the *Phoenix* justified publication on the three grounds we list. Pearl's wife, Mariane Pearl, was quoted in various newspapers as condemning the "heartless decision to air this despicable video," and a spokeswoman for the Pearl family, when asked for comment, referred reporters to a statement issued earlier, which said that broadcasters who show the video

fall without shame into the terrorists' plan. . . . Danny believed that journalism was a tool to report the truth and foster understanding—not

perpetuate propaganda and sensationalize tragedy. We had hoped that
no part of this tape would ever see the light of day. . . . We urge all
networks and news outlets to exercise responsibility and not aid the
terrorists in spreading their message of hate and murder.[1]

Although some journalists expressed regret that Pearl's family was distressed, they insisted that journalists have a right to reproduce such material and that the images can serve the valuable purpose of shocking
viewers into awareness.

TOPIC FOR CRITICAL THINKING AND WRITING

Marvin Kalb, a distinguished journalist, was quoted as saying that the
public has a right to see the tape of Daniel Pearl's murder but that "common sense, decency, [and] humanity would encourage editors . . . to say
'no, it is not necessary to put this out.' There is no urgent demand on the
part of the American people to see Daniel Pearl's death." Your view?

Query In June 2006 two American soldiers were captured in Iraq.
Later their bodies were found, dismembered and beheaded. Should
newspapers have shown photographs of the mutilated bodies? Why, or
why not? (In July 2006 insurgents in Iraq posted images on the Internet,
showing a soldier's severed head beside his body.)

Another issue concerning the appropriateness or inappropriateness
of showing images occurred early in 2006. In September 2005 a Danish
newspaper, accused of being afraid to show political cartoons that were
hostile to Muslim terrorists, responded by publishing twelve cartoons.
One cartoon, for instance, showed the Prophet Muhammad wearing a
turban that looked like a bomb. The images at first did not arouse much
attention, but when in January 2006 they were reprinted in Norway
they attracted worldwide attention and outraged Muslims, most of
whom regard any depiction of the Prophet as blasphemous. The upshot
is that some Muslims in various Islamic nations burned Danish em-
bassies and engaged in other acts of violence. Most non-Muslims agreed
that the images were in bad taste, and apparently in deference to Islamic
sensibilities (but possibly also out of fear of reprisals) very few Western
newspapers reprinted the cartoons when they covered the news events.
Most newspapers (including the *New York Times*) were content merely to
describe the images. These papers believed that readers had to be told
the news but because the drawings were so offensive to some persons
they should be described rather than reprinted. A controversy then
arose: Do readers of a newspaper deserve to *see* the evidence for them-

---

[1]Quoted in the *Hartford Courant*, June 5, 2002, and reproduced on the Internet by the Freedom of Information Center, under the heading "Boston Paper Creates Controversy."

selves, or can a newspaper adequately fulfill its function by offering only a verbal description?

Persons who argued that the images should be reproduced generally made these points:

- Newspapers should yield neither to the delicate sensibilities of some readers nor to threats of violence.

- Jews for the most part do not believe that God should be depicted (the prohibition against "graven images" is found in Exodus 20.3), but they raise no objections to such Christian images as Michelangelo's painting of God awakening Adam, on the roof of the Sistine Chapel. Further, when Andres Serrano (a Christian) in 1989 exhibited a photograph of a small plastic crucifix submerged in urine, it outraged a wider public—several U.S. senators condemned it because the artist had received federal funds—but virtually all newspapers showed the image, and many even printed its title, *Piss Christ*. That is, the subject was judged to be newsworthy, and the fact that some viewers would regard the image as blasphemous was not considered highly relevant.

- We value freedom of speech, and newspapers should not be intimidated. When certain pictures are a matter of news, the pictures should be shown to readers.

On the other hand, opposing voices were heard:

- Newspapers should—must—recognize deep-seated religious beliefs. They should indeed report the news, but there is no reason to *show* images that some people regard as blasphemous. The images can be adequately *described* in words.

- The Jewish response to Christian images of God and even the tolerant Christian's response to Serrano's image of Christ immersed in urine are simply irrelevant to the issue of whether images of the Prophet Muhammad should be represented in a Western newspaper. Virtually all Muslims regard depictions of the Prophet as blasphemous, and that is what counts.

- Despite all the Western talk about freedom of the press, the press does *not* reproduce all images that become matters of news. For instance, news items about the sale of child pornography do not include images of the pornographic photos.

EXERCISES: THINKING ABOUT IMAGES

1. Does the display of the cartoons constitute an argument? If so, what is the conclusion, and what are the premises? If not, then what sort of statement, if any, does publishing these cartoons constitute?

2. Hugh Hewitt, an evangelical Christian, offered a comparison to the cartoon of Muhammad with a bomblike turban. Suppose, he asked, an abortion clinic had been bombed by someone who said he was an Evangelical Christian. Would newspapers publish "a cartoon of Christ's crown of thorns transformed into sticks of TNT?" Do you think they would? If you were the editor of a paper, would you? Why, or why not?

3. One American newspaper, the *Boston Phoenix*, did not publish any of the cartoons "out of fear of retaliation from the international brotherhood of radical and bloodthirsty Islamists who seek to impose their will on those who do not believe as they do. . . . We could not in good conscience place the men and women who work at the *Phoenix* and its related companies in physical jeopardy." Evaluate this position.

READING ADVERTISEMENTS

Advertising is one of the most common forms of visual persuasion we encounter in everyday life. None of us is so unsophisticated these days as to believe everything we see in an ad, yet the influence of advertising in our culture is pervasive and subtle. Consider, for example, a much-reproduced poster sponsored by Gatorade and featuring Michael Jordan. Such an image costs an enormous amount to produce and disseminate, and nothing in it is left to chance. The photograph of Jordan is typical, his attitude simultaneously strained and graceful, his face exultant, as he performs the feat for which he is so well known and about which most of us could only dream. We are aware of a crowd watching him, but the people in this crowd appear tiny, blurred, and indistinct compared to the huge image in the foreground; the photograph, like the crowd, focuses solely on Jordan. He is a legend, an icon of American culture. He is dressed not in his Chicago Bulls uniform but in a USA jersey, connecting his act of gravity-defying athleticism with the entire nation and with our sense of patriotism. The red, white, and blue of the uniform strengthens this impression in the original color photograph of the advertisement.

What do we make of the verbal message boldly written along the left-hand margin of the poster, "Be like Mike"? We are certainly not foolish enough to believe that drinking Gatorade will enable us to perform like Michael Jordan on the basketball court. But who among us wouldn't like to "Be like Mike" in some small way, to enjoy even a glancing association with his athletic grace and power—to say nothing of his fame, wealth, and sex appeal? Though the makers of Gatorade surely know we will not all rush out to buy their drink to improve our game, they are banking on the expectation that the association of their name with Jordan, and our memory of their logo in association with Jordan's picture, will create a positive impression of their product. If

Mike drinks Gatorade—well, why shouldn't I give it a try? The good feelings and impressions created by the ad will, the advertisers hope, travel with us the next time we consider buying a sports drink.

As we discuss the power of advertising, it is appropriate to say a few words about the corporate logos that appear everywhere these days—on billboards, in newspapers and magazines, on television, and on T-shirts. It is useful to think of a logo as a sort of advertisement in shorthand. It is a single, usually simple, image that carries with it a world of associations and impressions. (The makers of Gatorade would certainly hope that we will be reminded of Michael Jordan and his slam dunk when we see their product name superimposed over the orange lightning bolt.)

Let's look at two advertisements—one that combines pictures with verbal text and another that relies almost entirely on a picture accompanied by only three words. The first ad has two head shots, pictures of the sort that show "Ten Most Wanted Men." Both faces are widely known—Martin Luther King Jr. and Charles Manson—and viewers may initially wonder why they are juxtaposed. Then the large type above the pictures captures our attention with its size and a bold statement of fact:

> The man on the left is 75 times more likely to be stopped by the police while driving than the man on the right.

We presume that the statement is true—that is, that dark-skinned people are stopped by police officers seventy-five times more often than whites—and we probably know why. Almost surely we do *not* conclude that dark people are far more likely than white to speed, go through red lights, or cross lanes. We have heard about racial profiling and racial prejudice, and we may also have heard about the wry offense of which all African Americans are guilty, "driving while black." The small print on this ad goes on to tell us that, every day, "Police stop drivers based on their skin color rather than for the way they are driving," and it supports this assertion with a fact: "For example, in Florida 80% of those stopped and searched were black and Hispanic, while they constituted only 5% of all drivers." We assume that these statistics are true and that most readers find the statement alarming. The poster might have had these very words without the two pictures, but would we then have read the small print?

Incidentally, the American Civil Liberties Union did not print this poster for any reason related to Martin Luther King Jr. or Charles Manson. The poster's purpose appears in very small letters at the end of the caption:

> Support the ACLU.

We think that this ad is highly effective, and we invite you to perform a thought experiment. Suppose that the two pictures were omitted and that the text of the large type at the top of the ad was different, something like this:

American Civil Liberties Union, *The Man on the Left*

Persons of color, notably African Americans and non-white Hispanics, are 75 times more likely than white people to be stopped by the police when driving.

And then suppose the rest of the text consisted of the words in the present ad. Do you think this alternate version would make nearly the impact that the ACLU ad makes? The text is essentially the same, the statistics are still shocking, but the impact is gone. When we see the ACLU ad, we are for only a tiny fraction of a second, puzzled: What can the two faces— a civil rights leader and a serial killer—have in common? The large print almost immediately lets us know why these faces are paired, and we are probably hooked by (a) the shocking juxtaposition of faces and (b) the astounding fact that is asserted. So we probably go on to read the small print, though ordinarily we would not bother to read such tiny writing.

Incidentally, the writing beneath the picture could have been as large, or almost as large, as the print above the picture, merely by reducing the blank space at the top and bottom of the page. Why do you sup-

---

✓ A CHECKLIST FOR ANALYZING IMAGES (ESPECIALLY ADVERTISEMENTS)

☐ What is the overall effect of the design? Colorful and busy (suggesting activity)? Quiet and understated (for instance, chiefly white and grays, with lots of empty space)? Old fashioned or cutting edge?

☐ What about the image immediately gets your attention? Size? Position on the page? Beauty of the image? Grotesqueness of the image? Humor?

☐ Who is the audience for the image? Affluent young men? Housewives? Retired persons?

☐ What is the argument?

☐ Does the text make a rational appeal (*logos*) ("Tests at a leading university prove that . . . ," "If you believe X, you should vote 'No' on this referendum")?

☐ Does the image appeal to the emotions, to dearly held values (*pathos*)? Examples: Images of starving children or maltreated animals appeal to our sense of pity; images of military valor may appeal to our patriotism; images of luxury may appeal to our envy; images of sexually attractive people may appeal to our desire to be like them; images of violence or of extraordinary ugliness (as, for instance, in some ads showing a human fetus being destroyed) may seek to shock us.

☐ Does the image make an ethical appeal—that is, does it appeal to our character as a good human being (*ethos*)? Ads by charitable organizations often appeal to our sense of decency, fairness, and pity, but ads that appeal to our sense of prudence (ads for insurance companies or for investment houses) also essentially are making an ethical appeal.

☐ What is the relation of print to image? Does the image do most of the work, or does it serve to attract us and to lead us on to read the text?

pose the writing beneath the pictures is small? Do you think the ad would have been as compelling if the type above and below were of approximately equal size? Why, or why not?

One other point: The pictures of King and Manson catch the interest of a wide audience, an audience much wider than the group that would normally be targeted as persons who might contribute money or energy to an association chiefly concerned with civil liberties. That is, this ad speaks to almost anyone who may be concerned with fairness or decency.

The second ad uses only three words, "American Cancer Society." Here the picture does almost all of the work of communicating a message. At first glance the picture may be puzzling, since it is not a picture of anything we have seen. But a second glance and a look at the caption

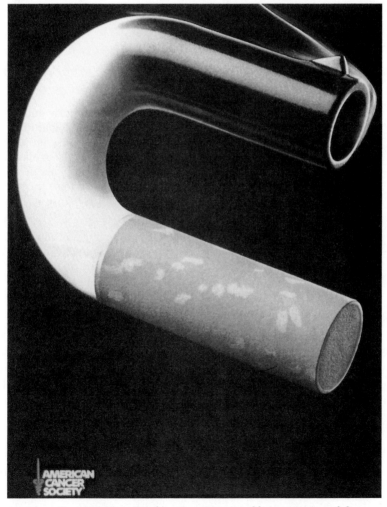

American Cancer Society, *Smoking Gun*. (Reprinted by permission of the American Cancer Society. All rights reserved.)

make everything clear. This image is a sort of visual pun, and if we don't get it just by looking at the picture, the caption gives us a big hint. The picture shows a cigarette that turns into a gun. Knowing that the American Cancer Society campaigns against smoking, we get the point: Cigarettes are killers; smoking a cigarette is like pointing a gun at your head. There is no request for money (though conceivably some viewers say to themselves, "Yes, I must support the American Cancer Society"). The ad is aimed (if we can use a word that is most unpleasant in association with this picture) at smokers. No verbal text is needed; the picture says, "Smokers are killing themselves." Highly effective ads could also be constructed in which a picture of a hospitalized patient or of someone coughing violently supports a lengthy text that gives viewers statistics on how many people died of lung cancer last year, but we doubt that any text (beyond the words "American Cancer Society") would strengthen the message that this powerful image conveys.

Topics for Critical Thinking and Writing

1. Imagine that you work for a business that advertises in a publication such as *Time* or *Newsweek,* for instance, a vacation resort, a manufacturer of clothes, or an automaker. Design an advertisement: Describe the picture and write the text, and then, in an essay of 500 words, explain who your target audience is (college students? young couples about to buy their first home? retired persons?) and explain why you use the sorts of appeals (for instance, to reason, to the emotions, to a sense of humor) that you do.

2. It is often said that colleges, like businesses, are selling a product. Examine a brochure or catalog that is sent to prospective applicants at a college, and analyze the kinds of appeals that some of the images make.

WRITING ABOUT A POLITICAL CARTOON

Most editorial pages print political cartoons as well as editorials. Like the writers of editorials, cartoonists seek to persuade, but they rarely use words to *argue* a point. True, they may use a few words in speech balloons or in captions, but generally the drawing does most of the work. Because their aim usually is to convince the viewer that some person's action or proposal is ridiculous, cartoonists almost always **caricature** their subjects:

- They exaggerate the subject's distinctive features to the point where
- The subject becomes grotesque and ridiculous—absurd, laughable, contemptible.

True, it is scarcely fair to suggest that because, say, the politician who proposes such-and-such is short, fat, and bald his proposal is ridiculous, but that is the way cartoonists work. Further, cartoonists are concerned with producing a striking image, not with exploring an issue, so they almost always oversimplify, implying that there really is no other sane view.

In the course of saying that (a) the figures in the cartoon are ridiculous and *therefore* their ideas are contemptible, and (b) there is only one side to the issue, cartoonists often use **symbolism**, for instance:

- Symbolic figures (Uncle Sam),
- Animals (the Democratic donkey and the Republican elephant),
- Buildings (the White House stands symbolically for the president of the United States),
- Things (a bag with a dollar sign on it usually symbolizes a bribe).

For anyone brought up in our culture, these symbols (like the human figures who are represented) are obvious, and cartoonists assume that viewers will instantly recognize the symbols and figures, will get the joke, will see the absurdity of whatever it is that the cartoonist is seeking to demolish.

In writing about the argument presented in a cartoon, normally you will

- Lead into your analysis with a sentence or two that sets the context: the date, the publication, the cartoonist's name. Then,
- Even though you will include a photocopy of the cartoon with your paper, you will offer a brief but clear *description* of the picture. From your description your reader ought to have a pretty good idea of what the picture looks like. You will then
- offer some *exposition*, that is, you will explain (interpret) the drawing by identifying the persons depicted and the event or the issue the cartoonist comments on. You will then
- Devote most of the essay to an *analysis* of the cartoon.

That is, you will discuss the ways in which the cartoon makes its point. Caricature, we have said, usually says, "This is ridiculous, as you can plainly see by the absurdity of the figures depicted." "What X's proposal adds up to, despite its apparent complexity, is nothing more than . . ."). As we have already said, this sort of persuasion, chiefly by ridicule, probably is unfair: A funny-looking person *can offer* a thoughtful political proposal, and almost certainly the issue is more complicated than the cartoonist indicates. But this is largely the way cartoons work, by ridicule and by omitting counterarguments, and we should not reject the possibility that the cartoonist has indeed put his or her finger on the absurdity of the issue.

Probably your essay will include an *evaluation* of the cartoon; indeed, the *thesis* underlying your analytic/argumentative essay may be (for

---

✓ A CHECKLIST FOR ANALYZING POLITICAL CARTOONS

☐ Is a lead-in provided?

☐ Is a brief but accurate description of the drawing provided?

☐ Is the source of the cartoon cited (and perhaps commented on)?

☐ Is a brief report of the event or issue that the cartoon is dealing with, and explanation of all of the symbols included?

☐ Is there a statement of the cartoonist's claim (point, thesis)?

☐ Is there an analysis of the evidence, if any, that the image offers in support of the claim?

☐ Is there an analysis of the ways in which the content and style of the drawing help to convey the message?

☐ Is there adequate evaluation of the effectiveness of the drawing?

☐ Is there adequate evaluation of the effectiveness of the text (caption or speech balloons) and of the fairness of the cartoon?

---

instance) that the cartoon is effective (persuasive) for such-and-such reasons, but it is also unfair for such-and-such reasons.

In analyzing the cartoon—in grasping the attitude of the cartoonist—consider such things as

- The relative size of the figures in the image;
- The quality of the lines—thin and spidery, or thick and seemingly aggressive;
- The amount of empty space in comparison with the amount of heavily inked space (a drawing with lots of inky areas will convey a more oppressive sense than a drawing that is largely open);
- The degree to which text is important, and what the text says—is it witty? Heavy-handed?

Caution: If your instructor lets you choose a cartoon, be sure to choose one with sufficient complexity to make the exercise worthwhile.

Let's look at an example. Jackson Smith wrote this essay in a composition course at Tufts University.

Jackson Smith

Pledging Nothing?

Gary Markstein's cartoon about the Pledge of Allegiance is one of dozens that can be retrieved by a search engine. It happens that every one of the cartoons that I retrieved mocked the courts for ruling that schools cannot require students to recite the Pledge of Allegiance in its present form, which includes the words "under God." I personally object to these words, so the cartoons certainly do not speak for me, but I'll try as impartially as possible to analyze the strength of Markstein's cartoon.

Markstein shows us, in the cartoon, four school children reciting the Pledge. Coming out of all four mouths is a speech balloon with the words, "One nation under nothing in particular." The children are facing a furled American flag, and to the right of the flag is a middle-aged female teacher, whose speech balloon is in the form of a cloud, indicating that she is *thinking* rather than saying the words, "God help us."

Certainly the image grabs us: Little kids lined up reciting the Pledge of Allegiance, an American flag, a maternal-looking teacher, and, in fact, if one examines the cartoon closely, one sees an apple on the teacher's desk. It's almost a Norman Rockwell scene, except, of course, it is a cartoon, so the figures are all a bit grotesque—but, still, they are nice folks. What is *not* nice, Markstein says, is what these kids must recite, "One nation under nothing in particular." In fact the cartoon is far from telling the truth. Children who recite the Pledge without the words "under God" will still be saying that they are pledging allegiance to something quite specific—the United States:

> I pledge allegiance to the flag of the United States of America, and to the Republic for which it stands: one nation indivisible, with Liberty and Justice for all.

That's really quite a lot, very far from Markstein's "under nothing in particular." But no one, I suppose, expects fairness in a political cartoon—and of course this cartoon *is* political, because the issue of the Pledge has become a political football, with liberals on the whole wanting the words "under God" removed and conservatives on the whole wanting the words retained.

Let's now look at some of the subtleties of the cartoon. First, although, as I have said, cartoons present grotesque caricatures, the figures here are all affectionately presented. None of these figures is menacing. The teacher, with her spectacles and her rather dumpy figure, is clearly a benevolent figure, someone who in the eyes of the cartoonist rightly is disturbed about the fate of these little kids who are not allowed to say the words "under God." (Nothing, of course, prevents the children from speaking about God when they are not in the classroom. Those who believe in God can say grace at mealtime, can go to Sunday School, can go to church regularly, can pray before they go to bed, etc.) Markstein suggests that the absence of these words makes the entire Pledge meaningless ("under nothing in particular"), and in a master stroke he has conveyed this idea of impoverishment by showing a tightly furled flag, a flag that is presented as minimally as possible. After all, the flag could have been shown more fully, perhaps hanging from a pole that extended from a wall into the classroom, or the flag could have been displayed

extended against a wall. Instead we get the narrowest of flags, something that is not much more than a furled umbrella, identifiable as the American flag by its stripes and a few stars in the upper third. Markstein thus cleverly suggests that with the loss of the words "under God," the flag itself is reduced to almost nothing.

Fair? No. Effective? Yes, and that's the job of a cartoonist. Readers probably give cartoons no more than three or four seconds, and Markstein has made the most of those few seconds. The reader gets his point, and if the reader already holds this view, he or she probably says, "Hey, here's a great cartoon." I don't hold that view, but I am willing to grant that it is a pretty good cartoon, effectively making a point that I think is wrong-headed.

VISUALS AS AIDS TO CLARITY: MAPS, GRAPHS, TABLES, AND PIE CHARTS

Maps were obviously part of the argument in the debate over drilling in the Arctic National Wildlife Refuge.

- Advocates of drilling argued that drilling would take place only in such a tiny area. Their map showed Alaska, with an indication (in gray) of the much smaller part of Alaska that was the Refuge, and a further indication (cross-hatched) of what these advocates of drilling emphasized was a minuscule part of the Refuge.

- Opponents, however, showed maps indicating the path of migrating caribou and the roads that would have to be constructed across the refuge to get to the area where the drilling would take place.

COMING TO AMERICA . . .

Both the percentage and number of foreign-born people in the United States dropped during much of the twentieth century, but after 1970, the tide was turning again.

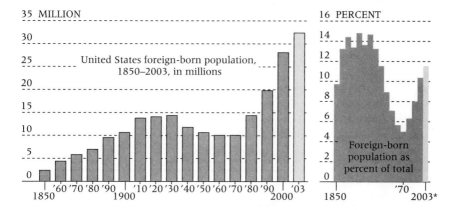

Graphs, tables, and pie charts usually present quantitative data in visual form, helping writers clarify mind-numbing statistical assertions. For instance, a line graph may tell us how many immigrants came to the United States in each decade of the last century.

A bar graph (the bars can run either horizontally or vertically) offers similar information; we can see at a glance that, say, the second bar is almost double the length of the first, indicating that the number is almost double.

. . . FROM NEAR AND FAR

Central America, Mexico, and Asia contribute most to the foreign-born population.

Other
South
America

Caribbean

Europe

Central
America
and
Mexico

Asia

8%
6%
10%
14%
36%
26%

Foreign-born population by
region of birth, 2002

*Most recent estimate
Source: United States Census Bureau

A pie chart is a circle divided into wedges so that we can see—literally see—how a whole is divided into its parts. We can see, for instance, that of the entire pie—which may represent registered voters in a certain state—one-fourth are registered Democrats, one-fifth are registered Republicans, and the remainder do not give a party affiliation.

✓ A CHECKLIST FOR CHARTS AND GRAPHS

☐ Is the source authoritative?
☐ Is the source cited?
☐ Will the chart or graph be intelligible to the imagined audience?
☐ Is the caption, if any, clear and helpful?

A NOTE ON USING VISUALS IN YOUR OWN PAPER

Every paper uses some degree of visual persuasion, merely in its appearance: perhaps a title page, certainly margins (ample—but not so wide that they tell the reader that the writer is unable to write a paper of the assigned length), double-spacing for the convenience of the reader, paragraphing (again for the convenience of the reader), and so on. But you may also want to use images—for example, pictures, graphs, or pie charts. Keep a few guidelines in mind as you begin to work with images, "writing" visuals into your own argument with at least as much care as you would read them in others':

- Consider the needs and attitudes of your audience, and select the type of visuals—graphs, drawings, photographs—likely to be most persuasive to that audience.

- Consider the effect of color, composition, and placement within your document. Because images are most effective when they appear near the text that supplements them, do not group all of your images at the end of the paper.

Remember especially that images are almost never self-supporting or self-explanatory. They may be evidence for your argument (Ut's photograph of napalm victims is *very* compelling evidence of suffering), but they are not arguments themselves.

- Be sure to explain each image that you use, integrating it into the verbal text that provides the logic and principal support of your thesis.

- Be sure to cite the source of any image, for instance, a graph or a pie chart, that you paste into your argument.

(DILBERT © Scott Adams. Distributed by permission of United Features Syndicate, Inc.)

A NOTE ON FORMATTING YOUR PAPER: DOCUMENT DESIGN

Even if you do not use pictures or graphs or charts, the format you use—the margins, the font, the headings and subheadings, if any, will still give your paper a visual aspect. NoonewantstoreadapaperthatlookslikethisOR LIKETHIS*ORLIKETHIS*ANDCERTAINLYNOT**LIKETHIS**ORLIKETHIS. For academic papers, margins (one inch on each side), spacing (double-spaced), and font and size (Times New Roman, 12 point) are pretty well standardized, and it is usually agreed that the text should be justified at the left rather than centered (to avoid rivers of white down the page), but you are still in charge of some things, notably headings and bulleted or numbered lists—as well as, of course, the lengths of your paragraphs.

Headings in a long paper (more than five pages) are functional, helping to guide the reader from unit to unit, but the extra white space—a decorative element—is also functional, giving the reader's eye a moment of rest. Longish academic papers often use one, two, or even three levels of headings, normally distinguished by type size, position, and highlighting ("highlighting" includes the use of CAPITALS, **boldface**, and *italic*). Here are examples of three levels:

FIRST-LEVEL HEADING

Second-Level Heading

Third-Level Heading

If you use headings, you must be consistent in the form. For instance, if you use a noun phrase (for instance "the present system") printed in CAPITAL LETTERS for the first of your first-level headings, you must use noun phrases and caps for the rest of your first-level headings, thus:

THE PRESENT SYSTEM
THE NEED TO CHANGE

But you need not use noun phases and you need not use capitals. You may use, for instance, -*ing* headings (gerund phrases), and you may decide to capitalize only the first letter of each word other than prepositions and articles, thus:

Thinking about Immigration

Reviewing the Past

Thinking about the Future

Reconsidering Legislation

And here are headings that use a single word:

Problems

Answers

Strengths

Weaknesses

Finally, headings that consist of questions can be effective:

What Are We Now Doing?

Why Should We Change?

Caution: Although headings can be useful in a paper of moderate or considerable length, they almost never are useful in a paper of five or fewer pages.

ADDITIONAL IMAGES FOR ANALYSIS

In 1936, photographer Dorothea Lange (1895–1965) took a series of pictures, including the two below, of a migrant mother and her children. Widely reprinted in the nation's newspapers, these photographs helped to dramatize for the American public the poverty of displaced workers during the Great Depression.

Topics for Critical Thinking and Writing

1. Lange drew increasingly near to her subject as she took a series of pictures. Make a list of details gained and lost by framing the mother and children more closely. The final shot in the series (above) became the most famous and most widely reprinted. Do you find it more effective than the other? Why, or why not?

2. Note the expression on the mother's face, the position of her body, and the way she interacts with her children. What sorts of relationships are implied? Why is it significant that she does not look at her children or at the camera? How is the effect of the photographs altered based on how much we can see of the children's faces?

3. As we mentioned earlier in this chapter, these photographs constitute a sort of persuasive "speech." Of what, exactly, might the photographer be trying to persuade her viewers? Try to state the purpose of Lange's photograph by completing this sentence, "Lange would like the viewers of her photographers to . . ." Write a brief essay (250 words) making the same case. Compare your written argument to Lange's visual one. Which form of persuasion do you find more effective? Why?

4. Whom do you think Lange had in mind as her original audience? What assumptions does she make about that audience? What sorts of evidence does she use to reach them?

During World War II, the U.S. government produced a series of posters bearing the legend "This is the enemy." These posters depicted racially stereotyped images of both German and Japanese soldiers, generally engaged in acts of savage violence.

TOPICS FOR CRITICAL THINKING AND WRITING

1. It has been claimed that one role of propaganda is to dehumanize the enemy so that (a) soldiers will feel less remorse about killing opposing soldiers and (b) civilians will continue to support the war effort. What specific features of this poster contribute to this propaganda function?

2. Some would claim that such a racially provocative image of a Japanese soldier should never have been used because of the potential harm to all Asians, including patriotic Asian Americans. (Consisting solely of Japanese American volunteers, the 442nd Regimental Combat Team was by

war's end the most decorated unit in U.S. military history for its size and length of service.) Others believe that the ordinary rules do not apply in times of national crisis and that, as the old saying has it, "All's fair in love and war." In an essay of 500 words, argue for one or the other of these propositions. Refer to this poster as one piece of your evidence.

From ancient times until the eighteenth century, when newspapers began to be read widely, public posting was about the only way to reach a large audience. The invention of movable type in the fifteenth century made the dissemination of posted bills and handbills inexpensive, and such bills (along with newspaper advertisements) were the most common forms of advertising until well into the twentieth century. (Commercial radio broadcasting began only in 1920, and television was not an important medium before 1945.) I Want You is by James Montgomery Flagg.

TOPICS FOR CRITICAL THINKING AND WRITING

1. Imagine that this figure of Uncle Sam were in profile, pointing either to the right or left. Would the effect be the same? Why? Imagine the figure as a three-quarter view. Again, would the effect be different? Why? Which of the three versions do you think would be the most effective? Explain your reasons.

2. Approximately what is the date of this poster? What makes you give it this date?

ADDITIONAL TOPICS FOR CRITICAL THINKING AND WRITING

Gather some of the graphic materials used to promote and reflect your college or university — including a screen shot of its Web site, the college catalog, and the brochures and other materials sent to prospective students.

1. What is the dominant image that your college or university administration seems to be putting forth? Are there different, maybe even competing, images of your school at work? How accurate a story do these materials tell about your campus? Write an essay (250 words) in which you explain to prospective students the ways in which the promotional materials capture, or fail to capture, the true spirit of your campus.

2. Compare the Web site of your institution to one or two from very different institutions — perhaps a community college, a large state university, or an elite private college. How do you account for the similarities and differences among the sites?

Nora Ephron

Nora Ephron, born in 1941, attended Wellesley College. She worked as a reporter for the New York Post *and as a columnist and senior editor for* Esquire. *Ephron has written screenplays and directed films, including* Sleepless in Seattle *(1993), and has continued to write essays on a wide variety of topics. "The Boston Photographs" is from her collection* Scribble, Scribble: Notes on the Media *(1978).*

The Boston Photographs

"I made all kinds of pictures because I thought it would be a good rescue shot over the ladder . . . never dreamed it would be anything else. . . . I kept having to move around because of the light set. The sky was bright and they were in deep shadow. I was making pictures with a motor drive and he, the fire fighter, was reaching up and, I don't know, everything started falling. I followed the girl down taking pictures. . . . I made three or four frames. I realized what was going on and I completely turned around, because I didn't want to see her hit."

You probably saw the photographs. In most newspapers, there were three of them. The first showed some people on a fire escape—a fireman, a woman, and a child. The fireman had a nice strong jaw and looked very brave. The woman was holding the child. Smoke was pouring from the building behind them. A rescue ladder was approaching, just a few feet away, and the fireman had one arm around the woman and one arm reaching out toward the ladder. The second picture showed the fire escape slipping off the building. The child had fallen on the escape and seemed about to slide off the edge. The woman was grasping desperately at the legs of the fireman, who had managed to grab the ladder. The third picture showed the woman and child in midair, falling to the ground. Their arms and legs were outstretched, horribly distended. A potted plant was falling too. The caption said that the woman, Diana Bryant, nineteen, died in the fall. The child landed on the woman's body and lived.

The pictures were taken by Stanley Forman, thirty, of the *Boston Herald American*. He used a motor-driven Nikon F set at 1/250, f5.6-S. Because of the motor, the camera can click off three frames a second. More than four hundred newspapers in the United States alone carried the photographs: The tear sheets from overseas are still coming in. The *New York Times* ran them on the first page of its second section; a paper in south Georgia gave them nineteen columns; the *Chicago Tribune,* the *Washington Post,* and the *Washington Star* filled almost half their front pages, the *Star* under a somewhat redundant headline that read: SENSATIONAL PHOTOS OF RESCUE ATTEMPT THAT FAILED.

The photographs are indeed sensational. They are pictures of death in action, of that split second when luck runs out, and it is impossible to

look at them without feeling their extraordinary impact and remembering, in an almost subconscious way, the morbid fantasy of falling, falling
off a building, falling to one's death. Beyond that, the pictures are clas-
sics, old-fashioned but perfect examples of photojournalism at its most
spectacular. They're throwbacks, really, fire pictures, 1930s tabloid shots;
at the same time they're technically superb and thoroughly modern —
the sequence could not have been taken at all until the development of
the motor-driven camera some sixteen years ago.

Most newspaper editors anticipate some reader reaction to photo-   5
graphs like Forman's; even so, the response around the country was
enormous, and almost all of it was negative. I have read hundreds of the
letters that were printed in letters-to-the-editor sections, and they repeat
the same points. "Invading the privacy of death." "Cheap sensationalism." "I thought I was reading the *National Enquirer.*" "Assigning the
agony of a human being in terror of imminent death to the status of a
side-show act." "A tawdry way to sell newspapers." The *Seattle Times* received sixty letters and calls; its managing editor even got a couple of
them at home. A reader wrote the *Philadelphia Inquirer: "Jaws* and *Tower-
ing Inferno* are playing downtown; don't take business away from people
who pay good money to advertise in your own paper." Another reader
wrote the *Chicago Sun-Times:* "I shall try to hide my disappointment that
Miss Bryant wasn't wearing a skirt when she fell to her death. You could
have had some award-winning photographs of her underpants as her
skirt billowed over her head, you voyeurs." Several newspaper editors
wrote columns defending the pictures: Thomas Keevil of the *Costa Mesa*
(California) *Daily Pilot* printed a ballot for readers to vote on whether
they would have printed the pictures; Marshall L. Stone of Maine's *Ban-
gor Daily News,* which refused to print the famous assassination picture of
the Vietcong prisoner in Saigon, claimed that the Boston pictures showed
the dangers of fire escapes and raised questions about slumlords. (The
burning building was a five-story brick apartment house on Marlbor-
ough Street in the Back Bay section of Boston.)

For the last five years, the *Washington Post* has employed various
journalists as ombudsmen, whose job is to monitor the paper on behalf
of the public. The *Post's* current ombudsman is Charles Seib, former
managing editor of the *Washington Star;* the day the Boston photographs
appeared, the paper received over seventy calls in protest. As Seib later
wrote in a column about the pictures, it was "the largest reaction to
a published item that I have experienced in eight months as the *Post's*
ombudsman. . . .

"In the *Post's* newsroom, on the other hand, I found no doubts, no
second thoughts . . . the question was not whether they should be
printed but how they should be displayed. When I talked to editors . . .
they used words like 'interesting' and 'riveting' and 'gripping' to describe
them. The pictures told of something about life in the ghetto, they said
(although the neighborhood where the tragedy occurred is not a ghetto,

I am told). They dramatized the need to check on the safety of fire escapes. They dramatically conveyed something that had happened, and that is the business we're in. They were news. . . .

"Was publication of that [third] picture a bow to the same taste for the morbidly sensational that makes gold mines of disaster movies? Most papers will not print the picture of a dead body except in the most unusual circumstances. Does the fact that the final picture was taken a millisecond before the young woman died make a difference? Most papers will not print a picture of a bare female breast. Is that a more inappropriate subject for display than the picture of a human being's last agonized instant of life?" Seib offered no answers to the questions he raised, but he went on to say that although as an editor he would probably have run the pictures, as a reader he was revolted by them.

In conclusion, Seib wrote: "Any editor who decided to print those pictures without giving at least a moment's thought to what purpose they served and what their effect was likely to be on the reader should ask another question: Have I become so preoccupied with manufacturing a product according to professional traditions and standards that I have forgotten about the consumer, the reader?"

It should be clear that the phone calls and letters and Seib's own reaction were occasioned by one factor alone: the death of the woman. Obviously, had she survived the fall, no one would have protested; the pictures would have had a completely different impact. Equally obviously, had the child died as well—or instead—Seib would undoubtedly have received ten times the phone calls he did. In each case, the pictures would have been exactly the same—only the captions, and thus the responses, would have been different.

But the questions Seib raises are worth discussing—though not exactly for the reasons he mentions. For it may be that the real lesson of the Boston photographs is not the danger that editors will be forgetful of reader reaction, but that they will continue to censor pictures of death precisely because of that reaction. The protests Seib fielded were really a variation on an old theme—and we saw plenty of it during the Nixon-Agnew years—the "Why doesn't the press print the good news?" argument. In this case, of course, the objections were all dressed up and cleverly disguised as righteous indignation about the privacy of death. This is a form of puritanism that is often justifiable; just as often it is merely puritanical.

Seib takes it for granted that the widespread though fairly recent newspaper policy against printing pictures of dead bodies is a sound one; I don't know that it makes any sense at all. I recognize that printing pictures of corpses raises all sorts of problems about taste and titillation and sensationalism; the fact is, however, that people die. Death happens to be one of life's main events. And it is irresponsible—and more than that, inaccurate—for newspapers to fail to show it, or to show it only when an astonishing set of photos comes in over the Associated Press wire. Most papers covering fatal automobile accidents will print pictures of mangled cars. But the significance of fatal automobile accidents is not that a great deal of steel is twisted but that people die. Why not show it? That's what accidents are about. Throughout the Vietnam war, editors were reluctant to print atrocity pictures. Why *not* print them? That's what that was about. Murder victims are almost never photographed; they are granted their privacy. But their relatives are relentlessly pictured on their way in and out of hospitals and morgues and funerals.

I'm not advocating that newspapers print these things in order to teach their readers a lesson. The *Post* editors justified their printing of the Boston pictures with several arguments in that direction; every one of them is irrelevant. The pictures don't show anything about slum life; the incident could have happened anywhere, and it did. It is extremely unlikely that anyone who saw them rushed out and had his fire escape strengthened. And the pictures were not news — at least they were not national news. It is not news in Washington, or New York, or Los Angeles that a woman was killed in a Boston fire. The only newsworthy thing about the pictures is that they were taken. They deserve to be printed because they are great pictures, breathtaking pictures of something that happened. That they disturb readers is exactly as it should be: that's why photojournalism is often more powerful than written journalism.

TOPICS FOR CRITICAL THINKING AND WRITING

1. In paragraph 5 Ephron refers to "the famous assassination picture of the Vietcong prisoner in Saigon" (see p. 147). The photo shows the face of a prisoner who is about to be shot in the head at close range. Jot down the reasons why you would or would not approve of printing this photo in a newspaper. Think, too, about this: If the photo on page 146 were not about a war — if it did not include the soldiers and the burning village in the rear but instead showed children fleeing from an abusive parent or from an abusive sibling — would you approve of printing it in a newspaper?

2. In paragraph 9 Ephron quotes a newspaperman as saying that before printing Forman's pictures of the woman and the child falling from the fire escape, editors should have asked themselves "what purpose they served and what their effect was likely to be on the reader." If you were an editor, what would your answers be? By the way, the pictures were *not* taken in a poor neighborhood, and they did *not* expose slum conditions.

3. In 50 words or so, write a precise description of what you see in the third of the Boston photographs. Do you think readers of your description would be "revolted" by the picture (para. 8), as were many viewers, the *Washington Post*'s ombudsman among them? Why, or why not?

4. Ephron thinks it would be a good thing if more photographs of death and dying were published by newspapers (paras. 11–13). In an essay of 500 words, state her reasons and your evaluation of them.

PART TWO

CRITICAL WRITING

5

Writing an Analysis
of an Argument

*This is what we can all do to nourish and strengthen one another: listen
to one another very hard, ask questions, too, send one another away to
work again, and laugh in all the right places.*

—NANCY MAIRS

*I don't wait for moods. You accomplish nothing if you do that. Your
mind must know it has got to get down to work.*

—PEARL S. BUCK

Fear not those who argue but those who dodge.

—MARIE VON EBNER-ESCHENBACH

ANALYZING AN ARGUMENT

Examining the Author's Thesis

Most of your writing in other courses will require you to write an analysis of someone else's writing. In a course in political science you may
have to analyze, say, an essay first published in *Foreign Affairs*, perhaps
reprinted in your textbook, that argues against raising tariff barriers to
foreign trade. Or a course in sociology may require you to analyze a report on the correlation between fatal accidents and drunk drivers under
the age of twenty-one. Much of your writing, in short, will set forth reasoned responses to your reading as preparation for making an argument
of your own.

Obviously you must understand an essay before you can analyze
it thoughtfully. You must read it several times—not just skim it—and
(the hard part) you must think about it. Again, you'll find that your
thinking is stimulated if you take notes and if you ask yourself questions
about the material. Notes will help you to keep track of the writer's
thoughts and also of your own responses to the writer's thesis. The

writer probably *does* have a thesis, a claim, a point, and if so, you must try to locate it. Perhaps the thesis is explicitly stated in the title or in a sentence or two near the beginning of the essay or in a concluding paragraph, but perhaps you will have to infer it from the essay as a whole.

Notice that we said the writer *probably* has a thesis. Much of what you read will indeed be primarily an argument; the writer explicitly or implicitly is trying to support some thesis and to convince you to agree with it. But some of what you read will be relatively neutral, with the argument just faintly discernible — or even with no argument at all. A work may, for instance, chiefly be a report: Here are the data, or here is what *X, Y,* and *Z* said; make of it what you will. A report might simply state how various ethnic groups voted in an election. In a report of this sort, of course, the writer hopes to persuade readers that the facts are correct, but no thesis is advanced, at least not explicitly or perhaps even consciously; the writer is not evidently arguing a point and trying to change our minds. Such a document differs greatly from an essay by a political analyst who presents similar findings to persuade a candidate to sacrifice the votes of this ethnic bloc and thereby get more votes from other blocs.

Examining the Author's Purpose

While reading an argument, try to form a clear idea of the author's **purpose.** Judging from the essay or the book, was the purpose to persuade, or was it to report? An analysis of a pure report (a work apparently without a thesis or argumentative angle) on ethnic voting will deal chiefly with the accuracy of the report. It will, for example, consider whether the sample poll was representative.

Much material that poses as a report really has a thesis built into it, consciously or unconsciously. The best evidence that the prose you are reading is argumentative is the presence of two kinds of key terms:

- **Transitions that imply the drawing of a conclusion:** *therefore, because, for the reason that, consequently;*
- **Verbs that imply proof:** *confirms, verifies, accounts for, implies, proves, disproves, is (in)consistent with, refutes, it follows that.*

Keep your eye out for such terms, and scrutinize their precise role whenever, or whatever they appear. If the essay does not advance a thesis, think of a thesis (a hypothesis) that it might support or some conventional belief that it might undermine.

Examining the Author's Methods

If the essay advances a thesis, you will want to analyze the strategies or methods of argument that allegedly support the thesis.

- Does the writer quote authorities? Are these authorities really competent in this field? Are equally competent authorities who take a different view ignored?

- Does the writer use statistics? If so, are they appropriate to the point being argued? Can they be interpreted differently?

- Does the writer build the argument by using examples or analogies? Are they satisfactory?

- Are the writer's assumptions acceptable?

- Does the writer consider all relevant factors? Has he or she omitted some points that you think should be discussed? For instance, should the author recognize certain opposing positions and perhaps concede something to them?

- Does the writer seek to persuade by means of ridicule? If so, is the ridicule fair: Is it supported also by rational argument?

In writing your analysis, you will want to tell your reader something about the author's purpose and something about the author's **methods.** It is usually a good idea at the start of your analysis—if not in the first paragraph then in the second or third—to let the reader know the purpose (and thesis, if there is one) of the work you are analyzing and then to summarize the work briefly.

Next you will probably find it useful (your reader will certainly find it helpful) to write out *your* thesis (your evaluation or judgment). You might say, for instance, that the essay is impressive but not conclusive, or is undermined by convincing contrary evidence, or relies too much on unsupported generalizations, or is wholly admirable, or whatever. Remember, because your paper is itself an argument, it needs its own thesis.

And then, of course, comes the job of setting forth your analysis and the support for your thesis. There is no one way of going about this work. If, say, your author gives four arguments (for example, an appeal to common sense, the testimony of authorities, the evidence of comparisons, and an appeal to self-interest), you might want to do one of the following:

- Take up these four arguments in sequence.

- Discuss the simplest of the four and then go on to the more difficult ones.

- Discuss the author's two arguments that you think are sound and then turn to the two that you think are not sound (or perhaps the reverse).

- Take one of these approaches and then clinch your case by constructing a fifth argument that is absent from the work under scrutiny but in your view highly important.

In short, the organization of your analysis may or may not follow the organization of the work you are analyzing.

Examining the Author's Persona

You will probably also want to analyze something a bit more elusive than the author's explicit arguments: the author's self-presentation. Does the author seek to persuade readers partly by presenting himself or herself as conscientious, friendly, self-effacing, authoritative, tentative, or in some other light? Most writers do two things:

- They present evidence, and
- They present themselves (or, more precisely, they present the image of themselves that they wish us to behold).

In some persuasive writing this **persona** or **voice** or presentation of the self may be no less important than the presentation of evidence.

In establishing a persona, writers adopt various rhetorical strategies, ranging from the use of characteristic words to the use of a particular form of organization. For instance, the writer who speaks of an opponent's "gimmicks" instead of "strategy" is trying to downgrade the opponent and also to convey the self-image of a streetwise person. On a larger scale, consider the way in which evidence is presented and the kind of evidence offered. One writer may first bombard the reader with facts and then spend relatively little time drawing conclusions. Another may rely chiefly on generalizations, waiting until the end of the essay to bring the thesis home with a few details. Another may begin with a few facts and spend most of the space reflecting on these. One writer may seem professorial or pedantic, offering examples of an academic sort; another, whose examples are drawn from ordinary life, may seem like a regular guy. All such devices deserve comment in your analysis.

The writer's persona, then, may color the thesis and help it develop in a distinctive way. If we accept the thesis, it is partly because the writer has won our goodwill by persuading us of his or her good character (*ethos,* in Aristotle's terms). Later we talk more about the appeal to the character of the speaker—the so-called *ethical appeal.*

The author of an essay may, for example, seem fair minded and open minded, treating the opposition with great courtesy and expressing interest in hearing other views. Such a tactic is itself a persuasive device. Or take an author who appears to rely on hard evidence such as statistics. This reliance on seemingly objective truths is itself a way of seeking to persuade—a rational way, to be sure, but a mode of persuasion nonetheless.

Especially in analyzing a work in which the author's persona and ideas are blended, you will want to spend some time commenting on the persona. Whether you discuss it near the beginning of your analysis or near the end will depend on your own sense of how you want to construct your essay, and this decision will partly depend on the work you are analyzing. For example, if the author's persona is kept in the background and is thus relatively invisible, you may want to make that point fairly early to get it out of the way and then concentrate on more interesting matters. If, however, the persona is interesting—and perhaps seductive, whether because it seems so scrupulously objective or so engagingly subjective—you may want to hint at this quality early in your essay and then develop the point while you consider the arguments.

Summary

In the last few pages we have tried to persuade you that, in writing an analysis of your reading, you must do the following:

- Read and reread thoughtfully. Writing notes will help you to think about what you are reading.
- Be aware of the purpose of the material to which you are responding.

We have also tried to point out these facts:

- Most of the nonliterary material that you will read is designed to argue, to report, or to do both.
- Most of this material also presents the writer's personality, or voice, and this voice usually merits attention in an analysis. An essay on, say, nuclear war, in a journal devoted to political science, may include a voice that moves from an objective tone to a mildly ironic tone to a hortatory tone, and this voice is worth commenting on.

Possibly all this explanation is obvious. There is yet another point, equally obvious but often neglected by students who begin by writing an analysis and end up by writing only a summary, a shortened version of the work they have read: Although your essay is an analysis of someone else's writing, and you may have to include a summary of the work you are writing about, your essay is *your* essay. The thesis, the organization, and the tone are yours.

- Your thesis, for example, may be that although the author is convinced she has presented a strong case, her case is far from proved.
- Your organization may be deeply indebted to the work you are analyzing, but it need not be. The author may have begun with specific examples and then gone on to make generalizations and to draw conclusions, but you may begin with the conclusions.
- Your tone, similarly, may resemble your subject's (let's say the voice is courteous academic), but it will nevertheless have its own ring, its own tone of, say, urgency, caution, or coolness.

Most of the essays that we have printed thus far are more or less in an academic style, and indeed several are by students and by professors. But argumentative writing is not limited to academicians—if it were, your college would not be requiring you to take a course in the subject. The following essay, in a breezy style, comes from a columnist who writes for the *New York Times*.

✓ A CHECKLIST FOR ANALYZING A TEXT

Have I considered all of the following matters?

☐ Who is the author?

☐ Is the piece aimed at a particular audience? A neutral audience? Persons who are already sympathetic to the author's point of view? A hostile audience?

☐ What is the author's thesis (argument, main point, claim)?

☐ What assumptions does the author make? Do I share them? If not, why not?

☐ Does the author ever confuse facts with beliefs or opinions?

☐ What appeals does the author make? To reason (*logos*), for instance, with statistics, the testimony of authorities, and personal experience? To the emotions (*pathos*), for instance, by an appeal to "our better nature," or to widely shared values? To our sense that the speaker is trustworthy (*ethos*)?

☐ How convincing is the evidence?

☐ Are significant objections and counterevidence adequately discussed?

☐ How is the text organized, and is the organization effective? Are the title, the opening paragraphs, and the concluding paragraphs effective? In what ways?

☐ If visual materials such as graphs, pie charts, or pictures are used, how persuasive are they? Do they make a logical appeal? (Charts and graphs presumably make a logical appeal.) Do they make an emotional appeal?

☐ What is the author's tone? Is it appropriate?

☐ To what extent has the author convinced me? Why?

AN ARGUMENT, ITS ELEMENTS, AND A STUDENT'S ANALYSIS OF THE ARGUMENT

Nicholas D. Kristof

Nicholas D. Kristof grew up on a farm in Oregon. After graduating from Harvard, he was awarded a Rhodes scholarship to Oxford, where he studied law. In 1984 he joined the New York Times *as a correspondent, and since 2001 he has written as a columnist. He has won two Pulitzer Prizes.*

For Environmental Balance, Pick Up a Rifle

Here's a quick quiz: Which large American mammal kills the most humans each year?

It's not the bear, which kills about two people a year in North America. Nor is it the wolf, which in modern times hasn't killed anyone in this country. It's not the cougar, which kills one person every year or two.

Rather, it's the deer. Unchecked by predators, deer populations are exploding in a way that is profoundly unnatural and that is destroying the ecosystem in many parts of the country. In a wilderness, there might be 10 deer per square mile; in parts of New Jersey, there are up to 200 per square mile.

One result is ticks and Lyme disease, but deer also kill people more directly. A study for the insurance industry estimated that deer kill about 150 people a year in car crashes nationwide and cause $1 billion in damage. Granted, deer aren't stalking us, and they come out worse in these collisions—but it's still true that in a typical year, an American is less likely to be killed by Osama bin Laden than by Bambi.

If the symbol of the environment's being out of whack in the 1960s 5 was the Cuyahoga River in Cleveland catching fire, one such symbol today is deer congregating around what they think of as salad bars and what we think of as suburbs.

So what do we do? Let's bring back hunting.

Now, you've probably just spilled your coffee. These days, among the university-educated crowd in the cities, hunting is viewed as barbaric.

The upshot is that towns in New York and New Jersey are talking about using birth control to keep deer populations down. (Liberals presumably support free condoms, while conservatives back abstinence education.) Deer contraception hasn't been very successful, though.

Meanwhile, the same population bomb has spread to bears. A bear hunt has been scheduled for this week in New Jersey—prompting outrage from some animal rights groups (there's also talk of bear contraception: make love, not cubs).

As for deer, partly because hunting is perceived as brutal and vaguely 10 psychopathic, towns are taking out contracts on deer through discreet private companies. Greenwich, Connecticut, budgeted $47,000 this year to pay a company to shoot eighty deer from raised platforms over four nights—as well as $8,000 for deer birth control.

Look, this is ridiculous.

We have an environmental imbalance caused in part by the decline of hunting. Humans first wiped out certain predators—like wolves and cougars—but then expanded their own role as predators to sustain a rough ecological balance. These days, though, hunters are on the decline.

According to "Families Afield: An Initiative for the Future of Hunting," a report by an alliance of shooting organizations, for every hundred hunters who die or stop hunting, only sixty-nine hunters take their place.

I was raised on *Bambi*—but also, as an Oregon farm boy, on venison and elk meat. But deer are not pets, and dead deer are as natural as live deer. To wring one's hands over them, perhaps after polishing off a hamburger, is soggy sentimentality.

What's the alternative to hunting? Is it preferable that deer die of 15 disease and hunger? Or, as the editor of *Adirondack Explorer* magazine suggested, do we introduce wolves into the burbs?

To their credit, many environmentalists agree that hunting can be green. The New Jersey Audubon Society this year advocated deer hunting as an ecological necessity.

There's another reason to encourage hunting: it connects people with the outdoors and creates a broader constituency for wilderness preservation. At a time when America's wilderness is being gobbled away for logging, mining, or oil drilling, that's a huge boon.

Granted, hunting isn't advisable in suburban backyards, and I don't expect many soccer moms to install gun racks in their minivans. But it's an abdication of environmental responsibility to eliminate other predators and then refuse to assume the job ourselves. In that case, the collisions with humans will simply get worse.

In October, for example, Wayne Goldsberry was sitting in a home in northwestern Arkansas when he heard glass breaking in the next room. It was a home invasion—by a buck.

Mr. Goldsberry, who is six feet one inch and weighs two hundred 20 pounds, wrestled with the intruder for forty minutes. Blood spattered the walls before he managed to break the buck's neck.

So it's time to reestablish a balance in the natural world—by accepting the idea that hunting is as natural as bird-watching.

In a moment we will talk at some length about Kristof's essay, but first you may want to think about the following questions.

1. What is Kristof's chief thesis? (State it in one sentence.)
2. Does Kristof make any assumptions—tacit or explicit—with which you disagree? With which you agree?
3. Is the slightly humorous tone of Kristof's essay inappropriate for a discussion of deliberately killing wild animals? Why, or why not?
4. If you are familiar with *Bambi*, does the story make any *argument* against killing deer, or does the story appeal only to our emotions?
5. Do you agree that "hunting is as natural as bird-watching" (para. 21)? In any case, do you think that an appeal to what is "natural" is a good argument for expanding the use of hunting?

OK, time's up. Let's examine Kristof's essay with an eye to identifying those elements we mentioned earlier in this chapter (pp. 177–81) that deserve notice when examining *any* argument: the author's *thesis, purpose, methods,* and *persona.* And while we're at it, let's also notice some other features of Kristof's essay that will help us appreciate its effects and evaluate it. We will thus be in a good position to write an evaluation or an argument that confirms, extends, or even rebuts Kristof's argument.

But first, a caution: Kristof's essay appeared in a newspaper where paragraphs are customarily very short, partly to allow for easy reading and partly because the columns are narrow and even short paragraphs may extend for an inch or two. If his essay were to appear in a book, doubtless the author would join many of the paragraphs, making longer units.

Title   By combining "Environmental Balance" with "Rifle"—terms that don't seem to go together—Kristof starts off with a bang. He gives a hint of his *topic* (something about the environment) and of his thesis (some sort of way of introducing ecological balance). He also conveys something of his persona by introducing a rifle into the environment. He is, the title suggests, a no-nonsense, hard-hitting guy.

Opening Paragraphs   Kristof immediately grabs hold of us ("Here's a quick quiz") and asks a simple question, but one that we probably have not thought much about: "Which large American mammal kills the most humans each year?" In his second paragraph he tells us it is *not* the bear—the answer most readers probably come up with—nor is it the cougar. Not until the third paragraph does Kristof give us the answer, the deer. But remember, Kristof is writing in a newspaper, where paragraphs customarily are very short. It takes us only a few seconds to get to the third paragraph and the answer.

Thesis   What is the basic thesis Kristof is arguing? Somewhat unusually, Kristof does *not* announce it in its full form until his sixth paragraph ("Let's bring back hunting"), but, again, his paragraphs are very short, and if the essay were published in a book, Kristof's first two paragraphs probably would be combined, as would the third and fourth.

Purpose   Kristof's purpose is clear: He wants to *persuade* readers to adopt his view. This amounts to trying to persuade us that his thesis (stated above) is *true*. Kristof, however, does not show that his essay is argumentative or persuasive by using many of the key terms that normally mark argumentative prose. He doesn't call anything his *conclusion*, none of his statements is labeled *my premises*, and he doesn't connect clauses or sentences with *therefore* or *because*. Almost the only traces of the language of argument are "Granted" (para. 18) and "So" (that is, *therefore*) in his final paragraph.

Despite the lack of argumentative language, the argumentative nature of his essay is clear. He has a thesis—one that will strike many readers as highly unusual—and he wants readers to accept it, so he must go on to *support* it; accordingly, after his introductory paragraphs, in which he calls attention to a problem and offers a solution (his thesis), he must offer evidence, and that is what much of the rest of the essay seeks to do.

Methods   Although Kristof will have to offer evidence, he begins by recognizing the folks on the other side, "the university-educated crowd in the cities, [for whom] hunting is viewed as barbaric" (para. 7). He goes on to spoof this "crowd" when, speaking of methods of keeping the deer population down, he says in paragraph 8, "Liberals presumably support free condoms, while conservatives back abstinence education." Ordinarily it is a bad idea to make fun of persons who hold views other than your own — after all, they just may be on to something, they just might know something you don't know, and, in any case, impartial readers rarely want to align themselves with someone who mocks others. In the essay we are looking at, however, Kristof gets away with this smart-guy tone because he (a) has loyal readers and (b) has written the entire essay in a highly informal or playful manner. Think again about the first paragraph, which begins "Here's a quick quiz." The informality is not only in the contraction (*Here's* versus *Here is*), but in the very idea of beginning by grabbing the readers and thrusting a quiz at them. The playfulness is evident throughout: For instance, immediately after Kristof announces his thesis, "Let's bring back hunting," he begins a new paragraph (6) with, "Now, you've probably just spilled your coffee."

Kristof's methods of presenting evidence include providing **statistics** (paras. 3, 4, 10, and 13), giving **examples** (paras. 10, 19–20), and citing **authorities** (paras. 13 and 16).

Persona   Kristof presents himself as a confident, no-nonsense fellow, a persona that not many writers can get away with, but that probably is acceptable in a journalist who regularly writes a newspaper column. His readers know what to expect, and they read him with pleasure. But it probably would be inadvisable for an unknown writer to adopt this persona, unless perhaps he or she were writing for an audience that could be counted on to be friendly (in this instance, an audience of hunters). If this essay appeared in a hunting magazine, doubtless it would please and entertain its audience. It would not convert anybody, but conversion would not be its point if it were published in a magazine read by hunters. In the *New York Times,* where the essay originally appeared, Kristof could count on a moderately sympathetic audience because he has a large number of faithful readers, but one can guess that many of these readers — chiefly city dwellers — read him for entertainment rather than for information about how they should actually behave.

Closing Paragraphs   The first two of the last three paragraphs report an episode (the two hundred pound buck inside the house) that Kristof presumably thinks is pretty conclusive evidence. The final paragraph begins with "So," strongly implying a logical conclusion to the essay.

Let's now turn to a student's analysis of Kristof's essay and then to our analysis of the student's analysis. (We should say that the analysis that you have just read, of Kristof's essay, is partly indebted to the student's essay that you are about to read.)

Betsy Swinton

Professor Knowles

English 101B

March 12, 2007

Tracking Kristof

Nicholas D. Kristof's "For Environmental Balance, Pick Up a Rifle" is an engaging piece of writing, but whether it is convincing is something I am not sure about. And I am not sure about it for two reasons: (1) I don't know much about the deer problem, and that's my fault; (2) I don't know much about the deer problem, and that's Kristof's fault. The first point needs no explanation, but let me explain the second.

Kristof is making an argument, offering a thesis: Deer are causing destruction, and the best way to reduce the destruction is to hunt deer. For all that I know, he may be correct both in his comment about what deer are doing and also in his comment about what must be done about deer. My ignorance of the situation is regrettable, but I don't think that I am the only reader from Chicago who doesn't know much about the deer problems in New Jersey, Connecticut, and Arkansas, the states that Kristof specifically mentions in connection with the deer problem. He announces his thesis early enough, in his sixth paragraph, and he is entertaining throughout his essay, but does he make a convincing case? To ask "Does he make a convincing case?" is to ask "Does he offer adequate evidence?" and "Does he show that his solution is better than other possible solutions?"

To take the first question: In a short essay Kristof can hardly give overwhelming evidence, but he does convince me that there is a problem. The most convincing evidence he gives appears in paragraph 16, where he says that the New Jersey Audubon Society "advocated deer hunting as an ecological necessity." I don't really know anything about the New Jersey Audubon Society, but I suppose that they are

Swinton 2

people with a deep interest in nature and in conservation, and if even such a group advocates deer hunting, there must be something to this solution.

I am even willing to accept his argument that, in this nation of meat-eaters, "to wring one's hands over them [dead deer], perhaps after polishing off a hamburger, is soggy sentimentality" (para. 14). According to Kristof, the present alternative to hunting deer is that we leave the deer to "die of disease and hunger" (para. 15). But what I am not convinced of is that there is no way to reduce the deer population other than by hunting. I don't think Kristof adequately explains why some sort of birth control is inadequate. In his eighth paragraph he makes a joke about controlling the birth of deer ("Liberals presumably support free condoms, while conservatives back abstinence education"), and the joke is funny, but it isn't an argument, it's just a joke. Why can't food containing some sort of sterilizing medicine be put out for the starving deer, food that will nourish them and yet make them unreproductive? In short, I don't think he has fairly informed his readers of alternatives to his own positions, and because he fails to look at counterproposals, he weakens his own proposal.

Although Kristof occasionally uses a word or phrase that suggests argument, such as "Granted" (para. 18), "So" (final paragraph), and "There's another reason" (para. 17), he relies chiefly on forceful writing rather than on reasoning. And the second of his two reasons for hunting seems utterly unconvincing to me. His first, as we have seen, is that the deer population (and apparently the bear population) is out of control. His second (para. 17) is that hunting "connects people with the outdoors and creates a broader constituency for wilderness preservation." I am not a hunter and I have never been one. Perhaps that's my misfortune, but I don't think I

am missing anything. And when I hear Kristof say, in his final
sentence--the climactic place in his essay--that "hunting is as natural
as bird-watching," I rub my eyes in disbelief. If he had me at least
half-convinced by his statistics and his citation of the Audubon
Society, he now loses me when he argues that hunting is "natural."
One might as well say that war is natural, rape is natural, bribery is
natural--all these terrible things occur, but we ought to deplore them
and we ought to make every effort to see that they disappear.

In short, I think that Kristof has written an engaging essay,
and he may well have an important idea, but I think that in his glib
final paragraph, where he tells us that "hunting is as natural as bird-
watching," he utterly loses the reader's confidence.

AN ANALYSIS OF THE STUDENT'S ANALYSIS

Swinton's essay seems to us to be excellent, doubtless the product of a good deal of thoughtful revision. She does not cover every possible aspect of Kristof's essay—she concentrates on his reasoning and she says very little about his style—but we think that, given the limits of space (about 500 words), she does a good job. What makes this student's essay effective?

- The essay has a title ("Tracking Kristof") that is of at least a little interest; it picks up Kristof's point about hunting, and it gives a hint of what is to come.

✓ A CHECKLIST FOR WRITING AN ANALYSIS
OF AN ARGUMENT

Have I asked myself the following questions?

☐ Early in my essay have I fairly stated the writer's thesis (claim) and summarized his or her supporting reasons? Have I explained to my reader any disagreement about definitions of important terms?

☐ Have I, again fairly early in my essay, indicated where I will be taking my reader, i.e., have I indicated my general response to the essay I are analyzing?

☐ Have I called attention to the strengths, if any, and the weaknesses, if any, of the essay?

☐ Have I commented not only on the *logos* (logic, reasoning) but also on the *ethos* (character of the writer, as presented in the essay)? For instance, has the author convinced me that he or she is well-informed and is a person of goodwill? Or, on the other hand, does the writer seem to be chiefly concerned with ridiculing those who hold a different view?

☐ If there is an appeal to *pathos* (emotion, originally meaning "pity for suffering," but now interpreted more broadly to include appeals to patriotism, humor, or loyalty to family, for example), is it acceptable? If not, why not?

☐ Have I used occasional brief quotations to let my reader hear the author's tone and to ensure fairness and accuracy?

☐ Is my analysis effectively organized?

☐ Does my essay, perhaps in the concluding paragraphs, indicate my agreement or disagreement with the writer and but also my view of the essay as a piece of argumentative writing?

☐ Is my tone appropriate?

- The author promptly identifies her subject (she names the writer and the title of his essay) early.

- Early in the essay she gives us a hint of where she will be going (in her first paragraph she tells us that Kristof's essay is "engaging . . . *but . . ."*).

- She uses a few brief quotations, to give us a feel for Kristof's essay and to let us hear the evidence for itself, but she does not pad her essay with long quotations.

- She takes up all of Kristof's main points.

- She gives her essay a reasonable organization, letting us hear Kristof's thesis, letting us know the degree to which she accepts it, and finally letting us know her specific reservations about the essay.

- She concludes without the formality of "in conclusion"; "in short" nicely does the trick.

- Notice, finally, that she sticks closely to Kristof's essay. She does not go off on a tangent about the virtues of vegetarianism or the dreadful politics of the *New York Times,* the newspaper that published Kristof's essay. She was asked to analyze the essay, and she has done so.

EXERCISE

Take one of the essays not yet discussed in class or an essay assigned now by your instructor, and in an essay of 500 words analyze and evaluate it.

ARGUMENTS FOR ANALYSIS

Jeff Jacoby

Jeff Jacoby is a columnist for the Boston Globe, *where this essay was originally published on the op-ed page on February 20, 1997.*

Bring Back Flogging

Boston's Puritan forefathers did not indulge miscreants lightly.

For selling arms and gunpowder to Indians in 1632, Richard Hopkins was sentenced to be "whipt, & branded with a hott iron on one of his cheekes." Joseph Gatchell, convicted of blasphemy in 1684, was ordered "to stand in pillory, have his head and hand put in & have his toung drawne forth out of his mouth, & peirct through with a hott iron." When Hannah Newell pleaded guilty to adultery in 1694, the court ordered "fifteen stripes Severally to be laid on upon her naked back at the Common Whipping post." Her consort, the aptly named Lambert Despair, fared worse: He was sentenced to 25 lashes "and that on the next Thursday Immediately after Lecture he stand upon the Pillory for . . . a full hower with Adultery in Capitall letters written upon his brest."

Corporal punishment for criminals did not vanish with the Puritans—Delaware didn't get around to repealing it until 1972—but for all relevant purposes, it has been out of fashion for at least 150 years. The day is long past when the stocks had an honored place on the Boston Common, or when offenders were publicly flogged. Now we practice a more enlightened, more humane way of disciplining wrongdoers: We lock them up in cages.

Imprisonment has become our penalty of choice for almost every offense in the criminal code. Commit murder; go to prison. Sell cocaine; go to prison. Kite checks; go to prison. It is an all-purpose punishment, suitable—or so it would seem—for crimes violent and nonviolent, motivated by hate or by greed, plotted coldly or committed in a fit of passion. If anything, our preference for incarceration is deepening—behold the slew of mandatory minimum sentences for drug crimes and "three-strikes-you're-out" life terms for recidivists. Some 1.6 million Americans are behind bars today. That represents a 250 percent increase since 1980, and the number is climbing.

We cage criminals at a rate unsurpassed in the free world, yet few of 5 us believe that the criminal justice system is a success. Crime is out of control, despite the deluded happy talk by some politicians about how "safe" cities have become. For most wrongdoers, the odds of being arrested, prosecuted, convicted, and incarcerated are reassuringly long. Fifty-eight percent of all murders do *not* result in a prison term. Likewise 98 percent of all burglaries.

Many states have gone on prison-building sprees, yet the penal system is choked to bursting. To ease the pressure, nearly all convicted felons are released early—or not locked up at all. "About three of every four convicted criminals," says John DiIulio, a noted Princeton criminologist, "are on the streets without meaningful probation or parole supervision." And while everyone knows that amateur thugs should be deterred before they become career criminals, it is almost unheard of for judges to send first- or second-time offenders to prison.

Meanwhile, the price of keeping criminals in cages is appalling—a common estimate is $30,000 per inmate per year. (To be sure, the cost to society of turning many inmates loose would be even higher.) For tens of thousands of convicts, prison is a graduate school of criminal studies: They emerge more ruthless and savvy than when they entered. And for many offenders, there is even a certain cachet to doing time—a stint in prison becomes a sign of manhood, a status symbol.

But there would be no cachet in chaining a criminal to an outdoor post and flogging him. If young punks were horsewhipped in public after their first conviction, fewer of them would harden into lifelong felons. A humiliating and painful paddling can be applied to the rear end of a crook for a lot less than $30,000 — and prove a lot more educational than ten years' worth of prison meals and lockdowns.

Are we quite certain the Puritans have nothing to teach us about dealing with criminals?

Of course, their crimes are not our crimes: We do not arrest blas-   10 phemers or adulterers, and only gun control fanatics would criminalize the sale of weapons to Indians. (They would criminalize the sale of weapons to anybody.) Nor would the ordeal suffered by poor Joseph Gatchell — the tongue "peirct through" with a hot poker — be regarded today as anything less than torture.

But what is the objection to corporal punishment that doesn't maim or mutilate? Instead of a prison term, why not sentence at least some criminals — say, thieves and drunk drivers — to a public whipping?

"Too degrading," some will say. "Too brutal." But where is it written that being whipped is more degrading than being caged? Why is it more brutal to flog a wrongdoer than to throw him in prison — where the risk of being beaten, raped, or murdered is terrifyingly high?

The *Globe* reported in 1994 that more than two hundred thousand prison inmates are raped each year, usually to the indifference of the guards. "The horrors experienced by many young inmates, particularly those who . . . are convicted of nonviolent offenses," former Supreme Court Justice Harry Blackmun has written, "border on the unimaginable." Are those horrors preferable to the short, sharp shame of corporal punishment?

Perhaps the Puritans were more enlightened than we think, at least on the subject of punishment. Their sanctions were humiliating and painful, but quick and cheap. Maybe we should readopt a few.

TOPICS FOR CRITICAL THINKING AND WRITING

1. When Jacoby says (para. 3) that today we are more "enlightened" than our Puritan forefathers because where they used flogging, "We lock them up in cages," is he being ironic? Explain.

2. Suppose you agree with Jacoby. Explain precisely (a) what you mean by *flogging* (does Jacoby explain what he means?) and (b) how much flogging is appropriate for the crimes of housebreaking, rape, robbery, and murder.

3. In an essay of 250 words, explain why you think that flogging would be more (or less) degrading and brutal than imprisonment.

4. At the end of his essay Jacoby draws to our attention the terrible risk of being raped in prison as an argument in favor of replacing imprisonment

with flogging. Do you think he mentions this point at the end because he believes it is the strongest or most persuasive of all those he mentions? Why, or why not?

5. It is often said that corporal punishment does not have any effect or, if it does, that the effect is the negative one of telling the recipient that violence is an acceptable form of behavior. But suppose it were demonstrated that the infliction of physical pain reduced at least certain kinds of crimes, perhaps shoplifting or unarmed robbery. Should we adopt the practice?

6. Jacoby draws the line (para. 11) at punishment that would "maim or mutilate." Why draw the line here? Some societies punish thieves by amputating a hand. Suppose we knew that this practice really did seriously reduce theft. Should we adopt it? How about adopting castration (surgical or chemical) for rapists? For child molesters?

John Irving

John Irving won an Academy Award for his screenplay of The Cider House Rules, *adapted from his 1985 novel. He competed in or coached wrestling for over thirty years and was inducted into the National Wrestling Hall of Fame in 1992. As Irving explains in his first paragraph, Title IX is a federal law prohibiting sex discrimination in educational programs that receive federal aid.*

Wrestling with Title IX

Title IX, the federal law that prohibits sex discrimination in educational programs receiving federal assistance, may be in for an overhaul. This week a committee appointed by the Bush administration will hold its final meetings before submitting its recommendations for changing the law to Secretary of Education Rod Paige. Since Title IX was enacted in 1972, it has been the subject of debate — much of it misguided — about its application to college athletics. At issue now is how to alter the law — or not — so that, as Secretary Paige has put it, we can find ways of "expanding opportunities to ensure fairness for all college athletes."

I hope the commission will realize that what's wrong with Title IX isn't Title IX. What's wrong is that, in practice, there are two Title IX's. The first Title IX was the one passed by Congress in 1972 to put an end to sex discrimination in schools — good for the original Title IX! The second Title IX, the one currently enforced, is the product of a policy interpretation in 1979 by the Department of Education's Office for Civil Rights (but never debated or approved by Congress) — and which is functioning as a gender quota law.

In its prohibition against sex discrimination, the 1972 law expressly states as "exceptions" any "preferential or disparate treatment because of imbalance in participation" or any "statistical evidence of imbalance." In English, this means that Congress recognized that the intent of Title IX was not to establish gender quotas or require preferential treatment as reparation for past discrimination. Smart thinking—after all, the legislation was intended to prohibit discrimination against either sex.

But what happened in 1979—and in subsequent re-evaluations of the law—has invited discrimination against male athletes. The 1979 interpretation required colleges to meet at least one of the following three criteria: that the number of athletes from each sex be roughly equivalent to the number of students enrolled; that colleges demonstrate a commitment to adding women's sports; and that they prove that the athletic interests of female students are effectively accommodated. The problems lie in complying with the first criterion. In order to achieve gender proportionality, men's collegiate sports are being undermined and eliminated. This was never the intention of Title IX.

The proportionality rule stipulates that the ratio of male to female 5 athletes be proportionate to the ratio of male to female students at a particular college. On average, females make up about 56 percent of college enrollment, males 44 percent; for most colleges to be in compliance with proportionality, more than half the athletes on team rosters must be women. Can you imagine this rule being applied to all educational programs—classes in science, engineering, accounting, medicine, or law? What about dance, drama, or music—not to mention women's studies?

In 1996, the Department of Education further bolstered the proportionality zealots by requiring colleges to count every name on a team's roster—scholarship and nonscholarship athletes, starters and nonstarters. It is this ruling that has prompted a lawsuit by the National Wrestling Coaches Association, the Committee to Save Bucknell Wrestling, the Marquette Wrestling Club, the Yale Wrestling Association, and the National Coalition for Athletics Equity, all of whom argue that the 1996 rules exceed the Department of Education's statutory authority "by effectively mandating the very discrimination that Title IX prohibits."

Why are wrestlers so upset about this? The number of collegiate wrestling programs lost to Title IX compliance is staggering; this is especially alarming because, since 1993, wrestling has been a rapidly growing sport at the high-school level. Data compiled by Gary Abbott, director of special projects at USA Wrestling, indicates that in 2001, there were 244,984 athletes wrestling in high school; only 5,966 got to wrestle in the National Collegiate Athletic Association. Not to put too fine a point on it: there is only one N.C.A.A. spot for every 41 high-school wrestlers. The numbers have been going downhill for a while. In 1982, there were 363 N.C.A.A. wrestling teams with 7,914 wrestlers competing; in 2001, there were only 229 teams with fewer than 6,000 wrestlers. Yet, in that same period, the number of N.C.A.A. institutions has increased from 787 to 1,049. No wonder wrestlers are unhappy.

As for the virtual elimination of walk-ons (nonscholarship athletes) in many men's sports, and the unrealistic capping of male team rosters— again, to make the number of male athletes proportional to the number of females—the problem is that athletic programs are going to absurd lengths to fill the unfilled rosters for women's teams. But women, statistically, aren't interested in participating in intercollegiate athletics to the degree that men are. J. Robinson, wrestling coach at the University of Minnesota, cites intramural sports, which are wholly interest driven, as an example. In a column about Title IX published in the *Chronicle of Higher Education*, Robinson wrote that "men outnumber women 3–1 or 4–1 on the intramural field."

Don't we need to know the exact numbers for how many women are interested in playing college sports now? But the Women's Sports Foundation, an advocacy group that favors maintaining proportionality, opposes conducting surveys of incoming students—that is, expressly to gauge interest in athletics. These surveys, they say, would force "female athletes to prove their interest in sports in order to obtain the right to participate and be treated fairly." But men would fill out the same surveys.

One suggestion that the presidential commission is considering is 10 counting the available spots on teams, rather than the actual participants. The Women's Sports Foundation rejects this idea, arguing that it counts "ghost female participants." However, the foundation has no objection to counting interest that isn't there.

In fact, those women's groups opposed to tampering with either the 1979 interpretation or the 1996 ruling, which endorses the proportionality arm of Title IX, often argue that there are three ways (at least on paper) for an institution to comply with Title IX—not just proportionality. But only proportionality can be measured concretely. A 1996 clarification letter from the Department of Education refers to the proportionality test as a "safe harbor"—meaning that this simple-to-apply numerical formula can assure an athletic director and a university president that their institution is in compliance and not subject to legal action. In other words, proportionality is not only wrong—it's lazy.

Some women's advocates argue that it is not proportionality that forces athletic directors to cut men's teams; they blame the budget excesses of Division I football and men's basketball. But there are countless examples where money was not the issue in the case of the sport that was dropped. Marquette University had a wrestling team that was completely financed by alumni and supporters; yet the sport was dropped in 2001, to comply with gender equity. (Marquette has no football team.)

Boston College dropped three sports that had only part-time coaches and offered no scholarships; these sports could easily have been sponsored by fund-raising. Keep in mind, too, that the majority of male college teams dropped in the 1990's were from Division II and Division III programs, which don't have big-time football or men's basketball.

Furthermore, many Division I football and basketball programs earn millions of dollars a year, enough to support all the other sports programs—men's and women's. Moreover, most schools with high-profile football programs are schools where women's teams have thrived. (Wit-

ness the Big 10, the S.E.C., the Big 12 and other Division I athletic con-
ferences, which have produced both winning football teams as well as
great women's teams in other sports.)

While eliminating men's sports like wrestling, where the interest in 15
participation is increasing, athletic programs go begging to find women athletes to fill the vacancies on an ever-expanding number of women's teams.

One of the most ludicrous examples of this was the attempt by Arizona State University in Tempe — a cactus-studded campus in the middle
of the Sonoran Desert — to add a competitive women's rowing team.
There's not a lot of water in Arizona. But the school asked the city to create a body of water (by flooding a dry gulch) on which the team could
practice. Because of a lack of funds, the school had to drop the plan. This
is probably just as well; taxpayer dollars would have financed scholarships either to rowers from out of state or to teach Arizona women
(most of whom have never held an oar) how to row. But Arizona State is
to be commended. It not only worked to meet the numerical demands
of proportionality, it tried to adhere to the original spirit of Title IX by
adding opportunities for women, not by cutting opportunities for men.

To apply the rule of proportionality to men's and women's collegiate
athletics amounts to a feminist form of sex discrimination. And I won't
be dismissed by that other argument I've heard (ad nauseam) from those
women's advocates unwilling to let proportionality go — namely, that to
oppose proportionality, or even the crudest enforcement of Title IX to
eliminate men's sports programs, is tantamount to being antifeminist
and hostile to women in sports. Don't try to lay that on me.

I *am* a women's advocate. I have long been active in the pro-choice
movement; my principal political commitment is my longstanding and
continuing role as an abortion-rights advocate. But I'm also an advocate
of fairness. What is unfair is not Title IX — it is Title IX's enforcement of
proportionality, which discriminates against men.

In 1992, Brian Picklo, a walk-on, asked the Michigan State Wrestling
coach, Tom Minkel, if he could try out for the team. Picklo had wrestled
for only two years in high school and never qualified for state tour-
naments. Minkel thought Picklo's chances of wrestling in the Big 10
were "slim to none." But Picklo became a two-time Division I All-
American, and he won the Big 10 title at 190 pounds. In most wrestling
programs across the country today, Brian Picklo wouldn't be allowed to
be a walk-on.

Title IX, the original legislation, was conceived as a fairness-for-all 20
law; it has been reinvented as a tool to treat men unfairly. Advocates of
proportionality claim that universities that are not "proportional" are
breaking the law, but they're not breaking the original law.

The Women's Sports Foundation has accused the presidential commission of politicizing Title IX. But Title IX was politicized by the
Department of Education in 1979 and 1986 — during Democratic admin-
istrations. Is it only now political because a Republican administration is

taking a closer look at the way Title IX is applied? (I make this criticism, by the way, as a Democrat. I'd have a hard time being an abortion rights advocate in the Bush administration, wouldn't I?)

Based on 2001 membership data—raw data from the National Federation of State High Schools, and from the N.C.A.A.—for every single N.C.A.A. sports opportunity for a woman, there are seventeen high school athletes available to fill the spot; for a man, there are eighteen. Isn't that equal enough? In fact, women have more opportunity to compete in college than men do. Yet the attitude represented by the Women's Sports Foundation, and other women's groups, is that women are far from achieving gender equity; by their continuing endorsement of proportionality in collegiate athletics, these women's advocates are being purely vindictive.

Years ago, I was playing in a Little League baseball game when an umpire made what I thought was a memorable mistake. Later, in another game, he made it again. I realized it was no mistake at all—he meant to say it. Instead of hollering "Play ball!" at the start of the game, this umpire shouted "Play fair!"

Keep Title IX; eliminate proportionality. Play fair.

TOPICS FOR CRITICAL THINKING AND WRITING

1. Interview a coach of a men's team, and find out his or her views of Title IX. (Be sure to ask if any men's varsity sports have been dropped at the coach's school.) Do you think the coach's position (whatever it is) is reasonable? Interview a coach of a women's team, and find out his or her views. Do you think they are reasonable?

2. Let's assume that you attend a college or university with a highly popular (money-making) football team or basketball team. You learn that your college spends twice as much on men's athletics as it does on women's athletics. Are you distressed? Why, or why not?

3. It is a fact—though possibly not at your school—that fewer dollars are spent on scholarships for female athletes than for male athletes. Are you distressed by this fact? Why, or why not?

4. Reread the essay, taking careful note of Irving's tone throughout—in his presentation of himself and in the *ethos* he conveys. Does he consistently retain your sympathy, or does he sometimes sound a bit churlish with the result that he turns you off? If he does reveal some grumpiness, do you feel that the facts of the matter are such that he is entitled to be grumpy?

Peter Singer

Peter Singer is the Ira W. DeCamp Professor of Bioethics at Princeton University. A native of Australia, he is a graduate of the University of Melbourne and Oxford University and the author or editor of more than two dozen books, including Animal Liberation *(1975),* Practical Ethics *(1979),* Rethinking Life and Death

(1995), and One World: The Ethics of Globalization *(2002). He has written on a variety of ethical issues, but he is especially known for caring about the welfare of animals.*

This essay originally appeared in the New York Review of Books *(April 5, 1973), as a review of* Animals, Men and Morals, *edited by Stanley and Roslind Godlovitch and John Harris.*

Animal Liberation

I

We are familiar with Black Liberation, Gay Liberation, and a variety of other movements. With Women's Liberation some thought we had come to the end of the road. Discrimination on the basis of sex, it has been said, is the last form of discrimination that is universally accepted and practiced without pretense, even in those liberal circles which have long prided themselves on their freedom from racial discrimination. But one should always be wary of talking of "the last remaining form of discrimination." If we have learned anything from the liberation movements, we should have learned how difficult it is to be aware of the ways in which we discriminate until they are forcefully pointed out to us. A liberation movement demands an expansion of our moral horizons, so that practices that were previously regarded as natural and inevitable are now seen as intolerable.

Animals, Men and Morals is a manifesto for an Animal Liberation movement. The contributors to the book may not all see the issue this way. They are a varied group. Philosophers, ranging from professors to graduate students, make up the largest contingent. There are five of them, including the three editors, and there is also an extract from the unjustly neglected German philosopher with an English name, Leonard Nelson, who died in 1927. There are essays by two novelist/critics, Brigid Brophy and Maureen Duffy, and another by Muriel the Lady Dowding, widow of Dowding of Battle of Britain fame and the founder of "Beauty without Cruelty," a movement that campaigns against the use of animals for furs and cosmetics. The other pieces are by a psychologist, a botanist, a sociologist, and Ruth Harrison, who is probably best described as a professional campaigner for animal welfare.

Whether or not these people, as individuals, would all agree that they are launching a liberation movement for animals, the book as a whole amounts to no less. It is a demand for a complete change in our attitudes to nonhumans. It is a demand that we cease to regard the exploitation of other species as natural and inevitable, and that, instead, we see it as a continuing moral outrage. Patrick Corbett, Professor of Philosophy at Sussex University, captures the spirit of the book in his closing words:

> We require now to extend the great principles of liberty, equality, and fraternity over the lives of animals. Let animal slavery join human slavery in the graveyard of the past.

The reader is likely to be skeptical. "Animal Liberation" sounds more like a parody of liberation movements than a serious objective. The reader may think: We support the claims of blacks and women for equality because blacks and women really are equal to whites and males—equal in intelligence and in abilities, capacity for leadership, rationality, and so on. Humans and nonhumans obviously are not equal in these respects. Since justice demands only that we treat equals equally, unequal treatment of humans and nonhumans cannot be an injustice.

This is a tempting reply, but a dangerous one. It commits the non- 5 racist and nonsexist to a dogmatic belief that blacks and women really are just as intelligent, able, etc., as whites and males—and no more. Quite possibly this happens to be the case. Certainly attempts to prove that racial or sexual differences in these respects have a genetic origin have not been conclusive. But do we really want to stake our demand for equality on the assumption that there are no genetic differences of this kind between the different races or sexes? Surely the appropriate response to those who claim to have found evidence for such genetic differences is not to stick to the belief that there are no differences, whatever the evidence to the contrary; rather one should be clear that the claim to equality does not depend on IQ. Moral equality is distinct from factual equality. Otherwise it would be nonsense to talk to the equality of human beings, since humans, as individuals, obviously differ in intelligence and almost any ability one cares to name. If possessing greater intelligence does not entitle one human to exploit another, why should it entitle humans to exploit nonhumans?

Jeremy Bentham expressed the essential basis of equality in his famous formula: "Each to count for one and none for more than one." In other words, the interests of every being that has interests are to be taken into account and treated equally with the like interests of any other being. Other moral philosophers, before and after Bentham, have made the same point in different ways. Our concern for others must not depend on whether they possess certain characteristics, though just what that concern involves may, of course, vary according to such characteristics.

Bentham, incidentally, was well aware that the logic of the demand for racial equality did not stop at the equality of humans. He wrote:

> The day *may* come when the rest of the animal creation may acquire those rights which never could have been withholden from them but by the hand of tyranny. The French have already discovered that the blackness of the skin is no reason why a human being should be abandoned without redress to the caprice of a tormentor. It may one day come to be recognized that the number of the legs, the villosity of the skin, or the termination of the *os sacrum,* are reasons equally insufficient for abandoning a sensitive being to the same fate. What else is it that should trace the insuperable line? Is it the faculty of reason, or perhaps the faculty of discourse? But a full-grown horse or dog is

beyond comparison a more rational, as well as a more conversable animal, than an infant of a day, or a week, or even a month, old. But suppose they were otherwise, what would it avail? The question is not, Can they *reason*? nor Can they *talk*? but, Can they *suffer*?[1]

Surely Bentham was right. If a being suffers, there can be no moral justification for refusing to take that suffering into consideration, and, indeed, to count it equally with the like suffering (if rough comparisons can be made) of any other being.

So the only question is: Do animals other than man suffer? Most people agree unhesitatingly that animals like cats and dogs can and do suffer, and this seems also to be assumed by those laws that prohibit wanton cruelty to such animals. Personally, I have no doubt at all about this and find it hard to take seriously the doubts that a few people apparently do have. The editors and contributors of *Animals, Men and Morals* seem to feel the same way, for although the question is raised more than once, doubts are quickly dismissed each time. Nevertheless, because this is such a fundamental point, it is worth asking what grounds we have for attributing suffering to other animals.

It is best to begin by asking what grounds any individual human has for supposing that other humans feel pain. Since pain is a state of consciousness, a "mental event," it can never be directly observed. No observations, whether behavioral signs such as writhing or screaming or physiological or neurological recordings, are observations of pain itself. Pain is something one feels, and one can only infer that others are feeling it from various external indications. The fact that only philosophers are ever skeptical about whether other humans feel pain shows that we regard such inference as justifiable in the case of humans.

Is there any reason why the same inference should be unjustifiable 10 for other animals? Nearly all the external signs which lead us to infer pain in other humans can be seen in other species, especially "higher" animals such as mammals and birds. Behavioral signs—writhing, yelping, or other forms of calling, attempts to avoid the source of pain, and many others—are present. We know, too, that these animals are biologically similar in the relevant respects, having nervous systems like ours which can be observed to function as ours do.

So the grounds for inferring that these animals can feel pain are nearly as good as the grounds for inferring other humans do. Only nearly, for there is one behavioral sign that humans have but nonhumans, with the exception of one or two specially raised chimpanzees, do not have. This, of course, is a developed language. As the quotation from Bentham indicates, this has long been regarded as an important distinction

[1] *The Principles of Morals and Legislation,* ch. XVII, sec. 1, footnote to paragraph 4. [All notes are the author's unless otherwise specified.]

between man and other animals. Other animals may communicate with each other, but not in the way we do. Following Chomsky,[2] many people now mark this distinction by saying that only humans communicate in a form that is governed by rules of syntax. (For the purposes of this argument, linguists allow those chimpanzees who have learned a syntactic sign language to rank as honorary humans.) Nevertheless, as Bentham pointed out, this distinction is not relevant to the question of how animals ought to be treated, unless it can be linked to the issue of whether animals suffer.

This link may be attempted in two ways. First, there is a hazy line of philosophical thought, stemming perhaps from some doctrines associated with Wittgenstein, which maintains that we cannot meaningfully attribute states of consciousness to beings without language. I have not seen this argument made explicit in print, though I have come across it in conversation. This position seems to me very implausible, and I doubt that it would be held at all if it were not thought to be a consequence of a broader view of the significance of language. It may be that the use of a public, rule-governed language is a precondition of conceptual thought. It may even be, although personally I doubt it, that we cannot meaningfully speak of a creature having an intention unless that creature can use a language. But states like pain, surely, are more primitive than either of these, and seem to have nothing to do with language.

Indeed, as Jane Goodall points out in her study of chimpanzees, when it comes to the expression of feelings and emotions, humans tend to fall back on nonlinguistic modes of communication which are often found among apes, such as a cheering pat on the back, an exuberant embrace, a clasp of hands, and so on.[3] Michael Peters makes a similar point in his contribution to *Animals, Men and Morals* when he notes that the basic signals we use to convey pain, fear, sexual arousal, and so on are not specific to our species. So there seems to be no reason at all to believe that a creature without language cannot suffer.

The second, and more easily appreciated way of linking language and the existence of pain is to say that the best evidence that we can have that another creature is in pain is when he tells us that he is. This is a distinct line of argument, for it is not being denied that a non-language-user conceivably could suffer, but only that we could know that he is suffering. Still, this line of argument seems to me to fail, and for reasons similar to those just given. "I am in pain" is not the best possible evidence that the speaker is in pain (he might be lying) and it is certainly not the only possible evidence. Behavioral signs and knowledge of the animal's biological similarity to ourselves together provide adequate evidence that animals do suffer. After all, we would not accept linguistic

---

[2]**Chomsky** Noam Chomsky (b. 1928), a professor of linguistics and the author of (among other books) *Language and Mind* (1972). [Editors' note.]
[3]Jane van Lawick-Goodall, *In the Shadow of Man* (Houghton Mifflin, 1971), p. 225.

evidence if it contradicted the rest of the evidence. If a man was severely burned, and behaved as if he were in pain, writhing, groaning, being very careful not to let his burned skin touch anything, and so on, but later said he had not been in pain at all, we would be more likely to conclude that he was lying or suffering from amnesia than that he had not been in pain.

Even if there were stronger grounds for refusing to attribute pain to those who do not have a language, the consequences of this refusal might lead us to examine these grounds unusually critically. Human infants, as well as some adults, are unable to use language. Are we to deny that a year-old infant can suffer? If not, how can language be crucial? Of course, most parents can understand the responses of even very young infants better than they understand the responses of other animals, and sometimes infant responses can be understood in the light of later development. 15

This, however, is just a fact about the relative knowledge we have of our own species and other species, and most of this knowledge is simply derived from closer contact. Those who have studied the behavior of other animals soon learn to understand their responses at least as well as we understand those of an infant. (I am not referring to Jane Goodall's and other well-known studies of apes. Consider, for example, the degree of understanding achieved by Tinbergen from watching herring gulls.[4]) Just as we can understand infant human behavior in the light of adult human behavior, so we can understand the behavior of other species in the light of our own behavior (and sometimes we can understand our own behavior better in the light of the behavior of other species).

The grounds we have for believing that other mammals and birds suffer are, then, closely analogous to the grounds we have for believing that other humans suffer. It remains to consider how far down the evolutionary scale this analogy holds. Obviously it becomes poorer when we get further away from man. To be more precise would require a detailed examination of all that we know about other forms of life. With fish, reptiles, and other vertebrates the analogy still seems strong, with molluscs like oysters it is much weaker. Insects are more difficult, and it may be that in our present state of knowledge we must be agnostic about whether they are capable of suffering.

If there is no moral justification for ignoring suffering when it occurs, and it does occur in other species, what are we to say of our attitudes toward these other species? Richard Ryder, one of the contributors to *Animals, Men and Morals,* uses the term "speciesism" to describe the belief that we are entitled to treat members of other species in a way in which it would be wrong to treat members of our own species. The term is not euphonious, but it neatly makes the analogy with racism. The nonracist would do well to bear the analogy in mind when he is inclined to defend human behavior toward nonhumans. "Shouldn't we worry

[4]N. Tinbergen, *The Herring Gull's World* (Basic Books, 1961).

about improving the lot of our own species before we concern ourselves with other species?" he may ask. If we substitute "race" for "species" we shall see that the question is better not asked. "Is a vegetarian diet nutritionally adequate?" resembles the slaveowner's claim that he and the whole economy of the South would be ruined without slave labor. There is even a parallel with skeptical doubts about whether animals suffer, for some defenders of slavery professed to doubt whether blacks really suffer in the way whites do.

I do not want to give the impression, however, that the case for Animal Liberation is based on the analogy with racism and no more. On the contrary, *Animals, Men and Morals* describes the various ways in which humans exploit nonhumans, and several contributors consider the defenses that have been offered, including the defense of meat-eating mentioned in the last paragraph. Sometimes the rebuttals are scornfully dismissive, rather than carefully designed to convince the detached critic. This may be a fault, but it is a fault that is inevitable, given the kind of book this is. The issue is not one on which one can remain detached. As the editors state in their Introduction:

> Once the full force of moral assessment has been made explicit there can be no rational excuse left for killing animals, be they killed for food, science, or sheer personal indulgence. We have not assembled this book to provide the reader with yet another manual on how to make brutalities less brutal. Compromise, in the traditional sense of the term, is simple unthinking weakness when one considers the actual reasons for our crude relationships with the other animals.

The point is that on this issue there are few critics who are genuinely 20 detached. People who eat pieces of slaughtered nonhumans every day find it hard to believe that they are doing wrong; and they also find it hard to imagine what else they could eat. So for those who do not place nonhumans beyond the pale of morality, there comes a stage when further argument seems pointless, a stage at which one can only accuse one's opponent of hypocrisy and reach for the sort of sociological account of our practices and the way we defend them is attempted by David Wood in his contribution to his book. On the other hand, to those unconvinced by the arguments, and unable to accept that they are merely rationalizing their dietary preferences and their fear of being thought peculiar, such sociological explanations can only seem insultingly arrogant.

II

The logic of speciesism is most apparent in the practice of experimenting on nonhumans in order to benefit humans. This is because the issue is rarely obscured by allegations that nonhumans are so different from humans that we cannot know anything about whether they suffer.

The defender of vivisection cannot use this argument because he needs to stress the similarities between man and other animals in order to justify the usefulness to the former of experiments on the latter. The researcher who makes rats choose between starvation and electric shocks to see if they develop ulcers (they do) does so because he knows that the rat has a nervous system very similar to man's, and presumably feels an electric shock in a similar way.

Richard Ryder's restrained account of experiments on animals made me angrier with my fellow men than anything else in this book. Ryder, a clinical psychologist by profession, himself experimented on animals before he came to hold the view he puts forward in his essay. Experimenting on animals is now a large industry, both academic and commercial. In 1969, more than 5 million experiments were performed in Britain, the vast majority without anesthetic (though how many of these involved pain is not known). There are no accurate U.S. figures, since there is no federal law on the subject, and in many cases no state law either. Estimates vary from 20 million to 200 million. Ryder suggests that 80 million may be the best guess. We tend to think that this is all for vital medical research, but of course it is not. Huge numbers of animals are used in university departments from Forestry to Psychology, and even more are used for commercial purposes, to test whether cosmetics can cause skin damage, or shampoos eye damage, or to test food additives or laxatives or sleeping pills or anything else.

A standard test for foodstuffs is the "LD50." The object of this test is to find the dosage level at which 50 percent of the test animals will die. This means that nearly all of them will become very sick before finally succumbing or surviving. When the substance is a harmless one, it may be necessary to force huge doses down the animals, until in some cases sheer volume or concentration causes death.

Ryder gives a selection of experiments, taken from recent scientific journals. I will quote two, not for the sake of indulging in gory details, but in order to give an idea of what normal researchers think they may legitimately do to other species. The point is not that the individual researchers are cruel men, but that they are behaving in a way that is allowed by our speciesist attitudes. As Ryder points out, even if only 1 percent of the experiments involve severe pain, that is 50,000 experiments in Britain each year, or nearly 150 every day (and about fifteen times as many in the United States, if Ryder's guess is right). Here then are two experiments:

O. S. Ray and R. J. Barrett of Pittsburgh gave electric shocks to the feet of 1,042 mice. They then caused convulsions by giving more intense shocks through cup-shaped electrodes applied to the animals' eyes or through pressure spring clips attached to their ears. Unfortunately some of the mice who "successfully completed Day One training were found sick or dead prior to testing on Day Two." [*Journal of Comparative and Physiological Psychology,* 1969, vol. 67, pp. 110-116]

At the National Institute for Medical Research, Mill Hill, London, W. Feldberg and S. L. Sherwood injected chemicals into the brains of cats—"with a number of widely different substances, recurrent patterns of reaction were obtained. Retching, vomiting, defecation, increased salivation and greatly accelerated respiration leading to panting were common features." . . .

The injection into the brain of a large dose of Tubocuraine caused the cat to jump "from the table to the floor and then straight into its cage, where it started calling more and more noisily whilst moving about restlessly and jerkily . . . finally the cat fell with legs and neck flexed, jerking in rapid clonic movements, the condition being that of a major [epileptic] convulsion . . . within a few seconds the cat got up, ran for a few yards at high speed, and fell in another fit. The whole process was repeated several times within the next ten minutes, during which the cat lost faeces and foamed at the mouth."

This animal finally died thirty-five minutes after the brain injection. [*Journal of Physiology,* 1954, vol. 123, pp. 148-167]

There is nothing secret about these experiments. One has only to open 25 any recent volume of a learned journal, such as the *Journal of Comparative and Physiological Psychology,* to find full descriptions of experiments of this sort, together with the results obtained—results that are frequently trivial and obvious. The experiments are often supported by public funds.

It is a significant indication of the level of acceptability of these practices that, although these experiments are taking place at this moment on university campuses throughout the country, there has, so far as I know, not been the slightest protest from the student movement. Students have been rightly concerned that their universities should not discriminate on grounds of race or sex, and that they should not serve the purposes of the military or big business. Speciesism continues undisturbed, and many students participate in it. There may be a few qualms at first, but since everyone regards it as normal, and it may even be a required part of a course, the student soon becomes hardened and, dismissing his earlier feelings as "mere sentiment," comes to regard animals as statistics rather than sentient beings with interests that warrant consideration.

Argument about vivisection has often missed the point because it has been put in absolutist terms: Would the abolitionist be prepared to let thousands die if they could be saved by experimenting on a single animal? The way to reply to this purely hypothetical question is to pose another: Would the experimenter be prepared to experiment on a human orphan under six months old, if it were the only way to save many lives? (I say "orphan" to avoid the complication of parental feelings, although in doing so I am being overfair to the experimenter, since the nonhuman subjects of experiments are not orphans.) A negative answer to this question indicates that the experimenter's readiness to use nonhumans is simple discrimination, for adult apes, cats, mice, and other mammals are more conscious of what is happening to them, more self-directing, and, so far as we can tell, just as sensitive to pain as a human infant. There is no characteristic that human infants possess that adult mammals do not have to the same or a higher degree.

(It might be possible to hold that what makes it wrong to experiment on a human infant is that the infant will in time develop into more than the nonhuman, but one would then, to be consistent, have to oppose abortion, and perhaps contraception, too, for the fetus and the egg and sperm have the same potential as the infant. Moreover, one would still have no reason for experimenting on a nonhuman rather than a human with brain damage severe enough to make it impossible for him to rise above infant level.)

The experimenter, then, shows a bias for his own species whenever he carries out an experiment on a nonhuman for a purpose that he would not think justified him in using a human being at an equal or lower level of sentience, awareness, ability to be self-directing, etc. No one familiar with the kind of results yielded by these experiments can have the slightest doubt that if this bias were eliminated the number of experiments performed would be zero or very close to it.

III

If it is vivisection that shows the logic of speciesism most clearly, it is 30 the use of other species for food that is at the heart of our attitudes toward them. Most of *Animals, Men and Morals* is an attack on meat eating—an attack which is based solely on concern for nonhumans, without reference to arguments derived from consideration of ecology, macrobiotics, health, or religion.

The idea that nonhumans are utilities, means to our ends, pervades our thought. Even conservationists who are concerned about the slaughter of wildfowl but not about the vastly greater slaughter of chickens for our tables are thinking in this way—they are worried about what we would lose if there were less wildlife. Stanley Godlovitch, pursuing the Marxist idea that our thinking is formed by the activities we undertake in satisfying our needs, suggests that man's first classification of his environment was into Edibles and Inedibles. Most animals came into the first category, and there they have remained.

Man may always have killed other species for food, but he has never exploited them so ruthlessly as he does today. Farming has succumbed to business methods, the objective being to get the highest possible ratio of output (meat, eggs, milk) to input (fodder, labor costs, etc.). Ruth Harrison's essay "On Factory Farming" gives an account of some aspects of modern methods, and of the unsuccessful British campaigns for effective controls, a campaign which was sparked off by her *Animal Machines* (London: Stuart, 1964).

Her article is in no way a substitute for her earlier book. This is a pity since, as she says, "Farm produce is still associated with mental pictures of animals browsing in the fields . . . of hens having a last forage before going to roost. . . ." Yet neither in her article nor elsewhere in *Animals, Men and Morals* is this false image replaced by a clear idea of the nature and extent of factory farming. We learn of this only indirectly, when we hear of the code of reform proposed by an advisory committee set up by the British government.

Among the proposals, which the government refused to implement on the grounds that they were too idealistic, were: *"Any animal should at least have room to turn around freely."*

Factory farm animals need liberation in the most literal sense. Veal 35 calves are kept in stalls 5 feet by 2 feet. They are usually slaughtered when about four months old, and have been too big to turn in their stalls for at least a month. Intensive beef herds, kept in stalls only proportionately larger for much longer periods, account for a growing percentage of beef production. Sows are often similarly confined when pregnant, which, because of artificial methods of increasing fertility, can be most of the time. Animals confined in this way do not waste food by exercising, nor do they develop unpalatable muscle.

"A dry bedded area should be provided for all stock." Intensively kept animals usually have to stand and sleep in slatted floors without straw, because this makes cleaning easier.

"Palatable roughage must be readily available to all calves after one week of age." In order to produce the pale veal housewives are said to prefer, calves are fed on an all-liquid diet until slaughter, even though they are long past the age at which they would normally eat grass. They develop a craving for roughage, evidenced by attempts to gnaw wood from their stalls. (For the same reason, their diet is deficient in iron.)

"Battery cages for poultry should be large enough for a bird to be able to stretch one wing at a time." Under current British practice, a cage for four or five laying hens has a floor area of 20 inches by 18 inches, scarcely larger than a double page of the *New York Review of Books*. In this space, on a sloping wire floor (sloping so the eggs roll down, wire so the dung drips through) the birds live for a year or eighteen months while artificial lighting and temperature conditions combine with drugs in their food to squeeze the maximum number of eggs out of them. Table birds are also sometimes kept in cages. More often they are reared in sheds, no less crowded. Under these conditions all the birds' natural activities are frustrated, and they develop "vices" such as pecking each other to death. To prevent this, beaks are often cut off, and the sheds kept dark.

How many of those who support factory farming by buying its produce know anything about the way it is produced? How many have heard something about it, but are reluctant to check up for fear that it will make them uncomfortable? To nonspeciesists, the typical consumer's mixture of ignorance, reluctance to find out the truth, and vague belief that nothing really bad could be allowed seems analogous to the attitudes of "decent Germans" to the death camps.

There are, of course, some defenders of factory farming. Their argu- 40 ments are considered, though again rather sketchily, by John Harris. Among the most common: "Since they have never known anything else, they don't suffer." This argument will not be put by anyone who knows anything about animal behavior, since he will know that not all behavior has to be learned. Chickens attempt to stretch wings, walk around, scratch, and even dustbathe or build a nest, even though they have never lived under conditions that allowed these activities. Calves can suffer from maternal deprivation no matter at what age they were taken from their mothers. "We need these intensive methods to provide protein for a growing population." As ecologists and famine relief organizations know, we can produce far more protein per acre if we grow the right vegetable crop, soy beans for instance, than if we use the land to grow crops to be converted into protein by animals who use nearly 90 percent of the protein themselves, even when unable to exercise.

There will be many readers of this book who will agree that factory farming involves an unjustifiable degree of exploitation of sentient creatures, and yet will want to say that there is nothing wrong with rearing animals for food, provided it is done "humanely." These people are saying, in effect, that although we should not cause animals to suffer, there is nothing wrong with killing them.

There are two possible replies to this view. One is to attempt to show that this combination of attitudes is absurd. Roslind Godlovitch takes this course in her essay, which is an examination of some common attitudes to animals. She argues that from the combination of "animal suffering is to be avoided" and "there is nothing wrong with killing animals" it follows that all animal life ought to be exterminated (since all sentient creatures will suffer to some degree at some point in their lives). Euthanasia is a contentious issue only because we place some value on living. If we did not, the least amount of suffering would justify it. Accordingly, if we deny that we have a duty to exterminate all animal life, we must concede that we are placing some value on animal life.

This argument seems to me valid, although one could still reply that the value of animal life is to be derived from the pleasures that life can have for them, so that, provided their lives have a balance of pleasure over pain, we are justified in rearing them. But this would imply that we ought to produce animals and let them live as pleasantly as possible, without suffering.

At this point, one can make the second of the two possible replies to the view that rearing and killing animals for food is all right so long as it is done humanely. This second reply is that so long as we think that a nonhuman may be killed simply so that a human can satisfy his taste for meat, we are still thinking of nonhumans as means rather than as ends in themselves. The factory farm is nothing more than the application of technology to this concept. Even traditional methods involve castration, the separation of mothers and their young, the breaking up of herds, branding or earpunching, and of course transportation to the abattoirs and the final moments of terror when the animal smells blood and senses danger. If we were to try rearing animals so that they lived and died without suffering, we should find that to do so on anything like the scale of today's meat industry would be a sheer impossibility. Meat would become the prerogative of the rich.

I have been able to discuss only some of the contributions to this 45 book, saying nothing about, for instance, the essays on killing for furs and for sport. Nor have I considered all the detailed questions that need to be asked once we start thinking about other species in the radically different way presented by this book. What, for instance, are we to do about genuine conflicts of interest like rats biting slum children? I am not sure of the answer, but the essential point is just that we *do* see this as a conflict of interests, that we recognize that rats have interests too. Then we may begin to think about other ways of resolving the conflict — perhaps by leaving out rat baits that sterilize the rats instead of killing them.

I have not discussed such problems because they are side issues compared with the exploitation of other species for food and for experimental purposes. On these central matters, I hope that I have said enough to show that this book, despite its flaws, is a challenge to every human to recognize his attitudes to nonhumans as a form of prejudice no less objectionable than racism or sexism. It is a challenge that demands not just a change of attitudes, but a change in our way of life, for it requires us to become vegetarians.

Can a purely moral demand of this kind succeed? The odds are certainly against it. The book holds out no inducements. It does not tell us that we will become healthier, or enjoy life more, if we cease exploiting animals. Animal Liberation will require greater altruism on the part of mankind than any other liberation movement, since animals are incapable of demanding it for themselves, or of protesting against their exploitation by votes, demonstrations, or bombs. Is man capable of such genuine altruism? Who knows? If this book does have a significant effect, however, it will be a vindication of all those who have believed that man has within himself the potential for more than cruelty and selfishness.

Topics for Critical Thinking and Writing

1. In his fourth paragraph Singer formulates an argument on behalf of the skeptical reader. Examine that argument closely, restate it in your own words, and evaluate it. Which of its premises is most vulnerable to criticism? Why?

2. Singer quotes with approval (para. 7) Bentham's comment, "The question is not, Can they *reason*? nor Can they *talk*? but, Can they *suffer*?" Do you find this argument persuasive? Can you think of any effective challenge to it?

3. Singer allows that although developed linguistic capacity is not necessary for a creature to have pain, perhaps such a capacity is necessary for "having an intention" (para. 12). Do you think this concession is correct? Have you ever seen animal behavior that you would be willing to describe or explain as evidence that the animal has an intention to do something, despite knowing that the animal cannot talk?

4. Singer thinks that the readiness to experiment on animals argues against believing that animals don't suffer pain (see para. 21). Do you agree with this reasoning?

5. Singer confesses (para. 22) to being made especially angry "with my fellow men" after reading the accounts of animal experimentation. What is it that aroused his anger? Do such feelings, and the acknowledgment that one has them, have any place in a sober discussion about the merits of animal experimentation? Why, or why not?

6. What is "factory farming" (paras. 32–40)? Why is Singer opposed to it?

7. To the claim that there is nothing wrong with "rearing animals for food," provided it is done "humanely" (para. 41), Singer offers two replies (paras. 42–44). In an essay of 250 words summarize them briefly, and then indicate whether either persuades you and why or why not.

8. Suppose someone were to say to Singer: "You claim that capacity to suffer is the relevant factor in deciding whether a creature deserves to be treated as my moral equal. But you're wrong. The relevant factor is whether the creature is *alive*. Being alive is what matters, not being capable of feeling pain." In one or two paragraphs declare what you think would be Singer's reply.

9. Do you think it is worse to kill an animal for its fur than to kill, cook, and eat an animal? Is it worse to kill an animal for sport than to kill it for medical experimentation? What is Singer's view? Explain your view, making use of Singer's if you wish, in an essay of 500 words.

10. Are there any arguments, in your opinion, that show the immorality of eating human flesh (cannibalism) but that do not show a similar objection to eating animal flesh? Write a 500-word essay in which you discuss the issue.

Jonathan Swift

Jonathan Swift (1667–1745) was born in Ireland of English stock. An Anglican clergyman, he became Dean of St. Patrick's in Dublin in 1723, but the post he really wanted, one of high office in England, was never given to him. A prolific pamphleteer on religious and political issues, Swift today is known not as a churchman but as a satirist. His best-known works are Gulliver's Travels

(1726, a serious satire but now popularly thought of as a children's book) and "A Modest Proposal" (1729). In "A Modest Proposal," which was published anonymously, Swift addresses the great suffering that the Irish endured under the British.

A Modest Proposal

For Preventing the Children of Poor People in Ireland from Being a Burden to Their Parents or Country, and for Making Them Beneficial to the Public

It is a melancholy object to those who walk through this great town or travel in the country, when they see the streets, the roads, and cabin doors, crowded with beggars of the female sex, followed by three, four, or six children, all in rags and importuning every passenger for an alms. These mothers, instead of being able to work for their honest livelihood, are forced to employ all their time in strolling to beg sustenance for their helpless infants: who as they grow up either turn thieves for want of work, or leave their dear native country to fight for the Pretender in Spain, or sell themselves to the Barbadoes.

I think it is agreed by all parties that this prodigious number of children in the arms, or on the backs, or at the heels of their mothers, and frequently of their fathers, is in the present deplorable state of the kingdom a very great additional grievance; and, therefore, whoever could find out a fair, cheap, and easy method of making these children sound, useful members of the commonwealth, would deserve so well of the public as to have his statue set up for a preserver of the nation.

But my intention is very far from being confined to provide only for the children of professed beggars; it is of a much greater extent, and shall take in the whole number of infants at a certain age who are born of parents in effect as little able to support them as those who demand our charity in the streets.

As to my own part, having turned my thoughts for many years upon this important subject, and maturely weighed the several schemes of our projectors,[1] I have always found them grossly mistaken in their computation. It is true, a child just dropped from its dam may be supported by her milk for a solar year, with little other nourishment; at most not above the value of 2s.,[2] which the mother may certainly get, or the value in scraps, by her lawful occupation of begging; and it is exactly at one year old that I propose to provide for them in such a manner as instead of being a charge upon their parents or the parish, or wanting food and raiment for the rest of their lives, they shall on the contrary contribute to the feeding, and partly to the clothing, of many thousands.

[1]**projectors** Persons who devise plans. [All notes are the editors'.]
[2]**2s** Two shillings.

There is likewise another great advantage in my scheme, that it will prevent those voluntary abortions, and that horrid practice of women murdering their bastard children, alas! too frequent among us! sacrificing the poor innocent babes I doubt more to avoid the expense than the shame, which would move tears and pity in the most savage and inhuman breast.

The number of souls in this kingdom being usually reckoned one million and a half, of these I calculate there may be about 200,000 couple whose wives are breeders; from which number I subtract 30,000 couple who are able to maintain their own children (although I apprehend there cannot be so many, under the present distress of the kingdom); but this being granted, there will remain 170,000 breeders. I again subtract 50,000 for those women who miscarry, or whose children die by accident or disease within the year. There only remain 120,000 children of poor parents annually born. The question therefore is, how this number shall be reared and provided for? which, as I have already said, under the present situation of affairs, is utterly impossible by all the methods hitherto proposed. For we can neither employ them in handicraft or agriculture; we neither build houses (I mean in the country) nor cultivate land; they can very seldom pick up a livelihood by stealing, till they arrive at six years old, except where they are of towardly parts; although I confess they learn the rudiments much earlier; during which time they can, however, be properly looked upon only as probationers; as I have been informed by a principal gentleman in the county of Cavan, who protested to me that he never knew above one or two instances under the age of six, even in a part of the kingdom so renowned for the quickest proficiency in that art.

I am assured by our merchants, that a boy or a girl before twelve years old is no salable commodity; and even when they come to this age they will not yield above 3£. or 3£. 2s. 6d.[3] at most on the exchange; which cannot turn to account either to the parents or kingdom, the charge of nutriment and rags having been at least four times that value.

I shall now therefore humbly propose my own thoughts, which I hope will not be liable to the least objection.

I have been assured by a very knowing American of my acquaintance in London, that a young healthy child well nursed is at a year old a most delicious, nourishing, and wholesome food, whether stewed, roasted, baked, or broiled; and I make no doubt that it will equally serve in a fricassee or a ragout.

I do therefore humbly offer it to public consideration that of the 120,000 children already computed, 20,000 may be reserved for breed, whereof only one-fourth part to be males; which is more than we allow to sheep, black cattle, or swine; and my reason is, that these children are seldom the fruits of marriage, a circumstance not much regarded by our

---

[3]**£. . . . d** £ is an abbreviation for "pound sterling" and *d.*, for "pence."

savages; therefore one male will be sufficient to serve four females. That the remaining 100,000 may, at a year old, be offered in sale to the persons of quality and fortune through the kingdom; always advising the mother to let them suck plentifully in the last month, so as to render them plump and fat for a good table. A child will make two dishes at an entertainment for friends; and when the family dines alone, the fore or hind quarter will make a reasonable dish, and seasoned with a little pepper or salt will be very good boiled on the fourth day, especially in winter.

I have reckoned upon a medium that a child just born will weigh twelve pounds, and in a solar year, if tolerably nursed, will increase to twenty-eight pounds.

I grant this food will be somewhat dear, and therefore very proper for landlords, who, as they have already devoured most of the parents, seem to have the best title to the children.

Infant's flesh will be in season throughout the year, but more plentiful in March, and a little before and after: for we are told by a grave author, an eminent French physician, that fish being a prolific diet, there are more children born in Roman Catholic countries about nine months after Lent than at any other season; therefore, reckoning a year after Lent, the markets will be more glutted than usual, because the number of popish infants is at least three to one in this kingdom: and therefore it will have one other collateral advantage, by lessening the number of papists among us.

I have already computed the charge of nursing a beggar's child (in which list I reckon all cottagers, laborers, and four-fifths of the farmers) to be about 2s. per annum, rags included; and I believe no gentleman would repine to give 10s. for the carcass of a good fat child, which, as I have said, will make four dishes of excellent nutritive meat, when he has only some particular friend or his own family to dine with him. Thus the squire will learn to be a good landlord, and grow popular among the tenants; the mother will have 8s. net profit, and be fit for work till she produces another child.

Those who are more thrifty (as I must confess the times require) may flay the carcass; the skin of which artificially dressed will make admirable gloves for ladies, and summer boots for fine gentlemen.   15

As to our city of Dublin, shambles[4] may be appointed for this purpose in the most convenient parts of it, and butchers we may be assured will not be wanting: although I rather recommend buying the children alive, and dressing them hot from the knife as we do roasting pigs.

A very worthy person, a true lover of his country, and whose virtues I highly esteem, was lately pleased in discoursing on this matter to offer a refinement upon my scheme. He said that many gentlemen of this kingdom, having of late destroyed their deer, he conceived that the want

[4]**shambles** Slaughterhouses.

of venison might be well supplied by the bodies of young lads and maidens, not exceeding fourteen years of age nor under twelve; so great a number of both sexes in every country being now ready to starve for want of work and service; and these to be disposed of by their parents, if alive, or otherwise by their nearest relations. But with due deference to so excellent a friend and so deserving a patriot, I cannot be altogether in his sentiments; for as to the males, my American acquaintance assured me from frequent experience that their flesh was generally tough and lean, like that of our schoolboys by continual exercise, and their taste disagreeable; and to fatten them would not answer the charge. Then as to the females, it would, I think, with humble submission be a loss to the public, because they soon would become breeders themselves: and besides, it is not improbable that some scrupulous people might be apt to censure such a practice (although indeed very unjustly), as a little bordering upon cruelty; which, I confess, has always been with me the strongest objection against any project, how well soever intended.

But in order to justify my friend, he confessed that this expedient was put into his head by the famous Psalmanazar[5] a native of the island Formosa, who came from thence to London about twenty years ago: and in conversation told my friend, that in his country when any young person happened to be put to death, the executioner sold the carcass to persons of quality as a prime dainty; and that in his time the body of a plump girl of fifteen, who was crucified for an attempt to poison the emperor, was sold to his imperial majesty's prime minister of state, and other great mandarins of the court, in joints from the gibbet, at 400 crowns. Neither indeed can I deny, that if the same use were made of several plump young girls in this town, who without one single groat to their fortunes cannot stir abroad without a chair, and appear at the playhouse and assemblies in foreign fineries which they never will pay for, the kingdom would not be the worse.

Some persons of a depending spirit are in great concern about the vast number of poor people, who are aged, diseased, or maimed, and I have been desired to employ my thoughts what course may be taken to ease the nation of so grievous an encumbrance. But I am not in the least pain upon that matter, because it is very well known that they are every day dying and rotting by cold and famine, and filth and vermin, as fast as can be reasonably expected. And as to the young laborers, they are now in as hopeful a condition: They cannot get work, and consequently pine away for want of nourishment, to a degree that if at any time they are accidentally hired to common labor, they have not strength to perform it; and thus the country and themselves are happily delivered from the evils to come.

---

[5]**Psalmanazar** George Psalmanazar (c. 1679–1763), a Frenchman who claimed to be from Formosa (now Taiwan); he wrote *An Historical and Geographical Description of Formosa* (1704). The hoax was exposed soon after publication.

I have too long digressed, and therefore shall return to my subject. I 20
think the advantages by the proposal which I have made are obvious
and many, as well as of the highest importance.

For first, as I have already observed, It would greatly lessen the
number of papists, with whom we are yearly overrun, being the principal breeders of the nation as well as our most dangerous enemies; and
who stay at home on purpose to deliver the kingdom to the Pretender,
hoping to take their advantage by the absence of so many good Protestants, who have chosen rather to leave their country than stay at home
and pay tithes against their conscience to an Episcopal curate.

Secondly, The poor tenants will have something valuable of their
own, which by law may be made liable to distress and help to pay their
landlord's rent, their corn and cattle being already seized, and money a
thing unknown.

Thirdly, Whereas the maintenance of 100,000 children from two
years old and upward, cannot be computed at less than 10s. apiece per
annum, the nation's stock will be thereby increased £50,000 per annum,
beside the profit of a new dish introduced to the tables of all gentlemen
of fortune in the kingdom who have any refinement in taste. And the
money will circulate among ourselves, the goods being entirely of our
own growth and manufacture.

Fourthly, The constant breeders beside the gain of 8s. sterling per
annum by the sale of their children, will be rid of the charge of maintaining them after the first year.

Fifthly, This food would likewise bring great custom to taverns, 25
where the vintners will certainly be so prudent as to procure the best
receipts for dressing it to perfection, and consequently have their
houses frequented by all the fine gentlemen, who justly value themselves upon their knowledge in good eating; and a skilful cook who understands how to oblige his guests, will contrive to make it as expensive
as they please.

Sixthly, This would be a great inducement to marriage, which all
wise nations have either encouraged by rewards or enforced by laws and
penalties. It would increase the care and tenderness of mothers toward
their children, when they were sure of a settlement for life to the poor
babes, provided in some sort by the public, to their annual profit instead
of expense. We should see an honest emulation among the married
women, which of them would bring the fattest child to the market. Men
would become as fond of their wives during the time of their pregnancy
as they are now of their mares in foal, their cows in calf, their sows
when they are ready to farrow; nor offer to beat or kick them (as is too
frequent a practice) for fear of a miscarriage.

Many other advantages might be enumerated. For instance, the addition of some thousand carcasses in our exportation of barreled beef,
the propagation of swine's flesh, and improvement in the art of making
good bacon, so much wanted among us by the great destruction of pigs,

too frequent at our table; which are no way comparable in taste or magnificence to a well-grown, fat, yearling child, which roasted whole will make a considerable figure at a lord mayor's feast or any other public entertainment. But this and many others I omit, being studious of brevity.

Supposing that 1,000 families in this city would be constant customers for infants' flesh, besides others who might have it at merry-meetings, particularly at weddings and christenings, I compute that Dublin would take off annually about 20,000 carcasses; and the rest of the kingdom (where probably they will be sold somewhat cheaper) the remaining 80,000.

I can think of no one objection that will possibly be raised against this proposal, unless it should be urged that the number of people will be thereby much lessened in the kingdom. This I freely own, and it was indeed one principal design in offering it to the world. I desire the reader will observe, that I calculate my remedy for this one individual kingdom of Ireland and for no other that ever was, is, or I think ever can be upon earth. Therefore let no man talk to me of other expedients: of taxing our absentees at 5s. a pound; of using neither clothes nor household furniture except what is of our own growth and manufacture; of utterly rejecting the materials and instruments that promote foreign luxury; of curing the expensiveness of pride, vanity, idleness, and gaming in our women; of introducing a vein of parsimony, prudence, and temperance; of learning to love our country, in the want of which we differ even from Laplanders and the inhabitants of Topinamboo; of quitting our animosities and factions, nor acting any longer like the Jews, who were murdering one another at the very moment their city was taken; of being a little cautious not to sell our country and conscience for nothing; of teaching landlords to have at least one degree of mercy toward their tenants; lastly, of putting a spirit of honesty, industry, and skill into our shopkeepers; who, if a resolution could now be taken to buy only our native goods, would immediately unite to cheat and exact upon us in the price the measure, and the goodness, nor could ever yet be brought to make one fair proposal of just dealing, though often and earnestly invited to it.

Therefore I repeat, let no man talk to me of these and the like expedients, till he has at least some glimpse of hope that there will be ever some hearty and sincere attempt to put them in practice.

But as to myself, having been wearied out for many years with offering vain, idle, visionary thoughts, and at length utterly despairing of success, I fortunately fell upon this proposal; which, as it is wholly new, so it has something solid and real, of no expense and little trouble, full in our own power, and whereby we can incur no danger in disobliging England. For this kind of commodity will not bear exportation, the flesh being of too tender a consistence to admit a long continuance in salt, although perhaps I could name a country which would be glad to eat up our whole nation without it.

After all, I am not so violently bent upon my own opinion as to reject any offer proposed by wise men, which shall be found equally innocent, cheap, easy, and effectual. But before something of that kind shall be advanced in contradiction to my scheme, and offering a better, I desire the author or authors will be pleased maturely to consider two points. First, as things now stand, how they will be able to find food and raiment for 100,000 useless mouths and backs. And secondly, there being a round million of creatures in human figure throughout this kingdom, whose subsistence put into a common stock would leave them in debt 2,000,000£. sterling, adding those who are beggars by profession to the bulk of farmers, cottagers, and laborers, with the wives and children who are beggars in effect; I desire those politicians who dislike my overture, and may perhaps be so bold as to attempt an answer, that they will first ask the parents of these mortals, whether they would not at this day think it a great happiness to have been sold for food at a year old in the manner I prescribe, and thereby have avoided such a perpetual scene of misfortunes as they have since gone through by the oppression of landlords, the impossibility of paying rent without money or trade, the want of common sustenance, with neither house nor clothes to cover them from the inclemencies of the weather, and the most inevitable prospect of entailing the like or greater miseries upon their breed for ever.

I profess, in the sincerity of my heart, that I have not the least personal interest in endeavoring to promote this necessary work, having no other motive than the public good of my country, by advancing our trade, providing for infants, relieving the poor, and giving some pleasure to the rich. I have no children by which I can propose to get a single penny; the youngest being nine years old, and my wife past childbearing.

Topics for Critical Thinking and Writing

1. In paragraph 4 the speaker of the essay mentions proposals set forth by "projectors" — that is, by advocates of other proposals or projects. On the basis of the first two paragraphs of "A Modest Proposal," how would you characterize *this* projector, the speaker of the essay? Write your characterization in one paragraph. Then, in a second paragraph, characterize the projector as you understand him, having read the entire essay. In your second paragraph, indicate what *he thinks he is* and also what the reader sees he really is.

2. The speaker or persona of "A Modest Proposal" is confident that selling children "for a good table" (para. 10) is a better idea than any of the then current methods of disposing of unwanted children, including abortion and infanticide. Can you think of any argument that might favor abortion or infanticide for parents in dire straits, rather than the projector's scheme?

3. In paragraph 29 the speaker considers, but dismisses out of hand, several other solutions to the wretched plight of the Irish poor. Write a 500-

word essay in which you explain each of these ideas and their combined merits as an alternative to the solution he favors.

4. What does the projector imply are the causes of the Irish poverty he deplores? Are there possible causes he has omitted? If so, what are they?

5. Imagine yourself as one of the poor parents to whom Swift refers, and write a 250-word essay explaining why you prefer not to sell your infant to the local butcher.

6. The modern version of the problem to which the proposal is addressed is called "population policy." How would you describe our nation's current population policy? Do we have a population policy, in fact? If not, what would you propose? If we do have one, would you propose any changes in it? Why, or why not?

7. It is sometimes suggested that just as persons need to get a license to drive a car, to hunt with a gun, or to marry, a husband and wife ought to be required to get a license to have a child. Would you favor this idea, assuming that it applied to you as a possible parent? Would Swift? Explain your answers in an essay of 500 words.

8. Consider the six arguments advanced in paragraphs 21 to 26, and write a 1,000-word essay criticizing all of them. Or if you find that one or more of the arguments is really unanswerable, explain why you find it so compelling.

9. Write your own "modest proposal," ironically suggesting a solution to a problem. Possible topics: health care or schooling for the children of illegal immigrants, overcrowded jails, children who have committed a serious crime, homeless people.

6

Developing an Argument of Your Own

The difficult part in an argument is not to defend one's opinion but to know what it is.

— ANDRÉ MAUROIS

Imagine that you enter a parlor. You come late. When you arrive, others have long preceded you, and they are engaged in a heated discussion, a discussion too heated for them to pause and tell you exactly what it is about. In fact, the discussion had already begun long before any of them got there, so that no one present is qualified to retrace for you all the steps that had gone before. You listen for a while, until you decide that you have caught the tenor of the argument; then you put in your oar. Someone answers; you answer him; another comes to your defense; another aligns himself against you, to either the embarrassment or gratification of your opponent, depending upon the quality of your ally's assistance. However, the discussion is interminable. The hour grows late, you must depart. And you do depart, with the discussion still vigorously in progress.

— KENNETH BURKE

No greater misfortune could happen to anyone than that of developing a dislike for argument.

— PLATO

PLANNING, DRAFTING, AND REVISING AN ARGUMENT

First, hear the wisdom of Mark Twain: "When the Lord finished the world, He pronounced it good. That is what I said about my first work, too. But Time, I tell you, Time takes the confidence out of these incautious early opinions."

All of us, teachers and students, have our moments of confidence, but for the most part we know that it takes considerable effort to write clear, thoughtful, seemingly effortless prose. In a conversation we can cover ourselves with such expressions as "Well, I don't know, but I sort of think...," and we can always revise our position ("Oh, well, I didn't mean it that way"), but once we have handed in the final version of our writing, we are helpless. We are (putting it strongly) naked to our enemies.

Getting Ideas

In Chapter 1 we quoted Robert Frost, "To learn to write is to learn to have ideas," and we offered suggestions about getting ideas, a process traditionally called **invention.** A moment ago we said that we often improve our ideas when we try to explain them to someone else. Partly, of course, we are responding to questions or objections raised by our companion in the conversation. But partly we are responding to ourselves: Almost as soon as we hear what we have to say, we may find that it won't do, and, if we are lucky, we may find a better idea surfacing. One of the best ways of getting ideas is to talk things over.

The process of talking things over usually begins with the text that you are reading: Your marginal notes, your summary, and your queries parenthetically incorporated within your summary are a kind of dialogue between you and the author you are reading. More obviously, when you talk with friends about your topic, you are trying out and developing ideas. Finally, after reading, taking notes, and talking, you may feel that you now have clear ideas and need only put them into writing. And so you take a sheet of blank paper, and perhaps a paralyzing thought suddenly strikes: "I have ideas but just can't put them into words."

Despite what many people believe,

- Writing is not only a matter of putting one's ideas into words.
- Just as talking with others is a way of getting ideas, *writing is a way of getting and developing ideas.*

Writing, in short, can be an important part of critical thinking. One big reason we have trouble writing is our fear of putting ourselves on record, but another big reason is our fear that we have no ideas worth putting down. But by jotting down notes—or even free associations—and by writing a draft, however weak, we can help ourselves to think our way toward good ideas.

Freewriting   Writing for five or six minutes, nonstop, without censoring what you produce is one way of getting words down on paper that will help to lead to improved thoughts. Some people who write on a computer find it useful to dim the screen so they won't be tempted to look up and fiddle too soon with what they have just written. Later they illuminate the screen, scroll back, and notice some keywords or passages that can be used later in drafting a paper.

Listing   Jotting down items, just as you do when you make a shopping list, is another way of getting ideas. When you make a shopping list, you write *ketchup,* and the act of writing it reminds you that you also need hamburger rolls—and *that* in turn reminds you (who knows how or why?) that you also need a can of tuna fish. Similarly, when you prepare a list of ideas for a paper, jotting down one item will generate another. Of course, when you look over the list, you will probably drop some of these ideas—the dinner menu will change—but you are making progress.

Diagramming   Sketching some sort of visual representation of an essay is a kind of listing. Three methods of diagramming are especially common:

- **Clustering**   Write, in the middle of a sheet of paper, a word or phrase summarizing your topic (for instance, *health care;* see diagram, below), circle it, and then write down and circle a related word (for example, *gov't-provided*). Perhaps this leads you to write *higher taxes,* and you then circle this phrase and connect it to *gov't-provided.* The next thing that occurs to you is *employer-provided*— and so you write this down and circle it. You will not connect this to *higher taxes,* but you will connect it to *health care* because it is a sort of parallel to *gov't-provided.* The next thing that occurs to you is *unemployed people.* This category does not connect easily with *employer-provided,* so you won't connect these two terms with a line, but you probably will connect *unemployed people* with *health care* and maybe also with *gov't-provided.* Keep going, jotting down ideas, and making connections where possible, indicating relationships.
- **Branching**   Some writers find it useful to build a tree, moving from the central topic to the main branches (chief ideas) and then to the twigs (aspects of the chief ideas).
- **Comparing in columns**   Draw a line down the middle of the page, and then set up two columns showing oppositions. For instance, if you are concerned with health care, you might head one column *gov't-provided* and the other *employer-provided.* Under the first column, you might write *covers unemployed,* and under the second column, you might write *omits unemployed.* You might go on to write, under the first column, *higher taxes,* and under the second, *higher prices*—or whatever else relevant comes to mind.

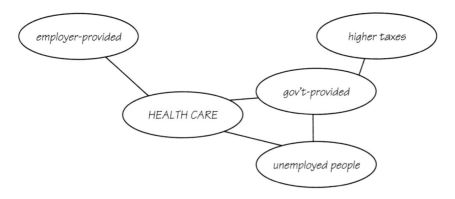

All of these methods can, of course, be executed with pen and paper, but you may also be able to use them on your computer depending on the capabilities of your software.

Whether you are using a computer or a pen, you put down some words and almost immediately see that they need improvement, not simply a little polishing but a substantial overhaul. You write, "Race should be counted in college admissions for two reasons," and as soon as you write these words, a third reason comes to mind. Or perhaps one of those "two reasons" no longer seems very good. As E. M. Forster said, "How can I know what I think till I see what I say?" We have to see what we say, we have to get something down on paper, before we realize that we need to make it better.

Writing, then, is really **rewriting**—that is, **revising**—and a revision is a *re-vision,* a second look. The paper that you hand in should be clear and may even seem effortless to the reader, but in all likelihood the clarity and apparent ease are the result of a struggle with yourself, a struggle during which you greatly improved your first thoughts. You begin by putting down your ideas, such as they are, perhaps even in the random order in which they occurred, but sooner or later comes the job of looking at them critically, developing what is useful in them and chucking out what is not. If you follow this procedure you will be in the company of Picasso, who said that he "advanced by means of destruction."

Whether you advance bit by bit (writing a sentence, revising it, writing the next, and so on) or whether you write an entire first draft and then revise it and revise it again and again is chiefly a matter of temperament. Probably most people combine both approaches, backing up occasionally but trying to get to the end fairly soon so that they can see rather quickly what they know, or think they know, and can then start the real work of thinking, of converting their initial ideas into something substantial.

Asking Questions   Getting ideas, we said when we talked about **topics** and **invention** strategies in Chapter 1 (p. 11) is mostly a matter of asking (and then thinking about) questions. We append questions to the end of each argumentative essay in this book, not to torment you but to help you to think about the arguments—for instance, to turn your attention to especially important matters. If your instructor asks you to write an answer to one of these questions, you are lucky: Examining the question will stimulate your mind to work in a definite direction.

If a topic is not assigned, and you are asked to write an argument, you will find that some ideas (possibly poor ones, at this stage, but that doesn't matter because you will soon revise) will come to mind if you ask yourself questions. You can begin finding where you stand on an issue (**stasis**) by asking the following five basic questions:

1. What is X?
2. What is the value of X?

3. What are the causes (or the consequences) of *X*?
4. What should (or ought or must) we do about *X*?
5. What is the evidence for my claims about *X*?

Let's spend a moment looking at each of these questions.

1. **What is *X*?** We can hardly argue about the number of people sentenced to death in the United States in 2000—a glance at the appropriate government report will give the answer—but we can argue about whether capital punishment as administered in the United States is discriminatory. Does the evidence, we can ask, support the view that in the United States the death penalty is unfair? Similarly, we can ask whether a human fetus is a human being (in saying what something is, must we take account of its potentiality?), and, even if we agree that a fetus is a human being, we can further ask about whether it is a person. In *Roe v. Wade* the U.S. Supreme Court ruled that even the "viable" unborn human fetus is not a "person" as that term is used in the Fifth and Fourteenth Amendments. Here the question is this: Is the essential fact about the fetus that it is a person?

An argument of this sort makes a claim—that is, it takes a stand, but notice that it does not also have to argue for an action. Thus, it may argue that the death penalty is administered unfairly—that's a big enough issue—but it need not go on to argue that the death penalty should be abolished. After all, another possibility is that the death penalty should be administered fairly. The writer of the essay may be doing enough if he or she establishes the truth of the claim and leaves to others the possible responses.

2. **What is the value of *X*?** College courses often call for literary judgments. No one can argue with you if you say you prefer the plays of Tennessee Williams to those of Arthur Miller. But academic papers are not mere declarations of preferences. As soon as you say that Williams is a better playwright than Miller, you have based your preference on implicit standards, and it is incumbent on you to support your preference by giving evidence about the relative skill, insight, and accomplishments of Williams and of Miller. Your argument is an evaluation. The question now at issue is the merits of the two authors and the standards appropriate for such an appraisal. (For a discussion of literary evaluations, see pp. 467–70.)

In short, an essay offering an evaluation normally has two purposes:

• To set forth an assessment, and
• To convince the reader that the assessment is reasonable.

In writing an evaluation, you will have to rely on criteria, and these will vary depending on your topic. For instance, if you are comparing the artistic merit of the plays by Williams and by Miller, you may want to talk about the quality of the characterization, the importance of the theme, and so on. But if the topic is "Which playwright is more suitable to be taught in high school?," other criteria may be appropriate, such as

- The difficulty of the author's language,
- The sexual content of some scenes, and
- The presence of obscene words.

Or consider a nonliterary issue: On balance, are college fraternities and sororities good or bad? If good, how good? If bad, how bad? What criteria can we use in making our evaluation? Probably some or all of the following:

- Testimony of authorities (for instance, persons who can offer first-hand testimony about the good or bad effects),
- Inductive evidence (we can collect examples of good or bad effects),
- Appeals to logic ("it follows, therefore, that . . ."), and
- Appeals to emotion (for instance, an appeal to our sense of fairness).

3. **What are the causes (or the consequences) of *X*?** Why did the rate of auto theft increase during a specific period? If we abolish the death penalty, will that cause the rate of murder to increase? Notice, by the way, that such problems may be complex. The phenomena that people usually argue about—say, such things as inflation, war, suicide, crime—have many causes, and it is therefore often a mistake to speak of *the* cause of *X*. A writer in *Time* mentioned that the life expectancy of an average American male is about sixty-seven years, a figure that compares unfavorably with the life expectancy of males in Japan and Israel. The *Time* writer suggested that an important cause of the relatively short life span is "the pressure to perform well in business." Perhaps. But the life expectancy of plumbers is no greater than that of managers and executives. Nutrition authority Jean Mayer, in an article in *Life*, attributed the relatively poor longevity of American males to a diet that is "rich in fat and poor in nutrients." Doubtless other authorities propose other causes, and in all likelihood no one cause accounts for the phenomenon.

What kinds of support usually accompany claims of cause?

- Factual data, especially statistics;
- Analogies ("The Roman Empire declined because of *X* and *Y*," "Our society exhibits *X* and *Y*, and therefore . . .");
- Inductive evidence.

4. **What should (or ought or must) we do about *X*?** Must we always obey the law? Should the law allow eighteen-year-olds to drink alcohol? Should eighteen-year-olds be drafted to do one year of social service? Should pornography be censored? Should steroid use by ath-

letes be banned? Ought there to be Good Samaritan laws, making it a legal duty for a stranger to intervene to save a person from death or great bodily harm, when one might do so with little or no risk to oneself? These questions involve conduct and policy; how we answer them will reveal our values and principles.

An essay answering questions of this sort usually

- Begins by explaining what the issue (the problem) is, then
- States why the reader should care about it, then
- Offers the proposed solution, then
- Considers alternative solutions, and finally
- Reaffirms the merit of the proposed solution, especially in the light of the audience's interests and needs.

Support for claims of policy usually include

- Statistics,
- Appeals to common sense and to the reader's moral sense, and
- Testimony of authorities.

5. **What is the evidence for my claims about *X*?** In commenting on the four previous topics, we have talked about the kinds of support that are commonly offered, but a few additional points can be made.

Critical reading, writing, and thinking depend essentially on identifying and evaluating the evidence for and against the claims one makes and encounters in the writings of others. It is not enough to have an *opinion* or belief one way or the other; you need to be able to support your opinions—the bare fact of your sincere belief in what you say or write is not itself any *evidence* that what you believe is true.

So what are good reasons for opinions, adequate evidence for one's beliefs? The answer, of course, depends on what kind of belief or opinion, assertion or hypothesis, claim or principle, you want to assert. For example, there is good evidence that President John F. Kennedy was assassinated on November 22, 1963, because this is the date for his death reported in standard almanacs. You could further substantiate the date by checking the back issues of the *New York Times.* But a different kind of evidence is needed to support the proposition that the chemical composition of water is H_2O. And you will need still other kinds of evidence to support your beliefs about the likelihood of rain tomorrow, the probability that the Red Sox will win the pennant this year, the twelfth digit in the decimal expansion of pi, the average cumulative grades of the graduating seniors over the past three years in your college, the relative merits of *Hamlet* and *Death of a Salesman,* and the moral dimensions of sexual harassment. None of these issues is merely a matter of opinion; yet on some of them, educated and informed people may disagree over the reasons and the evidence and what they show. Your job as a critical thinker is to be alert to the relevant reasons and evidence and to make the most of them as you present your views.

Again, an argument may take in two or more of these five issues. Someone who argues that pornography should (or should not) be censored will have to mark out the territory of the discussion by defining pornography (our first issue: What is X?). The argument probably will also need to examine the consequences of adopting the preferred policy (our third issue) and may even have to argue about its value (our second issue). Some people maintain that pornography produces crime, but others maintain that it provides a harmless outlet for impulses that otherwise might vent themselves in criminal behavior. Further, someone arguing about the wisdom of censoring pornography might have to face the objection that censorship, however desirable on account of some of its consequences, may be unconstitutional and that even if censorship were constitutional, it would (or might) have undesirable side effects, such as repressing freedom of political opinion. And one will always have to keep asking oneself the fifth question, What is the evidence for my claims?

Thinking about one or more of these questions may get you going. For instance, thinking about the first question, What is X?, will require you to produce a definition, and as you work at producing a satisfactory definition, you may find new ideas arising. If a question seems relevant, start writing, even if you write only a fragmentary sentence. You'll probably find that one word leads to another and that ideas begin to appear. Even if these ideas seem weak as you write them, don't be discouraged; you have put something on paper, and returning to these words, perhaps in five minutes or perhaps the next day, you will probably find that some are not at all bad and that others will stimulate you to better ones.

It may be useful to record your ideas in a special notebook reserved for the purpose. Such a **journal** can be a valuable resource when it comes time to write your paper. Many students find it easier to focus their thoughts on writing if during the period of gestation they have been jotting down relevant ideas on something more substantial than slips of paper or loose sheets. The very act of designating a notebook as your journal for a course can be the first step in focusing your attention on the eventual need to write a paper.

If what we have just said does not sound convincing, and you know from experience that you often have trouble getting started with your writing, don't despair; first aid is at hand in a sure-fire method that we will now explain.

The Thesis

Let's assume that you are writing an argumentative essay—perhaps an evaluation of an argument in this book—and you have what seems to be a pretty good draft or at least a bunch of notes that are the result of hard thinking. You really do have ideas now, and you want to present them effectively. How will you organize your essay? No one formula works best for every essayist and for every essay, but it is usually advisable to formulate a basic **thesis** (a claim, a central point, a chief position) and to state it early. Every essay that is any good, even a book-length one, has a thesis (a main point), which can be stated briefly, usually in a sentence. Remember Coolidge's remark on the preacher's sermon on sin: "He was against it." Don't confuse the **topic** (sin) with the thesis (sin is bad). The thesis is the argumentative theme, the author's primary claim or contention, the proposition that the rest of the essay will explain and defend. Of course, the thesis may sound commonplace, but the book or essay or sermon ought to develop it interestingly and convincingly.

Here are some sample theses:

- Smoking should be prohibited in all enclosed public places.
- Smoking should be limited to specific parts of enclosed public places and entirely prohibited in small spaces, such as elevators.
- Proprietors of public places such as restaurants and sports arenas should be free to determine whether they wish to prohibit, limit, or impose no limitations on smokers.

Imagining an Audience

Of course, the questions that you ask yourself to stimulate your thoughts will depend primarily on what you are writing about, but additional questions are always relevant:

- Who are my readers?
- What do they believe?
- What common ground do we share?
- What do I want my readers to believe?
- What do they need to know?
- Why should they care?

 A CHECKLIST FOR A THESIS STATEMENT

Consider the following questions:

☐ Does the statement make an arguable assertion rather than (a) merely assert an unarguable fact, (b) merely announce a topic, or (c) declare an unarguable opinion or belief?

☐ Is the statement broad enough to cover the entire argument that I will be presenting, and is it narrow enough for me to be able to cover the topic in the space allotted?

These questions require a little comment. The literal answer to the first probably is "my teacher," but (unless you are given instructions to the contrary) you should not write specifically for your teacher. Instead, you should write for an audience that is, generally speaking, like your classmates. In short, your imagined audience is literate, intelligent, and moderately well informed, but it does not know everything that you know, and it does not know your response to the problem that you are addressing.

The essays in this book are from many different sources, each with its own audience. An essay from the *New York Times* is addressed to the educated general reader; an essay from *Ms.* magazine is addressed to readers sympathetic to feminism. An essay from *Commonweal,* a Roman Catholic publication addressed to the nonspecialist, is likely to differ in point of view or tone from one in *Time,* even though both articles may advance approximately the same position. The writer of the article in *Commonweal* may, for example, effectively cite church fathers and distinguished Roman Catholic writers as authorities, whereas the writer of the *Time* article would probably cite few or even none of these figures because a non-Catholic audience might be unfamiliar with them or, even if familiar, might be unimpressed by their views.

The tone as well as the gist of the argument is in some degree shaped by the audience. For instance, popular journals, such as the *National Review* and *Ms.* magazine, are more likely to use ridicule than are journals chiefly addressed to, say, an academic audience.

The Audience as Collaborator

If you imagine an audience and keep asking yourself what this audience needs to be told and what it doesn't need to be told, you will find that material comes to mind, just as it comes to mind when a friend asks you what a film you saw was about, who was in it, and how you liked it.

Your readers do not have to be told that Thomas Jefferson was an American statesman in the early years of this country's history, but they do have to be told that Elizabeth Cady Stanton was a late-nineteenth-century American feminist. Why? You need to identify Stanton because it's your hunch that your classmates never heard of her, or even if they may have heard the name, they can't quite identify it. But what if your class has been assigned an essay by Stanton? In that case your imagined reader knows Stanton's name and knows at least a little about her, so you don't have to identify Stanton as an American of the nineteenth century. But you do still have to remind your reader about relevant aspects of her essay, and you do have to tell your reader about your responses to them.

After all, even if the instructor has assigned an essay by Stanton, you cannot assume that your classmates know the essay inside out. Obviously, you can't say, "Stanton's third reason is also unconvincing," without reminding the reader, by means of a brief summary, of her third reason. Again,

- Think of your classmates—people like you—as your imagined readers; and
- Be sure that your essay does not make unreasonable demands.

If you ask yourself,

- "What do my readers need to know?" and
- "What do I want them to believe?",

you will find some answers arising, and you will start writing.

We have said that you should imagine your audience as your classmates. But this is not the whole truth. In a sense, your argument is addressed not simply to your classmates but to the world interested in ideas. Even if you can reasonably assume that your classmates have read only one work by Stanton, you will not begin your essay by writing "Stanton's essay is deceptively easy." You will have to name the work; it is possible that a reader has read some other work by Stanton. And by precisely identifying your subject, you help to ease the reader into your essay.

Similarly, you won't begin by writing,

The majority opinion in <u>Walker v. City of Birmingham</u> held that . . .

Rather, you'll write something like this:

In <u>Walker v. City of Birmingham</u>, the U.S. Supreme Court ruled in 1966 that city authorities acted lawfully when they jailed Martin Luther King Jr. and other clergymen in 1963 for marching in Birmingham without a permit. Justice Potter Stewart delivered the majority opinion, which held that . . .

By the way, if you think you suffer from a writing block, the mere act of writing out such readily available facts will help you to get started. You will find that putting a few words down on paper, perhaps merely copying the essay's title or an interesting quotation from the essay, will stimulate you to jot down thoughts that you didn't know you had in you.

Here, again, are the questions about audience. If you write with a word processor, consider putting these questions into a file. For each assignment, copy (with the Copy command) the questions into the file you are currently working on, and then, as a way of generating ideas, *enter your responses, indented, under each question.*

- Who are my readers?
- What do they believe?
- What common ground do we share?

- What do I want my readers to believe?
- What do they need to know?
- Why should they care?

Thinking about your audience can help you to put some words on paper; even more important, it can help you to get ideas. Our second and third questions about the audience ("What do they believe?" and "How much common ground do we share?") will usually help you get ideas flowing.

- Presumably your imagined audience does not share your views, or at least does not fully share them. But why?
- How can these readers hold a position that to you seems unreasonable?

If you try to put yourself into your readers' shoes — and in your essay you will almost surely summarize the views that you are going to speak against — and if you think about what your audience knows or thinks it knows, you will find yourself getting ideas.

You do not believe (let's assume) that people should be allowed to smoke in enclosed public places, but you know that some people hold a different view. Why do they hold it? Try to state their view *in a way that would be satisfactory to them.* Having done so, you may come to perceive that your conclusions and theirs differ because they are based on different premises, perhaps different ideas about human rights. Examine the opposition's premises carefully, and explain, first to yourself and ultimately to your readers, why you find some premises unacceptable.

Possibly some facts are in dispute, such as whether nonsmokers may be harmed by exposure to tobacco. The thing to do, then, is to check the facts. If you find that harm to nonsmokers has not been proved, but you nevertheless believe that smoking should be prohibited in enclosed public places, of course you can't premise your argument on the wrongfulness of harming the innocent (in this case, the nonsmokers). You will have to develop arguments that take account of the facts, whatever they are.

Among the relevant facts there surely are some that your audience or your opponent will not dispute. The same is true of the values relevant to the discussion; the two of you are very likely to agree, if you stop to think about it, that you share belief in some of the same values (such as the principle mentioned above, that it is wrong to harm the innocent). These areas of shared agreement are crucial to effective persuasion in argument.

> **A RULE FOR WRITERS:** If you wish to persuade, you'll have to begin by finding premises you can share with your audience.

There are two good reasons why you should identify and isolate the areas of agreement:

- There is no point in disputing facts or values on which you and your readers really agree.

- It usually helps to establish goodwill between you and your opponent when you can point to beliefs, assumptions, facts, and values that the two of you share.

In a few moments we will return to the need to share some of the opposition's ideas.

Recall that in writing college papers it is usually best to write for a general audience, an audience rather like your classmates but without the specific knowledge that they all share as students enrolled in one course. If the topic is smoking in public places, the audience presumably consists of smokers and nonsmokers. Thinking about our fifth question on page 229 — "What do readers need to know?" — may prompt you to give statistics about the harmful effects of smoking. Or if you are arguing on behalf of smokers, it may prompt you to cite studies claiming that no evidence conclusively demonstrates that cigarette smoking is harmful to nonsmokers. If indeed you are writing for a general audience and you are not advancing a highly unfamiliar view, our second question ("What does the audience believe?") is less important here, but if the audience is specialized, such as an antismoking group, a group of restaurant owners who fear that antismoking regulations will interfere with their business,

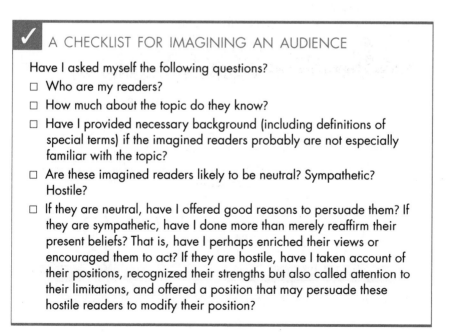

✓ A CHECKLIST FOR IMAGINING AN AUDIENCE

Have I asked myself the following questions?

☐ Who are my readers?

☐ How much about the topic do they know?

☐ Have I provided necessary background (including definitions of special terms) if the imagined readers probably are not especially familiar with the topic?

☐ Are these imagined readers likely to be neutral? Sympathetic? Hostile?

☐ If they are neutral, have I offered good reasons to persuade them? If they are sympathetic, have I done more than merely reaffirm their present beliefs? That is, have I perhaps enriched their views or encouraged them to act? If they are hostile, have I taken account of their positions, recognized their strengths but also called attention to their limitations, and offered a position that may persuade these hostile readers to modify their position?

or a group of civil libertarians, an effective essay will have to address their special beliefs.

In addressing their beliefs (let's assume that you do not share them or do not share them fully), you must try to establish some common ground. If you advocate requiring restaurants to provide nonsmoking areas, you should at least recognize the possibility that this arrangement will result in inconvenience for the proprietor. But perhaps (the good news) the restaurant will regain some lost customers or will attract some new customers. This thought should prompt you to think of kinds of evidence, perhaps testimony or statistics.

When you formulate a thesis and ask questions about it, such as who the readers are, what do they believe, what do they know, and what do they need to know, you begin to get ideas about how to organize the material or at least to see that some sort of organization will have to be worked out. The thesis may be clear and simple, but the reasons (the argument) may take many pages. The thesis is the point; the argument sets forth the evidence that is offered to support the thesis.

The Title

It's not a bad idea to announce your thesis in your **title.** If you scan the table of contents of this book, you will notice that a fair number of essayists use the title to let the readers know, at least in a very general way, what position will be advocated. Here are a few examples of titles that take a position:

Gay Marriages: Make Them Legal

"Diversity" Is a Smoke Screen for Discrimination

Why Handguns Must Be Outlawed

True, these titles are not especially engaging, but the reader welcomes them because they give some information about the writer's thesis.

Some titles do not announce the thesis, but they at least announce the topic:

CALVIN AND HOBBES. © 1993 Bill Watterson. Reprinted with permission of Universal Press Syndicate. All rights reserved.

Is All Discrimination Unfair?

On Racist Speech

Why Make Divorce Easy?

Although not clever or witty, these titles are informative.

Some titles seek to attract attention or to stimulate the imagination:

A First Amendment Junkie

A Crime of Compassion

Addicted to Health

All of these are effective, but a word of caution is appropriate here. In your effort to engage your reader's attention, be careful not to sound like a wise guy. You want to engage your readers, not turn them off.

Finally, be prepared to rethink your title *after* you have finished the last draft of your paper. A title somewhat different from your working title may be an improvement because the emphasis of your finished paper may have turned out to be rather different from what you expected when you first thought of a title.

The Opening Paragraphs

Opening paragraphs are difficult to write, so don't worry about writing an effective opening when you are drafting. Just get some words down on paper, and keep going. But when you revise your first draft—really a zero draft—you probably should begin to think seriously about the effect of your opening.

A good introduction arouses the reader's interest and helps prepare the reader for the rest of the paper. How? Opening paragraphs usually do at least one (and often all) of the following:

- Attract the reader's interest (often with a bold statement of the thesis or with an interesting statistic, quotation, or anecdote),
- Prepare the reader's mind by giving some idea of the topic and often of the thesis,
- Give the reader an idea of how the essay is organized, and
- Define a key term.

You may not wish to announce your thesis in your title, but if you don't announce it there, you should set it forth early in the argument, in your introductory paragraph or paragraphs. In her title "Human Rights and Foreign Policy," Jeanne J. Kirkpatrick merely announces her topic (subject) as opposed to her thesis (point), but she begins to hint at the thesis in her first paragraph, by deprecating President Jimmy Carter's policy:

> In this paper I deal with three broad subjects: first, the content and consequences of the Carter administration's human rights policy; second, the prerequisites of a more adequate theory of human rights; and third, some characteristics of a more successful human rights policy.

Or consider this opening paragraph from Peter Singer's "Animal Liberation" (p. 199):

> We are familiar with Black Liberation, Gay Liberation, and a variety of other movements. With Women's Liberation some thought we had come to the end of the road. Discrimination on the basis of sex, it has been said, is the last form of discrimination that is universally accepted and practiced without pretense, even in those liberal circles which have long prided themselves on their freedom from racial discrimination. But one should always be wary of talking of "the last remaining form of discrimination." If we have learned anything from the liberation movements, we should have learned how difficult it is to be aware of the ways in which we discriminate until they are forcefully pointed out to us. A liberation movement demands an expansion of our moral horizons, so that practices that were previously regarded as natural and inevitable are now seen as intolerable.

Although Singer's introductory paragraph nowhere mentions animal liberation, in conjunction with its title it gives us a good idea of what Singer is up to and where he is going. Singer knows that his audience will be skeptical, so he reminds them that many of us in previous years were skeptical of reforms that we now take for granted. He adopts a strategy used fairly often by writers who advance unconventional theses: Rather than beginning with a bold announcement of a thesis that may turn off some of his readers because it sounds offensive or absurd, Singer warms up his audience, gaining their interest by cautioning them politely that although they may at first be skeptical of animal liberation, if they stay with his essay they may come to feel that they have expanded their horizons.

Notice, too, that Singer begins by establishing common ground with his readers; he assumes, probably correctly, that they share his view that other forms of discrimination (now seen to be unjust) were once widely practiced and were assumed to be acceptable and natural. In this paragraph, then, Singer is not only showing himself to be fair-minded but is also letting us know that he will advance a daring idea. His opening wins our attention and our goodwill. A writer can hardly hope to do more. (In a few pages we will talk a little more about winning the audience.)

In your introductory paragraphs,

- You may have to give some background information that your readers will need to keep in mind if they are to follow your essay.

- You may wish to define some terms that are unfamiliar or that you use in an unusual sense.

> **A RULE FOR WRITERS:** In writing or at least in revising these paragraphs, keep in mind this question: What do my readers need to know? Remember, your aim throughout is to write *reader-friendly* prose, and keeping the needs and interests of your audience constantly in mind will help you achieve this goal.

After announcing the topic, giving the necessary background, and stating your position (and perhaps the opposition's) in as engaging a manner as possible, it is usually a good idea to give the reader an idea of *how* you will proceed—that is, what the organization will be. Look on page 236 at Kirkpatrick's opening paragraph for an obvious illustration. She tells us she will deal with three subjects, and she names them. Her approach in the paragraph is concise, obvious, and effective.

Similarly, you may, for instance, want to announce fairly early that there are four common objections to your thesis and that you will take them up one by one, beginning with the weakest (or most widely held, or whatever) and moving to the strongest (or least familiar), after which you will advance your own view in greater detail. Not every argument begins with refuting the other side, though many arguments do. The point to remember is that you usually ought to tell your readers where you will be taking them and by what route.

Organizing and Revising the Body of the Essay

We begin with a wise remark by a newspaper columnist, Robert Cromier: "The beautiful part of writing is that you don't have to get it right the first time—unlike, say, a brain surgeon."

In drafting your essay you will of course begin with an organization that seems to you to make sense, but you may well find, in rereading the draft, that some other organization is better. Here, for a start, is an organization that is common in argumentative essays.

1. Statement of the problem
2. Statement of the structure of the essay
3. Statement of alternative solutions
4. Arguments in support of the proposed solution
5. Arguments answering possible objections
6. A summary, resolution, or conclusion

Let's look at each of these six steps:

1. **Statement of the problem**   Whether the problem is stated briefly or at length depends on the nature of the problem and the writer's audience. If you haven't already defined unfamiliar terms or terms you use in a special way, probably now is the time to do so. In any case, it is advisable here to state the problem objectively

(thereby gaining the trust of the reader) and to indicate why the reader should care about the issue.

2. **Statement of the structure of the essay**   After stating the problem at the appropriate length, the writer often briefly indicates the structure of the rest of the essay. The commonest structure is suggested below, in points 3 and 4.

3. **Statement of alternative (but less adequate) solutions**   In addition to stating the alternatives fairly, the writer probably conveys willingness to recognize not only the integrity of the proposals but also the (partial) merit of at least some of the alternative solutions.

The point made in the previous sentence is important and worth amplifying. Because it is important to convey your goodwill—your sense of fairness—to the reader, it is advisable to let your reader see that you are familiar with the opposition and that you recognize the integrity of those who hold that view. This you do by granting its merits as far as you can. (For more about this approach, see the essay by Carl R. Rogers on p. 455.)

The next stage, which constitutes most of the body of the essay, usually is this:

4. **Arguments in support of the proposed solution**   The evidence offered will, of course, depend on the nature of the problem. Relevant statistics, authorities, examples, or analogies may come to mind or be available. This is usually the longest part of the essay.

5. **Arguments answering possible objections**   These arguments may suggest that
   a. The proposal won't work (perhaps it is alleged to be too expensive, to make unrealistic demands on human nature, or to fail to get to the heart of the problem).
   b. The proposed solution will create problems greater than the difficulty to be resolved. (A good example of a proposal that produced dreadful unexpected results is the law mandating a prison term for anyone over eighteen in possession of an illegal drug. Heroin dealers then began to use children as runners, and cocaine importers followed the practice. And while we are on the subject of children, consider this: Five states have statutes that allow the death penalty for adults who molest children. A chief argument *against* this penalty is that the molesters, having nothing further to lose, may kill their victims. A second argument is that victims of sex crimes by family members may be less likely to report the crimes. In your view, how valid are these arguments about unintended consequences? You can see examples of the importance of answering possible objections to an argument in Martin Luther King Jr.'s "Letter from Birmingham Jail" (p. 910), where he says such things as "You may well ask," and "Some have asked.")

6. **A summary, resolution, or conclusion** Here the writer may seek to accommodate the views of the opposition as far as possible but clearly suggest that the writer's own position makes good sense. A conclusion—the word comes from the Latin *claudere*, "to shut"—ought to provide a sense of closure, but it can be much more than a restatement of the writer's thesis. It can, for instance, make a quiet emotional appeal by suggesting that the issue is important and that the ball is now in the reader's court.

Of course not every essay will follow this six-step pattern, but let's assume that in the introductory paragraphs you have sketched the topic (and have shown or nicely said, or implied, that the reader doubtless is interested in it) and have fairly and courteously set forth the opposition's view, recognizing its merits ("I grant that," "admittedly," "it is true that") and indicating the degree to which you can share part of that view. You now want to set forth your arguments explaining why you differ on some essentials.

In setting forth your own position, you can begin either with your strongest reasons or your weakest. Each method of organization has advantages and disadvantages.

- If you begin with your strongest, the essay may seem to peter out.
- If you begin with the weakest, you build to a climax, but your readers may not still be with you because they may have felt at the start that the essay was frivolous.

The solution to this last possibility is to make sure that even your weakest argument is an argument of some strength. You can, moreover, assure your readers that stronger points will soon be offered and you offer this point first only because you want to show that you are aware of it and that, slight though it is, it deserves some attention. The body of the essay, then, is devoted to arguing a position, which means offering not only supporting reasons but also refutations of possible objections to these reasons.

Doubtless you will sometimes be uncertain, as you draft your essay, whether to present a given point before or after another point. When you write, and certainly when you revise, try to put yourself into your reader's shoes: Which point do you think the reader needs to know first? Which point *leads to* which further point? Your argument should not be a mere list of points, of course; rather, it should clearly integrate one point with another in order to develop an idea. But in all likelihood you won't have a strong sense of the best organization until you have written a draft and have reread it.

> **A RULE FOR WRITERS:** When you revise, make sure that your organization is clear to your readers.

Checking Paragraphs   When you revise your draft, watch out also for short paragraphs. Although a paragraph of only two or three sentences (like some in this chapter) may occasionally be helpful as a transition between complicated points, most short paragraphs are undeveloped paragraphs. (Newspaper editors favor very short paragraphs because they can be read rapidly when printed in the narrow columns typical of newspapers. Many of the essays reprinted in this book originally were published in newspapers, hence they consist of very short paragraphs. There is no reason for you to imitate this style in the argumentative essays you will be writing.)

In revising, when you find a paragraph of only a sentence or two or three, check first to see if it should be joined to the paragraph that precedes or follows. Second, if on rereading you are certain that a given paragraph should not be tied to what comes before or after, think about amplifying the paragraph with supporting detail (this is not the same as mere padding).

Checking Transitions   Make sure, too, in revising, that the reader can move easily from the beginning of a paragraph to the end and from one paragraph to the next. Transitions help the reader to perceive the connections between the units of the argument. For example ("For example" is a transition, of course, indicating that an illustration will follow), they may

- **Illustrate:** *for example, for instance, consider this case;*
- **Establish a sequence:** *a more important objection, a stronger example, the best reason;*
- **Connect logically:** *thus, as a result, therefore, so, it follows;*
- **Amplify:** *further, in addition to, moreover;*
- **Compare:** *similarly, in like manner, just as, analogously;*
- **Contrast:** *on the other hand, in contrast, however, but;*
- **Summarize:** *in short, briefly;* or
- **Concede:** *admittedly, granted, to be sure.*

Expressions such as these serve as guideposts that enable your reader to move easily through your essay.

When writers revise an early draft, they chiefly

- **Unify** the essay by eliminating irrelevancies;
- **Organize** the essay by keeping in mind an imagined audience;
- **Clarify** the essay by fleshing out thin paragraphs, by making certain that the transitions are adequate, and by making certain that generalizations are adequately supported by concrete details and examples.

We are not talking about polish or elegance; we are talking about fundamental matters. Be especially careful not to abuse the logical connectives (*thus, as a result,* and so on). If you write several sentences followed by *therefore* or a similar word or phrase, be sure that what you write after the *therefore* really *does follow* from what has gone before. Logical connectives are not mere transitional devices used to link disconnected bits of prose. They are supposed to mark a real movement of thought — the essence of an argument.

The Ending

What about concluding paragraphs, in which you try to summarize the main points and reaffirm your position?

If you can look back over your essay and can add something that enriches it and at the same time wraps it up, fine, but don't feel compelled to say, "Thus, in conclusion, I have argued X, Y, and Z, and I have refuted Jones." After all, *conclusion* can have two meanings: (1) ending, or finish, as the ending of a joke or a novel; or (2) judgment or decision reached after deliberation. Your essay should finish effectively (the first sense), but it need not announce a judgment (the second).

If the essay is fairly short, so that a reader can more or less keep the whole thing in mind, you may not need to restate your view. Just make sure that you have covered the ground and that your last sentence is a good one. Notice that the student essay printed later in this chapter (p. 253) does not end with a formal conclusion, though it ends conclusively, with a note of finality.

By a note of finality we do *not* mean a triumphant crowing. It's usually far better to end with the suggestion that you hope you have by now indicated why those who hold a different view may want to modify it and accept yours.

If you study the essays in this book, or, for that matter, the editorials and op-ed pieces in a newspaper, you will notice that writers often provide a sense of closure by using one of the following devices:

- A return to something in the introduction,
- A glance at the wider implications of the issue (for example, if smoking is restricted, other liberties are threatened),
- An anecdote that engagingly illustrates the thesis, or
- A brief summary (but this sort of ending may seem unnecessary and even tedious, especially if the paper is short and if the summary merely repeats what has already been said).

> **A RULE FOR WRITERS:** Emulate John Kenneth Galbraith, a distinguished writer on economics. Galbraith said that in his fifth draft he introduced the note of spontaneity for which his writing was famous.

Two Uses of an Outline

The Outline as a Preliminary Guide   Some writers find it useful to sketch an **outline** as soon as they think they know what they want to say, even before they write a first draft. This procedure can be helpful in planning a tentative organization, but remember that in revising a draft new ideas will arise, and the outline may have to be modified. A preliminary outline is chiefly useful as a means of getting going, not as a guide to the final essay.

The Outline as a Way of Checking a Draft   Whether or not you use a preliminary outline, we strongly suggest that after you have written what you hope is your last draft, you make an outline of it; there is no better way of finding out whether the essay is well organized.

Go through the draft and jot down the chief points in the order in which you make them. That is, prepare a table of contents—perhaps a phrase for each paragraph. Next, examine your jottings to see what kind of sequence they reveal in your paper:

- Is the sequence reasonable? Can it be improved?
- Are any passages irrelevant?
- Does something important seem to be missing?

If no coherent structure or reasonable sequence clearly appears in the outline, then the full prose version of your argument probably doesn't have any either. Therefore, produce another draft, moving things around, adding or subtracting paragraphs—cutting and pasting into a new sequence, with transitions as needed—and then make another outline to see if the sequence now is satisfactory.

You are probably familiar with the structure known as a **formal outline.** Major points are indicated by I, II, III; points within major points are indicated by A, B, C; divisions within A, B, C are indicated by 1, 2, 3; and so on. Thus,

   I. Arguments for opening all Olympic sports to professionals
      A. Fairness
         1. Some Olympic sports are already open to professionals.
         2. Some athletes who really are not professionals are classified as professionals.
      B. Quality (achievements would be higher)

You may want to outline your draft according to this principle, or it may be enough if you simply jot down a phrase for each paragraph and indent the subdivisions. But keep these points in mind:

- It is not enough for the parts to be ordered reasonably.
- The order must be made clear to the reader, probably by means of transitions such as *for instance, on the other hand, we can now turn to an opposing view,* and so on.

Here is another way of thinking about an outline. For each paragraph, jot down

- What the paragraph *says*, and
- What the paragraph *does*.

An opening paragraph might be outlined thus:

- What the paragraph *says* is that the writer's thesis is that the words "under God" in the Pledge of Allegiance should be omitted.
- What the paragraph *does* is, first, it informs the reader of the thesis, and second, it *provides some necessary background*, for instance, that the words were not in the original wording of the Pledge.

A dual outline of this sort will help you to see whether you have a final draft or a draft that needs refinement.

Tone and the Writer's Persona

Although this book is chiefly about argument in the sense of rational discourse—the presentation of reasons in support of a thesis or conclusion—the appeal to reason is only one form of persuasion. Another form is the appeal to emotion—to pity, for example. Aristotle saw, in addition to the appeal to reason and the appeal to emotion, a third form of persuasion, the appeal to the character of the speaker. He called it the **ethical appeal** (the Greek word for this kind of appeal is **ethos,** "character"). The idea is that effective speakers convey the suggestion that they are

- Informed,
- Intelligent,
- Benevolent, and
- Honest.

Because they are perceived as trustworthy, their words inspire confidence in their listeners. It is, of course, a fact that when we read an argument we are often aware of the *person* or *voice* behind the words, and our assent to the argument depends partly on the extent to which we can share the speaker's assumptions, look at the matter from the speaker's point of view—in short, *identify* with this speaker.

How can a writer inspire the confidence that lets readers identify themselves with the writer? To begin with, the writer should possess the virtues Aristotle specified: intelligence or good sense, honesty, and benevolence or goodwill. As the Roman proverb puts it, "No one gives what he does not have." Still, possession of these qualities is not a guarantee that you will convey them in your writing. Like all other writers, you will have to revise your drafts so that these qualities become apparent, or, stated more moderately, you will have to revise so that nothing in the essay causes a reader to doubt your intelligence, honesty, and goodwill.

A blunder in logic, a misleading quotation, a snide remark, even an error in spelling—all such slips can cause readers to withdraw their sympathy from the writer.

But of course all good argumentative essays do not sound exactly alike; they do not all reveal the same speaker. Each writer develops his or her own voice or (as literary critics and teachers call it) **persona.** In fact, one writer will have several voices or personae, depending on the topic and the audience. The president of the United States delivering an address on the State of the Union has one persona; chatting with a reporter at his summer home he has another. This change is not a matter of hypocrisy. Different circumstances call for different language. As a French writer put it, there is a time to speak of "Paris" and a time to speak of "the capital of the nation." When Lincoln spoke at Gettysburg, he didn't say "Eighty-seven years ago," but "Four score and seven years ago." We might say that just as some occasions required him to be the folksy Honest Abe, the occasion of the dedication of hallowed ground required him to be formal and solemn, and so the president of the United States appropriately used biblical language. The election campaigns called for one persona, and the dedication of a military cemetery called for a different persona.

> **A RULE FOR WRITERS:** Present yourself so that your readers see you as knowledgeable, honest, open-minded, and interested in helping them to think about an issue of significance.

When we talk about a writer's persona, we mean the way in which the writer presents his or her attitudes

- Toward *the self,*
- Toward *the audience,* and
- Toward *the subject.*

Thus, if a writer says,

> I have thought long and hard about this subject, and I can say with assurance that . . .

we may feel that we are listening to a self-satisfied ass who probably is simply mouthing other people's opinions. Certainly he is mouthing clichés: "long and hard," "say with assurance."

Let's look at a slightly subtler example of an utterance that reveals an attitude. When we read that

> President Nixon was hounded out of office by journalists,

we hear a respectful attitude toward Nixon ("President Nixon") and a hostile attitude toward the press (they are beasts, curs who "hounded" our elected leader). If the writer's attitudes were reversed, she might have said something like this:

> The press turned the searchlight on Tricky Dick's criminal shenanigans.

"Tricky Dick" and "criminal" are obvious enough, but notice that "shenanigans" also implies the writer's contempt for Nixon, and of course, "turned the searchlight" suggests that the press is a source of illumination, a source of truth. The original version and the opposite version both say that the press was responsible for Nixon's resignation, but the original version ("President Nixon was hounded") conveys indignation toward journalists, whereas the revision conveys contempt for Nixon.

These two versions suggest two speakers who differ not only in their view of Nixon but also in their manner, including the seriousness with which they take themselves. Although the passage is very short, it seems to us that the first speaker conveys righteous indignation ("hounded"), whereas the second conveys amused contempt ("shenanigans"). To our ears the tone, as well as the point, differs in the two versions.

We are talking about **loaded words,** words that convey the writer's attitude and that by their connotations are meant to win the reader to the writer's side. Compare the words in the left-hand column with those in the right:

freedom fighter	terrorist
pro-choice	pro-abortion
pro-life	antichoice
economic refugee	illegal alien
terrorist-surveillance	domestic spying

The words in the left-hand column sound like good things; speakers who use these words are seeking to establish themselves as virtuous people who are supporting worthy causes. The **connotations** (associations, overtones) of these pairs of words differ, even though the **denotations** (explicit meanings, dictionary definitions) are the same, just as the connotations of *mother* and *female parent* differ, although the denotations are the same. Similarly, although Lincoln's "four score and seven" and "eighty-seven" both denote "thirteen less than one hundred," they differ in connotation.

Tone is not only a matter of connotations (*hounded out of office* versus, let's say, *compelled to resign*, or *pro-choice* versus *pro-abortion*); it is also a matter of such things as the selection and type of examples. A writer who offers many examples, especially ones drawn from ordinary life, conveys a persona different from that of a writer who offers no examples or only an occasional invented instance. The first of these probably is, one might say, friendlier, more down-to-earth.

Last Words on Tone   On the whole, when writing an argument, it is advisable to be courteous and respectful of your topic, of your audience, and of people who hold views you are arguing against. It is rarely good for one's own intellectual development to regard as villains or fools persons who hold views different from one's own, especially if some of them are in the audience. Keep in mind the story of the two strangers on a train who, striking up a conversation, found that both were clergymen, though of different faiths. Then one said to the other, "Well, why shouldn't we be friends? After all, we both serve God, you in your way and I in His."

Complacency is all right when telling a joke but not when offering an argument:

- Recognize opposing views.
- Assume they are held in good faith.
- State them fairly (if you don't, you do a disservice not only to the opposition but also to your own position because the perceptive reader will not take you seriously).
- Be temperate in arguing your own position: "If I understand their view correctly . . ."; "It seems reasonable to conclude that . . ."; "Perhaps, then, we can agree that . . ."

We, One, or I?

The use of *we* in the last sentence brings us to another point: May the first-person pronouns *I* and *we* be used? In this book, because two of us are writing, we often use *we* to mean the two authors. And we sometimes use *we* to mean the authors and the readers, as in phrases like the one that ends the previous paragraph. This shifting use of one word can be troublesome, but we hope (clearly the *we* here refers only to the authors) that we have avoided any ambiguity. But can, or should, or must, an individual use *we* instead of *I*? The short answer is no.

If you are simply speaking for yourself, use *I*. Attempts to avoid the first-person singular by saying things like "This writer thinks . . . ," and "It is thought that . . . ," and "One thinks that . . . ," are far more irritating (and wordy) than the use of *I*. The so-called editorial *we* is as odd-sounding in a student's argument as is the royal *we*. Mark Twain said that the only ones who can appropriately say *we* are kings, editors, and people with a tapeworm. And because one *one* leads to another, making the sentence sound (James Thurber's words) "like a trombone solo," it's best to admit that you are the author, and to use *I*. But there is no need to preface every sentence with "I think." The reader knows that the essay is yours; just write it, using *I* when you must, but not needlessly.

Avoiding Sexist Language

Courtesy as well as common sense requires that you respect the feelings of your readers. Many people today find offensive the implicit sexism in the use of male pronouns to denote not only men but also women ("As the reader follows the argument, he will find . . ."). And sometimes the use of the male pronoun to denote all people is ridiculous: "An individual, no matter what his sex, . . ."

In most contexts there is no need to use gender-specific nouns or pronouns. One way to avoid using *he* when you mean any person is to use *he or she* (or *she or he*) instead of *he*, but the result is sometimes a bit cumbersome — although it is superior to the overly conspicuous *he/she* and to *s/he*.

Here are two simple ways to solve the problem:

- *Use the plural* ("As readers follow the argument, they will find . . ."), or

- *Recast the sentence* so that no pronoun is required ("Readers following the argument will find . . .").

✓ A CHECKLIST FOR ATTENDING TO THE NEEDS OF THE AUDIENCE

☐ Do I have a sense of what the audience probably knows about the issue?

☐ Do I have a sense of what the audience probably thinks about the issue?

☐ Have I stated the thesis clearly and sufficiently early in the essay?

☐ How much common ground do we probably share?

☐ Have I, in the paper, tried to establish common ground and then moved on to advance my position?

☐ Have I supported my arguments with sufficient details?

☐ Have I used the appropriate language (for instance, defined terms that are likely to be unfamiliar)?

☐ Have I indicated *why* my readers should care about the issue and should accept or at least take seriously my views?

☐ Is the organization clear?

☐ Have I used transitions where they are needed?

☐ If visual material (charts, graphs, pictures) will enhance my arguments, have I used them?

☐ Have I presented myself as a person who is (a) fair, (b) informed, and (c) worth listening to?

Because *man* and *mankind* strike many readers as sexist when used in such expressions as "Man is a rational animal" and "Mankind has not yet solved this problem," consider using such words as *human being, person, people, humanity,* and *we. (Examples:* "Human beings are rational animals"; "We have not yet solved this problem.")

PEER REVIEW

Your instructor may suggest—or may even require—that you submit an early draft of your essay to a fellow student or small group of students for comment. Such a procedure benefits both author and readers: You get the responses of a reader and the student-reader gets experience in thinking about the problems of developing an argument, especially in thinking about such matters as the degree of detail that a writer needs to offer to a reader and the importance of keeping the organization evident to a reader.

Oral peer reviews allow for the give and take of discussion, but probably most students and most instructors find written peer reviews more helpful because reviewers think more carefully about their responses to the draft, and they help essayists to get beyond a knee-jerk response to criticism. Online reviews on a class Web site or through e-mail are especially helpful precisely because they are not face to face; the peer reviewer gets practice *writing,* and the essayist is not directly challenged.

A STUDENT'S ESSAY, FROM ROUGH NOTES TO FINAL VERSION

While we were revising this textbook, we asked the students in one of our classes to write a short essay (500–750 words) on some ethical problem that concerned them. Because this assignment was the first writing assignment in the course, we explained that a good way to get ideas is to ask oneself some questions, jot down responses, question those responses, and write freely for ten minutes or so, not worrying about contradictions. We invited our students to hand in their initial jottings along with the finished essay, so that we could get a sense of how they proceeded as writers. Not all of them chose to hand in their jottings, but we were greatly encouraged by those who did. What was encouraging was the confirmation of an old belief, the belief—we call it a fact—that students will hand in a thoughtful essay if before they prepare a final version they nag themselves, ask themselves *why* they think this or that, jot down their responses, and are not afraid to change their minds as they proceed.

A PEER REVIEW CHECKLIST FOR A DRAFT
OF AN ARGUMENT

Read the draft through quickly. Then read it again, with the following
questions in mind. Remember: You are reading a draft, a work in
progress. You are expected to offer suggestions, and it is also expected
that you will offer them courteously.

☐ Does the draft show promise of fulfilling the assignment?

☐ Is the writer's tone appropriate?

☐ Looking at the essay as a whole, what thesis (main idea) is
advanced?

☐ Are the needs of the audience kept in mind? For instance, do
some words need to be defined? Is the evidence (for instance,
the examples and the testimony of authorities) clear and
effective?

☐ Can I accept the assumptions? If not, why not?

☐ Is any obvious evidence (or counterevidence) overlooked?

☐ Is the writer proposing a solution? If so,

   ☐ Are other equally attractive solutions adequately examined?

   ☐ Has the writer overlooked some unattractive effects of the
proposed solution?

☐ Looking at each paragraph separately,

   ☐ What is the basic point?

   ☐ How does each paragraph relate to the essay's main idea or
to the previous paragraph?

   ☐ Should some paragraphs be deleted? Be divided into two or
more paragraphs? Be combined? Be put elsewhere? (If you outline
the essay by jotting down the gist of each paragraph,
you will get help in answering these questions.)

   ☐ Is each sentence clearly related to the sentence that precedes
and to the sentence that follows?

   ☐ Is each paragraph adequately developed? Are there sufficient
details, perhaps brief supporting quotations from the text?

   ☐ Are the introductory and concluding paragraphs effective?

☐ What are the paper's chief strengths?

☐ Make at least two specific suggestions that you think will assist the
author to improve the paper.

Here are the first jottings of a student, Emily Andrews, who elected to write about whether to give money to street beggars. She simply put down ideas, one after the other.

Help the poor? Why do I (sometimes) do it?

I feel guilty, and think I should help them: poor, cold, hungry (but also some of them are thirsty for liquor, and will spend the money on liquor, not on food).

I also feel annoyed by them--most of them:

Where does the expression "the deserving poor" come from?

And "poor but honest"? Actually, that sounds a bit odd. Wouldn't "rich but honest" make more sense?

Why don't they work? Fellow with red beard, always by bus stop in front of florist's shop, always wants a handout. He is a regular, there all day every day, so I guess he is in a way "reliable," so why doesn't he put the same time in on a job?

Or why don't they get help? Don't they know they need it? They <u>must</u> know they need it.

Maybe that guy with the beard is just a con artist. Maybe he makes more money by panhandling than he would by working, and it's a lot easier!

Kinds of poor--how to classify??
    drunks, druggies, etc.
    mentally ill (maybe drunks belong here too)
    decent people who have had terrible luck

Why private charity?

Doesn't it make sense to say we (fortunate individuals) should give some-thing--an occasional handout--to people who have had terrible luck? (I suppose some people might say that there is no need for any of us to give anything--the government takes care of the truly needy--but I <u>do</u> believe in giving charity. A month ago a friend of the family passed away, and the woman's children suggested that people might want to make a donation in her name, to a shelter for battered women. I know my parents made a donation.)

BUT how can I tell who is who, which are which? Which of these people asking for "spare change" really need (deserve???) help, and which are phonies? Impossible to tell.

Possibilities:
>   Give to no one
>   Give to no one but make an annual donation, maybe to United Way
>   Give a dollar to each person who asks. This would probably not cost me even a dollar a day
>   Occasionally do without something--maybe a CD--or a meal in a restaurant--and give the money I save to people who seem worthy.

WORTHY? What am I saying? How can I, or anyone, tell? The neat-looking guy who says he just lost his job may be a phony, and the dirty bum-- probably a drunk--may desperately need food. (OK, so what if he spends the money on liquor instead of food? At least he'll get a little pleasure in life. No! It's not all right if he spends it on drink.)

Other possibilities:
>   Do some volunteer work?
>   To tell the truth, I don't want to put in the time. I don't feel <u>that</u> guilty.

So what's the problem?

Is it, How I can help the very poor (handouts, or through an organization)? or

How I can feel less guilty about being lucky enough to be able to go to college, and to have a supportive family?

I can't quite bring myself to believe I should help every beggar who approaches, but I also can't bring myself to believe that I should do nothing, on the grounds that:
>   a. it's probably their fault
>   b. if they are deserving, they can get gov't help. No, I just can't believe that. Maybe some are too proud to look for government help, or don't know that they are entitled to it.

What to do?

On balance, it seems best to

    a. give to United Way

    b. maybe also give to an occasional individual, if I happen to be moved, without worrying about whether he or she is "deserving" (since it's probably impossible to know).

A day after making these notes Emily reviewed them, added a few points, and then made a very brief selection from them to serve as an outline for her first draft:

Opening para.: "poor but honest"? Deserve "spare change"?

Charity: private or through organizations?

    pros and cons

    guy at bus

    it wouldn't cost me much, but . . . better to give through organizations

Concluding para.: still feel guilty?

    maybe mention guy at bus again?

After writing and revising a draft, Emily Andrews submitted her essay to a fellow student for peer review. She then revised her work in light of the suggestions she received and in light of her own further thinking.

On the next page we give the final essay. If after reading the final version you reread the early jottings, you will notice that some of the jottings never made it into the final version. But without the jottings, the essay probably could not have been as interesting as it is. When the writer made the jottings, she was not so much putting down her ideas as *finding* ideas by the process of writing.

Emily Andrews

Professor Barnet

English 102

January 16, 2007

Why I Don't Spare "Spare Change"

"Poor but honest." "The deserving poor." I don't know the
origin of these quotations, but they always come to mind when I
think of "the poor." But I also think of people who, perhaps through
alcohol or drugs, have ruined not only their own lives but also the
lives of others in order to indulge in their own pleasure. Perhaps
alcoholism and drug addiction really are "diseases," as many people
say, but my own feeling--based, of course, not on any serious study--
is that most alcoholics and drug addicts can be classified with the
"undeserving poor." And that is largely why I don't distribute spare
change to panhandlers.

But surely among the street people there are also some who
can rightly be called "deserving." Deserving what? My spare change?
Or simply the government's assistance? It happens that I have been
brought up to believe that it is appropriate to make contributions to
charity--let's say a shelter for battered women--but if I give some
change to a panhandler, am I making a contribution to charity and
thereby helping someone, or, on the contrary, am I perhaps simply
encouraging someone not to get help? Or maybe even worse, am I
supporting a con artist?

If one believes in the value of private charity, one can give
either to needy individuals or to charitable organizations. In giving to
a panhandler one may indeed be helping a person who badly needs
help, but one cannot be certain that one is giving to a needy
individual. In giving to an organization such as the United Way, on
the other hand, one can feel that one's money is likely to be used
wisely. True, confronted by a beggar one may feel that this particular

Andrews 2

unfortunate individual needs help at this moment--a cup of coffee or
a sandwich--and the need will not be met unless I put my hand in my
pocket right now. But I have come to think that the beggars whom
I encounter can get along without my spare change, and indeed
perhaps they are actually better off for not having money to buy
liquor or drugs.

It happens that in my neighborhood I encounter few
panhandlers. There is one fellow who is always by the bus stop where I
catch the bus to the college, and I never give him anything precisely
because he is always there. He is such a regular that, I think, he ought
to be able to hold a regular job. Putting him aside, I probably don't
encounter more than three or four beggars in a week. (I'm not
counting street musicians. These people seem quite able to work for a
living. If they see their "work" as playing or singing, let persons who
enjoy their performances pay them. I do not consider myself among
their audience.) The truth of the matter is that, since I meet so few
beggars, I could give each one a dollar and hardly feel the loss. At
most, I might go without seeing a movie some week. But I know
nothing about these people, and it's my impression--admittedly based
on almost no evidence--that they simply prefer begging to working. I
am not generalizing about street people, and certainly I am not talking
about street people in the big urban centers. I am talking only about
the people whom I actually encounter.

That's why I usually do not give "spare change," and I don't
think I will in the future. These people will get along without me.
Someone else will come up with money for their coffee or their liquor, or,
at worst, they will just have to do without. I will continue to contribute
occasionally to a charitable organization, not simply (I hope) to salve
my conscience but because I believe that these organizations actually do
good work. But I will not attempt to be a mini-charitable organization,
distributing (probably to the unworthy) spare change.

THE ESSAY ANALYZED

Finally, here are a few comments about the essay:

- *The title is informative,* alerting the reader to the topic and the author's position. (By the way, the student told us that in her next-to-last draft the title was "Is It Right to Spare 'Spare Change'?" This title, like the revision, introduces the topic but not the author's position. The revised version seems to us to be more striking.)
- *The opening paragraph holds a reader's interest,* partly by alluding to the familiar phrase "the deserving poor" and partly by introducing the *un*familiar phrase "the *un*deserving poor." Notice, too, that this opening paragraph ends by clearly asserting the author's thesis. Of course, writers need not always announce their thesis early, but it is usually advisable to do so. Readers like to know where they are going.
- *The second paragraph* begins by voicing what probably is the reader's somewhat uneasy—perhaps even negative—response to the first paragraph. That is, *the writer has a sense of her audience;* she knows how her reader feels, and she takes account of the feeling.
- *The third paragraph clearly sets forth the alternatives.* A reader may disagree with the writer's attitude, but the alternatives seem to be stated fairly.
- *The last two paragraphs are more personal* than the earlier paragraphs. The writer, more or less having stated what she takes to be the facts, now is entitled to offer a highly personal response to them.
- *The final paragraph nicely wraps things up* by means of the words "spare change," which go back to the title and to the end of the first paragraph. The reader thus experiences a sensation of completeness. The essayist, of course, has not solved the problem for all of us for all time, but she presents a thoughtful argument and ends the essay effectively.

EXERCISE

In an essay of 500 words, state a claim and support it with evidence. Choose an issue in which you are genuinely interested and about which you already know something. You may want to interview a few experts and do some reading, but don't try to write a highly researched paper. Sample topics:

1. Students in laboratory courses should not be required to participate in the dissection of animals.
2. Washington, D.C., should be granted statehood.
3. Puerto Rico should be granted statehood.

4. Women should, in wartime, be exempted from serving in combat.
5. The annual Miss America contest is an insult to women.
6. The government should not offer financial support to the arts.
7. The chief fault of the curriculum in high school was . . .
8. Grades should be abolished in college and university courses.
9. No specific courses should be required in colleges or universities.

7

Using Sources

Research is formalized curiosity. It is poking and prying with a purpose.
——ZORA NEALE HURSTON

Life-transforming ideas have always come to me through books.
——BELL HOOKS

If you have knowledge, let others light their candles at it.
——MARGARET FULLER

A problem adequately stated is a problem on its way to being solved.
——R. BUCKMINSTER FULLER

*I have yet to see any problem, however complicated, which, when you
looked at it in the right way, did not become still more complicated.*
——POUL ANDERSON

WHY USE SOURCES?

We have pointed out that one gets ideas by writing. In the exercise of writing a draft, ideas begin to form, and these ideas stimulate further ideas, especially when one questions—when one *thinks* about—what one has written. But of course in writing about complex, serious questions, nobody is expected to invent all the answers. On the contrary, a writer is expected to be familiar with the chief answers already produced by others and to make use of them through selective incorporation and criticism. In short, writers are not expected to reinvent the wheel; rather, they are expected to make good use of it and perhaps round it off a bit or replace a defective spoke. In order to think out your own views in writing, you are expected to do some preliminary research into the views of others.

We use the word *research* broadly. It need not require taking copious notes on everything written on your topic; rather, it can involve no more than familiarizing yourself with at least some of the chief responses to your topic. In one way or another, almost everyone does some research. If we are going to buy a car, we may read an issue or two of a magazine or visit a Web site that rates cars, or we may talk to a few people who own models that we are thinking of buying, and then we visit a couple of dealers to find out who is offering the best price.

Research, in short, is not an activity conducted only by college professors or by students who visit the library in order to write research papers. It is an activity that all of us engage in to some degree. In writing a research paper, you will engage in it to a great degree. But doing research is not the whole of a research paper. The reader expects the writer to have *thought* about the research and to develop an argument based on the findings. Many businesses today devote an entire division to research and development. That's what is needed in writing, too. The reader wants not only a lot of facts but also a developed idea, a point to which the facts lead. Don't let your reader say of your paper what Gertrude Stein said of her hometown, Oakland, California: "When you get there, there isn't any *there* there."

Consider arguments about whether athletes should be permitted to take anabolic steroids, drugs that supposedly build up muscle, restore energy, and enhance aggressiveness. A thoughtful argument on this subject will have to take account of information that the writer can gather only by doing some research.

- Do steroids really have the effects commonly attributed to them?
- And are they dangerous?
- If they are dangerous, how dangerous are they?

After all, competitive sports are inherently dangerous, some of them highly so. Many boxers, jockeys, and football players have suffered severe injury, even death, from competing. Does anyone believe that anabolic steroids are more dangerous than the contests themselves? Obviously, again, a respectable argument about steroids will have to show awareness of what is known about them.

Or take this question:

Why did President Truman order that atomic bombs be dropped on Hiroshima and Nagasaki?

The most obvious answer is to end the war, but some historians believe he had a very different purpose. In their view, Japan's defeat was ensured before the bombs were dropped, and the Japanese were ready to surrender; the bombs were dropped not to save American (or Japanese) lives but to show Russia that the United States would not be pushed around. Scholars who hold this view, such as Gar Alperovitz in *Atomic Diplomacy* (1965), argue that Japanese civilians in Hiroshima and Nagasaki were incinerated not to save the lives of American soldiers who otherwise would have died in an invasion of Japan but to teach Stalin a lesson. Dropping the bombs, it is argued, marked not the end of the Pacific War but the beginning of the cold war.

One must ask: What evidence supports this argument or claim or thesis, which assumes that Truman could not have thought the bomb was needed to defeat the Japanese because the Japanese knew they were defeated and would soon surrender without a hard-fought defense that would cost hundreds of thousands of lives? What about the momentum that had built up to use the bomb? After all, years of effort and $2 billion had been expended to produce a weapon with the intention of using it to end the war against Germany. But Germany had been defeated without the use of the bomb. Meanwhile, the war in the Pacific continued unabated. If the argument we are considering is correct, all this background counted for little or nothing in Truman's decision, a decision purely diplomatic and coolly indifferent to human life. The task for the writer is to evaluate the evidence available and then to argue for or against the view that Truman's purpose in dropping the bomb was to impress the Soviet government.

A student writing on the topic will certainly want to consult the chief books on the subject (Alperovitz's, cited above, Martin Sherwin's *A World Destroyed* [1975], and John Toland's *The Rising Sun* [1970]) and perhaps reviews of them, especially the reviews in journals devoted to political science. (Reading a searching review of a serious scholarly book is a good way to identify quickly some of the book's main contributions and controversial claims.) Truman's letters and statements and books and articles about Truman are also clearly relevant, and doubtless important articles are to be found in recent issues of scholarly journals and electronic sources. In fact, even an essay on such a topic as whether Truman was morally justified in using the atomic bomb for *any* purpose will be a stronger essay if it is well informed about such matters as the estimated loss of life that an invasion would have cost, the international rules governing weapons, and Truman's own statements about the issue.

How does one go about finding the material needed to write a well-informed argument? We will provide help, but first we want to offer a few words about choosing a topic.

CHOOSING A TOPIC

We will be brief. If a topic is not assigned, choose one that

- Interests you and
- Can be researched with reasonable thoroughness in the allotted time.

Topics such as censorship, the environment, and sexual harassment obviously impinge on our lives, and it may well be that one such topic is of especial interest to you. But the scope of these topics makes researching them potentially overwhelming. Type the word *censorship* into an **Internet** search engine, and you will be referred to millions of information sources.

This brings us to our second point—a manageable topic. Any of the previous topics would need to be narrowed substantially before you could begin searching in earnest. Similarly, a topic such as the causes of World War II can hardly be mastered in a few weeks or argued in a ten-page paper. It is simply too big.

You can, however, write a solid paper analyzing, evaluating, and arguing for or against General Eisenhower's views on atomic warfare. What were they, and when did he hold them? (In his books of 1948 and 1963 Eisenhower says that he opposed the use of the bomb before Hiroshima and that he argued with Secretary of War Henry Stimson against dropping it, but what evidence supports these claims? Was Eisenhower attempting to rewrite history in his books?) Eisenhower's own writings and books and other information sources on Eisenhower will, of course, be the major sources for a paper on this topic, but you will also want to look at books and articles about Stimson and at publications that contain information about the views of other generals, so that, for instance, you can compare Eisenhower's view with Marshall's or MacArthur's.

Spend a little time exploring a topic to see if it will be interesting and manageable by taking one or more of these approaches.

- Do a Web search on the topic. Though you may not use any of the sites that turn up, you can quickly put your finger on the pulse of popular approaches to the issue by scanning the first page or two of results to see what issues are getting the most attention.

- Plug the topic into one of the library's article databases. Again, just by scanning titles you can get a sense of what questions are being raised.

- Browse the library shelves where books on the topic are kept. A quick check of the tables of contents of recently published books may give you ideas of how to narrow the topic.

- Ask a librarian to show you where specialized reference books on your topic are found. Instead of general encyclopedias, try sources like these:

   CQ Researcher
   Encyclopedia of Applied Ethics
   Encyclopedia of Bioethics
   Encyclopedia of Crime and Justice
   Encyclopedia of Science, Technology, and Ethics

- Talk to an expert. Members of the faculty who specialize in the area of your topic might be able to spell out some of the most significant controversies around a topic and may point you toward key sources.

FINDING MATERIAL

What strategy you use for finding good sources will depend on your topic. Researching a current issue in politics or popular culture may involve reading recent newspaper articles, scanning information on gov-

A WORD ABOUT WIKIPEDIA

Links to Wikipedia (*http://www.wikipedia.org*) often rise to the top of Web search results. This vast and decentralized site provides over a million articles on a wide variety of topics. However, anyone can contribute to the online encyclopedia, so the accuracy of articles varies, and, in some cases the coverage of a controversial issue is one-sided or disputed. Even when the articles are accurate, they provide only basic information. Wikipedia's founder, Jimmy Wales, cautions students against using it as a source, except for obtaining general background knowledge: "You're in college; don't cite the encyclopedia."[1]

ernment Web sites, and locating current statistics. Other topics may be best tackled by seeking out books and scholarly journal articles that are less up-to-the-minute, but more in-depth and analytical. You may want to supplement library and Web sources with your own field work, by conducting surveys or interviews.

Critical thinking is crucial to every step of the research process. Whatever strategy you use, remember that you will want to find material that is authoritative, represents a balanced approach to the issues, and is persuasive. As you choose your sources, bear in mind they will be serving as your "expert witnesses" as you make a case to your audience. Their quality and credibility are critical to your argument.

INTERVIEWING PEERS AND LOCAL AUTHORITIES

You ought to try to consult experts—for instance, members of the faculty or other local authorities on art, business, law, and so forth. You can also consult interested laypersons. Remember, however, that experts have their biases and that "ordinary" people may have knowledge that experts lack. When interviewing experts, keep in mind Picasso's comment: "You mustn't always believe what I say. Questions tempt you to tell lies, particularly when there is no answer."

If you are interviewing your peers, you will probably want to make an effort to get a representative sample. Of course, even within a group not all members share a single view—many African Americans favor affirmative action but not all do, and many gays favor legalizing gay marriage but, again, some don't. Make an effort to talk to a range of people who might be expected to offer varied opinions. You may learn some unexpected things.

Here we will concentrate, however, on interviews with experts.

[1]"Wikipedia Founder Discourages Academic Use of His Creation," *Chronicle of Higher Education: The Wired Campus*, 12 June 2006, 16 Nov. 2006 <http://chronicle.com/wiredcampus/article/1328/wikipedia-founder-discourages-academic-use-of-his-creation>.

1. **Finding subjects for interviews**   If you are looking for expert opinions, you may want to start with a faculty member on your campus. You may already know the instructor, or you may have to scan the catalog to see who teaches courses relevant to your topic. Department secretaries and college Web sites are good sources of information about the special interests of the faculty and also about lecturers who will be visiting the campus.

2. **Doing preliminary homework**   (1) Know something about the person whom you will be interviewing. Biographical reference works such as *Who's Who in America, Who's Who among Black Americans, Who's Who of American Women,* and *Directory of American Scholars* may include your interviewee, or, again, a departmental secretary may be able to provide a vita for a faculty member. (2) In requesting the interview, make evident your interest in the topic and in the person. (If you know something about the person, you will be able to indicate why you are asking him or her.) (3) Request the interview, preferably in writing, a week in advance, and ask for ample time—probably half an hour to an hour. Indicate whether the material will be confidential, and (if you want to use a recorder) ask if you may record the interview. (4) If the person accepts the invitation, ask if he or she recommends any preliminary reading, and establish a time and a suitable place, preferably not the cafeteria during lunchtime.

3. **Preparing thoroughly**   (1) If your interviewee recommended any reading or has written on the topic, read the material. (2) Tentatively formulate some questions, keeping in mind that (unless you are simply gathering material for a survey of opinions) you want more than yes or no answers. Questions beginning with *Why* and *How* will usually require the interviewee to go beyond yes and no.

Even if your subject has consented to let you bring a recorder, be prepared to take notes on points that strike you as especially significant; without written notes, you will have nothing if the recorder has malfunctioned. Further, by taking occasional notes you will give the interviewee some time to think and perhaps to rephrase or to amplify a remark.

4. **Conducting the interview**   (1) Begin by engaging in brief conversation, without taking notes. If the interviewee has agreed to let you use a recorder, settle on the place where you will put it. (2) Come prepared with an opening question or two, but as the interview proceeds, don't hesitate to ask questions that you had not anticipated asking. (3) Near the end (you and your subject have probably agreed on the length of the interview) ask the subject if he or she wishes to add anything, perhaps by way of clarifying some earlier comment. (4) Conclude by thanking the interviewee and by offering to provide a copy of the final version of your paper.

5. **Writing up the interview**   (1) As soon as possible—certainly within twenty-four hours after the interview—review your notes and

clarify them. At this stage, you can still remember the meaning of your abbreviated notes and shorthand devices (maybe you have been using *n* to stand for *nurses* in clinics where abortions are performed), but if you wait even a whole day you may be puzzled by your own notes. If you have recorded the interview, you may want to transcribe all of it—the laboriousness of this task is one good reason why many interviewers do not use recorders—and you may then want to scan the whole and mark the parts that now strike you as especially significant. If you have taken notes by hand, type them up, along with your own observations, for example, "Jones was very tentative on this matter, but she said she was inclined to believe that . . ." (2) Be especially careful to indicate which words are direct quotations. If in doubt, check with the interviewee.

FINDING QUALITY INFORMATION ON THE WEB

The Web is a valuable source of information for many topics and less helpful for others. In general, if you're looking for information on public policy, popular culture, current events, or legal affairs, or for any subject of interest to agencies of the federal or state government, the Web is likely to have useful material. If you're looking for literary criticism, scholarly analysis of historical or social issues, or scientific research reports, you will be better off using library databases, described below.

To make good use of the Web, try these strategies:

- Use the most specific terms possible when using a general search engine; put phrases in quotation marks or use the advanced search function to find phrases.

- If your topic is broad, try starting with one of the selective directories listed below instead of a general search engine.

- Consider which government agencies and organizations might be interested in your topic and go directly to their Web sites.

- Follow "about" links to see who or what organization has created the Web site, and why. If there is no "about" link, delete everything after the first slash in the URL to go to the parent site to see if it provides information.

- Use clues in URLs to see where sites originate. For example, URLs containing *.k12* are hosted at elementary and secondary schools, and so may be intended for a young audience; those ending in *.gov* are government agencies, and so tend to provide official information.

- Always bear in mind that the sources you choose must be persuasive to your audience. Avoid sites that may be dismissed as unreliable or biased.

Some useful Web sites include the following:

Selective Web Site Directories

- Infomine *<http://infomine.ucr.edu/>*
- Librarian's Internet Index *<http://lii.org>*
- WWW Virtual Library *<http://vlib.org>*

Current News Sources

- Google News *<http://news.google.com>*
- Kidon Media-Link *<http://www.kidon.com/media-link/index.php>*

Digital Primary Sources

- American Memory *<http://memory.loc.gov>*
- The Avalon Project at Yale Law School *<http://www.yale.edu/lawweb/avalon/avalon.htm>*

Government Information

- GPO Access *<http://www.gpoaccess.gov>*
- Thomas (federal legislation) *<http://thomas.loc.gov>*
- University of Michigan Documents Center *<http://www.lib.umich.edu/govdocs>*

Statistical Information

- American FactFinder *<http://factfinder.census.gov>*
- Fedstats *<http://www.fedstats.gov>*
- Pew Global Attitudes Project *<http://pewglobal.org>*
- U.S. Census Bureau *<http://www.census.gov>*

FINDING ARTICLES USING LIBRARY DATABASES

Your library has a wide range of general and specialized databases available through its Web site. Some databases provide references to articles (and perhaps abstracts, or summaries) or may provide direct links to the entire text of articles. General and interdisciplinary databases include Academic Search Premier (produced by the EBSCOhost company) and Expanded Academic Index (from InfoTrac).

More specialized databases include PsycINFO (for psychology research) and ERIC (focused on topics in education). Others, such as JSTOR, are full-text digital archives of scholarly journals. You probably will also have access to newspaper articles through LexisNexis or Proquest Newsstand, particularly useful for articles that are not available for free on the Web. Look at your library's Web site to see what your options are, or stop by the reference desk for a quick, personalized tutorial.

When using databases, first think through your topic using the listing and clustering techniques described on pages 222–23. List synonyms for your key search terms. As you search, look at words used in titles and descriptors for alternative ideas, and make use of the advanced search option so that you can easily combine multiple terms. Rarely will you find exactly what you're looking for right away. Try different search terms and different ways to narrow your topic.

As you find interesting sources, keep track of them by checking off specific articles in a list. Then you can print, save, or e-mail yourself the references you have selected. You may also have an option to export references to a citation management program such as RefWorks or EndNote. These programs allow you to create your own personal database of sources; you can store your references and take notes. Later, when you're ready to create a bibliography, these programs will automatically format your references in MLA, APA, or other style. Ask a librarian if one of these programs is available to students on your campus.

LOCATING BOOKS

The books your library owns are found through its online catalog. Typically, you can search by author or title or, if you don't have a specific book in mind, by keyword or subject. As with databases, think about different search terms to use, keeping an eye out for subject headings used for books that appear relevant. Take advantage of an advanced search option. You may, for example, be able to limit a search to books on a particular topic in English published within recent years. In addition to books, the catalog will list DVDs, sound recordings, and other formats.

Unlike articles, books tend to cover broad topics, so be prepared to broaden your search terms. It may be that a book has a chapter or ten pages that are precisely what you need, but the catalog typically doesn't index the contents of books in detail. Think instead of what kind of book might contain the information you need.

Once you've found some promising books in the catalog, note the call numbers, find them on the shelves, and then browse. Since books on the same topic are shelved together, you can quickly see what additional books are available by scanning the shelves. As you browse, be sure to look for books that have been published recently enough for your purposes. You do not have to read a book cover to cover to use it in your research. Instead, skim the introduction to see if it will be useful, and then use its table of contents and index to pinpoint the sections of the book that are most relevant.

EVALUATING YOUR SOURCES

Each step of the way, you will be making choices about your sources. As your research proceeds, from selecting promising items in a database search to browsing the book collection, you will want to use the techniques for previewing and skimming detailed on pages 31–32 to make your first selection. Ask yourself some basic questions:

- Is this source relevant?
- Is it current enough?
- Does the title and/or abstract suggest it will address an important aspect of my topic?
- Am I choosing sources that represent a range of ideas, not simply ones that support my opinion?

Once you have collected a number of likely sources, you will want to do further filtering. Examine each one with these questions in mind:

- *Is this source credible?* Does it include information about the author and his or her credentials that can help me decide whether to rely on it? In the case of books, you might check a database for book reviews for a second opinion. In the case of Web sites, find out where the site came from and why it has been posted on the Web. Don't use a Web source if you can't determine its authorship or purpose.

- *Will my audience find this source credible and persuasive?* Some publishers are more selective about which books they publish than others. University presses, for instance, have several experts read and comment on manuscripts before they decide which to publish. A story about U.S. politics from the *Washington Post,* whose writers conduct firsthand reporting in the nation's capital, carries more clout than a story from a small-circulation newspaper that is drawing its information from a wire service. A scholarly source may be more impressive than a magazine article.

- *Am I using the best evidence available?* Quoting directly from a government report may be more effective than quoting a news story that summarizes the report. Finding evidence that supports your claims in a president's speeches or letters is more persuasive than drawing your conclusions from a page or two of a history textbook.

- *Am I being fair to all sides?* Make sure you are prepared to address alternate perspectives, even if you ultimately take a position. Avoid sources that clearly promote an agenda in favor of ones that your audience will consider balanced and reliable.

- *Can I corroborate my key claims in more than one source?* Compare your sources to ensure that you aren't relying on facts that can't

> ✓ A CHECKLIST FOR EVALUATING PRINT SOURCES
>
> *For Books:*
>
> ☐ Is the book recent? If not, is the information I will be using from it likely or unlikely to change over time?
> ☐ How credible is the author?
> ☐ Is the book published by a respectable press?
> ☐ Is the book broad enough in its focus and written in a style I can understand?
> ☐ Does the book relate directly to my tentative thesis, or is it of only tangential interest?
> ☐ Do the arguments in the book seem sound, based on what I have learned about skillful critical reading and writing?
>
> *For Articles from Periodicals:*
>
> ☐ Is the periodical recent?
> ☐ Is the author's name given? Does he or she seem a credible source?
> ☐ Is the periodical respectable and serious?
> ☐ How directly does the article speak to my topic and tentative thesis?
> ☐ If the article is from a scholarly journal, am I sure I understand it?

be confirmed. If you're having trouble confirming a source, check with a librarian.

- *Do I really need this source?* It's tempting to use all the books and articles you have found, but if two sources say essentially the same thing, choose the one that is likely to carry the most weight with your audience.

TAKING NOTES

When it comes to taking notes, all researchers have their own habits that they swear by, and they can't imagine any other way of working. We still prefer to take notes on four- by six-inch index cards, while others use a notebook or a computer for note taking. If you use a citation management program, such as RefWorks or EndNote, you can store your personal notes and commentary with the citations you have saved. Using the program's search function, you can easily pull together related notes and citations, or you can create project folders for your references so that you can easily review what you've collected.

Whatever method you use, the following techniques should help you maintain consistency and keep organized during the research process:

A CHECKLIST FOR EVALUATING ELECTRONIC SOURCES

An enormous amount of valuable material is available on the World Wide Web—but so is an enormous amount of junk. True, there is also plenty of junk in books and journals, but most printed material has been subjected to a review process: Book publishers and editors of journals send manuscripts to specialized readers who evaluate them and recommend whether the material should or should not be published. Publishing on the Web is quite different. Anyone can publish on the Web with no review process: All that is needed is the right software. Ask yourself:

□ What person or organization produced the site (a commercial entity, a nonprofit entity, a student, an expert)? Check the electronic address to get a clue about the authorship. If there is a link to the author's homepage, check it out to learn about the author. Does the author have an affiliation with a respectable institution?

□ What is the purpose of the site? Is the site in effect an infomercial, or is it an attempt to contribute to a thoughtful discussion?

□ Are the sources of information indicated and verifiable? If possible, check the sources.

□ Is the site authoritative enough to use? (If it seems to contain review materials or class handouts, you probably don't want to take it too seriously.)

□ When was the page made available? Is it out of date?

1. If you use a notebook or cards, write in ink (pencil gets smudgy), and write on only one side of the card or paper. (Notes on the backs of cards tend to get lost, and writing on the back of paper will prevent you from later cutting up and rearranging your notes.)

2. Put only one idea in each notebook or computer entry or on each card (though an idea may include several facts).

3. Put a brief heading on each entry or card, such as "Truman's last words on A-bomb."

4. Summarize, for the most part, rather than quote at length.

5. Quote only passages in which the writing is especially effective, or passages that are in some way crucial.

6. Make sure that all quotations are exact. Enclose quoted words within quotation marks, indicate omissions by ellipses (three spaced periods: . . .), and enclose within square brackets ([ ]) any insertions or other additions you make.

7. *Never* copy a passage, changing an occasional word. *Either* copy it word for word, with punctuation intact, and enclose it within quotation marks, *or* summarize it drastically. If you copy a passage but change a word here and there, you may later make the

mistake of using your note verbatim in your essay, and you will be guilty of plagiarism.

8. Give the page number of your source, whether you summarize or quote. If a quotation you have copied runs in the original from the bottom of page 210 to the top of page 211, in your notes put a diagonal line (/) after the last word on page 210, so that later, if in your paper you quote only the material from page 210, you will know that you must cite 210 and not 210–11.

9. Indicate the source. The author's last name is enough if you have consulted only one work by the author; but if you consult more than one work by an author, you need further identification, such as the author's name and a short title.

10. Add your own comments about the substance of what you are recording. Such comments as "but contrast with Sherwin" or "seems illogical" or "evidence?" will ensure that you are thinking as well as writing and will be of value when you come to transform your notes into a draft. Be sure, however, to enclose such notes within double diagonals (//), or to mark them in some other way, so that later you will know they are yours and not your source's. If you use a computer for note taking, you may wish to write your comments in italics or in a different font.

11. In a separate computer file or notebook page or on separate index cards, write a bibliographic entry for each source. The information in each entry will vary, depending on whether the source is a book, a periodical, an electronic document, and so forth. The kind of information (for example, author and title) needed for each type of source can be found in the sections on MLA Format: The List of Works Cited (p. 284) or APA Format: The List of References (p. 295).

A NOTE ON PLAGIARIZING, PARAPHRASING, AND USING COMMON KNOWLEDGE

Plagiarism is the unacknowledged use of someone else's work. The word comes from a Latin word for "kidnapping," and plagiarism is indeed the stealing of something engendered by someone else. We won't deliver a sermon on the dishonesty (and folly) of plagiarism; we intend only to help you understand exactly what plagiarism is. The first thing to say is that plagiarism is not limited to the unacknowledged quotation of words.

A *paraphrase* is a sort of word-by-word or phrase-by-phrase translation of the author's language into your language. True, if you paraphrase you are using your own words, but you are also using someone else's ideas, and, equally important, you are using this other person's sequence of thoughts. Even if you change every third word in your source, and you give the author credit, you are plagiarizing. Here is an example of this sort of plagiarism, based on the previous sentence:

> Even if you alter every third or fourth word from your source, and you give credit to the author, you will be guilty of plagiarism.

Even if the writer of this paraphrase had cited a source after it, the writer would still be guilty of plagiarism because the passage borrows not only the idea but the shape of the presentation, the sentence structure. The writer of this passage hasn't really written anything; he or she has only adapted something. What the writer needs to do is to write something like this:

> Changing an occasional word does not free the writer from the obligation to cite a source.

And the source would still need to be cited, if the central idea were not a commonplace one.

You are plagiarizing if without giving credit you use someone else's ideas—even if you put these ideas entirely into your own words. When you use another's ideas, you must indicate your indebtedness by saying something like "Alperovitz points out that . . ." or "Secretary of War Stimson, as Martin Sherwin notes, never expressed himself on this point." Alperovitz and Sherwin pointed out something that you had not thought of, and so you must give them credit if you want to use their findings.

Again, even if after a paraphrase you cite your source, you are plagiarizing. How, you may wonder, can you be guilty of plagiarism if you cite a source? Easy. A reader assumes that the citation refers to information or an opinion, *not* to the presentation or development of the idea; and of course, in a paraphrase you are not presenting or developing the material in your own way.

Now consider this question: *Why* paraphrase? Often there is no good answer. Since a paraphrase is as long as the original, you may as well quote the original, if you think that a passage of that length is worth quoting. Probably it is *not* worth quoting in full; probably you should *not* paraphrase but rather should drastically *summarize* most of it, and perhaps quote a particularly effective phrase or two. As we explained on pages 36–38, the chief reason to paraphrase a passage is to clarify it—that is, to make certain that you and your readers understand a passage that— perhaps because it is badly written—is obscure.

Generally what you should do is to take the idea and put it entirely into your own words, perhaps reducing a paragraph of a hundred words to a sentence of ten words, but you must still give credit for the idea. If you believe that the original hundred words are so perfectly put that they cannot be transformed without great loss, you'll have to quote them and cite your source. But clearly there is no point in paraphrasing the

> ## ✓ A CHECKLIST FOR AVOIDING PLAGIARISM
>
> ☐ In my notes did I *always* put quoted material within quotation marks?
>
> ☐ In my notes did I summarize *in my own words* and give credit to the source for the idea?
>
> ☐ In my notes did I avoid paraphrasing, that is, did I avoid copying, keeping the structure of the source's sentences but using some of my own words? (Paraphrases of this sort, even with a footnote citing the source, are *not* acceptable, since the reader incorrectly assumes that the writing is essentially yours.)
>
> ☐ If in my paper I set forth a borrowed idea, do I give credit, even though the words and the shape of the sentences are entirely my own?
>
> ☐ If in my paper I quote directly, do I put the words within quotation marks and cite the source?
>
> ☐ Do I *not* cite material that can be considered common knowledge (material that can be found in numerous reference works, such as the date of a public figure's birth or the population of San Francisco or the fact that *Hamlet* is regarded as a great tragedy)?
>
> ☐ If I have the slightest doubt about whether I should or should not cite a source, have I taken the safe course and cited the source?

author's hundred words into a hundred of your own. Either quote or summarize, but cite the source.

Keep in mind, too, that almost all generalizations about human nature, no matter how common and familiar (for instance, "males are innately more aggressive than females") are not indisputable facts; they are at best hypotheses on which people differ and therefore should either not be asserted at all or should be supported by some cited source or authority. Similarly, because nearly all statistics (whether on the intelligence of criminals or the accuracy of lie detectors) are the result of some particular research and may well have been superseded or challenged by other investigators, it is advisable to cite a source for any statistics you use unless you are convinced they are indisputable, such as the number of registered voters in Memphis in 1988.

On the other hand, there is something called **common knowledge,** and the sources for such information need not be cited. The term does not, however, mean exactly what it seems to. It is common knowledge, of course, that Ronald Reagan was an American president (so you don't cite a source when you make that statement), and under the conventional interpretation of this doctrine, it is also common knowledge that he was born in 1911. In fact, of course, few people other than Reagan's wife and children know this date. Still, information that can be found in many places and that is indisputable belongs to all of us; therefore, a writer need not cite her source when she says that Reagan was born in 1911. Probably she checked a dictionary or an encyclopedia for the date, but the source doesn't matter. Dozens of sources will give exactly the same information, and in fact, no reader wants to be bothered with a citation on such a point.

Some students have a little trouble developing a sense of what is and what is not common knowledge. Although, as we have just said, readers don't want to hear about the sources for information that is indisputable and can be documented in many places, if you are in doubt about whether to cite a source, cite it. Better risk boring the reader a bit than risk being accused of plagiarism.

COMPILING AN ANNOTATED BIBLIOGRAPHY

When several sources have been identified and gathered, many researchers prepare an annotated bibliography. This is a list providing all relevant bibliographic information (just as it will appear in your Works Cited list or References list) as well as a brief descriptive and evaluative summary of each source—perhaps one to three sentences. Your instructor may ask you to provide an annotated bibliography for your research project.

An annotated bibliography serves four main purposes:

- First, constructing such a document helps you to master the material contained in any given source. To find the heart of the argument presented in an article or book, phrase it briefly, and comment on it, you must understand it fully.

- Second, creating an annotated bibliography helps you to think about how each portion of your research fits into the whole of your project, how you will use it, and how it relates to your topic and thesis.

- Third, an annotated bibliography helps your readers: They can quickly see which items may be especially helpful in their own research.

- Fourth, in constructing an annotated bibliography at this early stage, you will get some hands-on practice at bibliographic format, thereby easing the job of creating your final bibliography (the Works Cited list or References list for your paper).

Following are two examples of entries for an annotated bibliography in MLA (Modern Language Association) format for a project on the effect of violence in the media. The first is for a book, the second for an article from a periodical. Notice that each

- Begins with a bibliographic entry—author (last name first), title, and so forth—and then
- Provides information about the content of the work under consideration, suggesting how each may be of use to the final research paper.

Clover, Carol J. *Men, Women, and Chain Saws: Gender in the Modern Horror Film*. Princeton: Princeton UP, 1992. Print. The author focuses on Hollywood horror movies of the 1970s and 1980s. She studies representations of women and girls in these movies and the responses of male viewers to female characters, suggesting that this relationship is more complex and less exploitative than the common wisdom claims.

Winerip, Michael. "Looking for an Eleven O'Clock Fix." *New York Times Magazine* 11 Jan 1998: 30-40. Print. The article focuses on the rising levels of violence on local television news and highlights a station in Orlando, Florida, that tried to reduce its depictions of violence and lost viewers as a result. Winerip suggests that people only claim to be against media violence, while their actions prove otherwise.

WRITING THE PAPER

Organizing Your Notes

If you have read thoughtfully, taken careful (and, again, thoughtful) notes on your reading, and then (yet again) thought about these notes, you are well on the way to writing a good paper. You have, in fact, already written some of it, in your notes. By now you should clearly have in mind the thesis you intend to argue. But you still have to organize the material, and, doubtless, even as you set about organizing it, you will find points that will require you to do some additional research and much additional thinking.

Divide your notes into clusters, each devoted to one theme or point (for instance, one cluster on the extent of use of steroids, another on evidence that steroids are harmful, yet another on arguments that even if harmful they should be permitted). If your notes are in a computer file, use your word processor's Cut and Paste features to rearrange the notes into appropriate clusters. If you use index cards, simply sort them into packets. If you take notes in a notebook, either mark each note with a number or name indicating the cluster to which it belongs, or cut the notes apart and arrange them as you would cards. Put aside all notes that—however interesting—you now see are irrelevant to your paper.

Next, arrange the clusters or packets into a tentative sequence. In effect, you are preparing a **working outline.** At its simplest, say, you will give three arguments on behalf of *X* and then three counterarguments. (Or you might decide that it is better to alternate material from the two sets of three clusters each, following each argument with an objection. At this stage, you can't be sure of the organization you will finally use, but you can make a tentative decision.)

The First Draft

Draft the essay, without worrying much about an elegant opening paragraph. Just write some sort of adequate opening that states the topic and your thesis. When you revise the whole later, you can put some effort into developing an effective opening. (Most experienced writers find that the opening paragraph in the final version is almost the last thing they write.)

If your notes are on cards or notebook paper, carefully copy into the draft all quotations that you plan to use. If your notes are in a computer, you may simply cut and paste them from one file to another. Do keep in mind, however, that rewriting or retyping quotations will make you think carefully about them and may result in a more focused and thoughtful paper. (In the next section of this chapter we will talk briefly about leading into quotations and about the form of quotations.) Be sure to include citations in your drafts so that if you must check a reference later it will be easy to do so.

Later Drafts

Give the draft, and yourself, a rest—perhaps for a day or two—and then go back to it. Read it over, make necessary revisions, and then **outline** it. That is, on a sheet of paper chart the organization and development, perhaps by jotting down a sentence summarizing each paragraph or each group of closely related paragraphs. Your outline or map may now show you that the paper obviously suffers from poor organization. For instance, it may reveal that you neglected to respond to one argument or that one point is needlessly treated in two places. It may also help you to see that if you gave three arguments and then three counterarguments, you probably should instead have followed each argument with its rebuttal. On the other hand, if you alternated arguments and objections, it may now seem better to use two main groups, all the arguments and then all the criticisms.

No one formula is always right. Much will depend on the complexity of the material. If the arguments are highly complex, it is better to respond to them one by one than to expect a reader to hold three complex arguments in mind before you get around to responding. If, however, the arguments can be stated briefly and clearly, it is effective to state all three and then to go on to the responses. If you write on a word processor, you will find it easy, even fun, to move passages of text around.

Even so, you will probably want to print out a hard copy from time to time to review the structure of your paper. Allow enough time to produce several drafts.

A Few More Words about Organization

There is a difference between

- A paper that *has* an organization and
- A paper that helpfully lets the reader know what the organization is.

Write papers of the second sort, but (there is always a "but") take care not to belabor the obvious. Inexperienced writers sometimes either hide the organization so thoroughly that a reader cannot find it, or they so ploddingly lay out the structure ("Eighth, I will show . . .") that the reader becomes impatient. Yet it is better to be overly explicit than to be obscure.

The ideal, of course, is the middle route. Make the overall strategy of your organization evident by occasional explicit signs at the beginning of a paragraph ("We have seen . . . ," "It is time to consider the objections . . . ," "By far the most important . . ."); elsewhere make certain that the implicit structure is evident to the reader. When you reread your draft, if you try to imagine that you are one of your classmates, you will probably be able to sense exactly where explicit signs are needed and where they are not needed. Better still, exchange drafts with a classmate in order to exchange (tactful) advice.

Choosing a Tentative Title

By now a couple of tentative titles for your essay should have crossed your mind. If possible, choose a title that is both interesting and informative. Consider these three titles:

Are Steroids Harmful?

The Fuss over Steroids

Steroids: A Dangerous Game

"Are Steroids Harmful?" is faintly interesting, and it lets the reader know the gist of the subject, but it gives no clue about the writer's thesis, the writer's contention or argument. "The Fuss over Steroids" is somewhat better, for it gives information about the writer's position. "Steroids: A Dangerous Game" is still better; it announces the subject ("steroids") and the thesis ("dangerous"), and it also displays a touch of wit because "game" glances at the world of athletics.

Don't try too hard, however; better a simple, direct, informative title than a strained, puzzling, or overly cute one. And remember to make sure that everything in your essay is relevant to your title. In fact, your title should help you to organize the essay and to delete irrelevant material.

The Final Draft

When at last you have a draft that is for the most part satisfactory, check to make sure that **transitions** from sentence to sentence and from paragraph to paragraph are clear ("Further evidence," "On the other hand," "A weakness, however, is apparent"), and then worry about your opening and your closing paragraphs. Your **opening paragraph** should be clear, interesting, and focused; if neither the title nor the first paragraph announces your thesis, the second paragraph probably should do so.

The **final paragraph** need not say, "In conclusion, I have shown that . . ." It should effectively end the essay, but it need not summarize your conclusions. We have already offered a few words about final paragraphs (p. 241), but the best way to learn how to write such paragraphs is to study the endings of some of the essays in this book and to adopt the strategies that appeal to you.

Be sure that all indebtedness is properly acknowledged. We have talked about plagiarism; now we will turn to the business of introducing quotations effectively.

QUOTING FROM SOURCES

The Use and Abuse of Quotations

When is it necessary, or appropriate, to quote? Sometimes the reader must see the exact words of your source; the gist won't do. If you are arguing that Z's definition of *rights* is too inclusive, your readers have to know exactly how Z defined *rights*. Your brief summary of the definition may be unfair to Z; in fact, you want to convince your readers that you are being fair, and so you quote Z's definition, word for word. Moreover, if the passage is only a sentence or two long, or even if it runs to a paragraph, it may be so compactly stated that it defies summary. And to attempt to paraphrase it—substituting *natural* for *inalienable*, and so forth—saves no space and only introduces imprecision. There is nothing to do but to quote it, word for word.

Second, you may want to quote a passage that could be summarized but that is so effectively stated that you want your readers to have the pleasure of reading the original. Of course, readers will not give you credit for writing these words, but they will give you credit for your taste and for your effort to make especially pleasant the business of reading your paper.

In short, use (but don't overuse) quotations. Speaking roughly, quotations should occupy no more than 10 or 15 percent of your paper, and they may occupy much less. Most of your paper should set forth your ideas, not other people's ideas.

How to Quote

Long and Short Quotations   **Long quotations** (five or more lines of typed prose or three or more lines of poetry) are set off from your text. To set off material, start on a new line, indent one inch from the left margin, and type the quotation double-spaced. Do not enclose quotations within quotation marks if you are setting them off.

Short quotations are treated differently. They are embedded within the text; they are enclosed within quotation marks, but otherwise they do not stand out.

All quotations, whether set off or embedded, must be exact. If you omit any words, you must indicate the ellipsis by substituting three spaced periods for the omission; if you insert any words or punctuation, you must indicate the addition by enclosing it within square brackets, not to be confused with parentheses.

Leading into a Quotation   Now for a less mechanical matter, the way in which a quotation is introduced. To say that it is "introduced" implies that one leads into it, though on rare occasions a quotation appears without an introduction, perhaps immediately after the title. Normally one leads into a quotation by giving the name of the author and (no less important) clues or signals about the content of the quotation and the purpose it serves in the present essay. For example:

William James provides a clear answer to Huxley when he says that "..."

The writer has been writing about Huxley and now is signaling readers that they will be getting James's reply. The writer is also signaling (in "a clear answer") that the reply is satisfactory. If the writer believed that James's answer was not really acceptable, the lead-in might have run thus:

William James attempts to answer Huxley, but his response does not really meet the difficulty Huxley calls attention to. James writes, "..."

or thus:

William James provided what he took to be an answer to Huxley when he said that "..."

In this last example, clearly the words "what he took to be an answer" imply that the essayist will show, after the quotation from James, that the answer is in some degree inadequate. Or the essayist may wish to suggest the inadequacy even more strongly:

> William James provided what he took to be an answer to Huxley, but he
> used the word <u>religion</u> in a way that Huxley would not have allowed.
> James argues that ". . ."

If after reading something by Huxley the writer had merely given us "William James says . . . ," we wouldn't know whether we were getting confirmation, refutation, or something else. The essayist would have put a needless burden on the readers. Generally speaking, the more difficult the quotation, the more important is the introductory or explanatory lead-in, but even the simplest quotation profits from some sort of brief lead-in, such as "James reaffirms this point when he says . . ."

> **A RULE FOR WRITERS:** In introducing a quotation, it is usually advisable to signal the reader *why* you are using the quotation, by means of a lead-in consisting of a verb or a verb and adverb, such as *claims,* or *convincingly shows,* or *admits.*

DOCUMENTATION

In the course of your essay, you will probably quote or summarize material derived from a source. You must give credit, and although there is no one form of documentation to which all scholarly fields subscribe, you will probably be asked to use one of two. One, established by the Modern Language Association (MLA), is used chiefly in the humanities; the other, established by the American Psychological Association (APA), is used chiefly in the social sciences.

We include two papers that use sources. "Why Trials Should Not Be

---

 A CHECKLIST FOR USING QUOTATIONS RATHER THAN SUMMARIES

Ask yourself the following questions. If you cannot answer yes to at least one of the questions, consider *summarizing* the material rather than quoting it in full.

☐ Is the quotation given because it is necessary for the reader to see the exact wording of the original?

☐ Is the quotation given because the language is especially engaging?

☐ Is the quotation given because the author is a respected authority and the passage lends weight to my argument?

Televised" (p. 301) uses the MLA format. "The Role of Spirituality and Religion in Mental Health" (p. 315) follows the APA format. (You may notice that various styles are illustrated in other selections we have included.)

A Note on Footnotes (and Endnotes)

Before we discuss these two formats, a few words about footnotes are in order. Before the MLA and the APA developed their rules of style, citations commonly were given in footnotes. Although today footnotes are not so frequently used to give citations, they still may be useful for another purpose. (The MLA suggests endnotes rather than footnotes, but all readers know that, in fact, footnotes are preferable to endnotes. After all, who wants to keep shifting from a page of text to a page of notes at the rear?) If you want to include some material that may seem intrusive in the body of the paper, you may relegate it to a footnote. For example, in a footnote you might translate a quotation given in a foreign language, or you might demote from text to footnote a paragraph explaining why you are not taking account of such-and-such a point. By putting the matter in a footnote you are signaling the reader that it is dispensable; it is something relevant but not essential, something extra that you are, so to speak, tossing in. Don't make a habit of writing this sort of note, but there are times when it is appropriate.

MLA Format: Citations within the Text

Brief citations within the body of the essay give credit, in a highly abbreviated way, to the sources for material you quote, summarize, or make use of in any other way. These *in-text citations* are made clear by a list of sources, titled Works Cited, appended to the essay. Thus, in your essay you may say something like this:

> Commenting on the relative costs of capital punishment and life imprisonment, Ernest van den Haag says that he doubts "that capital punishment really is more expensive" (33).

The **citation,** the number 33 in parentheses, means that the quoted words come from page 33 of a source (listed in the Works Cited) written by van den Haag. Without a Works Cited, a reader would have no way of knowing that you are quoting from page 33 of an article that appeared in the February 8, 1985, issue of the *National Review.*

Usually the parenthetic citation appears at the end of a sentence, as in the example just given, but it can appear elsewhere; its position will depend chiefly on your ear, your eye, and the context. You might, for example, write the sentence thus:

Ernest van den Haag doubts that "capital punishment really is more expensive" than life imprisonment (33), but other writers have presented
figures that contradict him.

Five points must be made about these examples:

1. **Quotation marks**   The closing quotation mark appears after
the last word of the quotation, *not* after the parenthetic citation. Since
the citation is not part of the quotation, the citation is not included
within the quotation marks.

2. **Omission of words (ellipsis)**   If you are quoting a complete
sentence or only a phrase, as in the examples given, you do not need to
indicate (by three spaced periods) that you are omitting material before
or after the quotation. But if for some reason you want to omit an inte-
rior part of the quotation, you must indicate the omission by inserting an
ellipsis, the three spaced dots. To take a simple example, if you omit the
word "really" from van den Haag's phrase, you must alert the reader to
the omission:

Ernest van den Haag doubts that "capital punishment . . . is more expensive" than life imprisonment (33).

Suppose you are quoting a sentence but wish to omit material from the
end of the sentence. Suppose, also, that the quotation forms the end of
your sentence. Write a lead-in phrase, quote what you need from your
source, then type the bracketed ellipses for the omission, close the quotation, give the parenthetic citation, and finally type a fourth period to
indicate the end of your sentence.

Here's an example. Suppose you want to quote the first part of a
sentence that runs, "We could insist that the cost of capital punishment
be reduced so as to diminish the differences." Your sentence would incorporate the desired extract as follows:

Van den Haag says, "We could insist that the cost of capital punishment
be reduced . . ." (33).

3. **Punctuation with parenthetic citations**   In the preceding examples, the punctuation (a period or a comma in the examples) *follows* the citation. If, however, the quotation ends with a
question mark, include the question mark *within* the quotation,
since it is part of the quotation, and put a period *after* the citation:

Van den Haag asks, "Isn't it better--more just and more useful--that criminals, if they do not have the certainty of punishment, at least run the
risk of suffering it?" (35).

But if the question mark is your own and not in the source, put it after the citation, thus:

> What answer can be given to van den Haag's doubt that "capital punishment really is more expensive" (33)?

4. **Two or more works by an author**   If your list of Works Cited includes two or more works by an author, you cannot, in your essay, simply cite a page number because the reader will not know which of the works you are referring to. You must give additional information. You can give it in your lead-in, thus:

> In "New Arguments against Capital Punishment," van den Haag expresses doubt "that capital punishment really is more expensive" than life imprisonment (33).

Or you can give the title, in a shortened form, within the citation:

> Van den Haag expresses doubt that "capital punishment really is more expensive" than life imprisonment ("New Arguments" 33).

5. **Citing even when you do not quote**   Even if you don't quote a source directly, but use its point in a paraphrase or a summary, you will give a citation:

> Van den Haag thinks that life imprisonment costs more than capital punishment (33).

Note that in all of the previous examples, the author's name is given in the text (rather than within the parenthetic citation). But there are several other ways of giving the citation, and we shall look at them now. (We have already seen, in the example given under paragraph 4, that the title and the page number can be given within the citation.)

AUTHOR AND PAGE NUMBER IN PARENTHESES

> It has been argued that life imprisonment is more costly than capital punishment (van den Haag 33).

AUTHOR, TITLE, AND PAGE NUMBER IN PARENTHESES

We have seen that if the Works Cited list includes two or more works by an author, you will have to give the title of the work on which you are drawing, either in your lead-in phrase or within the parenthetic citation. Similarly, if you are citing someone who is listed more than once in the Works Cited, and for some reason you do not mention the name of the author or the work in your lead-in, you must add the information in your citation:

> Doubt has been expressed that capital punishment is as costly as life imprisonment (van den Haag, "New Arguments" 33).

A GOVERNMENT DOCUMENT OR A WORK
OF CORPORATE AUTHORSHIP

Treat the issuing body as the author. Thus, you will write something like this:

> The Commission on Food Control, in *Food Resources Today*, concludes that there is no danger (37–38).

A WORK BY TWO OR MORE AUTHORS

If a work is by *two or three authors,* give the names of all authors, either in the parenthetic citation (the first example below) or in a lead-in (the second example below):

> There is not a single example of the phenomenon (Smith, Dale, and Jones 182–83).

> Smith, Dale, and Jones insist there is not a single example of the phenomenon (182–83).

If there are *more than three authors,* give the last name of the first author, followed by *et al.* (an abbreviation for *et alii,* Latin for "and others"), thus:

> Gittleman et al. argue (43) that . . .

or

> On average, the cost is even higher (Gittleman et al. 43).

PARENTHETIC CITATION OF AN INDIRECT SOURCE
(CITATION OF MATERIAL THAT ITSELF WAS QUOTED
OR SUMMARIZED IN YOUR SOURCE)

Suppose you are reading a book by Jones in which she quotes Smith and you wish to use Smith's material. Your citation must refer the reader to Jones—the source you are using—but of course, you cannot attribute the words to Jones. You will have to make it clear that you are quoting Smith, and so after a lead-in phrase like "Smith says," followed by the quotation, you will give a parenthetic citation along these lines:

> (qtd. in Jones 324–25).

PARENTHETIC CITATION OF TWO OR MORE WORKS

The costs are simply too high (Smith 301; Jones 28).

Notice that a semicolon, followed by a space, separates the two sources.

A WORK IN MORE THAN ONE VOLUME

This is a bit tricky. If you have used only one volume, in the Works Cited you will specify the volume, and so in the parenthetic in-text citation you will not need to specify the volume. All that you need to include in the citation is a page number, as illustrated by most of the examples that we have given.

If you have used more than one volume, your parenthetic citation will have to specify the volume as well as the page, thus:

Jackson points out that fewer than one hundred fifty people fit this description (2: 351).

The reference is to page 351 in volume 2 of a work by Jackson.

If, however, you are citing not a page but an entire volume—let's say volume 2—your parenthetic citation will look like this:

Jackson exhaustively studies this problem (vol. 2).

or

Jackson (vol. 2) exhaustively studies this problem.

Notice the following points:

- In citing a volume and page, the volume number, like the page number, is given in arabic (not roman) numerals, even if the original used roman numerals to indicate the volume number.
- The volume number is followed by a colon, then a space, then the page number.
- If you cite a volume number without a page number, as in the last example quoted, the abbreviation is *vol.* Otherwise do *not* use such abbreviations as *vol.* and *p.* and *pg.*

AN ANONYMOUS WORK

For an anonymous work, give the title in your lead-in, or give it in a shortened form in your parenthetic citation:

A Prisoner's View of Killing includes a poll taken of the inmates on death row (32).

or

A poll is available (*Prisoner's View* 32).

AN INTERVIEW

Probably you won't need a parenthetic citation because you'll say something like

Vivian Berger, in an interview, said . . .

or

According to Vivian Berger, in an interview . . .

and when your reader turns to the Works Cited, he or she will see that Berger is listed, along with the date of the interview. But if you do not mention the source's name in the lead-in, you will have to give it in the parentheses, thus:

Contrary to popular belief, the death penalty is not reserved for serial killers and depraved murderers (Berger).

AN ELECTRONIC SOURCE

Electronic sources, such as those found on CD-ROMs or the Internet, are generally not divided into pages. Therefore, the in-text citation for such sources cite only the author's name (or, if a work is anonymous, the title):

According to the World Wide Web site for the American Civil Liberties Union . . .

If the source does use pages or breaks down further into paragraphs or screens, insert the appropriate identifier or abbreviation (*p.* or *pp.* for page or pages; *par.* or *pars.* for paragraph or paragraphs; *screen* or *screens*) before the relevant number:

The growth of day care has been called "a crime against posterity" by a spokesman for the Institute for the American Family (Terwilliger, screens 1–2).

MLA Format: The List of Works Cited

As the previous pages explain, parenthetic documentation consists of references that become clear when the reader consults the list titled Works Cited given at the end of an essay.

The list of Works Cited continues the pagination of the essay; if the last page of text is 10, then the Works Cited begins on its own page, in this case page 11. Type the page number in the upper right corner, a half inch from the top of the sheet and flush with the right margin. Next, type the heading Works Cited (*not* enclosed within quotation marks and not italic), centered, one inch from the top, and then double-space and type the first entry.

An Overview   Here are some general guidelines.

FORM ON THE PAGE

- Begin each entry flush with the left margin, but if an entry runs to more than one line, indent a half inch, for each succeeding line of the entry. This is known as a hanging indent, and most word processing programs can achieve this effect easily.
- Double-space each entry, and double-space between entries.
- Italicize titles of works published independently—for instance, books, pamphlets, and journals. Enclose within quotation marks a work not published independently—for instance, an article in a journal or a short story.
- If you are citing a book that includes the title of another book, italicize the main title, but do *not* italicize the title mentioned. Example:

    A Study of Mill's On Liberty

- In the sample entries below, pay attention to the use of commas, colons, and the space after punctuation.

ALPHABETIC ORDER

- Arrange the list alphabetically by author, with the author's last name first.
- For information about anonymous works, works with more than one author, and two or more works by one author, see below.

A Closer Look   Here is more detailed advice.

THE AUTHOR'S NAME

Notice that the last name is given first, but otherwise the name is given as on the title page. Do not substitute initials for names written out on the title page.

If your list includes two or more works by an author, do not repeat the author's name for the second title but represent it by three hyphens followed by a period. The sequence of the works is determined by the alphabetic order of the titles. Thus, Smith's book titled *Poverty* would be listed ahead of her book *Welfare*. See the example on page 287, listing two works by Roger Brown.

Anonymous works are listed under the first word of the title or the second word if the first is *A, An,* or *The* or a foreign equivalent. We discuss books by more than one author, government documents, and works of corporate authorship on pages 287 and 288.

THE TITLE

After the period following the author's name, allow one space and then give the title. Take the title from the title page, not from the cover or the spine, but disregard any unusual typography such as the use of all capital letters or the use of the ampersand (&) for *and.* Underline the title and subtitle (separate them by a colon) with one continuous underline to indicate italics, but do not underline the period that concludes this part of the entry.

- Capitalize the first word and the last word.
- Capitalize all nouns, pronouns, verbs, adjectives, adverbs, and subordinating conjunctions (for example, *although, if, because*).
- Do not capitalize (unless it's the first or last word of the title or the first word of the subtitle) articles (*a, an, the*), prepositions (for instance, *in, on, toward, under*), coordinating conjunctions (for instance, *and, but, or, for*), or the *to* in infinitives.

Examples:

The Death Penalty: A New View

On the Death Penalty: Toward a New View

On the Penalty of Death in a Democracy

PLACE OF PUBLICATION, PUBLISHER, DATE, AND MEDIUM OF PUBLICATION

For the place of publication, provide the name of the city; you can usually find it either on the title page or on the reverse of the title page. If a number of cities are listed, provide only the first. If the city is not likely to be known, or if it may be confused with another city of the same name (as is Oxford, Mississippi, with Oxford, England), add the name of the state, abbreviated using the two-letter postal code.

The name of the publisher is abbreviated. Usually the first word is enough (*Random House* becomes *Random*), but if the first word is a first name, such as in *Alfred A. Knopf,* the surname (*Knopf*) is used instead. University presses are abbreviated thus: *Yale UP, U of Chicago P, State U of New York P.*

The date of publication of a book is given when known; if no date appears on the book, write *n.d.* to indicate "no date."

Because you may find your sources in any number of places, each entry should end by indicating the Medium of Publication for each source ("Print" for books or periodicals, "Web," for sources found on the Internet, and so on).

SAMPLE ENTRIES   Here are some examples, illustrating the points we have covered thus far:

Brown, Roger. *Social Psychology.* New York: Free, 1965. Print.

---. *Words and Things.* Glencoe, IL: Free, 1958. Print.

Douglas, Ann. *The Feminization of American Culture.* New York: Knopf, 1977. Print.

Hartman, Chester. *The Transformation of San Francisco.* Totowa, NJ: Rowman, 1984. Print.

Kellerman, Barbara. *The Political Presidency: Practice of Leadership from Kennedy through Reagan.* New York: Oxford UP, 1984. Print.

Notice that a period follows the author's name and another period follows the title. If a subtitle is given, as it is for Kellerman's book, it is separated from the title by a colon and a space. A colon follows the place of publication, a comma follows the publisher, and a period follows the date.

A BOOK BY MORE THAN ONE AUTHOR

The book is alphabetized under the last name of the first author named on the title page. If there are *two or three authors,* the names of these are given (after the first author's name) in the normal order, *first name first:*

Gilbert, Sandra M., and Susan Gubar. *The Madwoman in the Attic: The Woman Writer and the Nineteenth-Century Literary Imagination.* New Haven: Yale UP, 1979. Print.

Notice, again, that although the first author's name is given *last name first,* the second author's name is given in the normal order, first name first. Notice, too, that a comma is put after the first name of the first author, separating the authors.

If there are *more than three authors,* give the name only of the first and then add (but *not* enclosed within quotation marks and not italic) *et al.* (Latin for "and others").

Altshuler, Alan, et al. *The Future of the Automobile.* Cambridge: MIT P, 1984. Print.

GOVERNMENT DOCUMENTS

If the writer is not known, treat the government and the agency as the author. Most federal documents are issued by the Government Printing Office (abbreviated to *GPO*) in Washington, D.C.

United States. Office of Technology Assessment. *Computerized Manufacturing
Automation: Employment, Education, and the Workplace.* Washington:
GPO, 1984. Print.

WORKS OF CORPORATE AUTHORSHIP

Begin the citation with the corporate author, even if the same body
is also the publisher, as in the first example:

American Psychiatric Association. *Psychiatric Glossary.* Washington: American
Psychiatric Association, 1984. Print.

Carnegie Council on Policy Studies in Higher Education. *Giving Youth a
Better Chance: Options for Educaton, Work, and Service.* San Francisco:
Jossey, 1980. Print.

A REPRINT (FOR INSTANCE, A PAPERBACK VERSION
OF AN OLDER CLOTHBOUND BOOK)

After the title, give the date of original publication (it can usually be
found on the reverse of the title page of the reprint you are using), then
a period, and then the place, publisher, and date of the edition you are
using. The example indicates that Gray's book was originally published
in 1970 and that the student is using the Vintage reprint of 1971.

Gray, Francine du Plessix. *Divine Disobedience: Profiles in Catholic Radi-
calism.* 1970. New York: Vintage, 1971. Print.

A BOOK IN SEVERAL VOLUMES

If you have used more than one volume, in a citation within your
essay you will (as explained on p. 283) indicate a reference to, say, page
250 of volume 3 thus: (3: 250).

If, however, you have used only one volume of the set—let's say
volume 3—in your entry in the Works Cited, specify which volume you
used, as in the next example:

Friedel, Frank. *Franklin D. Roosevelt.* Vol. 3. Boston: Little, 1973. Print. 4 vols.

With such an entry in the Works Cited, the parenthetic citation within
your essay would be to the page only, not to the volume and page, because a reader who consults the Works Cited will understand that you
used only volume 3. In the Works Cited, you may specify volume 3 and
not give the total number of volumes, or you may add the total number
of volumes, as in the preceding example.

ONE BOOK WITH A SEPARATE TITLE IN A SET OF VOLUMES

Sometimes a set with a title makes use also of a separate title for each
book in the set. If you are listing such a book, use the following form:

Churchill, Winston. *The Age of Revolution*. New York: Dodd, 1957. Vol. 3 of *History of English-Speaking Peoples*. Print. 4 vols. 1956-58.

A BOOK WITH AN AUTHOR AND AN EDITOR

Churchill, Winston and Franklin D. Roosevelt. *The Complete Correspodence.* Ed. Warren F. Kimball. 3 vols. Princeton: Princeton UP, 1985. Print.

Kant, Immanuel. *The Philosophy of Kant: Immanuel Kant's Moral and Political Writings*. Ed. Carl J. Friedrich. New York: Modern, 1949. Print.

If you are making use of the editor's introduction or other editorial material rather than of the author's work, list the book under the name of the editor rather than of the author, as shown below under An Introduction, Foreword, or Afterword.

A REVISED EDITION OF A BOOK

Arendt, Hannah. *Eichmann in Jerusalem*. Rev. and enlarged ed. New York: Viking, 1965. Print.

Honour, Hugh, and John Fleming. *The Visual Arts: A History*. 2nd ed. Englewood Cliffs: Prentice, 1986. Print.

A TRANSLATED BOOK

Franqui, Carlos. *Family Portrait with Fidel: A Memoir.* Trans. Alfred MacAdam. New York: Random, 1984. Print.

AN INTRODUCTION, FOREWORD, OR AFTERWORD

Goldberg, Arthur J. Foreword. *An Eye for an Eye? The Morality of Punishing by Death*. By Stephen Nathanson. Totowa, NJ: Rowman, 1987. v-vi. Print.

Usually an introduction or comparable material is listed under the name of the author of the book (here Nathanson) rather than under the name of the writer of the foreword (here Goldberg), but if you are referring to the apparatus rather than to the book itself, use the form just given. The words *Introduction, Preface, Foreword,* and *Afterword* are neither enclosed within quotation marks nor underlined.

A BOOK WITH AN EDITOR BUT NO AUTHOR

Let's assume that you have used a book of essays written by various people but collected by an editor (or editors), whose name(s) appears on the collection.

LaValley, Albert J., ed. *Focus on Hitchcock*. Englewood Cliffs: Prentice, 1972. Print.

If the book has one editor, the abbreviation is *ed.;* if two or more editors, *eds.*

A WORK WITHIN A VOLUME OF WORKS BY ONE AUTHOR

The following entry indicates that a short work by Susan Sontag, an essay called "The Aesthetics of Silence," appears in a book by Sontag titled *Styles of Radical Will.* Notice that the inclusive page numbers of the short work are cited, not merely page numbers that you may happen to refer to but the page numbers of the entire piece.

> Sontag, Susan. "The Aesthetics of Silence." *Styles of Radical Will.* New
> York: Farrar, 1969. 3-34. Print.

A BOOK REVIEW

Here is an example, citing Gerstein's review of Walker's book. Gerstein's review was published in a journal called *Ethics.*

> Gerstein, Robert S. Rev. of *Punishment, Danger, and Stigma: The Morality*
> *of Criminal Justice,* by Nigel Walker. *Ethics* 93 (1983): 408-10. Print.

If the review has a title, give the title between the period following the reviewer's name and *Rev.*

If a review is anonymous, list it under the first word of the title, or under the second word if the first is *A, An,* or *The.* If an anonymous review has no title, begin the entry with *Rev. of,* and then give the title of the work reviewed; alphabetize the entry under the title of the work reviewed.

AN ARTICLE OR ESSAY (NOT A REPRINT) IN A COLLECTION

A book may consist of a collection (edited by one or more persons) of new essays by several authors. Here is a reference to one essay in such a book. (The essay by Balmforth occupies pages 19 to 35 in a collection edited by Bevan.)

> Balmouth, Henry. "Science and Religion." *Steps to Christian Understanding.*
> Ed. R. J. W. Bevan. London: Oxford UP, 1958. 19-35. Print.

AN ARTICLE OR ESSAY REPRINTED IN A COLLECTION

The previous example (Balmforth's essay in Bevan's collection) was for an essay written for a collection. But some collections reprint earlier material, such as essays from journals or chapters from books. The following example cites an essay that was originally printed in a book called *The Cinema of Alfred Hitchcock.* This essay has been reprinted in a later collection of essays on Hitchcock, edited by Albert J. LaValley, and it was LaValley's collection that the student used.

> Bogdanovich, Peter. "Interviews with Alfred Hitchcock." *The Cinema of Alfred Hitchcock.* New York: Museum of Modern Art, 1963. 15-18. Rpt. in *Focus on Hitchcock.* Ed. Albert J. LaValley. Englewood Cliffs: Prentice, 1972. 28-31. Print.

The student has read Bogdanovich's essay or chapter, but not in Bogdanovich's book, where it occupied pages 15 to 18. The material was actually read on pages 28 to 31 in a collection of writings on Hitchcock, edited by LaValley. Details of the original publication—title, date, page numbers, and so forth—were found in LaValley's collection. Almost all editors will include this information, either on the copyright page or at the foot of the reprinted essay, but sometimes they do not give the original page numbers. In such a case, you need not include the original numbers in your entry.

Notice that the entry begins with the author and the title of the work you are citing (here, Bogdanovich's interviews), not with the name of the editor of the collection or the title of the collection.

AN ENCYCLOPEDIA OR OTHER ALPHABETICALLY ARRANGED REFERENCE WORK

The publisher, place of publication, volume number, and page number do *not* have to be given. For such works, list only the edition (if it is given) and the date.

For a *signed* article, begin with the author's last name. (If the article is signed with initials, check elsewhere in the volume for a list of abbreviations, which will inform you who the initials stand for, and use the following form.)

> Williams, Donald C. "Free Will and Determination." *Encyclopedia Americana.* 1987 ed. Print.

For an *unsigned article,* begin with the title of the article:

> "Automation." *The Business Reference Book.* 1977 ed. Print.

> "Tobacco." *Encyclopedia Britannica: Macropaedia.* 1988 ed. Print.

A TELEVISION OR RADIO PROGRAM

Be sure to include the title of the episode or segment (in quotation marks), the title of the show (underlined), the network, the call letters and city of the station, and the date of broadcast. Other information, such as performers, narrator, and so forth, may be included if pertinent.

> "Back to My Lai." *60 Minutes.* Narr. Mike Wallace. CBS. 29 Mar. 1998. Television.

> "Juvenile Justice." *Talk of the Nation.* Narr. Ray Suarez. Natl. Public Radio. WBUR, Boston. 15 Apr. 1998. Radio.

AN ARTICLE IN A SCHOLARLY JOURNAL   The title of the article is enclosed within quotation marks, and the title of the journal is underlined to indicate italics.

Some journals are paginated consecutively; the pagination of the second issue begins where the first issue leaves off. Other journals begin each issue with page 1.

A JOURNAL THAT IS PAGINATED CONSECUTIVELY

Vilas, Carlos M. "Popular Insurgency and Social Revolution in Central
America." *Latin American Perspectives* 15.1 (1988): 55-77. Print.

Vilas's article occupies pages 55 to 77 in volume 15, which was published in 1988. (Notice that the volume number is followed by a space, then by the year in parentheses, and then by a colon, a space, and the page numbers of the entire article.) When available, give the issue number.

A JOURNAL THAT BEGINS EACH ISSUE WITH PAGE 1

If the journal is, for instance, a quarterly, there will be four page 1's each year, so the issue number must be given. After the volume number, type a period and (without hitting the space bar) the issue number, as in the next example:

Greenberg, Jack. "Civil Rights Enforcement Activity of the Department of
Justice." *Black Law Journal* 8.1 (1983): 60-67. Print.

Greenberg's article appeared in the first issue of volume 8 of the *Black Law Journal*.

AN ARTICLE IN A WEEKLY, BIWEEKLY, MONTHLY, OR BIMONTHLY PUBLICATION

Do not include volume or issue numbers, even if given.

Lamar, Jacob V. "The Immigration Mess." *Time* 27 Feb. 1989: 14-15. Print.

Markowitz, Laura. "A Different Kind of Queer Marriage." *Utne Reader*
Sept.-Oct. 2000: 24-26. Print.

AN ARTICLE IN A NEWSPAPER

Because a newspaper usually consists of several sections, a section number or a capital letter may precede the page number. The example indicates that an article begins on page 1 of section 2 and is continued on a later page.

Chu, Harry. "Art Thief Defends Action." *New York Times* 8 Feb. 1989, sec.
2: 1+. Print.

AN UNSIGNED EDITORIAL

"The Religious Tyranny Amendment." Editorial. *New York Times* 15 Mar.
1998, sec. 4: 16. Print.

A LETTER TO THE EDITOR

Lasken, Douglas. Letter. *New York Times* 15 Mar. 1998, sec. 4: 16. Print.

A PUBLISHED OR BROADCAST INTERVIEW

Give the name of the interview subject and the interviewer, followed by
the relevant publication or broadcast information, in the following format:

Green, Al. Interview with Terry Gross. *Fresh Air.* Nat. Public Radion. WFCR,
Amherst, MA. 16 Oct. 2000. Radio.

AN INTERVIEW YOU CONDUCT

Jevgrafovs, Alexandre L. Personal [or Telephone] interview. 14 Dec. 2003.

PERSONAL CORRESPONDENCE

Add "TS" for a typed letter, "MS" for a handwritten letter, or "E-mail"
to the end of the citation.

Paso, Robert. Letter [or Message, in the case of E-mail] to the author. 6
Jan. 2004. TS.

CD-ROM

Books on CD-ROM are cited very much like their printed counterparts. For articles, to the usual print citation information, add (1) the title
of the database, underlined; (2) the medium (*CD-ROM*); (3) the vendor's
name; and (4) the date of electronic publication.

Louisberg, Margaret. *Charlie Brown Meets Godzilla: What Are Our Children
Watching?* Urbana: ERIC Clearinghouse on Elementary and Early
Childhood Education, 1990. CD-ROM.

"Pornography." *The Oxford English Dictionary.* 2nd ed. CD-ROM. Oxford:
Oxford UP, 1992.

A PERSONAL OR PROFESSIONAL WEB SITE

Include the following elements, separated by periods: site title (underlined), the name of the person who created the site (omit if not given,
as in the example below), date of electronic publication or of the latest
update (if given), name of any sponsoring institution or organization,
date of access, and electronic address.

School for Science and Technology. U of Massachusetts Dartmouth. Web.
   10 Oct. 2000.

AN ARTICLE IN AN ONLINE PERIODICAL

Give the same information as you would for a print article, plus the
date of access and electronic address.

Trammell, George W. "Cirque du O.J." *Court Technology Bulletin.* National
   Center for State Courts, July-Aug. 1995. Web. 12 Sept. 1996.

AN ONLINE POSTING

Citation includes the author's name, subject line of posting, description *Online posting* if the posting has no title, date material was posted,
name of the forum, date of access, and address.

Ricci, Paul. "Global Warming." Global Electronic Science Conference, 10
   June 1996. Web. 22 Sept. 1997.

A DATABASE SOURCE

Treat material obtained from a computer service, such as Bibliographic
Retrieval Service (BRS), like other printed material, but at the end of the
entry add (if available) the title of the database (italicized), publication medium (*Web*), name of the computer service, and date of access.

Jackson, Morton. "A Look at Profits." *Harvard Business Review* 40 (1962):
   106-13. *BRS.* Web. 23 Dec. 2006.

Caution: Although we have covered the most usual kinds of
sources, it is entirely possible that you will come across a source
that does not fit any of the categories that we have discussed. For
approximately two hundred pages of explanations of these matters, covering the proper way to cite all sorts of troublesome and
unbelievable (but real) sources, see *MLA Handbook for Writers of
Research Papers,* Seventh Edition (New York: Modern Language
Association of America, 2009).

APA Format: Citations within the Text

Your paper will conclude with a separate page headed References, in
which you list all of your sources. If the last page of your essay is numbered 10, number the first page of the References 11.

The APA style emphasizes the date of publication; the date appears not
only in the list of references at the end of the paper but also in the paper
itself, when you give a brief parenthetic citation of a source that you have
quoted or summarized or in any other way used. Here is an example:

Statistics are readily available (Smith, 1989, p. 20).

The title of Smith's book or article will be given at the end of your paper, in the list titled References. We discuss the form of the material listed in the References after we look at some typical citations within the text of a student's essay.

A SUMMARY OF AN ENTIRE WORK

Smith (1988) holds the same view.

or

Similar views are held widely (Smith, 1988; Jones & Metz, 1990).

A REFERENCE TO A PAGE OR TO PAGES

Smith (1988) argues that "the death penalty is a lottery, and blacks usually are the losers" (p. 17).

A REFERENCE TO AN AUTHOR WHO HAS MORE THAN ONE WORK IN THE LIST OF REFERENCES

If in the References you list two or more works that an author published in the same year, the works are listed in alphabetic order, by the first letter of the title. The first work is labeled *a*, the second *b*, and so on. Here is a reference to the second work that Smith published in 1989:

Florida presents "a fair example" of how the death penalty is administered (Smith, 1989b, p. 18).

APA Format: The List of References

Your brief parenthetic citations are made clear when the reader consults the list you give in the References. Type this list on a separate page, continuing the pagination of your essay.

An Overview   Here are some general guidelines.

FORM ON THE PAGE

- Begin each entry flush with the left margin, but if an entry runs to more than one line, indent five spaces for each succeeding line of the entry.
- Double-space each entry, and double-space between entries.

ALPHABETIC ORDER

- Arrange the list alphabetically by author.
- Give the author's last name first and then the initial of the first name and of the middle name (if any).

- If there is more than one author, name all of the authors up to seven, again inverting the name (last name first) and giving only initials for first and middle names. (But do not invert the editor's name when the entry begins with the name of an author who has written an article in an edited book.) When there are two or more authors, use an ampersand (&) before the name of the last author. Example (here, of an article in the tenth volume of a journal called *Developmental Psychology*):

Drabman, R. S., & Thomas, M. H. (1974). Does media violence increase children's tolerance of real-life aggression? *Developmental Psychology,* 10, 418–421.

- For eight or more authors, list the first six as explained above, then three periods, then the last author.

- If you list more than one work by an author, do so in the order of publication, the earliest first. If two works by an author were published in the same year, give them in alphabetic order by the first letter of the title, disregarding *A, An,* or *The,* and their foreign equivalent. Designate the first work as *a,* the second as *b.* Repeat the author's name at the start of each entry.

Donnerstein, E. (1980a). Aggressive erotica and violence against women. *Journal of Personality and Social Psychology, 39,* 269–277.

Donnerstein, E. (1980b). Pornography and violence against women. *Annals of the New York Academy of Sciences, 347,* 227–288.

Donnerstein, E. (1983). Erotica and human aggression. In R. Green and E. Donnerstein (Eds.), *Aggression: Theoretical and empirical reviews* (pp. 87–103). New York, NY: Academic Press.

FORM OF TITLE

- In references to books, capitalize only the first letter of the first word of the title (and of the subtitle, if any) and capitalize proper nouns. Italicize the complete title (but not the period at the end).

- In references to articles in periodicals or in edited books, capitalize only the first letter of the first word of the article's title (and subtitle, if any) and all proper nouns. Do not put the title within quotation marks. Type a period after the title of the article. For the title of the journal and the volume and page numbers, see the next instruction.

- In references to periodicals, give the volume number in arabic numerals, and italicize it. Do *not* use *vol.* before the number, and do not use *p.* or *pg.* before the page numbers.

Sample References   Here are some samples to follow.

A BOOK BY ONE AUTHOR

Pavlov, I. P. (1927). *Conditioned reflexes* (G. V. Anrep, Trans.). London, England: Oxford University Press.

A BOOK BY MORE THAN ONE AUTHOR

Belenky, M. F., Clinchy, B. M., Goldberger, N. R., & Torule, J. M. (1986). *Women's ways of knowing: The development of self, voice, and mind.* New York, NY: Basic Books.

A COLLECTION OF ESSAYS

Christ, C. P., & Plaskow, J. (Eds.). (1979). *Womanspirit rising: A feminist reader in religion.* New York, NY: Harper & Row.

A WORK IN A COLLECTION OF ESSAYS

Fiorenza, E. (1979). Women in the early Christian movement. In C. P. Christ & J. Plaskow (Eds.), *Woman-spirit rising: A feminist reader in religion* (pp. 84–92). New York, NY: Harper & Row.

GOVERNMENT DOCUMENTS

If the writer is not known, treat the government and the agency as the author. Most federal documents are issued by the Government Printing Office in Washington, D.C. If a document number has been assigned, insert that number in parentheses between the title and the following period.

United States Congress. Office of Technology Assessment. (1984). *Computerized manufacturing automation: Employment, education, and the workplace.* Washington, D.C.: Government Printing Office.

AN ARTICLE IN A JOURNAL WITH CONTINUOUS PAGINATION

Tversky, A., & Kahneman, D. (1981). The framing of decisions and the psychology of choice. *Science, 211,* 453–458.

**AN ARTICLE IN A JOURNAL THAT PAGINATES
EACH ISSUE SEPARATELY**

Foot, R. J. (1988-89). Nuclear coercion and the ending of the Korean conflict. *International Security, 13*(4), 92–112.

The reference informs us that the article appeared in issue number 4 of volume 13.

AN ARTICLE FROM A MONTHLY OR WEEKLY MAGAZINE

Greenwald, J. (1989, February 27). Gimme shelter. *Time, 133,* 50-51.

Maran, S. P. (1988, April). In our backyard, a star explodes. *Smithsonian, 19,* 46–57.

AN ARTICLE IN A NEWSPAPER

Connell, R. (1989, February 6). Career concerns at heart of 1980s' campus protests. *Los Angeles Times,* pp. 1, 3.

(*Note:* If no author is given, simply begin with the title followed by the date in parentheses.)

A BOOK REVIEW

Daniels, N. (1984). Understanding physician power [Review of the book *The social transformation of American medicine*]. *Philosophy and Public Affairs, 13,* 347–356.

Daniels is the reviewer, not the author of the book. The book under review is called *The Social Transformation of American Medicine,* but the review, published in volume 13 of *Philosophy and Public Affairs,* had its own title, "Understanding Physician Power."

If the review does not have a title, retain the square brackets, and use the material within as the title. Proceed as in the example just given.

A WEB SITE

American Psychological Association. (1995). Lesbian and gay parenting. Retrieved from http://www.apa.org/

AN ARTICLE IN AN ONLINE PERIODICAL

Carpenter, S. (2000, October). Biology and social environments jointly influence gender development. *Monitor on Psychology 31.* Retrieved from http://www.apa.org/

For a full account of the APA method of dealing with all sorts of unusual citations, see the sixth edition (2010) of the APA manual, *Publication Manual of the American Psychological Association.*

✓ A CHECKLIST FOR PAPERS USING SOURCES

Ask yourself the following questions:

☐ Are all borrowed words and ideas credited, including those from Internet sources?

☐ Are all summaries and paraphrases acknowledged as such?

☐ Are quotations and summaries not too long?

☐ Are quotations accurate? Are omissions of words indicated by three spaced periods? Are additions of words enclosed within square brackets?

☐ Are quotations provided with helpful lead-ins?

☐ Is documentation in proper form?

And of course, you will also ask yourself the questions that you would ask of a paper that did not use sources, such as:

☐ Is the topic sufficiently narrowed?

☐ Is the thesis (to be advanced or refuted) stated early and clearly, perhaps even in the title?

☐ Is the audience kept in mind? Are opposing views stated fairly and as sympathetically as possible? Are controversial terms defined?

☐ Are assumptions likely to be shared by readers? If not, are they argued rather than merely asserted?

☐ Is the focus clear (evaluation, recommendation of policy)?

☐ Is evidence (examples, testimony, statistics) adequate and sound?

☐ Are inferences valid?

☐ Is the organization clear (effective opening, coherent sequence of arguments, unpretentious ending)?

☐ Is all worthy opposition faced?

☐ Is the tone appropriate?

☐ Has the paper been carefully proofread?

☐ Is the title effective?

☐ Is the opening paragraph effective?

☐ Is the structure reader-friendly?

☐ Is the closing paragraph effective?

AN ANNOTATED STUDENT RESEARCH
PAPER IN MLA FORMAT

The following argument makes good use of sources. Early in the semester the students were asked to choose one topic from a list of ten, and to write a documented argument of 750 to 1,250 words (three to five pages of double-spaced typing). The completed paper was due two weeks after the topics were distributed. The assignment, a prelude to working on a research paper of 2,500 to 3,000 words, was in part designed to give students practice in finding and in using sources. Citations are given in the MLA form.

The *MLA Handbook* does not insist on a title page and outline, but many instructors prefer them.

Why Trials Should Not Be Televised

By

Theresa Washington

Title one-third down page

Professor Wilson

English 102

12 December 2006

All lines centered

Small roman
numerals for
page with
outline

Outline

Thesis: The televising of trials is a bad idea because it has several
negative effects on the First Amendment: It gives viewers a
deceptive view of particular trials and of the judicial system
in general, and it degrades the quality of media reporting
outside the courtroom.

I. Introduction

   A. Trend toward increasing trial coverage

   B. First Amendment versus Sixth Amendment

II. Effect of televising trials on First Amendment

   A. Provides deceptive version of truth

Roman numerals
for chief units
(I, II, etc.); capital
letters for chief
units within
these largest
units; for smaller
and smaller
units, arabic
numerals and
lowercase letters

      1. Confidence in verdicts misplaced

         a. William Smith trial

         b. Rodney King trial

      2. Nature of TV as a medium

         a. Distortion in sound bites

         b. Stereotyping trial participants

         c. Misleading camera angles

         d. Commentators and commercials

   B. Confuses viewers about judicial system

      1. Contradicts basic concept "innocent until proven guilty"

      2. Can't explain legal complexities

   C. Contributes to media circus outside of court

      1. Blurs truth and fiction

      2. Affects print media in negative ways

      3. Media makes itself the story

      4. Distracts viewers from other issues

III. Conclusion

Washington 1

Why Trials Should Not Be Televised

Although trials have been televised on and off since the 1950s,[1] in the last few years the availability of trials for a national audience has increased dramatically.[2] Media critics, legal scholars, social scientists, and journalists continue to debate the merits of this trend.

Proponents of cameras in the courtroom argue, falsely, I believe, that confidence in the fairness of our institutions, including the judicial system, depends on a free press, guaranteed by the First Amendment. Keeping trials off television is a form of censorship, they say. It limits the public's ability to understand (1) what is happening in particular trials and (2) how the judicial system operates, which is often confusing to laypeople. Opponents claim that televising trials threatens the defendant's Sixth Amendment rights to a fair trial because it can alter the behavior of the trial participants, including the jury ("Tale"; Thaler).

Regardless of its impact on due process of law,[3] TV in court does not serve the First Amendment well. Consider the first claim, that particular trials are easier to understand when televised. But does watching trials on television really allow the viewer to "see it like it is," to get the full scope and breadth of a trial? Steven Brill, founder of Court TV, would like us to believe so. He points out that most high-profile defendants in televised trials have been acquitted; he names William Kennedy Smith, Jimmy Hoffa, John Connally, and John Delorean as examples (Clark 821). "Imagine if [Smith's trial] had not been shown and he got off. Millions of people would have said the Kennedys fixed the case" (Brill qtd. in "Tale" 29). Polls taken after the trial seem to confirm this claim, since they showed the public by and large agreed with the jury's decision to acquit (Quindlen).

However, Thaler points out that the public can just as easily

Title is focused and announces the thesis.

Double-space between title and first paragraph — and throughout the essay.

←——→|

1″ margin on each side and at bottom

Summary of opposing positions

Parenthetic reference to an anonymous source and also to a source with a named author

Superscript numerals indicate endnotes.

Parenthetic reference to author and page

Parenthetic reference to an indirect source (a borrowed quotation)

Washington 2

disagree with the verdict as agree, and when this happens, the effects
can be catastrophic. One example is the Rodney King case. Four white
Los Angeles police officers were charged in 1991 with severely beating
African American Rodney King, who, according to the officers, had
been resisting arrest. At their first trial, all four officers were
acquitted. This verdict outraged many African Americans throughout
the country; they felt the evidence from watching the trial
overwhelmingly showed the defendants to be guilty. The black
community of south-central Los Angeles expressed its feelings by
rioting for days (Thaler 50–51).

Clearly the black community did not experience the trial the
same way the white community and the white jury did. Why? Marty
Rosenbaum, an attorney with the New York State Defenders
Association, points out that viewers cannot experience a trial the
same way trial participants do. "What you see at home 'is not what
jurors see' " (qtd. in Thaler 70). The trial process is slow, linear, and
methodical, as the defense and prosecution each builds its case, one
piece of information at a time (Thaler 11). The process is intended to
be thoughtful and reflective, with the jury weighing all the evidence
in light of the whole trial (Altheide 299–301). And it emphasizes
words--both spoken and written--rather than images (Thaler 11).

In contrast, TV's general strength is in handling visual images
that entertain or that provoke strong feelings. News editors and
reporters choose footage for its assumed visual and emotional impact
on viewers. Words are made to fit the images, not the other way
around, and they tend to be short catchy phrases, easy to understand
(Thaler 4, 7). As a result, the fifteen- to thirty-second "sound bites"
in nightly newscasts often present trial events out of context,
emphasizing moments of drama rather than of legal importance
(Thaler 7; Zoglin 62).

Although no words are quoted, the idea is borrowed, and so the source is cited.

Clear transition ("In contrast")

Parenthetic citation of two sources

Washington 3

Furthermore, this emphasis on emotional visuals leads to stereotyping the participants, making larger-than-life symbols out of them, especially regarding social issues (Thaler 9): abused children (the Menendez brothers), the battered wife (Hedda Nussbaum), the abusing husband (Joel Steinberg, O. J. Simpson), the jealous lover (Amy Fisher), the serial killer (Jeffrey Dahmer), and date rapist (William Smith). It becomes difficult for viewers to see defendants as ordinary human beings.

One can argue, as Brill has done, that gavel-to-gavel coverage of trials counteracts the distortions in sound-bite journalism (Clark 821). Yet even here a number of editorial assumptions and decisions affect what viewers see. Camera angles and movements reinforce in the viewer differing degrees of intimacy with the trial participant; close-ups are often used for sympathetic witnesses, three-quarter shots for lawyers, and profile shots for defendants (Entner 73–75).[4]

> Summary of an opposing view countered with a clear transition ("Yet")

On-air commentators also shape the viewers' experience. Several media critics have noted how much commentators' remarks often have the play-by-play tone of sportscasters informing viewers of what each side (the defense and the prosecution) needs to win (Cole 245; Thaler 71, 151). Continual interruptions for commercials add to the impression of watching a spectacle. "The CNN coverage [of the Smith trial] isn't so much gavel-to-gavel], actually, as gavel-to-commercial-to-gavel, with former CNN Gulf War correspondent Charles Jaco acting more as ringleader than reporter" (Bianculli 60). This encourages a sensationalistic tone to the proceedings that the jury does not experience. In addition, breaking for ads frequently occurs at important points in the trial (Thaler 48).

In-court proponents also believe that watching televised trials will help viewers understand the legal aspects of the judicial system. In June 1991, a month before Court TV went on the air, Vincent Blasi,

Washington 4

Author lets reader hear the opposition by means of a brief quotation

Omitted material indicated by three periods, with a fourth to mark the end of a sentence

Quotation of more than four lines, indented 1″ (ten spaces) from left margin, double-spaced, parenthetic reference set off from quotation

a law professor at Columbia University, told *Time* magazine, "Today most of us learn about judicial proceedings from lawyers' sound bites and artists' sketches. . . . Televised proceedings [such as Court TV] ought to dispel some of the myth and mystery that shroud our legal system" (qtd. in Zoglin 62).

But after several years of Court TV and CNN, we can now see this is not so. As a medium, TV is not good at educating the general public, either about concepts fundamental to our judicial system or about the complexities in particular cases.

For example, one basic concept--"innocent until proven guilty"--is contradicted in televised trials in numerous subtle ways: Commentators sometimes make remarks about (or omit comment on) actions of the defense or prosecution that show a bias against the defendant.

Media critic Lewis Cole, watching the trial of Lorena Bobbitt on Court TV in 1994, observed:

> Court TV commentators rarely challenged the state's characterization of what it was doing, repeating without comment, for instance, the prosecution's claims about protecting the reputation of Lorena Bobbitt and concentrating on the prosecution decision to pursue both cases as a tactical matter, rather than inquiring how the prosecution's view of the incident as a "barroom brawl" had limited its approach to and understanding of the case. (245)

Camera angles play a role also: Watching the defendant day after day in profile, which makes him or her seem either vulnerable or remote, tends to reinforce his or her guilt (Entner 158).

Thaler points out that these editorial effects arise because the goals of the media (print as well as electronic) differ from the goals of

Washington 5

the judicial system. His argument runs as follows: The court is interested in determining only whether the defendant broke the law. The media (especially TV) focus on acts to reinforce social values, whether they're codified into law or not. This can lead viewers to conclude that a defendant is guilty because pretrial publicity or courtroom testimony reveals he or she has transgressed against the community's moral code, even when the legal system later acquits. This happened in the case of Claus von Bulow, who between 1982 and 1985 was tried and acquitted twice for attempting to murder his wife and who clearly had behaved in reprehensible ways in the eyes of the public (35). It also happened in the case of Joel Steinberg, who was charged with murdering his daughter. Extended televised testimony by his former partner, Hedda Nussbaum, helped paint a portrait of "a monster" in the eyes of the public (140–42). Yet the jury chose to convict him on the lesser charge of manslaughter. When many viewers wrote to the prosecutor, Peter Casolaro, asking why the verdict was not first-degree murder, he had to conclude that TV does not effectively teach about due process of law (176).

Argument supported by specific examples

In addition to being poor at handling basic judicial concepts, television has difficulty conveying more complex and technical aspects of the law. Sometimes the legal nature of the case makes for a poor translation to the screen. Brill admitted that, despite attempts at hourly summaries, Court TV was unable to convey to its viewers any meaningful understanding of the case of Manuel Noriega (Thaler 61), the Panamanian leader who was convicted by the United States in 1992 of drug trafficking and money laundering ("Former"). In other cases, like the Smith trial, the "civics lesson" gets swamped by its sensational aspects (Thaler 45). In most cases print media are better at exploring and explaining legal issues than is TV (Thaler 4).

In addition to shaping the viewer's perceptions of trial reality

Washington 6

Transition
briefly
summarizes
and then
moves to a
new point.

directly, in-court TV also negatively affects the quality of trial
coverage outside of court, which in turn limits the public's "right to
know." Brill likes to claim that Court TV helps to counteract the
sensationalism of such tabloid TV shows as *A Current Affair* and *Hard
Copy*, which pay trial participants to tell their stories and publish
leaks from the prosecution and defense. "I think cameras in the

The author
uses "[*sic*]"
(Latin for
"thus") to
indicate that
the oddity is
in the source
and is not by
the author of
the paper.

courtroom is [sic] the best antidote to that garbage" (Brill qtd. in
Clark 821). However, as founder and editor of Court TV, he obviously
has a vested interest in affirming his network's social and legal worth.
There are several ways that in-court TV, rather than supplying a
sobering contrast, helps to feed the media circus surrounding high-
profile trials (Thaler 43).

One way is by helping to blur the line between reality and
fiction. This is an increasing trend among all media but is especially
true of TV, whose footage can be combined and recombined in so
many ways. An excellent example of this is the trial of Amy Fisher,
who pleaded guilty in September 1992 to shooting her lover's wife
and whose sentencing was televised by Court TV (Thaler 83). Three TV
movies about this love triangle appeared on network TV in the same
week, just one month after she had been sentenced to five to fifteen
years of jail (Thaler 82). Then Geraldo Rivera, the syndicated TV talk-
show host, held a mock grand jury trial of her lover, Joey Buttafuoco;
even though Buttafuoco had not at that point been charged with a
crime, Geraldo felt many viewers thought he ought to have been
(Thaler 83). Then *A Current Affair* had a series that "tried" Fisher for
events and behaviors that never got resolved in the actual trial. The
announcer on the program said, "When Ms. Fisher copped a plea and
went to jail, she robbed the public of a trial, leaving behind many
unanswered questions. Tonight we will try to . . . complete the
unwritten chapter" ("Trial"). Buttafuoco's lawyer from the trial served

Washington 7

as a consultant on this program (Thaler 84). This is also a good

example of how tabloid TV reinforces people's beliefs and plays on
people's feelings. Had her trial not been televised, the excitement
surrounding her case would not have been so high. Tabloid TV played
off the audience's expectation for what a televised trial should and
could reveal. Thus in-court television becomes one more ingredient in
the mix of docudramas, mock trials, talk shows, and tabloid
journalism. This limits the public's "right to know" by making it
difficult to keep fact separate from storytelling.

In-court TV also affects the quality of print journalism.
Proponents like to claim that "[f]rom the standpoint of the public's
right to know, there is no good reason why TV journalists should be
barred from trials while print reporters are not" (Zoglin 62). But when
TV is present, there is no level playing field among the media. Because
it provides images, sound, movement, and a greater sense of speed

and immediacy, TV can easily outcompete other media for audience
attention and thus for advertising dollars. In attempts to keep pace,
newspapers and magazines offer more and more of the kinds of stories
that once were beneath their standards, such as elaborate focus both
on sensational aspects of the case and on "personalities, analysis, and
prediction" rather than news (Thaler 45). While these attributes have
always been part of TV and the tabloid print press, this trend is
increasingly apparent in supposedly reputable papers like the *New
York Times*. During the Smith trial, for example, the *Times* violated
previously accepted boundaries of propriety by not only identifying
the rape victim but also giving lots of intimate details about her past
(Thaler 45).

Because the media are, for the most part, commercial, slow
periods--and all trials have them--must always be filled with some
"story." One such story is increasingly the media self-consciously

watching and analyzing itself, to see how it is handling (or mishandling) coverage of the trial (Thaler 43). At the Smith trial, for example, one group of reporters was covering the trial while another group covered the other reporters (Thaler 44).[5] As bizarre as this "media watching" is, there would be no "story" if the trial itself had not been televised.

Last but not least, televising trials distracts viewers from other important issues. Some of these are abstract and thus hard to understand (like the savings-and-loan scandal in the mid-1980s or the causes of lingering unemployment in the 1990s), while others are painful to contemplate (like overseas wars and famines). Yet we have to stay aware of these issues if we are to function as active citizens in a democracy.

Altogether, televising trials is a bad idea. Not only does it provide deceptive impressions about what's happening in particular trials; it also doesn't reveal much about our judicial system. In addition, televising trials helps to lower the quality of trial coverage outside of court, thus increasingly depriving the public of neutral, fact-based reporting. A healthy free press depends on balance and knowing when to accept limits. Saturating viewers with extended media coverage of sensational trials oversteps those limits. In this case, more is not better.

Yet it is unlikely that TV coverage will be legally removed from the courtroom, now that it is here. Only one state (New York) has ever legislated a return to nontelevised trials (in 1991), and even it changed its mind in 1992 (Thaler 78). Perhaps the best we can do is to educate ourselves about the pitfalls of televising the judicial system, as we struggle to do so with the televised electoral process.

Margin annotations:

No citation is needed for a point that can be considered common knowledge, but the second sentence *is* documented.

Useful summary of main points

Realistic appraisal of the current situation and a suggestion of what the reader can do

Washington 9

Notes

[1] Useful discussions of this history can be found in Clark (829–32) and Thaler (19–31).

[2] Cable networks have been showing trial footage to national audiences since at least 1982, when Cable News Network (CNN) covered the trial of Claus von Bulow (Thaler 33). It continues to show trials. In the first week of February 1995, four to five million homes accounted for the top fifteen most-watched shows on cable TV; all were CNN segments of the O. J. Simpson trial ("Cable TV"). In July 1991, Steven Brill founded the Courtroom Television Network, or "Court TV" (Clark 821). Like CNN, it broadcasts around the clock, showing gavel-to-gavel coverage. It now claims over fourteen million cable subscribers (Clark 821) and, as of January 1994, had televised over 280 trials ("In Camera" 27).

[3] Thaler's study *The Watchful Eye* is a thoughtful examination of the subtle ways in which TV in court can affect trial participants, inhibiting witnesses from coming forward, provoking grandstanding in attorneys and judges, and pressuring juries to come up with verdicts acceptable to a national audience.

[4] Sometimes legal restrictions determine camera angles. For example, in the Steinberg trial (1988), the audience and the jury were not allowed to be televised by New York state law. This required placing the camera so that the judge and witnesses were seen in "full frontal view" (generally a more neutral or positive stance). The lawyers could be seen only from the rear when questioning witnesses, and the defendant was shot in profile (Thaler 110–11). These camera angles, though not chosen for dramatic effect, still resulted in emotionally laden viewpoints not experienced by the jury. George W. Trammell, a Los Angeles Superior Court Judge, has written on how technology can interfere with the fairness of the trial system. He

Washington 10

claims that "[t]echnology, well managed, can be a great benefit. Technology poorly managed benefits no one."

[5] At the Smith trial a journalist from one German newspaper inadvertently filmed another German reporter from a competing newspaper watching the Smith trial in the pressroom outside the courtroom (Thaler 44).

Washington 11

Works Cited

Altheide, David. "TV News and the Social Construction of Justice." *Justice and the Media: Issues and Research.* Ed. Ray Surette. Springfield, IL: Thomas, 1984. 292-304 Print.

Bianculli, David. "Shame on You, CNN." *New York Post* 11 Dec. 1992: 60. Print.

"Cable TV Squeezes High Numbers and Aces Competition." *All Things Considered.* Natl Public Radio. 9 Feb 1994. Unedited Transcript. Segment 12. NPR Audience Services. Washington. Print.

Clark, Charles S. "Courts and the Media." *CQ Researcher* 23 Sept. 1994: 817-40. Print.

Cole, Lewis. "Court TV." *Nation* 21 Feb 1994: 243-45. Print.

Entner, Roberta. "Encoding the Image of the American Judiciary Institution: A Semiotic Analysis of Broadcast Trials to Ascertain Its Definition of the Court System." Diss. New York U, 1993. Print.

"Former Panamanian Leader Noriega Sentenced." *Facts on File* 16 July 1992: 526. CD-ROM. *InfoTrac: Magazine Index Plus 1992-Feb. 1995.* Information Access. Feb. 1995.

"In Camera with Court TV." *New Yorker* 24 Jan. 1994: 27-28. Print.

Quindlen, Anna. "The Glass Eye." *New York Times* 18 Dec. 1991: A29. Print.

"A Tale of a Rug." *Economist* 15 Jan. 1994: 28-29. Print.

Thaler, Paul. *The Watchful Eye: American Justice in the Age of the Television Trial.* Westport, CT: Praeger, 1994. Print.

Trammell, George W. "Cirque du O.J." *Court Technology Bulletin.* National Center for State Courts, July-Aug. 1995. Web. 12 Sept. 1996.

"The Trial That Had to Happen: The People versus Amy Fisher." *A Current Affair.* Fox. WFXT, Boston. 1-4 Feb. 1993. Television.

Zoglin, Richard. "Justice Faces a Screen Test." *Time* 17 June 1991: 62. Print.

Alphabetical by author's last name

Hanging indent 1/2"

Transcript of radio program

The title of an unpublished work is not italicized but is enclosed within quotation marks.

CD-ROM source

Anonymous source alphabetized under first word (or second if first is *A, An,* or *The*)

No page reference for this in-text Internet citation

Television program

AN ANNOTATED STUDENT RESEARCH PAPER IN APA FORMAT

The following paper is an example of a student paper that uses APA format.

The Role of Spirituality and Religion

in Mental Health

Laura DeVeau

The APA-style
cover page
gives title,
author, and
course
information.

English 102

Professor Gardner

October 12, 2009

Religion in Mental Health 1

The Role of Spirituality and Religion

in Mental Health

It has been called "a vestige of the childhood of mankind," "the feeling of something true, total and absolute," "an otherworldly answer as regards the meaning of life" (Jones, 1991, p. 1; Amaro, 2000; Kristeva, 1987, p. 27). It has been compared to medicine, described as a psychological cure for mental illness, and also referred to as the cause of a dangerous fanaticism. With so many differing opinions on the impact of religion in people's lives, where would one begin a search for the truth? Who has the answer: Christians, humanists, objectivists, atheists, psychoanalysts, Buddhists, philosophers, cults? This was my dilemma at the advent of my research into how religion and spirituality affect the mental health of society as a whole.

In this paper, I explore the claims, widely accepted by professionals in the field of psychology, that religious and spiritual practices have a negative impact on mental health. In addition, though, I cannot help but reflect on how this exploration has changed my beliefs as well. Religion is such a personal experience that one cannot be dispassionate in reporting it. One can, however, subject the evidence provided by those who have studied the issue to critical scrutiny. Having done so, I find myself in disagreement with those who claim religious feelings are incompatible with sound mental health. There is a nearly limitless number of beliefs regarding spirituality. Some are organized and involve rituals like mass or worship. Many are centered around the existence of a higher being, while others focus on the self. I have attempted to uncover the perfect set of values that lead to a better lifestyle, but my research has pointed me in an entirely different direction, where no single belief seems to be adequate but where spiritual belief in general

---

Short form of title and page number as running head

Citation of multiple works from references

Acknowledgment of opposing viewpoints

Religion in Mental Health 2

should be valued more highly than it is currently in mental health circles.

Thesis explicitly introduced

I grew up in a moderately devout Catholic family. Like many young people raised in a household where one religion is practiced by both parents, it never occurred to me to question those beliefs. I went through a spiritual cycle, which I believe much of Western society also experiences. I attended religious services because I had to. I possessed a blind, unquestioning acceptance of what I was being taught because the adults I trusted said it was so. Like many adolescents and young adults, though, I stopped going to church when I was old enough to decide because I thought I had better things to do. At this stage, we reach a point when we begin searching for a meaning to our existence. For some, this search is brought on by a major crisis or a feeling of emptiness in their daily lives, while for others it is simply a part of growing up. This is where we begin to make personal choices, but with the barrage of options, where do we turn?

Beginning with the holistic health movement in the eighties, there has been a mass shift from traditional religions to less structured spiritual practices such as meditation, yoga, the Cabala, and mysticism (Beyerman, 1989). They venture beyond the realm of conventional dogmatism and into the new wave of spirituality. Many of these practices are based on the notion that health of the mind and spirit equals health of the body. Associated with this movement is a proliferation of retreats offering a chance to get in touch with the beauty and silence of nature and seminars where we can take "a break from our everyday environment where our brains are bustling and our bodies are exhausting themselves" ("Psychological benefits," 1999). A major concept of the spiritual new wave is that it focuses inward toward the individual psyche, rather than outward toward another

Author and date cited for summary or paraphrase

Anonymous source cited by title and date

being like a god. Practitioners do not deny the existence of this being, but they believe that to fully love another, we must first understand ourselves. Many find this a preferable alternative to religions where the individual is seen as a walking dispenser of sin who is very fortunate to have a forgiving creator. It is also a relief from the scare tactics like damnation used by traditional religions to make people behave. Many, therefore, praise the potential psychological benefits of such spirituality.

Clear transition refers to previous paragraph

While I believe strongly in the benefits of the new wave, I am not willing to do away with structured religion, for I find that it also has its benefits. Without the existence of churches and temples, it would be harder to expose the public to values beneficial to mental stability. It is much more difficult to hand a child a copy of the Cabala and say "Read this, and then get back to me on it" than it is to bring a child to a service where the ideas are represented with concrete examples. My religious upbringing presented me with a set of useful morals and values, and it does the same for millions of others who are brought up in this manner. Many people, including some followers of the new wave, are bitter toward Christianity because of events in history like the Crusades, the Inquisition, the Salem witch trials, and countless other horrific acts supposedly committed in the name of God. But these events were based not on biblical teachings but on pure human greed and lust for power. We should not reject the benevolent possibilities of organized religion on the basis of historical atrocities any more than we should abandon public education because a few teachers are known to mistreat children.

Another factor contributing to the reluctance concerning religion is the existence of cults that seduce people into following their extreme teachings. The victims are often at vulnerable times in their lives, and the leaders are usually very charming, charismatic, and

Religion in Mental Health 4

sometimes also psychotic or otherwise mentally unstable. Many argue

that if we acknowledge these groups as dangerous cults, then we must

do the same for traditional religions such as Christianity and Islam,

which are likewise founded on the teachings of charismatic leaders.

Again, though, critics are too quick to conflate all religious and

spiritual practice; we must distinguish between those who pray and

attend services and those who commit group suicide because they

think that aliens are coming to take over the world. Cults have

provided many psychologists, who are eager to discount religion as a

factor in improving mental health, with an easy target. Ellis (1993),

the founder of rational-emotive therapy, cites many extreme examples

of religious commitment, such as cults and antiabortion killings, to

show that commitment is hazardous to one's sanity. Anomalies like

these should not be used to speak of religion as a whole, though.

Religion is clearly the least of these people's mental problems.

When the author's name appears in text, only the date is cited in parentheses.

Besides Ellis, there are many others in the field of psychology

who do not recognize religion as a potential aid for improving the

condition of the psyche. Actually, fewer than 45 percent of the

members of the American Psychiatric Association even believe in God.

The general American public has more than twice that percentage of

religious devotees (Larson, 1998). Going back to the days of Freud,

many psychologists have held atheist views. The father of

psychoanalysis himself called religion a "universal obsessional

neurosis." Psychologists have long rejected research that demon-

strates the benefits of spirituality by saying that this research is

biased. They claim that such studies are out to prove that religion

helps because the conductors are religious people who need to justify

their beliefs.

While this may be true in some instances, there is also some

quite empirical research available to support the claims of those who promote religion and spirituality. The *Journal for the Scientific Study of Religion* has conducted many studies examining the effects of religion on individuals and groups. In one example, the relationship between religious coping methods and positive recovery after major stressful events was observed. The results indicated not only that spirituality was not harmful to the mind but that "the positive religious coping pattern was tied to benevolent outcomes, including fewer symptoms of psychological distress, [and] reports of psychological and spiritual growth as a result of the stressor" (Pargament et al., 1998, p. 721). Clearly, the benefits of piety can, in fact, be examined empirically, and in some cases the results point to a positive correlation between religion and mental health.

Bracketed word in quotation not in original source

Author, date, and page number are cited for a direct quotation.

But let us get away from statistics and studies. If religion is both useless and dangerous, as so many psychologists claim, we must ask why has it remained so vital a part of humanity for so long. Even if it can be reduced to a mere coping method that humans use to justify their existence and explain incomprehensible events, is it futile? I would suggest that this alone represents a clear benefit to society. Should religion, if it cannot be proven as "true," be eliminated and life based on scientific fact alone? Surely many would find this a pointless existence. With all the conflicting knowledge I have gained about spirituality during my personal journey and my research, one idea is clear. It is not the depth of devotion, the time of life when one turns to religion, or even the particular combination of beliefs one chooses to adopt that will improve the quality of life. There is no right or wrong answer when it comes to self-fulfillment. It is whatever works for the individual, even if that means holding no religious or spiritual beliefs at all. But clearly there *are* benefits to be gained, at least for some individuals, and mental health professionals need to begin acknowledging this fact in their daily practice.

Conclusion restates and strengthens thesis

Religion in Mental Health 6

References

Amaro, J. (2000). Psychology, psychoanalysis and religious faith.

Nielsen's psychology of religion pages. Retrieved from

http://www.psywww.com/

Beyerman A. K. (1989). The holistic health movement. Tuscaloosa, AL:

Alabama University Press.

Ellis, A. (1993). Dogmatic devotion doesn't help, it hurts. In B. Slife

(Ed.), Taking sides: Clashing views on controversial psychological

issues (pp. 297–301). New York, NY: Scribner.

Jones, J. W. (1991). Contemporary psychoanalysis and religion:

Transference and transcendence. New Haven, CT: Yale University

Press.

Kristeva, J. (1987). In the beginning was love: Psychoanalysis and

faith. New York, NY: Columbia University Press.

Larson, D. (1998). Does religious commitment improve mental health?

In B. Slife (Ed.), Taking sides: Clashing views on controversial

psychological issues (pp. 292–296). New York, NY: Scribner.

Pargament, K. I., Smith, B. W., Koening, H. G., & Perez, L. (1998).

Patterns of positive and negative religious coping with major

life stressors. Journal for the Scientific Study of Religion, 37,

710–724.

"Psychological benefits." (1999). Walking the labyrinth. Retrieved from

http://www.labyrinthway.com/

Annotations (right margin):

References begin on a new page.

A World Wide Web source

A book

An article or a chapter in a book

An article in a journal

Anonymous source alphabetized by title

PART THREE

FURTHER VIEWS
on ARGUMENT

A Philosopher's View: The Toulmin Model

All my ideas hold together, but I cannot elaborate them all at once.
—JEAN-JACQUES ROUSSEAU

Clarity has been said to be not enough. But perhaps it will be time to go into that when we are within measurable distance of achieving clarity on some matter.
—J. L. AUSTIN

[Philosophy is] a peculiarly stubborn effort to think clearly.
—WILLIAM JAMES

Philosophy is like trying to open a safe with a combination lock: Each little adjustment of the dials seems to achieve nothing, only when everything is in place does the door open.
—LUDWIG WITTGENSTEIN

In Chapter 3, we explained the contrast between *deductive* and *inductive* arguments to focus on the two main ways in which we reason, either

- Making explicit something concealed in what we already accept (**deduction**) or
- Using what we have observed as a basis for asserting or proposing something new (**induction**).

Both types of reasoning share some structural features, as we also noticed. Thus, all reasoning is aimed at establishing some **thesis** (or conclusion) and does so by means of some **reasons.** These are two basic characteristics that any argument contains.

After a little scrutiny we can in fact point to several features shared by all arguments, deductive and inductive, good and bad alike. We use the vocabulary popularized by Stephen Toulmin, Richard Rieke, and Allan Janik in their book *An Introduction to Reasoning* (1979; second edition 1984) to explore the various elements of argument.

THE CLAIM

Every argument has a purpose, goal, or aim—namely, to establish a **claim** (*conclusion* or *thesis*). Suppose you were arguing in favor of equal rights for women. You might state your thesis or claim as follows:

> Men and women ought to have equal rights.

A more precise formulation of the claim might be

> Men and women ought to have equal legal rights.

A still more precise formulation might be

> Equal legal rights for men and women ought to be protected by our Constitution.

The third version of this claim states what the controversy in the 1970s over the Equal Rights Amendment was all about.

Consequently, in reading or analyzing someone else's argument, your first question should naturally be: What is the argument intended to prove or establish? *What claim is it making?* Has this claim been clearly and precisely formulated, so that it unambiguously asserts what its advocate wants to assert?

GROUNDS

Once we have the argument's purpose or point clearly in mind and thus know what the arguer is claiming to establish, then we can ask for the evidence, reasons, support—in short, for the **grounds**—on which that claim is based. In a deductive argument these grounds are the premises from which the claim is deduced; in an inductive argument the grounds are the evidence—a sample, an observation, or an experiment—that makes the claim plausible or probable.

Not every kind of claim can be supported by every kind of ground, and conversely, not every kind of ground gives equally good support for every kind of claim. Suppose I claim that half the students in the classroom are women. I can ground this claim in any of several ways.

1. I can count all the women and all the men. Suppose the total equals fifty. If the number of women is twenty-five and the number of men is twenty-five, I have vindicated my claim.
2. I can count a sample of, say, ten students and find that in the sample five of the students are women. I thus have inductive—plausible but not conclusive—grounds for my claim.
3. I can point out that the students in the college divide equally into men and women and claim that this class is a representative sample of the whole college.

Obviously, ground 1 is stronger than ground 2, and 2 is far stronger than ground 3.

So far we have merely restated points about premises and conclusions covered in Chapter 3. But now we want to consider four additional features of arguments.

WARRANTS

Once we have the claim or the point of an argument fixed in mind and the evidence or reasons offered in its support, the next question to ask is *why* these reasons support this conclusion. What is the **warrant,** or guarantee, that the reasons proffered do support the claim or lead to the conclusion? In simple deductive arguments, the warrant takes different forms, as we shall see. In the simplest cases, we can point to the way in which the *meanings* of the key terms are really equivalent. Thus, if John is taller than Bill, then Bill must be shorter than John because of the meaning in English of "is shorter than" and "is taller than." In this case, the warrant is something we can state quite literally and explicitly.

In other cases, we may need to be more resourceful. A reliable tactic is to think up a simple *parallel argument*—that is, an argument exactly parallel in form and structure to the argument we are trying to defend. We then point out that if we are ready to accept the simpler argument, then we must accept the more complex argument because both arguments have exactly the same structure. For example, in her much-discussed 1972 essay on the abortion controversy, "A Defense of Abortion," philosopher Judith Thomson argues that a pregnant woman has the right to an abortion to save her life, even if it involves the death of her unborn child. She anticipates that some readers may balk at her reasoning, and so she offers this parallel argument: Suppose you are locked in a tiny room with another human being, which through no fault of its own is growing uncontrollably, with the result that it is slowly crushing you to death. Of course, it would be morally permissible to kill the other person to save your own life. With the reader's presumed agreement on that conclusion, the parallel argument concerning the abortion situation—so Thomson hopes—is obvious and convincing.

In simple inductive arguments, we are likely to point to the way in which observations or sets of data constitute a *representative sample* of a whole (unexamined) population. Here, the warrant is the representativeness of the sample. For instance, in projecting a line on a graph through a set of points, we defend one projection over alternatives on the grounds that it makes the smoothest fit through most of the points. In this case, the warrant is *simplicity* and *inclusiveness*. Or in defending one explanation against competing explanations of a phenomenon, we appeal to the way in which the preferred explanation can be seen as a *special case* of generally accepted physical laws. Examples of such warrants for inductive reasoning will be offered in following pages (see Chapter 9, A Logician's View: Deduction, Induction, Fallacies, pp. 337–69).

Establishing the warrants for our reasoning—that is, explaining why our grounds really support our claims—can quickly become a highly technical and exacting procedure that goes far beyond what we can hope to explain in this book. Only a solid course or two in formal deductive logic and statistical methods can do justice to our current state of knowledge about these warrants. Developing a "feel" for why reasons or grounds are or are not relevant to what they are alleged to support is the most we can hope to do here without recourse to more rigorous techniques.

Even without formal training, however, one can sense that something is wrong with many bad arguments. Here is an example. British professor C. E. M. Joad found himself standing on a station platform, annoyed because he had just missed his train, when another train, making an unscheduled stop, pulled up to the platform in front of him. He decided to jump aboard, only to hear the porter say "I'm afraid you'll have to get off, sir. This train doesn't stop here." "In that case," replied Joad, "don't worry. I'm not on it."

BACKING

The kinds of reasons appropriate to support an amendment to the Constitution are completely different from the kinds appropriate to settle the question of what caused the defeat of Napoleon's invasion of Russia. Arguments for the amendment might be rooted in an appeal to fairness, whereas arguments about the military defeat might be rooted in letters and other documents in the French and Russian archives. The canons of good argument in each case derive from the ways in which the scholarly communities in law and history, respectively, have developed over the years to support, defend, challenge, and undermine a given kind of argument. Thus, the support or **backing** appropriate for one kind of argument might be quite inappropriate for another kind of argument.

Another way of stating this point is to recognize that once you have given reasons for a claim, you are then likely to be challenged to explain why these reasons are good reasons—why, that is, one should believe these reasons rather than regard them skeptically. Why (a simple example) should we accept the testimony of Dr. *X* when Dr. *Y,* equally renowned, supports the opposite side? Or why is it safe to rest a prediction on a small though admittedly carefully selected sample? Or why is it legitimate to argue that (1) if I dream I am the King of France, then I must exist, whereas it is illegitimate to argue that (2) if I dream I am the King of France, then the King of France must exist? To answer these kinds of challenges is to *back up* one's reasoning, and no argument is any better than its backing.

MODAL QUALIFIERS

As we have seen, all arguments are made up of assertions or propositions, which can be sorted into four categories:

- The *claim* (conclusion, thesis to be established),
- The *grounds* (explicit reasons advanced),
- The *warrant* (the principle that connects the ground to the claim), and
- The *backing* (implicit assumptions).

All these kinds of propositions have an explicit or tacit **modality** in
which they are asserted, indicating the scope and character with which
they are believed to hold true. Is the claim, for instance, believed to be
necessary—or only *probable*? Is the claim believed to be *plausible*—or
only *possible*? Of two reasons for a claim, both may be *good*, but one may
be *better* than the other. Indicating the modality with which an assertion
is advanced is crucial to any argument for or against it.

Empirical generalizations are typically *contingent* on various factors,
and it is important to indicate such contingencies to protect the generalization against obvious counterexamples. Thus, consider this empirical
generalization:

Students do best on final examinations if they study hard for them.

Are we really to believe that students who study regularly throughout
the whole course and so do not need to cram for the final will do less
well than students who neglect regular work in favor of several all-
nighters at the last minute? Probably not; what is really meant is that *all
other things being equal* (in Latin, *ceteris paribus*), concentrated study just
before an exam will yield good results. Alluding to the contingencies in
this way shows that the writer is aware of possible exceptions and that
they are conceded right from the start.

Assertions also have varying **scope,** and indicating their scope is equally
crucial to the role that an assertion plays in argument. Thus, suppose
you are arguing against smoking, and the ground for your claim is this:

Heavy smokers cut short their life span.

Such an assertion will be clearer, as well as more likely to be true, if it is
explicitly **quantified.** Here, there are three obvious alternative quantifi-
cations to choose among: *all* smokers cut short their life span, *most* do, or
only *some* do. Until the assertion is quantified in one of these ways, we
really do not know what is being asserted—and so we do not know
what degree and kind of evidence and counterevidence is relevant.
Other quantifiers include *few, rarely, many, often, sometimes, perhaps, usually, more or less, regularly, occasionally.*

In sum, sensitivity to the quantifiers and qualifiers appropriate for each of our assertions, whatever their role in an argument, will help prevent you from asserting exaggerations and other misguided generalizations.

REBUTTALS

Very few arguments of any interest are beyond dispute, conclusively knockdown affairs in which the claim of the argument is so rigidly tied to its grounds, warrants, and backing and its quantifiers and qualifiers so precisely orchestrated that it really proves its conclusion beyond any possibility of doubt. On the contrary, most arguments have many counterarguments, and sometimes one of these counterarguments is the most convincing.

Suppose one has taken a sample that appears to be random: An interviewer on your campus accosts the first ten students she encounters, and seven of them happen to be fraternity or sorority members. She is now ready to argue that seven-tenths of enrolled students belong to Greek organizations.

You believe, however, that the Greeks are in the minority and point out that she happens to have conducted her interview around the corner from the Panhellenic Society's office just off Sorority Row. Her random sample is anything but. The ball is now back in her court as you await her response to your rebuttal.

As this example illustrates, it is safe to say that we do not understand our own arguments very well until we have tried to get a grip on the places in which they are vulnerable to criticism, counterattack, or refutation. Edmund Burke (quoted in Chapter 3 but worth repeating) said, "He that wrestles with us strengthens our nerves, and sharpens our skill. Our antagonist is our helper." Therefore, cultivating alertness to such weak spots, girding one's loins to defend at these places, always helps strengthen one's position.

A MODEL ANALYSIS USING
THE TOULMIN METHOD

To see how the Toulmin method can be used, let's apply it to an argument in this book, Susan Jacoby's "A First Amendment Junkie" (p. 41).

The Claim   Jacoby's central thesis or claim is this: Any form of *censorship*—including feminist censorship of pornography in particular—*is wrong*.

Grounds   Jacoby offers six main reasons or grounds for her claim, roughly in this sequence (but arguably not in this order of importance).

First, feminists exaggerate the harm caused by pornography because they confuse expression of offensive ideas with harmful conduct.

Second, letting the government censor the expression of ideas and attitudes is the wrong response to the failure of parents to control the printed materials that get into the hands of their children.

Third, there is no unanimity even among feminists over what is pornography and what isn't.

Fourth, permitting censorship of pornography to please feminists could well lead to censorship on many issues of concern to feminists ("rape, abortion, menstruation, contraception, lesbianism").

Fifth, censorship under law shows a lack of confidence in the democratic process.

Finally, censorship of words and pictures is suppression of self-expression, and that violates the First Amendment.

Warrants   Each of these six grounds needs its own warrant, and the warrants vary considerably in their complexity. Jacoby (like most writers) is not so didactic as to make these warrants explicit. Taking them in order, this is what they look like.

First, since the First Amendment protects speech in the broadest sense, the censorship that the feminist attack on pornography advocates is *inconsistent* with the First Amendment.

Second, if feminists want to be consistent, then they must advocate censorship of *all* offensive self-expression, but such a radical interference with free speech (amounting virtually to repeal of the First Amendment) is indefensible.

Third, if feminists can't agree over what is pornographic, the censorship of pornography they propose is bound to be arbitrary.

Fourth, feminists ought to see that *they risk losing more than they can hope to gain* if they succeed in censoring pornography.

Fifth, the democratic process can be trusted to weed out harmful utterances.

Sixth, if feminists have a legal right to censor pornography, anti-feminists will claim the same right on other issues.

Backing   Why should the reader agree with Jacoby's grounds? She does not appeal to expert authority, the results of experimental tests or other statistical data, or the support of popular opinion. Instead, she relies principally on two things — but without saying so explicitly.

First, she assumes that the reader accepts the propositions that *freedom of self-expression is valuable* and that *censoring self-expression requires the strongest of reasons*. If there is no fundamental agreement on these propositions, several of her reasons cease to support her claim.

Second, she relies on the reader's open-mindedness and willingness to evaluate common sense (untechnical, ordinary, familiar) considerations at each step of the way. She relies also on the reader having had some personal experience with erotica, pornography, and art. Without that open-mindedness and experience, a reader is not likely to be persuaded by her rejection of the feminist demand for censorship.

Modal Qualifiers   Jacoby defends what she calls an "absolute interpretation" of the First Amendment—that is, the view that *all* censorship of words, pictures, and ideas is not only inconsistent with the First Amendment but is also politically unwise and morally objectionable. She allows that *some* pornography is highly offensive (it offends her, she insists); she allows that *some* pornography ("kiddie porn") may even be harmful to *some* viewers. But she also insists that *more* harm than good would result from the censorship of pornography. She points out that *some* paintings of nude women are art, not pornography; she implies that it is *impossible* to draw a sharp line between permissible erotic pornography and impermissible offensive pornography. She clearly believes that *all* Americans ought to understand and defend the First Amendment under the "absolute interpretation" she favors.

Rebuttals   Jacoby mentions several objections to her views, and perhaps the most effective aspect of her entire argument is her skill in identifying possible objections and meeting them effectively. (Notice the diversity of the objections and the various ways in which she replies.)

Objection: Some of her women friends tell her she is wrong.

Rebuttal: She admits she's a "First Amendment junkie," and she doesn't apologize for it.

Objection: "Kiddie porn" is harmful and deserves censorship.

Rebuttal: Such material is *not* protected by the First Amendment because it is an "abuse of power" of adults over children.

Objection: Pornography is a form of violence against women, and therefore it is especially harmful.

Rebuttal: (1) No, it really isn't harmful, but it is disgusting and offensive. (2) In any case, it's surely not as harmful as allowing American neo-Nazis to parade in Jewish neighborhoods. (Jacoby is referring to the march in Skokie, Illinois, in 1977, upheld by the courts as permissible political expression under the First Amendment despite its offensiveness to survivors of the Nazi concentration camps.)

Objection: Censoring pornography advances public respect for women.

Rebuttal: Censoring *Ms.* magazine, which antifeminists have already done, undermines women's freedom and self-expression.

Objection: Reasonable people can tell pornography when they see it, so censoring it poses no problems.

> ✓ A CHECKLIST FOR USING THE TOULMIN METHOD
>
> Have I asked the following questions?
>
> ☐ What claim does the argument make?
> ☐ What grounds are offered for the claim?
> ☐ What warrants the inferences from the grounds to the claim?
> ☐ What backing supports the claim?
> ☐ With what modalities are the claim and grounds asserted?
> ☐ To what rebuttals are the claim, grounds, and backing vulnerable?

Rebuttal: Yes, there are clear cases of gross pornography; but there are lots of borderline cases, as women themselves prove when they disagree over whether a photo in *Penthouse* is offensively erotic or "lovely" and "sensuous."

> See the companion Web site
> **bedfordstmartins.com/barnetbedau**
> for links related to the Toulmin model.

PUTTING THE TOULMIN METHOD TO WORK:
Responding to an Argument

Let's look at an argument—it happens to be a proposal concerning illegal immigration—and see how the Toulmin method can be applied.

Michael S. Dukakis and
Daniel J. B. Mitchell

Michael S. Dukakis, a professor of political science at Northeastern University, served as the governor of Massachusetts from 1975 to 1979 and from 1983 to 1991. Daniel J. B. Mitchell is a professor of management and public policy at the University of California at Los Angeles. The essay that follows originally appeared in the New York Times *(July 25, 2006).*

Raise Wages, Not Walls

There are two approaches to illegal immigration currently being debated in Congress. One, supported by the House, emphasizes border control and law enforcement, including a wall along the Mexican border and increased border patrols. The other, which is supported by the Bush administration and has been passed by the Senate, relies on employers to police the workplace. Both proposals have serious flaws.

As opponents of the House plan have rightly pointed out, walls rarely work; illegal immigrants will get around them one way or another. Unless we erect something akin to the Berlin Wall, which would cost billions to build and police, a barrier on the border would be monitored by largely symbolic patrols and easily evaded.

The Senate approach is more realistic but it, too, has problems. It creates a temporary worker program but requires employers first to attempt to recruit American workers to fill job openings. It allows for more border fencing, but makes no effort to disguise the basic futility of the enterprise. Instead, it calls on employers to enforce immigration laws in the workplace, a plan that can only succeed through the creation and distribution of a costly national identification card.

A national ID card raises serious questions about civil liberties, but they are not the sole concern. The cost estimates for producing and distributing a counterfeit-proof card for the roughly 150 million people currently in the labor force — and the millions more who will seek work in the near future — extend into the billions of dollars. Employers would have to verify the identity of every American worker, otherwise the program would be as unreliable as the one in place now. Anyone erroneously denied a card in this bureaucratic labyrinth would be unemployable.

There is a simpler alternative. If we are really serious about turning 5 back the tide of illegal immigration, we should start by raising the minimum wage from $5.15 per hour to something closer to $8. The Massachusetts legislature recently voted to raise the state minimum to $8 and California may soon set its minimum even higher. Once the minimum wage has been significantly increased, we can begin vigorously enforcing the wage law and other basic labor standards.

Millions of illegal immigrants work for minimum and even subminimum wages in workplaces that don't come close to meeting health and safety standards. It is nonsense to say, as President Bush did recently, that these jobs are filled by illegal immigrants because Americans won't do them. Before we had mass illegal immigration in this country, hotel beds were made, office floors were cleaned, restaurant dishes were washed and crops were picked — by Americans.

Americans will work at jobs that are risky, dirty, or unpleasant so long as they provide decent wages and working conditions, especially if employers also provide health insurance. Plenty of Americans now work in such jobs, from mining coal to picking up garbage. The difference is they are paid a decent wage and provided benefits for their labor.

However, Americans won't work for peanuts, and these days the national minimum wage is less than peanuts. For full-time work, it doesn't even come close to the poverty line for an individual, let alone provide a family with a living wage. It hasn't been raised since 1997 and isn't enforced even at its currently ridiculous level.

Yet enforcing the minimum wage doesn't require walling off a porous border or trying to distinguish yesterday's illegal immigrant from tomorrow's "guest worker." All it takes is a willingness by the federal government to inspect workplaces to determine which employers obey the law.

Curiously, most members of Congress who take a hard line on immigration also strongly oppose increasing the minimum wage, claiming it will hurt businesses and reduce jobs. For some reason, they don't seem eager to acknowledge that many of the jobs they claim to hold dear are held by the same illegal immigrants they are trying to deport.

But if we want to reduce illegal immigration, it makes sense to reduce the abundance of extremely low-paying jobs that fuels it. If we raise the minimum wage, it's possible some low-end jobs may be lost; but more Americans would also be willing to work in such jobs, thereby denying them to people who aren't supposed to be here in the first place. And tough enforcement of wage rules would curtail the growth of an underground economy in which both illegal immigration and employer abuses thrive.

Raising the minimum wage and increasing enforcement would prove far more effective and less costly than either proposal currently under consideration in Congress. If Congress would only remove its blinders about the minimum wage, it may see a plan to deal effectively with illegal immigration, too.

THINKING WITH TOULMIN'S METHOD

At first blush, what we have in this essay is a twelve-paragraph argument divided into two unequal parts. Paragraphs 1–4 offer some proposals for dealing with illegal immigration and reasons why these proposals won't work. This preliminary material is followed by paragraphs 5–12 in which the proposal favored by the authors is introduced, explained, and justified. So much for first impressions.

Let's now deconstruct this essay by identifying each of the six elements that constitute the Toulmin method.

- First and foremost, what is the **claim** being made, the main thesis of the essay? Is it in the title? Is it in paragraph 5? Or is it elsewhere? What kind of claim is it—a claim of fact? A claim of value? In any case, write down the claim for further reference.

- Second, what are the **grounds,** the evidence or reasons advanced in support of the claim? Partly they can be found in what the authors regard as ineffective alternative efforts in paragraphs 1–4. What are these alternatives? Why are they said to be ineffective?

Look also at paragraph 5 and later paragraphs. Write down the sentences you have discovered that are playing this role.

- Third, what are the **warrants** that Dukakis and Mitchell rely on to carry the burden of their argument? In paragraph 5, for example, the authors rely on examples from Massachusetts and California. The evidence they offer amounts to a minimal inductive argument. Could their argument of this sort be stronger? Paragraphs 6 and 7 rely on general knowledge, as do most of the rest of their argument. Is that the best one can do with this issue? Can you think of ways in which the authors' argument can be strengthened? Carefully look through the whole essay for whatever evidence you can find of the mention of and reliance on this or that warrant.

The essence of the Toulmin method lies in these three elements: the claim(s), the ground(s), and the warrant(s). If you have extracted these from the Dukakis-Mitchell essay, you will have identified most of what will suffice for a good grasp of the argument in question.

Of lesser importance are the three other elements of the Toulmin method: the backing, the modal qualifiers, and the rebuttal.

- Fourth, consider the **backing**—the reasons for one's reasons. The authors set out to argue for a claim, which they support on empirical or factual grounds, using warrants appropriate to an argument of that sort. But suppose Dukakis and Mitchell are challenged. How might they back up their reasons with further reasons? They are in effect answering the tacit questions "How do you know . . . ?" and "Why do you believe . . . ?" What might the authors offer in support of their views when confronted with such queries?

- Fifth, there are the **modal qualifiers**—or are there? Can you find any passages in which the authors qualify their assertions ("Perhaps if we tried . . .") ("Most, although not all, illegal immigration . . .")? Look at paragraph 11. There's at least one modal qualifier here—can you spot it?

- Finally, there are the **rebuttals,** the reasons advanced by someone who rejects the authors' claim, or who concedes their claim but rejects the grounds offered in its support, and so forth. Paragraphs 1–4 mention alternatives to the proposals favored by the authors, and the authors reply to these objections. Is their rebuttal convincing? Why, or why not?

9

A Logician's View:
Deduction, Induction,
Fallacies

Logic is the anatomy of thought.
—JOHN LOCKE

Logic takes care of itself; all we have to do is to look and see how it does it.
—LUDWIG WITTGENSTEIN

In Chapter 3 we introduced the terms *deduction, induction,* and *fallacy.* Here we discuss them in greater detail.

DEDUCTION

The basic aim of deductive reasoning is to start with some assumption or premise and extract from it a conclusion—a logical consequence—that is concealed but implicit in it. Thus, taking the simplest case, if I assert as a premise

    1a. Nuclear power poses more risks of harm to the environment than fossil fuels.

then it is a matter of simple deduction to infer the conclusion that

    1b. Fossil fuels pose fewer risks of harm to the environment than nuclear power.

Anyone who understands English would grant that 1b follows 1a—or equivalently, that 1b can be validly deduced from 1a—because whatever two objects, *A* and *B,* you choose, if *A* does *more things than B,* then *B* must do *fewer things than A.*

    Thus, in this and all other cases of valid deductive reasoning, we can say not only that we are entitled to *infer* the conclusion from the premise—

in this case, infer 1b from 1a—but that the premise *implies* the conclusion. Remember, too, the conclusion (1b) that fossil fuels pose fewer risks than nuclear power—inferred or deduced from the statement (1a) that nuclear power poses more risks—does not depend on the truth of the statement that nuclear power poses more risks. If the speaker (falsely) asserts that nuclear power poses more risks—does not depend on the truth of the statement that nuclear power poses more risks. If the speaker (falsely) asserts that nuclear power poses more risks, then the hearer validly (that is to say, logically) concludes that fossil fuels pose fewer risks. Thus, 1b follows from 1a whether or not 1a is true; consequently, if 1a is true, then so is 1b; but if 1a is false, then 1b must be false also.

Let's take another example—more interesting but comparably simple:

2a. President Truman was underrated by his critics.

Given 2a, a claim amply verified by events of the 1950s, one is entitled to infer

2b. His critics underrated President Truman.

On what basis can we argue that 2a implies 2b? The two propositions are equivalent because a rule of English grammar assures us that we can convert the position of subject and predicate phrases in a sentence by shifting from the passive to the active voice (or vice versa) without any change in the conditions that make the proposition true (or false).

Both pairs of examples illustrate that in deductive reasoning, our aim is to transform, reformulate, or restate in our conclusion some (or, as in the two examples above, all) of the information contained in our premises.

Remember, even though a proposition or statement follows from a previous proposition or statement, the statements need not be true. We can see why if we consider another example. Suppose someone asserts or claims that

3a. The Gettysburg Address is longer than the Declaration of Independence.

As every student of American history knows, 3a is false. But false or not, we can validly deduce from it that

3b. The Declaration of Independence is shorter than the Gettysburg Address.

This inference is valid (even though the conclusion is untrue) because the conclusion follows logically (more precisely, deductively) from 3a: In English, as we know, the meaning of "*A* is shorter than *B*," which appears in 3b, is simply the converse of "*B* is longer than *A*," which appears in 3a.

The deductive relation between 3a and 3b reminds us again that the idea of validity, which is so crucial to deduction, is not the same as the idea of truth. False propositions have implications—logical consequences— too, just as true propositions do.

In the three pairs of examples so far, what can we point to as the warrant for our claims? Well, look at the reasoning in each case; the arguments rely on rules of ordinary English, on the accepted meanings of words like on, under, and underrated.

In many cases, of course, the deductive inference or pattern of reasoning is much more complex than that which we have seen in the examples so far. When we introduced the idea of deduction in Chapter 3, we gave as our primary example the *syllogism*. Here is another example:

> 4. Texas is larger than California; California is larger than Arizona; therefore, Texas is larger than Arizona.

The conclusion in this syllogism is derivable from the two premises; that is, anyone who asserts the two premises is committed to accepting the conclusion as well, whether or not one thinks of it.

Notice again that the *truth* of the conclusion is not established merely by validity of the inference. The conclusion in this syllogism happens to be true. And the premises of this syllogism imply the conclusion. But the argument establishes the conclusion only because both of the premises on which the conclusion depends are true. Even a Californian admits that Texas is larger than California, which in turn is larger than Arizona. In other words, argument 4 is a *sound* argument because (as we explained in Chapter 3) it is valid and all its premises are true. All—and only—arguments that *prove* their conclusions have these two traits.

How might we present the warrant for the argument in 4? Short of a crash course in formal logic, either of two strategies might suffice. One is to argue from the fact that the validity of the inference depends on the meaning of a key concept, *being larger than*. This concept has the property of *transitivity,* a property that many concepts share (for example, *is equal to, is to the right of, is smarter than*—all are transitive concepts). Consequently, whatever *A, B,* and *C* are, if *A* is larger than *B,* and *B* is larger than *C,* then *A* will be larger than *C.* The final step is to substitute "Texas," "California," and "Arizona" for *A, B,* and *C,* respectively.

A second strategy, less abstract and more graphic, is to think of representing Texas, California, and Arizona by nested circles. Thus, the first premise in argument 4 would look like this:

The second premise would look like this:

The conclusion would look like this:

We can see that this conclusion follows from the premises because it amounts to nothing more than what one gets by superimposing the two premises on each other. Thus, the whole argument can be represented like this:

The so-called middle term in the argument—California—disappears from the conclusion; its role is confined to be the link between the other two terms, Texas and Arizona, in the premises. (This is an adaptation of the technique used in elementary formal logic known as Venn diagrams.) In this manner one can give graphic display to the important fact that the conclusion follows from the premises because one can literally *see* the conclusion represented by nothing more than a representation of the premises.

Both of these strategies bring out the fact that validity of deductive inference is a purely *formal* property of argument. Each strategy abstracts the form from the content of the propositions involved to show how the concepts in the premises are related to the concepts in the conclusion.

For the sake of illustration, here is another syllogistic argument with the same logical features as argument 4. (A nice exercise is to restate argument 5 using diagrams in the manner of argument 4.)

> 5. African American slaves were treated worse than white indentured servants. Indentured white servants were treated worse than free white labor. Therefore, African American slaves were treated worse than free white labor.

Not all deductive reasoning occurs in syllogisms, however, or at least not in syllogisms like the ones in 4 and 5. (The term *syllogism* is sometimes used to refer to any deductive argument of whatever form, provided only that it has two premises.) In fact, syllogisms such as 4 are not the commonest form of our deductive reasoning at all. Nor are they the simplest (and of course, not the most complex). For an argument that is even simpler, consider this:

> 6. If a youth is an African American slave, he is probably treated worse than a youth in indentured service. This youth is an African American slave. Therefore, he is probably treated worse than if he had been an indentured servant.

Here the pattern of reasoning has the form: If *A*, then *B; A;* therefore, *B*. Notice that the content of the assertions represented by *A* and *B* do not matter; any set of expressions having the same form or structure will do equally well, including assertions built out of meaningless terms, as in this example:

7. If the slithy toves, then the gyres gimble. The slithy toves. Therefore, the gyres gimble.

Argument 7 has the form: If *A*, then *B; A;* therefore *B*. As a piece of deductive inference it is every bit as good. Unlike 6, however, 7 is of no interest to us because none of its assertions make any sense (unless you are a reader of Lewis Carroll's "Jabberwocky," and even then the sense of 7 is doubtful). You cannot, in short, use a valid deductive argument to prove anything unless the premises and the conclusion are *true*, but they can't be true unless they *mean* something in the first place.

This parallel between arguments 6 and 7 shows once again that deductive validity in an argument rests on the *form* or structure of the argument, and not on its content or meaning. If all one can say about an argument is that it is valid—that is, its conclusion follows from the premises—one has not given a sufficient reason for accepting the argument's conclusion. It has been said that the Devil can quote Scripture; similarly, an argument can be deductively valid and of no further interest or value whatever because valid (but false) conclusions can be drawn from false or even meaningless assumptions. For example,

8. New York's Metropolitan Museum of Art has the finest collection of abstract impressionist painting in the world. The finest collection of abstract impressionist paintings includes dozens of canvases by Winslow Homer. Therefore, the Metropolitan Museum of Art has dozens of paintings by Winslow Homer.

Here, the conclusion follows validly from the premises, even though all three propositions are false. Nevertheless, although validity by itself is not enough, it is a necessary condition of any deductive argument that purports to establish its conclusion.

Now let us consider another argument with the same form as 8, only more interesting.

9. If President Truman knew the Japanese were about to surrender, then it was immoral of him to order that atom bombs be dropped on Hiroshima and Nagasaki. Truman knew the Japanese were about to surrender. Therefore, it was immoral of him to order dropping those bombs.

As in the two previous examples, anyone who assents to the premises in argument 9 must assent to the conclusion; the form of arguments 8 and 9 is identical. But do the premises of argument 9 *prove* the conclusion? That depends on whether both premises are true. Well, are they? This turns on a number of considerations, and it is worthwhile pausing to examine this argument closely to illustrate the kinds of things that are involved in answering this question.

Let us begin by examining the second (minor) premise. Its truth is controversial even to this day. Autobiography, memoranda, other documentary evidence—all are needed to assemble the evidence to back up the grounds for the thesis or claim made in the conclusion of this valid argument. Evaluating this material effectively will probably involve not only further deductions, but inductive reasoning as well.

Now consider the first (major) premise in argument 9. Its truth doesn't depend on what history shows but on the moral principles one accepts. The major premise has the form of a hypothetical proposition ("if . . . then . . .") and asserts a connection between two very different kinds of things. The antecedent of the hypothetical (the clause following "if") mentions facts about Truman's *knowledge,* and the consequent of the hypothetical (the clause following "then") mentions facts about the *morality* of his conduct in light of such knowledge. The major premise as a whole can thus be seen as expressing *a principle of moral responsibility.*

Such principles can, of course, be controversial. In this case, for instance, is the principle peculiarly relevant to the knowledge and conduct of a president of the United States? Probably not; it is far more likely that this principle is merely a special case of a more general proposition about anyone's moral responsibility. (After all, we know a great deal more about the conditions of our own moral responsibility than we do about those of high government officials.) We might express this more general principle in this way: If we have knowledge that would make our violent conduct unnecessary, then we are immoral if we deliberately act violently anyway. Thus, accepting this general principle can serve as a basis for defending the major premise of argument 9.

We have examined this argument in some detail because it illustrates the kinds of considerations needed to test whether a given argument is not only valid but whether its premises are true—that is, whether its premises really prove the conclusion.

The great value of the form of argument known as hypothetical syllogism, exemplified by arguments 6 and 7, is that the structure of the argument is so simple and so universally applicable in reasoning that it is often both easy and worthwhile to formulate one's claims so that they can be grounded by an argument of this sort.

Before leaving the subject of deductive inference, consider three other forms of argument, each of which can be found in actual use elsewhere in the readings in this volume. The simplest of these is **disjunctive syllogism,** so called because its major premise is a **disjunction.** For example,

10. Either censorship of television shows is overdue, or our society is indifferent to the education of its youth. Our society is not indif-

ferent to the education of its youth. Therefore, censorship of television is overdue.

Notice, by the way, that the validity of an argument, as in this case, does not turn on pedantic repetition of every word or phrase as the argument moves along; nonessential elements can be dropped, or equivalent expressions substituted for variety without adverse effect on the reasoning. Thus, in conversation or in writing, the argument in 10 might actually be presented like this:

11. Either censorship of television is overdue, or our society is indifferent to the education of its youth. But, of course, we aren't indifferent; it's censorship that's overdue.

The key feature of disjunctive syllogism, as example 11 suggests, is that the conclusion is whichever of the disjuncts is left over after the others have been negated in the minor premise. Thus, we could easily have a very complex disjunctive syllogism, with a dozen disjuncts in the major premise, and seven of them denied in the minor premise, leaving a conclusion of the remaining five. Usually, however, a disjunctive argument is formulated in this manner: Assert a disjunction with two or more disjuncts in the major premise; then *deny all but one* in the minor premise; and infer validly the remaining disjunct as the conclusion. That was the form of argument 11.

Another type of argument, especially favored by orators and rhetoricians, is the **dilemma.** Ordinarily we use the term *dilemma* in the sense of an awkward predicament, as when we say, "His dilemma was that he didn't have enough money to pay the waiter." But when logicians refer to a dilemma, they mean a forced choice between two or more equally unattractive alternatives. For example, the predicament of the U.S. government during the mid-1980s as it faced the crisis brought on by terrorist attacks on American civilian targets, which were believed, during that time, to be inspired and supported by the Libyan government, can be formulated in a dilemma:

12. If the United States bombs targets in Libya, innocent people will be killed, and the Arab world will be angered. If the United States doesn't bomb Libyan targets, then terrorists will go unpunished, and the United States will lose respect among other governments. Either the United States bombs Libyan targets, or it doesn't. Therefore, in either case unattractive consequences will follow: The innocent will be killed, or terrorists will go unpunished.

Notice first the structure of the argument: two conditional propositions asserted as premises, followed by another premise that states a **necessary truth.** (The premise, "Either we bomb the Libyans, or we don't," is a disjunction; since its two alternatives are exhaustive, one of the two alternatives must be true. Such a statement is often called analytically true, or a *tautology*.) No doubt the conclusion of this dilemma follows from its premises.

But does the argument prove, as it purports to do, that whatever the U.S. government does, it will suffer "unattractive consequences"? It is customary to speak of "the horns of the dilemma," as though the challenge posed by the dilemma were like a bull ready to gore you whichever direction you turn. But if the two conditional premises failed to exhaust the possibilities, then one can escape from the dilemma by going "between the horns"; that is, by finding a third alternative. If (as in this case) that is not possible, one can still ask whether both of the main premises are true. (In this argument, it should be clear that neither of these main premises spells out all or even most of the consequences that could be foreseen.) Even so, in cases where both these conditional premises are true, it may be that the consequences of one alternative are nowhere nearly so bad as those of the other. If that is true, but our reasoning stops before evaluating that fact, we may be guilty of failing to distinguish between the greater and the lesser of two admitted evils. The logic of the dilemma itself cannot decide this choice for us. Instead, we must bring to bear empirical inquiry and imagination to the evaluation of the grounds of the dilemma itself.

Writers commonly use the term *dilemma* without explicitly formulating the dilemma to which they refer, leaving it for the readers to do. And sometimes, what is called a dilemma really isn't one. (Remember the dog's tail? Calling it a leg doesn't make it a leg.) As an example, consider the plight of Sophie in William Stryon's novel, *Sophie's Choice*. The scene is Birkenau, the main Nazi extermination camp during World War II. Among the thousands arriving at the prison gates are Sophie and her two children, Jan and Eva. On the train platform they are confronted by a Nazi SS medical officer. He will decide which are the lucky ones; they will live to work in the camp. The rest will go to their death in the gas chambers. When Sophie insists she is Polish but not Jewish, the officer says she may choose one of her children to be saved. Which of the two ought to be saved? On what basis ought Sophie resolve her dilemma? It looks as if she has only two alternatives, each of which presents her with an agonizing outcome. Or is there a third way out?

Finally, one of the most powerful and dramatic forms of argument is **reductio ad absurdum** (from the Latin, meaning "reduction to absurdity"). The idea of a reductio argument is to disprove a proposition by showing the absurdity of its inevitable conclusion. It is used, of course, to refute your opponent's position and prove your own. For example, in Plato's *Republic*, Socrates asks an old gentleman, Cephalus, to define what right conduct is. Cephalus says that it consists of paying your debts and keeping your word. Socrates rejects this answer by showing that it leads to a contradiction. He argues that Cephalus cannot have given the correct answer because if we believe that he did, we will be quickly led into contradictions; in some cases when you keep your word you will nonetheless be doing the wrong thing. For suppose, says Socrates, that you borrowed a weapon from a man, promising to return it when he asks for it. One day he comes to your door, demanding his weapon and swearing angrily that he intends to murder a neighbor. Keeping your word under those circumstances is absurd, Socrates implies, and the reader of the dialogue is left to infer that Cephalus's definition, which led to this result, is refuted.

Let's take a closer look at another example. Suppose you are opposed to any form of gun control, whereas I am in favor of gun control. I might try to refute your position by attacking it with a reductio argument. To do that, I start out by assuming the very opposite of what I believe or favor and try to establish a contradiction that results from following out the consequences of this initial assumption. My argument might look like this:

13. Let's assume your position—namely, that there ought to be no legal restrictions whatever on the sale and ownership of guns. That means that you'd permit having every neighborhood hardware store sell pistols and rifles to whoever walks in the door. But that's not all. You apparently also would permit selling machine guns to children, antitank weapons to lunatics, small-bore cannons to the nearsighted, as well as guns and the ammunition to go with them to anyone with a criminal record. But this is utterly preposterous. No one could favor such a dangerous policy. So the only question worth debating is what kind of gun control is necessary.

Now in this example, my reductio of your position on gun control is not based on claiming to show that you have strictly contradicted yourself, for there is no purely logical contradiction in opposing all forms of gun control. Instead, what I have tried to do is to show that there is a contradiction between what you profess—no gun controls whatever—and what you probably really believe, if only you will stop to think about it—no lunatic should be allowed to buy a loaded machine gun.

My refutation of your position rests on whether I succeed in establishing an inconsistency among your own beliefs. If it turns out that you really believe lunatics should be free to purchase guns and ammunition, then my attempted refutation fails.

In explaining reductio ad absurdum, we have had to rely on another idea fundamental to logic, that of **contradiction,** or inconsistency. (We used this idea, remember, to define validity in Chapter 3. A deductive argument is valid if and only if affirming the premises and denying the conclusion results in a contradiction.) The opposite of contradiction is **consistency,** a notion of hardly less importance to good reasoning than validity. These concepts deserve a few words of further explanation and illustration. Consider this pair of assertions:

14. Abortion is homicide.
15. Racism is unfair.

No one would plausibly claim that we can infer or deduce 15 from 14, or, for that matter, 14 from 15. This almost goes without saying, because there is no evident connection between these two assertions. They are unrelated assertions; logically speaking, they are *independent* of each other. In such cases the two assertions are mutually *consistent;* that is, both could be true—or both could be false. But now consider another proposition:

16. Euthanasia is not murder.

Could a person assert 14 (*Abortion is homicide*) and also assert 16 (*Euthanasia is not murder*) and be consistent? This question is equivalent to asking whether one could assert the **conjunction** of these two propositions—namely,

17. Abortion is homicide, and euthanasia is not murder.

It is not so easy to say whether 17 is consistent or inconsistent. The kinds of moral scruples that might lead a person to assert one of these conjuncts (that is, one of the two initial propositions, *Abortion is homicide* and *Euthanasia is not murder*) might lead to the belief that the other one must be false and thus to the conclusion that 17 is inconsistent. (Notice that if 14 were the assertion that *Abortion is murder,* instead of *Abortion is homicide,* the problem of asserting consistently both 14 and 15 would be more acute.) Yet if we think again, we might imagine someone being convinced that there is no inconsistency in asserting that *Abortion is homicide,* say, and that *Euthanasia is not murder,* or even the reverse. (For instance, suppose you believed that the unborn deserve a chance to live and that putting elderly persons to death in a painless manner and with their consent confers a benefit on them.)

Let us generalize: We can say of any set of propositions that they are *consistent* if and only if *all could be true together.* (Notice that it follows from this definition that propositions that mutually imply each other, as do *Seabiscuit was America's fastest racehorse* and *America's fastest racehorse was Seabiscuit.* Remember that, once again, the truth of the assertions in question does not matter. Two propositions can be consistent or not, quite apart from whether they are true. Not so with falsehood: It follows from our definition of consistency that an *inconsistent* proposition must be *false.* (We have relied on this idea in explaining how a reductio ad absurdum works.)

Assertions or claims that are not consistent can take either of two forms. Suppose you assert proposition 14, that abortion is homicide, early in an essay you are writing, but later you assert that

18. Abortion is harmless.

You have now asserted a position on abortion that is strictly contrary to the one with which you began; contrary in the sense that both assertions 14 and 18 cannot be true. It is simply not true that if an abortion involves killing a human being (which is what *homicide* strictly means), then it causes no one any harm (killing a person always causes harm — even if it is excusable, justifiable, not wrong, the best thing to do in the circumstances, and so on). Notice that although 14 and 18 cannot both be true, they can both be false. In fact, many people who are perplexed about the morality of abortion believe precisely this. They concede that abortion does harm the fetus, so 18 must be false; but they also believe that abortion doesn't kill a person, so 14 must also be false.

Or consider another, simpler case. If you describe the glass as half empty and I describe it as half full, both of us can be right; the two assertions are consistent, even though they sound vaguely incompatible. (This is the reason that disputing over whether the glass is half full or half empty has become the popular paradigm of a futile, purely *verbal disagreement*.) But if I describe the glass as half empty whereas you insist that it is two-thirds empty, then we have a real disagreement; your description and mine are strictly contrary, in that both cannot be true — although both can be false. (Both are false if the glass is only one-quarter full.)

This, by the way, enables us to define the difference between a pair of **contradictory** propositions and a pair of **contrary** propositions. Two propositions are contrary if and only if both cannot be true (though both can be false); two propositions are contradictory if and only if they are such that if one is true the other must be false, and vice versa. Thus, if Jack says that Alice Walker's *The Color Purple* is a better novel than Mark Twain's *Huckleberry Finn*, and Jill says, "No, *Huckleberry Finn* is better than *The Color Purple*," she is contradicting Jack. If what either one of them says is true, then what the other says must be false.

A more subtle case of contradiction arises when two or more of one's own beliefs implicitly contradict each other. We may find ourselves saying "Travel is broadening," and saying an hour later, "People don't really change." Just beneath the surface of these two beliefs lies a self-contradiction: How can travel broaden us unless it influences — and changes — our beliefs, values, and outlook? But if we can't really change ourselves, then traveling to new places won't change us, either. (Indeed, there is a Roman saying to the effect that travelers change the skies above them, not their hearts.) "Travel is broadening" and "People don't change" collide with each other; something has to give.

Our point, of course, is not that you must never say today something that contradicts something you said yesterday. Far from it; if you think you were mistaken yesterday, of course you will take a different position today. But what you want to avoid is what George Orwell called *doublethink* in his novel *1984*: "*Doublethink* means the power of holding two contradictory beliefs in one's mind simultaneously, and accepting them both."

Genuine contradiction, and not merely contrary assertion, is the situation we should expect to find in some disputes. Someone advances a thesis—such as the assertion in 14, *Abortion is homicide*—and someone else flatly contradicts it by the simple expedient of negating it, thus:

19. Abortion is not homicide.

If we can trust public opinion polls, many of us are not sure whether to agree with 14 or with 19. But we should agree that whichever is true, *both* cannot be true, and *both* cannot be false. The two assertions, between them, exclude all other possibilities; they pose a forced choice for our belief. (Again, we have met this idea, too, in a reductio ad absurdum.)

Now it is one thing for Jack and Jill in a dispute or argument to contradict each other. It is quite another matter for Jack to contradict himself. One wants (or should want) to avoid self-contradiction because of the embarrassing position in which one then finds oneself. Once I have contradicted myself, what are others to believe I really believe? What, indeed, *do* I believe, for that matter?

It may be, as Emerson observed, that a "foolish consistency is the hobgoblin of little minds"—that is, it may be shortsighted to purchase a consistency in one's beliefs at the expense of flying in the face of common sense. But making an effort to avoid a foolish inconsistency is the hallmark of serious thinking.

While we are speaking of inconsistency, we should spend a moment on **paradox.** The word refers to two different things:

- An assertion that is essentially self-contradictory and therefore cannot be true and

- A seemingly contradictory assertion that nevertheless may be true.

An example of the first might be, "Evaluations concerning quality in literature are all a matter of personal judgment, but Shakespeare is the world's greatest writer." It is hard to make any sense out of this assertion. Contrast it with a paradox of the second sort, a *seeming* contradiction that may make sense, such as "The longest way round is the shortest way home," or "Work is more fun than fun," or "The best way to find happiness is not to look for it." Here we have assertions that are striking because as soon as we hear them we realize that although they seem inconsistent and self-defeating, they contain (or may contain) profound truths. Paradoxes of this second sort are especially common in religious texts, where they may imply a mysterious reality concealed by a world of contradictory appearances. Examples are "Some who are last shall be first, and some who are first shall be last" (Jesus, quoted in Luke 13:30), and "Death, thou shalt die" (the poet John Donne, alluding to the idea that the person who has faith in Jesus dies to this world but lives eternally). If you use the word *paradox* in your own writing—for instance, to characterize an argument that you are reading—be sure that your reader will understand in which sense you are using the word. (And, of course, you will not want to write paradoxes of the first, self-contradictory sort.)

INDUCTION

Deduction involves logical thinking that applies to any assertion or claim whatever—because every possible statement, true or false, has its deductive logical consequences. Induction is relevant to one kind of assertion only; namely, to **empirical** or *factual* claims. Other kinds of assertions (such as definitions, mathematical equations, and moral or legal norms) simply are not the product of inductive reasoning and cannot serve as a basis for further inductive thinking.

And so, in studying the methods of induction, we are exploring tactics and strategies useful in gathering and then using **evidence**—empirical, observational, experimental—in support of a belief as its ground. Modern scientific knowledge is the product of these methods, and they differ somewhat from one science to another because they depend on the theories and technology appropriate to each of the sciences. Here, all we can do is discuss generally the more abstract features common to inductive inquiry generally. For fuller details, you must eventually consult your local physicist, chemist, geologist, or their colleagues and counterparts in other scientific fields.

Observation and Inference

Let us begin with a simple example. Suppose we have evidence (actually we don't, but that will not matter for our purposes) in support of the claim that

1. In a sample of 500 smokers, 230 persons observed have cardiovascular disease.

The basis for asserting 1—the evidence or ground—would be, presumably, straightforward physical examination of the 500 persons in the sample, one by one.

With this claim in hand, we can think of the purpose and methods of induction as being pointed in both of two opposite directions: toward establishing the basis or ground of the very empirical proposition with which we start (in this example the observation stated in 1) or toward understanding what that observation indicates or suggests as a more general, inclusive, or fundamental fact of nature.

In each case, we start from something we *do* know (or take for granted and treat as a sound starting point)—some fact of nature, perhaps a striking or commonplace event that we have observed and recorded—and then go on to something we do *not* fully know and perhaps cannot directly observe. In example 1, only the second of these two orientations is of any interest, and so let us concentrate exclusively on it. Let us also generously treat as a *method* of induction any regular pattern or style of nondeductive reasoning that we could use to support a claim such as that in 1.

Anyone truly interested in the observed fact that *230 of 500 smokers have cardiovascular disease* is likely to start speculating about, and thus be interested in finding out, whether any or all of several other propositions are also true. For example, one might wonder whether

> 2. *All* smokers have cardiovascular disease or will develop it during their lifetimes.

This claim is a straightforward generalization of the original observation as reported in claim 1. When we think inductively about the linkage between 1 and 2, we are reasoning from an observed sample (some smokers—that is, 230 of the 500 *observed*) to the entire membership of a more inclusive class (*all* smokers, whether observed or not). The fundamental question raised by reasoning from the narrower claim 1 to the broader claim 2 is whether we have any ground for believing that what is true of *some* members of a class is true of them *all*. So the difference between 1 and 2 is that of *quantity* or scope.

We can also think inductively about the *relation* between the factors mentioned in 1. Having observed data as reported in 1, we may be tempted to assert a different and profounder kind of claim:

> 3. Smoking *causes* cardiovascular disease.

Here our interest is not merely in generalizing from a sample to a whole class; it is the far more important one of *explaining* the observation with which we began in claim 1. Certainly the preferred, even if not the only, mode of explanation for a natural phenomenon is a *causal* explanation. In proposition 3, we propose to explain the presence of one phenomenon (cardiovascular disease) by the prior occurrence of an independent phenomenon (smoking). The observation reported in 1 is now being used as evidence or support for this new conjecture stated in 3.

Our original claim in 1 asserted no causal relation between anything and anything else; whatever the cause of cardiovascular disease may be, that cause is not observed, mentioned, or assumed in assertion 1. Similarly, the observation asserted in claim 1 is consistent with many explanations. For example, the explanation of 1 might not be 3, but some other, undetected, carcinogenic factor unrelated to smoking—for instance, exposure to high levels of radon. The question one now faces is what can be added to 1, or teased out of it, to produce an adequate ground for claiming 3. (We shall return to this example for closer scrutiny.)

But there is a third way to go beyond 1. Instead of a straightforward generalization, as we had in 2, or a pronouncement on the cause of a phenomenon, as in 3, we might have a somewhat more complex and cautious further claim in mind, such as this:

4. Smoking is a factor in the causation of cardiovascular disease in some persons.

This proposition, like 3, advances a claim about causation. But 4 is obviously a weaker claim than 3. That is, other observations, theories, or evidence that would require us to reject 3 might be consistent with 4; evidence that would support 4 could easily fail to be enough to support 3. Consequently, it is even possible that 4 is true although 3 is false, because 4 allows for other (unmentioned) factors in the causation of cardiovascular disease (genetic or dietary factors, for example) which may not be found in all smokers.

Propositions 2, 3, and 4 differ from proposition 1 in an important respect. We began by assuming that 1 states an empirical fact based on direct observation, whereas these others do not. Instead, they state empirical *hypotheses* or conjectures—tentative generalizations not fully confirmed—each of which goes beyond the observed facts asserted in 1. Each of 2, 3, and 4 can be regarded as an *inductive inference* from 1. We can also say that 2, 3, and 4 are hypotheses relative to 1, even if relative to some other starting point (such as all the information that scientists today really have about smoking and cardiovascular disease) they are not.

Probability

Another way of formulating the last point is to say that whereas proposition 1, a statement of observed fact (*230 out of 500 smokers have cardiovascular disease*), has a **probability** of 1.0—that is, it is absolutely certain—the probability of each of the hypotheses stated in 2, 3, and 4, *relative* to 1 is smaller than 1.0. (We need not worry here about how much smaller than 1.0 the probabilities are, nor about how to calculate these probabilities precisely.) Relative to some starting point other than 1, however, the probability of these same three hypotheses might be quite different. Of course, it still would not be 1.0, absolute certainty. But it takes only a moment's reflection to realize that, whatever may be the probability of 2 or 3 or 4 relative to 1, those probabilities in each case will be quite different relative to different information, such as this:

5. Ten persons observed in a sample of 500 smokers have cardiovascular disease.

The idea that a *given proposition can have different probabilities* relative to different bases is fundamental to all inductive reasoning. It can be convincingly illustrated by the following example. Suppose we want to consider the probability of this proposition being true:

6. Susanne Smith will live to be eighty.

Taken as an abstract question of fact, we cannot even guess what the probability is with any assurance. But we can do better than guess; we can in fact even calculate the answer, if we are given some further information. Thus, suppose we are told that

> 7. Susanne Smith is seventy-nine.

Our original question then becomes one of determining the probability that 6 is true given 7; that is, relative to the evidence contained in proposition 7. No doubt, if Susanne Smith really is seventy-nine, then the probability that she will live to be eighty is greater than if we know only that

> 8. Susanne Smith is more than nine years old.

Obviously, a lot can happen to Susanne in the seventy years between nine and seventy-nine that is not very likely to happen to her in the one year between seventy-nine and eighty. And so, proposition 6 is more probable relative to proposition 7 than it is relative to proposition 8.

Let us disregard 7 and instead further suppose for the sake of the argument that the following is true:

> 9. Ninety percent of the women alive at seventy-nine live to be eighty.

Given this additional information, we now have a basis for answering our original question about proposition 6 with some precision. But suppose, in addition to 8, we are also told that

> 10. Susanne Smith is suffering from inoperable cancer.

and also that

> 11. The survival rate for women suffering from inoperable cancer is 0.6 years (that is, the average life span for women after a diagnosis of inoperable cancer is about seven months).

With this new information, the probability that 6 will be true has dropped significantly, all because we can now estimate the probability in relation to a new body of evidence.

The probability of an event, thus, is not a fixed number but one that varies because it is always relative to some evidence—and given different evidence, one and the same event can have different probabilities. In other words, the probability of any event is always relative to how much is known (assumed, believed), and because different persons may know different things about a given event, or the same person may know different things at different times, one and the same event can have two or more probabilities. This conclusion is not a paradox but a logical consequence of the concept of what it is for an event to have (that is, to be assigned) a probability.

If we shift to the *calculation* of probabilities, we find that generally we have two ways to calculate them. One way to proceed is by the method of **a priori** or **equal probabilities**—that is, by reference to the relevant possibilities taken abstractly and apart from any other information.

Thus, in an election contest with only two candidates, Smith and Jones, each of the candidates has a fifty-fifty chance of winning (whereas in a three-candidate race, each candidate would have one chance in three of winning). Therefore, the probability that Smith will win is 0.5, and the probability that Jones will win is also 0.5. (The sum of the probabilities of all possible independent outcomes must always equal 1.0, which is obvious enough if you think about it.)

But in politics the probabilities are not reasonably calculated so abstractly. We know that many empirical factors affect the outcome of an election and that a calculation of probabilities in ignorance of those factors is likely to be drastically misleading. In our example of the two-candidate election, suppose Smith has strong party support and is the incumbent, whereas Jones represents a party long out of power and is further handicapped by being relatively unknown. No one who knows anything about electoral politics would give Jones the same chance of winning as Smith. The two events are not equiprobable in relation to all the information available.

Not only that, a given event can have more than one probability. This happens whenever we calculate a probability by relying on different bodies of data that report how often the event in question has been observed to happen. Probabilities calculated in this way are **relative frequencies.** Our earlier hypothetical example of Susanne Smith provides an illustration. If she is a smoker and we have observed that 100 out of a random set of 500 smokers are observed to have cardiovascular disease, we have a basis for claiming that she has a probability of 100 in 500, or 0.2 (one-fifth), of having this disease. However, if we had other data showing that 250 out of 500 women smokers aged eighty or older have cardiovascular disease, we have a basis for believing that there is a probability of 250 in 500, or 0.5 (one-half), that she has this disease. Notice, of course, that in both calculations we assume that Susanne Smith is not among the persons we have examined. In both cases we infer the probability with which she has this disease from observing its frequency in populations that exclude her.

Both methods of calculating probabilities are legitimate; in each case the calculation is relative to observed circumstances. But as the examples show, it is most reasonable to have recourse to the method of equiprobabilities only when few or no other factors affecting possible outcomes are known.

Mill's Methods

Let us return to our earlier discussion of smoking and cardiovascular disease and consider in greater detail the question of a causal connection between the two phenomena. We began thus:

1. In a sample of 500 smokers, 230 persons observed have cardiovascular disease.

We regarded 1 as an observed fact, though in truth, of course, it is mere supposition. Our question now is, how might we augment this information so as to strengthen our confidence that

> 3. Smoking *causes* cardiovascular disease.

or at least

> 4. Smoking is a factor in the causation of cardiovascular disease in some persons.

Suppose further examination showed that

> 12. In the sample of 230 smokers with cardiovascular disease, no other suspected factor (such as genetic predisposition, lack of physical exercise, age over fifty) was also observed.

Such an observation would encourage us to believe 3 or 4 is true. Why? We are encouraged to believe it because we are inclined to believe also that whatever the cause of a phenomenon is, it must *always* be present when its effect is present. Thus, the inference from 1 to 3 or 4 is supported by 12, using **Mill's Method of Agreement,** named after the British philosopher, John Stuart Mill (1806–1873), who first formulated it. It is called a method of agreement because of the way in which the inference relies on *agreement* among the observed phenomena where a presumed cause is thought to be *present.*

Let us now suppose that in our search for evidence to support 3 or 4 we conduct additional research and discover that

> 13. In a sample of 500 nonsmokers, selected to be representative of both sexes, different ages, dietary habits, exercise patterns, and so on, none is observed to have cardiovascular disease.

This observation would further encourage us to believe that we had obtained significant additional confirmation of 3 or 4. Why? Because we now know that factors present (such as male sex, lack of exercise, family history of cardiovascular disease) in cases where the effect is absent (no cardiovascular disease observed) cannot be the cause. This is an example of **Mill's Method of Difference,** so called because the cause or causal factor of an effect must be *different* from whatever the factors are that are present when the effect is *absent.*

Suppose now that, increasingly confident we have found the cause of cardiovascular disease, we study our first sample of 230 smokers ill with the disease, and discover this:

> 14. Those who smoke two or more packs of cigarettes daily for ten or more years have cardiovascular disease either much younger or much more severely than those who smoke less.

This is an application of **Mill's Method of Concomitant Variation,** perhaps the most convincing of the three methods. Here we deal not merely with the presence of the conjectured cause (smoking) or the absence of the effect we are studying (cardiovascular disease), as we were previously, but with the more interesting and subtler matter of the *degree and regularity of the correlation* of the supposed cause and effect. According to the observations reported in 14, it strongly appears that the more we have of the "cause" (smoking), the sooner or the more intense the onset of the "effect" (cardiovascular disease).

Notice, however, what happens to our confirmation of 3 and 4 if, instead of the observation reported in 14, we had observed

15. In a representative sample of 500 nonsmokers, cardiovascular disease was observed in 34 cases.

(Let us not pause here to explain what makes a sample more or less representative of a population, although the representativeness of samples is vital to all statistical reasoning.) Such an observation would lead us almost immediately to suspect some other or additional causal factor: Smoking might indeed be *a* factor in causing cardiovascular disease, but it can hardly be *the* cause because (using Mill's Method of Difference) we cannot have the effect, as we do in the observed sample reported in 15, unless we also have the cause.

An observation such as the one in 15, however, is likely to lead us to think our hypothesis that *smoking causes cardiovascular disease* has been disconfirmed. But we have a fallback position ready; we can still defend a weaker hypothesis, namely 4, *Smoking is a factor in the causation of cardiovascular disease in some persons.* Even if 3 stumbles over the evidence in 15, 4 does not. It is still quite possible that smoking is a factor in causing this disease, even if it is not the *only* factor—and if it is, then 4 is true.

Confirmation, Mechanism, and Theory

Notice that in the discussion so far, we have spoken of the *confirmation* of a hypothesis, such as our causal claim in 4, but not of its *verification.* (Similarly, we have imagined very different evidence, such as that stated in 15, leading us to speak of the *dis*confirmation of 3, though not of its *falsi*fication.) Confirmation (getting some evidence for) is weaker than verification (getting sufficient evidence to regard as true); and our (imaginary) evidence so far in favor of 4 falls well short of conclusive support. Further research—the study of more representative or much larger samples, for example—might yield very different observations. It might lead us to conclude that although initial research had confirmed our hypothesis about smoking as the cause of cardiovascular disease, the additional information obtained subsequently disconfirmed the hypothesis. For most interesting hypotheses, both in detective stories and in modern science, there is both confirming and disconfirming evidence simultaneously. The challenge is to evaluate the hypothesis by considering such conflicting evidence.

As long as we confine our observations to *correlations* of the sort reported in our several (imaginary) observations, such as proposition 1, *230 smokers in a group of 500 have cardiovascular disease*, or 12, *230 smokers with the disease share no other suspected factors*, such as lack of exercise, any defense of a *causal* hypothesis such as claim 3, *Smoking causes cardiovascular disease*, or claim 4, *Smoking is a factor in causing the disease*, is not likely to convince the skeptic or lead those with beliefs alternative to 3 and 4 to abandon them and agree with us. Why is that? It is because a causal hypothesis without any account of the *underlying mechanism* by means of which the (alleged) cause produces the effect will seem superficial. Only when we can specify in detail *how* the (alleged) cause produces the effect will the causal hypothesis be convincing.

In other cases, in which no mechanism can be found, we seek instead to embed the causal hypothesis in a larger *theory*, one that rules out as incompatible any causal hypothesis except the favored one. (That is, we appeal to the test of consistency and thereby bring deductive reasoning to bear on our problem.) Thus, perhaps we cannot specify any mechanism—any underlying structure that generates a regular sequence of events, one of which is the effect we are studying—to explain why, for example, the gravitational mass of a body causes it to attract other bodies. But we can embed this claim in a larger body of physical theory that rules out as inconsistent any alternative causal explanation. To do that convincingly in regard to any given causal hypothesis, as this example suggests, requires detailed knowledge of the current state of the relevant body of scientific theory, something far beyond our aim or need to consider in further detail here.

FALLACIES

The straight road on which sound reasoning proceeds gives little latitude for cruising about. Irrationality, carelessness, passionate attachment to one's unexamined beliefs, and the sheer complexity of some issues, not to mention original sin, occasionally spoil the reasoning of even the best of us. Although in this book we reprint many varied voices and arguments, we hope we have reprinted no readings that exhibit the most flagrant errors or commit the graver abuses against the canons of good reasoning. Nevertheless, an inventory of those abuses and their close examination can be an instructive (as well as an amusing) exercise—instructive because the diagnosis and repair of error helps to fix more clearly the principles of sound reasoning on which such remedial labors depend; amusing because we are so constituted that our perception of the nonsense of others can stimulate our mind, warm our heart, and give us comforting feelings of superiority.

The discussion that follows, then, is a quick tour through the twisting lanes, mudflats, forests, and quicksands of the faults that one sometimes encounters in reading arguments that stray from the highway of clear thinking.

We can and do apply the term *fallacy* to many types of errors, mistakes, and confusions in oral and written discourse, in which our reasoning has gone awry. For convenience, we can group the fallacies by referring to the six aspects of reasoning identified in the Toulmin Method, described earlier (p. 325). Or, following the suggestion of S. Morris Engel in his book, *Without Good Reason* (2000), we can group fallacies according to whether they involve a crucial *ambiguity*, an *erroneous presumption*, or an *irrelevance*.

We ought not, however, take these categories too rigidly because it is often the case that a piece of fallacious thinking involves two or more fallacies. That is, it is possible (as we shall see) to find traces of faulty reasoning of several varieties, in which case we classify it under one rather than another of the headings above because we have chosen what in our judgment amounts to the dominant or most prominent of the fallacious features on display. Thus, most of the fallacies exhibit an irrelevant consideration. (Red herring is a good example. Is it best described as a fallacy of false presumption or as a fallacy of irrelevance? Same with erroneous presupposition.) In the end, classifying the fallacies under this or that system of headings is not very important. What is important is being able to spot the fallacious thinking no matter what it is called.

Fallacies of Ambiguity

Ambiguity   Near the center of the town of Concord, Massachusetts, is an empty field with a sign reading "Old Calf Pasture." Hmm. A pasture in former times in which calves grazed? A pasture now in use for old calves? An erstwhile pasture for old calves? These alternative readings arise because of **ambiguity;** brevity in the sign has produced a group of words that give rise to more than one possible interpretation, confusing the reader and (presumably) frustrating the sign writer's intentions.

Consider a more complex example. Suppose someone asserts *People have equal rights* and also *Everyone has a right to property.* Many people believe both these claims, but their combination involves an ambiguity. On one interpretation, the two claims entail that everyone has an *equal right* to property. (That is, you and I each have an equal right to whatever property we have.) But the two claims can also be interpreted to mean that everyone has a *right to equal property.* (That is, whatever property you have a right to, I have a right to the same, or at least equivalent, property.) The latter interpretation is radically revolutionary, whereas the former is not. Arguments over equal rights often involve this ambiguity.

Division   In the Bible, we are told that the apostles of Jesus were twelve and that Matthew was an apostle. Does it follow that Matthew was twelve? No. To argue in this way from a property of a group to a property of a member of that group is to commit the **fallacy of division.** The example of the apostles may not be a very tempting instance of this error; here is a classic version that is a bit more interesting. If it is true that the average American family has 1.8 children, does it follow that your brother and sister-in-law are likely to have 1.8 children? If you think it does, you have committed the fallacy of division.

Composition   Could an all-star team of professional basketball players beat the Boston Celtics in their heyday—say, the team of 1985 to 1986? Perhaps in one game or two, but probably not in seven out of a dozen games in a row. As students of the game know, teamwork is an indispensable part of outstanding performance, and the 1985 to 1986 Celtics were famous for their self-sacrificing style of play.

The **fallacy of composition** can be convincingly illustrated, therefore, in this argument: *A team of five NBA all-stars is the best team in basketball if each of the five players is the best at his position.* The fallacy is called composition because the reasoning commits the error of arguing from the true premise that each member of a group has a certain property to the not necessarily true conclusion that the group (the composition) itself has the property. (That is, because *A* is the best player at forward, *B* is the best center, and so on, therefore, the team of *A, B, . . .* is the best team.)

Equivocation   In a delightful passage in Lewis Carroll's *Through the Looking-Glass*, the king asks his messenger, "Who did you pass on the road?" and the messenger replies, "Nobody." This prompts the king to observe, "Of course, Nobody walks slower than you," provoking the messenger's sullen response: "I do my best. I'm sure nobody walks much faster than I do." At this the king remarks with surprise, "He can't do that or else he'd have been here first!" (This, by the way, is the classic predecessor of the famous comic dialogue "Who's on First?" between the comedians Bud Abbott and Lou Costello.) The king and the messenger are equivocating on the term *nobody.* The messenger uses it in the normal way as an indefinite pronoun equivalent to "not anyone." But the king uses the word as though it were a proper noun, *Nobody,* the rather odd name of some person. No wonder the king and the messenger talk right past each other.

Equivocation (from the Latin for "equal voice"— that is, giving utterance to two meanings at the same time in one word or phrase) can ruin otherwise good reasoning, as in this example: *Euthanasia is a good death; one dies a good death when one dies peacefully in old age; therefore, euthanasia is dying peacefully in old age.* The etymology of *euthanasia* is literally "a good death," and so the first premise is true. And the second premise is certainly plausible. But the conclusion of this syllogism is false. Euthanasia cannot be defined as a peaceful death in one's old age, for two reasons. First, euthanasia requires the intervention of another person who kills someone (or lets the person die); second, even a very young person can be euthanized. The problem arises because "a good death" is used in the second premise in a manner that does not apply to euthanasia. Both meanings of "a good death" are legitimate, but when used together, they constitute an equivocation that spoils the argument.

The fallacy of equivocation takes us from the discussion of confusions in individual claims or grounds to the more troublesome fallacies that infect the linkages between the claims we make and the grounds (or reasons) for them. These are the fallacies that occur in statements that, following the vocabulary of the Toulmin Method, are called the *warrant* of reasoning. Each fallacy is an example of reasoning that involves a **non sequitur** (Latin for "It does not follow"). That is, the *claim* (the conclusion) does not follow from the *grounds* (the premises).

For a start, here is an obvious non sequitur: "He went to the movies on three consecutive nights, so he must love movies." Why doesn't the claim ("He must love movies") follow from the grounds ("He went to the movies on three consecutive nights")? Perhaps the person was just fulfilling an assignment in a film course (maybe he even hated movies so much that he had postponed three assignments to see films and now had to see them all in quick succession), or maybe he went with a girlfriend who was a movie buff, or maybe . . . — well, one can think of any number of other possible reasons.

Fallacies of Presumption

Distorting the Facts   Facts can be distorted either intentionally (to deceive or mislead) or unintentionally, and in either case usually (but not invariably) to the benefit of whoever is doing the distortion. Consider this not entirely hypothetical case. A pharmaceutical company spends millions of dollars to develop a new drug that will help pregnant women avoid spontaneous abortion. The company reports its findings, but it does not also report that it has learned from its researchers of a serious downside for this drug in many cases, resulting in deformed limbs in the neonate. Had the company informed the public of this fact, the drug would not have been certified for use.

Here is another case. Half a century ago the surgeon general reported that smoking cigarettes increased the likelihood that smokers would eventually suffer from lung cancer. The cigarette manufacturers vigorously protested that the surgeon general relied on inconclusive research and was badly misleading the public about the health risks of smoking. It later turned out that the tobacco companies knew that smoking increased the risk of lung cancer — a fact established by the company's own laboratories but concealed from the public. Today, thanks to public access to all the facts, it is commonplace knowledge that inhaled smoke — including secondhand smoke — is a risk factor for many illnesses.

Post Hoc, Ergo Propter Hoc   One of the most tempting errors in reasoning is to ground a claim about causation on an observed temporal sequence;

that is, to argue "after this, therefore because of this" (which is what the phrase **post hoc, ergo propter hoc** means in Latin). Nearly forty years ago, when the medical community first announced that smoking tobacco caused lung cancer, advocates for the tobacco industry replied that doctors were guilty of this fallacy.

These industry advocates argued that medical researchers had merely noticed that in some people, lung cancer developed *after* considerable smoking, indeed, years after; but (they insisted) this correlation was not at all the same as a causal relation between smoking and lung cancer. True enough. The claim that *A causes B* is not the same as the claim that *B* comes after *A*. After all, it was possible that smokers as a group had some other common trait and that this factor was the true cause of their cancer.

As the long controversy over the truth about the causation of lung cancer shows, to avoid the appearance of fallacious *post hoc* reasoning one needs to find some way to link the observed phenomena (the correlation of smoking and the onset of lung cancer). This step requires some further theory and preferably some experimental evidence for the exact sequence or physical mechanism, in full detail, of how ingestion of tobacco smoke is a crucial factor — and is not merely an accidental or happenstance prior event — in the subsequent development of the cancer.

Many Questions   The old saw, "When did you stop beating your wife?" illustrates the **fallacy of many questions.** This question, as one can readily see, is unanswerable unless all three of its implicit presuppositions are true. The questioner presupposes that (1) the addressee has or had a wife, (2) he has beaten her, and (3) he has stopped beating her. If any of these presuppositions is false, then the question is pointless; it cannot be answered strictly and simply with a date.

Hasty Generalization   From a logical point of view, **hasty generalization** is the precipitous move from true assertions about *one* or a *few* instances to dubious or even false assertions about *all*. For example, while it may be true, based on your personal experience, that the only native Hungarians you personally know do not speak English very well, that is no basis for asserting that Hungarians do not speak English very well. Or if the clothes you recently ordered by mail turn out not to fit very well, it doesn't follow that *all* mail-order clothes turn out to be too large or too small. A hasty generalization usually lies behind a **stereotype** — that is, a person or event treated as typical of a whole class. Thus, in 1914, after the German invasion of Belgium, during which some atrocities were committed by the invaders, the German troops were quickly stereotyped by the Allies as brutal savages who skewered helpless babies on their bayonets.

The Slippery Slope   One of the most familiar arguments against any type of government regulation is that if it is allowed, then it will be just the first step down the path that leads to ruinous interference, overregulation, and totalitarian control. Fairly often we encounter this mode of argument in the public debates over handgun control, the censorship of pornography, and physician-assisted suicide. The argument is called the **slippery slope argument** (or the **wedge argument,** from the way we use the thin end of a wedge to split solid things apart; it is also called, rather colorfully, "letting the camel's nose under the tent"). The fallacy here is in implying that the first step necessarily leads to the second, and so on down the slope to disaster, when in fact there is no necessary slide from the first step to the second. (Would handgun registration lead to a police state? Well, it hasn't in Switzerland.) Sometimes the argument takes the form of claiming that a seemingly innocent or even attractive principle that is being applied in a given case (censorship of pornography, to avoid promoting sexual violence) requires one for the sake of consistency to apply the same principle in other cases, only with absurd and catastrophic results (censorship of everything in print, to avoid hurting anyone's feelings).

Here's an extreme example of this fallacy in action:

> Automobiles cause more deaths than handguns do. If you oppose handguns on the ground that doing so would save lives of the innocent, you'll soon find yourself wanting to outlaw the automobile.

Does opposition to handguns have this consequence? Not necessarily. Most people accept without dispute the right of society to regulate the operation of motor vehicles by requiring drivers to have a license, a greater restriction than many states impose on gun ownership. Besides, a gun is a lethal weapon designed to kill, whereas an automobile or truck is a vehicle designed for transportation. Private ownership and use in both cases entail risks of death to the innocent. But there is no inconsistency in a society's refusal to tolerate this risk in the case of guns and its willingness to do so in the case of automobiles.

Closely related to the slippery slope is what lawyers call a **parade of horrors,** an array of examples of terrible consequences that will or might follow if we travel down a certain path. A good example appears in Justice William Brennan's opinion for the Supreme Court in *Texas v. Johnson* (p. 425), concerned with a Texas law against burning the American flag in political protest. If this law is allowed to stand, Brennan suggests, we may next find laws against burning the presidential seal, state flags, and the Constitution.

False Analogy   Argument by analogy, as we point out in Chapter 3 and as many of the selections in this book show, is a familiar and even indispensable mode of argument. But it can be treacherous because it runs the risk of the **fallacy of false analogy.** Unfortunately, we have no simple or foolproof way of distinguishing between the useful, legitimate analogies and the others. The key question to ask yourself is this: Do the two things put into analogy differ in any essential and relevant respect, or are they different only in unimportant and irrelevant aspects?

In a famous example from his discussion in support of suicide, philosopher David Hume rhetorically asked: "It would be no crime in me to divert the Nile or Danube from its course, were I able to effect such purposes. Where then is the crime of turning a few ounces of blood from their natural channel?" This is a striking analogy, except that it rests on a false assumption. No one has the right to divert the Nile or the Danube or any other major international watercourse; it would be a catastrophic crime to do so without the full consent of people living in the region, their government, and so forth. Therefore, arguing by analogy, one might well say that no one has the right to take his or her own life, either. Thus, Hume's own analogy can be used to argue against his thesis that suicide is no crime. But let us ignore the way in which his example can be turned against him. The analogy is a terrible one in any case. Isn't it obvious that the Nile, whatever its exact course, would continue to nourish Egypt and the Sudan, whereas the blood flowing out of someone's veins will soon leave that person dead? The fact that the blood is the same blood, whether in one's body or in a pool on the floor (just as the water of the Nile is the same body of water whatever path it follows to the sea) is, of course, irrelevant to the question of whether one has the right to commit suicide.

Let us look at a more complex example. During the 1960s, when the United States was convulsed over the purpose and scope of its military involvement in Southeast Asia, advocates of more vigorous U.S. military participation appealed to the so-called domino effect, supposedly inspired by a passing remark from President Eisenhower in the 1950s. The analogy refers to the way in which a row of standing dominoes will collapse, one after the other, if the first one is pushed. If Vietnam turns Communist, according to this analogy, so too will its neighbors, Laos and Cambodia, followed by Thailand and then Burma, until the whole region is as communist as China to the north. The domino analogy (or metaphor) provided, no doubt, a vivid illustration and effectively portrayed the worry of many anti-Communists. But did it really shed any light on the likely pattern of political and military developments in the region? The history of events there during the 1970s and 1980s did not bear out the domino analogy.

Straw Man   It is often tempting to reframe or report your opponent's thesis to make it easier to attack and perhaps refute it. If you do this in the course of an argument, you are creating a straw man, a thing of no substance and easily blown away. The straw man you've constructed is usually a radically conservative or extremely liberal thesis, which few if any would want to defend. That is why it is easier to refute than the view your opponent actually holds. "So you defend the death penalty—and all the horrible things done in its name. No one in his right mind would hold such a view." It's highly unlikely that your friend supports *everything* that has been done in the name of capital punishment—crucifixion and beheading, for example, or execution of the children of the guilty offender.

Special Pleading We all have our favorites—relatives, friends, and neighbors—and we are all too likely to show that favoritism in unacceptable ways. How about this: "Yes, I know Billy hit Sally first, but he's my son. He's a good boy, and I know he must have had a good reason." Or this: "True, she's late for work again—the third time this week!—but her uncle's my friend, and it will be embarrassing to me if she is fired, so we'll just ignore it." Special pleading inevitably leads to unmerited advantages, as illustrated above.

Begging the Question The argument over whether the death penalty is a deterrent illustrates another fallacy. From the fact that you live in a death-penalty state and were not murdered yesterday, we cannot infer that the death penalty was a deterrent. Yet it is tempting to make this inference, perhaps because—all unawares—we are relying on the **fallacy of begging the question.** If someone tacitly assumes from the start that the death penalty is an effective deterrent, then the fact that you weren't murdered yesterday certainly looks like evidence for the truth of that assumption. But it isn't, so long as there are competing but unexamined alternative explanations, as in this case. (The fallacy is called "begging the question," *petitio principii* in Latin, because the conclusion of the argument is hidden among its assumptions—and so the conclusion, not surprisingly, follows from the premises.)

Of course, the fact that you weren't murdered is *consistent* with the claim that the death penalty is an effective deterrent, just as someone else's being murdered is also consistent with that claim (for an effective deterrent need not be a *perfect* deterrent). In general, from the fact that two propositions are consistent with each other, we cannot infer that either is evidence for the other.

Note: The term "begging the question" is often wrongly used to mean "raises the question," as in "His action of burning the flag begs the question, What drove him to do such a thing?"

False Dichotomy Sometimes oversimplification takes a more complex form, in which contrary possibilities are wrongly presented as though they were exhaustive and exclusive. "Either we get tough with drug users, or we must surrender and legalize all drugs." Really? What about doing neither and instead offering education and counseling, detoxification programs, and incentives to "Say no"? A favorite of debaters, **either/or** reasoning always runs the risk of ignoring a third (or fourth) possibility. Some disjunctions are indeed exhaustive: "Either we get tough with drug users, or we do not." This proposition, though vague (what does "get tough" really mean?), is a tautology; it cannot be false, and there is no third alternative. But most disjunctions do not express a pair of *contradictory* alternatives: They offer only a pair of *contrary* alternatives, and mere contraries do not exhaust the possibilities (recall our discussion of contraries versus contradictories on p. 347).

An example of **false dichotomy** can be found in the essay by Jeff Jacoby on flogging (p. 183). His entire discussion is built on the relative superiority of whipping over imprisonment, as though there was no alternative punishment worth considering. But of course, there is, notably community service (especially for white-collar offenders, juveniles, and many first offenders).

Oversimplification   "Poverty causes crime," "Taxation is unfair," "Truth is stranger than fiction"—these are examples of generalizations that exaggerate and therefore oversimplify the truth. Poverty as such can't be the sole cause of crime because many poor people do not break the law. Some taxes may be unfairly high, others unfairly low—but there is no reason to believe that *every* tax is unfair to all those who have to pay it. Some true stories do amaze us as much or more than some fictional stories, but the reverse is true, too. (In the language of the Toulmin Method, **oversimplification** is the result of a failure to use suitable modal qualifiers in formulating one's claims or grounds or backing.)

Red Herring   The fallacy of **red herring,** less colorfully named irrelevant thesis, occurs when one tries to distract one's audience by invoking a consideration that is irrelevant to the topic under discussion. (This fallacy probably gets its name from the fact that a rotten herring, or a cured herring, which is reddish, will throw pursuing hounds off the right track.) Consider this case. Some critics, seeking to defend our government's refusal to sign the Kyoto accords to reduce global warming, argue that signing is supported mainly by left-leaning scientists. This argument supposedly shows that global warming—if there is such a thing—is not a serious, urgent issue. But claiming that the supporters of these accords are left-inclined is a red herring, an irrelevant thesis. By raising doubts about the political views of the advocates of signing, it distracts attention from the scientific question (Is there global warming?) and also from the separate political question (Ought the United States sign these accords?). The refusal of a government to sign these accords does not show there is no such thing as global warming. And even if all of the advocates of signing were left-leaning (they aren't), this fact (if it were a fact, but it isn't) would not show that worries about global warming are exaggerated.

Fallacies of Relevance

Tu Quoque   The Romans had a word for it: *Tu quoque* means "you, too." Consider this: "You're a fine one, trying to persuade me to give up smoking when you indulge yourself with a pipe and a cigar from time to time.

Maybe I should quit, but then so should you. As things stand now, however, it's hypocritical of you to complain about my smoking when you persist in the same habit." The fallacy is this: The merit of a person's argument has nothing to do with the person's character or behavior. Here, the assertion that smoking is bad for one's health is *not* weakened by the fact that a smoker offers the argument.

The Genetic Fallacy   A member of the family of fallacies that includes poisoning the well and ad hominem is the **genetic fallacy.** Here the error takes the form of arguing against some claim by pointing out that its origin (genesis) is tainted or that it was invented by someone deserving our contempt. Thus, one might attack the ideas of the Declaration of Independence by pointing out that its principal author, Thomas Jefferson, was a slaveholder. Assuming that it is not anachronistic and inappropriate to criticize a public figure of two centuries ago for practicing slavery, and conceding that slavery is morally outrageous, it is nonetheless fallacious to attack the ideas or even the sincerity of the Declaration by attempting to impeach the credentials of its author. Jefferson's moral faults do not by themselves falsify, make improbable, or constitute counterevidence to the truth or other merits of the claims made in his writings. At most, one's faults cast doubt on one's integrity or sincerity if one makes claims at odds with one's practice.

The genetic fallacy can take other forms less closely allied to ad hominem argument. For example, an opponent of the death penalty might argue,

> Capital punishment arose in barbarous times; but we claim to be civilized; therefore, we should discard this relic of the past.

Such reasoning shouldn't be persuasive because the question of the death penalty for our society must be decided by the degree to which it serves our purposes—justice and defense against crime, presumably—to which its historic origins are irrelevant. The practices of beer- and wine-making are as old as human civilization, but their origin in antiquity is no reason to outlaw them in our time. The curious circumstances in which something originates usually play no role whatever in its validity. Anyone who would argue that nothing good could possibly come from molds and fungi is refuted by Sir Alexander Fleming's discovery of penicillin in 1928.

Poisoning the Well   During the 1970s some critics of the Equal Rights Amendment (ERA) argued against it by pointing out that Marx and Engels, in their *Communist Manifesto*, favored equality of women and men—and therefore the ERA was immoral, undesirable, and perhaps even a Communist plot. This kind of reasoning is an attempt to **poison the well;** that is, an attempt to shift attention from the merits of the argument—the validity of the reasoning, the truth of the claims—to the source or origin of the argument. Such criticism deflects attention from the real issue; namely, whether the view in question is true and what the quality of evidence is in its support. The mere fact that Marx (or Hitler, for that matter) believed something does not show that the belief is false or immoral; just because some scoundrel believes the world is round, that is no reason for you to believe it is flat.

Appeal to Ignorance   In the controversy over the death penalty, the issues of deterrence and executing the innocent are bound to be raised. Because no one knows how many innocent persons have been convicted for murder and wrongfully executed, it is tempting for abolitionists to argue that the death penalty is too risky. It is equally tempting for the proponent of the death penalty to argue that since no one knows how many people have been deterred from murder by the threat of execution, we abolish it at our peril.

Each of these arguments suffers from the same flaw: the **fallacy of appeal to ignorance.** Each argument invites the audience to draw an inference from a premise that is unquestionably true—but what is that premise? It asserts that there is something "we don't know." But what we *don't* know cannot be *evidence* for (or against) anything. Our ignorance is no reason for believing anything, except perhaps that we ought to try to undertake an appropriate investigation in order to reduce our ignorance and replace it with reliable information.

Ad Hominem   Closely allied to poisoning the well is another fallacy, **ad hominem** argument (from the Latin for "against the person"). A critic can easily yield to the temptation to attack an argument or theory by trying to impeach or undercut the credentials of its advocates.

Example: Jones is arguing that prayer should not be permitted in public schools, and Smith responds by pointing out that Jones has twice been convicted of assaulting members of the clergy. Jones's behavior doubtless is reprehensible, but the issue is not Jones, it is prayer in school, and what must be scrutinized is Jones's argument, not his police record or his character.

Appeal to Authority   The example of Jefferson given to illustrate the genetic fallacy can be turned around to illustrate another fallacy. One might easily imagine someone from the South in 1860 defending the slave-owning society of that day by appealing to the fact that no less a person than Jefferson—a brilliant public figure, thinker, and leader by any measure—owned slaves. Or today one might defend capital punishment on the ground that Abraham Lincoln, surely one of the nation's greatest presidents, signed many death warrants during the Civil War, authorizing the execution of Union soldiers. No doubt the esteem in which such figures as Jefferson and Lincoln are deservedly held amounts to impressive endorsement for whatever acts and practices, policies and institutions, they supported. But the **authority** of these figures in itself is not evidence for the truth of their views, and so their authority cannot be a reason for anyone to agree with them. Obviously, Jefferson and Lincoln themselves could not support their beliefs by pointing to the fact that they held them. Because their own authority is no reason for them to believe what they believe, it is no reason for anyone else, either.

Sometimes the appeal to authority is fallacious because the authoritative person is not an expert on the issue in dispute. The fact that a high-energy physicist has won the Nobel Prize is no reason for attaching any special weight to her views on the causes of cancer, the reduction of traffic accidents, or the legalization of marijuana. On the other hand, one would be well advised to attend to her views on the advisability of ballistic missile-defense systems, for there may be a connection between the kind of research for which she received the prize and the defense research projects.

All of us depend heavily on the knowledge of various experts and authorities, and so we tend not to ignore their views. Conversely, we should resist the temptation to accord their views on diverse subjects the same respect that we grant them in the area of their expertise.

Appeal to Fear   The Romans called this fallacy *ad baculum*, "resorting to violence" (*baculum* means "stick," or "club"). Trying to persuade people to agree with you by threatening them with painful consequences is obviously an appeal that no rational person would contemplate. The violence need not be physical; if you threaten someone with the loss of a job, for instance, you are still using a stick. Violence or the threat of harmful consequences in the course of an argument is beyond reason and always shows the haste or impatience of those who appeal to it. It is also an indication that the argument on its merits would be unpersuasive, inconclusive, or worse. President Teddy Roosevelt's epigrammatic doctrine for the kind of foreign policy he favored—"Speak softly but carry a big stick"—illustrates an attempt to have it both ways, an appeal to reason for starters, but a recourse to coercion, or the threat of coercion, as a backup if needed.

Finally, we add two fallacies, not easily embraced by Engel's three categories that have served us well thus far (ambiguity, erroneous presumption, and irrelevance): death by a thousand qualifications and protecting the hypothesis.

Death by a Thousand Qualifications   In a letter of recommendation, sent in support of an applicant for a job on your newspaper, you find this sentence: "Young Smith was the best student I've ever taught in an English course." Pretty strong endorsement, you think, except that you do not know, because you have not been told, the letter writer is a very junior faculty member, has been teaching for only two years, is an instructor in the history department, taught a section of freshman English as a courtesy for a sick colleague, and had only eight students enrolled in the course. Thanks to these implicit qualifications, the letter writer did not lie or exaggerate in his praise; but the effect of his sentence on you, the unwitting reader, is quite misleading. The explicit claim in the letter, and its impact on you, is quite different from the tacitly qualified claim in the mind of the writer.

Death by a thousand qualifications gets its name from the ancient torture of death by a thousand small cuts. Thus, a bold assertion can be virtually killed, its true content reduced to nothing, bit by bit, as all the appropriate or necessary qualifications are added to it. Consider another example. Suppose you hear a politician describing another country (let's call it Ruritania so as not to offend anyone) as a "democracy"—except it turns out that Ruritania doesn't have regular elections, lacks a written constitution, has no independent judiciary, prohibits religious worship except of the state-designated deity, and so forth. So what is left of the original claim that Ruritania is a democracy is little or nothing. The qualifications have taken all the content out of the original description.

Protecting the Hypothesis   In Chapter 3, we contrasted *reasoning* and *rationalization* (or the finding of bad reasons for what one intends to believe anyway). Rationalization can take subtle forms, as the following example indicates. Suppose you're standing with a friend on the shore or on a pier, and you watch as a ship heads out to sea. As it reaches the horizon, it slowly disappears—first the hull, then the upper decks, and finally the tip of the mast. Because the ship (you both assume) isn't sinking, it occurs to you that you have in this sequence of observations convincing evidence that the earth's surface is curved. Nonsense, says your companion. Light waves sag, or bend down, over distances of a few miles, and so a flat surface (such as the ocean) can intercept them. Hence the ship, which appears to be going "over" the horizon, really isn't: It's just moving steadily farther and farther away in a straight line. Your friend, you discover to your amazement, is a card-carrying member of the Flat Earth Society (yes, there really is such an organization). Now most of us would regard the idea that light rays bend down in the manner required by the Flat Earther's argument as a rationalization whose sole purpose is to protect the flat-earth doctrine against counterevidence. We would be convinced it was a rationalization, and not a very good one at that, if the Flat Earther held to it despite a patient and thorough explanation from a physicist that showed modern optical theory to be quite incompatible with the view that light waves sag.

This example illustrates two important points about the *backing* of arguments. First, it is always possible to protect a hypothesis by abandoning adjacent or connected hypotheses; this is the tactic our Flat Earth friend has used. This maneuver is possible, however, only because—and this is the second point—whenever we test a hypothesis, we do so by taking for granted (usually quite unconsciously) many other hypotheses

---

✓ A CHECKLIST FOR EVALUATING AN ARGUMENT
FROM A LOGICAL POINT OF VIEW

☐ Is the argument purely deductive, purely inductive, or a mixture of the two?
☐ If it is deductive, is it valid?
☐ If it is valid, are all its premises and assumptions true?
☐ If it is not valid, what fallacy does it commit?
☐ If it is not valid, are the claims at least consistent with each other?
☐ If it is not valid, can you think of additional plausible assumptions that would make it valid?
☐ If the argument is inductive, on what observations is it based?
☐ If the argument is inductive, how probable are its premises and its conclusion?
☐ In any case, can you think of evidence that would further confirm the conclusion? Disconfirm the conclusion?

---

as well. So the evidence for the hypothesis we think we are confirming is impossible to separate entirely from the adequacy of the connected hypotheses. As long as we have no reason to doubt that light rays travel in straight lines (at least over distances of a few miles), our Flat Earth friend's argument is unconvincing. But once that hypothesis is itself put in doubt, the idea that looked at first to be a pathetic rationalization takes on an even more troublesome character.

There are, then, not one but two fallacies exposed by this example. The first and perhaps graver is in rigging your hypothesis so that *no matter what* observations are brought against it, you will count nothing as falsifying it. The second and subtler is in thinking that as you test one hypothesis, all of your other background beliefs are left safely to one side, immaculate and uninvolved. On the contrary, our beliefs form a corporate structure, intertwined and connected to each other with great complexity, and no one of them can ever be singled out for unique and isolated application, confirmation, or disconfirmation, to the world around us.

EXERCISE: FALLACIES — OR NOT?

Here, for diversion and practice, are some fallacies in action. Some of these statements, however, are not fallacies. Can you tell which is which? Can you detect *what* has gone wrong in the cases where something has gone wrong? Please explain your reasoning.

1. Abortion is murder—and it doesn't matter whether we're talking about killing a human embryo or a human fetus.

2. Euthanasia is not a good thing, it's murder—and it doesn't matter how painful one's dying may be.
3. Never loan a tool to a friend. I did once and never got it back.
4. If the neighbors don't like our loud music, that's just too bad. After all, we have a right to listen to the music we like when and where we want to play it.
5. The Good Samaritan in the Bible was pretty foolish; he was taking grave risks with no benefits for him in sight.
6. "Shoot first and ask questions afterward" is a good epigram for the kind of foreign policy we need.
7. "You can fool some of the people all of the time, and you can fool all the people some of the time, but you can't fool all the people all of the time." That's what Abraham Lincoln said, and he was right.
8. It doesn't matter whether Shakespeare wrote the plays attributed to him. What matters is whether the plays are any good.
9. The Golden Gate Bridge in San Francisco ought to be closed down. After all, just look at all the suicides that have occurred there.
10. Reparations for African Americans are way overdue; it's just another version of the reparations eventually paid to the Japanese Americans who were wrongly interned in 1942 during World War II.
11. Animals don't have rights any more than do trees or stones. They don't have desires, either. What they have are feelings and needs.
12. The average American family is said to have 2.1 children. This is absurd—did you ever meet 2.1 children?
13. My marriage was a failure, which just proves my point: Don't ever get married in the first place.
14. The Red Queen in *Alice in Wonderland* was right: Verdict first, evidence later.
15. Not until astronauts sailed through space around the moon and could see its back side for themselves did we have adequate reason to believe that the moon even had a back side.
16. If you start out with a bottle of beer a day and then go on to a glass or two of wine on the weekends, you're well on your way to becoming a hopeless drunk.
17. Two Indians are sitting on a fence. The small Indian is the son of the big Indian, but the big Indian is not the small Indian's father. How is that possible?
18. If you toss a coin five times and each time it come up heads, it is more likely than not that on the sixth throw you'll come up heads again—or is it more likely that you'll come up tails? Or is neither more likely?
19. Going to church on a regular basis is bad for your health. Instead of sitting in a pew for an hour each Sunday you'd be better off taking an hour's brisk walk.
20. You can't trust anything he says. When he was young he was an avid Communist.
21. Since 9/11 we've tried and convicted few terrorists, so our defense systems must be working.
22. We can trust the White House in its press releases because it's a reliable source of information.
23. Intelligent design must be true because the theory of evolution can't explain how life began.

24. Andreas Serrano's notorious photograph called *Piss Christ* (1989), showing a small plastic crucifix submerged in a glass of urine, never should have been put on public display, let alone financed by public funds.

25. Doubting Thomas was right—you need more than somebody's say-so to support a claim of resurrection.

26. You are a professional baseball player and you have a good-luck charm. When you wear it the team wins. When you don't wear it the team loses. What do you infer?

27. Resolve the following dilemma: When it rains you can't fix the hole in the roof. When it's not raining there is no need to mend the roof. Conclusion: Leave the roof as it is.

28. You are at the beach and you watch a ship steaming toward the horizon. Bit by bit it disappears from view—first the masts, then the upper deck, then the main deck, then the stern, and then it's gone. Why would it be wrong to infer that the ship is sinking?

29. How can it be true that "it's the exception that proves the rule"? If anything, isn't it the exception that *dis*proves the rule?

30. How come herbivores don't eat herbs?

31. In the 1930s it was commonplace to see ads announcing "More Doctors Smoke Camels." What do you make of such an ad?

32. Suppose the only way you could save five innocent people was by killing one of them. Would you do it? Suppose the only way you could save one innocent person was by killing five others. Would you do it?

Max Shulman

Having read about proper and improper arguments, you are now well equipped to read a short story on the topic.

Max Shulman (1919–1988) began his career as a writer when he was a journalism student at the University of Minnesota. Later he wrote humorous novels, stories, and plays. One of his novels, Barefoot Boy with Cheek *(1943), was made into a musical, and another,* Rally Round the Flag, Boys! *(1957), was made into a film starring Paul Newman and Joanne Woodward. The Tender Trap *(1954), a play he wrote with Robert Paul Smith, still retains its popularity with theater groups.*

"Love Is a Fallacy" was first published in 1951, when demeaning stereotypes about women and minorities were widely accepted in the marketplace as well as the home. Thus, jokes about domineering mothers-in-law or about dumb blondes routinely met with no objection.

Love Is a Fallacy

Cool was I and logical. Keen, calculating, perspicacious, acute, and astute—I was all of these. My brain was as powerful as a dynamo, as precise as a chemist's scales, as penetrating as a scalpel. And—think of it!—I was only eighteen.

It is not often that one so young has such a giant intellect. Take, for example, Petey Bellows, my roommate at the university. Same age, same background, but dumb as an ox. A nice enough fellow, you understand, but nothing upstairs. Emotional type. Unstable. Impressionable. Worst of all, a faddist. Fads, I submit, are the very negation of reason. To be swept up in every new craze that comes along, to surrender yourself to idiocy just because everybody else is doing it—this, to me, is the acme of mindlessness. Not, however, to Petey.

One afternoon I found Petey lying on his bed with an expression of such distress on his face that I immediately diagnosed appendicitis. "Don't move," I said. "Don't take a laxative. I'll call a doctor."

"Raccoon," he mumbled thickly.

"Raccoon?" I said, pausing in my flight.   5

"I want a raccoon coat," he wailed.

I perceived that his trouble was not physical, but mental. "Why do you want a raccoon coat?"

"I should have known it," he cried, pounding his temples. "I should have known they'd come back when the Charleston came back. Like a fool I spent all my money for textbooks, and now I can't get a raccoon coat."

"Can you mean," I said incredulously, "that people are actually wearing raccoon coats again?"

"All the Big Men on Campus are wearing them. Where've you 10 been?"

"In the library," I said, naming a place not frequented by Big Men on Campus.

He leaped from the bed and paced the room. "I've got to have a raccoon coat," he said passionately. "I've got to!"

"Petey, why? Look at it rationally. Raccoon coats are unsanitary. They shed. They smell bad. They weigh too much. They're unsightly. They——"

"You don't understand," he interrupted impatiently. "It's the thing to do. Don't you want to be in the swim?"

"No," I said truthfully.   15

"Well, I do," he declared. "I'd give anything for a raccoon coat. Anything!"

My brain, that precision instrument, slipped into high gear. "Anything?" I asked, looking at him narrowly.

"Anything," he affirmed in ringing tones.

I stroked my chin thoughtfully. It so happened that I knew where to get my hands on a raccoon coat. My father had had one in his undergraduate days; it lay now in a trunk in the attic back home. It also happened that Petey had something I wanted. He didn't *have* it exactly, but at least he had first rights on it. I refer to his girl, Polly Espy.

I had long coveted Polly Espy. Let me emphasize that my desire for 20 this young woman was not emotional in nature. She was, to be sure, a girl who excited the emotions, but I was not one to let my heart rule my head. I wanted Polly for a shrewdly calculated, entirely cerebral reason.

I was a freshman in law school. In a few years I would be out in practice. I was well aware of the importance of the right kind of wife in furthering a lawyer's career. The successful lawyers I had observed were, almost without exception, married to beautiful, gracious, intelligent women. With one omission, Polly fitted these specifications perfectly.

Beautiful she was. She was not yet of pin-up proportions, but I felt sure that time would supply the lack. She already had the makings.

Gracious she was. By gracious I mean full of graces. She had an erectness of carriage, an ease of bearing, a poise that clearly indicated the best of breeding. At table her manners were exquisite. I had seen her at the Kozy Kampus Korner eating the specialty of the house — a sandwich that contained scraps of pot roast, gravy, chopped nuts, and a dipper of sauerkraut — without even getting her fingers moist.

Intelligent she was not. In fact, she veered in the opposite direction. But I believed that under my guidance she would smarten up. At any rate, it was worth a try. It is, after all, easier to make a beautiful dumb girl smart than to make an ugly smart girl beautiful.

"Petey," I said, "are you in love with Polly Espy?"   25

"I think she's a keen kid," he replied, "but I don't know if you'd call it love. Why?"

"Do you," I asked, "have any kind of formal arrangement with her? I mean are you going steady or anything like that?"

"No. We see each other quite a bit, but we both have other dates. Why?"

"Is there," I asked, "any other man for whom she has a particular fondness?"

"Not that I know of. Why?"   30

I nodded with satisfaction. "In other words, if you were out of the picture, the field would be open. Is that right?"

"I guess so. What are you getting at?"

"Nothing, nothing," I said innocently, and took my suitcase out of the closet.

"Where you going?" asked Petey.

"Home for the week end." I threw a few things into the bag.   35

"Listen," he said, clutching my arm eagerly, "while you're home, you couldn't get some money from your old man, could you, and lend it to me so I can buy a raccoon coat?"

"I may do better than that," I said with a mysterious wink and closed my bag and left.

"Look," I said to Petey when I got back Monday morning. I threw open the suitcase and revealed the huge, hairy, gamy object that my father had worn in his Stutz Bearcat in 1925.

"Holy Toledo!" said Petey reverently. He plunged his hands into the raccoon coat and then his face. "Holy Toledo!" he repeated fifteen or twenty times.

"Would you like it?" I asked.   40

"Oh yes!" he cried, clutching the greasy pelt to him. Then a canny look came into his eyes. "What do you want for it?"

"Your girl," I said, mincing no words.

"Polly?" he said in a horrified whisper. "You want Polly?"

"That's right."

He flung the coat from him. "Never," he said stoutly.   45

I shrugged. "Okay. If you don't want to be in the swim, I guess it's your business."

I sat down in a chair and pretended to read a book, but out of the corner of my eye I kept watching Petey. He was a torn man. First he looked at the coat with the expression of a waif at a bakery window. Then he turned away and set his jaw resolutely. Then he looked back at the coat, with even more longing in his face. Then he turned away, but with not so much resolution this time. Back and forth his head swiveled, desire waxing, resolution waning. Finally he didn't turn away at all; he just stood and stared with mad lust at the coat.

"It isn't as though I was in love with Polly," he said thickly. "Or going steady or anything like that."

"That's right," I murmured.

"What's Polly to me, or me to Polly?"   50

"Not a thing," said I.

"It's just been a casual kick—just a few laughs, that's all."

"Try on the coat," said I.

He complied. The coat bunched high over his ears and dropped all the way down to his shoe tops. He looked like a mound of dead raccoons. "Fits fine," he said happily.

I rose from my chair. "Is it a deal?" I asked, extending my hand.   55

He swallowed. "It's a deal," he said and shook my hand.

I had my first date with Polly the following evening. This was in the nature of a survey; I wanted to find out just how much work I had to do to get her mind up to the standard I required. I took her first to dinner. "Gee, that was a delish dinner," she said as we left the restaurant. Then I took her to a movie. "Gee, that was a marvy movie," she said as we left the theater. And then I took her home. "Gee, I had a sensaysh time," she said as she bade me good night.

I went back to my room with a heavy heart. I had gravely underestimated the size of my task. This girl's lack of information was terrifying. Nor would it be enough merely to supply her with information. First she had to be taught to *think*. This loomed as a project of no small dimensions, and at first I was tempted to give her back to Petey. But then I got to thinking about her abundant physical charms and about the way she entered a room and the way she handled a knife and fork, and I decided to make an effort.

I went about it, as in all things, systematically. I gave her a course in logic. It happened that I, as a law student, was taking a course in logic myself, so I had all the facts at my fingertips. "Polly," I said to her when I picked her up on our next date, "tonight we are going over to the Knoll and talk."

"Oo, terrif," she replied. One thing I will say for this girl: You would go far to find another so agreeable.

We went to the Knoll, the campus trysting place, and we sat down under an old oak, and she looked at me expectantly: "What are we going to talk about?" she asked.

"Logic."

She thought this over for a minute and decided she liked it. "Magnif," she said.

"Logic," I said, clearing my throat, "is the science of thinking. Before we can think correctly, we must first learn to recognize the common fallacies of logic. These we will take up tonight."

"Wow-dow!" she cried, clapping her hands delightedly.

I winced, but went bravely on. "First let us examine the fallacy called Dicto Simpliciter."

"By all means," she urged, batting her lashes eagerly.

"Dicto Simpliciter means an argument based on an unqualified generalization. For example: Exercise is good. Therefore everybody should exercise."

"I agree," said Polly earnestly. "I mean exercise is wonderful. I mean it builds the body and everything."

"Polly," I said gently, "the argument is a fallacy. *Exercise is good* is an unqualified generalization. For instance, if you have heart disease, exercise is bad, not good. Many people are ordered by their doctors *not* to exercise. You must *qualify* the generalization. You must say exercise is *usually* good, or exercise is good *for most people*. Otherwise you have committed a Dicto Simpliciter. Do you see?"

"No," she confessed. "But this is marvy. Do more! Do more!"

"It will be better if you stop tugging at my sleeve," I told her, and when she desisted, I continued. "Next we take up a fallacy called Hasty Generalization. Listen carefully: You can't speak French. I can't speak French. Petey Bellows can't speak French. I must therefore conclude that nobody at the University of Minnesota can speak French."

"Really?" said Polly, amazed. "*Nobody?*"

I hid my exasperation. "Polly, it's a fallacy. The generalization is reached too hastily. There are too few instances to support such a conclusion."

"Know any more fallacies?" she asked breathlessly. "This is more fun than dancing even."

I fought off a wave of despair. I was getting nowhere with this girl, absolutely nowhere. Still, I am nothing if not persistent. I continued. "Next comes Post Hoc. Listen to this: Let's not take Bill on our picnic. Every time we take him out with us, it rains."

"I know somebody just like that," she exclaimed. "A girl back home — Eula Becker, her name is. It never fails. Every single time we take her on a picnic —— "

"Polly," I said sharply, "it's a fallacy. Eula Becker doesn't *cause* the rain. She has no connection with the rain. You are guilty of Post Hoc if you blame Eula Becker."

"I'll never do it again," she promised contritely. "Are you mad at me?"

I sighed. "No, Polly, I'm not mad."   80

"Then tell me some more fallacies."

"All right. Let's try Contradictory Premises."

"Yes, let's," she chirped, blinking her eyes happily.

I frowned, but plunged ahead. "Here's an example of Contradictory Premises: If God can do anything, can He make a stone so heavy that He won't be able to lift it?"

"Of course," she replied promptly.   85

"But if He can do anything, He can lift the stone," I pointed out.

"Yeah," she said thoughtfully. "Well, then I guess He can't make the stone."

"But He can do anything," I reminded her.

She scratched her pretty, empty head. "I'm all confused," she admitted.

"Of course you are. Because when the premises of an argument con- 90
tradict each other, there can be no argument. If there is an irresistible force, there can be no immovable object. If there is an immovable object, there can be no irresistible force. Get it?"

"Tell me some more of this keen stuff," she said eagerly.

I consulted my watch. "I think we'd better call it a night. I'll take you home now, and you go over all the things you've learned. We'll have another session tomorrow night."

I deposited her at the girls' dormitory, where she assured me that she had had a perfectly terrif evening, and I went glumly home to my room. Petey lay snoring in his bed, the raccoon coat huddled like a great hairy beast at his feet. For a moment I considered waking him and telling him that he could have his girl back. It seemed clear that my project was doomed to failure. The girl simply had a logic-proof head.

But then I reconsidered. I had wasted one evening; I might as well waste another. Who knew? Maybe somewhere in the extinct crater of her mind a few embers still smoldered. Maybe somehow I could fan them into flame. Admittedly it was not a prospect fraught with hope, but I decided to give it one more try.

Seated under the oak the next evening I said, "Our first fallacy 95
tonight is called Ad Misericordiam."

She quivered with delight.

"Listen closely," I said. "A man applies for a job. When the boss asks him what his qualifications are, he replies that he has a wife and six children at home, the wife is a helpless cripple, the children have nothing to eat, no clothes to wear, no shoes on their feet, there are no beds in the house, no coal in the cellar, and winter is coming."

A tear rolled down each of Polly's pink cheeks. "Oh, this is awful, awful," she sobbed.

"Yes, it's awful," I agreed, "but it's no argument. The man never answered the boss's question about his qualifications. Instead he appealed to the boss's sympathy. He committed the fallacy of Ad Misericordiam. Do you understand?"

"Have you got a handkerchief?" she blubbered.   100

I handed her a handkerchief and tried to keep from screaming while she wiped her eyes. "Next," I said in a carefully controlled tone, "we will discuss False Analogy. Here is an example: Students should be allowed to look at their textbooks during examinations. After all, surgeons have X rays to guide them during an operation, lawyers have briefs to guide them during a trial, carpenters have blueprints to guide them when they are building a house. Why, then, shouldn't students be allowed to look at their textbooks during an examination?"

"There now," she said enthusiastically, "is the most marvy idea I've heard in years."

"Polly," I said testily, "the argument is all wrong. Doctors, lawyers, and carpenters aren't taking a test to see how much they have learned, but students are. The situations are altogether different, and you can't make an analogy between them."

"I still think it's a good idea," said Polly.

"Nuts," I muttered. Doggedly I pressed on. "Next we'll try Hypothe-   105
sis Contrary to Fact."

"Sounds yummy," was Polly's reaction.

"Listen: If Madame Curie had not happened to leave a photographic plate in a drawer with a chunk of pitchblende, the world today would not know about radium."

"True, true," said Polly, nodding her head. "Did you see the movie? Oh, it just knocked me out. That Walter Pidgeon is so dreamy. I mean he fractures me."

"If you can forget Mr. Pidgeon for a moment," I said coldly, "I would like to point out that the statement is a fallacy. Maybe Madame Curie would have discovered radium at some later date. Maybe somebody else would have discovered it. Maybe any number of things would have happened. You can't start with a hypothesis that is not true and then draw any supportable conclusions from it."

"They ought to put Walter Pidgeon in more pictures," said Polly. "I   110
hardly ever see him any more."

One more chance, I decided. But just one more. There is a limit to what flesh and blood can bear. "The next fallacy is called Poisoning the Well."

"How cute!" she gurgled.

"Two men are having a debate. The first one gets up and says, 'My opponent is a notorious liar. You can't believe a word that he is going to say.' . . . Now, Polly, think. Think hard. What's wrong?"

I watched her closely as she knit her creamy brow in concentration. Suddenly a glimmer of intelligence — the first I had seen — came into her eyes. "It's not fair," she said with indignation. "It's not a bit fair. What chance has the second man got if the first man calls him a liar before he even begins talking?"

"Right!" I cried exultantly. "One hundred percent right. It's not fair. 115 The first man has *poisoned the well* before anybody could drink from it. He has hamstrung his opponent before he could even start. . . . Polly, I'm proud of you."

"Pshaw," she murmured, blushing with pleasure.

"You see, my dear, these things aren't so hard. All you have to do is concentrate. Think — examine — evaluate. Come now, let's review everything we have learned."

"Fire away," she said with an airy wave of her hand.

Heartened by the knowledge that Polly was not altogether a cretin, I began a long, patient review of all I had told her. Over and over and over again I cited instances, pointed out flaws, kept hammering away without letup. It was like digging a tunnel. At first everything was work, sweat, and darkness. I had no idea when I would reach the light, or even *if* I would. But I persisted. I pounded and clawed and scraped, and finally I was rewarded. I saw a chink of light. And then the chink got bigger and the sun came pouring in and all was bright.

Five grueling nights this took, but it was worth it. I had made a logi- 120 cian out of Polly; I had taught her to think. My job was done. She was worthy of me at last. She was a fit wife for me, a proper hostess for my many mansions, a suitable mother for my well-heeled children.

It must not be thought that I was without love for this girl. Quite the contrary. Just as Pygmalion loved the perfect woman he had fashioned, so I loved mine. I decided to acquaint her with my feelings at our very next meeting. The time had come to change our relationship from academic to romantic.

"Polly," I said when next we sat beneath our oak, "tonight we will not discuss fallacies."

"Aw, gee," she said, disappointed.

"My dear," I said, favoring her with a smile, "we have now spent five evenings together. We have gotten along splendidly. It is clear that we are well matched."

"Hasty Generalization," said Polly brightly.   125

"I beg your pardon," said I.

"Hasty Generalization," she repeated. "How can you say that we are well matched on the basis of only five dates?"

I chuckled with amusement. The dear child had learned her lessons well. "My dear," I said, patting her hand in a tolerant manner, "five dates is plenty. After all, you don't have to eat a whole cake to know that it's good."

"False Analogy," said Polly promptly. "I'm not a cake. I'm a girl."

I chuckled with somewhat less amusement. The dear child had 130 learned her lesson perhaps too well. I decided to change tactics. Obviously the best approach was a simple, strong, direct declaration of love. I paused for a moment while my massive brain chose the proper words. Then I began:

"Polly, I love you. You are the whole world to me, and the moon and the stars and the constellations of outer space. Please, my darling, say that you will go steady with me, for if you will not, life will be meaningless. I will languish. I will refuse my meals. I will wander the face of the earth, a shambling, hollow-eyed hulk."

There, I thought, folding my arms, that ought to do it.

"Ad Misericordiam," said Polly.

I ground my teeth. I was not Pygmalion; I was Frankenstein, and my monster had me by the throat. Frantically I fought back the tide of panic surging through me. At all costs I had to keep cool.

"Well, Polly," I said, forcing a smile, "you certainly have learned your fallacies." 135

"You're darn right," she said with a vigorous nod.

"And who taught them to you, Polly?"

"You did."

"That's right. So you do owe me something, don't you, my dear? If I hadn't come along you never would have learned about fallacies."

"Hypothesis Contrary to Fact," she said instantly. 140

I dashed perspiration from my brow. "Polly," I croaked, "You mustn't take all these things so literally. I mean this is just classroom stuff. You know that the things you learn in school don't have anything to do with life."

"Dicto Simpliciter," she said, wagging her finger at me playfully.

That did it. I leaped to my feet, bellowing like a bull. "Will you or will you not go steady with me?"

"I will not," she replied.

"Why not?" I demanded. 145

"Because this afternoon I promised Petey Bellows that I would go steady with him."

I reeled back, overcome with the infamy of it. After he promised, after he made a deal, after he shook my hand! "That rat!" I shrieked, kicking up great chunks of turf. "You can't go with him, Polly. He's a liar. He's a cheat. He's a rat."

"Poisoning the Well," said Polly, "and stop shouting. I think shouting must be a fallacy too."

With an immense effort of will, I modulated my voice. "All right," I said. "You're a logician. Let's look at this thing logically. How could you choose Petey Bellows over me? Look at me—a brilliant student, a tremendous intellectual, a man with an assured future. Look at Petey—a knothead, a jitterbug, a guy who'll never know where his next meal is coming from. Can you give me one logical reason why you should go steady with Petey Bellows?"

"I certainly can," declared Polly. "He's got a raccoon coat." 150

Topic for Critical Thinking and Writing

After you have finished reading "Love Is a Fallacy," you may want to write an argumentative essay of 500 to 750 words on one of the following topics: (1) the story, rightly understood, is not antiwoman; (2) if the story is antiwoman, it is equally antiman; (3) the story is antiwoman but nevertheless belongs in this book; or (4) the story is antiwoman and does not belong in the book.

See the companion Web site
bedfordstmartins.com/barnetbedau
for a series of brain teasers and links related to
the logical point of view in argument.

10

A Moralist's View: Ways of Thinking Ethically

About morals, I know only that what is moral is what you feel good after and what is immoral is what you feel bad after.

— ERNEST HEMINGWAY

Our whole life is startlingly moral. There is never an instant's truth between virtue and vice.

— HENRY DAVID THOREAU

Elsewhere in this book we explain *deductive reasoning* (p. 77, 337), *inductive reasoning* (p. 77, 349), and *legal reasoning* (p. 417). More familiar and probably more important is **moral reasoning.** If truth be told, virtually every essay reprinted in this book is an example of more or less self-conscious moral reasoning. (In passing, at the outset we note that we do not draw any distinction between morals and ethics or between moral reasoning and ethical reasoning. Apart from insignificant connotations, the terms *moral* and *ethical* differ mainly in their origins, *ethical* deriving from the Greek *ethos,* meaning "custom" or "manners," and *moral* deriving from the Latin *moralis,* meaning "moral" or "ethical.")

Moral reasoning has various purposes, particularly guidance for conduct — for what someone actually does or fails to do. In this light, consider the parable Jesus tells of the Good Samaritan (Luke 10:30–37). On a journey from Jerusalem to Jericho, a man is robbed by thieves, beaten, and left nearly dead. First a priest came along, "looked on him, and passed by on the other side." Then a Levite (an assistant to a temple priest) does the same thing. (Implied in the story is that both the priest and the Levite are fellow countrymen of the victim and so might well be expected to come to the man's aid.) "But a certain Samaritan . . . came where he was and when he saw him, he had compassion on him." The Samaritan bound up his wounds, took him to an inn, and paid for his lodging.

Jesus tells this story to answer the question, Who is my neighbor? In context, this amounts to the question, Which of the three passersby acts

"Which entrée raises the fewest ethical issues?"

toward the beaten man in a truly neighborly manner? The answer, of course, is that only the Samaritan—a person from a different culture—does.

Most of the moral reasoning in this parable is left implicit by the Gospel writer. To understand the indifference of the priest and Levite to the plight of the victim, we might imagine them thinking as follows: "Nothing I have done or failed to do caused the victim to be robbed and assaulted, so I have no responsibility to interrupt my travels to care for him. Nothing binds him to me as kinship would; he and I are not neighbors in the ordinary sense of that term (persons who live nearby, in the same neighborhood), so I do not owe him assistance as I would to my kin and my immediate neighbors. His need gives him no claim on my attention. Finally, why put myself at uncertain risk in trying to help him? Perhaps the thieves are still in the vicinity, just waiting to pounce on anyone foolish enough to stop and give aid."

Clearly, Jesus implies that none of these reasons is adequate. His parable is intended in part to stretch our ordinary notion of what it means to be someone's neighbor. Jesus is in effect telling us that the beaten stranger ought to elicit the same concern and care that we would give to an assaulted family member, close friend, or immediate neighbor.

What makes Jesus' parable a story told from the moral point of view is that his implicit evaluation of the conduct of the three passersby depends on an unspoken moral principle that he believes but that he knows is not widely shared: *We ought to help the needy even at some cost or risk to ourselves.*

As a next step in the effort to deepen our grasp of moral reasoning, it is useful to be clear about what it *isn't*. To do that we need to think about two kinds of reasoning sharply contrasted to moral reasoning: *amoral* reasoning and *immoral* reasoning.

AMORAL REASONING

Amorality consists of conduct of no moral significance — that is, conduct not to be evaluated by reference to moral considerations. For example, suppose you are in the market for a used car. You want a two-door car and have narrowed your choices to three: a 2005 Honda, a 2006 Subaru, and a 2007 Toyota. No moral consideration enters your deliberation over which car to choose; morality is silent on your choice. Daily life is filled with examples of this sort, situations in which nothing of moral relevance seems to be involved, and so our decisions and choices can be made without worry over their morality or immorality. In short, for most of us, morality just does not control or pervade everything we do in life. And when we judge moral considerations to be irrelevant, we are dealing with what we regard as amoral matters.

Let us examine another example in greater detail. You are about to dine with a friend at a nice restaurant. The waiter brings you the menu, and you look it over, pondering whether to have an appetizer, order a bottle of white or red wine, choose fish or poultry for the main dish, and top it all off with dessert and coffee. Since the restaurant is noted for its cuisine, you are trying to design a meal for yourself worthy of the occasion. There is nothing particularly moral or immoral in your deliberations as you study the menu and make your choices. By eating in this restaurant, you are not depriving anyone else of their dinner, much less depriving them unfairly. You are not coercing others to turn over their food to you. You have not stolen the money to pay for your food. You are not breaking a promise to anyone to avoid this restaurant or to avoid rich and expensive restaurant food. You have no intention of leaving without paying the bill. Thus, various standard and familiar ways of acting immorally can be seen to play no role in your dinner deliberations.

On the other hand, there is no moral requirement that you dine in this restaurant or that you order this rather than that from the menu. You have no moral duty to have a feast, no obligation to anyone to have an expensive dinner. You have not promised anyone to dine in this restaurant. Your failure to dine there would flout no moral rule or principle.

Situations such as this, which call for reasoning and decision but where no moral principle or rule is involved, are without moral significance whichever way they are decided. To put this another way, in cases such as this, moral reasoning tells us we are *permitted* (neither prohibited nor required by morality) to go ahead with our restaurant meal as planned, and in this regard we may do whatever we like.

So the first of several questions that capture the idea of moral reasoning can be put this way:

- Is your (or someone else's) conduct prohibited or required by a moral rule or principle? If not, then it is probably not morally wrong: Morality permits you to act as you please.

Two kinds of considerations raised by this example deserve a closer look. First, if you are on a diet that forbids rich food, you are at risk in doing yourself some harm unless you read the menu carefully and order accordingly (no steak or other red meat, for example, and no fatty custards or sauces). The best way to treat yourself, we can probably agree, dictates caution in what you select to eat. But suppose you fail to act cautiously. Well, you are not acting immorally—although your behavior is imprudent, ill advised, and contrary to your best interests. We break no moral rule when we choose not to act in our own rational self-interest. The rule "Act always to promote your own rational self-interest" is not a moral rule.

Unless, of course, one's morality does consist of some form of self-interest, as in, for example, the views of the novelist-turned-philosopher Ayn Rand in her widely read book *The Virtue of Selfishness* (1965). Her defense of selfishness is exceptional and somewhat misleading—exceptional because very few moralists agree with her, and somewhat misleading because her main thesis—*everyone would do better if each of us pursued only our own rational self-interest*—is obviously contestable. Most moralists would insist that all of us do *not* do better if each of us acts without ever taking into account the needs of others except where they impinge on our own welfare. (For another version of a morality of selfishness, see the essay by Garrett Hardin, p. 402.) Of course, any given moral code or moral principle is subject to criticism on moral grounds. Not all moralities—sets of moral principles that a person or a society holds—are equally reasonable, fair, or free of some other moral defect.

Second, if, for example, you are concerned about animal rights, you may see the choice between a meatless salad and a chef's salad as a moral issue. That is not the only way the choice of a meal may turn out to conceal a moral issue. The more expensive the dinner, the more you may feel uneasy about such self-indulgence when you could eat an adequate dinner elsewhere at one-third the cost and donate the difference to Oxfam or UNESCO. Many moralists would insist that we who are well fed in fact have a responsibility to see to it that the starving are fed. Some influential moral thinkers in recent years have gone even further, arguing that the best moral principles, preeminently the utilitarian principle that one always ought to act so as to maximize the net benefits among the available choices, require those of us in affluent nations to reduce radically our standard of living to improve the standard of living of people in the poorest nations. (See the essay by Peter Singer, p. 390.) This example nicely illustrates how something as seemingly harmless and amoral as having an expensive meal in a nice restaurant can turn out, after all, to pose a moral choice—because one's moral principles turn out to be applicable to the case in question, even if the moral principles acknowledged by others are not.

IMMORAL REASONING

The most obvious reasoning to be contrasted with moral reasoning is *immoral* reasoning. Immorality, defined abstractly, is conduct contrary to what morality requires or prohibits. Hence a person is reasoning immorally whenever he or she is contemplating judgment or conduct that violates or disregards some relevant moral rule or principle.

We are acting immorally when we use *force or fraud* in our dealings with other people and when we treat them *unfairly*. Typically we act in these ways toward others when our motives are *selfish*—that is, when we act in ways intended to gain advantage for ourselves without regard to the effects that advantage will have on others. For example,

Suppose you are short of cash and try to borrow some from a friend. You don't expect your friend simply to give you the money, so

You know you will have to promise to repay her as soon as you can, say, in a week.

But you know you really have no intention of keeping your promise to pay her back.

Nonetheless, you make the promise—well, you utter words such as "Sure, you can rely on me; I'll pay you back in a few days"—and she loans you the money. Weeks go by. Eventually your paths cross and she reminds you that you haven't yet paid her back.

What to say? Some of your options:

Laugh in her face for being so naive as to loan you the money in the first place?

Make up some phony excuse, and hope she'll accept it?

Renew your promise to pay her back but without any change in your intention not to do so?

Act tough, and threaten her if she doesn't lay off?

Each of these is an immoral tactic, and deliberating among them to choose the most effective is immoral reasoning. Why? Because each of them violates a familiar moral principle (albeit rarely formulated expressly in words). First, *promises are fraudulent if they are made with no intention to keep them.* (Underlying that principle is another one: Fraud is morally wrong.) Second, *promises ought to be kept.* Whatever else morality is, it is a constraint on acting purely out of self-interest and in a manner heedless of the consequences for others. Making fraudulent promises and unfairly breaking genuine promises are actions usually done out of selfish intentions and are likely to cause harm to others.

The discussion so far yields this important generalization:

- If the reasons for your proposed judgment and conduct are purely selfish, they are not moral reasons.

Of course, there are exceptions to the two principles mentioned in the previous paragraph. Neither principle is a rigid moral rule. Why? Because on some occasions making a fraudulent promise or breaking a sincere promise can be *excused,* and on other occasions such conduct can be *justified.* (Or so most of us in our society think when we reflect on the matter.) Both invoking a legitimate excuse or justification for breaking a moral rule and rejecting illegitimate excuses or justifications, are crucial features of everyday moral reasoning. For example, you ought to be excused for breaking a sincere promise — say, a promise to meet a friend for lunch at a certain time and place — if your car gets a flat tire on the way. On the other hand, you would be justified in breaking your promise if, for example, while driving on the way to your lunch date you are late because you stopped to help a stranded motorist change his flat tire. In general,

- We *excuse* violating a moral rule when we argue that we know breaking it was wrong but it couldn't be helped, whereas
- We *justify* violating a moral rule when we argue that doing so was the right or the best thing to do in the circumstances.

We have now identified two more questions to keep in mind as you try to assess the morality of your own or someone else's reasoning. The first is this:

- Are the reasons you offer an attempt to excuse wrongful conduct? If so, is the excuse a legitimate one?

Typical excuses include these: "It was an *accident;* he *couldn't help* it; she *didn't know it was wrong;* they did it *by mistake;* we were *forced* to do it; I was *provoked.*" The legitimacy of an excuse in any given case depends on the facts of the matter. Claiming that the harm you caused, for example, was an accident doesn't *make* it an accident. (Children are quick to learn these excuses and can be quite adept at misusing them to their own advantage.)

The second question to ask is this:

- Are the reasons you offer an attempt to justify breaking a moral rule knowingly? If so, is the proposed justification really convincing?

Typical justifications include these: "It was the *best* thing to do in the circumstances; the *sacrifice* was necessary to protect something else of greater value; *little or no harm to others will be done* if the rule is ignored;

superior orders required me to do what I did." A justification is convincing in a given case just to the extent that it invokes a moral rule or principle of greater weight or scope than the rule or principle being violated.

MORAL REASONING: A CLOSER LOOK

What does this brief excursion into amoral and immoral reasoning teach us about *moral* reasoning? Just this: Moral reasoning involves (1) reasoning from *moral* rules, principles, or standards and (2) resolving conflicts among them, thereby placing limits on what one may do with a clear conscience.

This point can be restated as follows:

- Do the reasons you propose for your conduct violate any of the relevant moral rules you accept? If not, then your morality raises no objection to your conduct.

Morality and moral reasoning can be conveniently subdivided into several narrower areas. We are sexual beings, and our pursuit of sexual experience will inevitably raise questions about the morality of our conduct. Hence we often have occasion to think about *sexual* morality—our own and that of others. *Sexual* morality can be defined as the moral rules, principles, and standards relevant to judgment and conduct in which someone's sexual behavior is at issue. Similarly, *political* morality concerns the moral rules, principles, and standards with which people ought to conduct and evaluate political activities, practices, and institutions. *Professional* ethics all involve special rules, norms, principles relevant to judgment and conduct, and these rules are often stated in the form of a *code* of ethics suitable to the judgments and conduct more or less unique to each profession (such as business, medicine, journalism, law). What is common to all such codes are prohibitions against coercion and misrepresentation, unfair advantage, and the failure to obtain informed voluntary consent from one's clients, patients, witnesses, and employees.

Second, the rules, principles, and standards that constitute a morality differ in different religions and cultures, just as they differ historically. The morality of ancient Greece was not the morality of feudal Europe or contemporary America; the morality of the Trobriand Islanders is not the same as the morality of the Kwakiutl Indians. This does not imply *moral relativism*—that is, the view that there is no rational ground on which to choose among alternative moralities. (The purely descriptive thesis that *different cultures endorse different moral codes* does not imply the evaluative thesis that *one moral code is as good as another.*) The fact that different cultures endorse different moral codes does, however, imply that there may be a need for tolerance of moral standards other than one's own.

Third, in the morality most widely shared in our society, moral rules are not rigid; they permit exceptions (as we have seen above), and they are of different importance and weight. For example, few would deny that it is more important to help a stranded motorist than to keep a lunch date. Unlike the ancient Hebrews, however, who were guided by the Ten Commandments, most of us have no book or engraved tablet where our moral principles are listed for all to study at their leisure and violate at their peril. Where, then, do a society's moral rules come from? How do we learn these rules? They come from the collective experience of peoples and cultures in their search for stability, continuity, and harmony among persons of diverse interests, talents, and preferences. And we learn them in our youth (unless we have the misfortune to be neglected by our parents and teachers) in the daily processes of socialization.

What gives these rules authority over our conduct and judgment? Indeed, what makes a rule, principle, or standard a *moral* rule, standard, or principle? These are serious philosophical questions that we cannot adequately discuss and answer here. Suffice it to say that a person's *principles* guide that person's conduct and judgment; a rule or principle counts as a *moral* rule or principle when it gives guidance regarding rational constraints on self-interested conduct. A rule or principle gives such guidance when it takes into account the legitimate and relevant interests of people generally—not just one's own interests, those of one's friends and relatives, clan, or tribe, or those of one's fellow citizens but the interests of persons generally—and does so in a manner neither deliberately nor negligently indifferent to the interests of others.

This constraining function of moral rules is most evident in the best-known Western moral code, the Ten Commandments. Apart from the first three of the Commandments, which concern people's behavior toward God, the rest—Honor thy father and thy mother, Do not kill, Do not covet thy neighbor's property, and so on—clearly amount to constraints on the pursuit of self-interest regardless of its cost to others. The immoralist flouts all such constraints; the amoralist believes that most of his and our conduct involves no moral considerations one way or the other. The rest of us, however, recognize that there are constraints on our conduct. The *moral skeptic* needs to be reminded of certain indisputable facts: Does anyone seriously believe that lying and cheating are never wrong? Or that murder, rape, assault, arson, and kidnapping are wrong only because they are against the law? Or that it is merely a matter of personal opinion or taste that we ought to help the needy and ought not to take unfair advantage of others?

To be sure, honesty requires us to admit that we do not always comply with the constraints we acknowledge—we are not saints—hence the familiar experience of feeling guilty over having knowingly done the wrong thing to somebody who deserved better of us. If morality involves constraints on the pursuit of self-interest, moral reasoning involves identifying and weighing those constraints and being prepared to explain, when appropriate, why one has not complied with them.

CRITERIA FOR MORAL RULES

Philosophers and moralists over the centuries have developed various tests or criteria against which to measure the adequacy of a moral rule. Presupposed by all these criteria is the answer to this question:

- What is the rule, principle, or standard on which you propose to act?

If you can't formulate such a rule, then the rationality of your proposed action is in doubt. (In the excerpts later in this chapter, we identify some relevant moral principles and show how they are used in practice.)

Among the questions worth asking in the evaluation of someone's conduct and the rule or rules on which it relies is this:

- Would you be willing to argue for the general adoption of whatever rules you profess?

This principle is a version of the Categorical Imperative proposed by Immanuel Kant (1724–1804): Always act so that the principle of your action could be the principle on which everyone else acts in similar situations. Could a society of utterly selfish persons accept such a principle? Surely, a general practice of fraudulent promise-making could never pass this test.

Here's another criterion:

- Would you be willing to argue openly for the general adoption of whatever reasons you accept?

Here's yet another criterion:

- Do the reasons for your proposed conduct take into account the greatest good for the greatest number?

This is a version of the utilitarian principle (for an alternative version, see p. 385; for an application, see the essay by Peter Singer, p. 390).

Still other criteria include the following:

- Do the reasons for your proposed conduct take into account the relevant moral rights of others?
- Would an unbiased observer, fully informed of what you regard as all the relevant facts, approve of your reasons for your proposed conduct?

Which one of these criteria is the best? Or do they all come to the same thing in practice? Answering such questions involves reasoning *about* moral principles, whereas up to now we have been discussing only reasoning *with* such principles. Reasoning about moral principles arises naturally out of reflection on reasoning with such principles. *Meta-ethics*— thinking about the nature of moral concepts, values, and norms—has been a matter of immense philosophical interest since Socrates and Plato. We must leave further development of these issues to their heirs.

✓ A CHECKLIST FOR MORAL REASONING

☐ Is my (or someone else's) conduct prohibited or required by a moral rule or principle? If not, then it is probably not morally right or wrong: Morality permits me to act as I please.

☐ If the reasons for my proposed judgment or conduct are purely selfish, they are not moral reasons.

☐ Are my reasons an attempt to excuse wrongful conduct? If so, is the excuse a legitimate one?

☐ Are my reasons an attempt to justify breaking a moral rule knowingly? If so, is the proposed justification convincing?

☐ Do the reasons I propose for my conduct violate any of the relevant moral rules I accept? If not, then my morality raises no objection to your conduct.

☐ What is the rule, principle, or standard on which I propose to act?

☐ Would I be willing to argue openly for the general adoption of whatever rules I accept?

☐ Would I be willing to argue openly for the general adoption of whatever reasons I accept?

☐ Do the reasons for my proposed conduct take into account the greatest good for the greatest number?

☐ Do the reasons for my proposed conduct take into account the relevant moral rights of others?

☐ Would an unbiased observer, fully informed of what I regard as all the relevant facts, approve of my reasons for my proposed conduct?

Peter Singer

Peter Singer is the Ira W. DeCamp Professor of Bioethics at Princeton University. A native of Australia, he is a graduate of the University of Melbourne and Oxford University and the author or editor of more than two dozen books, including Animal Liberation *(1975),* Practical Ethics *(1979),* Rethinking Life and Death *(1995), and* One World: The Ethics of Globalization *(2002). His views on several life-and-death issues have been the source of much public and scholarly controversy. This essay originally appeared in* Philosophy and Public Affairs *(Spring 1972).*

Famine, Affluence, and Morality

As I write this, in November 1971, people are dying in East Bengal from lack of food, shelter, and medical care. The suffering and death that are occurring there now are not inevitable, not unavoidable in any fatalistic sense of the term. Constant poverty, a cyclone, and a civil war have turned at least nine million people into destitute refugees; nevertheless, it is not beyond the capacity of the richer nations to give enough assistance to reduce any further suffering to very small proportions. The decisions and actions of human beings can prevent this kind of suffering. Unfortunately, human beings have not made the necessary decisions. At the individual level, people have, with very few exceptions, not responded to the situation in any significant way. Generally speaking, people have not given large sums to relief funds; they have not written to their parliamentary representatives demanding increased government assistance; they have not demonstrated in the streets, held symbolic fasts, or done anything else directed toward providing the refugees with the means to satisfy their essential needs. At the government level, no government has given the sort of massive aid that would enable the refugees to survive for more than a few days. Britain, for instance, has given rather more than most countries. It has, to date, given £14,750,000. For comparative purposes, Britain's share of the nonrecoverable development costs of the Anglo-French Concorde project is already in excess of £275,000,000, and on present estimates will reach £440,000,000. The implication is that the British government values a supersonic transport more than thirty times as highly as it values the lives of the 9 million refugees. Australia is another country which, on a per capita basis, is well up in the "aid to Bengal" table. Australia's aid, however, amounts to less than one-twelfth of the cost of Sydney's new opera house. The total amount given, from all sources, now stands at about £65,000,000. The estimated cost of keeping the refugees alive for one year is £464,000,000. Most of the refugees have now been in the camps for more than six months. The World Bank has said that India needs a minimum of £300,000,000 in assistance from other countries before the end of the year. It seems obvious that assistance on this scale will not be forthcoming. India will be forced to choose between letting the refugees starve or diverting funds from her own development program, which will mean that more of her own people will starve in the future.[1]

These are the essential facts about the present situation in Bengal. So far as it concerns us here, there is nothing unique about this situation except its magnitude. The Bengal emergency is just the latest and most acute of a series of major emergencies in various parts of the world, arising both from natural and from man-made causes. There are also many parts of the world in which people die from malnutrition and lack of food independent of any special emergency. I take Bengal as my example only because it is the present concern, and because the size of the problem has ensured that it has been given adequate publicity. Neither individuals nor governments can claim to be unaware of what is happening there.

---

[1] There was also a third possibility: that India would go to war to enable the refugees to return to their lands. Since I wrote this paper, India has taken this way out. The situation is no longer that described above, but this does not affect my argument, as the next paragraph indicates. [All notes are Singer's.]

What are the moral implications of a situation like this? In what follows, I shall argue that the way people in relatively affluent countries react to a situation like that in Bengal cannot be justified; indeed, the whole way we look at moral issues — our moral conceptual scheme — needs to be altered, and with it, the way of life that has come to be taken for granted in our society.

In arguing for this conclusion I will not, of course, claim to be morally neutral. I shall, however, try to argue for the moral position that I take, so that anyone who accepts certain assumptions, to be made explicit, will, I hope, accept my conclusion.

I begin with the assumption that suffering and death from lack of 5 food, shelter, and medical care are bad. I think most people will agree about this, although one may reach the same view by different routes. I shall not argue for this view. People can hold all sorts of eccentric positions, and perhaps from some of them it would not follow that death by starvation is in itself bad. It is difficult, perhaps impossible, to refute such positions, and so for brevity I will henceforth take this assumption as accepted. Those who disagree need read no further.

My next point is this: If it is in our power to prevent something bad from happening, without thereby sacrificing anything of comparable moral importance, we ought, morally, to do it. By "without sacrificing anything of comparable moral importance" I mean without causing anything else comparably bad to happen, or doing something that is wrong in itself, or failing to promote some moral good, comparable in significance to the bad thing that we can prevent. This principle seems almost as uncontroversial as the last one. It requires us only to prevent what is bad, and not to promote what is good, and it requires this of us only when we can do it without sacrificing anything that is, from the moral point of view, comparably important. I could even, as far as the application of my argument to the Bengal emergency is concerned, qualify the point so as to make it: If it is in our power to prevent something very bad from happening, without thereby sacrificing anything morally significant, we ought, morally, to do it. An application of this principle would be as follows: If I am walking past a shallow pond and see a child drowning in it, I ought to wade in and pull the child out. This will mean getting my clothes muddy, but this is insignificant, while the death of the child would presumably be a very bad thing.

The uncontroversial appearance of the principle just stated is deceptive. If it were acted upon, even in its qualified form, our lives, our society, and our world would be fundamentally changed. For the principle takes, firstly, no account of proximity or distance. It makes no moral difference whether the person I can help is a neighbor's child ten yards from me or a Bengali whose name I shall never know, ten thousand miles away. Secondly, the principle makes no distinction between cases in which I am the only person who could possibly do anything and cases in which I am just one among millions in the same position.

I do not think I need to say much in defense of the refusal to take proximity and distance into account. The fact that a person is physically near to us, so that we have personal contact with him, may make it more likely that we *shall* assist him, but this does not show that we *ought* to help him rather than another who happens to be further away. If we accept any principle of impartiality, universalizability, equality, or whatever, we cannot discriminate against someone merely because he is far away from us (or we are far away from him). Admittedly, it is possible that we are in a better position to judge what needs to be done to help a person near to us than one far away, and perhaps also to provide the assistance we judge to be necessary. If this were the case, it would be a reason for helping those near to us first. This may once have been a justification for being more concerned with the poor in one's own town than with famine victims in India. Unfortunately for those who like to keep their moral responsibilities limited, instant communication and swift transportation have changed the situation. From the moral point of view, the development of the world into a "global village" has made an important, though still unrecognized, difference to our moral situation. Expert observers and supervisors, sent out by famine relief organizations or permanently stationed in famine-prone areas, can direct our aid to a refugee in Bengal almost as effectively as we could get it to someone in our own block. There would seem, therefore, to be no possible justification for discriminating on geographical grounds.

There may be a greater need to defend the second implication of my principle—that the fact that there are millions of other people in the same position, in respect to the Bengali refugees, as I am, does not make the situation significantly different from a situation in which I am the only person who can prevent something very bad from occurring. Again, of course, I admit that there is a psychological difference between the cases; one feels less guilty about doing nothing if one can point to others, similarly placed, who have also done nothing. Yet this can make no real difference to our moral obligations.[2] Should I consider that I am less obliged to pull the drowning child out of the pond if on looking around I see other people, no further away than I am, who have also noticed the child but are doing nothing? One has only to ask this question to see the absurdity of the view that numbers lessen obligation. It is a view that is an ideal excuse for inactivity; unfortunately most of the major evils— poverty, overpopulation, pollution—are problems in which everyone is almost equally involved.

[2]In view of the special sense philosophers often give to the term, I should say that I use "obligation" simply as the abstract noun derived from "ought," so that "I have an obligation to" means no more, and no less, than "I ought to." This usage is in accordance with the definition of "ought" given by the *Shorter Oxford English Dictionary:* "the general verb to express duty or obligation." I do not think any issue of substance hangs on the way the term is used; sentences in which I use "obligation" could all be rewritten, although somewhat clumsily, as sentences in which a clause containing "ought" replaces the term "obligation."

The view that numbers do make a difference can be made plausible if 10 stated in this way: If everyone in circumstances like mine gave £5 to the Bengal Relief Fund, there would be enough to provide food, shelter, and medical care for the refugees; there is no reason why I should give more than anyone else in the same circumstances as I am; therefore I have no obligation to give more than £5. Each premise in this argument is true, and the argument looks sound. It may convince us, unless we notice that it is based on a hypothetical premise, although the conclusion is not stated hypothetically. The argument would be sound if the conclusion were: If everyone in circumstances like mine were to give £5, I would have no obligation to give more than £5. If the conclusion were so stated, however, it would be obvious that the argument has no bearing on a situation in which it is not the case that everyone else gives £5. This, of course, is the actual situation. It is more or less certain that not everyone in circumstances like mine will give £5. So there will not be enough to provide the needed food, shelter, and medical care. Therefore by giving more than £5 I will prevent more suffering than I would if I gave just £5.

It might be thought that this argument has an absurd consequence. Since the situation appears to be that very few people are likely to give substantial amounts, it follows that I and everyone else in similar circumstances ought to give as much as possible, that is, at least up to the point at which by giving more one would begin to cause serious suffering for oneself and one's dependents—perhaps even beyond this point to the point of marginal utility, at which by giving more one would cause oneself and one's dependents as much suffering as one would prevent in Bengal. If everyone does this, however, there will be more than can be used for the benefit of the refugees, and some of the sacrifice will have been unnecessary. Thus, if everyone does what he ought to do, the result will not be as good as it would be if everyone did a little less than he ought to do, or if only some do all that they ought to do.

The paradox here arises only if we assume that the actions in question—sending money to the relief funds—are performed more or less simultaneously, and are also unexpected. For if it is to be expected that everyone is going to contribute something, then clearly each is not obliged to give as much as he would have been obliged to had others not been giving too. And if everyone is not acting more or less simultaneously, then those giving later will know how much more is needed, and will have no obligation to give more than is necessary to reach this amount. To say this is not to deny the principle that people in the same circumstances have the same obligations, but to point out that the fact that others have given, or may be expected to give, is a relevant circumstance: Those giving after it has become known that many others are giving and those giving before are not in the same circumstances. So the seemingly absurd consequence of the principle I have put forward can occur only if people are in error about the actual circumstances—that is, if they think they are giving when others are not, but in fact they are giving when others are. The result of everyone doing what he really ought to do cannot be worse than the result of everyone doing less than he ought to do, although the result of everyone doing what he reasonably believes he ought to do could be.

If my argument so far has been sound, neither our distance from a preventable evil nor the number of other people who, in respect to that evil, are in the same situation as we are, lessens our obligation to mitigate or prevent that evil. I shall therefore take as established the principle I asserted earlier. As I have already said, I need to assert it only in its qualified form: If it is in our power to prevent something very bad from happening, without thereby sacrificing anything else morally significant, we ought, morally, to do it.

The outcome of this argument is that our traditional moral categories are upset. The traditional distinction between duty and charity cannot be drawn, or at least, not in the place we normally draw it. Giving money to the Bengal Relief Fund is regarded as an act of charity in our society. The bodies which collect money are known as "charities." These organizations see themselves in this way—if you send them a check, you will be thanked for your "generosity." Because giving money is regarded as an act of charity, it is not thought that there is anything wrong with not giving. The charitable man may be praised, but the man who is not charitable is not condemned. People do not feel in any way ashamed or guilty about spending money on new clothes or a new car instead of giving it to famine relief. (Indeed, the alternative does not occur to them.) This way of looking at the matter cannot be justified. When we buy new clothes not to keep ourselves warm but to look "well-dressed" we are not providing for any important need. We would not be sacrificing anything significant if we were to continue to wear our old clothes, and give the money to famine relief. By doing so, we would be preventing another person from starving. It follows from what I have said earlier that we ought to give money away, rather than spend it on clothes which we do not need to keep us warm. To do so is not charitable, or generous. Nor is it the kind of act which philosophers and theologians have called "supererogatory"—an act which it would be good to do, but not wrong not to do. On the contrary, we ought to give the money away, and it is wrong not to do so.

I am not maintaining that there are no acts which are charitable, or that there are no acts which it would be good to do but not wrong not to do. It may be possible to redraw the distinction between duty and charity in some other place. All I am arguing here is that the present way of drawing the distinction, which makes it an act of charity for a man living at the level of affluence which most people in the "developed nations" enjoy to give money to save someone else from starvation, cannot be supported. It is beyond the scope of my argument to consider whether the distinction should be redrawn or abolished altogether. There would be many other possible ways of drawing the distinction—for instance, one might decide that it is good to make other people as happy as possible, but not wrong not to do so.

Despite the limited nature of the revision in our moral conceptual scheme which I am proposing, the revision would, given the extent of both affluence and famine in the world today, have radical implications. These implications may lead to further objections, distinct from those I have already considered. I shall discuss two of these.

One objection to the position I have taken might be simply that it is too drastic a revision of our moral scheme. People do not ordinarily judge in the way I have suggested they should. Most people reserve their moral condemnation for those who violate some moral norm, such as the norm against taking another person's property. They do not condemn those who indulge in luxury instead of giving to famine relief. But given that I did not set out to present a morally neutral description of the way people make moral judgments, the way people do in fact judge has nothing to do with the validity of my conclusion. My conclusion follows from the principle which I advanced earlier, and unless that principle is rejected, or the arguments shown to be unsound, I think the conclusion must stand, however strange it appears.

It might, nevertheless, be interesting to consider why our society, and most other societies, do judge differently from the way I have suggested they should. In a well-known article, J. O. Urmson suggests that the imperatives of duty, which tell us what we must do, as distinct from what it would be good to do but not wrong not to do, function so as to prohibit behavior that is intolerable if men are to live together in society.[3] This may explain the origin and continued existence of the present division between acts of duty and acts of charity. Moral attitudes are shaped by the needs of society, and no doubt society needs people who will observe the rules that make social existence tolerable. From the point of view of a particular society, it is essential to prevent violations of norms against killing, stealing, and so on. It is quite inessential, however, to help people outside one's own society.

If this is an explanation of our common distinction between duty and supererogation, however, it is not a justification of it. The moral point of view requires us to look beyond the interests of our own society. Previously, as I have already mentioned, this may hardly have been feasible, but it is quite feasible now. From the moral point of view, the prevention of the starvation of millions of people outside our society must be considered at least as pressing as the upholding of property norms within our society.

It has been argued by some writers, among them Sidgwick and 20

---

[3] J. O. Urmson, "Saints and Heroes," in *Essays in Moral Philosophy*, ed. Abraham I. Melden (Seattle and London, 1958), p. 214. For a related but significantly different view see also Henry Sidgwick, *The Methods of Ethics*, 7th ed. (London, 1907), pp. 220–21, 492–93.

Urmson, that we need to have a basic moral code which is not too far beyond the capacities of the ordinary man, for otherwise there will be a general breakdown of compliance with the moral code. Crudely stated, this argument suggests that if we tell people that they ought to refrain from murder and give everything they do not really need to famine relief, they will do neither, whereas if we tell them that they ought to refrain from murder and that it is good to give to famine relief but not wrong not to do so, they will at least refrain from murder. The issue here is: Where should we draw the line between conduct that is required and conduct that is good although not required, so as to get the best possible result? This would seem to be an empirical question, although a very difficult one. One objection to the Sidgwick-Urmson line of argument is that it takes insufficient account of the effect that moral standards can have on the decisions we make. Given a society in which a wealthy man who gives 5 percent of his income to famine relief is regarded as most generous, it is not surprising that a proposal that we all ought to give away half our incomes will be thought to be absurdly unrealistic. In a society which held that no man should have more than enough while others have less than they need, such a proposal might seem narrow-minded. What it is possible for a man to do and what he is likely to do are both, I think, very greatly influenced by what people around him are doing and expecting him to do. In any case, the possibility that by spreading the idea that we ought to be doing very much more than we are to relieve famine we shall bring about a general breakdown of moral behavior seems remote. If the stakes are an end to widespread starvation, it is worth the risk. Finally, it should be emphasized that these considerations are relevant only to the issue of what we should require from others, and not to what we ourselves ought to do.

The second objection to my attack on the present distinction between duty and charity is one which has from time to time been made against utilitarianism. It follows from some forms of utilitarian theory that we all ought, morally, to be working full time to increase the balance of happiness over misery. The position I have taken here would not lead to this conclusion in all circumstances, for if there were no bad occurrences that we could prevent without sacrificing something of comparable moral importance, my argument would have no application. Given the present conditions in many parts of the world, however, it does follow from my argument that we ought, morally, to be working full time to relieve great suffering of the sort that occurs as a result of famine or other disasters. Of course, mitigating circumstances can be adduced — for instance, that if we wear ourselves out through overwork, we shall be less effective than we would otherwise have been. Nevertheless, when all considerations of this sort have been taken into account, the conclusion remains: We ought to be preventing as much suffering as we can without sacrificing something else of comparable moral importance. This conclusion is one which we may be reluctant to face. I cannot see, though, why it should be regarded as a criticism of the position for which I have argued, rather than a criticism of our ordinary standards of behavior. Since most people are self-interested to some degree, very few of us are likely to do everything that we ought to do. It would, however, hardly be honest to take this as evidence that it is not the case that we ought to do it.

It may still be thought that my conclusions are so wildly out of line with what everyone else thinks and has always thought that there must be something wrong with the argument somewhere. In order to show that my conclusions, while certainly contrary to contemporary Western moral standards, would not have seemed so extraordinary at other times and in other places, I would like to quote a passage from a writer not normally thought of as a way-out radical, Thomas Aquinas.

> Now, according to the natural order instituted by divine providence, material goods are provided for the satisfaction of human needs. Therefore the division and appropriation of property, which proceeds from human law, must not hinder the satisfaction of man's necessity from such goods. Equally, whatever a man has in superabundance is owed, of natural right, to the poor for their sustenance. So Ambrosius says, and it is also to be found in the *Decretum Gratiani:* "The bread which you withhold belongs to the hungry; the clothing you shut away, to the naked; and the money you bury in the earth is the redemption and freedom of the penniless."[4]

I now want to consider a number of points, more practical than philosophical, which are relevant to the application of the moral conclusion we have reached. These points challenge not the idea that we ought to be doing all we can to prevent starvation, but the idea that giving away a great deal of money is the best means to this end.

It is sometimes said that overseas aid should be a government responsibility, and that therefore one ought not to give to privately run charities. Giving privately, it is said, allows the government and the non-contributing members of society to escape their responsibilities.

This argument seems to assume that the more people there are who [25] give to privately organized famine relief funds, the less likely it is that the government will take over full responsibility for such aid. This assumption is unsupported, and does not strike me as at all plausible. The opposite view—that if no one gives voluntarily, a government will assume that its citizens are uninterested in famine relief and would not wish to be forced into giving aid—seems more plausible. In any case, unless there were a definite probability that by refusing to give one would be helping to bring about massive government assistance, people who do refuse to make voluntary contributions are refusing to prevent a certain amount of suffering without being able to point to any tangible

---

[4]*Summa Theologica*, II–II, Question 66, Article 7, in *Aquinas, Selected Political Writings*, ed. A. P. d'Entreves, trans. J. G. Dawson (Oxford, 1948), p. 171.

beneficial consequence of their refusal. So the onus of showing how their refusal will bring about government action is on those who refuse to give.

I do not, of course, want to dispute the contention that governments of affluent nations should be giving many times the amount of genuine, no-strings-attached aid that they are giving now. I agree, too, that giving privately is not enough, and that we ought to be campaigning actively for entirely new standards for both public and private contributions to famine relief. Indeed, I would sympathize with someone who thought that campaigning was more important than giving oneself, although I doubt whether preaching what one does not practice would be very effective. Unfortunately, for many people the idea that "it's the government's responsibility" is a reason for not giving which does not appear to entail any political action either.

Another, more serious reason for not giving to famine relief funds is that until there is effective population control, relieving famine merely postpones starvation. If we save the Bengal refugees now, others, perhaps the children of these refugees, will face starvation in a few years' time. In support of this, one may cite the now well-known facts about the population explosion and the relatively limited scope for expanded production.

This point, like the previous one, is an argument against relieving suffering that is happening now, because of a belief about what might happen in the future; it is unlike the previous point in that very good evidence can be adduced in support of this belief about the future. I will not go into the evidence here. I accept that the earth cannot support indefinitely a population rising at the present rate. This certainly poses a problem for anyone who thinks it important to prevent famine. Again, however, one could accept the argument without drawing the conclusion that it absolves one from any obligation to do anything to prevent famine. The conclusion that should be drawn is that the best means of preventing famine, in the long run, is population control. It would then follow from the position reached earlier that one ought to be doing all one can to promote population control (unless one held that all forms of population control were wrong in themselves, or would have significantly bad consequences). Since there are organizations working specifically for population control, one would then support them rather than more orthodox methods of preventing famine.

A third point raised by the conclusion reached earlier relates to the question of just how much we all ought to be giving away. One possibility, which has already been mentioned, is that we ought to give until we reach the level of marginal utility—that is, the level at which, by giving more, I would cause as much suffering to myself or my dependents as I would relieve by my gift. This would mean, of course, that one would reduce oneself to very near the material circumstances of a Bengali refugee. It will be recalled that earlier I put forward both a strong and a moderate version of the principle of preventing bad occurrences. The strong version, which required us to prevent bad things from happening unless in doing so we would be sacrificing something of comparable moral significance, does seem to require reducing ourselves to the level of marginal utility. I should also say that the strong version seems to me to be the correct one. I proposed the more moderate version—that we should prevent bad occurrences unless, to do so, we had to sacrifice something morally significant—only in order to show that even on this surely undeniable principle a great change in our way of life is required. On the more moderate principle, it may not follow that we ought to reduce ourselves to the level of marginal utility, for one might hold that to reduce oneself and one's family to this level is to cause something significantly bad to happen. Whether this is so I shall not discuss, since, as I have said, I can see no good reason for holding the moderate version of the principle rather than the strong version. Even if we accepted the principle only in its moderate form, however, it should be clear that we would have to give away enough to ensure that the consumer society, dependent as it is on people spending on trivia rather than giving to famine relief, would slow down and perhaps disappear entirely. There are several reasons why this would be desirable in itself. The value and necessity of economic growth are now being questioned not only by conservationists, but by economists as well.[5] There is no doubt, too, that the consumer society has had a distorting effect on the goals and purposes of its members. Yet looking at the matter purely from the point of view of overseas aid, there must be a limit to the extent to which we should deliberately slow down our economy; for it might be the case that if we gave away, say, 40 percent of our Gross National Product, we would slow down the economy so much that in absolute terms we would be giving less than if we gave 25 percent of the much larger GNP that we would have if we limited our contribution to this smaller percentage.

I mention this only as an indication of the sort of factor that one would have to take into account in working out an ideal. Since Western societies generally consider 1 percent of the GNP an acceptable level for overseas aid, the matter is entirely academic. Nor does it affect the question of how much an individual should give in a society in which very few are giving substantial amounts.

It is sometimes said, though less often now than it used to be, that philosophers have no special role to play in public affairs, since most public issues depend primarily on an assessment of facts. On questions of fact, it is said, philosophers as such have no special expertise, and so it has been possible to engage in philosophy without committing one-

[5]See, for instance, John Kenneth Galbraith, *The New Industrial State* (Boston, 1967); and E. J. Mishan, *The Costs of Economic Growth* (London, 1967).

self to any position on major public issues. No doubt there are some issues of social policy and foreign policy about which it can truly be said that a really expert assessment of the facts is required before taking sides or acting, but the issue of famine is surely not one of these. The facts about the existence of suffering are beyond dispute. Nor, I think, is it disputed that we can do something about it, either through orthodox methods of famine relief or through population control or both. This is therefore an issue on which philosophers are competent to take a position. The issue is one which faces everyone who has more money than he needs to support himself and his dependents, or who is in a position to take some sort of political action. These categories must include practically every teacher and student of philosophy in the universities of the Western world. If philosophy is to deal with matters that are relevant to both teachers and students, this is an issue that philosophers should discuss.

Discussion, though, is not enough. What is the point of relating philosophy to public (and personal) affairs if we do not take our conclusions seriously? In this instance, taking our conclusion seriously means acting upon it. The philosopher will not find it any easier than anyone else to alter his attitudes and way of life to the extent that, if I am right, is involved in doing everything that we ought to be doing. At the very least, though, one can make a start. The philosopher who does so will have to sacrifice some of the benefits of the consumer society, but he can find compensation in the satisfaction of a way of life in which theory and practice, if not yet in harmony, are at least coming together.

TOPICS FOR CRITICAL THINKING AND WRITING

1. How does Singer tell when one thing we might do is more or less "morally significant" (para. 6) than something else we might do? Do you agree with him on this point?

2. Explain whether you agree with Singer that, morally speaking, there is no difference between my coming to the aid of someone I know and love (say, my child or my parent) and coming to the aid of a stranger thousands of miles away, someone "whose name I shall never know" (para. 7)—perhaps someone whom I would thoroughly dislike if I did know him or her?

3. What is the view that "numbers lessen obligation" (para. 9), and why does Singer refer to it as an "absurdity"?

4. What does Singer mean by the affluent giving money or other resources to the needy up to the point or level of "marginal utility" (paras. 11 and 29)?

5. What does Singer mean by "the traditional distinction between duty and charity" (para. 14)? Why does he think this distinction collapses? Does he in fact contradict himself on this point in paragraph 15?

6. Suppose that a gift of large-scale resources by the affluent to the currently starving in some nation reduces what can be given to their successors, the next generation, when the next famine hits that nation (see paras. 27 and 28). Would Singer favor giving those resources to the currently starving or to their descendants?

7. Singer considers two objections to his position (paras. 16–21). What are they, and how does he respond to them? In an essay of 1,000 words, state concisely those objections, his replies, and your evaluation.

8. Singer refers to "the principle which I advanced earlier" (para. 17). State in a sentence what that principle is. (Hint: A version is found in para. 21.)

9. Suppose someone were to object to Singer that the plight of starving people in Africa, Asia, or elsewhere in the world is to a large extent their own fault, a result of uncontrolled overpopulation, leading to their destruction of their physical habitat and aggravated by corrupt self-government. How might Singer reply?

10. What is Singer's answer to the question of "how much we all ought to be giving away" (para. 29)?

Garrett Hardin

Garrett Hardin (1915–2003) was Emeritus Professor of Human Ecology at the University of California, Santa Barbara. Born in Dallas, Texas, he received his Ph.D. in biology from Stanford in 1941 and is the author of several books, including The Limits of Altruism *(1977),* Managing the Commons *(1977),* Filters Against Folly *(1988), and* The Ostrich Factor *(1998). The essay reprinted here originally appeared in* Psychology Today *(September 1974).*

Lifeboat Ethics:
The Case against Helping the Poor

Environmentalists use the metaphor of the earth as a "spaceship" in trying to persuade countries, industries, and people to stop wasting and polluting our natural resources. Since we all share life on this planet, they argue, no single person or institution has the right to destroy, waste, or use more than a fair share of its resources.

But does everyone on earth have an equal right to an equal share of its resources? The spaceship metaphor can be dangerous when used by misguided idealists to justify suicidal policies for sharing our resources through uncontrolled immigration and foreign aid. In their enthusiastic but unrealistic generosity, they confuse the ethics of a spaceship with those of a lifeboat.

A true spaceship would have to be under the control of a captain, since no ship could possibly survive if its course were determined by committee. Spaceship Earth certainly has no captain; the United Nations is merely a toothless tiger, with little power to enforce any policy upon its bickering members.

If we divide the world crudely into rich nations and poor nations, two thirds of them are desperately poor, and only one third comparatively rich, with the United States the wealthiest of all. Metaphorically each nation can be seen as a lifeboat full of comparatively rich people. In the ocean outside each lifeboat swim the poor of the world, who would like to get in, or at least to share some of the wealth. What should the lifeboat passengers do?

First, we must recognize the limited capacity of any lifeboat. For 5 example, a nation's land has a limited capacity to support a population and as the current energy crisis has shown us, in some ways we have already exceeded the carrying capacity of our land.

ADRIFT IN A MORAL SEA

So here we sit, say fifty people in our lifeboat. To be generous, let us assume it has room for ten more, making a total capacity of sixty. Suppose the fifty of us in the lifeboat see 100 others swimming in the water outside, begging for admission to our boat or for handouts. We have several options: We may be tempted to try to live by the Christian ideal of being "our brother's keeper," or by the Marxist ideal of "to each according to his needs." Since the needs of all in the water are the same, and since they can all be seen as "our brothers," we could take them all into our boat, making a total of 150 in a boat designed for sixty. The boat swamps, everyone drowns. Complete justice, complete catastrophe.

Since the boat has an unused excess capacity of ten more passengers, we could admit just ten more to it. But which ten do we let in? How do we choose? Do we pick the best ten, the neediest ten, "first come, first served"? And what do we say to the ninety we exclude? If we do let an extra ten into our lifeboat, we will have lost our "safety factor," an engineering principle of critical importance. For example, if we don't leave room for excess capacity as a safety factor in our country's agriculture, a new plant disease or a bad change in the weather could have disastrous consequences.

Suppose we decide to preserve our small safety factor and admit no more to the lifeboat. Our survival is then possible, although we shall have to be constantly on guard against boarding parties.

While this last solution clearly offers the only means of our survival, it is morally abhorrent to many people. Some say they feel guilty about their good luck. My reply is simple: "Get out and yield your place to others." This may solve the problem of the guilt-ridden person's conscience, but it does not change the ethics of the lifeboat. The needy person to whom the guilt-ridden person yields his place will not himself feel guilty about his good luck. If he did, he would not climb aboard. The net result of conscience-stricken people giving up their unjustly held seats is the elimination of that sort of conscience from the lifeboat.

This is the basic metaphor within which we must work out our 10 solutions. Let us now enrich the image, step by step, with substantive additions from the real world, a world that must solve real and pressing problems of overpopulation and hunger.

The harsh ethics of the lifeboat become even harsher when we consider the reproductive differences between the rich nations and the poor nations. The people inside the lifeboats are doubling in numbers every eighty-seven years; those swimming around outside are doubling, on the average, every thirty-five years, more than twice as fast as the rich. And since the world's resources are dwindling, the difference in prosperity between the rich and the poor can only increase.

As of 1973, the United States had a population of 210 million people, who were increasing by 0.8 percent per year. Outside our lifeboat, let us imagine another 210 million people (say the combined populations of Colombia, Ecuador, Venezuela, Morocco, Pakistan, Thailand, and the Philippines), who are increasing at a rate of 3.3 percent year. Put differently, the doubling time for this aggregate population is twenty-one years, compared to eighty-seven years for the United States.

MULTIPLYING THE RICH AND THE POOR

Now suppose the United States agreed to pool its resources with those seven countries, with everyone receiving an equal share. Initially the ratio of Americans to non-Americans in this model would be one-to-one. But consider what the ratio would be after eighty-seven years, by which time the Americans would have doubled to a population of 420 million. By then, doubling every twenty-one years, the other group would have swollen to 354 billion. Each American would have to share the available resource with more than eight people.

But, one could argue, this discussion assumes that current population trends will continue, and they may not. Quite so. Most likely the rate of population increase will decline much faster in the United States than it will in the other countries, and there does not seem to be much we can do about it. In sharing with "each according to his needs," we must recognize that needs are determined by population size, which is determined by the rate of reproduction, which at present is regarded as a sovereign right of every nation, poor or not. This being so, the philanthropic load created by the sharing ethic of the spaceship can only increase.

THE TRAGEDY OF THE COMMONS

The fundamental error of spaceship ethics, and the sharing it requires, is that it leads to what I call "the tragedy of the commons." Under a system of private property, the men who own property recognize their responsibility to care for it, for if they don't they will eventu- 15 ally suffer. A farmer, for instance, will allow no more cattle in a pasture than its carrying capacity justifies. If he overloads it, erosion sets in, weeds take over, and he loses the use of the pasture.

If a pasture becomes a commons open to all, the right of each to use it may not be matched by a corresponding responsibility to protect it. Asking everyone to use it with discretion will hardly do, for the considerate herdsman who refrains from overloading the commons suffers more than a selfish one who says his needs are greater. If everyone would restrain himself, all would be well; but it takes only one less than everyone to ruin a system of voluntary restraint. In a crowded world of less than perfect human beings, mutual ruin is inevitable if there are no controls. This is the tragedy of the commons.

One of the major tasks of education today should be the creation of such an acute awareness of the dangers of the commons that people will recognize its many varieties. For example, the air and water have become polluted because they are treated as commons. Further growth in the population or per-capita conversion of natural resources into pollutants will only make the problem worse. The same holds true for the fish of the oceans. Fishing fleets have nearly disappeared in many parts of the world, technological improvements in the art of fishing are hastening the day of complete ruin. Only the replacement of the system of the commons with a responsible system of control will save the land, air, water, and oceanic fisheries.

THE WORLD FOOD BANK

In recent years there has been a push to create a new commons called a World Food Bank, an international depository of food reserves to which nations would contribute according to their abilities and from which they would draw according to their needs. This humanitarian proposal has received support from many liberal international groups, and from such prominent citizens as Margaret Mead, U.N. Secretary General Kurt Waldheim, and Senators Edward Kennedy and George McGovern.

A world food bank appeals powerfully to our humanitarian impulses. But before we rush ahead with such a plan, let us recognize where the greatest political push comes from, lest we be disillusioned later. Our experience with the "Food for Peace program," or Public Law 480, gives us the answer. This program moved billions of dollars' worth of U.S. surplus grain to food-short, population-long countries during the past two decades. But when PL 480 first became law, a headline in the business magazine *Forbes* revealed the real power behind it: "Feeding the World's Hungry Millions: How It Will Mean Billions for U.S. Business."

And indeed it did. In the years 1960 to 1970, U.S. taxpayers spent a total of $7.9 billion on the Food for Peace program. Between 1948 and 1970, they also paid an additional $50 billion for other economic-aid 20 programs, some of which went for food and food-producing machinery and technology. Though all U.S. taxpayers were forced to contribute to the cost of PL 480, certain special interest groups gained handsomely under the program. Farmers did not have to contribute the grain; the government, or rather the taxpayers, bought it from them at full market prices. The increased demand raised prices of farm products generally. The manufacturers of farm machinery, fertilizers, and pesticides benefited by the farmers' extra efforts to grow more food. Grain elevators profited from storing the surplus until it could be shipped. Railroads made money hauling it to ports, and shipping lines profited from carrying it overseas. The implementation of PL 480 required the creation of a vast government bureaucracy, which then acquired its own vested interest in continuing the program regardless of its merits.

EXTRACTING DOLLARS

Those who proposed and defended the Food for Peace program in public rarely mentioned its importance to any of these special interests. The public emphasis was always on its humanitarian effects. The combination of silent selfish interests and highly vocal humanitarian apologists made a powerful and successful lobby for extracting money from taxpayers. We can expect the same lobby to push now for the creation of a World Food Bank.

However great the potential benefit to selfish interests, it should not be a decisive argument against a truly humanitarian program. We must ask if such a program would actually do more good than harm, not only momentarily but also in the long run. Those who propose the food bank usually refer to a current "emergency" or "crisis" in terms of world food supply. But what is an emergency? Although they may be infrequent and sudden, everyone knows that emergencies will occur from time to time. A well-run family, company, organization, or country prepares for the likelihood of accidents and emergencies. It expects them, it budgets for them, it saves for them.

LEARNING THE HARD WAY

What happens if some organizations or countries budget for accidents and others do not? If each country is solely responsible for its own well-being, poorly managed ones will suffer. But they can learn from experience. They may mend their ways, and learn to budget for infrequent but certain emergencies. For example, the weather varies from year to year, and periodic crop failures are certain. A wise and competent government saves out of the production of the good years in anticipation of bad years to come. Joseph taught this policy to Pharaoh in Egypt more than 2,000 years ago. Yet the great majority of the governments in the world today do not follow such a policy. They lack either the wisdom or the competence, or both. Should those nations that do manage to put something aside be forced to come to the rescue each time an emergency occurs among the poor nations?

"But it isn't their fault!" some kindhearted liberals argue. "How can we blame the poor people who are caught in an emergency? Why must they suffer for the sins of their governments?" The concept of blame is simply not relevant here. The real question is, what are the operational consequences of establishing a world food bank? If it is open to every country every time a need develops, slovenly rulers will not be motivated to take Joseph's advice. Someone will always come to their aid. Some countries will deposit food in the world food bank, and others will withdraw it. There will be almost no overlap. As a result of such solutions to food shortage emergencies, the poor countries will not learn to mend their ways, and will suffer progressively greater emergencies as their populations grow.

POPULATION CONTROL THE CRUDE WAY

On the average, poor countries undergo a 2.5 percent increase in 25 population each year; rich countries, about 0.8 percent. Only rich countries have anything in the way of food reserves set aside, and even they do not have as much as they should. Poor countries have none. If poor countries received no food from the outside, the rate of their population growth would be periodically checked by crop failures and famines. But if they can always draw on a world food bank in time of need, their populations can continue to grow unchecked, and so will their "need" for aid. In the short run, a world food bank may diminish that need, but in the long run it actually increases the need without limit.

Without some system of worldwide food sharing, the proportion of people in the rich and poor nations might eventually stabilize. The overpopulated poor countries would decrease in numbers, while the rich countries that had room for more people would increase. But with a well-meaning system of sharing, such as a world food bank, the growth differential between the rich and the poor countries will not only persist, it will increase. Because of the higher rate of population growth in the poor countries of the world, 88 percent of today's children are born poor, and only 12 percent rich. Year by year the ratio becomes worse, as the fast-reproducing poor outnumber the slow-reproducing rich.

A world food bank is thus a commons in disguise. People will have more motivation to draw from it than to add to any common store. The less provident and less able will multiply at the expense of the abler and more provident, bringing eventual ruin upon all who share in the commons. Besides, any system of "sharing" that amounts to foreign aid from the rich nations to the poor nations will carry the taint of charity, which will contribute little to the world peace so devoutly desired by those who support the idea of a world food bank.

As past U.S. foreign-aid programs have amply and depressingly demonstrated, international charity frequently inspires mistrust and antagonism rather than gratitude on the part of the recipient nation.

CHINESE FISH AND MIRACLE RICE

The modern approach to foreign aid stresses the export of technology and advice, rather than money and food. As an ancient Chinese proverb goes: "Give a man a fish and he will eat for a day; teach him how to fish and he will eat for the rest of his days." Acting on this advice, the Rockefeller and Ford foundations have financed a number of programs for improving agriculture in the hungry nations. Known as the "Green Revolution," these programs have led to the development of "miracle rice" and "miracle wheat," new strains that offer bigger harvests and greater resistance to crop damage. Norman Borlaug, the Nobel Prize–winning agronomist who, supported by the Rockefeller Foundation, developed "miracle wheat," is one of the most prominent advocates of a world food bank.

Whether or not the Green Revolution can increase food production 30 as much as its champions claim is a debatable but possibly irrelevant point. Those who support this well-intended humanitarian effort should first consider some of the fundamentals of human ecology. Ironically, one man who did was the late Alan Gregg, a vice president of the Rockefeller Foundation. Two decades ago he expressed strong doubts about the wisdom of such attempts to increase food production. He likened the growth and spread of humanity over the surface of the earth to the spread of cancer in the human body, remarking that "cancerous growths demand food; but, as far as I know, they have never been cured by getting it."

OVERLOADING THE ENVIRONMENT

Every human born constitutes a draft on all aspects of the environment: food, air, water, forests, beaches, wildlife, scenery, and solitude. Food can, perhaps, be significantly increased to meet a growing demand. But what about clean beaches, unspoiled forests, and solitude? If we satisfy a growing population's need for food, we necessarily decrease its per-capita supply of the other resources needed by men.

India, for example, now has a population of 600 million, which increases by 15 million each year. This population already puts a huge load on a relatively impoverished environment. The country's forests are now only a small fraction of what they were three centuries ago, and floods and erosion continually destroy the insufficient farmland that remains. Every one of the 15 million new lives added to India's population puts an additional burden on the environment, and increases the economic and social costs of crowding. However humanitarian our intent, every

Indian life saved through medical or nutritional assistance from abroad diminishes the quality of life for those who remain, and for subsequent generations. If rich countries make it possible, through foreign aid, for 600 million Indians to swell to 1.2 billion in a mere twenty-eight years, as their current growth rate threatens, will future generations of Indians thank us for hastening the destruction of their environment? Will our good intentions be sufficient excuse for the consequences of our actions?

My final example of a commons in action is one for which the public has the least desire for rational discussion—immigration. Anyone who publicly questions the wisdom of current U.S. immigration policy is promptly charged with bigotry, prejudice, ethnocentrism, chauvinism, isolationism, or selfishness. Rather than encounter such accusations, one would rather talk about other matters, leaving immigration policy to wallow in the crosscurrents of special interests that take no account of the good of the whole, or the interest of posterity.

Perhaps we still feel guilty about things we said in the past. Two generations ago the popular press frequently referred to Dagos, Wops, Polacks, Chinks, and Krauts, in articles about how America was being "overrun" by foreigners of supposedly inferior genetic stock. But because the implied inferiority of foreigners was used then as justification for keeping them out, people now assume that restrictive policies could only be based on such misguided notions. There are no other grounds.

A NATION OF IMMIGRANTS

Just consider the numbers involved. Our government acknowledges 35 a net inflow of 400,000 immigrants a year. While we have no hard data on the extent of illegal entries, educated guesses put the figure at about 600,000 a year. Since the natural increase (excess of births over deaths) of the resident population now runs about 1.7 million per year, the yearly gain from immigration amounts to at least 19 percent of the total annual increase, and may be as much as 37 percent if we include the estimate for illegal immigrants. Considering the growing use of birth-control devices, the potential effect of educational campaigns by such organizations as Planned Parenthood Federation of America and Zero Population Growth, and the influence of inflation and the housing shortage, the fertility rate of American women may decline so much that immigration could account for all the yearly increase in population. Should we not at least ask if that is what we want?

For the sake of those who worry about whether the "quality" of the average immigrant compares favorably with the quality of the average resident, let us assume that immigrants and native-born citizens are of exactly equal quality, however one defines that term. We will focus here only on quantity; and since our conclusions will depend on nothing else, all charges of bigotry and chauvinism become irrelevant.

IMMIGRATION VS. FOOD SUPPLY

World food banks *move food to the people,* hastening the exhaustion of the environment of the poor countries. Unrestricted immigration, on the other hand, *moves people to the food,* thus speeding up the destruction of the environment of the rich countries. We can easily understand why poor people should want to make this latter transfer, but why should rich hosts encourage it?

As in the case of foreign-aid programs, immigration receives support from selfish interests and humanitarian impulses. The primary selfish interest in unimpeded immigration is the desire of employers for cheap labor, particularly in industries and trades that offer degrading work. In the past, one wave of foreigners after another was brought into the United States to work at wretched jobs for wretched wages. In recent years, the Cubans, Puerto Ricans, and Mexicans have had this dubious honor. The interests of the employers of cheap labor mesh well with the guilty silence of the country's liberal intelligentsia. White Anglo-Saxon Protestants are particularly reluctant to call for a closing of the doors to immigration for fear of being called bigots.

But not all countries have such reluctant leadership. Most educated Hawaiians, for example, are keenly aware of the limits of their environment, particularly in terms of population growth. There is only so much room on the islands, and the islanders know it. To Hawaiians, immigrants from the other forty-nine states present as great a threat as those from other nations. At a recent meeting of Hawaiian government officials in Honolulu, I had the ironic delight of hearing a speaker, who like most of his audience was of Japanese ancestry, ask how the country might practically and constitutionally close its doors to further immigration. One member of the audience countered: "How can we shut the doors now? We have many friends and relatives in Japan that we'd like to bring here some day so that they can enjoy Hawaii too." The Japanese-American speaker smiled sympathetically and answered: "Yes, but we have children now, and someday we'll have grandchildren too. We can bring more people here from Japan only by giving away some of the land that we hope to pass on to our grandchildren some day. What right do we have to do that?"

At this point, I can hear U.S. liberals asking: "How can you justify slamming the door once you're inside? You say that immigrants should be kept out. But aren't we all immigrants, or the descendants of immigrants? If we insist on staying, must we not admit all others?" Our craving for intellectual order leads us to seek and prefer symmetrical rules and morals: a single rule for me and everybody else; the same rule yesterday, today, and tomorrow. Justice, we feel, should not change with time and place.

We Americans of non-Indian ancestry can look upon ourselves as the descendants of thieves who are guilty morally, if not legally, of stealing this land from its Indian owners. Should we then give back the land to the now living American descendants of those Indians? However morally or logically sound this proposal may be, I, for one, am unwilling to live by it and I know no one else who is. Besides, the logical consequence would be absurd. Suppose that, intoxicated with a sense of pure justice, we should decide to turn our land over to the Indians. Since all our wealth has also been derived from the land, wouldn't we be morally obliged to give that back to the Indians too?

PURE JUSTICE VS. REALITY

Clearly, the concept of pure justice produces an infinite regression to absurdity. Centuries ago, wise men invented statutes of limitations to justify the rejection of such pure justice, in the interest of preventing continual disorder. The law zealously defends property rights, but only relatively recent property rights. Drawing a line after an arbitrary time has elapsed may be unjust, but the alternatives are worse.

We are all descendants of thieves, and the world's resources are inequitably distributed. But we must begin the journey to tomorrow from the point where we are today. We cannot remake the past. We cannot safely divide the wealth equitably among all peoples so long as people reproduce at different rates. To do so would guarantee that our grandchildren, and everyone else's grandchildren, would have only a ruined world to inhabit.

To be generous with one's own possessions is quite different from being generous with those of posterity. We should call this point to the attention of those who, from a commendable love of justice and equality, would institute a system of the commons, either in the form of a world food bank, or of unrestricted immigration. We must convince them if we wish to save at least some parts of the world from environmental ruin.

Without a true world government to control reproduction and the 45 use of available resources, the sharing ethic of the spaceship is impossible. For the foreseeable future, our survival demands that we govern our actions by the ethics of a lifeboat, harsh though they may be. Posterity will be satisfied with nothing less.

TOPICS FOR CRITICAL THINKING AND WRITING

1. Hardin says that "in some ways we have already exceeded the carrying capacity of our land" (para. 5). Does he tell us later what some of those ways are? Can you think of others?

2. The central analogy on which Hardin's argument rests is that human life on planet Earth is like living in an overcrowded lifeboat. Evaluate this analogy.

3. What does Hardin mean by "ethics" in the title of his essay? What, if any, ethical principle does Hardin believe should guide our conduct in lifeboat Earth?

4. What is "the tragedy" and what is "the commons" in what Hardin calls "the tragedy of the commons" (paras. 15–17)?

5. What does Hardin mean by "a truly humanitarian program" (para. 22) to alleviate future problems of hunger and starvation? Why does he think a World Food Bank would aggravate, rather than alleviate, the problem?

6. How do you react to the analogy that compares the growth of the human race over the earth to "the spread of cancer in the human body" (para. 30)?

7. Hardin's view of the relationship between population growth and available resources can be described (though he doesn't) as a zero-sum game. Do you agree with such a description? Why, or why not?

8. Hardin refers to an organization named Zero Population Growth (para. 35). In your public or college library find out about this organization, and then write a 250-word essay describing its origin and aims.

9. Hardin offers a reductio ad absurdum argument (see pp. 410–11) against large-scale restitution by the current nonnative American population to the surviving native Americans (para. 41). Evaluate this argument in an essay of 250 words.

10. Hardin refers frequently (for example, para. 42) and unsympathetically to what he calls "pure justice." To what principle, exactly, is he referring by this phrase? Would you agree that this principle is, indeed, well described as "pure justice"? Why, or why not?

11. Suppose someone, after reading Hardin's essay, described it as nothing more than selfishness on a national scale. Would Hardin agree? Would he consider this a serious criticism of his analysis and proposals?

Randy Cohen

Since 1999, the New York Times Magazine *has been publishing a column called "The Ethicist," in which Randy Cohen or occasionally a guest writer responds to a reader's letter that poses an ethical question. Some of these letters and responses have been collected in a book called* The Good, the Bad, and the Difference *(2002). The letters have posed such questions as these:*

1. *I am a lesbian who will become a freshman college student in the autumn. Should I inform my roommates?*
2. *On the subway I saw a mother slap her child for crying. Should I have spoken up?*
3. *As a police officer, I handle phone inquiries about persons who have just been arrested. When a wife asks about her husband, who has been arrested for soliciting prostitution, can I withhold the truth?*

Below, we give three letters on other topics, with Cohen's responses.

Three Letters (to an Ethicist)

DYING WISH

Recently at the hospice where I work, the family of an African-American patient requested an African-American nursing assistant rather than the Latino we had planned to assign. I feel uncomfortable when a white patient requests a white care provider, but this seems different. After all, the requests of female patients for female nursing assistants seem reasonable on the basis of modesty. What should I do here?—Anonymous

Your proclivity to accede to any request of a dying patient does you credit. Yet, though your intentions are benign, you should not assign jobs simply on the basis of race. If the former segregationist Strom Thurmond demanded a white nurse's aide, few hospices would comply. And while the victims of racism confront different circumstances than its beneficiaries do, that is not sufficient reason to establish a race-based jobs policy. To do so would be to discriminate against members of your staff, and that rejected Latino aide would have grounds to complain if you did.

You could honor a request for a particular aide: I want Rosa. She's capable and kind, and I love beating her at gin. And going further, a hospice can consider race as one of many factors—age, experience, geographic background, temperament, sense of humor—when deciding which aide would be a great match for a particular patient. Indeed, given America's history, how could race not be a factor in such decisions? This is akin to what some university admissions officers do, treating race as one of many factors that inform them about prospective students. Thus, after considering all criteria, you may well decide to grant the request of your African-American patient.

As for sex and health care, here too we meet some demands but not others. Most of us would consent to a woman's request for a female gynecologist, deferring to her sense of sexual modesty. But few would honor her request for a female heart surgeon. And while a nurse's aide does perform intimate tasks—bathing a patient, for example—the analogy of race and sex has only limited application here, given the essential similarity of all human bodies.

Follow up: Anonymous later learned that an episode in the patient's past had instilled in her a fear of white faces. This new information makes assigning her an African-American aide not racism but compassion, an honorable response to her individual circumstances.

SUFFER THE LITTLE CHILDREN

I am a university researcher using magnetic resonance imaging to study how children learn to speak and read. All such work is monitored by a review board to

assess its safety. Our board has given me permission to study children as young as 7. There is as yet no evidence at all that M.R.I. is harmful, but I worry about later discoveries, and so I may not let my own 7-year-old participate. Can I run other children in this study if I wouldn't run my own?—Anonymous

Different people accept different levels of risk. That this study entails more than you find palatable does not mean others will concur. Some let their kids drive dirt bikes; others don't. (Although few would allow their 7-year-old to drive a motorcycle through an M.R.I.) Forbidding your child to be a research subject does not make you a hypocrite. Your duty as a researcher is to be a responsible scientist, not a model father.

It is your obligation to make sure that potential participants understand the current risks as well as the dangers that might be confirmed in the future—not just statistical possibilities, but information meaningful to a lay person. You must be alert to the deference we civilians sometimes show doctors and scientists, which inhibits us from asking pertinent questions. And your volunteers must be truly that: you must avoid offering, for example, the sort of payments to participants that exploit the desperation of the financially hard pressed.

After that, it is up to other parents to decide. If anyone asks if you'd allow your child to participate, you must of course answer calmly and honestly. That is, you should not shriek, unprompted: "I'd never let my kid within 50 feet of an M.R.I. Those things could blow sky high!" By appealing to parents' emotions rather than to their reasoned judgment, by manipulating their regard for you as an authority figure, you would undermine not only this valuable research but your respect for science itself.

COLLEGE PARKING

At the public university where I used to work, it was first-arrive, first-park. (The later you came to work, the more likely you had to park in the satellite lot and ride the shuttle.) Recently, just before I left, a number of closer spots were reserved for particular deans and vice presidents. I then had fewer spots to choose from, even when I arrived before them. Is it ethical for them to get preferred parking?—Andrew Feldman, Long Island

Sure, rank has its privileges. I've even heard of cases in which some high-ranking people make more money than we hoi polloi—and talk about scarce resources.

But while this policy is not unethical, it is unwise. To elevate administrators to a privileged class is contrary to the American ideal of an egalitarian society. Why bestow parking perks on a dean rather than a math professor or a grad student or, for that matter, a cafeteria worker? What's more—or perhaps less—it will not improve a dean's ability to do his job if his experience of campus life has little in common with the people who work and study there.

However, if your university is eager to create a petty aristocracy, it could instead force students with lower than a C average to carry administrators around the campus in sedan chairs, providing both an incentive to excel academically and a public display of the university's values.

TOPICS FOR CRITICAL THINKING AND WRITING

The following letters were *not* sent to Randy Cohen, but the problems they raise are real. Choose one letter, and write your response.

1. Assume that *you* hold Cohen's job. Write a response to one letter. Or, alternatively, write a response to one of Cohen's letters.

2. Following my instructor's advice, I submitted the draft of an essay to my roommate for peer review. She corrected numerous spelling errors, pointed out some wordy sentences, and gave me some ideas that I think are really better than my own. Is it enough if in a note I merely thank her for "reading the draft and making suggestions"?

3. In my high school course in biology, we are required to dissect frogs. I think this is cruel and pointless. Whatever we learn about a frog's anatomy can be learned from a book. My teacher says that I must dissect the frog.

4. My high school requires that we dissect frogs. I am a vegetarian because I believe in reverence for life, but the teacher says that I cannot be exempted. What should I do?

5. My high school requires that we dissect frogs. I am a Buddhist, and we Buddhists have a reverence for all living creatures. I do not even swat mosquitos. My teacher says that I must do the work to pass the course. What should I do?

6. My friend was a sperm donor in the days when donors were assured of anonymity. I happen to know the young woman—she is sixteen—who was born from this sperm, and she now is deeply concerned with finding her biological father. Should I tell the father? Should I tell the daughter? Should I at least let the mother know that I know? Or should I keep my mouth shut?

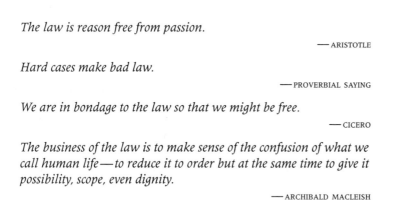

A Lawyer's View:
Steps toward Civic Literacy

The law is reason free from passion.

— ARISTOTLE

Hard cases make bad law.

— PROVERBIAL SAYING

We are in bondage to the law so that we might be free.

— CICERO

The business of the law is to make sense of the confusion of what we call human life — to reduce it to order but at the same time to give it possibility, scope, even dignity.

— ARCHIBALD MACLEISH

When John Adams in 1774 said that ours is "a government of law, and not of men," he meant that much of public conduct is regulated, rightly, by principles of law that by general agreement ought to be enforced and that can be altered only by our duly elected representatives, whose power is derived from our consent. In a democracy, laws, not individuals (for instance, kings or tyrants), govern. Adams and other early Americans rejected the view attributed to Louis XIV, "I am the state" (*L'état c'est moi*).

But what exactly the law in a given situation is often causes hot debate (as we know from watching the TV news). Whether we are ever personally called on to decide the law — as are legislators, judges, jurors, or lawyers — all of us find our daily lives constantly affected by the law. It is fitting, therefore, and even necessary that we develop **civic literacy,** the ability to understand the principles by which our government and its courts operate so that we can act appropriately. (In today's global community, our civic literacy must also include a knowledge of the ways our and others' governments function.)

From the time of Plato's *Apology*, reporting Socrates' trial before the Athenian assembly in 399 B.C. on charges of corrupting the young and preaching false gods, courtroom argument has been a staple of dramatic verbal cut-and-thrust. (Think of popular television shows such as *Boston Legal* and *Law and Order*.) Probably no profession prides itself more on the ability of its members to argue than does the legal profession. The uninitiated are easily intimidated by the skill with which a lawyer can marshal relevant considerations to support a client's interests. But legal argument is, after all, *argument*, and so its main features are those already discussed in Chapter 3 (such as definition, assumption, premise, deduction, conclusion, evidence, validity). What is distinctive about legal reasoning is fairly straightforward in all but the most unusual cases.

CIVIL AND CRIMINAL CASES

Legal cases are divided into civil and criminal. In a *civil* case one party (the plaintiff) brings suit against another party (the defendant), claiming that he or she has suffered some wrong at the hands of the defendant and deserves some remedy (for instance, due to a dispute over a property boundary or over fault in a multicar accident). The judge or jury decides for or against the plaintiff based on the evidence and the relevant law. All crimes are wrongs, but not all wrongs are crimes. For instance, an automobile accident that involves negligence on the part of one of the drivers and results in harm to another is surely a wrong, but the driver responsible for the accident, even if found guilty, does not face a prison sentence (that could happen only if the accident were in fact the result of driving with gross recklessness or driving while intoxicated or were no "accident" at all). Why? Because the harm inflicted was not criminal; that is, it was not intentional, deliberate, malicious, or premeditated.

Criminal cases involve someone (the defendant) charged either with a *felony* (a serious crime like assault or battery) or with a *misdemeanor* (a less serious crime, as in *Texas v. Johnson*, p. 425). In criminal cases the state, through its prosecutor, seeks to convict the defendant as charged; the defendant, through his or her attorney, seeks an acquittal or, at worst, a conviction on a lesser charge (manslaughter instead of murder) and a milder punishment. The decision to convict or acquit on the basis of the facts submitted in evidence and the relevant law is the duty of the jury (or the judge, if there is no jury). The prosecutor and defense lawyer present what they believe are the relevant facts. Defining the relevant law is the responsibility of the trial judge. Public interest in criminal cases is often high, especially when the crime is particularly heinous. (Think of the 1995 trial of O. J. Simpson, charged with the murder of his wife and one of her friends, and the 1997 trial of Timothy McVeigh for the Oklahoma City federal building bombing.)

As you begin reading a legal case, therefore, you will want to be sure you can answer this question:

- Is the court trying to decide whether someone accused of a crime is guilty as charged, or is the court trying to resolve some noncriminal (civil) dispute?

TRIAL AND APPEAL

Most cases (civil or criminal) never go to *trial* at all. Most civil cases are settled out of court, and most criminal cases are settled with a plea bargain in which the prosecutor and the defense attorney persuade the judge to accept the defendant's guilty plea in exchange for a less severe sentence. Of the cases that are settled by trial, the losing party usually does not try to reopen, or *appeal*, the case. If, however, the losing party believes that he or she should have won, the case may be appealed for review by a higher appellate court (provided, of course, the loser can finance the appeal). The party bringing the appeal (the appellant) typically argues that because the relevant law was misstated or misapplied during the trial, the decision must be reversed and a new trial ordered. On rare occasion the issue in dispute is appealed all the way to the highest court in the nation—the U.S. Supreme Court—for a final decision. (The cases we reprint for discussion in this chapter are all cases decided by the Supreme Court.)

A pair of useful questions to answer as you work your way through a reported case are these:

- What events gave rise to the legal controversy in this case?
- What intermediate steps did the case go through before reaching the final court of appeal?

DECISION AND OPINION

With rare exceptions, only cases decided by the appellate courts are *reported*—that is, published. A reported case consists of two very different elements: (1) the court's decision, or *holding*, and (2) the court's *opinion* in support of its decision. Typically, a court's decision can be stated in a sentence; it amounts to the conclusion of the court's argument. The opinion, however, is more complex and lengthy; as with most arguments, the premises of judicial reasoning and their linkages with each other involve several steps.

To illustrate, in *Texas v. Johnson* (p. 425), the U.S. Supreme Court considered a Texas statute that made it a crime to burn the American flag in political protest. The Court decided that the statute was an unconstitutional interference with freedom of speech. (The decision, as you see, can be stated concisely.)

The Court's opinion, however, runs to several pages. The gist is this: The purpose of the First Amendment (reprinted in the headnote on p. 425) prohibiting abridgment of speech by the government is to protect personal expression, especially where there is a political intention or significance to the speech. Previous decisions of the Court interpreting the amendment have established that the protection of "speech" applies also to nonverbal acts; flag burning in political protest is such an act. Under certain conditions the state may regulate "speech," but in no case may the state prohibit "speech" because of its content or meaning. The Texas statute did not merely regulate the circumstances of "speech"; rather, it regulated the content or meaning of the "speech." Therefore, the statute is unconstitutional.

Thus, in reading the report of a decided case, you will want to be able to answer these two questions:

- What did the court decide?
- What reasons did the court offer to justify its decision?

MAJORITY, CONCURRING, AND DISSENTING OPINIONS

Not all appellate court decisions are unanimous ones. A court's *majority opinion* contains the ruling and reasoning of a majority of its judges. In *Texas v. Johnson*, for example, Justice William Brennan wrote the majority opinion in which four of his colleagues joined. Occasionally one or more of the judges in the majority files a *concurring opinion*; in such cases the judge agrees with the majority's decision but disagrees with its reasoning. Justice John Paul Stevens wrote a concurring opinion in *Johnson*.

In any appellate court decision, at least one judge is likely to dissent from the majority opinion and file a *dissenting opinion* explaining why. (Throughout this book we make the point that intelligent, honorable people may differ on issues of importance.) In the *Johnson* case, four judges dissented but joined in one dissenting opinion. Minority opinions have much to offer for reflection, and in many instances today's dissenting opinion becomes tomorrow's law. The most famous example is Justice John Marshall Harlan's solitary dissent in *Plessy v. Ferguson* (1896), the case that upheld "separate but equal" racial segregation; Harlan's dissent was eventually vindicated by a unanimous vote of the Supreme Court in *Brown v. Board of Education* (1954).

Thus, where there are majority, concurring, and minority opinions, you will want to think about these questions:

- On what issues do the majority and concurring opinions agree?
- On what issues do they disagree?
- Where does the minority in its dissenting opinion(s) disagree with the majority?
- Which opinion is more convincing, the majority or the minority?

FACTS AND LAW

Every court's decision is based on the relevant facts and the relevant law. What the relevant facts are is often in dispute at the trial but not on appeal; appellate court judges rarely reexamine the facts as decided by the trial court. The appellate court, however, usually restates the relevant facts in the opening paragraphs of its opinion. An old joke told among lawyers is appropriate here: "Argue the facts if the facts are on your side, argue the law if the law is on your side; if neither the law nor the facts are on your side, pound the table!"

Unfortunately, a sharp distinction between facts and law cannot always be maintained. For example, if we describe the defendant's conduct as "careless," is that a matter of fact? Or is it in part a matter of law because "careless" conduct may also be judged "negligent" conduct, and the law defines what counts as negligence?

As you read through the reported case, keep in mind these two questions:

- What are the relevant facts in the case, insofar as they can be determined by what the appellate court reported?
- Are there issues of fact omitted or ignored by the appellate court that, had they been addressed, might have shed light on the decision?

For instance, consider a case in which a cattle rancher finds one of her cows dead after it collided with a railroad train. She decides to sue for negligence and wins, and the defendant (the railroad company) appeals. Why did she sue the railroad in the first place, rather than the engineer of the train that killed her cow? Suppose the appellate court's opinion fails to mention whether there was a fence at the edge of the field to keep her cattle off the tracks; wouldn't that be relevant to deciding whether she was partly at fault for the accident? (Ought the railroad to have erected a fence on its property parallel to the track?) Information about such facts could well shed light on the strength and correctness of the court's opinion and decision.

Appellate court judges are almost entirely preoccupied with what they believe is the relevant law to deciding the case at hand. The law can come in any of several different forms: *common law principles* ("No one may enlist the courts to assist him in profiting from his own wrong"), *statutes* enacted by a legislature ("As of January 1, 2004, income taxes shall be levied according to the following formula . . ."), *ordinances* enacted by a town council ("Dogs must be leashed in public places"), a *precedent* found in a prior case decided by some appellate court ("The decision in the case before us is governed by the Supreme Court's earlier holding in . . ."), *executive orders* ("All persons of Japanese extraction currently resident in California shall be removed inland to a relocation center"), *administrative regulations* ("Milk shipped interstate must have a butterfat content not less than . . ."), as well as *constitutional interpretations* ("Statements critical of a public official but not malicious or uttered by one who knows they are false are not libelous and are permitted under the First Amendment"). Not all laws are of equal weight; as *Texas v. Johnson* shows, a state statute inconsistent with the federal Bill of Rights will be nullified, not the other way around.

Appellate court judges devote much of their attention to **interpretation,** trying to decide exactly what the relevant statute, regulation, or prior decision really means and whether it applies to the case before the court. For example, does a local ordinance prohibiting "four-wheeled vehicles" in the park apply to a nanny pushing a baby carriage? The answer often turns on what was the *purpose* of the law or the *intention* of the lawmaker.

It is not easy to decide what the lawmakers' **intention** was; lawmakers are rarely available to state for the courts what their intention was. Can we confidently infer what a legislature's intention was from the legislative history left behind in the form of debates or hearings? From what the relevant committee chairperson says it was? What if (as is typically true) the legislature never declared its intentions when it enacted a law? When a legislature creates a statute, do all those who vote for it act with the same intention? If not, which of the many intentions involved should dominate? How do we find out what those intentions were? What counts as relevant evidence for ascribing this rather than that as someone's intention?

Accordingly, as you read a reported legal case, your study of the court's opinion should lead you to ask these questions:

- Exactly what law or laws is the court trying to interpret?
- What evidence does the court cite in favor of its interpretation?

BALANCING INTERESTS

In U.S. Supreme Court cases, the decision often turns on how competing interests are to be *balanced* or weighed. This pattern of reasoning is especially relevant when one of the conflicting interests is apparently protected by the Constitution. The majority opinion in *New Jersey v. T.L.O.*

(1985) (p. 434) is a good example of such balancing; there, the privacy interests of high school students are weighed (metaphorically speaking, of course—no one can literally "weigh" or "balance" anyone's interests) against the competing interest of school officials responsible for maintaining an orderly environment for teaching. The Court decided that the latter ought to prevail and concluded that "reasonable" searches are not forbidden under the Fourth Amendment's prohibition of "unreasonable searches and seizures."

This leads directly to several other questions you will want to try to answer in the legal cases you study:

- In a constitutional case, what are the conflicting interests?
- How does the Supreme Court propose to balance them?
- Why does it strike the balance one way rather than the other?

A WORD OF CAUTION

Lawyers are both officers of the court and champions for their clients' causes. In the first role they share with judges and other officials the duty to seek justice by honorable means. But in the second role lawyers often see their job as one in which they ought to bend every rule as far as they can in pursuit of their clients' interests (after all, it is the client who pays the bills). This attitude is nicely conveyed in the title of a book, *How to Argue and Win Every Time* (1995), by Gerry Spence, one of the nation's leading trial lawyers. And it is reinforced by a comment from defense attorney Alan Dershowitz: "All sides in a trial want to hide at least some of the truth."

Yet it would be wrong to see lawyers as motivated only by a ruthless desire to win at any cost. Lawyers have a civic duty to present their clients' cases in the most favorable light and to challenge whatever evidence and testimony is offered in court against them. (If you were hiring a lawyer to defend you, would you settle for anything less?) In a society such as ours—a society of law rather than of powerful individuals—it is right that accused persons be found guilty as charged only after the strongest defenses have been mounted.

To be sure, everyone concerned to argue on behalf of any claim, whether in or out of court, whether as a lawyer or in some other capacity, ought to take the challenge seriously. But it is too much to hope to "win every time"—and in fact winning is not the only, much less the highest, goal. Sometimes the other side does have the better argument, and in such cases we should be willing, indeed eager, to see the merits and to enlarge our minds.

In any case, in this book we think of argument not as a weapon for use in mortal combat but as a device for exploring the controversy or dispute under discussion, a tool for isolating the issues in contention and

> ✓ A CHECKLIST FOR ANALYZING LEGAL ARGUMENTS
>
> ☐ Is the court trying to decide whether someone accused of a crime is guilty as charged, or is the court trying to resolve some noncriminal (civil) dispute?
>
> ☐ What events gave rise to the legal controversy in this case?
>
> ☐ What intermediate steps did the case go through before reaching the final court of appeal?
>
> ☐ What did the court decide?
>
> ☐ What reasons did the court offer to justify its decision?
>
> ☐ On what issues do the majority and concurring opinions agree?
>
> ☐ On what issues do they disagree?
>
> ☐ Where does the minority in its dissenting opinion(s) disagree with the majority?
>
> ☐ Which opinion is more convincing, the majority or the minority?
>
> ☐ What are the relevant facts in the case, insofar as they can be determined by what the appellate court reported?
>
> ☐ Are there issues of fact omitted or ignored by the appellate court that, had they been addressed, might have shed light on the decision?
>
> ☐ Exactly what law or laws is the court trying to interpret?
>
> ☐ What evidence does the court cite in favor of its interpretation?
>
> ☐ In constitutional cases, what are the conflicting interests?
>
> ☐ How does the Supreme Court propose to balance them?
>
> ☐ Why does it strike the balance one way rather than the other?

for helping in the evaluation of different possible outcomes. We expect you will use argument to persuade your audience to accept your views, just as a lawyer typically does; but we hope you will use argument sometimes—even often—to clarify your ideas *for yourself;* when you develop arguments for effective presentation to your colleagues and associates, you will probably improve the quality of your ideas.

A CASEBOOK ON THE LAW AND SOCIETY:
What Rights Do the Constitution
and the Bill of Rights Protect?

William J. Brennan Jr. and
William H. Rehnquist

William J. Brennan Jr. (1906–1990), appointed to the U.S. Supreme Court in 1956 by President Dwight D. Eisenhower, established himself as a strong supporter of individual liberties. William H. Rehnquist (1924–2005), appointed in 1971 by President Richard M. Nixon because of his emphasis on law and order, was regarded as one of the most conservative members of the Court.

Texas v. Johnson (1989) concerns the right to burn the American flag in political protest. (Recall that the First Amendment to the Constitution holds that "Congress shall make no law respecting an establishment of religion, or prohibiting the free exercise thereof; or abridging the freedom of speech, or of the press; or the right of the people peaceably to assemble, and to petition the government for a redress of grievances.") The case was decided by a vote of five to four. Immediately after the Court's decision was announced, a resolution was drafted and filed in Congress to condemn the Court's decision. Also filed was the Flag Protection Act of 1989, making it a criminal offense to "knowingly mutilate, deface, burn, or trample upon" the flag. Another bill was designed to amend the Constitution so that criminal penalties for desecration of the flag would not violate the First Amendment. To date, none of these bills has left the congressional committees charged with examining them. In the excerpt that follows, legal citations have been deleted and portions of the text omitted.

Texas v. Johnson

Associate Justice Brennan delivered the opinion of the Court.

After publicly burning an American flag as a means of political protest, Gregory Lee Johnson was convicted of desecrating a flag in violation of Texas law. This case presents the question whether his conviction is consistent with the First Amendment. We hold that it is not.

I

While the Republican National Convention was taking place in Dallas in 1984, respondent Johnson participated in a political demonstration dubbed the "Republican War Chest Tour." As explained in literature distributed by the demonstrators and in speeches made by them, the purpose of this event was to protest the policies of the Reagan administration and of certain Dallas-based corporations. The demonstrators marched through the Dallas streets, chanting political slogans and stopping at several corporate locations to stage "die-ins" intended to dramatize the consequences of nuclear war. On several occasions they spray-painted the walls of buildings and overturned potted plants, but Johnson himself took no part in such activities. He did, however, accept an American flag handed to him by a fellow protestor who had taken it from a flag pole outside one of the targeted buildings.

The demonstration ended in front of Dallas City Hall, where Johnson unfurled the American flag, doused it with kerosene, and set it on fire. While the flag burned, the protestors chanted, "America, the red, white, and blue, we spit on you." After the demonstrators dispersed, a witness to the flag burning collected the flag's remains and buried them in his backyard. No one was physically injured or threatened with injury, though several witnesses testified that they had been seriously offended by the flag burning.

Of the approximately 100 demonstrators, Johnson alone was charged with a crime. The only criminal offense with which he was charged was the desecration of a venerated object in violation of Tex. Penal Code Ann.[1] After a trial, he was convicted, sentenced to one year in prison, and fined $2,000. The Court of Appeals for the Fifth District of Texas at Dallas affirmed Johnson's conviction, but the Texas Court of Criminal Appeals reversed, holding that the state could not, consistent with the First Amendment, punish Johnson for burning the flag in these circumstances. . . .

II

. . . The First Amendment literally forbids the abridgment only of 5 "speech," but we have long recognized that its protection does not end at the spoken or written word. While we have rejected "the view that an apparently limitless variety of conduct can be labeled 'speech' whenever the person engaging in the conduct intends thereby to express an idea," we have acknowledged that conduct may be "sufficiently imbued with the elements of communication to fall within the scope of the First and Fourteenth Amendments." . . .

IV

It remains to consider whether the state's interest in preserving the flag as a symbol of nationhood and national unity justifies Johnson's conviction.

---

[1]Tex. Penal Code Ann. §42.09 (1989) ["Desecration of a Venerated Object"] provides in full:

"(a) A person commits an offense if he intentionally or knowingly desecrates: (1) a public monument; (2) a place of worship or burial; or (3) a state or national flag.

"(b) For purposes of this section, 'desecrate' means deface, damage, or otherwise physically mistreat in a way that the actor knows will seriously offend one or more persons likely to observe or discover his action.

"(c) An offense under this section is a Class A misdemeanor." [Court's note.]

As in *Spence* [*v. Washington*], "we are confronted with a case of prosecution for the expression of an idea through activity," and "accordingly, we must examine with particular care the interests advanced by [petitioner] to support its prosecution." Johnson was not, we add, prosecuted for the expression of just any idea; he was prosecuted for his expression of dissatisfaction with the policies of this country, expression situated at the core of our First Amendment values.

Moreover, Johnson was prosecuted because he knew that his politically charged expression would cause "serious offense." If he had burned the flag as a means of disposing of it because it was dirty or torn, he would not have been convicted of flag desecration under this Texas law: Federal law designates burning as the preferred means of disposing of a flag "when it is in such condition that it is no longer a fitting emblem for display," and Texas has no quarrel with this means of disposal. The Texas law is thus not aimed at protecting the physical integrity of the flag in all circumstances, but is designed instead to protect it only against impairments that would cause serious offense to others. Texas concedes as much: "Section 42.09(b) reaches only those severe acts of physical abuse of the flag carried out in a way likely to be offensive. The statute mandates intentional or knowing abuse, that is, the kind of mistreatment that is not innocent, but rather is intentionally designed to seriously offend other individuals."

Whether Johnson's treatment of the flag violated Texas law thus depended on the likely communicative impact of his expressive conduct. Our decision in *Boos v. Barry* tells us that this restriction on Johnson's expression is content based. In *Boos,* we considered the constitutionality of a law prohibiting "the display of any sign within 500 feet of a foreign embassy if that sign tends to bring that foreign government into 'public odium' or 'public disrepute.'" Rejecting the argument that the law was content neutral because it was justified by "our international law obligation to shield diplomats from speech that offends their dignity," we held that "the emotive impact of speech on its audience is not a 'secondary effect'" unrelated to the content of the expression itself. . . .

Texas argues that its interest in preserving the flag as a symbol of nationhood and national unity survives this close analysis. Quoting extensively from the writings of this Court chronicling the flag's historic and symbolic role in our society, the state emphasizes the "'special place'" reserved for the flag in our nation. The state's argument is not that it has an interest simply in maintaining the flag as a symbol of something, no matter what it symbolizes; indeed, if that were the state's position, it would be difficult to see how that interest is endangered by highly symbolic conduct such as Johnson's. Rather, the state's claim is that it has an interest in preserving the flag as a symbol of *nationhood* and *national unity*, a symbol with a determinate range of meanings. According to Texas, if one physically treats the flag in a way that would tend to cast

10

doubt on either the idea that nationhood and national unity are the flag's referents or that national unity actually exists, the message conveyed thereby is a harmful one and therefore may be prohibited.

If there is a bedrock principle underlying the First Amendment, it is that the government may not prohibit the expression of an idea simply because society finds the idea itself offensive or disagreeable.

We have not recognized an exception to this principle even where our flag has been involved. In *Street v. New York,* we held that a state may not criminally punish a person for uttering words critical of the flag. Rejecting the argument that the conviction could be sustained on the ground that Street had "failed to show the respect for our national symbol which may properly be demanded of every citizen," we concluded that "the constitutionally guaranteed 'freedom to be intellectually . . . diverse or even contrary,' and the 'right to differ as to things that touch the heart of the existing order,' encompass the freedom to express publicly one's opinions about our flag, including those opinions which are defiant or contemptuous." Nor may the government, we have held, compel conduct that would evince respect for the flag. "To sustain the compulsory flag salute we are required to say that a Bill of Rights which guards the individual's right to speak his own mind, left it open to public authorities to compel him to utter what is not in his mind." . . .

Texas's focus on the precise nature of Johnson's expression, moreover, misses the point of our prior decisions: their enduring lesson, that the government may not prohibit expression simply because it disagrees with its message, is not dependent on the particular mode in which one chooses to express an idea. If we were to hold that a state may forbid flag burning wherever it is likely to endanger the flag's symbolic role, but allow it wherever burning a flag promotes that role—as where, for example, a person ceremoniously burns a dirty flag—we would be saying that when it comes to impairing the flag's physical integrity, the flag itself may be used as a symbol—as a substitute for the written or spoken word or a "short cut from mind to mind"—only in one direction. We would be permitting a state to "prescribe what shall be orthodox" by saying that one may burn the flag to convey one's attitude toward it and its referents only if one does not endanger the flag's representation of nationhood and national unity.

We never before have held that the government may ensure that 15 a symbol be used to express only one view of that symbol or its referents. Indeed, in *Schacht v. United States,* we invalidated a federal statute permitting an actor portraying a member of one of our armed forces to "'wear the uniform of that armed force if the portrayal does not tend to discredit that armed force.'" This proviso, we held, "which leaves Americans free to praise the war in Vietnam but can send persons like Schacht to prison for opposing it, cannot survive in a country which has the First Amendment."

We perceive no basis on which to hold that the principle underlying our decision in *Schacht* does not apply to this case. To conclude that the government may permit designated symbols to be used to communicate only a limited set of messages would be to enter territory having no discernible or defensible boundaries. Could the government, on this theory, prohibit the burning of state flags? Of copies of the presidential seal? Of the Constitution? In evaluating these choices under the First Amendment, how would we decide which symbols were sufficiently special to warrant this unique status? To do so, we would be forced to consult our own political preferences, and impose them on the citizenry, in the very way that the First Amendment forbids us to do.

There is, moreover, no indication—either in the text of the Constitution or in our cases interpreting it—that a separate juridical category exists for the American flag alone. Indeed, we would not be surprised to learn that the persons who framed our Constitution and wrote the Amendment that we now construe were not known for their reverence for the Union Jack. The First Amendment does not guarantee that other concepts virtually sacred to our nation as a whole—such as the principle that discrimination on the basis of race is odious and destructive—will go unquestioned in the marketplace of ideas. We decline, therefore, to create for the flag an exception to the joust of principles protected by the First Amendment.

It is not the state's ends, but its means, to which we object. It cannot be gainsaid that there is a special place reserved for the flag in this nation, and thus we do not doubt that the government has a legitimate interest in making efforts to "preserve the national flag as an unalloyed symbol of our country." We reject the suggestion, urged at oral argument by counsel for Johnson, that the government lacks "any state interest whatsoever" in regulating the manner in which the flag may be displayed. Congress has, for example, enacted precatory regulations describing the proper treatment of the flag, and we cast no doubt on the legitimacy of its interest in making such recommendations. To say that the government has an interest in encouraging proper treatment of the flag, however, is not to say that it may criminally punish a person for burning a flag as a means of political protest. "National unity as an end which officials may foster by persuasion and example is not in question. The problem is whether under our Constitution compulsion as here employed is a permissible means for its achievement." . . .

We are tempted to say, in fact, that the flag's deservedly cherished place in our community will be strengthened, not weakened, by our holding today. Our decision is a reaffirmation of the principles of freedom and inclusiveness that the flag best reflects, and of the conviction that our toleration of criticism such as Johnson's is a sign and source of our strength. Indeed, one of the proudest images of our flag, the one immortalized in our own national anthem, is of the bombardment it survived at Fort McHenry. It is the nation's resilience, not its rigidity, that Texas sees reflected in the flag—and it is that resilience that we reassert today.

The way to preserve the flag's special role is not to punish those who 20 feel differently about these matters. It is to persuade them that they are wrong. "To courageous, self-reliant men, with confidence in the power of free and fearless reasoning applied through the processes of popular government, no danger flowing from speech can be deemed clear and present, unless the incidence of the evil apprehended is so imminent that it may befall before there is opportunity for full discussion. If there be time to expose through discussion the falsehood and fallacies, to avert the evil by the processes of education, the remedy to be applied is more speech, not enforced silence." And, precisely because it is our flag that is involved, one's response to the flag burner may exploit the uniquely persuasive power of the flag itself. We can imagine no more appropriate response to burning a flag than waving one's own, no better way to counter a flag burner's message than by saluting the flag that burns, no surer means of preserving the dignity even of the flag that burned than by—as one witness here did—according its remains a respectful burial. We do not consecrate the flag by punishing its desecration, for in doing so we dilute the freedom that this cherished emblem represents. . . .

Chief Justice Rehnquist dissented.

. . . Both Congress and the states have enacted numerous laws regulating misuse of the American flag. Until 1967, Congress left the regulation of misuse of the flag up to the states. Now, however, Title 18 U.S.C. §700(a) provides that:

> Whoever knowingly casts contempt upon any flag of the United States by publicly mutilating, defacing, defiling, burning, or trampling upon it shall be fined not more than $1,000 or imprisoned for not more than one year, or both.

Congress has also prescribed, inter alia, detailed rules for the design of the flag, the time and occasion of flag's display, the position and manner of its display, respect for the flag, and conduct during hoisting, lowering, and passing of the flag. With the exception of Alaska and Wyoming, all of the states now have statutes prohibiting the burning of the flag. Most of the state statutes are patterned after the Uniform Flag Act of 1917, which in §3 provides: "No person shall publicly mutilate, deface, defile, defy, trample upon, or by word or act cast contempt upon any such flag, standard, color, ensign or shield." Most were passed by the states at about the time of World War I. . . .

The American flag, then, throughout more than two hundred years of our history, has come to be the visible symbol embodying our nation. It does not represent the views of any particular political party, and it does not represent any particular political philosophy. The flag is not simply another "idea" or "point of view" competing for recognition in the marketplace of ideas. Millions and millions of Americans regard it with an almost mystical reverence regardless of what sort of social, political, or philosophical beliefs they may have. I cannot agree that the First Amendment invalidates the act of Congress, and the laws of forty-eight of the fifty states, which make criminal the public burning of the flag.

More than eighty years ago in *Halter v. Nebraska*, this Court upheld the constitutionality of a Nebraska statute that forbade the use of representations of the American flag for advertising purposes upon articles of merchandise. The Court there said:

> For that flag every true American has not simply an appreciation but a deep affection. . . . Hence, it has often occurred that insults to a flag have been the cause of war, and indignities put upon it, in the presence of those who revere it, have often been resented and sometimes punished on the spot. . . .

But the Court insists that the Texas statute prohibiting the public burn- 25 ing of the American flag infringes on respondent Johnson's freedom of expression. Such freedom, of course, is not absolute. In *Chaplinsky v. New Hampshire*, a unanimous Court said:

> Allowing the broadest scope to the language and purpose of the Fourteenth Amendment, it is well understood that the right of free speech is not absolute at all times and under all circumstances. There are certain well-defined and narrowly limited classes of speech, the prevention and punishment of which have never been thought to raise any Constitutional problem. These include the lewd and obscene, the profane, the libelous, and the insulting or "fighting" words—those which by their very utterance inflict injury or tend to incite an immediate breach of the peace. It has been well observed that such utterances are no essential part of any exposition of ideas, and are of such slight social value as a step to truth that any benefit that may be derived from them is clearly outweighed by the social interest in order and morality. . . .

The result of the Texas statute is obviously to deny one in Johnson's frame of mind one of many means of "symbolic speech." Far from being a case of "one picture being worth a thousand words," flag burning is the equivalent of an inarticulate grunt or roar that, it seems fair to say, is most likely to be indulged in not to express any particular idea, but to antagonize others. . . . The Texas statute deprived Johnson of only one rather inarticulate symbolic form of protest—a form of protest that was profoundly offensive to many—and left him with a full panoply of other symbols and every conceivable form of verbal expression to express his deep disapproval of national policy. Thus, in no way can it be said that Texas is punishing him because his hearers—or any other group of people—were profoundly opposed to the message that he sought to convey. Such opposition is no proper basis for restricting speech or expression under the First Amendment. It was Johnson's use of this particular symbol, and not the idea that he sought to convey by it or by his many other expressions, for which he was punished.

Our prior cases dealing with flag desecration statutes have left open the question that the Court resolves today. In *Street v. New York*, the defendant burned a flag in the street, shouting "We don't need no damned flag" and, "if they let that happen to Meredith we don't need an American flag." The Court ruled that since the defendant might have been convicted solely on the basis of his words, the conviction could not stand, but it expressly reserved the question whether a defendant could constitutionally be convicted for burning the flag. . . .

In *Spence v. Washington*, the Court reversed the conviction of a college student who displayed the flag with a peace symbol affixed to it by means of removable black tape from the window of his apartment. Unlike the instant case, there was no risk of a breach of the peace, no one other than the arresting officers saw the flag, and the defendant owned the flag in question. The Court concluded that the student's conduct was protected under the First Amendment, because "no interest the state may have in preserving the physical integrity of a privately owned flag was significantly impaired on these facts." The Court was careful to note, however, that the defendant "was not charged under the desecration statute, nor did he permanently disfigure the flag or destroy it."

In another related case, *Smith v. Goguen*, the appellee, who wore a small flag on the seat of his trousers, was convicted under a Massachusetts flag-misuse statute that subjected to criminal liability anyone who "publicly . . . treats contemptuously the flag of the United States." The Court affirmed the lower court's reversal of appellee's conviction, because the phrase "treats contemptuously" was unconstitutionally broad and vague. The Court was again careful to point out that "certainly nothing prevents a legislature from defining with substantial specificity what constitutes forbidden treatment of United States flags." ("The flag is a national property, and the Nation may regulate those who would make, imitate, sell, possess, or use it. I would not question those statutes which proscribe mutilation, defacement, or burning of the flag or which otherwise protect its physical integrity, without regard to whether such conduct might provoke violence. . . . There would seem to be little question about the power of Congress to forbid the mutilation of the Lincoln Memorial. . . . The flag is itself a monument, subject to similar protection"); ("Goguen's punishment was constitutionally permissible for harming the physical integrity of the flag by wearing it affixed to the seat of his pants").

But the Court today will have none of this. The uniquely deep awe 30 and respect for our flag felt by virtually all of us are bundled off under the rubric of "designated symbols" that the First Amendment prohibits the government from "establishing." But the government has not "established" this feeling; two hundred years of history have done that. The government is simply recognizing as a fact the profound regard for the American flag created by that history when it enacts statutes prohibiting the disrespectful public burning of the flag.

The Court concludes its opinion with a regrettably patronizing civics lecture, presumably addressed to the members of both houses of Congress, the members of the forty-eight state legislatures that enacted prohibitions against flag burning, and the troops fighting under that flag in Vietnam who objected to its being burned: "The way to preserve the flag's special role is not to punish those who feel differently about these matters. It is to persuade them that they are wrong." The Court's role as the final expositor of the Constitution is well established, but its role as a platonic guardian admonishing those responsible to public opinion as if they were truant school children has no similar place in our system of government. The cry of "no taxation without representation" animated those who revolted against the English Crown to found our nation—the idea that those who submitted to government should have some say as to what kind of laws would be passed. Surely one of the high purposes of a democratic society is to legislate against conduct that is regarded as evil and profoundly offensive to the majority of people—whether it be murder, embezzlement, pollution, or flag burning.

Our Constitution wisely places limits on powers of legislative majorities to act, but the declaration of such limits by this Court "is, at all times, a question of much delicacy, which ought seldom, if ever, to be decided in the affirmative, in a doubtful case." Uncritical extension of constitutional protection to the burning of the flag risks the frustration of the very purpose for which organized governments are instituted. The Court decides that the American flag is just another symbol, about which not only must opinions pro and con be tolerated, but for which the most minimal public respect may not be enjoined. The government may conscript men into the armed forces where they must fight and perhaps die for the flag, but the government may not prohibit the public burning of the banner under which they fight. I would uphold the Texas statute as applied in this case.

Topics for Critical Thinking and Writing

1. State the facts of this case describing Johnson's illegal conduct and the events in court, beginning with his arrest and culminating in the decision of the Supreme Court.

2. What does Justice Brennan state are the interests in conflict?

3. Why does Brennan describe Johnson's conduct as "highly symbolic" (para. 11)? What would count as less symbolic, or nonsymbolic, conduct having the same purpose as flag burning?

4. Chief Justice Rehnquist suggests (para. 26) that Johnson's flag burning is "equivalent" to "an inarticulate grunt or roar," with the intention "not

to express any particular idea, but to antagonize others." Explain why you agree or disagree with these judgments.

5. Brennan cites the prior cases of *Street v. New York* and *Schacht v. United States* in his favor; Rehnquist cites several cases supporting his dissenting opinion. Which of these precedents (if any) do you find most relevant to the proper outcome of this case, and why?

6. Would it be a desecration of the flag to print the Stars and Stripes on paper towels to be sold for Fourth of July picnics? On toilet paper? Write a 250-word essay on the topic: "Desecration of the Flag: What It Is and What It Isn't."

7. In paragraph 16, Brennan uses a version of the slippery slope argument (see p. 360) in support of striking down the Texas statute. Explain whether you think this argument is effective and relevant.

8. In First Amendment cases, it is often said that the government may not restrict "speech" because of its "content" but may restrict speech in the "time, place, and manner" of expression. What might be plausible restrictions of these sorts on flag burning for political purposes?

Byron R. White and John Paul Stevens

In January 1985, a majority of the U.S. Supreme Court, in a case called New Jersey v. T.L.O. *(a student's initials), ruled six to three that a school official's search of a student who was suspected of disobeying a school regulation does not violate the Fourth Amendment's protection against unreasonable searches and seizures.*

The case originated thus: An assistant principal in a New Jersey high school opened the purse of a fourteen-year-old girl who had been caught violating school rules by smoking in the lavatory. The girl denied that she ever smoked, and the assistant principal thought that the contents of her purse would show whether she was lying. The purse was found to contain cigarettes, marijuana, and some notes that seemed to indicate that she sold marijuana to other students. The school then called the police.

The case went through three lower courts; almost five years after the event occurred, the case reached the Supreme Court. Associate Justice Byron R. White wrote the majority opinion, joined by Chief Justice Warren E. Burger and by Associate Justices Lewis F. Powell Jr., William H. Rehnquist, and Sandra Day O'Connor. Associate Justice Harry A. Blackmun concurred in a separate opinion. Associate Justices William J. Brennan Jr., John Paul Stevens, and Thurgood Marshall dissented in part. In the excerpt that follows, legal citations have been omitted.

New Jersey v. T.L.O.

Justice White delivered the opinion of the Court.

In determining whether the search at issue in this case violated the Fourth Amendment, we are faced initially with the question whether that amendment's prohibition on unreasonable searches and seizures applies to searches conducted by public school officials. We hold that it does.

It is now beyond dispute that "the Federal Constitution, by virtue of the Fourteenth Amendment, prohibits unreasonable searches and seizures by state officers." Equally indisputable is the proposition that the Fourteenth Amendment protects the rights of students against encroachment by public school officials.

On reargument, however, the State of New Jersey has argued that the history of the Fourth Amendment indicates that the amendment was intended to regulate only searches and seizures carried out by law enforcement officers; accordingly, although public school officials are concededly state agents for purposes of the Fourteenth Amendment, the Fourth Amendment creates no rights enforceable against them.

But this Court has never limited the amendment's prohibition on 5 unreasonable searches and seizures to operations conducted by the police. Rather, the Court has long spoken of the Fourth Amendment's strictures as restraints imposed upon "governmental action" — that is, "upon the activities of sovereign authority." Accordingly, we have held the Fourth Amendment applicable to the activities of civil as well as criminal authorities: building inspectors, OSHA inspectors, and even firemen entering privately owned premises to battle a fire, are all subject to the restraints imposed by the Fourth Amendment.

Notwithstanding the general applicability of the Fourth Amendment to the activities of civil authorities, a few courts have concluded that school officials are exempt from the dictates of the Fourth Amendment by virtue of the special nature of their authority over schoolchildren. Teachers and school administrators, it is said, act *in loco parentis* [that is, in place of a parent] in their dealings with students: Their authority is that of the parent, not the state, and is therefore not subject to the limits of the Fourth Amendment.

Such reasoning is in tension with contemporary reality and the teachings of this Court. We have held school officials subject to the commands of the First Amendment, and the Due Process Clause of the Fourteenth Amendment. If school authorities are state actors for purposes of the constitutional guarantees of freedom of expression and due process, it is difficult to understand why they should be deemed to be exercising parental rather than public authority when conducting searches of their students.

In carrying out searches and other disciplinary functions pursuant to such policies, school officials act as representatives of the state, not merely as surrogates for the parents, and they cannot claim the parents' immunity from the strictures of the Fourth Amendment.

To hold that the Fourth Amendment applies to searches conducted by school authorities is only to begin the inquiry into the standards governing such searches. Although the underlying command of the Fourth Amendment is always that searches and seizures be reasonable, what is reasonable depends on the context within which a search takes place.

[STANDARD OF REASONABLENESS]

The determination of the standard of reasonableness governing any   10
specific class of searches requires balancing the need to search against
the invasion which the search entails. On one side of the balance are
arrayed the individual's legitimate expectations of privacy and personal
security; on the other, the government's need for effective methods to
deal with breaches of public order.

We have recognized that even a limited search of the person is a substantial invasion of privacy. A search of a child's person or of a closed
purse or other bag carried on her person, no less than a similar search
carried out on an adult, is undoubtedly a severe violation of subjective
expectations of privacy.

Of course, the Fourth Amendment does not protect subjective expectations of privacy that are unreasonable or otherwise "illegitimate."
The State of New Jersey has argued that because of the pervasive supervision to which children in the schools are necessarily subject, a child
has virtually no legitimate expectation of privacy in articles of personal
property "unnecessarily" carried into a school. This argument has two
factual premises: (1) the fundamental incompatibility of expectations of
privacy with the maintenance of a sound educational environment; and
(2) the minimal interest of the child in bringing any items of personal
property into the school. Both premises are severely flawed.

Although this Court may take notice of the difficulty of maintaining
discipline in the public schools today, the situation is not so dire that students in the schools may claim no legitimate expectations of privacy.

[PRIVACY AND DISCIPLINE]

Against the child's interest in privacy must be set the substantial interest of teachers and administrators in maintaining discipline in the
classroom and on school grounds. Maintaining order in the classroom
has never been easy, but in recent years, school disorder has often taken
particularly ugly forms; drug use and violent crime in the schools have
become major social problems. Accordingly, we have recognized that
maintaining security and order in the schools requires a certain degree of
flexibility in school disciplinary procedures, and we have respected the
value of preserving the informality of the student-teacher relationship.

How, then, should we strike the balance between the schoolchild's   15
legitimate expectations of privacy and the school's equally legitimate
need to maintain an environment in which learning can take place? It is
evident that the school setting requires some easing of the restrictions to
which searches by public authorities are ordinarily subject. The warrant
requirement, in particular, is unsuited to the school environment; requiring a teacher to obtain a warrant before searching a child suspected
of an infraction of school rules (or of the criminal law) would unduly in-

terfere with the maintenance of the swift and informal disciplinary procedures needed in the schools. We hold today that school officials need not obtain a warrant before searching a student who is under their authority.

The school setting also requires some modification of the level of suspicion of illicit activity needed to justify a search. Ordinarily, a search—even one that may permissibly be carried out without a warrant—must be based upon "probable cause" to believe that a violation of the law has occurred. However, "probable cause" is not an irreducible requirement of a valid search.

[BALANCING OF INTERESTS]

The fundamental command of the Fourth Amendment is that searches and seizures be reasonable, and although "both the concept of probable cause and the requirement of a warrant bear on the reasonableness of a search, . . . in certain limited circumstances neither is required." Thus, we have in a number of cases recognized the legality of searches and seizures based on suspicions that, although "reasonable," do not rise to the level of probable cause. Where a careful balancing of governmental and private interests suggests that the public interest is best served by a Fourth Amendment standard of reasonableness that stops short of probable cause, we have not hesitated to adopt such a standard.

We join the majority of courts that have examined this issue in concluding that the accommodation of the privacy interests of schoolchildren with the substantial need of teachers and administrators for freedom to maintain order in the schools does not require strict adherence to the requirement that searches be based on probable cause to believe that the subject of the search has violated or is violating the law.

Rather, the legality of a search of a student should depend simply on the reasonableness, under all the circumstances, of the search. Determining the reasonableness of any search involves a twofold inquiry; first, one must consider "whether the . . . action was justified at its inception," second, one must determine whether the search as actually conducted "was reasonably related in scope to the circumstances which justified the interference in the first place."

Under ordinary circumstances, a search of a student by a teacher or 20 other school official will be "justified at its inception" when there are reasonable grounds for suspecting that the search will turn up evidence that the student has violated or is violating either the law or the rules of the school. Such a search will be permissible in its scope when the measures adopted are reasonably related to the objectives of the search and not excessively intrusive in light of the age and sex of the student and the nature of the infraction.

This standard will, we trust, neither unduly burden the efforts of school authorities to maintain order in their schools nor authorize unrestrained intrusions upon the privacy of schoolchildren. By focusing attention on the question of reasonableness, the standard will spare teachers and school administrators the necessity of schooling themselves in the niceties of probable cause and permit them to regulate their conduct according to the dictates of reason and common sense. At the same time, the reasonableness standard should insure that the interests of students will be invaded no more than is necessary to achieve the legitimate end of preserving order in the schools.

There remains the question of the legality of the search in this case. We recognize that the "reasonable grounds" standard applied by the New Jersey Supreme Court in its consideration of this question is not substantially different from the standard that we have adopted today. Nonetheless, we believe that the New Jersey court's application of that standard to strike down the search of T.L.O.'s purse reflects a somewhat crabbed notion of reasonableness. Our review of the facts surrounding the search leads us to conclude that the search was in no sense unreasonable for Fourth Amendment purposes.

Justice Stevens, dissenting.

The majority holds that "a search of a student by a teacher or other school official will be 'justified at its inception' when there are reasonable grounds for suspecting that the search will turn up evidence *that the student has violated or is violating either the law or the rules of the school."*

This standard will permit teachers and school administrators to search   25 students when they suspect that the search will reveal evidence of [violation of] even the most trivial school regulation or precatory guideline for students' behavior. For the Court, a search for curlers and sunglasses in order to enforce the school dress code is apparently just as important as a search for evidence of heroin addiction or violent gang activity.

A standard better attuned to this concern would permit teachers and school administrators to search a student when they have reason to believe that the search will uncover *evidence that the student is violating the law or engaging in conduct that is seriously disruptive of school order, or the educational process.*

A standard that varies the extent of the permissible intrusion with the gravity of the suspected offense is also more consistent with common-law experience and this Court's precedent. Criminal law has traditionally recognized a distinction between essentially regulatory offenses and serious violations of the peace, and graduated the response of the criminal justice system depending on the character of the violation.

Topics for Critical Thinking and Writing

1. In the majority opinion Justice White says that "it is evident that the school setting requires some easing of the restrictions to which searches

by public authorities are ordinarily subject" (para. 15). Does White offer evidence supporting what he says is "evident"? List any evidence that White gives or any that you can think of.

2. What argument does White give to show that the Fourth Amendment prohibition against "unreasonable searches and seizures" (para. 3) applies to the behavior of school officials? Do you think his argument is reasonable? Explain.

3. On what ground does White argue that school students have "legitimate expectations of privacy" (para. 15) and so New Jersey is wrong in arguing the contrary?

4. What are the conflicting interests involved in the case, according to White? How does the Supreme Court resolve this conflict?

5. Why does White argue (para. 16) that school authorities may search students without first obtaining a search warrant? (By the way, who issues a search warrant? Who seeks one?) What does he mean when he says that the requirement of "probable cause" is "not an irreducible requirement of a valid search" (para. 16)?

6. Could a search undertaken on the principle enunciated by the Court's majority mean that whenever authorities perceive what they choose to call "disorder"—perhaps in the activity of an assembly of protesters in the streets of a big city—they may justify otherwise unlawful searches and seizures?

7. Some forty years before this case, Justice Robert H. Jackson argued that the schools have a special responsibility for adhering to the Constitution: "That they are educating the young for citizenship is reason for scrupulous protection of constitutional freedoms of the individual, if we are not to strangle the free mind at its source and teach youth to discount important principles of our government as mere platitudes." Similarly, in 1967 in an analogous case involving another female pupil, Justice Brennan argued that "schools cannot expect their students to learn the lessons of good citizenship when the school authorities themselves disregard the fundamental principles underpinning our constitutional freedoms." Do you find these arguments compelling? Why, or why not?

8. Let's admit that maintaining order in schools may be extremely difficult. In your opinion, does the difficulty justify diminishing the rights of citizens? Smoking is not an illegal activity, yet in this instance a student suspected of smoking—that is, merely of violating a school rule—was searched. In an essay of 250 words, consider whether the maintenance of school discipline in such a matter justifies a search.

9. White relies on a standard of "reasonableness." Do you think this criterion is too subjective to be a proper standard to distinguish between permissible and impermissible searches? Write a 500-word essay on the standard of reasonable searches and seizures, giving a hypothetical but plausible example of a reasonable search and seizure and then of an unreasonable search and seizure.

Harry Blackmun and William H. Rehnquist

The first important case in which the U.S. Supreme Court decided a controversy by appeal to our "right of privacy" was in 1965 in Griswold v. Connecticut. *Plaintiffs argued that the state statute forbidding the sale of birth control devices, as well as birth control information from a licensed physician, was an unconstitutional invasion of privacy. The Court ruled in their favor, a controversial ruling because there is no explicit "right of privacy" in the Bill of Rights or elsewhere in the Constitution. The seven Justices in the majority divided over the best way to locate this right in the interstices of prior rulings, and they invoked the "penumbra" of recognized constitutional provisions as the locus of this protection.*

The storm aroused by the Court's ruling in Griswold *was as nothing compared to the raging protest eight years later caused by the Court's ruling (again, by a vote of seven to two) supporting a woman's right to choose whether to carry her pregnancy to completion or, instead, to arrange to terminate her pregnancy by abortion under the direction of a licensed physician. In 1973, when* Roe v. Wade *was decided, abortion (except in special cases) was illegal in most states in the nation; the decision in* Roe *effectively nullified all such statutes. Justice Harry Blackmun, who wrote the opinion for the Court majority, proposed dividing pregnancy into three trimesters of equal length. During the first trimester, a woman's right to have an abortion was virtually absolute; not so in the second and third trimesters.*

The decision provoked a sharp and deep division between those who embraced it because it recognized a woman's autonomy and the finality of her choice and those who deplored the decision as a violation of the unborn's right to life. The struggle between "right-to-life" advocates (who would, typically, limit abortion to those rare cases where it is medically necessary to save the life of the mother) and the advocates of a "right to choose" (who favor leaving all questions of pregnancy and its termination to the decision of the pregnant woman) rages unabated. Now, more than three decades later, it can be said that Roe v. Wade *ranks as the most controversial decision by the Supreme Court in the past century. While it is not likely to be overturned in any future ruling by the Court, influential political forces are manifestly at work to limit its scope. Many observers have noted that, were* Roe v. Wade *up for decision today before a more conservative Supreme Court, it would be decided differently.*

Roe v. Wade

Mr. Justice Blackmun delivered the opinion of the Court. . . .

We forthwith acknowledge our awareness of the sensitive and emotional nature of the abortion controversy, of the vigorous opposing views, even among physicians, and of the deep and seemingly absolute convictions that the subject inspires. One's philosophy, one's experiences, one's exposure to the raw edges of human existence, one's religious training, one's attitudes toward life and family and their values, and the moral standards one establishes and seeks to observe, are all likely to influence and to color one's thinking and conclusions about abortion.

In addition, population growth, pollution, poverty, and racial overtones tend to complicate and not to simplify the problem.

Our task, of course, is to resolve the issue by constitutional measurement, free of emotion and of predilection. We seek earnestly to do this, and, because we do, we have inquired into, and in this opinion place some emphasis upon, medical and medical-legal history and what that history reveals about man's attitudes toward the abortion procedure over the centuries. . . .

The Texas statutes that concern us here are Articles 1191–1194 and 5 1196 of the State's Penal Code. These make it a crime to "procure an abortion," as therein defined, or to attempt one, except with respect to "an abortion procured or attempted by medical advice for the purpose of saving the life of the mother." Similar statutes are in existence in a majority of the states. . . .

The principal thrust of appellant's attack on the Texas statutes is that they improperly invade a right, said to be possessed by the pregnant woman, to choose to terminate her pregnancy. Appellant would discover this right in the concept of personal "liberty" embodied in the Fourteenth Amendment's Due Process Clause; or in personal, marital, familial, and sexual privacy said to be protected by the Bill of Rights or its penumbras, see *Griswold v. Connecticut*, 381 U.S. 479 (1965); *Eisenstadt v. Baird*, 405 U.S. 438 (1972); id., at 460 (White, J., concurring in result); or among those rights reserved to the people by the Ninth Amendment, *Griswold v. Connecticut*, 381 U.S., at 486 (Goldberg, J., concurring). Before addressing this claim, we feel it desirable briefly to survey, in several aspects, the history of abortion, for such insight as that history may afford us, and then to examine the state purposes and interests behind the criminal abortion laws.

It perhaps is not generally appreciated that the restrictive criminal abortion laws in effect in a majority of states today are of relatively recent vintage. Those laws, generally proscribing abortion or its attempt at any time during pregnancy except when necessary to preserve the pregnant woman's life, are not of ancient or even of common-law origin. Instead, they derive from statutory changes effected, for the most part, in the latter half of the nineteenth century. . . .

THE AMERICAN LAW

In this country, the law in effect in all but a few states until midnineteenth century was the pre-existing English common law. Connecticut, the first state to enact abortion legislation, adopted in 1821 that part of Lord Ellenborough's Act [in England] that related to a woman "quick with child." The death penalty was not imposed. Abortion before quickening was made a crime in that state only in 1860. In 1828, New York enacted legislation that, in two respects, was to serve as a model for early anti-abortion statutes. First, while barring destruction of an unquickened fetus as well as a quick fetus, it made the former only a misdemeanor, but the latter second-degree manslaughter. Second, it incorporated a concept of therapeutic abortion by providing that an abortion was excused if it "shall have been necessary to preserve the life of such mother, or shall have been advised by two physicians to be necessary for such purpose." By 1840, when Texas had received the common law, only eight American states had statutes dealing with abortion. It was not until after the War Between the States that legislation began generally to replace the common law. Most of these initial statutes dealt severely with abortion after quickening but were lenient with it before quickening. Most punished attempts equally with completed abortions. While many statutes included the exception for an abortion thought by one or more physicians to be necessary to save the mother's life, that provision soon disappeared and the typical law required that the procedure actually be necessary for that purpose.

Gradually, in the middle and late nineteenth century the quickening distinction disappeared from the statutory law of most states and the degree of the offense and the penalties were increased. By the end of the 1950s, a large majority of the jurisdictions banned abortion, however and whenever performed, unless done to save or preserve the life of the mother. The exceptions, Alabama and the District of Columbia, permitted abortion to preserve the mother's health. Three states permitted abortions that were not "unlawfully" performed or that were not "without lawful justification," leaving interpretation of those standards to the courts. In the past several years, however, a trend toward liberalization of abortion statutes has resulted in adoption, by about one-third of the states, of less stringent laws, most of them patterned after the ALI Model Penal Code, §230.3. . . .

It is thus apparent that at common law, at the time of the adoption 10 of our Constitution, and throughout the major portion of the nineteenth century, abortion was viewed with less disfavor than under most American statutes currently in effect. Phrasing it another way, a woman enjoyed a substantially broader right to terminate a pregnancy than she does in most states today. At least with respect to the early stage of pregnancy, and very possibly without such a limitation, the opportunity to make this choice was present in this country well into the nineteenth century. Even later, the law continued for some time to treat less punitively an abortion procured in early pregnancy.

THE POSITION OF THE AMERICAN MEDICAL ASSOCIATION

The anti-abortion mood prevalent in this country in the late nineteenth century was shared by the medical profession. Indeed, the attitude of the profession may have played a significant role in the enactment of stringent criminal abortion legislation during that period. . . .

In 1970, after the introduction of a variety of proposed resolutions, and of a report from its Board of Trustees, a reference committee noted "polarization of the medical profession on this controversial issue"; division among those who had testified; a difference of opinion among AMA councils and committees; "the remarkable shift in testimony" in six months, felt to be influenced "by the rapid changes in state laws and by the judicial decisions which tend to make abortion more freely available;" and a feeling "that this trend will continue." On June 25, 1970, the House of Delegates adopted preambles and most of the resolutions proposed by the reference committee. The preambles emphasized "the best interests of the patient," "sound clinical judgment," and "informed patient consent," in contrast to "mere acquiescence to the patient's demand." The resolutions asserted that abortion is a medical procedure that should be performed by a licensed physician in an accredited hospital only after consultation with two other physicians and in conformity with state law, and that no party to the procedure should be required to violate personally held moral principles. Proceedings of the AMA House of Delegates 200 (June 1970). The AMA Judicial Council rendered a complementary opinion.

THE POSITION OF THE AMERICAN PUBLIC HEALTH ASSOCIATION

In October 1970, the Executive Board of the APHA adopted Standards for Abortion Services. These were five in number:

a. Rapid and simple abortion referral must be readily available through state and local public health departments, medical societies, or other nonprofit organizations.
b. An important function of counseling should be to simplify and expedite the provision of abortion services; it should not delay the obtaining of these services.
c. Psychiatric consultation should not be mandatory. As in the case of other specialized medical services, psychiatric consultation should be sought for definite indications and not on a routine basis.
d. A wide range of individuals from appropriately trained, sympathetic volunteers to highly skilled physicians may qualify as abortion counselors.
e. Contraception and/or sterilization should be discussed with each abortion patient.

Among factors pertinent to life and health risks associated with abortion were three that "are recognized as important":

a. the skill of the physician,
b. the environment in which the abortion is performed, and above all
c. the duration of pregnancy, as determined by uterine size and confirmed by menstrual history.

It was said that "a well-equipped hospital" offers more protection "to cope with unforeseen difficulties than an office or clinic without such resources. . . . The factor of gestational age is of overriding importance."

Thus, it was recommended that abortions in the second trimester and early abortions in the presence of existing medical complications be performed in hospitals as inpatient procedures. For pregnancies in the first trimester, abortion in the hospital with or without overnight stay "is probably the safest practice." An abortion in an extramural facility, however, is an acceptable alternative "provided arrangements exist in advance to admit patients promptly if unforeseen complications develop." Standards for an abortion facility were listed. It was said that at present abortions should be performed by physicians or osteopaths who are licensed to practice and who have "adequate training."

THE POSITION OF THE AMERICAN BAR ASSOCIATION

At its meeting in February 1972 the ABA House of Delegates approved, with 17 opposing votes, the Uniform Abortion Act that had been drafted and approved the preceding August by the Conference of Commissioners on Uniform State Laws (1972). . . .   15

Three reasons have been advanced to explain historically the enactment of criminal abortion laws in the nineteenth century and to justify their continued existence.

It has been argued occasionally that these laws were the product of a Victorian social concern to discourage illicit sexual conduct. Texas, however, does not advance this justification in the present case, and it appears that no court or commentator has taken the argument seriously. The appellants and *amici* [friends of the court] contend, moreover, that this is not a proper state purpose at all and suggest that, if it were, the Texas statutes are overbroad in protecting it since the law fails to distinguish between married and unwed mothers.

A second reason is concerned with abortion as a medical procedure. When most criminal abortion laws were first enacted, the procedure was a hazardous one for the woman. This was particularly true prior to the development of antisepsis. Antiseptic techniques, of course, were based on discoveries by Lister, Pasteur, and others first announced in 1867, but were not generally accepted and employed until about the turn of the century. Abortion mortality was high. Even after 1900, and perhaps until as late as the development of antibiotics in the 1940s, standard modern techniques such as dilation and curettage were not nearly so safe as they are today. Thus, it has been argued that a state's real concern in enacting a criminal abortion law was to protect the pregnant woman, that is, to restrain her from submitting to a procedure that placed her life in serious jeopardy.

Modern medical techniques have altered this situation. Appellants and various *amici* refer to medical data indicating that abortion in early pregnancy, that is, prior to the end of the first trimester, although not without its risk, is now relatively safe. Mortality rates for women undergoing early abortions, where the procedure is legal, appear to be as low as or lower than the rates for normal childbirth. Consequently, any interest of the state in protecting the woman from an inherently hazardous procedure, except when it would be equally dangerous for her to forgo it, has largely disappeared. Of course, important state interests in the areas of health and medical standards do remain. . . . The prevalence of high mortality rates at illegal "abortion mills" strengthens, rather than weakens, the state's interest in regulating the conditions under which abortions are performed. Moreover, the risk to the woman increases as her pregnancy continues. Thus, the state retains a definite interest in protecting the woman's own health and safety when an abortion is proposed at a late stage of pregnancy.

The third reason is the state's interest—some phrase it in terms of duty—in protecting prenatal life. Some of the argument for this justification rests on the theory that a new human life is present from the moment of conception. The state's interest and general obligation to protect life then extends, it is argued, to prenatal life. Only when the life of the pregnant mother herself is at stake, balanced against the life she carries within her, should the interest of the embryo or fetus not prevail. Logically, of course, a legitimate state interest in this area need not stand or fall on acceptance of the belief that life begins at conception or at some other point prior to live birth. In assessing the state's interest, recognition may be given to the less rigid claim that as long as at least *potential* life is involved, the state may assert interests beyond the protection of the pregnant woman alone. . . .

The Constitution does not explicitly mention any right of privacy. In a line of decisions, however, going back perhaps as far as *Union Pacific R. Co. v. Botsford*, 141 U.S. 250, 251 (1891), the Court has recognized that a right of personal privacy, or a guarantee of certain areas or zones of privacy, does exist under the Constitution. In varying contexts, the Court or individual Justices have, indeed, found at least the roots of that right in the First Amendment, in the Fourth and Fifth Amendments, in the Ninth Amendment, or in the concept of liberty guaranteed by the first section of the Fourteenth Amendment. These decisions make it clear that only personal rights that can be deemed "fundamental" or "implicit in the concept of ordered liberty" are included in this guarantee of personal privacy. They also make it clear that the right has some extension to activities relating to marriage, procreation, contraception, family relationships, and child rearing and education.

This right of privacy, whether it be founded in the Fourteenth Amendment's concept of personal liberty and restrictions upon state action, as we feel it is, or, as the District Court determined, in the Ninth Amendment's reservation of rights to the people, is broad enough to encompass a woman's decision whether or not to terminate her pregnancy. The detriment that the state would impose upon the pregnant woman by denying this choice altogether is apparent. Specific and direct harm medically diagnosable even in early pregnancy may be involved. Maternity, or additional offspring, may force upon the woman a distressful life and future. Psychological harm may be imminent. Mental and physical health may be taxed by child care. There is also the distress, for all concerned, associated with the unwanted child, and there is the problem of bringing a child into a family already unable, psychologically and otherwise, to care for it. In other cases, as in this one, the additional difficulties and continuing stigma of unwed motherhood may be involved. All these are factors the woman and her responsible physician necessarily will consider in consultation.

On the basis of elements such as these, appellant and some *amici* argue that the woman's right is absolute and that she is entitled to terminate her pregnancy at whatever time, in whatever way, and for whatever reason she alone chooses. With this we do not agree. Appellant's arguments that Texas either has no valid interest at all in regulating the abortion decision, or no interest strong enough to support any limitation upon the woman's sole determination, are unpersuasive. The Court's decisions recognizing a right of privacy also acknowledge that some state regulation in areas protected by that right is appropriate. As noted above, a state may properly assert important interests in safeguarding health, in maintaining medical standards, and in protecting potential life. At some point in pregnancy, these respective interests become sufficiently compelling to sustain regulation of the factors that govern the abortion decision. The privacy right involved, therefore, cannot be said to be absolute. In fact, it is not clear to us that the claim asserted by some *amici* that one has an unlimited right to do with one's body as one pleases bears a close relationship to the right of privacy previously articulated in the Court's decisions. . . .

We, therefore, conclude that the right of personal privacy includes the abortion decision, but that this right is not unqualified and must be considered against important state interests in regulation.

Where certain "fundamental rights" are involved, the Court has held 25 that regulation limiting these rights may be justified only by a "compelling state interest" . . . and that legislative enactments must be narrowly drawn to express only the legitimate state interests at stake. . . .

In the recent abortion cases, cited above, courts have recognized these principles. Those striking down state laws have generally scrutinized the state's interests in protecting health and potential life, and have concluded that neither interest justified broad limitations on the reasons for which a physician and his pregnant patient might decide that she should have an abortion in the early stages of pregnancy. Courts sustaining state laws have held that the state's determinations to protect health or prenatal life are dominant and constitutionally justifiable.

A

The appellee and certain *amici* argue that the fetus is a "person" within the language and meaning of the Fourteenth Amendment. In support of this, they outline at length and in detail the well-known facts of fetal development. If this suggestion of personhood is established, the appellant's case, of course, collapses, for the fetus' right to life would then be guaranteed specifically by the Amendment. The appellant conceded as much on reargument. On the other hand, the appellee conceded on reargument that no case could be cited that holds that a fetus is a person within the meaning of the Fourteenth Amendment.

The Constitution does not define "person" in so many words. Section 1 of the Fourteenth Amendment contains three references to "person." The first, in defining "citizens," speaks of "persons born or naturalized in the United States." The word also appears both in the Due Process Clause and in the Equal Protection Clause. "Person" is used in other places in the Constitution. . . . But in nearly all these instances, the use of the word is such that it has application only postnatally. None indicates, with any assurance, that it has any possible prenatal application.

This conclusion, however, does not of itself fully answer the contentions raised by Texas, and we pass on to other considerations.

B

The pregnant woman cannot be isolated in her privacy. She carries 30 an embryo and, later, a fetus, if one accepts the medical definitions of the developing young in the human uterus. The situation therefore is inherently different from marital intimacy, or bedroom possession of obscene material, or marriage, or procreation, or education, with which [several decided cases] were respectively concerned. As we have intimated above, it is reasonable and appropriate for a state to decide that at some point in time another interest, that of health of the mother or that of potential human life, becomes significantly involved. The woman's privacy is no longer sole and any right of privacy she possesses must be measured accordingly.

Texas urges that, apart from the Fourteenth Amendment, life begins at conception and is present throughout pregnancy, and that, therefore, the state has a compelling interest in protecting that life from and after conception. We need not resolve the difficult question of when life begins. When those trained in the respective disciplines of medicine, philosophy, and theology are unable to arrive at any consensus, the judiciary, at this point in the development of man's knowledge, is not in a position to speculate as to the answer. . . .

In areas other than criminal abortion, the law has been reluctant to endorse any theory that life, as we recognize it, begins before live birth or to accord legal rights to the unborn except in narrowly defined situations and except when the rights are contingent upon live birth. For example, the traditional rule of tort law denied recovery for prenatal injuries even though the child was born alive. That rule has been changed in almost every jurisdiction. In most states, recovery is said to be permitted only if the fetus was viable, or at least quick, when the injuries were sustained, though few courts have squarely so held. In a recent development, generally opposed by the commentators, some states permit the parents of a stillborn child to maintain an action for wrongful death because of prenatal injuries. Such an action, however, would appear to be one to vindicate the parents' interest and is thus consistent with the view that the fetus, at most, represents only the potentiality of life. Similarly, unborn children have been recognized as acquiring rights or interests by way of inheritance or other devolution of property, and have been represented by guardians *ad litem* [for the purpose of this lawsuit]. Perfection of the interests involved, again, has generally been contingent upon live birth. In short, the unborn have never been recognized in the law as persons in the whole sense.

To summarize and to repeat:

1. A state criminal abortion statute of the current Texas type, that excepts from criminality only a *lifesaving* procedure on behalf of the mother, without regard to pregnancy stage and without recognition of the other interests involved, is violative of the Due Process Clause of the Fourteenth Amendment.

   (a) For the stage prior to approximately the end of the first trimester, the abortion decision and its effectuation must be left to the medical judgment of the pregnant woman's attending physician.

   (b) For the stage subsequent to approximately the end of the first trimester, the state, in promoting its interest in the health of the mother, may, if it chooses, regulate the abortion procedure in ways that are reasonably related to maternal health.

   (c) For the stage subsequent to viability, the state in promoting its interest in the potentiality of human life may, if it chooses, regulate, and even proscribe, abortion except where it is necessary, in appropriate medical judgment, for the preservation of the life or health of the mother.

2. The state may define the term "physician," as it has been employed in the preceding paragraphs of this . . . opinion, to mean only a physician currently licensed by the state, and may proscribe any abortion by a person who is not a physician as so defined. . . .

This holding, we feel, is consistent with the relative weights of the respective interests involved, with the lessons and examples of medical and legal history, with the lenity of the common law, and with the demands of the profound problems of the present day. The decision leaves the state free to place increasing restrictions on abortion as the period of pregnancy lengthens, so long as those restrictions are tailored to the recognized state interests. The decision vindicates the right of the physician to administer medical treatment according to his professional judgment up to the points where important state interests provide compelling justifications for intervention. Up to those points, the abortion decision in all its aspects is inherently, and primarily, a medical decision, and basic responsibility for it must rest with the physician. If an individual practitioner abuses the privilege of exercising proper medical judgment, the usual remedies, judicial and intra-professional, are available.

Our conclusion that Article 1196 is unconstitutional means, of course, that the Texas abortion statutes, as a unit, must fall. . . .

Mr. Justice Rehnquist, dissenting.

The Court's opinion brings to the decision of this troubling question 35 both extensive historical fact and a wealth of legal scholarship. While the opinion thus commands my respect, I find myself nonetheless in fundamental disagreement with those parts of it that invalidate the Texas statute in question, and therefore dissent.

I

The Court's opinion decides that a state may impose virtually no restriction on the performance of abortions during the first trimester of pregnancy. Our previous decisions indicate that a necessary predicate for such an opinion is a plaintiff who was in her first trimester of pregnancy at some time during the pendency of her lawsuit. While a party may vindicate his own constitutional rights, he may not seek vindication for the rights of others. . . . The Court's statement of facts in this case makes clear, however, that the record in no way indicates the presence of such a plaintiff. We know only that plaintiff Roe at the time of filing her complaint was a pregnant woman; for aught that appears in this record, she may have been in her *last* trimester of pregnancy as of the date the complaint was filed.

Nothing in the Court's opinion indicates that Texas might not constitutionally apply its proscription of abortion as written to a woman in that stage of pregnancy. Nonetheless, the Court uses her complaint against the Texas statute as a fulcrum for deciding that states may impose virtually no restrictions on medical abortions performed during the *first* trimester of pregnancy. In deciding such a hypothetical lawsuit, the Court departs from the longstanding admonition that it should never "formulate a rule of constitutional law broader than is required by the precise facts to which it is to be applied."

II

Even if there were a plaintiff in this case capable of litigating the 40 issue which the Court decides, I would reach a conclusion opposite to that reached by the Court. I have difficulty in concluding, as the Court does, that the right of "privacy" is involved in this case. Texas, by the statute here challenged, bars the performance of a medical abortion by a licensed physician on a plaintiff such as Roe. A transaction resulting in an operation such as this is not "private" in the ordinary usage of that word. Nor is the "privacy" that the Court finds here even a distant relative of the freedom from searches and seizures protected by the Fourth Amendment to the Constitution, which the Court has referred to as embodying a right to privacy.

If the Court means by the term "privacy" no more than that the claim of a person to be free from unwanted state regulation of consensual transactions may be a form of "liberty" protected by the Fourteenth Amendment, there is no doubt that similar claims have been upheld in our earlier decisions on the basis of that liberty. I agree with the statement of Mr. Justice Stewart in his concurring opinion[1] that the "liberty," against deprivation of which without due process the Fourteenth Amendment protects, embraces more than the rights found in the Bill of Rights. But that liberty is not guaranteed absolutely against deprivation, only against deprivation without due process of law. The test traditionally applied in the area of social and economic legislation is whether or not a law such as that challenged has a rational relation to a valid state objective. . . . The Due Process Clause of the Fourteenth Amendment undoubtedly does place a limit, albeit a broad one, on legislative power to enact laws such as this. If the Texas statute were to prohibit an abortion even where the mother's life is in jeopardy, I have little doubt that such a statute would lack a rational relation to a valid state objective under the test stated in *Williamson, supra.* But the Court's sweeping invalidation of any restrictions on abortion during the first trimester is impossible to justify under that standard, and the conscious weighing of competing factors that the Court's opinion apparently substitutes for the established test is far more appropriate to a legislative judgment than to a judicial one.

The Court eschews the history of the Fourteenth Amendment in its reliance on the "compelling state interest" test. . . . But the Court adds a new wrinkle to this test by transposing it from the legal considerations associated with the Equal Protection Clause of the Fourteenth Amendment to this case arising under the Due Process Clause of the Fourteenth Amendment. Unless I misapprehend the consequences of this transplanting of the "compelling state interest test," the Court's opinion will accomplish the seemingly impossible feat of leaving this area of the law more confused than it found it.

While the Court's opinion quotes from the dissent of Mr. Justice Holmes in *Lochner v. New York,* 198 U.S. 45, 74 (1905), the result it reaches is more closely attuned to the majority opinion of Mr. Justice Peckham in that case. As in *Lochner* and similar cases applying substantive due process standards to economic and social welfare legislation, the

---

[1] Omitted here. [Editors' note.]

adoption of the compelling state interest standard will inevitably require this Court to examine the legislative policies and pass on the wisdom of these policies in the very process of deciding whether a particular state interest put forward may or may not be "compelling." The decision here to break pregnancy into three distinct terms and to outline the permissible restrictions the state may impose in each one, for example, partakes more of judicial legislation than it does of a determination of the intent of the drafters of the Fourteenth Amendment.

The fact that a majority of the states reflecting, after all, the majority sentiment in those states, have had restrictions on abortions for at least a century is a strong indication, it seems to me, that the asserted right to an abortion is not "so rooted in the traditions and conscience of our people as to be ranked as fundamental." . . . Even today, when society's views on abortion are changing, the very existence of the debate is evidence that the "right" to an abortion is not so universally accepted as the appellant would have us believe.

To reach its result, the Court necessarily has had to find within the 45 scope of the Fourteenth Amendment a right that was apparently completely unknown to the drafters of the Amendment. As early as 1821, the first state law dealing directly with abortion was enacted by the Connecticut Legislature. . . . By the time of the adoption of the Fourteenth Amendment in 1868, there were at least thirty-six laws enacted by state or territorial legislatures limiting abortion. While many states have amended or updated their laws, twenty-one of the laws on the books in 1868 remain in effect today. Indeed, the Texas statute struck down today was, as the majority notes, first enacted in 1857 and "has remained substantially unchanged to the present time."

There apparently was no question concerning the validity of this provision or of any of the other state statutes when the Fourteenth Amendment was adopted. The only conclusion possible from this history is that the drafters did not intend to have the Fourteenth Amendment withdraw from the states the power to legislate with respect to this matter.

III

Even if one were to agree that the case that the Court decides were here, and that the enunciation of the substantive constitutional law in the Court's opinion were proper, the actual disposition of the case by the Court is still difficult to justify. The Texas statute is struck down *in toto*, even though the Court apparently concedes that at later periods of pregnancy Texas might impose these selfsame statutory limitations on abortion. My understanding of past practice is that a statute found to be invalid as applied to a particular plaintiff, but not unconstitutional as a whole, is not simply "struck down" but is, instead, declared unconstitutional as applied to the fact situation before the Court. . . .

For all of the foregoing reasons, I respectfully dissent.

Topics for Critical Thinking and Writing

1. Abortion is nowhere mentioned in the federal Bill of Rights. Is that an insurmountable obstacle for both opponents and defenders of a woman's right to abortion who seek constitutional support for their position?

2. What does it mean for a pregnant woman to be "'quick with child'" (para. 8)?

3. Can a person consistently believe that (a) a woman has no right to an abortion, (b) a human embryo or fetus has an inviolable right to life, and (c) a woman may have an abortion if it is necessary to save her own life? Explain in an essay of 500 words why you think these three propositions are or are not inconsistent.

4. Blackmun cites three reasons to explain the enactment of anti-abortion laws in nineteenth-century America (paras. 17–20). How would you rank these reasons in order of their decreasing relevance today? Write an essay of 500 words in which you state succinctly these reasons and your evaluation of them for present policy on abortion.

5. What is a "trimester" in a pregnancy (para. 14)? How, if at all, does this concept relate to the older idea of "quickening"?

6. What is a "state interest" (paras. 19–20), and why is there any such interest concerning human pregnancy and abortion?

7. Suppose someone argued that Blackmun's opinion is hopelessly confused because the issue is not the *privacy* of the pregnant woman but her *autonomy*—that is, her capacity and right to make fundamental decisions about her own life as she sees fit. Write a 250-word opinion for this case in which you defend or attack Roe's autonomy as the fundamental basis for her decision whether to abort.

8. Do you agree with the Supreme Court that a woman's right to abort a pregnancy is not an "absolute" right (paras. 23–24)? Do you agree with the Court's reasons for this conclusion? Explain.

9. Blackmun is unwilling to "endorse any theory that life . . . begins before live birth" (para. 32). Do you share his refusal? Why, or why not?

10. Do you think the unborn human fetus is a "person" in any sense of that term (see paras. 27–28)? How about a month-old human embryo? Suppose we grant that an embryo and a fetus are *alive* (that is, neither dead nor inert) and *human* (that is, not animal or vegetable or inhuman). What do you think needs to be added to establish the personhood of the living but unborn human offspring? Or do you think it is impossible that a human embryo or fetus could be a person? Explain.

11. Rehnquist, in a dissenting opinion, argues that an abortion is "not 'private' in the ordinary usage of that word" (para. 40). What is his reason for this view? Do you agree or not? Explain.

12. Rehnquist remarks that the complex position on abortion taken by the majority of the Court (see especially para. 33) "is far more appropriate to a legislative judgment than to a judicial one" (para. 41). Why does he say this, do you think? Do you agree or not? Explain.

A Psychologist's View: Rogerian Argument

Real communication occurs . . . when we listen with understanding.
—CARL ROGERS

The first duty of a wise advocate is to convince his opponents that he understands their arguments, and sympathizes with their just feelings.
—SAMUEL TAYLOR COLERIDGE

ROGERIAN ARGUMENT: AN INTRODUCTION

Carl R. Rogers (1902–1987), perhaps best known for his book entitled *On Becoming a Person* (1961), was a psychotherapist, not a teacher of writing. This short essay by Rogers has, however, exerted much influence on instructors who teach argument. Written in the 1950s, this essay reflects the political climate of the cold war between the United States and the Soviet Union, which dominated headlines for more than forty years (1947–1989). Several of Rogers's examples of bias and frustrated communication allude to the tensions of that era.

On the surface, many arguments seem to show *A* arguing with *B*, presumably seeking to change *B's* mind; but *A's* argument is really directed not to *B* but to *C*. This attempt to persuade a nonparticipant is evident in the courtroom, where neither the prosecutor (*A*) nor the defense lawyer (*B*) is really trying to convince the opponent. Rather, both are trying to convince a third party, the jury (*C*). Prosecutors do not care whether they convince defense lawyers; they don't even mind infuriating defense lawyers because their only real goal is to convince the jury. Similarly, the writer of a letter to a newspaper, taking issue with an editorial, does not expect to change the paper's policy. Rather, the writer hopes to convince a third party, the reader of the newspaper.

But suppose *A* really does want to bring *B* around to *A's* point of view. Suppose Mary really wants to persuade the teacher to allow her little lamb to stay in the classroom. Rogers points out that when we engage in an argument, if we feel our integrity or our identity is threatened, we will stiffen our position. (The teacher may feel that his or her dignity is compromised by the presence of the lamb and will scarcely attend to Mary's argument.) The sense of threat may be so great that we are unable to consider the alternative views being offered, and we therefore remain unpersuaded. Threatened, we may defend ourselves rather than our argument, and little communication takes place. Of course, a third party might say that we or our opponent presented the more convincing case, but we, and perhaps the opponent, have scarcely listened to each other, and so the two of us remain apart.

Rogers suggests, therefore, that a writer who wishes to communicate with someone (as opposed to convincing a third party) needs to reduce the threat. In a sense, the participants in the argument need to become partners rather than adversaries. Rogers writes, "Mutual communication tends to be pointed toward solving a problem rather than toward attacking a person or group." Thus, an essay on whether schools should test students for use of drugs, need not—and probably should not—see the issue as black or white, *either/or.* Such an essay might indicate that testing is undesirable because it may have bad effects, *but in some circumstances* it may be acceptable. This qualification does not mean that one must compromise. Thus, the essayist might argue that the potential danger to liberty is so great that no circumstances justify testing students for drugs. But even such an essayist should recognize the merit (however limited) of the opposition and should grant that the position being advanced itself entails great difficulties and dangers.

A writer who wishes to reduce the psychological threat to the opposition and thus facilitate the partnership in the study of some issue can do several things:

- One can show sympathetic understanding of the opposing argument,
- One can recognize what is valid in it, and
- One can recognize and demonstrate that those who take the other side are nonetheless persons of goodwill.

Advocates of Rogerian argument are likely to contrast it with Aristotelian argument, saying that the style of argument associated with Aristotle (384–322 B.C., Greek philosopher and rhetorician)

- Is adversarial, seeking to refute other views; and
- Sees the listener as wrong, someone who now must be overwhelmed by evidence.

In contrast to the confrontational Aristotelian style, which allegedly seeks to present an airtight case that compels belief, Rogerian argument (it is said)

- Is nonconfrontational, collegial, and friendly;
- Respects other views and allows for plural truths; and
- Seeks to achieve some degree of assent rather than convince utterly.

Thus a writer who takes Rogers seriously will, usually, in the first part of an argumentative essay

1. State the problem,
2. Give the opponent's position, and
3. Grant whatever validity the writer finds in that position — for instance, will recognize the circumstances in which the position would indeed be acceptable.

Next, the writer will, if possible,

4. Attempt to show how the opposing position will be improved if the writer's own position is accepted.

Sometimes, of course, the differing positions may be so far apart that no reconciliation can be proposed, in which case the writer will probably seek to show how the problem can best be solved by adopting the writer's own position. We have discussed these matters in Chapter 6, but not from the point of view of a psychotherapist, and so we reprint Rogers's essay here.

Carl R. Rogers

Communication: Its Blocking and Its Facilitation

It may seem curious that a person whose whole professional effort is devoted to psychotherapy should be interested in problems of communication. What relationship is there between providing therapeutic help to individuals with emotional maladjustments and the concern of this conference with obstacles to communication? Actually the relationship is very close indeed. The whole task of psychotherapy is the task of dealing with a failure in communication. The emotionally maladjusted person, the "neurotic," is in difficulty first because communication within himself has broken down, and second because as a result of this his communication with others has been damaged. If this sounds somewhat strange, then let me put it in other terms. In the "neurotic" individual, parts of himself which have been termed unconscious, or repressed, or denied to awareness, become blocked off so that they no longer communicate themselves to the conscious or managing part of himself. As long as this is true, there are distortions in the way he communicates himself to others, and so he suffers both within himself, and in his interpersonal relations. The task of psychotherapy is to help the person achieve, through a special relationship with a therapist, good communication within himself. Once this is achieved he can communicate more freely and more effectively with others. We may say then that psychotherapy is good communication, within and between men. We may also turn that statement around and it will still be true. Good communication, free communication, within or between men, is always therapeutic.

It is, then, from a background of experience with communication in counseling and psychotherapy that I want to present here two ideas. I wish to state what I believe is one of the major factors in blocking or impeding communication, and then I wish to present what in our experience has proven to be a very important way to improving or facilitating communication.

I would like to propose, as an hypothesis for consideration, that the major barrier to mutual interpersonal communication is our very natural tendency to judge, to evaluate, to approve or disapprove, the statement of the person, or the other group. Let me illustrate my meaning with some very simple examples. As you leave the meeting tonight, one of the statements you are likely to hear is, "I didn't like that man's talk." Now what do you respond? Almost invariably your reply will be either approval or disapproval of the attitude expressed. Either you respond, "I didn't either. I thought it was terrible," or else you tend to reply, "Oh, I thought it was really good." In other words, your primary reaction is to evaluate what has just been said to you, to evaluate it from *your* point of view, your own frame of reference.

Or take another example. Suppose I say with some feeling, "I think the Republicans are behaving in ways that show a lot of good sound sense these days," what is the response that arises in your mind as you listen? The overwhelming likelihood is that it will be evaluative. You will find yourself agreeing, or disagreeing, or making some judgment about me such as "He must be a conservative," or "He seems solid in his thinking." Or let us take an illustration from the international scene. Russia says vehemently, "The treaty with Japan is a war plot on the part of the United States." We rise as one person to say "That's a lie!"

This last illustration brings in another element connected with my 5 hypothesis. Although the tendency to make evaluations is common in almost all interchange of language, it is very much heightened in those situations where feelings and emotions are deeply involved. So the stronger our feelings, the more likely it is that there will be no mutual element in the communication. There will be just two ideas, two feelings, two judgments, missing each other in psychological space. I'm sure you recognize this from your own experience. When you have not been emotionally involved yourself, and have listened to a heated discussion, you often go away thinking, "Well, they actually weren't talking about the same thing." And they were not. Each was making a judgment, an evaluation, from his own frame of reference. There was really nothing which could be called communication in any genuine sense. This tendency to react to any emotionally meaningful statement by forming an evaluation of it from our own point of view, is, I repeat, the major barrier to interpersonal communication.

But is there any way of solving this problem, of avoiding this barrier? I feel that we are making exciting progress toward this goal and I would like to present it as simply as I can. Real communication occurs, and this evaluative tendency is avoided, when we listen with understanding. What does that mean? It means *to see the expressed idea and attitude from the other person's point of view, to sense how it feels to him, to achieve his frame of reference in regard to the thing he is talking about.*

Stated so briefly, this may sound absurdly simple, but it is not. It is an approach which we have found extremely potent in the field of psychotherapy. It is the most effective agent we know for altering the basic personality structure of an individual, and improving his relationships and his communications with others. If I can listen to what he can tell me, if I can understand how it seems to him, if I can see its personal meaning for him, if I can sense the emotional flavor which it has for him, then I will be releasing potent forces of change in him. If I can really understand how he hates his father, or hates the university, or hates communists—if I can catch the flavor of his fear of insanity, or his fear of atom bombs, or of Russia—it will be of the greatest help to him in altering those very hatreds and fears, and in establishing realistic and harmonious relationships with the very people and situations toward which he has felt hatred and fear. We know from our research that such empathic understanding—understanding *with* a person, not *about* him—is such an effective approach that it can bring about major changes in personality.

Some of you may be feeling that you listen well to people, and that you have never seen such results. The chances are very great indeed that your listening has not been of the type I have described. Fortunately I can suggest a little laboratory experiment which you can try to test the quality of your understanding. The next time you get into an argument with your wife, or your friend, or with a small group of friends, just stop the discussion for a moment and for an experiment, institute this rule. "Each person can speak up for himself only *after* he has first restated the ideas and feelings of the previous speaker accurately, and to that speaker's satisfaction." You see what this would mean. It would simply mean that before presenting your own point of view, it would be necessary for you to really achieve the other speaker's frame of reference—to understand his thoughts and feelings so well that you could summarize them for him. Sounds simple, doesn't it? But if you try it you will discover it one of the most difficult things you have ever tried to do. However, once you have been able to see the other's point of view, your own comments will have to be drastically revised. You will also find the emotion going out of the discussion, the differences being reduced, and those differences which remain being of a rational and understandable sort.

Can you imagine what this kind of an approach would mean if it were projected into larger areas? What would happen to a labor-management dispute if it was conducted in such a way that labor, without necessarily agreeing, could accurately state management's point of view in a way that management could accept; and management, without approving labor's stand, could state labor's case in a way that labor agreed was accurate? It would mean that real communication was established, and one could practically guarantee that some reasonable solution would be reached.

If then this way of approach is an effective avenue to good commu- 10 nication and good relationships, as I am quite sure you will agree if you try the experiment I have mentioned, why is it not more widely tried and used? I will try to list the difficulties which keep it from being utilized.

In the first place it takes courage, a quality which is not too widespread. I am indebted to Dr. S. I. Hayakawa, the semanticist, for pointing out that to carry on psychotherapy in this fashion is to take a very real risk, and that courage is required. If you really understand another person in this way, if you are willing to enter his private world and see the way life appears to him, without any attempt to make evaluative judgments, you run the risk of being changed yourself. You might see it his way, you might find yourself influenced in your attitudes or your personality. This risk of being changed is one of the most frightening prospects most of us can face. If I enter, as fully as I am able, into the private world of a neurotic or psychotic individual, isn't there a risk that I might become lost in that world? Most of us are afraid to take that risk. Or if we had a Russian communist speaker here tonight, or Senator Joe McCarthy, how many of us would dare to try to see the world from each of these points of view? The great majority of us could not *listen;* we would find ourselves compelled to *evaluate,* because listening would seem too dangerous. So the first requirement is courage, and we do not always have it.

But there is a second obstacle. It is just when emotions are strongest that it is most difficult to achieve the frame of reference of the other person or group. Yet it is the time the attitude is most needed, if communication is to be established. We have not found this to be an insuperable obstacle in our experience in psychotherapy. A third party, who is able to lay aside his own feelings and evaluations, can assist greatly by listening with understanding to each person or group and clarifying the views and attitudes each holds. We have found this very effective in small groups in which contradictory or antagonistic attitudes exist. When the parties to a dispute realize that they are being understood, that someone sees how the situation seems to them, the statements grow less exaggerated and less defensive, and it is no longer necessary to maintain the attitude, "I am 100 percent right and you are 100 percent wrong." The influence of such an understanding catalyst in the group permits the members to come closer and closer to the objective truth involved in the relationship. In this way mutual communication is established and some type of agreement becomes much more possible. So we may say that though heightened emotions make it much more difficult to understand *with* an opponent, our experience makes it clear that a neutral, understanding, catalyst type of leader or therapist can overcome this obstacle in a small group.

This last phrase, however, suggests another obstacle to utilizing the approach I have described. Thus far all our experience has been with small face-to-face groups—groups exhibiting industrial tensions, religious tensions, racial tensions, and therapy groups in which many personal tensions are present. In these small groups our experience, confirmed by a limited amount of research, shows that this basic approach leads to improved communication, to greater acceptance of others and by others, and to attitudes which are more positive and more problem-solving in nature. There is a decrease in defensiveness, in exaggerated statements, in evaluative and critical behavior. But these findings are from small groups. What about trying to achieve understanding between larger groups that are geographically remote? Or between face-to-face groups who are not speaking for themselves, but simply as representatives of others, like the delegates at Kaesong?[1] Frankly we do not know the answers to these questions. I believe the situation might be put this way. As social scientists we have a tentative test-tube solution of the problem of breakdown in communication. But to confirm the validity of this test-tube solution, and to adapt it to the enormous problems of communication breakdown between classes, groups, and nations, would involve additional funds, much more research, and creative thinking of a high order.

Even with our present limited knowledge we can see some steps which might be taken, even in large groups, to increase the amount of listening *with,* and to decrease the amount of evaluation *about.* To be imaginative for a moment, let us suppose that a therapeutically oriented international group went to the Russian leaders and said, "We want to achieve a genuine understanding of your views and even more important, of your attitudes and feelings, toward the United States. We will summarize and resummarize the views and feelings if necessary, until you agree that our description represents the situation as it seems to you." Then suppose they did the same thing with the leaders in our own country. If they then gave the widest possible distribution to these two views, with the feelings clearly described but not expressed in name-calling, might not the effect be very great? It would not guarantee the type of understanding I have been describing, but it would make it much more possible. We can understand the feelings of a person who hates us much more readily when his attitudes are accurately described to us by a neutral third party, than we can when he is shaking his fist at us.

But even to describe such a first step is to suggest another obstacle to 15 this approach of understanding. Our civilization does not yet have enough faith in the social sciences to utilize their findings. The opposite is true of

[1]**the delegates at Kaesong** Representatives of North and South Korea met at the border town of Kaesong to arrange terms for an armistice to hostilities during the Korean War (1950–1953). [All notes are the editors'.]

the physical sciences. During the war[2] when a test-tube solution was found to the problem of synthetic rubber, millions of dollars and an army of talent was turned loose on the problem of using that finding. If synthetic rubber could be made in milligrams, it could and would be made in the thousands of tons. And it was. But in the social science realm, if a way is found of facilitating communication and mutual understanding in small groups, there is no guarantee that the finding will be utilized. It may be a generation or more before the money and the brains will be turned loose to exploit that finding.

In closing, I would like to summarize this small-scale solution to the problem of barriers in communication, and to point out certain of its characteristics.

I have said that our research and experience to date would make it appear that breakdowns in communication, and the evaluative tendency which is the major barrier to communication, can be avoided. The solution is provided by creating a situation in which each of the different parties come to understand the other from the *other's* point of view. This has been achieved, in practice, even when feelings run high, by the influence of a person who is willing to understand each point of view empathically, and who thus acts as a catalyst to precipitate further understanding.

This procedure has important characteristics. It can be initiated by one party, without waiting for the other to be ready. It can even be initiated by a neutral third person, providing he can gain a minimum of cooperation from one of the parties.

This procedure can deal with the insincerities, the defensive exaggerations, the lies, the "false fronts" which characterize almost every failure in communication. These defensive distortions drop away with astonishing speed as people find that the only intent is to understand, not judge.

This approach leads steadily and rapidly toward the discovery of the truth, toward a realistic appraisal of the objective barriers to communication. The dropping of some defensiveness by one party leads to further dropping of defensiveness by the other party, and truth is thus approached. 20

This procedure gradually achieves mutual communication. Mutual communication tends to be pointed toward solving a problem rather than toward attacking a person or group. It leads to a situation in which I see how the problem appears to you, as well as to me, and you see how it appears to me, as well as to you. Thus accurately and realistically defined, the problem is almost certain to yield to intelligent attack, or if it is in part insoluble, it will be comfortably accepted as such.

This then appears to be a test-tube solution to the breakdown of communication as it occurs in small groups. Can we take this small-scale answer, investigate it further, refine it; develop it and apply it to the

[2]**the war** World War II.

✓ A CHECKLIST FOR ANALYZING ROGERIAN ARGUMENT

☐ Have I stated the problem and indicated that a dialogue is possible?
☐ Have I stated at least one other point of view in a way that would satisfy its proponents?
☐ Have I been courteous to those who hold views other than mine?
☐ Have I enlarged my own understanding to the extent that I can grant validity, at least in some circumstances, to at least some aspects of other positions?
☐ Have I stated my position and indicated the contexts in which I believe it is valid?
☐ Have I pointed out the ground that we share?
☐ Have I shown how other positions will be strengthened by accepting some aspects of my position?

---

tragic and well-nigh fatal failures of communication which threaten the very existence of our modern world? It seems to me that this is a possibility and a challenge which we should explore.

See the companion Web site **bedfordstmartins.com/barnetbedau** for links related to Rogerian argument.

The following essay was submitted in a first-year course at Tufts University.

Jane Willy

Is the College Use of American Indian Mascots Racist?

In Tallahassee, where I grew up, everyone thinks of the athletic teams of Florida State University as the Seminoles. At the beginning of every home game of the football team, a student impersonating Chief Osceola, dressed in Indian regalia and riding on a spotted horse (an Appaloosa), plants a flaming spear at the midpoint of the field. White people such as me thought of this action as not only a moment of pageantry and fun but also as a tribute to the greatness of the Seminole people, past and present. I continue to think of it this way, but now I know that many other people have a different view.

A few years ago I read in the newspapers that the National Collegiate Athletic Association (NCAA) ordered colleges to stop using American

Indian nicknames. Several dozen universities were involved. Thus, Arkansas State University was told to stop calling itself the Indians, the University of Louisiana at Monroe was told to drop the name Warhawks, the University of Illinois at Champaign-Urbana was told to drop the name Illini, and the University of Utah was told to drop the name Utes. And of course Florida State University was told to stop calling its teams the Seminoles. Apparently the NCAA was responding to a report issued by the U.S. Commission on Civil Rights, which in 2001 characterized American Indian nicknames and mascots at colleges as "inappropriate" and "disrespectful," and urged that they be eliminated (Wills A29).

Persons who argue that the names are disrespectful and racist point out that no one today would call a team the Krauts, or the Jewboys, or the Chinks or Japs, or whatever (Pewewardy). At least two exceptions comes to my mind—the "Fighting Irish" of Notre Dame and the Yankees—but clearly there is considerable merit to the argument that some names can be hurtful, and surely we can agree that if they are hurtful, they should be eliminated, just as the U.S. Commission on Civil Rights and the NCAA recommend. Those who argue that the names are hurtful should be listened to, and it is not up to us outsiders to tell them that they shouldn't be offended, that they are too thin-skinned, too eager to be Politically Correct. For instance, if persons of African descent say they do *not* want to be called "colored" or "Negro," and that they prefer to be called "African Americans," we should (and we do) honor their preference. We can write all the essays we wish, explaining that "white" is as misleading as "colored" (white people certainly are *not* white but are a sort of pinkish-buff color), that "Negro" has a good Latin root meaning "black," and so forth, but if the people in question prefer to be called African Americans, we outsiders ought to defer to their wishes.

But what *are* the wishes of the people in question? In the case of the Florida Seminoles, we have a pretty good idea. The Seminole Tribe of Florida in June 2005 passed a resolution supporting Florida State University's use of the name Seminole ("NCAA"). It happens—things never are as simple as one can wish them to be!—that the Seminoles of Oklahoma have objected, but it seems to me that when we are speaking of a Florida university, the response of the Florida Seminoles must be decisive. An article in the *New York Times* by a member of the Seminole tribe and the general counsel for the tribe sets forth the good relations between the university and the tribe, and reports that "the Tribal Council voted unanimously to support the university in its efforts to keep the Seminole name" (Shore A25).

But what of the fighting Sioux, at the University of North Dakota? The university petitioned the NCAA for permission to retain the nickname, but the NCAA denied the petition after a Sioux leader informed the NCAA that his tribe opposed the university's use of the name (Wolverton A43). It apparently is not entirely clear if the unnamed leader did have the authority to speak for the tribe, but this is a matter that can be settled.

As I have already indicated, I think the voice of the Indians is the voice that should, finally, be listened to, though of course the Indians must first listen to the voices of the universities that wish to use the Indian imagery. Do these universities, Indians might well ask, really value the American Indian heritage or are they presenting racist stereotypes, Indians as painted savages who utter war whoops as they go about scalping imaginary innocent whites? The Seminoles of Florida are convinced that FSU's values are right, that (for instance) the university actively recruits students from among the Seminoles, and that it gives courses in Indian culture. And the Athletic Department's use of the image of the Seminole is seen as *not* degrading, but as a symbol of fortitude.

Perhaps the University of North Dakota can persuade the Sioux—not by words but by actions—that its use of the "Fighting Sioux" is similarly affirmative rather than racist. If it can, and if the Sioux then agree to let the university use their image, the NCAA ought to withdraw its objections. If the university cannot persuade the Sioux, well, the Fighting Sioux will just have to agree that they have lost this fight, and they can take the name of the Hawks or the Eagles or of any other group that won't object.

WORKS CITED

"NCAA American Indian Mascot Ban Will Begin Feb. 1." *ESPN.com*. ESPN, 12 Aug. 2005. Web. 9 Mar. 2007.

Pewewardy, Cornel. "Will Another School Year Bring Insult or Honor?" *Canku Ota*. Canku Ota, 7 Oct. 2000. Web. 9 Mar. 2007.

Shore, Jim. "Play with Our Name." *New York Times*, 27 Aug. 2005, natl. ed.: A25. Print.

Wills, Eric. "Pride or Prejudice?" *Chronicle of Higher Education* 3 June 2005: A29. Print.

Wolverton, Brad. "Mascot Dispute Escalates." *Chronicle of Higher Education* 12 May 2006: A43. Print.

A Literary Critic's View: Arguing about Literature

Literary criticism [is] a reasoned account of the feeling produced upon the critic by the book he is reading.

—D. H. LAWRENCE

A writer is someone for whom writing is more difficult than it is for other people.

—THOMAS MANN

You can never draw the line between aesthetic criticism and social criticism. . . . You start with literary criticism, and however rigorous an aesthete you may be, you are over the frontier into something else sooner or later. The best you can do is to accept these conditions and know what you are doing when you are doing it.

—T. S. ELIOT

Nothing is as easy as it looks.

—MURPHY'S LAW #23

Everything is what it is and not another thing.

—BISHOP JOSEPH BUTLER

You might think that literature—fiction, poetry (including songs), drama—is meant only to be enjoyed, not to be argued about. Yet literature is constantly the subject of argumentative writing—not all of it by teachers of English. For instance, if you glance at the current issue of *Time* or *Newsweek*, you probably will find a review of a play suggesting that the play is worth seeing or is not worth seeing. Or in the same magazine you may find an article reporting that a senator or member of Congress argued that the National Endowment for the Humanities wasted its grant money by funding research on such-and-such an author or that the National Endowment for the Arts insulted taxpayers by making an award to a writer who defamed the American family.

Probably most writing about literature, whether done by college students, their professors, journalists, members of Congress, or whomever, is devoted to interpreting, judging (evaluating), and theorizing. Let's look at each of these, drawing our examples chiefly from comments about Shakespeare's *Macbeth*.

INTERPRETING

Interpreting is a matter of setting forth the *meaning* or the meanings of a work. For some readers, a work has *a* meaning, the one intended by the writer, which we may or may not perceive. For most critics today, however, a work has *many* meanings—for instance, the meaning it had for the writer, the meanings it has accumulated over time, and the meanings it has for each of today's readers. Take *Macbeth*, a play about a Scottish king, written soon after a Scot—James VI of Scotland—had been installed as James I, King of England. The play must have meant something special to the king—we know that it was presented at court—and something a little different to the ordinary English citizen. And surely it means something different to us. For instance, few if any people today believe in the divine right of kings, although James I certainly did; and few if any people today believe in malignant witches, although witches play an important role in the tragedy. What *we* see in the play must be rather different from what Shakespeare's audience saw in it.

Many interpretations of *Macbeth* have been offered. Let's take two fairly simple and clearly opposed views:

1. Macbeth is a villain who, by murdering his lawful king, offends God's rule, so he is overthrown by God's earthly instruments, Malcolm and Macduff. Macbeth is justly punished; the reader or spectator rejoices in his defeat.

One can offer a good deal of evidence—and if one is taking this position in an essay, of course one must *argue* it—by giving supporting reasons rather than merely assert the position.

Here is a second view.

2. Macbeth is a hero-villain, a man who commits terrible crimes but who never completely loses the reader's sympathy; although he is justly punished, the reader believes that with the death of Macbeth the world has become a smaller place.

Again, one *must* offer evidence in an essay that presents this thesis or indeed presents any interpretation. For instance, one might offer as evidence the fact that the survivors, especially Macduff and Malcolm, have not interested us nearly as much as Macbeth has. One might argue, too, that although Macbeth's villainy is undeniable, his conscience never deserts him—here one would point to specific passages and would offer some brief quotations. Macbeth's pained awareness of what he has done, it can be argued, enables the reader to sympathize with him continually.

Or consider an interpretation of Lady Macbeth. Is she simply evil through and through, or are there mitigating reasons for her actions? Might one argue, perhaps in a feminist interpretation, that despite her intelligence and courage she had no outlet for expression except through her husband? To make this argument, the writer might want to go beyond the text of the play, offering as evidence Elizabethan comments about the proper role of women.

JUDGING (OR EVALUATING)

Literary criticism is also concerned with such questions as these: Is *Macbeth* a great tragedy? Is *Macbeth* a greater tragedy than *Romeo and Juliet*? The writer offers an opinion about the worth of the literary work, but the opinion must be supported by an argument, expressed in sentences that offer supporting evidence.

Let's pause for a moment to think about evaluation in general. When we say "This is a great play," are we in effect saying only "I like this play"? That is, are we merely *expressing* our taste rather than *asserting* anything about something out there—something independent of our tastes and feelings? (The next few paragraphs will not answer this question, but they may start you thinking about your own answer.) Consider these three sentences:

1. It's raining outside.
2. I like vanilla.
3. This is a really good book.

If you are indoors and you say that it is raining outside, a hearer may ask for verification. Why do you say what you say? "Because," you reply, "I'm looking out the window." Or "Because Jane just came in, and she is drenched." Or "Because I just heard a weather report." If, on the other hand, you say that you like vanilla, it's almost unthinkable that anyone would ask you why. No one expects you to justify—to support, to give a reason for—an expression of taste.

Now consider the third statement, "This is a really good book." It is entirely reasonable, we think, for someone to ask you *why* you say that. And you reply, "Well, the characters are realistic, and the plot held my interest," or "It really gave me an insight into what life among the rich [or the poor] must be like," or some such thing.

That is, statement 3 at least seems to be stating a fact, and it seems to be something we can discuss, even argue about, in a way that we cannot argue about a personal preference for vanilla. Almost everyone would agree that when we offer an aesthetic judgment we ought to be able to give reasons for it. At the very least, we might say, we hope to show *why* we evaluate the work as we do, and to suggest that if our readers try to see it from our point of view they may then accept our evaluation.

Evaluations are always based on assumptions, although these assumptions may be unstated, and in fact the writer may even be unaware of them. Some of these assumptions play the role of criteria; they control the sort of evidence the writer believes is relevant to the evaluation. What sorts of assumptions may underlie value judgments? We will mention a few, merely as examples. Other assumptions are possible, and all of these assumptions can themselves become topics of dispute:

1. A good work of art, although fictional, says something about real life.
2. A good work of art is complex yet unified.
3. A good work of art sets forth a wholesome view of life.
4. A good work of art is original.
5. A good work of art deals with an important subject.

Let's look briefly at these views, one by one.

1. *A good work of art, although fictional, says something about real life.* If you hold the view that literature is connected to life and believe that human beings behave in fairly consistent ways—that is, that each of us has an enduring "character"—you probably will judge as inferior a work in which the figures behave inconsistently or seem not to be adequately motivated. (The point must be made, however, that different literary forms or genres are governed by different rules. For instance, consistency of character is usually expected in tragedy but not in melodrama or in comedy, where last-minute reformations may be welcome and greeted with applause. The novelist Henry James said, "You will not write a good novel unless you possess the sense of reality." He is probably right—but does his view hold for the writer of farces?) In the case of *Macbeth* you might well find that the characters are consistent: Although the play begins by showing Macbeth as a loyal defender of King Duncan, Macbeth's later treachery is understandable, given the temptation and the pressure. Similarly, Lady Macbeth's descent into madness, although it may come as a surprise, may strike you as entirely plausible: At the beginning of the play she is confident that she can become an accomplice to a murder, but she has overestimated herself (or, we might say, she has underestimated her own humanity, the power of her guilty conscience, which drives her to insanity).

2. *A good work of art is complex yet unified.* If Macbeth is only a "tyrant" (Macduff's word) or a "butcher" (Malcolm's word), he is a unified character but he may be too simple and too uninteresting a character to be the subject of a great play. But, one argument holds, Macbeth in fact is a complex character, not simply a villain but a hero-villain, and the play as a whole is complex. *Macbeth* is a good work of art, one might argue, partly because it shows us so many aspects of life (courage, fear, loyalty, treachery, for a start) through a richly varied language (the diction

ranges from a grand passage in which Macbeth says that his bloody hands will "incarnadine," or make red, "the multitudinous seas" to colloquial passages such as the drunken porter's "Knock, knock"). The play shows us the heroic Macbeth tragically destroying his own life, and it shows us the comic porter making coarse jokes about deceit and damnation, jokes that (although the porter doesn't know it) connect with Macbeth's crimes.

3. *A good work of art sets forth a wholesome view of life.* The idea that a work should be judged partly or largely on the moral view that it contains is widely held by the general public. (It has also been held by esteemed philosophers, notably Plato.) Thus, a story that demeans women — perhaps one that takes a casual view of rape — would be given a low rating and so would a play that treats a mass murderer as a hero.

Implicit in this approach is what is called an *instrumentalist* view — the idea that a work of art is an instrument, a means, to some higher value. Thus, many people hold that reading great works of literature makes us better — or at least does not make us worse. In this view, a work that is pornographic or in some other way thought to be immoral will be given a low value. At the time we are writing this chapter, a law requires the National Endowment for the Arts to take into account standards of decency when making awards.

Moral judgments, it should be noted, do not come only from the conservative right; the liberal left has been quick to detect political incorrectness. In fact, except for those people who subscribe to the now unfashionable view that a work of art is an independent aesthetic object with little or no connection to the real world — something like a pretty floral arrangement or a wordless melody — most people judge works of literature largely by their content, by what the works seem to say about life.

- Marxist critics, for instance, have customarily held that literature should make the reader aware of the political realities of life.

- Feminist critics are likely to hold that literature should make us aware of gender relationships — for example, aware of patriarchal power and of female accomplishments.

4. *A good work of art is original.* This assumption puts special value on new techniques and new subject matter. Thus, the *first* playwright who introduces a new subject (say, AIDS) gets extra credit, so to speak. Or to return to Shakespeare, one sign of his genius, it is held, is that he was so highly varied; none of his tragedies seems merely to duplicate another, each is a world of its own, a new kind of achievement. Compare, for instance, *Romeo and Juliet*, with its two youthful and innocent heroes, with *Macbeth*, with its deeply guilty hero. Both plays are tragedies, but we can hardly imagine two more different plays — even if a reader perversely argues that the young lovers are guilty of impetuosity and of disobeying appropriate authorities.

5. *A good work of art deals with an important subject.* Here we are concerned with theme: Great works, in this view, must deal with great themes. Love, death, patriotism, and God, say, are great themes; a work that deals with these may achieve a height, an excellence, that, say, a work describing a dog scratching for fleas may not achieve. (Of course, if the reader feels that the dog is a symbol of humanity plagued by invisible enemies, then the poem about the dog may reach the heights, but then, too, it is *not* a poem about a dog and fleas: It is really a poem about humanity and the invisible.)

The point: In writing an evaluation you must let your reader know *why* you value the work as you do. Obviously, it is not enough just to keep saying that *this* work is great whereas *that* work is not so great; the reader wants to know *why* you offer the judgments that you do, which means that you

- Must set forth your criteria and then
- Offer evidence that is in accord with them.

THEORIZING

Some literary criticism is concerned with such theoretical questions as these:

✔ A CHECKLIST FOR AN ARGUMENT ABOUT LITERATURE

☐ Is my imagined reader like a typical classmate of mine, someone who is not a specialist in literature but who is open-minded and interested in hearing my point of view about a work?

☐ Is the essay supported with evidence, usually from the text itself but conceivably from other sources (such as a statement by the author, a statement by a person regarded as an authority, or perhaps the evidence of comparable works)?

☐ Is the essay inclusive? Does it take into account all relevant details (which is not to say that it includes everything the writer knows about the work—for instance, that it was made into a film or that the author died poor)?

☐ Is the essay focused? Does the thesis stay steadily before the reader?

☐ Does the essay use quotations, but as evidence, not as padding? Whenever possible, does it abridge or summarize long quotations?

☐ Are all sources fully acknowledged? (For the form of documentation, see Chapter 7.)

What is tragedy? Can the hero be a villain? How does tragedy differ from melodrama?

Why do tragedies—works showing good or at least interesting people destroyed—give us pleasure?

Does a work of art—a play or a novel, say, a made-up world with imagined characters—offer anything that can be called "truth"? Does an experience of a work of art affect our character?

Does a work of art have meaning in itself, or is the meaning simply whatever anyone wishes to say it is? Does *Macbeth* tell us anything about life, or is it just an invented story?

And, yet again, one hopes that anyone asserting a thesis concerned with any of these topics will offer evidence—will, indeed, *argue* rather than merely assert.

EXAMPLES:
Two Students Interpret Robert Frost's "Mending Wall"

Let's consider two competing interpretations of a poem, Robert Frost's "Mending Wall." We say "competing" because these interpretations clash head-on. Differing interpretations need not be incompatible, of course. For instance, a historical interpretation of *Macbeth*, arguing that an understanding of the context of English-Scottish politics around 1605 helps us to appreciate the play, need not be incompatible with a psychoanalytic interpretation that tells us that Macbeth's murder of King Duncan is rooted in an Oedipus complex, the king being a father figure. Different approaches thus can illuminate different aspects of the work, just as they can emphasize or subordinate different elements in the plot or characters portrayed. But, again, in the next few pages we will deal with mutually incompatible interpretations of the meaning of Frost's poem—of what Frost's poem is about.

After reading the poem and the two interpretations written by students, spend a few minutes thinking about the questions that we raise after the second interpretation.

Robert Frost

Robert Frost (1874–1963) studied for part of one term at Dartmouth College in New Hampshire, then did odd jobs (including teaching), and from 1897 to 1899 was enrolled as a special student at Harvard. He then farmed in New Hampshire, published a few poems in newspapers, did some more teaching, and in 1912 left for England, where he hoped to achieve success as a writer. By 1915 he was known in England, and he returned to the United States. By the time of his death he was the nation's unofficial poet laureate. "Mending Wall" was first published in 1914.

Mending Wall

Something there is that doesn't love a wall,
That sends the frozen-ground-swell under it,
And spills the upper boulders in the sun;
And makes gaps even two can pass abreast.
The work of hunters is another thing: 5
I have come after them and made repair
Where they have left not one stone on a stone,
But they would have the rabbit out of hiding,
To please the yelping dogs. The gaps I mean,
No one has seen them made or heard them made,   10
But at spring mending-time we find them there.
I let my neighbor know beyond the hill;
And on a day we meet to walk the line
And set the wall between us once again.
We keep the wall between us as we go.   15
To each the boulders that have fallen to each.
And some are loaves and some so nearly balls
We have to use a spell to make them balance:
"Stay where you are until our backs are turned!"
We wear our fingers rough with handling them.   20
Oh, just another kind of outdoor game,
One on a side. It comes to little more:
There where it is we do not need the wall:
He is all pine and I am apple orchard.
My apple trees will never get across   25
And eat the cones under his pines, I tell him.
He only says, "Good fences make good neighbors."
Spring is the mischief in me, and I wonder
If I could put a notion in his head:
"*Why* do they make good neighbors? Isn't it   30
Where there are cows? But here there are no cows.
Before I built a wall I'd ask to know
What I was walling in or walling out,
And to whom I was like to give offense.
Something there is that doesn't love a wall,   35
That wants it down." I could say "Elves" to him,
But it's not elves exactly, and I'd rather
He said it for himself. I see him there

Bringing a stone grasped firmly by the top
In each hand, like an old-stone savage armed.   40
He moves in darkness as it seems to me,
Not of woods only and the shade of trees.
He will not go behind his father's saying,
And he likes having thought of it so well
He says again, "Good fences make good neighbors."   45

Jonathan Deutsch

Professor Walton

English 102

5 March 2004

The Deluded Speaker in Frost's "Mending Wall"

Our discussions of "Mending Wall" in high school showed that most people think Frost is saying that walls between people are a bad thing and that we should not try to separate ourselves from each other unnecessarily. Perhaps the wall, in this view, is a symbol for race prejudice or religious differences, and Frost is suggesting that these differences are minor and that they should not keep us apart. In this common view, the neighbor's words, "Good fences make good neighbors" (lines 27 and 45) show that the neighbor is shortsighted. I disagree with this view, but first I want to present the evidence that might be offered for it, so that we can then see whether it really is substantial.

First of all, someone might claim that in lines 23 to 26 Frost offers a good argument against walls:

There where it is we do not need the wall:

He is all pine and I am apple orchard.

My apple trees will never get across

And eat the cones under his pines, I tell him.

The neighbor does not offer a valid reply to this argument; in fact, he doesn't offer any argument at all but simply says, "Good fences make good neighbors."

Another piece of evidence supposedly showing that the neighbor is wrong, it is said, is found in Frost's description of him as "an old-stone savage" and someone who "moves in darkness" (40, 41). And a third piece of evidence is said to be that the neighbor "will not go behind his father's saying" (43), but he merely repeats the saying.

There is, however, another way of looking at the poem. As I see it, the speaker is a very snide and condescending person. He is confident that he knows it all and that his neighbor is an ignorant savage; he is even willing to tease his supposedly ignorant neighbor. For instance, the speaker admits to "the mischief in me" (28), and he is confident that he could tell the truth to the neighbor but arrogantly thinks that it would be a more effective form of teaching if the neighbor "said it for himself" (38).

The speaker is not only unpleasantly mischievous and condescending toward his neighbor, but he is also shallow, for he does not see the great wisdom that there is in proverbs. The American Heritage Dictionary of the English Language, Third Edition, defines a proverb as "A short, pithy saying in frequent and widespread use that expresses a basic truth." Frost, or at least the man who speaks this poem, does not seem to realize that proverbs express truths. He just dismisses them, and he thinks the neighbor is wrong not to "go behind his father's saying" (43). But there is a great deal of wisdom in the sayings of our fathers. For instance, in the Bible (in the Old Testament) there is a whole book of proverbs, filled with wise sayings such as "Reprove not a scorner, lest he hate thee: rebuke a wise man, and he will love thee" (9:8); "He that trusteth in his riches shall fall" (11:28); "The way of a fool is right in his own eyes" (12:15; this might be said of the speaker of "Mending Wall"); "A soft answer turneth away wrath" (15:1); and (to cut short what could be a list many pages long), "Whoso diggeth a pit shall fall therein" (26:27).

The speaker is confident that walls are unnecessary and probably bad, but he doesn't realize that even where there are no cattle, walls serve the valuable purpose of clearly marking out our territory. They help us to preserve our independence and our individuality. Walls--man-made structures--are a sign of civilization. A wall more or less says, "This is mine, but I respect that as yours."

Frost's speaker is so confident of his shallow view that he makes fun of his neighbor for repeating that "Good fences make good neighbors" (27, 45). But he himself repeats his own saying, "Something there is that doesn't love a wall" (1, 35). And at least the neighbor has age-old tradition on his side, since the proverb is the saying of his father. On the other hand, the speaker has only his own opinion, and he can't even say what the "something" is.

It may be that Frost meant for us to laugh at the neighbor and to take the side of the speaker, but I think it is much more likely that he meant for us to see that the speaker is mean-spirited (or at least given to unpleasant teasing), too self-confident, foolishly dismissing the wisdom of the old times, and entirely unaware that he has these unpleasant characteristics.

Felicia Alonso

Professor Walton

English 102

5 March 2004

The Debate in Robert Frost's "Mending Wall"

I think the first thing to say about Frost's "Mending Wall" is this: The poem is not about a debate over whether good fences do or do not make good neighbors. It is about two debaters: One of the debaters is on the side of vitality, and the other is on the side of an unchanging, fixed--dead, we might say--tradition.

How can we characterize the speaker? For one thing, he is neighborly. Interestingly, it is <u>he</u>, and not the neighbor, who initiates the repairing of the wall: "I let my neighbor know beyond the hill" (line 12). This seems strange, since the speaker doesn't see any point in this wall, whereas the neighbor is all in favor of walls. Can we explain this apparent contradiction? Yes; the speaker is a good neighbor, willing to do his share of the work and willing (perhaps in order not to upset his neighbor) to maintain an old tradition even though he doesn't see its importance. It may not be important, he thinks, but it is really rather pleasant, "another kind of outdoor game" (21). In fact, sometimes he even repairs fences on his own, after hunters have destroyed them.

Second, we can say that the speaker is on the side of nature. "Something there is that doesn't love a wall," he says (1, 35), and of course, the "something" is nature itself. Nature "sends the frozen-ground-swell" under the wall and "spills the upper boulders in the sun; / And makes gaps even two can pass abreast" (2–4). Notice that nature itself makes the gaps and that "two can pass abreast"--that is, people can walk together in a companionable way. It is hard to imagine the neighbor walking side by side with anyone.

Third, we can say that the speaker has a sense of humor. When he thinks of trying to get his neighbor interested in the issue, he admits that "the mischief" is in him (28), and he amusingly attributes his playfulness to a natural force, the spring. He playfully toys with the obviously preposterous idea of suggesting to his neighbor that elves caused the stones to fall, but he stops short of making this amusing suggestion to his very serious neighbor. Still, the mere thought assures us that he has a playful, genial nature, and the idea also again implies that not only the speaker but also some sort of mysterious natural force dislikes walls.

Finally, though, of course, he thinks he is right and that his neighbor is mistaken, he at least is cautious in his view. He does not call his neighbor "an old-stone savage" (40); rather, he uses a simile ("like") and then adds that this is only his opinion, so the opinion is softened quite a bit. Here is the description of the neighbor, with underlining added to clarify my point. The neighbor is . . .

> like an old-stone savage armed. / He moves
>
> in darkness as it seems to me . . . (40–41)

Of course, the only things we know about the neighbor are those things that the speaker chooses to tell us, so it is not surprising that the speaker comes out ahead. He comes out ahead not because he is right about walls (real or symbolic) and his neighbor is wrong-- that's an issue that is not settled in the poem. He comes out ahead because he is a more interesting figure, someone who is neighborly, thoughtful, playful. Yes, maybe he seems to us to feel superior to his neighbor, but we can be certain that he doesn't cause his neighbor any embarrassment. Take the very end of the poem. The speaker tells us that the neighbor

> . . . will not go behind his father's saying,
>
> And he likes having thought of it so well
>
> He says again, "Good fences make good neighbors."

Alonso 3

The speaker is telling us that the neighbor is utterly unoriginal and that the neighbor confuses remembering something with thinking. But the speaker doesn't get into an argument; he doesn't rudely challenge his neighbor and demand reasons, which might force the neighbor to see that he can't think for himself. And in fact we probably like the neighbor just as he is, and we don't want him to change his mind. The words that ring in our ears are not the speaker's but the neighbor's: "Good fences make good neighbors." The speaker of the poem is a good neighbor. After all, one can hardly be more neighborly than to let the neighbor have the last word.

TOPICS FOR CRITICAL THINKING AND WRITING

1. State the thesis of each essay. Do you believe the theses are sufficiently clear and appear sufficiently early in the essays?

2. Consider the evidence that each essay offers by way of supporting its thesis. Do you find some of the evidence unconvincing? Explain.

3. Putting aside the question of which interpretation you prefer, comment on the organization of each essay. Is the organization clear? Do you want to propose some other pattern that you think might be more effective?

4. Consult the Checklist for Peer Review on page 249, and offer comments on one of the two essays. Or: If you were the instructor in the course in which these two essays were submitted, what might be your final comments on each of them? Or: Write an analysis (250–500 words) of the strengths and weaknesses of either essay.

EXERCISES: READING A POEM AND A STORY

Andrew Marvell

Andrew Marvell (1621–1678), born in Hull, England, and educated at Trinity College, Cambridge, was traveling in Europe when the civil war between the royalists and the puritans broke out in England in 1642. The puritans were victorious and established the Commonwealth (the monarchy was restored later, in 1660), and Marvell became a tutor to the daughter of the victorious Lord-General. In 1657 he became an assistant to the blind poet John Milton, who held the title of Latin Secretary (Latin was the language of international diplomacy). In 1659 Marvell was elected to represent Hull in Parliament. As a man of letters, during his lifetime he was known chiefly for some satiric prose and poetry; most of the writings for which he is now esteemed were published posthumously. The following poem was first published in 1681.

To His Coy Mistress°

Had we but world enough, and time,
This coyness,° Lady, were no crime.
We would sit down, and think which way
To walk, and pass our long love's day.
Thou by the Indian Ganges' side   5
Shouldst rubies find; I by the tide
Of Humber° would complain. I would
Love you ten years before the Flood,
And you should, if you please, refuse

Mistress Beloved woman.
coyness Reluctance.
Humber An estuary at Hull, Marvell's birthplace.

Till the Conversion of the Jews.°   10
My vegetable° love should grow
Vaster than empires and more slow;
An hundred years should go to praise
Thine eyes, and on thy forehead gaze;
Two hundred to adore each breast,   15
But thirty thousand to the rest;
An age at least to every part,
And the last age should show your heart.
For, Lady, you deserve this state,°
Nor would I love at lower rate.   20
    But at my back I always hear
Time's wingèd chariot hurrying near;
And yonder all before us lie
Deserts of vast eternity.
Thy beauty shall no more be found,   25
Nor, in thy marble vault, shall sound
My echoing song; then worms shall try°
That long-preserved virginity,
And your quaint° honour turn to dust,
And into ashes all my lust: 30
The grave's a fine and private place,
But none, I think, do there embrace.
    Now therefore, while the youthful hue
Sits on thy skin like morning dew,
And while thy willing soul transpires   35
At every pore with instant fires,
Now let us sport us while we may,
And now, like amorous birds of prey,
Rather at once our time devour
Than languish in his slow-chapt° power.   40
Let us roll all our strength and all
Our sweetness up into one ball,
And tear our pleasures with rough strife
Thorough° the iron gates of life:
Thus, though we cannot make our sun   45
Stand still,° yet we will make him run.

Conversion of the Jews Something that would take place in the remote future, at the
end of history.
vegetable Vegetative or growing.
state Ceremonious treatment.
try Test.
quaint Fastidious or finicky, with a pun on a coarse word defined in an Elizabethan dictionary as "a woman's privities."
slow-chapt Slow-jawed.
Thorough Through.
make our sun stand still An allusion to Joshua, the ancient Hebrew who, according to
the Book of Joshua (10.12–13), made the sun stand still.

Topics for Critical Thinking and Writing

1. The motif that life is short and that we should seize the day (Latin: Vita brevis *carpe diem*) is old. Marvell's poem, in fact, probably has its ultimate source in a classical text called *The Greek Anthology*, a collection of about six thousand short Greek poems composed between the first century B.C. and the tenth century A.D. One poem goes thus, in a fairly literal translation:

   > You spare your maidenhead, and to what profit? For when you come to Hades you will not find your lover, girl. Among the living are the delights of Venus, but, maiden, we shall lie in the underworld mere bones and dust.

   If you find Marvell's poem more impressive, offer reasons for your belief.

2. A student, working from the translation just given, produced this rhyming version:

   > You keep your virginity, but to what end?
   > Below, in Hades, you won't find your friend.
   > On earth we enjoy Venus' sighs and moans;
   > Buried below, we are senseless bones.

   What do you think of this version? Why? Prepare your own version — your instructor may divide the class into groups of four, and each group can come up with a collaborative version — and then compare it with other versions, giving reasons for your preferences.

3. Marvell's poem takes the form of a syllogism (see pp. 84–88). It can be divided into three parts:

   a. "Had we" (that is, "If we had") (line 1), a supposition, or suppositional premise;
   b. "But at my back" (line 21), a refutation;
   c. "Now therefore" (line 33), a deduction.

   Look closely at the poem and develop the argument using these three parts, devoting a few sentences to each part.

4. A student wrote of this poem:

   > As a Christian I can't accept the lover's statement that "yonder all before us lie / Deserts of vast eternity" (lines 23–24). The poem may contain beautiful lines, and it may offer clever reasoning, but the reasoning is based on what my religion tells me is wrong. I not only cannot accept the idea of the poem, but I also cannot enjoy the poem, since it presents a false view of reality.

   What assumptions is this student making about a reader's response to a work of literature? Do you agree or disagree? Why?

5. Here are three additional comments by students. For each, list the writer's assumptions, and then evaluate each comment. You may agree or disagree, in whole or in part, with any comment, but give your reasons.

   a. The poem is definitely clever, and that is part of what is wrong with it. It is a blatant attempt at seduction. The man seems to think he is smarter than the woman he is speaking to, and he "proves" that she should go to bed with him. Since we don't hear her side of the argument, Marvell implies that she has nothing to say and that his argument is sound. What the poet doesn't seem to understand is that there is such a thing as virtue, and a woman need not sacrifice virtue just because death is inevitable.

b. On the surface, "To His Coy Mistress" is an attempt to persuade a woman to go to bed with the speaker, but the poem is really less about sex than it is about the terrifying shortness of life.

c. This is not a love poem. The speaker admits that his impulse is "lust" (line 30), and he makes fun of the girl's conception of honor and virginity. If we enjoy this poem at all, our enjoyment must be in the hope that this would-be date-rapist is unsuccessful.

6. Read the poem several times slowly, perhaps even aloud. Do certain lines seem especially moving, especially memorable? If so, which ones? Give reasons for your belief.

7. In *On Deconstruction* (1982), a study of contemporary literary theory, Jonathan Culler remarks that feminist criticism has often stressed "reading as a woman." This concept, Culler says, affirms the "continuity between women's experience of social and familial structures and their experiences as readers." Do you agree with his suggestion that men and women often interpret literary works differently? Consider Marvell's poem in particular: Identify and discuss phrases and images in it to which men and women readers might (or might not) respond very differently.

8. A small point, but perhaps one of some interest. In the original text, line 34 ends with *glew*, not with *dew*. Most editors assume that the printer made an error, and—looking for a word to rhyme with *hue*—they replace *glew* with *dew*. Another possible emendation is *lew*, an archaic word meaning "warmth." But the original reading has been defended, as a variant of the word *glow*. Your preference? Your reasons?

Kate Chopin

Kate Chopin (1851–1904) was born in St. Louis and named Katherine O'Flaherty. At the age of nineteen she married a cotton broker in New Orleans, Oscar Chopin (the name is pronounced something like "show pan"), who was descended from the early French settlers in Louisiana. After her husband's death in 1883, Kate Chopin turned to writing fiction. The following story was first published in 1894.

The Story of an Hour

Knowing that Mrs. Mallard was afflicted with a heart trouble, great care was taken to break to her as gently as possible the news of her husband's death.

It was her sister Josephine who told her, in broken sentences, veiled hints that revealed in half concealing. Her husband's friend Richards was there, too, near her. It was he who had been in the newspaper office when intelligence of the railroad disaster was received, with Brently Mallard's name leading the list of "killed." He had only taken the time to assure himself of its truth by a second telegram, and had hastened to forestall any less careful, less tender friend in bearing the sad message.

She did not hear the story as many women have heard the same, with a paralyzed inability to accept its significance. She wept at once, with sudden, wild abandonment, in her sister's arms. When the storm of grief had spent itself she went away to her room alone. She would have no one follow her.

There stood, facing the open window, a comfortable, roomy arm-chair. Into this she sank, pressed down by a physical exhaustion that haunted her body and seemed to reach into her soul.

She could see in the open square before her house the tops of trees 5 that were all aquiver with the new spring life. The delicious breath of rain was in the air. In the street below a peddler was crying his wares. The notes of a distant song which some one was singing reached her faintly, and countless sparrows were twittering in the eaves.

There were patches of blue sky showing here and there through the clouds that had met and piled one above the other in the west facing her window.

She sat with her head thrown back upon the cushion of the chair, quite motionless, except when a sob came up into her throat and shook her, as a child who has cried itself to sleep continues to sob in its dreams.

She was young, with a fair, calm face, whose lines bespoke repression and even a certain strength. But now there was a dull stare in her eyes, whose gaze was fixed away off yonder on one of those patches of blue sky. It was not a glance of reflection, but rather indicated a suspension of intelligent thought.

There was something coming to her and she was waiting for it, fearfully. What was it? She did not know; it was too subtle and elusive to name. But she felt it, creeping out of the sky, reaching toward her through the sounds, the scents, the color that filled the air.

Now her bosom rose and fell tumultuously. She was beginning to 10 recognize this thing that was approaching to possess her, and she was striving to beat it back with her will—as powerless as her two white slender hands would have been.

When she abandoned herself a little whispered word escaped her slightly parted lips. She said it over and over under her breath: "Free, free, free!" The vacant stare and the look of terror that had followed it went from her eyes. They stayed keen and bright. Her pulses beat fast, and the coursing blood warmed and relaxed every inch of her body.

She did not stop to ask if it were not a monstrous joy that held her. A clear and exalted perception enabled her to dismiss the suggestion as trivial.

She knew that she would weep again when she saw the kind, tender hands folded in death; the face that had never looked save with love

upon her, fixed and gray and dead. But she saw beyond that bitter moment a long procession of years to come that would belong to her absolutely. And she opened and spread her arms out to them in welcome.

There would be no one to live for her during those coming years;
she would live for herself. There would be no powerful will bending her
in that blind persistence with which men and women believe they have
a right to impose a private will upon a fellow creature. A kind intention
or a cruel intention made the act seem no less a crime as she looked
upon it in that brief moment of illumination.

And yet she had loved him—sometimes. Often she had not. What   15
did it matter! What could love, the unsolved mystery, count for in face of
this possession of self-assertion which she suddenly recognized as the
strongest impulse of her being.

"Free! Body and soul free!" she kept whispering.

Josephine was kneeling before the closed door with her lips to the
keyhole, imploring for admission. "Louise, open the door! I beg; open
the door—you will make yourself ill. What are you doing, Louise? For
heaven's sake open the door."

"Go away. I am not making myself ill." No; she was drinking in a
very elixir of life through that open window.

Her fancy was running riot along those days ahead of her. Spring
days, and summer days, and all sorts of days that would be her own. She
breathed a quick prayer that life might be long. It was only yesterday she
had thought with a shudder that life might be long.

She arose at length and opened the door to her sister's importunities.   20
There was a feverish triumph in her eyes, and she carried herself unwittingly like a goddess of Victory. She clasped her sister's waist, and together they descended the stairs. Richards stood waiting for them at the
bottom.

Some one was opening the front door with a latchkey. It was Brently
Mallard who entered, a little travel-stained, composedly carrying his
gripsack and umbrella. He had been far from the scene of accident, and
did not even know there had been one. He stood amazed at Josephine's
piercing cry; at Richards' quick motion to screen him from the view of
his wife.

But Richards was too late.

When the doctors came they said she had died of heart disease—of
joy that kills.

Topics for Critical Thinking and Writing

Read the following assertions, and consider whether you agree or disagree, and
why. For each assertion, draft a paragraph with your arguments.

1. The railroad accident is a symbol of the destructiveness of the industrial
   revolution.

2. The story claims that women rejoice in the deaths of their husbands.
3. Mrs. Mallard's death at the end is a just punishment for the joy she takes in her husband's death.
4. The story is rich in irony. Some examples: (1) The other characters think she is grieving, but she is rejoicing; (2) she prays for a long life, but she dies almost immediately; (3) the doctors say she died of "the joy that kills," but they think her joy was seeing her husband alive.
5. The story is excellent because it has a surprise ending.

THINKING ABOUT THE EFFECTS OF LITERATURE

Works of art are artifacts—things constructed, made up, fashioned, just like chairs and houses and automobiles. In analyzing works of literature it is therefore customary to keep one's eye on the complex, constructed object and not simply tell the reader how one feels about it. Instead of reporting their feelings, critics usually analyze the relationships between the parts and the relationship of the parts to the whole.

For instance, in talking about literature we can examine the relationship of plot to character, of one character to another, or of one stanza in a poem to the next. Still, although we may try to engage in this sort of analysis as dispassionately as possible, we all know that inevitably

• We are not only examining something out there,
• But are also examining our own responses.

Why? Because literature has an effect on us. Indeed, it probably has several kinds of effects, ranging from short-range emotional responses ("I really enjoyed this," "I burst out laughing," "It revolted me") to long-range effects ("I have always tried to live up to a line in *Hamlet*, 'This above all, to thine own self be true'"). Let's first look at, very briefly, immediate emotional responses.

Analysis usually begins with a response: "This is marvelous," or "What a bore," and we then go on to try to account for our response. A friend mentions a book or a film to us, and we say, "I couldn't stay with it for five minutes." The friend expresses surprise, and we then go on to explain, giving reasons (to the friend and also to ourselves) why we couldn't stay with it. Perhaps the book seemed too remote from life, or perhaps, on the other hand, it seemed to be nothing more than a transcript of the boring talk that we can overhear on a bus or in an elevator.

In such discussions, when we draw on our responses, as we must, the work may disappear; we find ourselves talking about ourselves. Let's take two extreme examples: "I can't abide *Huckleberry Finn*. How am I expected to enjoy a so-called masterpiece that has a character in it called 'Nigger Jim?'" Or: "T. S. Eliot's anti-Semitism is too much for me to take. Don't talk to me about Eliot's skill with meter, when he has such lines as 'Rachel, *née* Rabinovitch / Tears at the grapes with murderous paws.'"

Although everyone agrees that literature can evoke this sort of strong emotional response, not everyone agrees on how much value we should put on our personal experience. Several of the Topics for Critical Thinking and Writing below invite you to reflect on this issue.

What about the *consequences of the effects* of literature? Does literature shape our character and therefore influence our behavior? It is generally believed that it does have an effect. One hears, for example, that literature (like travel) is broadening, that it makes us aware of, and tolerant of, kinds of behavior that differ from our own and from what we see around us. One of the chief arguments against pornography, for instance, is that it desensitizes us, makes us too tolerant of abusive relationships, relationships in which people (usually men) use other people (usually women) as mere things or instruments for pleasure. (A contrary view should be mentioned: Some people argue that pornography provides a relatively harmless outlet for fantasies that otherwise might be given release in the real world. In this view, pornography acts as a sort of safety valve.)

Discussions of the effects of literature that get into the popular press almost always involve pornography, but other topics are also the subjects of controversy. For instance, in recent decades parents and educators have been much concerned with fairy tales. Does the violence in some fairy tales ("Little Red Riding Hood," "The Three Little Pigs") have a bad effect on children? Do some of the stories teach the wrong lessons, implying that women should be passive, men active ("Sleeping Beauty," for instance, in which the sleeping woman is brought to life by the action of the handsome prince)? The Greek philosopher Plato (427–347 B.C.) strongly believed that the literature we hear or read shapes our later behavior, and since most of the ancient Greek traditional stories (notably Homer's *Odyssey* and *Iliad*) celebrate acts of love and war rather than of justice, he prohibited the reading of such material in his ideal society. (We reprint a relevant passage from Plato on page 489.)

TOPICS FOR CRITICAL THINKING AND WRITING

1. If you have responded strongly (favorably or unfavorably) to some aspect of the social content of a literary work—for instance, its depiction of women or of a particular minority group—in an essay of 250 to 500 words analyze the response, and try to determine whether you are talking chiefly about yourself or the work. (Two works widely regarded as literary masterpieces but nonetheless often banned from classrooms are Shakespeare's *The Merchant of Venice* and Mark Twain's *Huckleberry Finn*. If you have read either of these, you may want to write about it and your response.) Can we really see literary value—*really* see it—in a work that deeply offends us?

2. Most people believe that literature influences life—that in some perhaps mysterious way it helps to shape character. Certainly anyone who

believes that some works should be censored, or at least should be made unavailable to minors, assumes that they can have a bad influence, so why not assume that other works can have a good influence?

Read the following brief claims about literature, then choose one and write a 250-word essay offering support or taking issue with it.

The pen is mightier than the sword. — ANONYMOUS

The writer isn't made in a vacuum. Writers are witnesses. The reason we need writers is because we need witnesses to this terrifying century. — E. L. DOCTOROW

When we read of human beings behaving in certain ways, with the approval of the author, who gives his benedictions to this behavior by his attitude towards the result of the behavior arranged by himself, we can be influenced towards behaving in the same way. — T. S. ELIOT

Poetry makes nothing happen. — W. H. AUDEN

Literature is *without proofs*. By which it must be understood that it cannot prove, not only *what* it says, but even that it is worth the trouble of saying it. — ROLAND BARTHES

Of course the illusion of art is to make one believe that great literature is very close to life, but exactly the opposite is true. Life is amorphous, literature is formal. — FRANÇOISE SAGAN

3. At least since the time of Plato (see the piece directly following) some thoughtful people have wanted to ban certain works of literature because they allegedly stimulate the wrong sorts of pleasure or cause us to take pleasure in the wrong sorts of things. Consider, by way of comparison, bullfighting and cockfighting. Of course, they cause pain to the animals, but branding animals also causes pain and is not banned. Bullfighting and cockfighting probably are banned in the United States largely because most of us believe that people should not take pleasure in these activities. Now to return to literature: Should some kinds of writing be prohibited because they offer the wrong sorts of pleasure?

Plato

Plato (427–347 B.C.), an Athenian aristocrat by birth, was the student of one great philosopher (Socrates) and the teacher of another (Aristotle). His legacy of more than two dozen dialogues — imaginary discussions between Socrates and one or more other speakers, usually young Athenians — has been of such influence that the whole of Western philosophy can be characterized, A. N. Whitehead wrote, as "a series of footnotes to Plato." Plato's interests encompassed the full range of topics in philosophy: ethics, politics, logic, metaphysics, epistemology, aesthetics, psychology, and education.

This selection from Plato's Republic, *one of his best-known and longest dialogues, is about the education suitable for the rulers of an ideal society. The Re-*

public *begins, typically, with an investigation into the nature of justice. Socrates (who speaks for Plato) convincingly explains to Glaucon that we cannot reasonably expect to achieve a just society unless we devote careful attention to the moral education of the young men who are scheduled in later life to become the rulers. (Here as elsewhere, Plato's elitism and aristocratic bias shows itself; as readers of* The Republic *soon learn, Plato is no admirer of democracy or of a classless society.) Plato cares as much about what the educational curriculum should exclude as what it should include. His special target was the common practice in his day of using for pedagogy the Homeric tales and other stories about the gods. He readily embraces the principle of censorship, as the excerpt explains, because he thinks it is a necessary means to achieve the ideal society.*

"The Greater Part of the Stories Current Today We Shall Have to Reject"

"What kind of education shall we give them then? We shall find it difficult to improve on the time-honored distinction between the physical training we give to the body and the education we give to the mind and character."

"True."

"And we shall begin by educating mind and character, shall we not?"

"Of course."

"In this education you would include stories, would you not?"   5

"Yes."

"These are of two kinds, true stories and fiction.[1] Our education must use both, and start with fiction."

"I don't know what you mean."

"But you know that we begin by telling children stories. These are, in general, fiction, though they contain some truth. And we tell children stories before we start them on physical training."

"That is so."   10

"That is what I meant by saying that we must start to educate the mind before training the body."

"You are right," he said.

"And the first step, as you know, is always what matters most, particularly when we are dealing with those who are young and tender. That is the time when they are easily molded and when any impression we choose to make leaves a permanent mark."

"That is certainly true."

---

[1]The Greek word *pseudos* and its corresponding verb meant not only "fiction"—stories, tales—but also "what is not true" and so, in suitable contexts, "lies": and this ambiguity should be borne in mind. [Editors' note: All footnotes are by the translator, but some have been omitted.]

"Shall we therefore readily allow our children to listen to any 15
stories made up by anyone, and to form opinions that are for the most
part the opposite of those we think they should have when they
grow up?"

"We certainly shall not."

"Then it seems that our first business is to supervise the production
of stories, and choose only those we think suitable, and reject the rest.
We shall persuade mothers and nurses to tell our chosen stories to their
children, and by means of them to mold their minds and characters
which are more important than their bodies. The greater part of the stories current today we shall have to reject."

"Which are you thinking of?"

"We can take some of the major legends as typical. For all, whether
major or minor, should be cast in the same mold and have the same effect. Do you agree?"

"Yes: but I'm not sure which you refer to as major."   20

"The stories in Homer and Hesiod and the poets. For it is the poets
who have always made up fictions and stories to tell to men."

"What sort of stories do you mean and what fault do you find in
them?"

"The worst fault possible," I replied, "especially if the fiction is an
ugly one."

"And what is that?"

"Misrepresenting the nature of gods and heroes, like a portrait 25
painter whose portraits bear no resemblance to their originals."

"That is a fault which certainly deserves censure. But give me more
details."

"Well, on the most important of subjects, there is first and foremost the foul story about Ouranos[2] and the things Hesiod says he did, and
the revenge Cronos took on him. While the story of what Cronos did, and
what he suffered at the hands of his son, is not fit as it is to be lightly repeated to the young and foolish, even if it were true; it would be best to
say nothing about it, or if it must be told, tell it to a select few under oath
of secrecy, at a rite which required, to restrict it still further, the sacrifice
not of a mere pig but of something large and difficult to get."

"These certainly are awkward stories."

"And they shall not be repeated in our state, Adeimantus," I said.
"Nor shall any young audience be told that anyone who commits horrible crimes, or punishes his father unmercifully, is doing nothing out of
the ordinary but merely what the first and greatest of the gods have
done before."

"I entirely agree," said Adeimantus, "that these stories are unsuitable." 30

---

[2]**Ouranos** The sky, the original supreme god. Ouranos was castrated by his son Cronos to
separate him from Gaia (mother earth). Cronos was in turn deposed by Zeus in a struggle
in which Zeus was helped by the Titans.

"Nor can we permit stories of wars and plots and battles among the gods; they are quite untrue, and if we want our prospective guardians to believe that quarrelsomeness is one of the worst of evils, we must certainly not let them be told the story of the Battle of the Giants or embroider it on robes, or tell them other tales about many and various quarrels between gods and heroes and their friends and relations. On the contrary, if we are to persuade them that no citizen has ever quarreled with any other, because it is sinful, our old men and women must tell children stories with this end in view from the first, and we must compel our poets to tell them similar stories when they grow up. But we can admit to our state no stories about Hera being tied up by her son, or Hephaestus being flung out of Heaven by his father for trying to help his mother when she was getting a beating, nor any of Homer's Battles of the Gods, whether their intention is allegorical or not. Children cannot distinguish between what is allegory and what isn't, and opinions formed at that age are usually difficult to eradicate or change; we should therefore surely regard it as of the utmost importance that the first stories they hear shall aim at encouraging the highest excellence of character."

"Your case is a good one," he agreed, "but if someone wanted details, and asked what stories we were thinking of, what should we say?"

To which I replied, "My dear Adeimantus, you and I are not engaged on writing stories but on founding a state. And the founders of a state, though they must know the type of story the poet must produce, and reject any that do not conform to that type, need not write them themselves."

"True: but what are the lines on which our poets must work when they deal with the gods?"

"Roughly as follows," I said. "God must surely always be represented 35 as he really is, whether the poet is writing epic, lyric, or tragedy."

"He must."

"And in reality of course god is good, and he must be so described."

"Certainly."

"But nothing good is harmful, is it?"[3]

"I think not."   40

"Then can anything that is not harmful do harm?"

"No."

"And can what does no harm do evil?"

"No again."

"And can what does no evil be the cause of any evil?"   45

"How could it?"

---

[3]The reader of the following passage should bear the following ambiguities in mind: (1) the Greek word for good (*agathos*) can mean (a) morally good, (b) beneficial or advantageous; (2) the Greek word for evil (*kakos*) can also mean harm or injury; (3) the adverb of *agathos* (*eu*—the well) can imply either morally right or prosperous. The word translated "cause of" could equally well be rendered "responsible for."

"Well then; is the good beneficial?"

"Yes."

"So it must be the cause of well-being."

"Yes."   50

"So the good is not the cause of everything, but only of states of well-being and not of evil."

"Most certainly," he agreed.

"Then god, being good, cannot be responsible for everything, as is commonly said, but only for a small part of human life, for the greater part of which he has no responsibility. For we have a far smaller share of good than of evil, and while god must be held to be the sole cause of good, we must look for some factors other than god as cause of the evil."

"I think that's very true," he said.

"So we cannot allow Homer or any other poet to make such a stupid   55 mistake about the gods, as when he says that

> Zeus has two jars standing on the floor of his palace, full of fates, good in one and evil in the other

and that the man to whom Zeus allots a mixture of both has 'varying fortunes sometimes good and sometimes bad,' while the man to whom he allots unmixed evil is `chased by ravening despair over the face of the earth.'[4] Nor can we allow references to Zeus as `dispenser of good and evil.' And we cannot approve if it is said that Athene and Zeus prompted the breach of solemn treaty and oath by Pandarus, or that the strife and contentions of the gods were due to Themis and Zeus. Nor again can we let our children hear from Aeschylus that

> God implants a fault in man, when he wishes to destroy a house utterly.

No: We must forbid anyone who writes a play about the sufferings of Niobe (the subject of the play from which these last lines are quoted), or the house of Pelops, or the Trojan war, or any similar topic, to say they are acts of god; or if he does he must produce the sort of interpretation we are now demanding, and say that god's acts were good and just, and that the sufferers were benefited by being punished. What the poet must not be allowed to say is that those who were punished were made wretched through god's action. He may refer to the wicked as wretched because they needed punishment, provided he makes it clear that in punishing them god did them good. But if a state is to be run on the right lines, every possible step must be taken to prevent anyone, young or old, either saying or being told, whether in poetry or prose, that god, being good, can cause harm or evil to any man. To say so would be sinful, inexpedient, and inconsistent."

---

[4]Quotations from Homer are generally taken from the translations by Dr. Rieu in the Penguin series. At times (as here) the version quoted by Plato differs slightly from the accepted text.

"I should approve of a law for this purpose and you have my vote for it," he said.

"Then of our laws laying down the principles which those who write or speak about the gods must follow, one would be this: *God is the cause, not of all things, but only of good.*"

"I am quite content with that," he said.

TOPICS FOR CRITICAL THINKING AND WRITING

1. In the beginning of the dialogue Plato says that adults recite fictions to very young children and that these fictions help to mold character. Think of some stories that you heard or read when young, such as "Snow White and the Seven Dwarfs" or "Ali Baba and the Forty Thieves." Try to think of a story that, in the final analysis, is not in accord with what you consider to be proper morality, such as a story in which a person triumphs through trickery or a story in which evil actions—perhaps murders—are set forth without unfavorable comment. (Was it naughty of Jack to kill the giant?) On reflection, do you think children should not be told such stories? Why, or why not? Or think of the early film westerns, in which, on the whole, the Indians (except for an occasional Uncle Tonto) are depicted as bad guys and the whites (except for an occasional coward or rustler) are depicted as good guys. Many people who now have gray hair enjoyed such films in their childhood. Are you prepared to say that such films are not damaging? Or on the other hand, are you prepared to say they are damaging and should be prohibited?

2. It is often objected that censorship of reading matter and of television programs available to children underrates their ability to think for themselves and to discount the dangerous, obscene, and tawdry. Do you agree with this objection? Does Plato?

3. Plato says that allowing poets to say what they please about the gods in his ideal state would be "inconsistent." Explain what he means by this criticism, and then explain why you agree or disagree with it.

4. Do you believe that parents should censor the "fiction" their children encounter (literature, films, pictures, music) but that the community should not censor the "fiction" of adults? Write an essay of 500 words on one of these topics: "Censorship and Rock Lyrics"; "X-rated Films"; "Ethnic Jokes." (These topics are broadly worded; you can narrow one and offer whatever thesis you wish.)

5. Were you taught that any of the founding fathers ever acted disreputably, or that any American hero had any serious moral flaw? Or that America ever acted immorally in its dealings with other nations? Do you think it appropriate for children to hear such things?

THINKING ABOUT GOVERNMENT
FUNDING FOR THE ARTS

Our government supports the arts, including writers, by giving grants to numerous institutions. On the other hand, the amount that the government contributes is extremely small when compared to the amounts given to the arts by most European governments. Consider the following questions.

1. Should taxpayers' dollars be used to support the arts? Why, or why not?
2. What possible public benefit can come from supporting the arts? Can one argue that we should support the arts for the same reasons that we support the public schools, that is, to have a civilized society?
3. If dollars are given to the arts, should the political content of the works be taken into account, or only the aesthetic merit? Can we separate content from aesthetic merit? (The best way to approach this issue probably is to begin by thinking of a strongly political work.)
4. Is it censorship not to award public funds to writers whose work is not approved of, or is it simply a matter of refusing to reward them with taxpayers' dollars?
5. Should decisions about grants to writers be made chiefly by government officials or chiefly by experts in the field? Why?

A Forensic View: Oral Presentation and Debate

He who knows only his own side of the case knows little of that.
— JOHN STUART MILL

A philosopher who is not taking part in discussions is like a boxer who never goes into the ring.
— LUDWIG WITTGENSTEIN

Freedom is hammered out on the anvil of dissension, dissent, and debate.
— HUBERT HUMPHREY

Forensic comes from a Latin word, *foris,* meaning "out of doors," which also produced the word *forum,* an open space in front of a public building. In such a place, loiterers inevitably assembled, marketplaces developed, people got into arguments—and trials were publicly conducted. The English word *forensic,* meaning the practice or study of formal debate, comes from this activity; *forensic medicine,* for instance, is the branch of medicine that, in legal cases, establishes the medical facts: Did the patient die of the knife wound or of a subsequent heart attack?

It would be nice if all arguments ended with everyone, participants and spectators, agreeing that the facts are clear, that one presentation is more reasonable than the other, and therefore that one side is right and the other side is wrong. But in life, most issues are complicated. High school students may earnestly debate—this is a real topic in a national debate—

Resolved: That education has failed its mission in the United States,

but it takes only a moment of reflection to see that neither the affirmative nor the negative can be true. Yes, education has failed its mission in many ways, but, No, it has succeeded in many ways. Its job now is (in the words of Samuel Beckett) to try again: "Fail. Fail again. Fail better."

Debates of this sort, conducted before a judge and guided by strict rules concerning "Constructive Speeches," "Rebuttal Speeches," and "Cross-Examinations" are not attempts to get at the truth; like lawsuits, they are attempts to win a case. Each speaker seeks not to persuade the opponent but only to convince the judge. Although most of this chapter is devoted not to forensics in the strictest sense but more generally to the presentation of oral arguments, we begin with the standard format.

STANDARD DEBATE FORMAT

Formal debates occur within a structure that governs the number of speeches, the order of the speeches, and the maximum time for each speech. The format may vary from place to place, but there is always a structure. In most debates, a formal resolution states the reason for the debate ("Resolved: That capital punishment be abolished in juvenile cases"). The affirmative team supports the resolution; the negative team denies its legitimacy. The basic structure has three parts:

- *The constructive phase,* in which the debaters construct their cases and develop their arguments (usually for ten minutes);
- *The rebuttal,* in which debaters present their responses and also present their final summary (usually for five minutes); and
- *The preparation,* in which the debater prepares for presenting the next speech. (During the preparation—a sort of time-out—the debater is not addressing the opponent or audience. The total time allotted to a team is usually six or eight minutes, which the individual debaters divide as they wish.)

We give, very briefly, the usual structure of each part, though it should be mentioned that another common format calls for a cross-examination of the First Affirmative Construction by the Second Negative, a cross-examination of the First Negative Construction by the First Affirmative, a cross-examination of the Second Affirmative by the First Negative, and a cross-examination of the Second Negative by the Second Affirmative:

First Affirmative Constructive Speech: Serves as introduction, giving summary overview, definitions, criteria for resolution, major claims and evidence, statement, and intention to support the resolution.

First Negative Constructive Speech: Responds by introducing the basic position, challenges the definitions and criteria, suggests the line of attack, emphasizes that the burden of proof lies with the affirmative, rejects the resolution as unnecessary or dangerous, and supports the status quo.

Second Affirmative Constructive: Rebuilds the affirmative case; refutes chief attacks, especially concerning definitions, criteria, and rationale (philosophic framework); and further develops the affirmative case.

Second Negative Constructive: Completes the negative case, if possible advances it by rebuilding portions of the first negative construction, and contrasts the entire negative case with the entire affirmative case.

First Negative Rebuttal: Attacks the opponents' arguments and defends the negative constructive arguments (but a rebuttal may *not* introduce new constructive arguments).

First Affirmative Rebuttal: Usually responds first to the second negative construction and then to the first negative rebuttal.

Second Negative Rebuttal: Constitutes final speech for the negative, summarizing the case and explaining to the judge why the negative should be declared the winner.

Second Affirmative Rebuttal: Summarizes the debate, responds to issues pressed by the second negative rebuttal, and suggests to the judge that the affirmative team should win.

We turn now to our chief topic, oral presentation of an argument.

THE AUDIENCE

It is not merely because topics are complicated that we cannot agree that one side is reasonable and right and the other side irrational and wrong. The truth is, we are swayed not only by reason (*logos*) but also by appeals to the emotions (*pathos*) and by the character of the speaker (*ethos*). We can combine these last two things and put it this way: Sometimes we are inclined to agree with *X* rather than with *Y* because *X* strikes us as a more appealing person (perhaps more open-minded, more intelligent, better informed, more humane, and less cold). *X* is the sort of person we want to have as a friend. We disagree with *Y*—or at least we are unwilling to associate ourselves with *Y*—because *Y* is, well, *Y* just isn't the sort of person we want to agree with. *Y*'s statistics don't sound right, or *Y* seems like a bully; for some reason, we just don't have confidence in *Y*. Confidence is easily lost: Alas, even a mispronunciation will diminish the audience's confidence in *Y*. As Peter de Vries said, "You can't be happy with someone who pronounces both *d*'s in Wednesday."

Earlier in the book we talked about the importance of **tone** and of the writer's **persona**. And we have made the point that the writer's tone will depend partly on the audience. A person who is writing for a conservative journal whose readership is almost entirely conservatives can adopt a highly satiric manner in talking about liberals and will meet with much approval. But if this conservative writer is writing in a liberal journal and hopes to get at least a sympathetic hearing, he or she will have to avoid satire and wisecracks and will have to present himself or herself as a person of goodwill who is open-minded and eager to address the issue seriously.

The **language** that you use—the degree to which it is formal as opposed to colloquial, and the degree to which it is technical as opposed to general—will also depend on the audience. Speaking a bit broadly, in oral argument speak politely but not formally. You do *not* want to be one of those people who "talk like a book." But you also don't want to be overly colloquial. Choose a middle course, probably a notch below the style you would use if you were handing in a written paper. For instance, in an oral presentation you might say, "We'll consider this point in a minute or two," whereas in a written paper you probably will write "We will consider this point shortly."

Technical language is entirely appropriate *if* your audience is familiar with it. If you are arguing before members of Amnesty International about the use of torture—we include essays in this book that support the use of torture to prevent a disaster like that of September 11—you can assume certain kinds of specialized knowledge. You can, for instance, breezily speak of the DRC and of KPCS, and your hearers will know what you are talking about because Amnesty International has been active with issues concerning the Democratic Republic of Congo and the Kimberley Process Certification Scheme. On the other hand, if you are arguing the same case before a general public, you will have to explain these abbreviations, and you may even have to explain what Amnesty International is.

If you are arguing before your classmates, you probably have a pretty good idea of what you can assume they know and what you can assume they do not know.

DELIVERY

Your audience will in some measure determine not only your tone but also the way you appear when you give the speech. Part of the delivery is the speaker's **appearance.** The medium is part of the message. The president can appear in jeans when he chats about his reelection plans, but he wears a suit and a tie when he delivers the State of the Union address. Just as we wear one kind of **clothing** when we play tennis, another when we attend classes, and yet another when we go for a job interview, an effective speaker dresses appropriately. A lawyer arguing before the Supreme Court wears a dark suit or dress, and if the lawyer is male he wears a necktie. The same lawyer, arguing at a local meeting, speaking as a community resident who objects to a proposal to allow a porno store to open near a school, may well dress informally, maybe in jeans, to show that he or she is not at all stuffy but still feels that a porno store goes too far.

Your appearance when you speak is not merely a matter of your clothing; it includes your **facial expressions,** your **posture,** your **gestures,** your general demeanor. All that we can say here is that you should avoid those bodily motions—swaying, thumping the table, putting on and taking off eyeglasses, craning your neck, smirking—that are so distracting that they cause the audience to concentrate on the distraction rather than on the argument. ("That's the third time he straightened his necktie. I wonder how many more times he will—oops, that's the fourth!"). Most of us are not aware of our annoying habits; if you are lucky, a friend, when urged, will tell you about them. You may lose a friend, but you will gain some good advice.

You probably can't do much about your **voice**—it may be high-pitched, or it may be gravelly—but you can make sure that you speak loudly enough for the audience to hear you, slowly enough for it to understand you, and clearly enough for it to understand you.

The text of an oral presentation ought not to be identical with the text of a written presentation. Both must have a clear **organization,** but oral presentations usually require that the organization be made a bit more obvious, with abundant **signposts** such as "Before I talk about *X*," "When I discussed *Y*, I didn't mention such-and-such because I wanted to concentrate on a single instance, but now is the time to consider *Y*," and so on. You will also have to repeat a bit more than you would in a written presentation. After all, a reader can turn back to check a sentence or a statistic but an auditor cannot, so rather than saying (as one might in a printed text), "When we think further about Smith's comment, we realize. . . ," you will repeat what Smith said before you go on to analyze the statement.

Speaking of **quotations,** we have some advice. First, if possible, use an effective quotation or two, partly because—we will be frank—the quotations probably are more impressively worded than anything you can come up with on your own. A quotation may be the chief thing that your audience comes away with: "Hey, yes, I liked that: 'War is too important to be left to the generals'" or "When it comes down to it, I agree with that Frenchman who said 'If we are to abolish the death penalty, I should like to see the first step taken by the murderers'" or "You know, I think it was all summed up in that line by Margaret Mead, something like, 'No one would remember the Good Samaritan if he'd had only good intentions. He had money as well.' Yes, that's pretty convincing. Morality isn't enough. You need money." You didn't invent the words that you quote, but you did bring them to the attention of your listeners, and your listeners will be grateful to you.

A second bit of advice about quotations: When you quote, do *not* begin by saying "quote," and do not end by saying "end quote" (or as we once heard a speaker endlessly say, quotation after quotation, "unquote") and do not hook the air with your fingers. How do you make it clear that you are quoting, and how do you make it clear that you have finished quoting? Begin with a clear lead-in ("In *Major Barbara* George Bernard Shaw touches on this issue, when Barbara says, . . ."), slightly pause, and then slightly change (for instance, elevate) your voice. When you have finished quoting—again a slight pause and a return to your normal voice—be sure to use words that clearly indicate the quotation is finished, such as "Shaw here says what everyone thinks," or "Shaw's comment is witty but short-sighted," or "Barbara's point, then, is . . ."

Our third and last piece of advice concerning quotations is this: If the quotation is only a phrase or a brief sentence, you can memorize it and can be confident that you will remember it, but if it is longer than a sentence, write it on a sheet in your notes or on a four- by six-inch card in print large enough for you to read easily. You have chosen these words because they are effectively put, so you don't want to misquote them or even hesitate in delivering them.

You may want to use **visual aids**—for instance, handouts, graphs, projected slides, or even a PowerPoint program that lets you project images from a computer. Fine, we have only two suggestions.

- First, if you use machinery, be sure that you have some backup. We have seen more than one talk end miserably when the bulb in the slide projector burned out.

- Second, although visual material may be extremely useful, it can also be trivial, irrelevant, and annoying.

The writer of this page recently sat through a scholarly lecture on the use of quotations in certain famous speeches in which the lecturer projected his own name on the screen for the first three or four minutes. When the lecturer got around to the 1858 Lincoln-Douglas debates, this is what appeared on the screen:

Abraham Lincoln
Stephen A. Douglas

The effect of these and other similar slides was that we in the audience assumed (rightly) that the speaker assumed (wrongly) that we were simpletons. Furthermore, we assumed (rightly) that *he* was a simpleton. For a delightful parody of PowerPoint presentations, see *http://www.norvig.com/Gettysburg/*.

Some visual bits are inspired. President Reagan in his first televised budget speech used a handful of small coins to illustrate the decline of the dollar. Brilliant. (A wit later said that President Carter would have emphasized the wrong words, President Ford would have dropped some of the coins, and President Nixon would have pocketed them.) For this sort of visual persuasion we can offer no advice whatsoever; it is the touch of a master.

THE TALK

As for the talk itself, well, we have been touching on it in our discussion of such matters as the speaker's relation to the audience, the speaker's need to provide signposts, and the use of quotations. All of our comments in earlier chapters about developing a written argument are relevant also to oral arguments, but here we should merely emphasize that because the talk is oral and the audience cannot look back to an earlier page to remind itself of some point, the speaker may have to repeat and summarize a bit more than is usual in a written essay.

Remember, too, that a reader can *see* when the essay ends—there is blank space at the end of the page—but a listener depends on aural cues. Nothing is more embarrassing—and less effective as argument—than a speaker who seems (to the audience) to suddenly stop and sit down. In short, give your hearers ample clues that you are ending (post such signs as "Finally" or "Last" or "Let me end by saying"), and be sure to end with a strong sentence. It probably won't be as good as the end of the Gettysburg address ("government of the people, by the people, for the people, shall not perish from the earth"), nor will it be as good as the end of Martin Luther King's "I Have a Dream" speech ("Free at last! Free at last! Thank God Almighty, we are free at last!"), but those are the models to emulate.

✓ A CHECKLIST FOR PREPARING FOR A DEBATE

- ☐ Have I done adequate preparation in research?
- ☐ Are my notes legible, with accurate quotations and impressive sources?
- ☐ Am I prepared to take good notes during the debate?
- ☐ Is my proposition clearly stated?
- ☐ Do I have adequate evidence to support the thesis (main point)?
- ☐ Do I have backup points in mind?
- ☐ Have I given thought to issues opponents may raise?
- ☐ Does the opening properly address the instructor, the audience, the opponents? (Remember, you are addressing an audience, not merely the opponents.)
- ☐ Are my visual aids focused on major points?
- ☐ Is my demeanor professional, and is my dress appropriate?

PART FOUR

A CASEBOOK
on the STATE and
the INDIVIDUAL

What Is the Ideal Society?

Thomas More

The son of a prominent London lawyer, More (1478–1535) served as a page in the household of the Archbishop of Canterbury, went to Oxford University, and then studied law in London. More's charm, brilliance, and gentle manner caused Erasmus, the great Dutch humanist who became his friend during a visit to London, to write to a friend: "Did nature ever create anything kinder, sweeter, or more harmonious than the character of Thomas More?"

More served in Parliament, became a diplomat, and after holding several important positions in the government of Henry VIII, rose to become Lord Chancellor. But when Henry married Anne Boleyn, broke from the Church of Rome, and established himself as head of the Church of England, More refused to subscribe to the Act of Succession and Supremacy. Condemned to death as a traitor, he was executed in 1535, nominally for treason but really because he would not recognize the king rather than the pope as the head of his church. A moment before the ax fell, More displayed a bit of the whimsy for which he was known: When he put his head on the block, he brushed his beard aside, commenting that his beard had done no offense to the king. In 1886 the Roman Catholic Church beatified More, and in 1935, the four-hundredth anniversary of his death, it canonized him as St. Thomas More.

More wrote Utopia *(1514–15) in Latin, the international language of the day. The book's name, however, is Greek for "no place" (*ou topos*), with a pun on "good place" (*eu topos*). *Utopia *owes something to Plato's* Republic *and something to then-popular accounts of voyagers such as Amerigo Vespucci.* Utopia *purports to record an account given by a traveler named Hytholodaeus (Greek for "learned in nonsense"), who allegedly visited Utopia. The work is playful, but it is also serious. In truth, it is hard to know exactly where it is serious and how serious it is. One inevitably wonders, for example, if More the devoted Roman Catholic could really have advocated euthanasia. And could More the persecutor of heretics really have approved of the religious tolerance practiced in Utopia? Is he perhaps in effect saying, "Let's see what reason, unaided by Christian revelation, can tell us about an ideal society"? But if so, is he nevertheless also saying, very strongly, that Christian countries, though blessed with the revelation of Christ's teachings, are far behind these unenlightened pagans?* Utopia *has been widely praised by all sorts of readers—from Roman Catholics to communists—but for all sorts of reasons. The selection presented here is about one-twelfth of the book (in a translation by Paul Turner).*

From *Utopia*

[A DAY IN UTOPIA]

And now for their working conditions. Well, there's one job they all do, irrespective of sex, and that's farming. It's part of every child's education. They learn the principles of agriculture at school, and they're taken for regular outings into the fields near the town, where they not only watch farm work being done, but also do some themselves, as a form of exercise.

Besides farming which, as I say, is everybody's job, each person is taught a special trade of his own. He may be trained to process wool or flax, or he may become a stonemason, a blacksmith, or a carpenter. Those are the only trades that employ any considerable quantity of labor. They have no tailors or dressmakers, since everyone on the island wears the same sort of clothes—except that they vary slightly according to sex and marital status—and the fashion never changes. These clothes are quite pleasant to look at, they allow free movement of the limbs, they're equally suitable for hot and cold weather—and the great thing is, they're all home-made. So everybody learns one of the other trades I mentioned, and by everybody I mean the women as well as the men—though the weaker sex are given the lighter jobs, like spinning and weaving, while the men do the heavier ones.

Most children are brought up to do the same work as their parents, since they tend to have a natural feeling for it. But if a child fancies some other trade, he's adopted into a family that practices it. Of course, great care is taken, not only by the father, but also by the local authorities, to see that the foster father is a decent, respectable type. When you've learned one trade properly, you can, if you like, get permission to learn another—and when you're an expert in both, you can practice whichever you prefer, unless the other one is more essential to the public.

The chief business of the Stywards[1]—in fact, practically their only business—is to see that nobody sits around doing nothing, but that everyone gets on with his job. They don't wear people out, though, by keeping them hard at work from early morning till late at night, like cart horses. That's just slavery—and yet that's what life is like for the working classes nearly everywhere else in the world. In Utopia they have a six-hour working day—three hours in the morning, then lunch—then a two-hour break—then three more hours in the afternoon, followed by supper. They go to bed at 8 P.M., and sleep for eight hours. All the rest of the twenty-four they're free to do what they like—not to waste their

---

[1]**Stywards**   In Utopia, each group of thirty households elects a styward; each town has two hundred stywards, who elect the mayor. [All notes are the editors'.]

time in idleness or self-indulgence, but to make good use of it in some congenial activity. Most people spend these free periods on further education, for there are public lectures first thing every morning. Attendance is quite voluntary, except for those picked out for academic training, but men and women of all classes go crowding in to hear them—I mean, different people go to different lectures, just as the spirit moves them. However, there's nothing to stop you from spending this extra time on your trade, if you want to. Lots of people do, if they haven't the capacity for intellectual work, and are much admired for such public-spirited behavior.

After supper they have an hour's recreation, either in the gardens 5 or in the communal dining-halls, according to the time of year. Some people practice music, others just talk. They've never heard of anything so silly and demoralizing as dice, but they have two games rather like chess. The first is a sort of arithmetical contest, in which certain numbers "take" others. The second is a pitched battle between virtues and vices, which illustrates most ingeniously how vices tend to conflict with one another, but to combine against virtues. It also shows which vices are opposed to which virtues, how much strength vices can muster for a direct assault, what indirect tactics they employ, what help virtues need to overcome vices, what are the best methods of evading their attacks, and what ultimately determines the victory of one side or the other.

But here's a point that requires special attention, or you're liable to get the wrong idea. Since they only work a six-hour day, you may think there must be a shortage of essential goods. On the contrary, those six hours are enough, and more than enough to produce plenty of everything that's needed for a comfortable life. And you'll understand why it is, if you reckon up how large a proportion of the population in other countries is totally unemployed. First you have practically all the women—that gives you nearly 50 percent for a start. And in countries where the women *do* work, the men tend to lounge about instead. Then there are all the priests, and members of so-called religious orders—how much work do they do? Add all the rich, especially the landowners, popularly known as nobles and gentlemen. Include their domestic staffs—I mean those gangs of armed ruffians that I mentioned before. Finally, throw in all the beggars who are perfectly hale and hearty, but pretend to be ill as an excuse for being lazy. When you've counted them up, you'll be surprised to find how few people actually produce what the human race consumes.

And now just think how few of these few people are doing essential work—for where money is the only standard of value, there are bound to be dozens of unnecessary trades carried on, which merely supply luxury goods or entertainment. Why, even if the existing labor force were distributed among the few trades really needed to make life reasonably comfortable, there'd be so much overproduction that prices would fall too low for the workers to earn a living. Whereas, if you took all those engaged in nonessential trades, and all who are too lazy to work—each of whom consumes twice as much of the products of other people's labor as any of the producers themselves—if you put the whole lot of them on to something useful, you'd soon see how few hours' work a day would be amply sufficient to supply all the necessities and comforts of life—to which you might add all real and natural forms of pleasure.

[THE HOUSEHOLD]

But let's get back to their social organization. Each household, as I said, comes under the authority of the oldest male. Wives are subordinate to their husbands, children to their parents, and younger people generally to their elders. Every town is divided into four districts of equal size, each with its own shopping center in the middle of it. There the products of every household are collected in warehouses, and then distributed according to type among various shops. When the head of a household needs anything for himself or his family, he just goes to one of these shops and asks for it. And whatever he asks for, he's allowed to take away without any sort of payment, either in money or in kind. After all, why shouldn't he? There's more than enough of everything to go round, so there's no risk of his asking for more than he needs—for why should anyone want to start hoarding, when he knows he'll never have to go short of anything? No living creature is naturally greedy, except from fear of want—or in the case of human beings, from vanity, the notion that you're better than people if you can display more superfluous property than they can. But there's no scope for that sort of thing in Utopia.

[UTOPIAN BELIEFS]

The Utopians fail to understand why anyone should be so fascinated by the dull gleam of a tiny bit of stone, when he has all the stars in the sky to look at—or how anyone can be silly enough to think himself better than other people, because his clothes are made of finer woollen thread than theirs. After all, those fine clothes were once worn by a sheep, and they never turned it into anything better than a sheep.

Nor can they understand why a totally useless substance like gold 10 should now, all over the world, be considered far more important than human beings, who gave it such value as it has, purely for their own convenience. The result is that a man with about as much mental agility as a lump of lead or a block of wood, a man whose utter stupidity is paralleled only by his immorality, can have lots of good, intelligent people at his beck and call, just because he happens to possess a large pile of gold coins. And if by some freak of fortune or trick of the law—two equally effective methods of turning things upside down—the said coins were suddenly transferred to the most worthless member of his domestic staff, you'd soon see the present owner trotting after his money, like an extra piece of currency, and becoming his own servant's servant. But what puzzles and disgusts the Utopians even more is the idiotic way some people have of practically worshipping a rich man, not because they owe him money or are otherwise in his power, but simply because he's rich—although they know perfectly well that he's far too mean to let a single penny come their way, so long as he's alive to stop it.

They get these ideas partly from being brought up under a social system which is directly opposed to that type of nonsense, and partly from their reading and education. Admittedly, no one's allowed to become a full-time student, except for the very few in each town who appear as children to possess unusual gifts, outstanding intelligence, and a special aptitude for academic research. But every child receives a primary education, and most men and women go on educating themselves all their lives during those free periods that I told you about. . . .

In ethics they discuss the same problems as we do. Having distinguished between three types of "good," psychological, physiological, and environmental, they proceed to ask whether the term is strictly applicable to all of them, or only to the first. They also argue about such things as virtue and pleasure. But their chief subject of dispute is the nature of human happiness—on what factor or factors does it depend? Here they seem rather too much inclined to take a hedonistic view, for according to them human happiness consists largely or wholly in pleasure. Surprisingly enough, they defend this self-indulgent doctrine by arguments drawn from religion—a thing normally associated with a more serious view of life, if not with gloomy asceticism. You see, in all their discussions of happiness they invoke certain religious principles to supplement the operations of reason, which they think otherwise ill-equipped to identify true happiness.

The first principle is that every soul is immortal, and was created by a kind God, Who meant it to be happy. The second is that we shall be rewarded or punished in the next world for our good or bad behavior in this one. Although these are religious principles, the Utopians find rational grounds for accepting them. For suppose you didn't accept them? In that case, they say, any fool could tell you what you ought to do. You should go all out for your own pleasure, irrespective of right and wrong. You'd merely have to make sure that minor pleasures didn't interfere with major ones, and avoid the type of pleasure that has painful aftereffects. For what's the sense of struggling to be virtuous, denying yourself the pleasant things of life, and deliberately making yourself uncomfortable, if there's nothing you hope to gain by it? And what *can* you hope to gain by it, if you receive no compensation after death for a thoroughly unpleasant, that is, a thoroughly miserable life?

Not that they identify happiness with every type of pleasure—only with the higher ones. Nor do they identify it with virtue—unless they belong to a quite different school of thought. According to the normal view, happiness is the *summmum bonum*[2] toward which we're naturally impelled by virtue—which in their definition means following one's natural impulses, as God meant us to do. But this includes obeying the instinct to be reasonable in our likes and dislikes. And reason also teaches us, first to love and reverence Almighty God, to Whom we owe our existence and our potentiality for happiness, and secondly to get through life as comfortably and cheerfully as we can, and help all other members of our species to do so too.

The fact is, even the sternest ascetic tends to be slightly inconsistent in his condemnation of pleasure. He may sentence *you* to a life of hard labor, inadequate sleep, and general discomfort, but he'll also tell you to do your best to ease the pains and privations of others. He'll regard all such attempts to improve the human situation as laudable acts of humanity—for obviously nothing could be more humane, or more natural for a human being, than to relieve other people's sufferings, put an end to their miseries, and restore their *joie de vivre*, that is, their capacity for pleasure. So why shouldn't it be equally natural to do the same thing for oneself?

Either it's a bad thing to enjoy life, in other words, to experience pleasure—in which case you shouldn't help anyone to do it, but should try to save the whole human race from such a frightful fate—or else, if it's good for other people, and you're not only allowed, but positively obliged to make it possible for them, why shouldn't charity begin at home? After all, you've a duty to yourself as well as to your neighbor, and, if Nature says you must be kind to others, she can't turn round the next moment and say you must be cruel to yourself. The Utopians therefore regard the enjoyment of life—that is, pleasure—as the natural object of all human efforts, and natural, as they define it, is synonymous with virtuous. However, Nature also wants us to help one another to enjoy life, for the very good reason that no human being has a monopoly of her affections. She's equally anxious for the welfare of every member of the species. So of course she tells us to make quite sure that we don't pursue our own interests at the expense of other people's.

On this principle they think it right to keep one's promises in private life, and also to obey public laws for regulating the distribution of "goods"—by which I mean the raw materials of pleasure—provided such laws have been properly made by a wise ruler, or passed by common consent of a whole population, which has not been subjected to any form of violence or deception. Within these limits they say it's sensible to consult one's own interests, and a moral duty to consult those of the community as well. It's wrong to deprive someone else of a pleasure so that you can enjoy one yourself, but to deprive yourself of a pleasure so that you can add to someone else's enjoyment is an act of humanity

[2]*summmum bonum* Latin for "the highest good."

by which you always gain more than you lose. For one thing, such benefits are usually repaid in kind. For another, the mere sense of having done somebody a kindness, and so earned his affection and goodwill, produces a spiritual satisfaction which far outweighs the loss of a physical one. And lastly—a belief that comes easily to a religious mind—God will reward us for such small sacrifices of momentary pleasure, by giving us an eternity of perfect joy. Thus they argue that, in the final analysis, pleasure is the ultimate happiness which all human beings have in view, even when they're acting most virtuously.

Pleasure they define as any state or activity, physical or mental, which is naturally enjoyable. The operative word is *naturally*. According to them, we're impelled by reason as well as an instinct to enjoy ourselves in any natural way which doesn't hurt other people, interfere with greater pleasures, or cause unpleasant aftereffects. But human beings have entered into an idiotic conspiracy to call some things enjoyable which are naturally nothing of the kind—as though facts were as easily changed as definitions. Now the Utopians believe that, so far from contributing to happiness, this type of thing makes happiness impossible—because, once you get used to it, you lose all capacity for real pleasure, and are merely obsessed by illusory forms of it. Very often these have nothing pleasant about them at all—in fact, most of them are thoroughly disagreeable. But they appeal so strongly to perverted tastes that they come to be reckoned not only among the major pleasures of life, but even among the chief reasons for living.

In the category of illusory pleasure addicts they include the kind of person I mentioned before, who thinks himself better than other people because he's better dressed than they are. Actually he's just as wrong about his clothes as he is about himself. From a practical point of view, why is it better to be dressed in fine woollen thread than in coarse? But he's got it into his head that fine thread is naturally superior, and that wearing it somehow increases his own value. So he feels entitled to far more respect than he'd ever dare to hope for, if he were less expensively dressed, and is most indignant if he fails to get it.

Talking of respect, isn't it equally idiotic to attach such importance to 20 a lot of empty gestures which do nobody any good? For what real pleasure can you get out of the sight of a bared head or a bent knee? Will it cure the rheumatism in your own knee, or make you any less weak in the head? Of course, the great believers in this type of artificial pleasure are those who pride themselves on their "nobility." Nowadays that merely means that they happen to belong to a family which has been rich for several generations, preferably in landed property. And yet they feel every bit as "noble" even if they've failed to inherit any of the said property, or if they have inherited it and then frittered it all away.

Then there's another type of person I mentioned before, who has a passion for jewels, and feels practically superhuman if he manages to get hold of a rare one, especially if it's a kind that's considered particularly precious in his country and period—for the value of such things varies according to where and when you live. But he's so terrified of being taken in by appearances that he refuses to buy any jewel until he's stripped off all the gold and inspected it in the nude. And even then he won't buy it without a solemn assurance and a written guarantee from the jeweler that the stone is genuine. But my dear sir, why shouldn't a fake give you just as much pleasure, if you can't, with your own eyes, distinguish it from a real one? It makes no difference to you whether it's genuine or not—any more than it would to a blind man!

And now, what about those people who accumulate superfluous wealth, for no better purpose than to enjoy looking at it? Is their pleasure a real one, or merely a form of delusion? The opposite type of psychopath buries his gold, so that he'll never be able to use it, and may never even see it again. In fact, he deliberately loses it in his anxiety not to lose it—for what can you call it but lost, when it's put back into the earth, where it's no good to him, or probably to anyone else? And yet he's tremendously happy when he's got it stowed away. Now, apparently, he can stop worrying. But suppose the money is stolen, and ten years later he dies without ever knowing it has gone. Then for a whole ten years he has managed to survive his loss, and during that period what difference has it made to him whether the money was there or not? It was just as little use to him either way.

Among stupid pleasures they include not only gambling—a form of idiocy that they've heard about but never practiced—but also hunting and hawking. What on earth is the fun, they ask, of throwing dice onto a table? Besides, you've done it so often that, even if there was some fun in it at first, you must surely be sick of it by now. How can you possibly enjoy listening to anything so disagreeable as the barking and howling of dogs? And why is it more amusing to watch a dog chasing a hare than to watch one dog chasing another? In each case the essential activity is running—if running is what amuses you. But if it's really the thought of being in at the death, and seeing an animal torn to pieces before your eyes, wouldn't pity be a more appropriate reaction to the sight of a weak, timid, harmless little creature like a hare being devoured by something so much stronger and fiercer?

So the Utopians consider hunting below the dignity of free men, and leave it entirely to butchers, who are, as I told you, slaves. In their view hunting is the vilest department of butchery, compared with which all the others are relatively useful and honorable. An ordinary butcher slaughters livestock far more sparingly, and only because he has to, whereas a hunter kills and mutilates poor little creatures purely for his own amusement. They say you won't find that type of blood lust even among animals, unless they're particularly savage by nature, or have become so by constantly being used for this cruel sport.

There are hundreds of things like that, which are generally regarded 25 as pleasures, but everyone in Utopia is quite convinced that they've got nothing to do with real pleasure, because there's nothing naturally enjoyable about them. Nor is this conviction at all shaken by the argument that most people do actually enjoy them, which would seem to indicate an appreciable pleasure content. They say this is a purely subjective reaction caused by bad habits, which can make a person prefer unpleasant things to pleasant ones, just as pregnant women sometimes lose their sense of taste, and find suet or turpentine more delicious than honey. But however much one's judgment may be impaired by habit or ill health, the nature of pleasure, as of everything else, remains unchanged.

Real pleasures they divide into two categories, mental and physical. Mental pleasures include the satisfaction that one gets from understanding something, or from contemplating truth. They also include the memory of a well-spent life, and the confident expectation of good things to come. Physical pleasures are subdivided into two types. First there are those which fill the whole organism with a conscious sense of enjoyment. This may be the result of replacing physical substances which have been burnt up by the natural heat of the body, as when we eat or drink. Or else it may be caused by the discharge of some excess, as in excretion, sexual intercourse, or any relief of irritation by rubbing or scratching. However, there are also pleasures which satisfy no organic need, and relieve no previous discomfort. They merely act, in a mysterious but quite unmistakable way, directly on our senses, and monopolize their reactions. Such is the pleasure of music.

Their second type of physical pleasure arises from the calm and regular functioning of the body—that is, from a state of health undisturbed by any minor ailments. In the absence of mental discomfort, this gives one a good feeling, even without the help of external pleasures. Of course, it's less ostentatious, and forces itself less violently on one's attention than the cruder delights of eating and drinking, but even so it's often considered the greatest pleasure in life. Practically everyone in Utopia would agree that it's a very important one, because it's the basis of all the others. It's enough by itself to make you enjoy life, and unless you have it, no other pleasure is possible. However, mere freedom from pain, without positive health, they would call not pleasure but anesthesia.

Some thinkers used to maintain that a uniformly tranquil state of health couldn't properly be termed a pleasure since its presence could only be detected by contrast with its opposite—oh yes, they went very thoroughly into the whole question. But that theory was exploded long ago, and nowadays nearly everybody subscribes to the view that health is most definitely a pleasure. The argument goes like this—illness involves pain, which is the direct opposite of pleasure, and illness is the direct opposite of health, therefore health involves pleasure. They don't think it matters whether you say that illness *is* or merely *involves* pain. Either way it comes to the same thing. Similarly, whether health *is* a pleasure, or merely *produces* pleasure as inevitably as fire produces heat, it's equally logical to assume that where you have an uninterrupted state of health you cannot fail to have pleasure.

Besides, they say, when we eat something, what really happens is this. Our failing health starts fighting off the attacks of hunger, using the food as an ally. Gradually it begins to prevail, and, in this very process of winning back its normal strength, experiences the sense of enjoyment which we find so refreshing. Now, if health enjoys the actual battle, why shouldn't it also enjoy the victory? Or are we to suppose that when it has finally managed to regain its former vigor — the one thing that it has been fighting for all this time — it promptly falls into a coma, and fails to notice or take advantage of its success? As for the idea that one isn't conscious of health except through its opposite, they say that's quite untrue. Everyone's perfectly aware of feeling well, unless he's asleep or actually feeling ill. Even the most insensitive and apathetic sort of person will admit that it's delightful to be healthy — and what is delight, but a synonym for pleasure?

They're particularly fond of mental pleasures, which they consider of 30 primary importance, and attribute mostly to good behavior and a clear conscience. Their favorite physical pleasure is health. Of course, they believe in enjoying food, drink, and so forth, but purely in the interests of health, for they don't regard such things as very pleasant in themselves — only as methods of resisting the stealthy onset of disease. A sensible person, they say, prefers keeping well to taking medicine, and would rather feel cheerful than have people trying to comfort him. On the same principle it's better not to need this type of pleasure than to become addicted to it. For, if you think that sort of thing will make you happy, you'll have to admit that your idea of perfect felicity would be a life consisting entirely of hunger, thirst, itching, eating, drinking, rubbing, and scratching — which would obviously be most unpleasant as well as quite disgusting. Undoubtedly these pleasures should come right at the bottom of the list, because they're so impure. For instance, the pleasure of eating is invariably diluted with the pain of hunger, and not in equal proportions either — for the pain is both more intense and more prolonged. It starts before the pleasure, and doesn't stop until the pleasure has stopped too.

So they don't think much of pleasures like that, except insofar as they're necessary. But they enjoy them all the same, and feel most grateful to Mother Nature for encouraging her children to do things that have to be done so often, by making them so attractive. For just think how dreary life would be, if those chronic ailments, hunger and thirst, could only be cured by foul-tasting medicines, like the rarer types of disease!

They attach great value to special natural gifts such as beauty, strength, and agility. They're also keen on the pleasures of sight, hearing, and smell, which are peculiar to human beings — for no other species admires the beauty of the world, enjoys any sort of scent, except as a method of locating food, or can tell the difference between a harmony and a discord. They say these things give a sort of relish to life.

However, in all such matters they observe the rule that minor pleasures mustn't interfere with major ones, and that pleasure mustn't cause pain—which they think is bound to happen, if the pleasure is immoral. But they'd never dream of despising their own beauty, overtaxing their strength, converting their agility into inertia, ruining their physique by going without food, damaging their health, or spurning any other of Nature's gifts, unless they were doing it for the benefit of other people or of society, in the hope of receiving some greater pleasure from God in return. For they think it's quite absurd to torment oneself in the name of an unreal virtue, which does nobody any good, or in order to steel oneself against disasters which may never occur. They say such behavior is merely self-destructive, and shows a most ungrateful attitude toward Nature—as if one refused all her favors, because one couldn't bear the thought of being indebted to her for anything.

Well, that's their ethical theory, and short of some divine revelation, they doubt if the human mind is capable of devising a better one. We've no time to discuss whether it's right or wrong—nor is it really necessary, for all I undertook was to describe their way of life, not to defend it.

[TREATMENT OF THE DYING]

As I told you, when people are ill, they're looked after most sympathetically, and given everything in the way of medicine or special food that could possibly assist their recovery. In the case of permanent invalids, the nurses try to make them feel better by sitting and talking to them, and do all they can to relieve their symptoms. But if, besides being incurable, the disease also causes constant excruciating pain, some priests and government officials visit the person concerned, and say something like this:

"Let's face it, you'll never be able to live a normal life. You're just a nuisance to other people and a burden to yourself—in fact you're really leading a sort of posthumous existence. So why go on feeding germs? Since your life's a misery to you, why hesitate to die? You're imprisoned in a torture chamber—why don't you break out and escape to a better world? Or say the word, and we'll arrange for your release. It's only common sense to cut your losses. It's also an act of piety to take the advice of a priest, because he speaks for God."

If the patient finds these arguments convincing, he either starves himself to death, or is given a soporific and put painlessly out of his misery. But this is strictly voluntary, and, if he prefers to stay alive, everyone will go on treating him as kindly as ever.

[THE SUMMING UP]

Well, that's the most accurate account I can give you of the Utopian Republic. To my mind, it's not only the best country in the world, but the only one that has any right to call itself a republic. Elsewhere, people are always talking about the public interest, but all they really care about is private property. In Utopia, where's there's no private property, people take their duty to the public seriously. And both attitudes are perfectly reasonable. In other "republics" practically everyone knows that, if he doesn't look out for himself, he'll starve to death, however prosperous his country may be. He's therefore compelled to give his own interests priority over those of the public; that is, of other people. But in Utopia, where everything's under public ownership, no one has any fear of going short, as long as the public storehouses are full. Everyone gets a fair share, so there are never any poor men or beggars. Nobody owns anything, but everyone is rich—for what greater wealth can there be than cheerfulness, peace of mind, and freedom from anxiety? Instead of being worried about his food supply, upset by the plaintive demands of his wife, afraid of poverty for his son, and baffled by the problem of finding a dowry for his daughter, the Utopian can feel absolutely sure that he, his wife, his children, his grandchildren, his great-grandchildren, his great-great-grandchildren, and as long a line of descendants as the proudest peer could wish to look forward to, will always have enough to eat and enough to make them happy. There's also the further point that those who are too old to work are just as well provided for as those who are still working.

Now, will anyone venture to compare these fair arrangements in Utopia with the so-called justice of other countries?—in which I'm damned if I can see the slightest trace of justice or fairness. For what sort of justice do you call this? People like aristocrats, goldsmiths, or money-lenders, who either do no work at all, or do work that's really not essential, are rewarded for their laziness or their unnecessary activities by a splendid life of luxury. But laborers, coachmen, carpenters, and farmhands, who never stop working like cart horses, at jobs so essential that, if they *did* stop working, they'd bring any country to a standstill within twelve months—what happens to them? They get so little to eat, and have such a wretched time, that they'd be almost better off if they *were* cart horses. Then at least, they wouldn't work quite such long hours, their food wouldn't be very much worse, they'd enjoy it more, and they'd have no fears for the future. As it is, they're not only ground down by unrewarding toil in the present, but also worried to death by the prospect of a poverty-stricken old age—since their daily wages aren't enough to support them for one day, let alone leave anything over to be saved up when they're old.

Can you see any fairness or gratitude in a social system which lav- 40
ishes such great rewards on so-called noblemen, goldsmiths, and people like that, who are either totally unproductive or merely employed in producing luxury goods or entertainment, but makes no such kind provision for farmhands, coal heavers, laborers, carters, or carpenters, without whom society couldn't exist at all? And the climax of ingratitude comes when they're old and ill and completely destitute. Having taken

advantage of them throughout the best years of their lives, society now forgets all the sleepless hours they've spent in its service, and repays them for all the vital work they've done, by letting them die in misery. What's more, the wretched earnings of the poor are daily whittled away by the rich, not only through private dishonesty, but through public legislation. As if it weren't unjust enough already that the man who contributes most to society should get the least in return, they make it even worse, and then arrange for injustice to be legally described as justice.

In fact, when I consider any social system that prevails in the modern world, I can't, so help me God, see it as anything but a conspiracy of the rich to advance their own interests under the pretext of organizing society. They think up all sorts of tricks and dodges, first for keeping safe their ill-gotten gains, and then for exploiting the poor by buying their labor as cheaply as possible. Once the rich have decided that these tricks and dodges shall be officially recognized by society—which includes the poor as well as the rich—they acquire the force of law. Thus an unscrupulous minority is led by its insatiable greed to monopolize what would have been enough to supply the needs of the whole population. And yet how much happier even these people would be in Utopia! There, with the simultaneous abolition of money and the passion for money, how many other social problems have been solved, how many crimes eradicated! For obviously the end of money means the end of all those types of criminal behavior which daily punishments are powerless to check: fraud, theft, burglary, brawls, riots, disputes, rebellion, murder, treason, and black magic. And the moment money goes, you can also say goodbye to fear, tension, anxiety, overwork, and sleepless nights. Why, even poverty itself, the one problem that has always seemed to need money for its solution, would promptly disappear if money ceased to exist.

Let me try to make this point clearer. Just think back to one of the years when the harvest was bad, and thousands of people died of starvation. Well, I bet if you'd inspected every rich man's barn at the end of that lean period you'd have found enough corn to have saved all the lives that were lost through malnutrition and disease, and prevented anyone from suffering any ill effects whatever from the meanness of the weather and the soil. Everyone could so easily get enough to eat, if it weren't for that blessed nuisance, money. There you have a brilliant invention which was designed to make food more readily available. Actually it's the only thing that makes it unobtainable.

I'm sure that even the rich are well aware of all this, and realize how much better it would be to have everything one needed, than lots of things one didn't need—to be evacuated altogether from the danger area, than to dig oneself in behind a barricade of enormous wealth. And I've no doubt that either self-interest, or the authority of our Savior Christ—Who was far too wise not to know what was best for us, and far too kind to recommend anything else—would have led the whole world to adopt the Utopian system long ago, if it weren't for that beastly root of all evils, pride. For pride's criterion of prosperity is not what you've got yourself, but what other people haven't got. Pride would refuse to set foot in paradise, if she thought there'd be no underprivileged classes there to gloat over and order about—nobody whose misery could serve as a foil to her own happiness, or whose poverty she could make harder to bear, by flaunting her own riches. Pride, like a hellish serpent gliding through human hearts—or shall we say, like a sucking-fish that clings to the ship of state?—is always dragging us back, and obstructing our progress toward a better way of life.

But as this fault is too deeply ingrained in human nature to be easily eradicated, I'm glad that at least one country has managed to develop a system which I'd like to see universally adopted. The Utopian way of life provides not only the happiest basis for a civilized community, but also one which, in all human probability, will last forever. They've eliminated the root causes of ambition, political conflict, and everything like that. There's therefore no danger of internal dissension, the one thing that has destroyed so many impregnable towns. And as long as there's unity and sound administration at home, no matter how envious neighboring kings may feel, they'll never be able to shake, let alone to shatter, the power of Utopia. They've tried to do so often enough in the past, but have always been beaten back.

Topics for Critical Thinking and Writing

1. More, writing early in the sixteenth century, was living in a primarily agricultural society. Laborers were needed on farms, but might More have had any other reason for insisting (para. 1) that all people should do some farming and that farming should be "part of every child's education"? Do you think everyone should put in some time as a farmer? Why, or why not?

2. More indicates that in the England of his day many people loafed or engaged in unnecessary work (producing luxury goods, for one thing), putting an enormous burden on those who engaged in useful work. Is this condition, or any part of it, true of our society? Explain.

3. The Utopians cannot understand why the people of other nations value gems, gold, and fine clothes. If you value any of these, can you offer an explanation?

4. What arguments can you offer against the Utopians' treatment of persons who are incurably ill and in pain?

5. Take three or four paragraphs to summarize More's report of the Utopians' idea of pleasure.

6. More's Utopians cannot understand why anyone takes pleasure in gambling or in hunting. If either activity gives you pleasure, in an essay of 500 words explain why, and offer an argument on behalf of your view.

7. As More makes clear in the part we entitle "The Summing Up," in Utopia there is no private property. In a sentence or two summarize the reasons he gives for this principle, and then in a paragraph evaluate them.

Niccolò Machiavelli

Niccolò Machiavelli (1469–1527) was born in Florence at a time when Italy was divided into five major states: Venice, Milan, Florence, the Papal States, and Naples. Although these states often had belligerent relations with one another as well as with lesser Italian states, under the Medici family in Florence they achieved a precarious balance of power. In 1494, however, Lorenzo de' Medici, who had ruled from 1469 to 1492, died, and two years later Lorenzo's successor was exiled when the French army arrived in Florence. Italy became a field where Spain, France, and Germany competed for power. From 1498 to 1512 Machiavelli held a high post in the diplomatic service of the Florentine Republic, but when the French army reappeared and the Florentines in desperation recalled the Medici, Machiavelli lost his post, was imprisoned, tortured, and then exiled. Banished from Florence, he nevertheless lived in comfort on a small estate nearby, writing his major works and hoping to obtain an office from the Medici. In later years he was employed in a few minor diplomatic missions, but even after the collapse and expulsion of the Medici in 1527 and the restoration of the republic, he did not regain his old position of importance. He died shortly after the restoration.

Our selection comes from The Prince, *which Machiavelli wrote in 1513 during his banishment hoping that it would interest the Medici and thus restore him to favor; but the book was not published until 1532, five years after his death. In this book of twenty-six short chapters, Machiavelli begins by examining different kinds of states, but the work's enduring power resides in the discussions (in Chapters 15–18, reprinted here) of qualities necessary to a prince—that is, a head of state. Any such examination obviously is based in part on assumptions about the nature of the citizens of the realm.*

This selection was taken from a translation edited by Peter Bondanella and Mark Musa.

From *The Prince*

ON THOSE THINGS FOR WHICH MEN, AND PARTICULARLY PRINCES, ARE PRAISED OR BLAMED

Now there remains to be examined what should be the methods and procedures of a prince in dealing with his subjects and friends. And because I know that many have written about this, I am afraid that by writing about it again I shall be thought of as presumptuous, since in discussing this material I depart radically from the procedures of others. But since my intention is to write something useful for anyone who understands it, it seemed more suitable to me to search after the effectual truth of the matter rather than its imagined one. And many writers have imagined for themselves republics and principalities that have never been seen nor known to exist in reality; for there is such a gap between how one lives and how one ought to live that anyone who abandons what is done for what ought to be done learns his ruin rather than his preservation: for a man who wishes to make a vocation of being good at all times will come to ruin among so many who are not good. Hence it is necessary for a prince who wishes to maintain his position to learn how not to be good, and to use this knowledge or not to use it according to necessity.

Leaving aside, therefore, the imagined things concerning a prince, and taking into account those that are true, I say that all men, when they are spoken of, and particularly princes, since they are placed on a higher level, are judged by some of these qualities which bring them either blame or praise. And this is why one is considered generous, another miserly (to use a Tuscan word, since "avaricious" in our language is still used to mean one who wishes to acquire by means of theft; we call "miserly" one who excessively avoids using what he has); one is considered a giver, the other rapacious; one cruel, another merciful; one treacherous, another faithful; one effeminate and cowardly, another bold and courageous; one humane, another haughty; one lascivious, another chaste; one trustworthy, another cunning; one harsh, another lenient; one serious, another frivolous; one religious, another unbelieving; and the like. And I know that everyone will admit that it would be a very praiseworthy thing to find in a prince, of the qualities mentioned above, those that are held to be good; but since it is neither possible to have them nor to observe them all completely, because human nature does not permit it, a prince must be prudent enough to know how to escape the bad reputation of those vices that would lose the state for him, and must protect himself from those that will not lose it for him, if this is possible; but if he cannot, he need not concern himself unduly if he ignores these less serious vices. And, moreover, he need not worry about incurring the bad reputation of those vices without which it would be difficult to hold his state; since, carefully taking everything into account, one will discover that something which appears to be a virtue, if pursued, will end in his destruction; while some other thing which seems to be a vice, if pursued, will result in his safety and his well-being.

ON GENEROSITY AND MISERLINESS

Beginning, therefore, with the first of the above-mentioned qualities, I say that it would be good to be considered generous; nevertheless, generosity used in such a manner as to give you a reputation for it will harm you; because if it is employed virtuously and as one should employ it, it will not be recognized and you will not avoid the reproach of its opposite. And so, if a prince wants to maintain his reputation for generosity among men, it is necessary for him not to neglect any possible means of lavish display; in so doing such a prince will always use up all his resources and he will be obliged, eventually, if he wishes to maintain his reputation for generosity, to burden the people with excessive taxes and to do everything possible to raise funds. This will begin to make him hateful to his subjects, and, becoming impoverished, he will not be much esteemed by anyone; so that, as a consequence of his generosity, having offended many and rewarded few, he will feel the effects of any slight unrest and will be ruined at the first sign of danger; recognizing this and wishing to alter his policies, he immediately runs the risk of being reproached as a miser.

A prince, therefore, unable to use this virtue of generosity in a manner which will not harm himself if he is known for it, should, if he is wise, not worry about being called a miser; for with time he will come to be considered more generous once it is evident that, as a result of his parsimony, his income is sufficient, he can defend himself from anyone who makes war against him, and he can undertake enterprises without overburdening his people, so that he comes to be generous with all those from whom he takes nothing, who are countless, and miserly with all those to whom he gives nothing, who are few. In our times we have not seen great deeds accomplished except by those who were considered miserly; all others were done away with. Pope Julius II, although he made use of his reputation for generosity in order to gain the papacy, then decided not to maintain it in order to be able to wage war; the present King of France has waged many wars without imposing extra taxes on his subjects, only because his habitual parsimony has provided for the additional expenditures; the present King of Spain, if he had been considered generous, would not have engaged in nor won so many campaigns.

Therefore, in order not to have to rob his subjects, to be able to defend himself, not to become poor and contemptible, and not to be forced to become rapacious, a prince must consider it of little importance if he incurs the name of miser, for this is one of those vices that permits him to rule. And if someone were to say: Caesar with his generosity came to rule the empire, and many others, because they were generous and known to be so, achieved very high positions; I reply: You are either already a prince or you are on the way to becoming one; in the first instance such generosity is damaging; in the second it is very necessary to be thought generous. And Caesar was one of those who wanted to gain the principality of Rome; but if, after obtaining this, he had lived and had not moderated his expenditures, he would have destroyed that empire. And if someone were to reply: There have existed many princes who have accomplished great deeds with their armies who have been reputed to be generous; I answer you: A prince either spends his own money and that of his subjects or that of others; in the first case he must be economical; in the second he must not restrain any part of his generosity. And for that prince who goes out with his soldiers and lives by looting, sacking, and ransoms, who controls the property of others, such generosity is necessary; otherwise he would not be followed by his troops. And with what does not belong to you or to your subjects you can be a more liberal giver, as were Cyrus, Caesar, and Alexander; for spending the wealth of others does not lessen your reputation but adds to it; only the spending of your own is what harms you. And there is nothing that uses itself up faster than generosity, for as you employ it you lose the means of employing it, and you become either poor or despised or, in order to escape poverty, rapacious and hated. And above all other things a prince must guard himself against being despised and hated; and generosity leads you to both one and the other. So it is wiser to live with the reputation of a miser, which produces reproach without hatred, than to be forced to incur the reputation of rapacity, which produces reproach along with hatred, because you want to be considered as generous.

ON CRUELTY AND MERCY AND WHETHER IT IS BETTER TO BE LOVED THAN TO BE FEARED OR THE CONTRARY

Proceeding to the other qualities mentioned above, I say that every prince must desire to be considered merciful and not cruel; nevertheless, he must take care not to misuse this mercy. Cesare Borgia[1] was considered cruel; nonetheless, his cruelty had brought order to Romagna, united it, restored it to peace and obedience. If we examine this carefully, we shall see that he was more merciful than the Florentine people, who, in order to avoid being considered cruel, allowed the destruction of Pistoia.[2] Therefore, a prince must not worry about the reproach of cruelty when it is a matter of keeping his subjects united and loyal; for with a very few examples of cruelty he will be more compassionate than those who, out of excessive mercy, permit disorders to continue, from which arise murders and plundering; for these usually harm the community at large, while the executions that come from the prince harm one individual in particular. And the new prince, above all other princes,

---

[1]**Cesare Borgia** The son of Pope Alexander VI, Cesare Borgia (1476–1507) was ruthlessly opportunistic. Encouraged by his father, in 1499 and 1500 he subdued the cities of **Romagna,** the region including Ferrara and Ravenna. [All notes are the editors' unless otherwise specified.]

[2]**Pistoia** A town near Florence; Machiavelli suggests that the Florentines failed to treat dissenting leaders with sufficient severity.

cannot escape the reputation of being called cruel, since new states are full of dangers. And Virgil, through Dido, states: "My difficult condition and the newness of my rule make me act in such a manner, and to set guards over my land on all sides."[3]

Nevertheless, a prince must be cautious in believing and in acting, nor should he be afraid of his own shadow; and he should proceed in such a manner, tempered by prudence and humanity, so that too much trust may not render him imprudent nor too much distrust render him intolerable.

From this arises an argument: whether it is better to be loved than to be feared, or the contrary. I reply that one should like to be both one and the other; but since it is difficult to join them together, it is much safer to be feared than to be loved when one of the two must be lacking. For one can generally say this about men: that they are ungrateful, fickle, simulators and deceivers, avoiders of danger, greedy for gain; and while you work for their good they are completely yours, offering you their blood, their property, their lives, and their sons, as I said earlier, when danger is far away; but when it comes nearer to you they turn away. And that prince who bases his power entirely in their words, finding himself stripped of other preparations, comes to ruin; for friendships that are acquired by a price and not by greatness and nobility of character are purchased but are not owned, and at the proper moment they cannot be spent. And men are less hesitant about harming someone who makes himself loved than one who makes himself feared because love is held together by a chain of obligation which, since men are a sorry lot, is broken on every occasion in which their own self-interest is concerned; but fear is held together by a dread of punishment which will never abandon you.

A prince must nevertheless make himself feared in such a manner that he will avoid hatred, even if he does not acquire love; since to be feared and not to be hated can very well be combined; and this will always be so when he keeps his hands off the property and the women of his citizens and his subjects. And if he must take someone's life, he should do so when there is proper justification and manifest cause; but, above all, he should avoid the property of others; for men forget more quickly the death of their father than the loss of their patrimony. Moreover, the reasons for seizing their property are never lacking; and he who begins to live by stealing always finds a reason for taking what belongs to others; on the contrary, reasons for taking a life are rarer and disappear sooner.

But when the prince is with his armies and has under his command 10 a multitude of troops, then it is absolutely necessary that he not worry about being considered cruel; for without that reputation he will never

---

[3]In *Aeneid* I, 563–64, **Virgil** (70–19 B.C.) puts this line into the mouth of **Dido,** the queen of Carthage.

keep an army united or prepared for any combat. Among the praiseworthy deeds of Hannibal[4] is counted this: that, having a very large army,
made up of all kinds of men, which he commanded in foreign lands,
there never arose the slightest dissension, neither among themselves nor
against their prince, both during his good and his bad fortune. This could
not have arisen from anything other than his inhuman cruelty, which,
along with his many other abilities, made him always respected and terrifying in the eyes of his soldiers; and without that, to attain the same effect, his other abilities would not have sufficed. And the writers of
history, having considered this matter very little, on the one hand admire
these deeds of his and on the other condemn the main cause of them.

And that it be true that his other abilities would not have been sufficient can be seen from the example of Scipio,[5] a most extraordinary man
not only in his time but in all recorded history, whose armies in Spain
rebelled against him; this came about from nothing other than his excessive compassion, which gave to his soldiers more liberty than military
discipline allowed. For this he was censured in the senate by Fabius
Maximus, who called him the corruptor of the Roman militia. The Locri-
ans, having been ruined by one of Scipio's officers, were not avenged by
him, nor was the arrogance of that officer corrected, all because of his
tolerant nature; so that someone in the senate who tried to apologize for
him said that there were many men who knew how not to err better
than they knew how to correct errors. Such a nature would have, in
time, damaged Scipio's fame and glory if he had maintained it during the
empire; but, living under the control of the senate, this harmful characteristic of his not only concealed itself but brought him fame.

I conclude, therefore, returning to the problem of being feared and
loved, that since men love at their own pleasure and fear at the pleasure
of the prince, a wise prince should build his foundation upon that which
belongs to him, not upon that which belongs to others: He must strive
only to avoid hatred, as has been said.

HOW A PRINCE SHOULD KEEP HIS WORD

How praiseworthy it is for a prince to keep his word and to live by
integrity and not by deceit everyone knows; nevertheless, one sees from
the experience of our times that the princes who have accomplished
great deeds are those who have cared little for keeping their promises
and who have known how to manipulate the minds of men by shrewd-
ness; and in the end they have surpassed those who laid their foundations upon honesty.

---

[4]**Hannibal** The Carthaginian general (247–183 B.C.) whose crossing of the Alps with ele-
phants and full baggage train is one of the great feats of military history.
[5]**Scipio** Publius Cornelius Scipio Africanus the Elder (235–183 B.C.), the conqueror of Hannibal in the Punic Wars. The mutiny of which Machiavelli speaks took place in 206 B.C.

You must, therefore, know that there are two means of fighting: one according to the laws, the other with force; the first way is proper to man, the second to beasts; but because the first, in many cases, is not sufficient, it becomes necessary to have recourse to the second. Therefore, a prince must know how to use wisely the natures of the beast and the man. This policy was taught to princes allegorically by the ancient writers, who described how Achilles and many other ancient princes were given to Chiron[6] the Centaur to be raised and taught under his discipline. This can only mean that, having a half-beast and half-man as a teacher, a prince must know how to employ the nature of the one and the other; and the one without the other cannot endure.

Since, then, a prince must know how to make good use of the nature of the beast, he should choose from among the beasts the fox and the lion; for the lion cannot defend itself from traps and the fox cannot protect itself from wolves. It is therefore necessary to be a fox in order to recognize the traps and a lion in order to frighten the wolves. Those who play only the part of the lion do not understand matters. A wise ruler, therefore, cannot and should not keep his word when such an observance of faith would be to his disadvantage and when the reasons which made him promise are removed. And if men were all good, this rule would not be good; but since men are a sorry lot and will not keep their promises to you, you likewise need not keep yours to them. A prince never lacks legitimate reasons to break his promises. Of this one could cite an endless number of modern examples to show how many pacts, how many promises have been made null and void because of the infidelity of princes; and he who has known best how to use the fox has come to a better end. But it is necessary to know how to disguise this nature well and to be a great hypocrite and a liar: and men are so simpleminded and so controlled by their present necessities that one who deceives will always find another who will allow himself to be deceived.

I do not wish to remain silent about one of these recent instances. Alexander VI[7] did nothing else, he thought about nothing else, except to deceive men, and he always found the occasion to do this. And there never was a man who had more forcefulness in his oaths, who affirmed a thing with more promises, and who honored his word less; nevertheless, his tricks always succeeded perfectly since he was well acquainted with this aspect of the world.

Therefore, it is not necessary for a prince to have all of the above-mentioned qualities, but it is very necessary for him to appear to have them. Furthermore, I shall be so bold as to assert this; that having them

15

---

[6]**Chiron** (Kī'ron) A centaur (half man, half horse) who was said in classical mythology to have been the teacher not only of Achilles but also of Theseus, Jason, Hercules, and other heroes.
[7]**Alexander VI** Pope from 1492 to 1503; father of Cesare Borgia.

and practicing them at all times is harmful; and appearing to have them useful; for instance, to seem merciful, faithful, humane, forthright, religious, and to be so; but his mind should be disposed in such a way that should it become necessary not to be so, he will be able and know how to change to the contrary. And it is essential to understand this: that a prince, and especially a new prince, cannot observe all those things by which men are considered good, for in order to maintain the state he is often obliged to act against his promise, against charity, against humanity, and against religion. And therefore, it is necessary that he have a mind ready to turn itself according to the way the winds of Fortune and the changeability of affairs require him; and, as I said above, as long as it is possible, he should not stray from the good, but he should know how to enter into evil when necessity commands.

A prince, therefore, must be very careful never to let anything slip from his lips which is not full of the five qualities mentioned above: He should appear, upon seeing and hearing him, to be all mercy, all faithfulness, all integrity, all kindness, all religion. And there is nothing more necessary than to seem to possess this last quality. And men in general judge more by their eyes than their hands; for everyone can see but few can feel. Everyone sees what you seem to be, few perceive what you are, and those few do not dare to contradict the opinion of the many who have the majesty of the state to defend them; and in the actions of all men, and especially of princes, where there is no impartial arbiter, one must consider the final result.[8] Let a prince therefore act to seize and to maintain the state; his methods will always be judged honorable and will be praised by all; for ordinary people are always deceived by appearances and by the outcome of a thing; and in the world there is nothing but ordinary people; and there is no room for the few, while the many have a place to lean on. A certain prince of the present day, whom I shall refrain from naming, preaches nothing but peace and faith, and to both one and the other he is entirely opposed; and both, if he had put them into practice, would have cost him many times over either his reputation or his state.

TOPICS FOR CRITICAL THINKING AND WRITING

1. In the opening paragraph, Machiavelli claims that a ruler who wishes to keep in power must "learn how not to be good" — that is, must know where and when to ignore the demands of conventional morality. In the rest of the excerpt, does he give any convincing evidence to support this claim? Can you think of any recent political event in which a political leader violated the requirements of morality, as Machiavelli advises?

[8]The Italian original, *si guarda al fine*, has often been mistranslated as "the ends justify the means," something Machiavelli never wrote. [Translators' note.]

2. Machiavelli says in paragraph 1 that "a man who wishes to make a vocation of being good at all times will come to ruin among so many who are not good." (By the way, the passage is ambiguous. "At all times" is, in the original, a squinting modifier. It may look backward to "being good" or forward to "will come to ruin," but Machiavelli probably means, "A man who at all times wishes to make a vocation of being good will come to ruin among so many who are not good.") Is this view realistic or cynical? (What is the difference between these two?) Assume for the moment that the view is realistic. Does it follow that society requires a ruler who must act according to the principles Machiavelli sets forth?

3. In his second paragraph Machiavelli claims that it is impossible for a ruler to exhibit *all* the conventional virtues (trustworthiness, liberality, and so on). Why does he make this claim? Do you agree with it?

4. In paragraph 4 Machiavelli cites as examples Pope Julius II, the King of France, the King of Spain, and other rulers. Is he using these examples to illustrate his generalizations or to provide evidence for them? If you think he is using them to provide evidence, how convincing do you find the evidence? (Consider: Could Machiavelli be arguing from a biased sample?)

5. In paragraphs 6 to 10 Machiavelli argues that it is sometimes necessary for a ruler to be cruel, and so he praises Cesare Borgia and Hannibal. What in human nature, according to Machiavelli, explains this need to have recourse to cruelty? (By the way, how do you think *cruelty* should be defined here?)

6. Machiavelli says that Cesare Borgia's cruelty brought peace to Romagna and that, on the other hand, the Florentines who sought to avoid being cruel in fact brought pain to Pistoia. Can you think of recent episodes supporting the view that cruelty can be beneficial to society? If so, restate Machiavelli's position, using these examples from recent history. Then go on to write two paragraphs, arguing on behalf of your two examples. Or if you believe that Machiavelli's point here is fundamentally wrong, explain why, again using current examples.

7. In *The Prince*, Machiavelli is writing about how to be a successful ruler. He explicitly says he is dealing with things as they are, not things as they should be. Do you think that in fact one can write usefully about statecraft without considering ethics? Explain. Or you may want to think about it in this way: The study of politics is often called *political science*. Machiavelli can be seen as a sort of scientist, objectively analyzing the nature of governing—without offering any moral judgments. In an essay of 500 words, argue for or against the view that the study of politics is rightly called *political science*.

8. In paragraph 18 Machiavelli declares that "one must consider the final result." Taking account of the context, do you think the meaning is that (a) any end, goal, or purpose of anyone justifies using any means to reach it or (b) the end of governing the state, nation, or country justifies using any means to achieve it? Or do you think Machiavelli means both? Something else entirely?

9. In 500 words, argue that an important contemporary political figure does or does not act according to Machiavelli's principles.

10. If you have read the selection from Thomas More's *Utopia* (p. 842), write an essay of 500 words on one of these two topics: (a) why More's book is or is not wiser than Machiavelli's or (b) why one of the books is more interesting than the other.

11. More and Machiavelli wrote their books at almost exactly the same time. Write a dialogue of two or three double-spaced typed pages in which the two men argue about the nature of the state. (During the argument, they will have to reveal their assumptions about the nature of human beings and the role of government.)

Thomas Jefferson

Thomas Jefferson (1743–1826) was a congressman, the governor of Virginia, the first secretary of state, and the president of the United States, but he said he wished to be remembered for only three things: drafting the Declaration of Independence, writing the Virginia Statute for Religious Freedom, and founding the University of Virginia. All three were efforts to promote freedom.

Jefferson was born in Virginia and educated at William and Mary College in Williamsburg, Virginia. After graduating he studied law, was admitted to the bar, and in 1769 was elected to the Virginia House of Burgesses, his first political office. In 1776 he went to Philadelphia as a delegate to the second Continental Congress, where he was elected to a committee of five to write the Declaration of Independence. Jefferson drafted the document, which was then subjected to some changes by the other members of the committee and by the Congress. Although he was unhappy with the changes (especially with the deletion of a passage against slavery), his claim to have written the Declaration is just.

The Declaration of Independence

When in the course of human events, it becomes necessary for one people to dissolve the political bands which have connected them with another, and to assume among the Powers of the earth, the separate and equal station to which the Laws of Nature and of Nature's God entitle them, a decent respect to the opinions of mankind requires that they should declare the causes which impel them to the separation.

We hold these truths to be self-evident, that all men are created equal, that they are endowed by their Creator with certain unalienable Rights, that among these are Life, Liberty and the pursuit of Happiness.

That to secure these rights, Governments are instituted among Men, deriving their just powers from the consent of the governed.

That whenever any Form of Government becomes destructive of these ends, it is the Right of the People to alter or to abolish it, and to institute a new Government, laying its foundation on such principles and organizing its powers in such form, as to them shall seem most likely to effect their Safety and Happiness. Prudence, indeed, will dictate that Governments long established should not be changed for light and transient causes; and accordingly all experience hath shown that mankind are more disposed to suffer, while evils are sufferable, than to right themselves by abolishing the forms to which they are accustomed. But when a long train of abuses and usurpations pursuing invariably the same Object evinces a design to reduce them under absolute Despotism, it is their right, it is their duty, to throw off such government, and to provide new Guards for their future security.

Such has been the patient sufferance of these Colonies; and such is 5 now the necessity which constrains them to alter their former Systems of Government. The history of the present King of Great Britain is a history of repeated injuries and usurpations, all having in direct object the establishment of an absolute Tyranny over these States. To prove this, let Facts be submitted to a candid world.

He has refused his Assent to Laws, the most wholesome and necessary for the public good.

He has forbidden his Governors to pass Laws of immediate and pressing importance, unless suspended in their operation till his Assent should be obtained; and when so suspended, he has utterly neglected to attend to them.

He has refused to pass over Laws for the accommodation of large districts of people, unless those people would relinquish the right of Representation in the Legislature, a right inestimable to them and formidable to tyrants only.

He has called together legislative bodies at places unusual, uncomfortable, and distant from the depository of their Public Records, for the sole purpose of fatiguing them into compliance with his measures.

He has dissolved Representative Houses repeatedly, for opposing 10 with manly firmness his invasions on the rights of the people.

He has refused for a long time, after such dissolutions, to cause others to be elected; whereby the Legislative Powers, incapable of Annihilation, have returned to the People at large for their exercise; the State remaining in the mean time exposed to all the dangers of invasion from without, and convulsions within.

He has endeavored to prevent the population of these States, for that purpose obstructing the Laws of Naturalization of Foreigners; refusing to pass others to encourage their migration hither, and raising the conditions of new Appropriations of Lands.

He has obstructed the Administration of Justice, by refusing his Assent to Laws for establishing Judiciary Powers.

He has made Judges dependent on his Will alone, for the tenure of their offices, and the amount and payment of their salaries.

He has erected a multitude of New Offices, and sent hither swarms 15 of Officers to harass our People, and eat out their substance.

He has kept among us, in time of peace, Standing Armies without the consent of our Legislature.

He has affected to render the Military independent of and superior to the Civil Power.

He has combined with others to subject us to jurisdictions foreign to our constitution, and unacknowledged by our laws; giving his Assent to their acts of pretended Legislation:

For quartering large bodies of armed troops among us:

For protecting them, by a mock Trial, from Punishment for any Mur- 20 ders which they should commit on the Inhabitants of these States:

For cutting off our Trade with all parts of the world:

For imposing Taxes on us without our Consent:

For depriving us in many cases, of the benefits of Trial by Jury:

For transporting us beyond Seas to be tried for pretended offenses:

For abolishing the free System of English Laws in a Neighbouring 25 Province, establishing therein an Arbitrary government, and enlarging its boundaries so as to render it at once an example and fit instrument for introducing the same absolute rule into these Colonies:

For taking away our Charters, abolishing our most valuable Laws, and altering fundamentally the Forms of our Governments.

For suspending our own Legislatures, and declaring themselves invested with Power to legislate for us in all cases whatsoever.

He has abdicated Government here, by declaring us out of his Protection and waging War against us.

He has plundered our seas, ravaged our Coasts, burnt our towns and destroyed the Lives of our people.

He is at this time transporting large Armies of foreign Mercenaries to 30 compleat the works of death, desolation and tyranny, already begun with circumstances of Cruelty & perfidy scarcely paralleled in the most barbarous ages, and totally unworthy the Head of a civilized nation.

He has constrained our fellow Citizens taken Captive on the high Seas to bear Arms against their Country, to become the executioners of their friends and Brethren, or to fall themselves by their Hands.

He has excited domestic insurrections amongst us, and has endeavored to bring on the inhabitants of our frontiers, the merciless Indian Savages, whose known rule of warfare is an undistinguished destruction of all ages, sexes and conditions.

In every stage of these Oppressions We Have Petitioned for Redress in the most humble terms: Our repeated petitions have been answered only by repeated injury. A Prince, whose character is thus marked by every act which may define a Tyrant, is unfit to be the ruler of a free People.

Nor have We been wanting in attention to our British brethren. We have warned them from time to time of attempts by their legislature to extend an unwarrantable jurisdiction over us. We have reminded them of the circumstances of our emigration and settlement here. We have appealed to their native justice and magnanimity and we have conjured them by the ties of our common kindred to disavow these usurpations, which would inevitably interrupt our connections and correspondence. They too have been deaf to the voice of justice and of consanguinity. We must, therefore, acquiesce in the necessity, which denounces our Separation, and hold them, as we hold the rest of mankind, Enemies in War, in Peace Friends.

We, therefore, the Representatives of the United States of America, 35 in General Congress, Assembled, appealing to the Supreme Judge of the world of the rectitude of our intentions, do, in the Name, and by Authority of the good People of these Colonies, solemnly publish and declare, That these United Colonies are, and of Right ought to be, Free and Independent States; that they are Absolved from all Allegiance to the British Crown, and that all political connection between them and the State of Great Britain, is and ought to be totally dissolved; and that as Free and Independent States, they have full power to levy War, conclude Peace, contract Alliances, establish Commerce, and so all the other Acts and Things which Independent States may of right do. And for the support of this Declaration, with a firm reliance on the protection of Divine Providence, we mutually pledge to each other our lives, our Fortunes and our sacred Honor.

TOPICS FOR CRITICAL THINKING AND WRITING

1. According to the first paragraph, for what audience was the Declaration written? What other audiences do you think the document was (in one way or another) addressed to?

2. The Declaration states that it is intended to "prove" that the acts of the government of George III had as their "direct object the establishment of an absolute Tyranny" in the American colonies (para. 5). Write an essay of 500 to 750 words showing whether the evidence offered in the Declaration "proves" this claim to your satisfaction. (You will, of course, want to define *absolute tyranny*.) If you think further evidence is needed to "prove" the colonists' point, indicate what this evidence might be.

3. Paying special attention to the paragraphs beginning "That whenever any Form of Government" (para. 4), "In every stage" (para. 33), and "Nor have We been wanting" (para. 34), in a sentence or two set forth the image of themselves that the colonists seek to convey.

4. In the Declaration of Independence it is argued that the colonists are entitled to certain things and that under certain conditions they may behave in a certain way. Make explicit the syllogism that Jefferson is arguing.

5. What evidence does Jefferson offer to support his major premise? His minor premise?

6. In paragraph 2 the Declaration cites "certain unalienable Rights" and mentions three: "Life, Liberty and the pursuit of Happiness." What is an unalienable right? If someone has an unalienable (or inalienable) right, does that imply that he or she also has certain duties? If so, what are these duties? John Locke, a century earlier (1690), asserted that all men have a natural right to "life, liberty, and property." Do you think the decision to drop "property" and substitute "pursuit of Happiness" improved Locke's claim? Explain.

7. The Declaration ends thus: "We mutually pledge to each other our lives, our Fortunes and our sacred Honor." Is it surprising that honor is put in the final, climactic position? Is this a better ending than "our Fortunes, our sacred Honor, and our lives," or than "our sacred Honor, our lives, and our Fortunes?" Why?

8. King George III has asked you to reply, on his behalf, to the colonists, in 500 to 750 words. Write his reply. (Caution: A good reply will probably require you to do some reading about the period.)

9. Write a declaration of your own, setting forth in 500 to 750 words why some group is entitled to independence. You may want to argue that adolescents should not be compelled to attend school, that animals should not be confined in zoos, or that persons who use drugs should be able to buy them legally. Begin with a premise, then set forth facts illustrating the unfairness of the present condition, and conclude by stating what the new condition will mean to society.

Elizabeth Cady Stanton

Elizabeth Cady Stanton (1815–1902), a lawyer's daughter and journalist's wife, proposed in 1848 a convention to address the "social, civil, and religious condition and rights of women." Responding to Stanton's call, women and men from all over the Northeast traveled to the Woman's Rights Convention held in the village of Seneca Falls, New York. Her Declaration, adopted by the Convention—but only after vigorous debate and some amendments by others—became the platform for the women's rights movement in this country.

Declaration of Sentiments and Resolutions

When, in the course of human events, it becomes necessary for one portion of the family of man to assume among the people of the earth a position different from that which they have hitherto occupied, but one to which the laws of nature and of nature's God entitle them, a decent respect to the opinions of mankind requires that they should declare the causes that impel them to such a course.

We hold these truths to be self-evident: that all men and women are created equal; that they are endowed by their Creator with certain inalienable rights; that among these are life, liberty and the pursuit of happiness; that to secure these rights governments are instituted, deriving their just powers from the consent of the governed. Whenever any form of government becomes destructive of these ends, it is the right of those who suffer from it to refuse allegiance to it, and to insist upon the institution of a new government, laying its foundation on such principles, and organizing its powers in such form, as to them shall seem most likely to effect their safety and happiness. Prudence, indeed, will dictate that governments long established should not be changed for light and transient causes; and accordingly all experience hath shown that mankind are more disposed to suffer, while evils are sufferable, than to right themselves by abolishing the forms to which they were accustomed. But when a long train of abuses and usurpations, pursuing invariably the same object, evinces a design to reduce them under absolute despotism, it is their duty to throw off such government, and to provide new guards for their future security. Such has been the patient sufferance of the women under this government, and such is now the necessity which constrains them to demand the equal station to which they are entitled.

The history of mankind is a history of repeated injuries and usurpations on the part of man toward woman, having in direct object the establishment of an absolute tyranny over her. To prove this, let facts be submitted to a candid world.

He has never permitted her to exercise her inalienable right to the elective franchise.

He has compelled her to submit to laws, in the formation of which 5 she had no voice.

He has withheld from her rights which are given to the most ignorant and degraded men — both natives and foreigners.

Having deprived her of this first right of a citizen, the elective franchise, thereby leaving her without representation in the halls of legislation, he has oppressed her on all sides.

He has made her, if married, in the eye of the law, civilly dead.

He has taken from her all right in property, even to the wages she earns.

He has made her, morally, an irresponsible being, as she can commit 10 many crimes with impunity, provided they be done in the presence of her husband. In the covenant of marriage, she is compelled to promise obedience to her husband, he becoming to all intents and purposes, her master — the law giving him power to deprive her of her liberty, and to administer chastisement.

He has so framed the laws of divorce, as to what shall be the proper causes, and in case of separation, to whom the guardianship of the children shall be given, as to be wholly regardless of the happiness of women — the law, in all cases, going upon a false supposition of the supremacy of man, and giving all power into his hands.

After depriving her of all rights as a married woman, if single, and the owner of property, he has taxed her to support a government which recognizes her only when her property can be made profitable to it.

He has monopolized nearly all the profitable employments, and from those she is permitted to follow, she receives but a scanty remuneration. He closes against her all the avenues to wealth and distinction which he considers most honorable to himself. As a teacher of theology, medicine, or law, she is not known.

He has denied her the facilities for obtaining a thorough education, all colleges being closed against her.

He allows her in Church, as well as State, but a subordinate position, 15 claiming Apostolic authority for her exclusion from the ministry, and, with some exceptions, from any public participation in the affairs of the Church.

He has created a false public sentiment by giving to the world a different code of morals for men and women, by which moral delinquencies which exclude women from society, are not only tolerated, but deemed of little account in man.

He has usurped the prerogative of Jehovah himself, claiming it as his right to assign for her a sphere of action, when that belongs to her conscience and to her God.

He has endeavored, in every way that he could, to destroy her confidence in her own powers, to lessen her self-respect, and to make her willing to lead a dependent and abject life.

Now, in view of this entire disfranchisement of one-half the people of this country, their social and religious degradation—in view of the unjust laws above mentioned, and because women do feel themselves aggrieved, oppressed, and fraudulently deprived of their most sacred rights, we insist that they have immediate admission to all the rights and privileges which belong to them as citizens of the United States.

In entering upon the great work before us, we anticipate no small 20 amount of misconception, misrepresentation, and ridicule; but we shall use every instrumentality within our power to effect our object. We shall employ agents, circulate tracts, petition the State and National legislatures, and endeavor to enlist the pulpit and the press in our behalf. We hope this Convention will be followed by a series of Conventions embracing every part of the country.

[The following resolutions were discussed by Lucretia Mott, Thomas and Mary Ann McClintock, Amy Post, Catharine A. F. Stebbins, and others, and were adopted:]

Whereas, The great precept of nature is conceded to be, that "man shall pursue his own true and substantial happiness." Blackstone in his Commentaries remarks, that this law of Nature being coeval with mankind, and dictated by God himself, is of course superior in obligation to any other. It is binding over all the globe, in all countries, and at all times; no human laws are of any validity if contrary to this, and such of them as are valid, derive all their force, and all their validity, and all their authority, mediately and immediately, from this original; therefore,

Resolved, That such laws as conflict, in any way, with the true and substantial happiness of woman, are contrary to the great precept of nature and of no validity, for this is "superior in obligation to any other."

Resolved, That all laws which prevent woman from occupying such a station in society as her conscience shall dictate, or which place her in a position inferior to that of man, are contrary to the great precept of nature, and therefore of no force or authority.

Resolved, That woman is man's equal—was intended to be so by the Creator, and the highest good of the race demands that she should be recognized as such.

Resolved, That the women of this country ought to be enlightened in regard to the laws under which they live, that they may no longer publish their degradation by declaring themselves satisfied with their present position, nor their ignorance, by asserting that they have all the rights they want.

Resolved, That inasmuch as man, while claiming for himself intellectual superiority, does accord to woman moral superiority, it is preeminently his duty to encourage her to speak and teach, as she has an opportunity, in all religious assemblies.

Resolved, That the same amount of virtue, delicacy, and refinement of behavior that is required of woman in the social state, should also be required of man, and the same transgressions should be visited with equal severity on both man and woman.

Resolved, That the objection of indelicacy and impropriety, which is so often brought against woman when she addresses a public audience, comes with a very ill-grace from those who encourage, by their attendance, her appearance on the stage, in the concert, or in feats of the circus.

Resolved, That woman has too long rested satisfied in the circumscribed limits which corrupt customs and a perverted application of the Scriptures have marked out for her, and that it is time she should move in the enlarged sphere which her great Creator has assigned her.

Resolved, That it is the duty of the women of this country to secure to themselves their sacred right to the elective franchise.

Resolved, That the equality of human rights results necessarily from the fact of the identity of the race in capabilities and responsibilities.

Resolved, therefore, That, being invested by the Creator with the same capabilities, and the same consciousness of responsibility for their exercise, it is demonstrably the right and duty of woman, equally with man, to promote every righteous cause by every righteous means; and especially in regard to the great subjects of morals and religion, it is self-evidently her right to participate with her brother in teaching them, both in private and in public, by writing and by speaking, by any instrumentalities proper to be used, and in any assemblies proper to be held; and this being a self-evident truth growing out of the divinely implanted principles of human nature, any custom or authority adverse to it, whether modern or wearing the hoary sanction of antiquity, is to be regarded as a self-evident falsehood, and at war with mankind.

[At the last session Lucretia Mott offered and spoke to the following resolution:]

Resolved, That the speedy success of our cause depends upon the zealous and untiring efforts of both men and women, for the overthrow of the monopoly of the pulpit, and for the securing to woman an equal participation with men in the various trades, professions, and commerce.

TOPICS FOR CRITICAL THINKING AND WRITING

1. Stanton echoes the Declaration of Independence because she wishes to associate her ideas and the movement she supports with a document and a movement that her readers esteem. And she must have believed that if readers esteem the Declaration of Independence, they must grant the justice of her goals. Does her strategy work, or does it backfire by making her essay seem strained?

2. When Stanton insists that women have an "inalienable right to the elective franchise" (para. 4), what does she mean by "inalienable"?

3. Stanton complains that men have made married women, "in the eye of the law, civilly dead" (para. 8). What does she mean by "civilly dead"? How is it possible for a person to be biologically alive and yet civilly dead?

4. Stanton objects that women are "not known" as teachers of "theology, medicine, or law" (para. 13). Is this still true today? Do some research in your library, and then write three 100-word biographical sketches, one each on well-known woman professors of theology, medicine, and law.

5. How might you go about proving (rather than merely asserting) that, as paragraph 24 says, "woman is man's equal—was intended to be so by the Creator"?

6. The Declaration claims that women have "the same capabilities" as men (para. 32). Yet in 1848 Stanton and the others at Seneca Falls knew, or should have known, that history recorded no example of a woman philosopher comparable to Plato or Kant, a composer comparable to Beethoven or Chopin, a scientist comparable to Galileo or Newton, or a mathematician comparable to Euclid or Descartes. Do these facts contradict the Declaration's claim? If not, why not? How else but by different intellectual capabilities do you think such facts can be explained?

7. Stanton's Declaration is over 155 years old. Have all of the issues she raised been satisfactorily resolved? If not, which ones remain?

8. In our society, children have very few rights. For instance, a child cannot decide to drop out of elementary school or high school, and a child

cannot decide to leave his or her parents to reside with some other family that he or she finds more compatible. Whatever your view of children's rights, compose the best Declaration of the Rights of Children that you can.

Martin Luther King Jr.

Martin Luther King Jr. (1929–1968) was born in Atlanta and educated at Morehouse College, Crozer Theological Seminary, and Boston University. In 1954 he was called to serve as a Baptist minister in Montgomery, Alabama. During the next two years he achieved national fame when, using a policy of nonviolent resistance, he successfully led the boycott against segregated bus lines in Montgomery. He then organized the Southern Christian Leadership Conference, which furthered civil rights, first in the South and then nationwide. In 1964 he was awarded the Nobel Peace Prize. Four years later he was assassinated in Memphis, Tennessee, while supporting striking garbage workers.

The speech presented here was delivered from the steps of the Lincoln Memorial, in Washington, D.C., in 1963, the hundredth anniversary of the Emancipation Proclamation. King's immediate audience consisted of more than two hundred thousand people who had come to demonstrate for civil rights.

I Have a Dream

I am happy to join with you today in what will go down in history as the greatest demonstration for freedom in the history of our nation.

Five score years ago, a great American, in whose symbolic shadow we stand today, signed the Emancipation Proclamation. This momentous decree came as a great beacon light of hope to millions of Negro slaves who had been seared in the flames of withering injustice. It came as a joyous daybreak to end the long night of their captivity. But one hundred years later, the Negro still is not free. One hundred years later, the life of the Negro is still sadly crippled by the manacles of segregation and the chains of discrimination. One hundred years later, the Negro lives on a lonely island of poverty in the midst of a vast ocean of material prosperity. One hundred years later, the Negro is still anguished in the corners of American society and finds himself in exile in his own land. And so we have come here today to dramatize a shameful condition.

In a sense we have come to our nation's capital to cash a check. When the architects of our republic wrote the magnificent words of the Constitution and the Declaration of Independence, they were signing a promissory note to which every American was to fall heir. This note was the promise that all men — yes, black men as well as white men — would be guaranteed the inalienable rights of life, liberty, and the pursuit of happiness.

It is obvious today that America has defaulted on this promissory note insofar as her citizens of color are concerned. Instead of honoring this sacred obligation, America has given the Negro people a bad check, a check which has come back marked "insufficient funds." But we refuse to believe that the bank of justice is bankrupt. We refuse to believe that there are insufficient funds in the great vaults of opportunity of this nation; and so we have come to cash this check, a check that will give us upon demand the riches of freedom and the security of justice.

We have also come to this hallowed spot to remind America of the fierce urgency of *now*. This is no time to engage in the luxury of cooling off or to take the tranquilizing drug of gradualism. *Now* is the time to make real promises of democracy. *Now* is the time to rise from the dark and desolate valley of segregation to the sunlit path of racial justice. *Now* is the time to lift our nation from the quicksands of racial injustice to the solid rock of brotherhood. *Now* is the time to make justice a reality for all of God's children.

It would be fatal for the nation to overlook the urgency of the moment. This sweltering summer of the Negro's legitimate discontent will not pass until there is an invigorating autumn of freedom and equality. Nineteen sixty-three is not an end, but a beginning. And those who hope that the Negro needed to blow off steam and will now be content will have a rude awakening if the nation returns to business as usual. There will be neither rest nor tranquility in America until the Negro is granted his citizenship rights. The whirlwinds of revolt will continue to shake the foundations of our nation until the bright day of justice emerges.

But there is something that I must say to my people who stand on the warm threshold which leads into the palace of justice. In the process of gaining our rightful place, we must not be guilty of wrongful deeds. Let us not seek to satisfy our thirst for freedom by drinking from the cup of bitterness and hatred. We must forever conduct our struggle on the high plane of dignity and discipline. We must not allow our creative protest to degenerate into physical violence. Again and again we must rise to the majestic heights of meeting physical force with soul force. And the marvelous new militancy which has engulfed the Negro community must not lead us to a distrust of all white people; for many of our white brothers, as evidenced by their presence here today, have come to realize that their destiny is tied up with our destiny, and they have come to realize that their freedom is inextricably bound to our freedom.

We cannot walk alone. And as we walk we must make the pledge that we shall always march ahead. We cannot turn back. There are those who are asking the devotees of civil rights, "When will you be satisfied?" We can never be satisfied as long as the Negro is the victim of the unspeakable horrors of police brutality. We can never be satisfied as long as our bodies, heavy with the fatigue of travel, cannot gain lodging in the motels of the highways and the hotels of the cities. We cannot be satisfied as long as the Negro's basic mobility is from a smaller ghetto to a larger one. We can never be satisfied as long as our children are stripped of their selfhood and robbed of their dignity by signs stating "For Whites Only." We cannot be satisfied as long as the Negro in Mississippi cannot vote and a Negro in New York believes he has nothing for which to vote. No, no, we are not satisfied, and we will not be satisfied until justice rolls down like waters and righteousness like a mighty stream.[1]

I am not unmindful that some of you have come here out of great trials and tribulations. Some of you have come fresh from narrow jail cells. Some of you have come from areas where your quest for freedom left you battered by the storms of persecution and staggered by the winds of police brutality. You have been the veterans of creative suffering. Continue to work with the faith that unearned suffering is redemptive.

Go back to Mississippi, and go back to Alabama. Go back to South 10 Carolina. Go back to Georgia. Go back to Louisiana. Go back to the slums and ghettos of our Northern cities, knowing that somehow this situation can and will be changed. Let us not wallow in the valley of despair.

I say to you today, my friends, even though we face the difficulties of today and tomorrow, I still have a dream. It is a dream deeply rooted in the American dream. I have a dream that one day this nation will rise up and live out the true meaning of its creed: "We hold these truths to be self-evident, that all men are created equal." I have a dream that one day, on the red hills of Georgia, sons of former slaves and the sons of former slave owners will be able to sit down together at the table of brotherhood. I have a dream that one day even the state of Mississippi, a state sweltering with the heat of injustice, sweltering with the heat of oppression, will be transformed into an oasis of freedom and justice. I have a dream that my four little children will one day live in a nation where they will not be judged by the color of their skin, but by the content of their character.

I have a dream today. I have a dream that one day down in Alabama — with its vicious racists, with its governor's lips dripping with the words of interposition and nullification — one day right there in Alabama, little black boys and black girls will be able to join hands with little white boys and white girls as sisters and brothers.

I have a dream today. I have a dream that one day every valley shall be exalted and every hill and mountain shall be made low, the rough places will be made plain and the crooked places will be made straight, and the glory of the Lord shall be revealed, and all flesh shall see it together.[2]

This is our hope. This is the faith that I go back to the South with. And with this faith we will be able to hew out of the mountain of despair a stone of hope. With this faith we will be able to transform the jangling discords of our nation into a beautiful symphony of brotherhood. With

---

[1]**justice . . . stream** A quotation from the Hebrew Bible: Amos 5:24. [All notes are the editors'.]

[2]**every valley . . . see it together** Another quotation from the Hebrew Bible: Isaiah 40:4–5.

this faith we will be able to work together, to play together, to struggle together, to go to jail together, to stand up for freedom together, knowing that we will be free one day.

And this will be the day — this will be the day when all of God's chil- 15
dren will be able to sing with new meaning:

> My country, 'tis of thee,
> Sweet land of liberty,
>   Of thee I sing;
> Land where my fathers died,
> Land of the Pilgrim's pride,
> From every mountainside
>   Let freedom ring.

And if America is to be a great nation, this must become true.

And so let freedom ring from the prodigious hilltops of New Hampshire. Let freedom ring from the mighty mountains of New York. Let freedom ring from the heightening Alleghenies of Pennsylvania. Let freedom ring from the snow-capped Rockies of Colorado. Let freedom ring from the curvaceous slopes of California.

But not only that. Let freedom ring from Stone Mountain of Georgia. Let freedom ring from Lookout Mountain of Tennessee. Let freedom ring from every hill and molehill of Mississippi. "From every mountainside let freedom ring."

And when this happens — when we allow freedom to ring, when we let it ring from every village and every hamlet, from every state and every city — we will be able to speed up that day when all of God's children, Black men and white men, Jews and Gentiles, Protestants and Catholics, will be able to join hands and sing in the words of the old Negro spiritual: "Free at last! Free at last! Thank God Almighty. We are free at last!"

Topics for Critical Thinking and Writing

1. Analyze the rhetoric — the oratorical art — of the second paragraph. What, for instance, is gained by saying "five score years ago" instead of "a hundred years ago"? By metaphorically calling the Emancipation Proclamation "a great beacon light of hope"? By saying that "Negro slaves . . . had been seared in the flames of withering injustice"? And what of the metaphors "daybreak" and "the long night of . . . captivity"?

2. Do the first two paragraphs make an effective opening? Why?

3. In the third and fourth paragraphs King uses the metaphor of a bad check. Rewrite the third paragraph *without* using any of King's metaphors, and then in a paragraph evaluate the differences between King's version and yours.

4. King's highly metaphoric speech appeals to emotions. But it also offers *reasons*. What reasons, for instance, does King give to support his belief

that African Americans should not resort to physical violence in their struggle against segregation and discrimination?

5. When King delivered the speech, his audience at the Lincoln Memorial was primarily African American. Do you think that the speech is also addressed to other Americans? Explain.

6. The speech can be divided into three parts: paragraphs 1 through 6; paragraphs 7 ("But there is") through 10; and paragraph 11 ("I say to you today, my friends") to the end. Summarize each of these three parts in a sentence or two so that the basic organization is evident.

7. King says (para. 11) that his dream is "deeply rooted in the American dream." First, what is the American dream, as King seems to understand it? Second, how does King establish his point—that is, what evidence does he use to convince us—that his dream is the American dream? (On this second issue, one might start by pointing out that in the second paragraph King refers to the Emancipation Proclamation. What other relevant documents does he refer to?)

8. King delivered his speech in 1963, more than forty years ago. In an essay of 500 words, argue that the speech still is—or is not—relevant. Or write an essay of 500 words in which you state what you take to be the "American dream," and argue that it now is or is not readily available to African Americans.

Ursula K. Le Guin

Ursula K. Le Guin was born in 1929 in Berkeley, California, the daughter of a distinguished mother (Theodora Kroeber, a folklorist) and father (Alfred L. Kroeber, an anthropologist). After graduating from Radcliffe College, she earned a master's degree at Columbia University; in 1952 she held a Fulbright Fellowship for study in Paris, where she met and married Charles Le Guin, a historian. She began writing in earnest while bringing up three children. Although her work is most widely known to buffs of science fiction, because it usually has larger moral or political dimensions, it interests many other readers who normally do not care for sci-fi.

Le Guin has said that she was prompted to write the following story by a remark she encountered in William James's "The Moral Philosopher and the Moral Life." James suggests there that if millions of people could be "kept permanently happy on the one simple condition that a certain lost soul on the far-off edge of things should lead a life of lonely torment," our moral sense "would make us immediately feel" it would be "hideous" to accept such a bargain. This story first appeared in New Dimensions 3 *(1973).*

The Ones Who Walk Away from Omelas

With a clamor of bells that set the swallows soaring, the Festival of Summer came to the city Omelas, bright-towered by the sea. The rigging of the boats in harbor sparkled with flags. In the streets between houses with red roofs and painted walls, between old moss-grown gardens and under avenues of trees, past great parks and public buildings, processions moved. Some were decorous: old people in long stiff robes of mauve and gray, grave master workmen, quiet, merry women carrying their babies and chatting as they walked. In other streets the music beat faster, a shimmering of gong and tambourine, and the people went dancing, the procession was a dance. Children dodged in and out, their high calls rising like the swallows' crossing flights over the music and the singing. All the processions wound towards the north side of the city, where on the great water-meadow called the Green Fields boys and girls, naked in the bright air, with mudstained feet and ankles and long, lithe arms, exercised their restive horses before the race. The horses wore no gear at all but a halter without bit. Their manes were braided with streamers of silver, gold, and green. They flared their nostrils and pranced and boasted to one another; they were vastly excited, the horse being the only animal who has adopted our ceremonies as his own. Far off to the north and west the mountains stood up half encircling Omelas on her bay. The air of morning was so clear that the snow still crowning the Eighteen Peaks burned with white-gold fire across the miles of sunlit air, under the dark blue of the sky. There was just enough wind to make the banners that marked the racecourse snap and flutter now and then. In the silence of the broad green meadows one could hear the music winding through the city streets, farther and nearer and ever approaching, a cheerful faint sweetness of the air that from time to time trembled and gathered together and broke out into the great joyous clanging of the bells.

Joyous! How is one to tell about joy? How describe the citizens of Omelas?

They were not simple folk, you see, though they were happy. But we do not say the words of cheer much any more. All smiles have become archaic. Given a description such as this one tends to make certain assumptions. Given a description such as this one tends to look next for the King, mounted on a splendid stallion and surrounded by his noble knights, or perhaps in a golden litter borne by great-muscled slaves. But there was no king. They did not use swords, or keep slaves. They were not barbarians. I do not know the rules and laws of their society, but I suspect that they were singularly few. As they did without monarchy and slavery, so they also got on without the stock exchange, the advertisement, the secret police, and the bomb. Yet I repeat that these were not simple folk, not dulcet shepherds, noble savages, bland utopians. They were not less complex than us. The trouble is that we have a bad habit, encouraged by pedants and sophisticates, of considering happiness as something rather stupid. Only pain is intellectual, only evil interesting. This is the treason of the artist: a refusal to admit the banality of evil and the terrible boredom of pain. If you can't lick 'em, join 'em. If it hurts, repeat it. But to praise despair is to condemn delight, to embrace violence is to lose hold of everything else. We have almost lost hold, we can no longer describe a happy man, nor make any celebration of joy. How can I tell you about the people of Omelas? They were not naïve and happy children—though their children were, in fact, happy. They were mature, intelligent, passionate adults whose lives were not wretched. O miracle! But I wish I could describe it better. I wish I could convince you. Omelas sounds in my words like a city in a fairy tale, long ago and far away, once upon a time. Perhaps it would be best if you imagined it as your own fancy bids, assuming it will rise to the occasion, for certainly I cannot suit you all. For instance, how about technology? I think that there would be no cars or helicopters in and above the streets; this follows from the fact that the people of Omelas are happy people. Happiness is based on a just discrimination of what is necessary, what is neither necessary nor destructive, and what is destructive. In the middle category, however—that of the unnecessary but undestructive, that of comfort, luxury, exuberance, etc.—they could perfectly well have central heating, subway trains, washing machines, and all kinds of marvelous devices not yet invented here, floating light-sources, fuelless power, a cure for the common cold. Or they could have none of that: it doesn't matter. As you like it. I incline to think that people from towns up and down the coast have been coming in to Omelas during the last days before the Festival on very fast little trains and double-decked trams, and that the train station of Omelas is actually the handsomest building in town, though plainer than the magnificent Farmers' Market. But even granted trains, I fear that Omelas so far strikes some of you as goody-goody. Smiles, bells, parades, horses, bleh. If so, please add an orgy. If an orgy would help, don't hesitate. Let us not, however, have temples from which issue beautiful nude priests and priestesses already half in ecstasy and ready to copulate with any man or woman, lover or stranger, who desires union with the deep godhead of the blood, although that was my first idea. But really it would be better not to have any temples in Omelas—at least, not manned temples. Religion yes, clergy no. Surely the beautiful nudes can just wander about, offering themselves like divine soufflés to the hunger of the needy and the rapture of the flesh. Let them join the processions. Let tambourines be struck above the copulations, and the glory of desire be proclaimed upon the gongs, and (a not unimportant point) let the offspring of these delightful rituals be beloved and looked after by all. One thing I know there is none of in Omelas is guilt. But what else should there be? I thought that first there were no drugs, but that is puritanical. For those who like it, the faint insistent sweetness of *drooz* may perfume the ways of the city, *drooz* which first brings a great lightness and brilliance to the mind and limbs, and then after some hours a dreamy languor, and wonderful visions at last of the very arcana and inmost secrets of the Universe, as well as exciting the pleasure of sex beyond all belief; and it is not habit-forming. For more modest tastes I think there ought to be beer. What else, what else belongs in the joyous city? The sense of victory, surely, the celebration of courage. But as we did without clergy, let us do without soldiers. The joy built upon successful slaughter is not the right kind of joy; it will not do; it is fearful and it is trivial. A boundless and generous contentment, a magnanimous triumph felt not against some outer enemy but in communion with the finest and fairest in the souls of all men everywhere and the splendor of the world's summer: this is what swells the hearts of the people of Omelas, and the victory they celebrate is that of life. I really don't think many of them need to take *drooz*.

Most of the processions have reached the Green Fields by now. A marvelous smell of cooking goes forth from the red and blue tents of the provisioners. The faces of small children are amiably sticky; in the benign grey beard of a man a couple of crumbs of rich pastry are entangled. The youths and girls have mounted their horses and are beginning to group around the starting line of the course. An old woman, small, fat, and laughing, is passing out flowers from a basket, and tall young men wear her flowers in their shining hair. A child of nine or ten sits at the edge of the crowd, alone, playing on a wooden flute. People pause to listen, and they smile, but they do not speak to him, for he never ceases playing and never sees them, his dark eyes wholly rapt in the sweet, thin magic of the tune.

He finishes, and slowly lowers his hands holding the wooden flute.   5

As if that little private silence were the signal, all at once a trumpet sounds from the pavilion near the starting line: imperious, melancholy, piercing. The horses rear on their slender legs, and some of them neigh in answer. Sober-faced, the young riders stroke the horses' necks and soothe them, whispering, "Quiet, quiet, there my beauty, my hope. . . ." They begin to form in rank along the starting line. The crowds along the racecourse are like a field of grass and flowers in the wind. The Festival of Summer has begun.

Do you believe? Do you accept the festival, the city, the joy? No? Then let me describe one more thing.

In a basement under one of the beautiful public buildings of Omelas, or perhaps in the cellar of one of its spacious private homes, there is a room. It has one locked door, and no window. A little light seeps in dustily between cracks in the boards, secondhand from a cobwebbed window somewhere across the cellar. In one corner of the little room a couple of mops, with stiff, clotted, foul-smelling heads, stand near a rusty bucket. The floor is dirt, a little damp to the touch, as cellar dirt usually is. The room is about three paces long and two wide: a mere broom closet or disused tool room. In the room a child is sitting. It could be a boy or a girl. It looks about six, but actually is nearly ten. It is feeble-minded. Perhaps it was born defective, or perhaps it has become imbecile through fear, malnutrition, and neglect. It picks its nose and occasionally fumbles vaguely with its toes or genitals, as it sits hunched in the corner farthest from the bucket and the two mops. It is afraid of the mops. It finds them horrible. It shuts its eyes, but it knows the mops are still standing there; and the door is locked; and nobody will come. The door is always locked; and nobody ever comes, except that sometimes—the child has no understanding of time or interval—sometimes the door rattles terribly and opens, and a person, or several people, are there. One of them may come in and kick the child to make it stand up. The others never come close, but peer in at it with frightened, disgusted eyes. The food bowl and the water jug are hastily filled, the door is locked, the eyes disappear. The people at the door never say anything, but the child, who has not always lived in the tool room, and can remember sunlight and its mother's voice, sometimes speaks. "I will be good," it says. "Please let me out. I will be good!" They never answer. The child used to scream for help at night, and cry a good deal, but now it only makes a kind of whining, "eh-haa, eh-haa," and it speaks less and less often. It is so thin there are no calves to its legs; its belly protrudes; it lives on a half-bowl of corn meal and grease a day. It is naked. Its buttocks and thighs are a mass of festered sores, as it sits in its own excrement continually.

They all know it is there, all the people of Omelas. Some of them have come to see it, others are content merely to know it is there. They all know that it has to be there. Some of them understand why, and some do not, but they all understand that their happiness, the beauty of their city, the tenderness of their friendships, the health of their children, the wisdom of their scholars, the skill of their makers, even the abundance of their harvest and the kindly weathers of their skies, depend wholly on this child's abominable misery.

This is usually explained to children when they are between eight 10 and twelve, whenever they seem capable of understanding; and most of those who come to see the child are young people, though often enough an adult comes, or comes back, to see the child. No matter how well the matter has been explained to them, these young spectators are always shocked and sickened at the sight. They feel disgust, which they had thought themselves superior to. They feel anger, outrage, impotence, despite all the explanations. They would like to do something for the child. But there is nothing they can do. If the child were brought up into the sunlight out of that vile place, if it were cleaned and fed and comforted, that would be a good thing, indeed; but if it were done, in that day and hour all the prosperity and beauty and delight of Omelas would wither and be destroyed. Those are the terms. To exchange all the goodness and grace of every life in Omelas for that single, small improvement: to throw away the happiness of thousands for the chance of the happiness of one: that would be to let guilt within the walls indeed.

The terms are strict and absolute; there may not even be a kind word spoken to the child.

Often the young people go home in tears, or in a tearless rage, when they have seen the child and faced this terrible paradox. They may brood over it for weeks or years. But as time goes on they begin to realize that even if the child could be released, it would not get much good of its freedom: a little vague pleasure of warmth and food, no doubt, but little more. It is too degraded and imbecile to know any real joy. It has been afraid too long ever to be free of fear. Its habits are too uncouth for it to respond to humane treatment. Indeed, after so long it would probably be wretched without walls about it to protect it, and darkness for its eyes, and its own excrement to sit in. Their tears at the bitter injustice dry when they begin to perceive the terrible justice of reality, and to accept it. Yet it is their tears and anger, the trying of their generosity and the acceptance of their helplessness, which are perhaps the true source of the splendor of their lives. Theirs is no vapid, irresponsible happiness. They know that they, like the child, are not free. They know compassion. It is the existence of the child, and their knowledge of its existence, that makes possible the nobility of their architecture, the poignancy of their music, the profundity of their science. It is because of the child that they are so gentle with children. They know that if the wretched one were not there snivelling in the dark, the other one, the flute-player, could make no joyful music as the young riders line up in their beauty for the race in the sunlight of the first morning of summer.

Now do you believe in them? Are they not more credible? But there is one more thing to tell, and this is quite incredible.

At times one of the adolescent girls or boys who go to see the child does not go home to weep or rage, does not, in fact, go home at all. Sometimes also a man or woman much older falls silent for a day or two, and then leaves home. These people go out into the street, and walk down the street alone. They keep walking, and walk straight out of the city of Omelas, through the beautiful gates. They keep walking across the farmlands of Omelas. Each one goes alone, youth or girl, man or woman. Night falls; the traveler must pass down village streets, between the houses with yellow-lit windows, and on out into the darkness of the fields. Each alone, they go west or north, towards the mountains. They go on. They leave Omelas, they walk ahead into the darkness, and they do not come back. The place they go towards is a place even less imaginable to most of us than the city of happiness. I cannot describe it at all. It is possible that it does not exist. But they seem to know where they are going, the ones who walk away from Omelas.

Topics for Critical Thinking and Writing

1. Summarize the point of the story—not the plot, but what the story adds up to, what the author is getting at. Next, set forth what you would probably do (and why) if you were born in Omelas.

2. Consider the narrator's assertion that happiness "is based on a just discrimination of what is necessary" (para. 3).

3. Do you think the story implies a criticism of contemporary American society? Explain.

Text (continued from p. iv)

Peter Singer. "Famine, Affluence, and Morality." From *Philosophy and Public Affairs*, Spring 1972. Copyright © 1972 by Princeton University Press. Reprinted by permission of Princeton University Press "Animal Liberation." From *New York Review of Books*, April 15, 1973. Copyright © 1973 by Peter Singer. Reprinted by permission of the author.

Deanne Stillman. "Last Roundup for Wild Horses." From the *Boston Globe*, March 5, 2005. Letters of Response by Holly Williams and Tom Burke. Reprinted by permission.

Nadine Strossen. "Everyone Is Watching You." From *www.intellectualCapital.com*. May 28, 1989 (ACLU website). Reprinted by permission of the American Civil Liberties Union. Email responses

Ronald Takaki. "The Harmful Myth of Asian Superiority." From *The New York Times*, June 16, 1990. Copyright © 1990 by The New York Times Company, Inc. Reprinted with permission.

George Will. "Being Green at Ben and Jerry's." Originally published in *Newsweek*, May 6, 2002, p. 72. Copyright © 2002 George F. Will. Reprinted by permission of the author.

James Q. Wilson. "Just Take Away Their Guns." From *The New York Times*, March 20. 1994. Copyright © 1994 by The New York Times Company, Inc. Reprinted by permisson.

Art

"Ad:" "Warning!" National Archives.

"Attention paid to poor, sick Negro." From Josiah Priest, Biblical Defense of Slavery.

A slave's back with scars. Massachusetts Historical Society.

"Calvin and Hobbes:" "I used to hate writing assignments . . ." Calvin and Hobbes © 1993 Watterson. Reprinted by permission of Universal Press Syndicate. All rights reserved.

Child at desk in classroom full of product placements. Copyright 2006 Samuel B. Whitehead.

Children running from napalm attack in Vietnam. AP Images.

"Department of Logic." © 2006 Robert Mankoff from cartoonbank.com. All Rights Reserved.

Diagram of slave ship. The Lundoff Collection.

"Dilbert:" "That concludes my two-hour presentation." DILBERT ©Scott Adams/Dist. by permission of United Feature Syndicate, Inc.

"Doonesbury:" "Poor lady . . . she looks so miserable . . ." DOONESBURY © 1998 G. B. Trudeau. Reprinted with permission of UNIVERSAL PRESS SYNDICATE. All rights reserved.

"It sort of makes you stop and think." ©The New Yorker Collection 2003 Sam Gross from cartoonbank.com. All Rights Reserved.

Martin Luther King giving speech. AP Images.

Mother and two children. Library of Congress.

Mother, child, and baby. Library of Congress.

"One nation, under nothing in particular. . . ." Gary Markstein/ Copley News Service.

Planned Parenthood banner. AP Images.

Police officer shooting a Viet Cong prisoner. AP Images.

Poster with Martin Luther King Jr. and Charles Manson. Courtesy DeVito/Verdi, New York, NY.

Poster with smoking gun/ cigarette. Reprinted by permission of the American Cancer Society. All rights reserved.

Sculpture of Ten Commandments. AP Images.

The Scream by Edvard Munch. © 2007 The Munch Museum/The Munch-Ellingsen Group/Artists Rights Society (ARS), NY. Digital Image © The Museum of Modern Art/Licensed by SCALA/Art Resource, NY.

"Uncle Sam," "I Want You." Library of Congress.

Veiled woman's eyes. AP Images.

"Which entrée raises the fewest ethical issues?" © The New Yorker Collection 2006 William Haefeli from cartoonbank.com. All Rights Reserved.

Wild horses in California desert. Index Stock Imagery/NewsCom.

Woman and child falling from fire escape. Stanley J. Forman.

Woman and fireman on fire escape. Stanley J. Forman.

Woman falling from fire escape. Stanley J. Forman.

Woman hanging on to fireman, falling off fire escape. Stanley J. Forman.

Index of Authors and Titles

Index of Terms

Date due slip
on previous pg.

Directory to Documentation Models in MLA Format